A JOURNEY THROUGH BRITAIN

Visitors to Britain from abroad, particularly those from much larger countries, are usually amazed by the diversity contained within a relatively small area – landscape, architecture, customs, accents and even that indistinct quality we call 'atmosphere' can all vary enormously within the space of a half-day on the road. And because of the lay of the land, many of these variations pop up suddenly to surprise you as you round a corner or crest a hill. Some of the most lonely and remote ranges of hills and moorland areas are, in fact, very close to our most vibrant cities, and in the middle of huge connurbations there are vast green areas of parkland.

This book brings together all the elements that make up the best of Britain, combining the famous places that absolutely should not be missed with lots of lesser-known delights, chosen and written about by writers who have a specialised knowledge and affinity with particular areas. Britain is well worth exploring, and the words and pictures you will find within the following pages offer the incentive and inspiration to set off – on wheels or on foot – and enjoy this lovely island.

THE WEST COUNTRY

THE WEST COUNTRY, WITH ITS dwindling peninsula reaching out into the Atlantic, inspires a greater sense of Island Britain than anywhere else in England. It is a land of diverse, yet complementary landscapes that retain strong elements of the ancient civilisations that were overtaken, but never submerged by successive conquests.

The farmed landscape of the West Country includes Dorset's serene and rolling acres and the unremitting flatness of the Somerset Levels. It embraces Devon's lush pastures, the tiny prehistoric fields of Cornwall's rugged Land's End Peninsula and the Mediterranean flower meadows of the Isles of Scilly. Within the farmed lowland are islands of high ground such as the slight, smooth Polden Hills and the Blackdown Hills of Somerset, the bulky Mendips, breached by craggy ravines, the tawny Quantocks, and the high, wild acres of Dartmoor, Exmoor, and Bodmin Moor.

The West Country is defined by its villages and country towns rather than by great cities or industrial conurbations. Even the metropolitan centres of the West reflect the culture of rural and maritime England. Exeter is identified with its glorious cathedral in a wide green space; Taunton's urban image is mellowed by county cricket and cider apples; Plymouth, with its powerful seagoing traditions turns its face towards the great gulf of Plymouth Sound and the open sea. In a thousand villages, centuries of complex history have created unique communities. Yet between the thatched serenity of wooded Selworthy in Somerset and the cobbled streets of Cornish St Ives lies unity within diversity.

There is always a sense of escape in the West Country, of there being enough land to go round, of an ancient landscape not yet overpowered by technology. Most strikingly there is the sea, the great element that makes the West Country so emphatically the heart of maritime England. From Devon and Cornish shores came the great adventurers of Elizabethan England – the Raleighs, the Drakes and the Grenvilles. Today, the colourful fishing boats and fishermen of numerous West Country ports retain a flavour of the old-time buccaneering spirit. Above all there is that sense of detachment that attracts all those who want to escape the rigours of an increasingly stressful urban Britain. Discover the marvellous contrasts of this favoured region, its beautiful and varied countryside, its outstanding beaches and resorts, its ancient market towns and secluded villages, and, above all, its friendly and accomplished people.

The scene at Fowey epitomises the seafaring flavour of the West Country

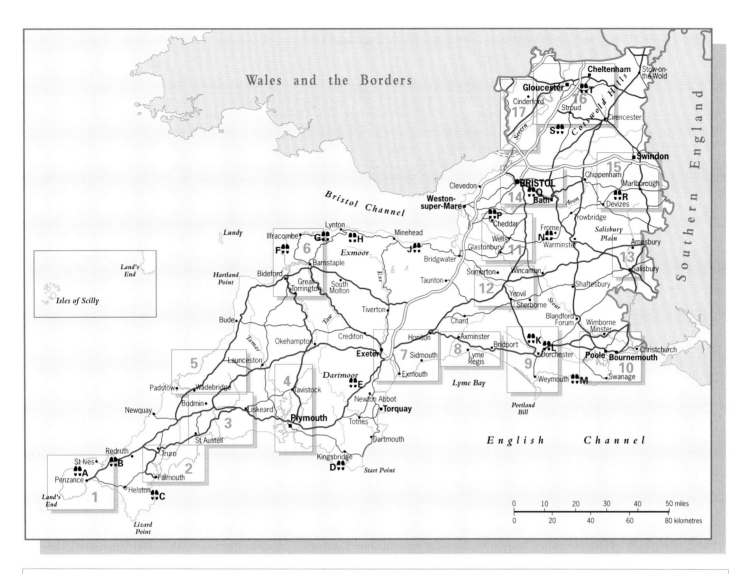

SECTION CONTENTS

FEATURES

WALKS

A GRANITE KINGDOM

Magnificent sea cliffs, golden beaches, tawny moorland and flower-filled lanes are the themes of the Land's End peninsula and the Isles of Scilly. This is an ancient landscape with a concentration of prehistoric remains which is unrivalled in Britain. The mainland towns of Penzance and St Ives have more than a hint of Mediterranean Europe about them, and the Isles of Scilly are known, deservedly, as the Fortunate Islands.

Tin Mining

The north coast of the Land's End peninsula is Cornwall's tin-mining coast, a landscape which is spectacular by nature, yet in places devastated by industry. Mining for copper, tin and other minerals in Cornwall began in pre-Roman times, when early 'tinners' dug out surface deposits and extracted mineral rich silt from moorland streams. Deep mining developed by the 17th and 18th centuries and reached its peak during the latter half of the 19th century. The ups and downs of the industry saw thousands of Cornish miners emigrating to Australia, South Africa and the Americas. Below ground, from St Just to St Ives, is a stygian maze of old workings, some running beneath the sea, and most now flooded. The enduring emblems of the industry are the granite mine stacks and treatment works that invest the raw landscape of the coast and moorlands with a haunting beauty. The last working coastal mine of Geevor, at Pendeen near St Just, closed in 1990 in spite of a spirited local campaign to save it. It is still called Geevor Tin Mine, but now has a fascinating Visitors Centre complete with museum and tours of parts of the mine.

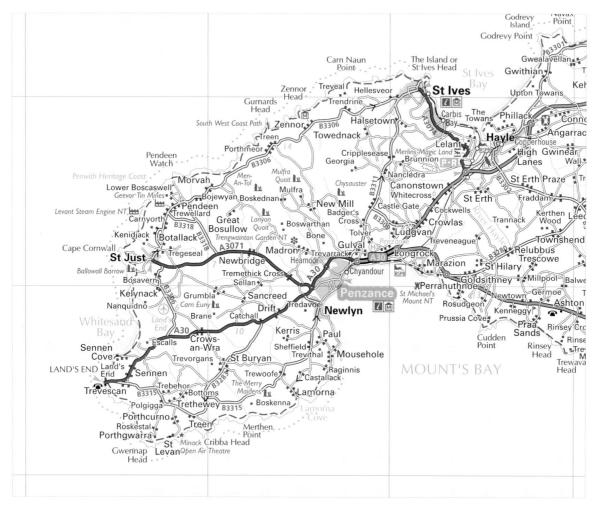

Cape Cornwall

Cape Cornwall lies on the rugged north coast of the Land's End peninsula. It is the only 'Cape' in England and is so by nature of its position at the meeting of the English Channel and St George's Channel. Most of the coastline to north and south of the Cape is in the care of the National Trust, which is promoting a fruitful programme of conservation of the area's Victorian tin mining relics. Just inland from the Cape is the sturdy little town of St Just, where tin mining and Methodism defined the heart of 19th-century Cornwall. It is also the most westerly town in England, and has a fine Norman church.

The Isles of Scilly

The Isles of Scilly lie 28 miles (17.5 km) south-west of Land's End and are reached by ferry or helicopter from Penzance. The five inhabited islands are St Mary's, St Agnes, St Martin's, Bryher and Tresco, each one uniquely different from the other. Travel by inter-island boats and aboard numerous pleasure launches is the best way of enjoying this beautiful mosaic of islands and dragon-backed reefs within their setting of blue sea and golden sands. The main island of St Mary's is the busy hub of island life, but all enjoy an extraordinary atmosphere of tranquillity, especially the smaller islands.

Tourist Information Centres

Penzance: Station Road (tel: 01736 362207)
St Ives: The Guildhall, Street-an-Pol (tel: 01736 796297)

Land's End

Land's End is the most westerly point in England. The top of the headland is broad and rather featureless except for the cluster of buildings that make up the modern 'Land's End Experience'. It is the flanking cliffs that make Land's End so astounding. They rise in enormous pinnacles and crumbling buttresses, which enclose boulder-strewn coves and echoing ravines called 'zawns'. Access on foot to the top of the headland is time-honoured and free; there is a charge for car parking and for entrance to the Land's End exhibitions, which offer diversions in plenty. The real diversion, in wild weather especially, is the head-on collision between the mighty Atlantic and the great cliffs.

The dramatic cliffs at Land's End: the headland may sometimes be fraught with danger in stormy weather, but it will always be a magnet to tourists from all over the world

Penzance

The friendly, bustling town of Penzance enjoys a sunny outlook across the broad waters of Mount's Bay, and the palm trees and brilliantly coloured shrubs of its parks and gardens enhance the 'Cornish Riviera' theme. At the top end of Market Jew Street, stands a statue of Humphry Davy, chemist, scientist and inventor of the miners' safety lamp. Chapel Street, with its mix of Georgian and Regency houses, pubs, antiques shops and art galleries, leads down to the busy harbour, an important focus for the midsummer festival of Golowan, two weeks of lively events that focus on Celtic traditions. Behind the town, lush fields and woods rise steadily to the ancient hills of Celtic Cornwall where stone circles and standing stones of the Bronze Age pepper the moors and where substantial remnants of Iron-Age villages are preserved at sites such as Chysauster and Carn Euny.

Porthcurno

Porthcurno Bay is flanked to the east by the rugged promontory of Treryn Dinas, with its remnants of Iron-Age defensive embankments and its massive Logan Rock, or 'rocking stone'. To the west is the astonishing open-air Minack Theatre, carved out of the cliffs in classical style and famous for its summer performances against the biggest backdrop the Atlantic can offer. Between both headlands is a glorious natural amphitheatre of granite pinnacles and towers, grassy cliffs and beaches of golden shell sand.

St Ives

The harbour area of St Ives draws you in through narrow alleyways and cobbled lanes that have intriguing names such as Salubrious Terrace, Teetotal Street, The Digey; they weave with random charm, dappled with sun and shade, amidst tightly packed granite cottages and houses, art galleries, craft markets, good pubs and restaurants.

The town's beaches are world class. Once it was pilchard fishing that ruled the St Ives harbour area of 'Downlong', but late 19th-century tourism coincided with the arrival of the group of talented English painters, who brought to St Ives the custom of painting outdoors that they had learnt in French painting schools. Today the importance of this artistic tradition is validated in the shape of the acclaimed St Ives Tate Gallery, a specially designed building above the magnificent Porthmeor Beach, which focuses on the mainly abstract work of the St Ives School of painters.

Mousehole

The village of Mousehole lies on the western edge of Mount's Bay. Clustered houses and cottages linked by narrow, sinuous alleyways crouch above a high-walled little harbour; the epitome of quaintness, yet with a robust Cornish identity still intact. The name is pronounced 'Mouzel' and its meaning is obscure. One hundred years ago Mousehole had such a large pilchard-fishing fleet that people walked across the harbour from boat to boat.

A sign of the times – this fishing boat for sale in Mousehole harbour is an all too familiar legacy of modern times for this Cornish village proud of its pilchard-fishing heritage

See Walk A page 52
Zennor and the
Spectacular Coast Path

See Walk B page 53
Hell's Mouth and the
North Cornwall Coast

The narrow backstreets of St Ives, with their typical guesthouses, offer a warm welcome to visitors to this ever-popular town

HIDDEN CORNWALL

Between Truro and Falmouth lies a hidden Cornwall of tidal rivers and creeks that merge into the great natural harbour of Falmouth Estuary. It is a country of mellow woods and lush fields. To the east is the beautiful Roseland Peninsula with its secluded coastline of sandy bays and quiet coves. While Truro maintains its position as the commercial and administrative centre of the county, Falmouth is the main port.

Once, pilchards were brought ashore in their thousands at Mevagissey, but these days sharks are a more common sight

In 1588 the Spanish Armada dropped anchor off Dodman Point before sailing into defeat at the hands of Sir Francis Drake's fleet. The coast path gives access to delightful little coves, with rock pools to explore, but swimming around the point is not safe

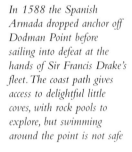

Tourist Information Centres

Falmouth: 28 Killigrew Street (tel: 01326 312300)
Truro: Municipal Buildings, Boscawen Street (tel: 01872 274555)

The Dodman

South of Mevagissey is mighty Dodman Point, a high blunt-headed promontory with a formidable Iron-Age earthwork lying across its broad neck. It encloses the headland's seaward area, which may have been used as a commercial and ceremonial centre in pre-Roman times. The earth banks are over 20ft (6m) high and are 2,000ft (609m) in length.

Falmouth

The estuary of the River Fal is one of the finest natural harbours in the world. Falmouth has seen hard times throughout its history, but vessels of all types and sizes still ply to and fro, and shipbuilding and repairs, cargo handling, and the fuelling and supply of ships still flourish. Falmouth prospered during the late 17th century when it became the packet station from where small, fast-sailing brigantines took mail to British colonies world-wide. The busy streets and narrow alleyways, known as 'Opes', retain a flavour of those salty times and the Falmouth Maritime Museum in Bell's Court outlines the port's maritime history. To the east of Falmouth is the 16th-century Pendennis Castle, while along the town's southern seafront are some fine hotels, and there are several pleasant

beaches. Visitors can make sea and river trips on pleasure launches from Falmouth's piers.

Mevagissey

Mevagissey is the archetypal Cornish fishing port, and pilchard fishing and processing was its main industry from Tudor times until the middle of the 20th century. At one time pilchards were known universally as 'Mevagissey Ducks'. Today, the village still has a busy fishing fleet, although tourism is now its main industry. The timeless charm of its narrow streets, old houses and harbour attracts large numbers of visitors during the busy summer months. A few miles inland from Mevagissey are the Heligan Gardens, remarkable Victorian gardens, rescued during the early 1990s after being totally overgrown for 80 years.

Mylor

Mylor lies on the west bank of the Upper Fal estuary, its boundaries defined by tidal creeks. Mylor Bridge is the gateway to twin peninsulas that have a serenity that is far removed from the unpredictability of the sea. North of Mylor Bridge, the famous Pandora Inn stands at the old ferry crossing of Restronguet Passage.

Helford and The Lizard

South of Falmouth lies The Lizard peninsula, a broad, flat landscape with large areas of heathland and coastal cliffs that support rare plants of international importance. Between Falmouth and The Lizard is the Helford Estuary, presenting a more serene face of maritime Cornwall than that of the exposed craggy Atlantic coasts of the west. The tree-lined muddy creeks of Helford are wonderfully reclusive; Daphne du Maurier based her romantic novel *Frenchman's Creek* on a quiet corner of the Helford. On the north bank of the river is the National Trust's exquisite Glendurgan Garden, and the equally ravishing privately-owned Trebah Garden. Both are open to the public.

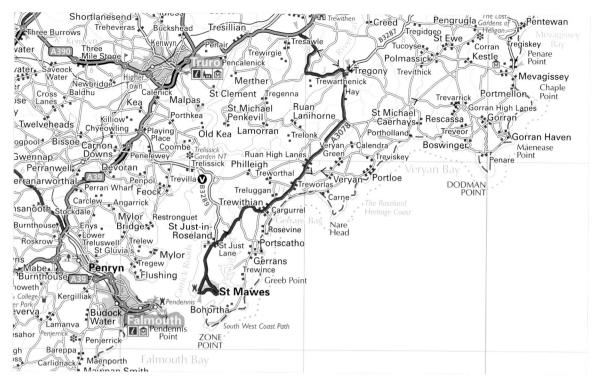

Fishing

Pilchards once shoaled through Cornish waters in their millions, and ports such as Mevagissey, Polperro, Mousehole, St Ives and Port Isaac owed their survival to the annual bounty. But the pilchard shoals decreased by the early decades of this century and Cornwall's fishermen were forced to diversify. They did so with great success, although the pressures of modern bureaucracy and of international competition are eroding the Cornish trade. Today, fishing of all types is carried out by Cornish vessels from the major port of Newlyn, and from smaller harbours such as Mevagissey and Padstow, and even from slipways and beaches at Penberth in Mount's Bay and Cadgwith on The Lizard. Methods used include baiting pots for crabs and lobsters, gill-netting for hake and dogfish, trawling for mackerel or for Dover sole, haddock and cod, and even 'ripping' for squid using multi-hooked weights. Cornish-caught fish are famous for their quality and variety.

St Mawes and the Roseland Peninsula

The Roseland Peninsula makes up the eastern arm of the Fal estuary. At its southern point is St Anthony Head and Zone Point and further north is the yachting haven of St Mawes, with the 16th-century St Mawes Castle close by. Access to The Roseland by road can be north from Truro along a circuitous route or, more directly, south across the River Fal via the King Harry vehicle ferry. There is a charming little church at St Just-in-Roseland, which stands above a narrow creek and is surrounded by exotic shrubs and palm trees.

Trelissick

The National Trust's Trelissick estate comprises 370 acres (150ha) of parkland on the shores of the River Fal, and its great glory lies in the superb ornamental gardens. There are various species of rhododendron, camellias, magnolias and hydrangeas and many South American shrubs of fragile and colourful beauty. The surrounding parkland has been laid out with delightful walks. Facilities for visitors here include a restaurant, a National Trust shop, and an art and craft gallery.

Truro

Cornwall's cathedral city has a reassuring small town atmosphere that enhances rather than diminishes its stature. It is a busy place, the commercial and administrative centre of the county, and the main shopping centre. Truro's Victorian cathedral has given a powerful focus to the city, its tall spires unchallenged by any of the surrounding domestic buildings, its pale stone reflecting the light. By the late 18th century Truro had become the political and cultural centre of Georgian Cornwall. The legacy includes such splendid features as Lemon Street, worthy of Bath and one of the most complete Georgian streets to survive in the country. The Royal Cornwall Museum is in River Street and has an important mineral collection, an art gallery, and displays on Cornish archaeology and mining. The deeply wooded countryside of the Truro and Tresillian Rivers is quickly reached from the city at the charming villages of St Clement and Malpas.

Veryan

The small village of Veryan lies just inland from the lofty Nare Head and the secluded beaches of Gerrans Bay. Veryan's Church of St Symphorian is darkly impressive, its churchyard dense with trees and shrubs. The village is famous for its unique round houses, five in number, with thatched roofs reminiscent of village huts in Africa, each crowned with a cross. They date from the early 19th century and may have been built as curiosities, although local legend claims that their circular design was planned so that the devil couldn't hide in corners.

This magnificent vaulting is a feature of Truro's fine Victorian cathedral

See Walk C page 54
Smugglers' Haunts on the Helford River

CLAY COUNTRY AND ANCIENT PORTS

The south-east coast of Cornwall has none of the raw grandeur of the north and west of the county. Here is a softer beauty of rounded headlands and wooded estuaries. Yet the coastal communities of Looe and Fowey are bustling places with a strong maritime heritage. Inland, at St Austell, and on the fringes of Bodmin Moor, the historic Cornish industries of copper-mining, quarrying and china clay have left their sometimes surreal marks on the landscape.

Clay Country

Around St Austell are the famous clay 'Alps', the white moonscape of ever-changing spoil heaps of the china clay industry. China clay is granite in which the feldspar crystals have decomposed into kaolin. It is found at various locations around Cornwall, but especially on Hensbarrow, the high plateau north of St Austell. Kaolin was used in China for the making of porcelain as early as AD 700. The pure kaolin is separated from quartz-sand and mica, and for years this waste was piled into great conical spoil tips, but concern about landslips saw them being transformed into flat-topped buttes and escarpments.

Clay was exported through the port of Par and from a custom-built dock at Charlestown to the south of St Austell. Today the modern industry produces about three million tons of clay annually.

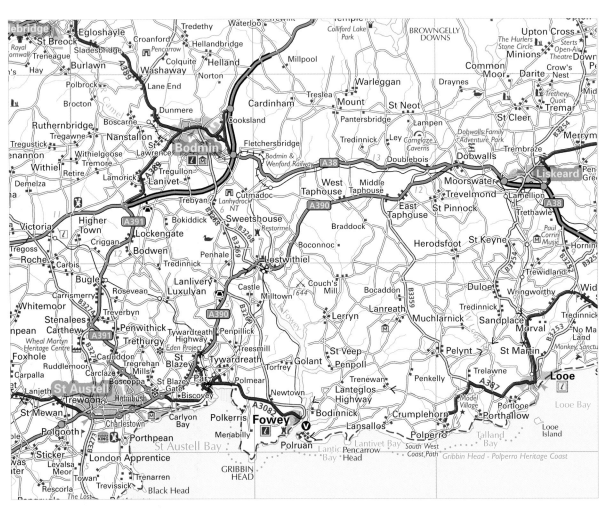

Bodmin

Bodmin was once the county town of Cornwall and although it has lost that status to Truro, it retains a strong Cornish identity. In the 10th century a monastery was founded here, and the enshrining of relics of St Petroc, Cornwall's most important Celtic saint, turned Bodmin into *the* major religious site in medieval times. Religious turbulence seems to have dominated historic Bodmin – the town still celebrates its 'Riding and Heritage Day' in July, an event that includes a mock hanging of the mayor. The tradition dates from the Prayer Book Rebellion of 1549 when Bodmin's mayor, Nicholas Boyer, was hanged for supporting a Cornish revolt against the Reformation. Legend tells that the unsuspecting Boyer first hosted a lavish dinner for the King's executioner, who had cruelly omitted to tell him of his post-prandial fate.

Fowey

Fowey (pronounced 'Foy') seems more of a riverside town than a seaport. Its jostling

The Eden Project

The Eden Project is a spectacular 'global garden' that was opened in March 2001 in what was once an old clay pit near St Austell. It is made up of a series of enormous geodesic domes called 'biomes', in which the environments of the world's major climate zones are re-created, complete with a huge collection of exotic plants and trees. Eden also features exhibitions, music and theatre events, arts projects and educational facilities.

houses look out across the sheltered estuary of the River Fowey to the hazy beauty of Polruan on the opposite shore. But ocean-going ships glide upstream to the clay-loading wharves at Golant and the estuary is full of yachts and pleasure boats in summer. Trafalgar Square, at the heart of the town, has a museum and aquarium, and the dark solidity of St Fimbarrus's Church, with its fine decorated tower, stands here in withdrawn seclusion. Beyond lies the busy Town Quay and the narrow Fore Street which leads on through the attractive streets. High above Fore Street the intriguing Gothic building of Place, home of the Treffry family since the 14th century, overlooks the town.

Tourist Information Centres

Bodmin: Shire House, Mount Folly Square (tel: 01208 76616)
Fowey: The Old Post Office, 4 Custom House Hill (tel: 01726 833616)
Looe: The Guildhall, Fore Street, East Looe (tel: 01503 262072)
Lostwithiel: Community Centre, Liddicoat Road (tel: 01208 872207)

Looe

The East and West Looe Rivers merge at Looe and divide the town into two parts that are connected by a graceful bridge. The sea unites both communities in the business of fishing and a busy fish market brings colour and liveliness to the quay.

East Looe is the larger of the two communities. Behind the harbour front, a maze of streets with connecting alleyways lies between tall colour-washed buildings, busy shops and good pubs and restaurants. A bathing machine for discreet undressing is said to have been sited at Looe Beach as early as 1800, when the Napoleonic Wars made rich British patrons seek home-grown 'Rivieras' as an alternative to the French original.

On the west bank of the West Looe River, Kilminorth Wood is a nature reserve with pleasant woodland walks.

Lostwithiel

Lostwithiel was a flourishing port until the upper reaches of the River Fowey became silted during the 14th century. A fine medieval bridge still spans the river, and another striking feature of the town is the elegant spire of the Church of St Bartholomew. To the north are the ruins of Restormel Castle, the best-preserved military building in Cornwall.

Restormel Castle, looking down over the Fowey Valley, is a remarkably well-preserved survivor from the 13th century, even though it was abandoned some 400 years ago

Minions

Minions, on the south-eastern edge of Bodmin Moor, was a mining village from the mid-19th century until well into the 20th. Near by is the Cheesewring Quarry, from which granite was sent nationwide to build docks, breakwaters and public works such as the Thames Embankment. On the lip of the quarry is The Cheesewring, a rock formation named after its resemblance to a cider press (cheese is the name given to apple pulp).

Polperro

Polperro lies at the seaward end of a steep, narrow valley, which is crammed with pixie-like houses and an enchanting tangle of narrow lanes, leading down to a boat-bobbing harbour. A stream tumbles through the village and into the harbour by an intriguing building known as the House on Props.

St Austell

In medieval times St Austell was just a village, but it was even then a commercial and industrial centre. The handsome Church of the Holy Trinity is a token of early prosperity and opposite the church is the grand Town Hall with its monumental Italianate façade, behind which is the old Market Hall, still intact and with massive wooden roof trusses. The heart of modern St Austell has been sensibly pedestrianised and is a convenient shopping centre for the area.

Wind and weather have eroded all but this fantastic granite pillar, called The Cheesewring, on Stowe's Hill, above the gaping chasm of the Cheesewring Quarry

The maritime heritage of Cornwall is very much apparent all along the coastline. This delightful figure of a sailor can be seen in Polperro

A Great River in the Shadow of Dartmoor

THE RIVER TAMAR is one of the great natural boundaries of the West Country. It provides an emphatic border between Devon and Cornwall, finally merging with Dartmoor's River Tavy to flow into the great gulf of Plymouth Sound. The historic town of Plymouth dominates the region, yet within a few miles of the city boundaries lies Dartmoor's magnificent wilderness, and to either side of Plymouth Sound are remote and beautiful coastlines.

This lofty viaduct spans the River Tamar at Calstock, once a busy industrial centre, but now a quiet and charming village

Calstock

Cornish Calstock faces the fields of Devon across the slow, muddy glide of the River Tamar, spanned here by a tall railway viaduct which dates from 1909 and has a surprising elegance. Calstock was a port, a railway town and an industrial and agricultural centre for hundreds of years. Its commercial stature has declined, but the village has survived and is now a delightful focus of river cruises and more leisurely rail journeys on the picturesque Tamar Valley Line. A short way upstream, and still on the Cornish side, is the National Trust's Cotehele, a well-preserved Elizabethan house of great charm.

Lydford

The village of Lydford lies on the wooded western fringes of Dartmoor. The ruins of Lydford's modest, yet prominent castle makes a pleasing group with the little Church of St Petroc on one side and the village pub on the other. A mile (1.6km) beyond the village is the National Trust's Lydford Gorge. Walkways, requiring some agility in places, lead into the atmospheric Devil's Cauldron, a series of fissures and hollows in the rock through which pours

the River Lyd. A mile downstream is the elegant ribbon of the White Lady Waterfall, which can be viewed by following more amenable pathways.

Noss Mayo

The River Yealm (pronounced 'Yam') reaches the sea between tree-muffled banks at Noss Mayo, an exquisite contrast to the great gaping mouth of Plymouth Sound only a mile (1.6km) or so to the west. The village lies on the south side of the subsidiary Newton Creek, while its larger counterpart, Newton Ferrers, occupies the north bank. Noss Mayo has the advantage of greater seclusion; at its heart is an even smaller creek, around which cottages and houses cluster and where two creekside pubs further enhance the peaceful well-being of it all.

Plymouth

Plymouth is Devon's largest urban area, and the modern city extends inland far beyond its historic waterfront. The original port of Sutton was insignificant until it became the base from which many of the great maritime adventures of the 16th century began. Since that time, Plymouth's naval dockyards have been its life, though they are now in decline. The famous Hoe stands above the breathtaking vista of Plymouth Sound and Drake's Island, while to the north, on the west side of Sutton harbour, is the Barbican area of the old town. It is an intriguing tangle of narrow old streets and alleys such as the cobbled New Street, an Elizabethan survival. The Barbican is further enhanced by its busy fishing harbour and yacht marina and by numerous excellent pubs and restaurants. Beyond the Barbican and The Hoe, the rebuilding of the war-devastated central Plymouth has produced a spacious, modern city centre.

Dartmoor

Dartmoor's status as a National Park indicates its importance as a substantial area of wild land. The moor is remote yet accessible, wild and rugged, yet with peaceful, wooded valleys and sheltered corners – an absorbing landscape of fascinating extremes. The National Park covers an area of 365sq miles (945sq km). The northern half, south of Okehampton and east of Tavistock, is the highest and wildest part, where the great hills of Yes Tor, High Willhays and Hangingstone Hill dominate a rolling wilderness of lonely moorland and granite outcrops. Here the endearing Dartmoor ponies graze amidst a landscape rich in prehistoric remains.

Southern Dartmoor has fewer well-defined summits but is just as wild and remote. It runs south from the bleak village of Princetown, with its grim-walled prison, across the marshy levels of typical *Hound of the Baskervilles* country, and then through the lonely wilderness of Erme Plains to Ivybridge. Eastern Dartmoor is a fascinating landscape where knuckly masses of granite protrude from grassy moorland at Haytor and Fox Tor and where the raw edge of the open moorland is blurred by green valleys. Nestling here are the lovely villages of Chagford, Buckland in the Moor, Widecombe in the Moor and Bovey Tracey.

The Rame Peninsula

The Rame Peninsula is the Cornish western arm of Plymouth Sound. On its eastern side, directly opposite Plymouth, is Mount Edgcumbe, a fine 18th-century house which was restored after it was bombed during the Plymouth blitz of 1941. The formal gardens are magnificent, and most of the large estate has been turned into a country park, with scenic walks along miles of beautiful coastline. To the south is Rame Head, crowned by the ruin of a small chapel. The headland was fortified during the Iron Age and its protective embankments are well preserved. Between Rame Head and Mount Edgcumbe are the linked villages of Cawsand and Kingsand, once great centres of both pilchard fishing and the famous 'free trade' of smuggling.

Shaugh Prior

The valley of the River Plym on Dartmoor's south-western edge is a ragged palimpsest of ancient remains, old tin mines and still active clay workings. The village of Shaugh Prior lies just south of the river and has a proud little church of granite and a good Devon pub. Just west of the village is Shaugh Bridge, at the junction of the Rivers Meavy and Plym, and the broad swathe of woodland that lies upstream from the bridge has a network of pathways. It is owned by the National Trust and includes the towering granite cliffs of The Dewerstone.

Tavistock

Tin, wool and copper brought prosperity to Tavistock over the years. Today, it is a busy market town of great charm, the western gateway to Dartmoor. At the heart of Tavistock is Bedford Square, flanked by some of the finest Victorian town buildings in the West Country, including the Town Hall and the Lloyds TSB Bank and HSBC Bank buildings. On the south side of the square is the Church of St Eustace, dating mainly from the early 16th century, on the site of a 10th-century Benedictine abbey. Fragments of the abbey still survive – within the churchyard, in a nearby gatehouse now known as Betsy Grimbal's Tower, and in the restored medieval gatehouse adjacent to the Town Hall. Behind the Town Hall is an attractive Pannier Market and there are good shops in the busy streets off Bedford Square. At the south-western end of Plymouth Road is a statue of Sir Francis Drake who was born at nearby Crowndale.

Tourist Information Centres

Plymouth: Island House, The Barbican (tel: 01752 304849)
Marsh Mills (tel: 01752 266030)
Tavistock: Town Hall, Bedford Square (seasonal) (tel: 01822 612938)

See Walk E page 56
Among the Tors of Dartmoor

A statue of Tavistock's most famous son, Sir Francis Drake, stands, appropriately, on the Plymouth road. This is the original; the more famous version on Plymouth Hoe is a replica

A LAND OF LEGENDS AND WILDERNESS

The granite wilderness of Bodmin Moor contrasts with spectacular coastal cliffs of dark slate in this dramatic corner of North Cornwall. It is a land that claims King Arthur for its own, and that inspired such poets as Hardy, Tennyson and Betjeman with its mix of wild countryside, wooded valleys and stormy seas.

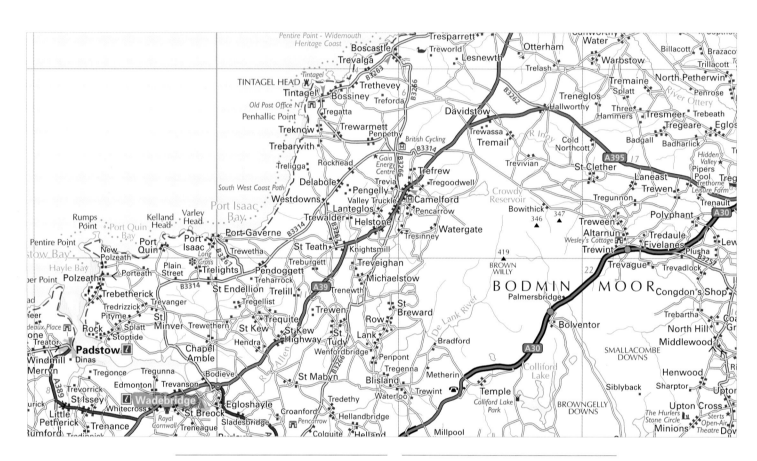

Bodmin Moor

Bodmin Moor is dissected by the busy ribbon of the A30. To the east is lower ground and the wooded folds of the valley of the River Fowey. To the west is true moorland, a surviving wilderness that culminates in the rock-crested hills of Rough Tor (pronounced 'Row Tor') and Brown Willy, both worthy of mountain status, though they are below 2,000ft (609.6m) in height. This is the granite roof of Cornwall, exhilarating country where smooth, whale-backed boulders, silvery white in the sun, protrude from the moorland grass and heather.

Brown Willy is the highest point, less dragon-backed than Rough Tor, but more remote. On the slopes of Rough Tor are numerous remains of ancient field boundaries and Bronze-Age hut circles.

Rough Tor, one of the highest points on Bodmin Moor, towers over a landscape which is best explored on foot or on horseback

Boscastle

At Boscastle harbour the sea fights to get in between high jagged cliffs, and when it does the narrow entrance to the channel reverberates with the crashing of the waves. It is the only natural harbour along 50 miles (80.5km) of savage coastline, but is not an easy one. In Victorian times, when Boscastle was a thriving port, ships were brought in safely by teams of men manipulating ropes that were strung from the vessel to stone bollards on either side of the harbour quays. Today, Boscastle is a popular tourist destination. To the south, Willapark is a high rounded headland, site of an Iron-Age fort. The Valency Valley runs inland from the harbour, its deep woods and singing river, hazy bluebells and dense greenery contrasting with the raw, rugged coast. A little way inland is the

The Rivers Valency and Jordan pour their combined waters into the picturesque and dramatic harbour at Boscastle

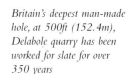

Pentire and The Rumps

The great promontory that makes up the northern arm of the Camel Estuary, and that culminates in Pentire Point and The Rumps, is in the care of the National Trust. The smaller promontory of The Rumps, with its eponymous twin hills, juts into the sea from the larger headland. The Rumps was the site of a substantial fortified settlement of the Iron Age and its earth embankments are visible across the narrow neck of the headland. The great pillow lava cliffs of Pentire are steep and spectacular. In spring and summer the cliffs are a glorious mass of pink thrift, saffron-coloured kidney vetch and the powder-blue squill.

peaceful church of St Juliot where Thomas Hardy met his future wife, Emma.

Launceston

Launceston (pronounced 'Lanson') was once a walled town, a frontier stronghold of the Normans, and the impressive ruins of its Norman motte and bailey castle dominate the surrounding countryside. The sturdy South Gate is a reminder of its former status. There are handsome Georgian buildings round the central area of The Square and there is a good museum in Castle Street. The Church of St Mary Magdalene is distinguished by the wealth of carving on its granite exterior.

Padstow

Padstow stands sheltered deep within the Camel Estuary. It has been a fair refuge for shipping for centuries, though reaching the port across the notorious sandbank, Doom Bar, has caused countless harrowing wrecks and loss of life. Padstow is still a busy fishing port of great character. The tightly-packed houses, in exposed stone or in bright colour-wash, rise in tiers towards the dignified Church of St Petroc. Above the church is Prideaux Place, a fine Tudor building that is still occupied, but is open to the public on certain days. Padstow is famous for its May Day celebration, the

wild processional dance of the 'Obby Oss' that takes place from dawn to dusk to welcome in the summer.

Port Isaac

Port Isaac is a compact little fishing village which, though hugely popular with visitors, has been spared the worst impact of traffic because of sensible parking arrangements. Port Isaac developed as a pilchard fishing port, and slate from the nearby Delabole Quarry was shipped out from the little beach. Narrow alleyways wriggle between the jostling houses.

Tintagel

The skeletal ruins of Tintagel Castle on the awesome headland known as The Island is attraction enough, but Tintagel also has the legendary King Arthur grafted on to its image and is awash with Arthurian enthusiasm. The area has seen much more daring enterprise than the King Arthur industry – when slate was quarried from the cliffs, men worked the sheer faces suspended on ropes. Tintagel is busy during the holiday season, when tolerance of crowds is needed if the undoubted attractions are to be enjoyed. The National Trust's Old Post Office in the main street is a delightfully eccentric building, originally a small manor house of the 14th or 15th century.

Britain's deepest man-made hole, at 500ft (152.4m), Delabole quarry has been worked for slate for over 350 years

No amount of cashing in on the Arthurian connection can detract from the natural splendours of Tintagel's spectacular coastline

Tourist Information Centres

Camelford: North Cornwall Museum, The Clease (seasonal) (tel: 01840 212954)
Launceston: Market House Arcade, Market Street (tel: 01566 772321)
Padstow: Red Brick Building, North Quay (seasonal) (tel: 01841 533449)

HISTORIC PORTS AND FAMOUS RESORTS

The great maritime past of North Devon is still evident today in the historic river ports of Barnstaple and Bideford and throughout the fascinating landscape of the estuary of the Rivers Taw and Torridge. Eastwards along the coast are the famous resorts of Ilfracombe and Combe Martin, within easy distance of the great rolling hills of Exmoor. It is an area of remarkable contrasts that never ceases to surprise and fascinate.

Appledore

Appledore, with its terraces of stone and colour-washed houses along narrow alleys, has a long quay on the broad estuary of the Rivers Taw and Torridge. The background to Appledore's great maritime traditions can be found at the excellent North Devon Maritime Museum in Odun Road.

Barnstaple

Barnstaple, on a crook of land between the Rivers Taw and Yeo, is a town besieged by traffic, but a bypass (due to open in 2004) will do much to enhance the charm and dignity of the old town. Barnstaple's High Street is partly pedestrianised and at its heart is the splendid Town Hall, behind which lies the Pannier Market with its great canopied roof and its arched side entrances facing the row of arcaded shops known as Butcher's Row. Near by, in a quiet leafy square, is the Church of St Peter and Mary Magdalene, with a wonderfully crooked spire. The Heritage Centre in the ornate Queen Anne's Building, and the North Devon Museum relate local history.

Bideford

Bideford once rivalled London as a port and eclipsed Barnstaple at various times throughout centuries of rivalry. The Long Bridge over the Torridge is impressive, and the size of the still active 17th-century quay reflects its importance in the days when Bideford ships sailed far and wide. One, the *Kathleen & May,* can now be seen under restoration at Brunswick Wharf.

Behind the tall buildings that line Quay Road is a network of narrow back streets. Bideford is a bustling little town, with regular pannier markets, and the Burton Art Gallery in the park is worth a visit. The town is one of the access points for the scenic Tarka Trail, recalling the area's link with Henry Williamson's *Tarka the Otter.*

Combe Martin

Combe Martin's main 'street', 1½ miles (2.4km) long, with five name changes, runs down a narrow valley to a pleasant beach between wings of slabby rock. This is a popular traditional seaside resort, and the adjoining coastline is magnificent, especially to the east.

Croyde

Croyde has a real flavour of rural Devon by the sea. A small stream runs alongside the main street, with small bridges to the thatched cottages, and to seaward is the wide Croyde Bay. To the south is the dune country of Braunton Burrows and Saunton Sands; north lies the protective arm of Baggy Point, where steep cliffs rise dramatically from the sea and the clamour of sea birds fills the air above a glittering sea.

Great Torrington

Great Torrington stands high above the Torridge, and the view of riverside fields and woods from the rim of the soaring escarpment is breathtaking. The town centre has the satisfying character of a market square, with a Georgian Town Hall and other fine old buildings. 'Torrington 1646' recalls the last major conflict of the Civil War, encapsulating 17th-century life, and Dartington Crystal offers factory tours, a shop and a restaurant. Just outside the town are the wonderful Rosemoor Gardens.

Exmoor and The Quantocks

Exmoor is an area of windswept high ground pierced by deep river valleys and dimpled with wooded combes. It is an invigoratingly open landscape of wild yet fragile beauty that is also a thriving working environment. Most of Exmoor is contained within the 267sq miles (693sq km) of the Exmoor National Park. To the east, beyond the Brendon Hills lie The Quantocks, a reprise of Exmoor's landscape within a single range of hills. The high ground rises dramatically from the smooth-browed coast, through the lonely heights of The Chains, Dunkery Beacon and Wills Neck, and its turbulent rivers rush to the coast down steep, wooded valleys. To the south the wild moorland merges imperceptibly with the (continued on page 27)

Appledore's strong maritime heritage goes back many centuries, top left; the spire of Barnstaple's church of St Peter and Mary Magdalene is curiously twisted, bottom left; Combe Martin has a delightful little bay at the foot of its long main street, above

(continued from page 26) wooded and cultivated countryside of Devon and Somerset and sends down, from its waterlogged heights, the Rivers Exe and Barle. Embedded in this remarkable landscape is an ancient pattern of prehistoric settlement, of small towns and villages, tiny hamlets and farmsteads. The high moorland is the domain of the red deer and the tough little Exmoor pony, the piping skylark and the circling buzzard. It is the country of the mythical robber barons, the Doones of Badgworthy Water, who inspired R D Blackmore's novel *Lorna Doone*, to which the real Exmoor provides an authentic background.

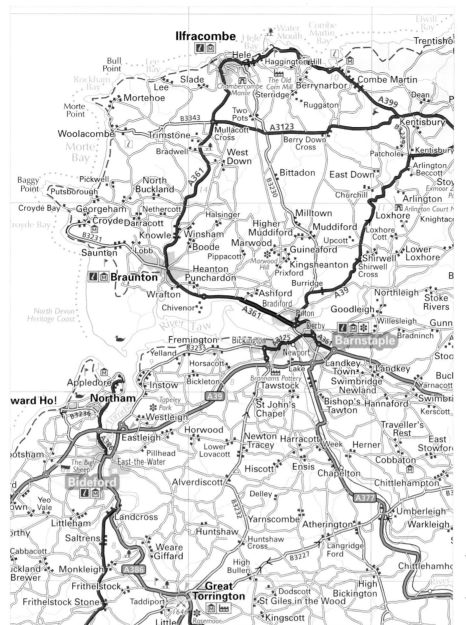

Tourist Information Centres

Barnstaple: 36 Boutport Street (tel: 0870 608 5531)
Bideford: Victoria Park, They Quay (tel: 01237 477676/421853)
Combe Martin: Seacot, Cross Street (seasonal) (tel: 01271 883319)
Ilfracombe: The Landmark, The Seafront (tel: 01271 863001)

See Walk F page 57
The Rocky Coast Beyond Woolacombe

See Walk G page 58
High Moors Above the River Exe

There are panoramic views over Ilfracombe and the beautiful north Devon coast from a number of high hills around the town – and some of them have 'user-friendly' zigzag paths to their summits, with seats along the way

Ilfracombe

High Victorian architecture reached ultimate expression in Ilfracombe's seafront hotels and the grand houses of Torrs Walk. The town is built round a number of distinctive hills, one of which – Lantern Hill – is topped by the tiny lighthouse chapel of St Nicholas. The heart of town is sheltered by Capstone Point, criss-crossed with pleasant walkways and overlooking a fine flower-filled promenade. Here is the aptly-named modern Landmark Theatre complex, and plans for a new pier are on the drawing board.

Old Ilfracombe is gathered round the harbour, the steep, narrow Fore Street and the busy High Street. The hilly nature of the coast denies Ilfracombe the advantages of wide beaches or panoramic views, but the intriguing Tunnels Beach is reached through tunnels in the cliff, and there are more beaches north of the harbour.

LITERARY SETTINGS:
WRITERS IN THE WEST COUNTRY

The poet John Heath-Stubbs captured, grudgingly it seems, both the inspiration and the awe of the wildest parts of the west of England, when he spoke of, '...a hideous and wicked country/Sloping to hateful sunsets and the end of time...' Most writers have been more happily captivated than that. For Heath-Stubbs, it seems, too much raw nature was unnerving. The poet's uneasy words were inspired by the powerful Atlantic coast of Gurnard's Head near Land's End, itself the *Belerium*, the 'Seat of Storms', of the Roman writer Tacitus, an early commentator within the literary setting.

From those Roman times until the present day, the West Country has continued to attract poets and writers. From the beautiful countryside of Dorset, Thomas Hardy created his own landscape of 'Wessex', at the gates of the West Country, yet Hardy too was drawn further west, to the spectacular coastline of North Cornwall. Here he met his wife Emma at the exquisite little church of St Juliot, near Boscastle, and much bitter-sweet romance ensued. The pair strolled out at Beeny Cliff just north of Boscastle and above 'the opal and the sapphire of that wandering western sea' – lines in which Hardy captured the essence of the Cornish coast better, perhaps, than generations of writers since. But before Hardy, the north coast of Devon gave inspiration to Charles Kingsley, who grew up at the exquisite village of Clovelly, lived later at Bideford, and gave the breezy name of Westward Ho! to his most famous novel – and subsequently to a seaside village.

EVOCATIVE LANDSCAPES

The coast of North Cornwall more recently inspired John Betjeman, whose lifelong association with Padstow, further south from Hardy's Beeny Cliff, added a richer, more robust tone to the poetry of suburbia. South of Padstow, the rugged tin-mining coast of St Agnes and Perranporth inspired Winston Graham's marvellous *Poldark* saga, epic narrative of life in 18th- and 19th-century Cornwall from the pen of a modern master.

The Atlantic coast of the west was ever inspirational, but so too were the high moors of Exmoor and the Quantocks. Amidst the wooded combes and soft rolling heaths of The Quantocks, the poet Samuel Taylor Coleridge and his friends, William and Dorothy Wordsworth, found the intensely pastoral inspiration for their great Romantic poems, even before the Lake District claimed them for its own.

Between Exmoor and the sea, Coleridge wrote his fevered, flawed masterpiece

Kubla Khan, its opium-induced fantasies rudely interrupted by the unannounced visit of 'a person from Porlock', who was thus immortalised as perhaps the most notorious full stop in literary history.

Directly inland from Porlock, amidst the heathland wastes of Badgworthy Water, is 'Doone Country', the inspiration for R D Blackmore's famously romantic novel *Lorna Doone*. The legends of the robber Doones of Badgworthy, said to originate from an exiled and disaffected Scottish noble family, was part of Exmoor lore long before Blackmore's masterly embellishment, but with all its lonely, compelling beauty, the moorland wilderness cried out for just such a rattling good tale. Blackmore's novel merged romance with reality and turned into shrines of literary pilgrimage such places as the little church at Oare where Lorna was shot and wounded by Carver Doone during her wedding to John Ridd.

Main picture: Thomas Hardy's study, in Dorchester's County Museum; above left: Samuel Taylor Coleridge; right: R D Blackmore

ROMANCE AND MYSTERY

R D Blackmore's 20th-century counterpart was undoubtedly Daphne du Maurier, whose grasp of the romantic and the picturesque gave rise to such popular novels as *Jamaica Inn* and *Frenchman's Creek*. The former borrowed some of its imagery from the forlorn heights of Cornwall's Bodmin Moor; the latter focused on the tree-shrouded creeks of the Helford River on the county's south-west coast. But du Maurier's true literary setting was the lovely landscape of the River Fowey. Here, amidst the wooded parkland of Menabilly House, were shaped the novels *My Cousin Rachel* and *Rebecca*, who woke and 'dreamt of Manderley'. It was here too that du Maurier was inspired to write the short story about predatory seabirds – subsequently filmed by Alfred Hitchcock as *The Birds* – after watching a cloud of screaming gulls foraging in the wake of a tractor as it drew its plough through the rich earth of the Cornish fields.

Similar inspiration for one of the greatest detective stories ever written, *The Hound of the Baskervilles*, was drawn from Dartmoor by Sir Arthur Conan Doyle. The novelist had stayed on the south-eastern edge of the moor, at Manaton, and had been gripped by the changing moods of its great waste, and by the Gothic atmosphere of the lonely granite tors that rise eerily like castles above the marshy low ground.

While R D Blackmore and Hardy gave us such enduring romantic novels as *Lorna Doone* and *Tess of the D'Urbervilles*, the 20th-century writer John Fowles has established Lyme Regis as the setting for his powerful novel, *The French Lieutenant's Woman*, with its more complex literary romanticism. The novel is now immortalised on film, most dra-

Jane Austen knew Lyme Regis

matically by the image of the tragic heroine, Sarah Woodruff, precarious in body and soul, on the storm-battered harbour wall of The Cobb at Lyme. Here also, the more formal romance of Jane Austen's *Persuasion* depicts Louisa Musgrove falling from the Higher Cobb, intent on landing in Captain Wentworth's arms, but knocking herself unconscious instead

CONTINUING INSPIRATION

The literary inspiration of the West Country continues today, its dramatic landscapes inspiring even those writers whose themes may not necessarily reflect a West-Country setting. Near Land's End lives the novelist John Le Carré, whose books range the cosmopolitan world of Europe and Asia, yet whose hard work of writing is often carried out against the background of the restless Atlantic. A near neighbour of Le Carré's is Derek Tangye, author of a gently sentimental series of autobiographical novels about his beloved West Cornwall. The novelist Mary Wesley lives in Totnes and writes more sophisticated novels than perhaps Daphne du Maurier would ever have dared. Wesley based her scintillating *Camomile Lawn* on Cornwall's Roseland Peninsula.

The popular novelist Rosamund Pilcher has strong connections with the north

Sir Arthur Conan Doyle wrote of the mysteries of brooding Dartmoor

coast of West Cornwall near St Ives, and the film version of her novel *The Shell Seekers* was filmed in the town.

Earlier literary figures connected with the St Ives area included Virginia Woolf, who based her novel *To The Lighthouse* on the nearby Godrevy lighthouse. D H Lawrence lived at Zennor for a period during World War I, hounded by the authorities because of his pacifist stance and his wife Frieda's German nationality. Lawrence described vividly his Cornish experiences in the nightmare sequence in his novel *Kangaroo*.

Locations in the West Country have inspired some of the most seminal works of English poetry and prose. Near Yeovil is East Coker, ancestral home of T S Eliot, whose ashes are buried here, and who attached the name of this archetypal English village to the second poem of his Four Quartets. Coleridge was born at Ottery St Mary. John Galsworthy lived

Top: the Boscastle coastline has romantic associations with Thomas Hardy; above: Doone Valley

for 18 years at Manaton in East Dartmoor, where he worked on *The Forsyte Saga*. At the unlikely setting of nearby Chagford, Evelyn Waugh wrote *Brideshead Revisited*, whose characters would have felt positively uneasy amidst Dartmoor's ruggedness. Torquay was the birthplace of Agatha Christie, who also lived on the inspiring Dart Estuary and wrote several of her famous crime novels on the nearby Burgh Island off Salcombe. And in the delightful valleys of the Rivers Taw and Torridge in North Devon Henry Williamson wrote *Tarka The Otter* and *Salar The Salmon*.

See Walk H page 59
In Search of Lorna Doone on Exmoor

REGENCY RESORTS AND A GREAT CATHEDRAL

T he south-east coast of Devon lies within the sheltering arm of Lyme Bay. The climate is benign, and there is a fascinating variety of coastal landscape, from the dazzling white of Beer's chalk cliffs to the long shingle beaches of Sidmouth and Budleigh Salterton, framed between great red cliffs. Inland are quiet, meandering lanes, sleepy villages and busy country towns. The focus of the region is the county town of Exeter, with its magnificent 14th-century cathedral and historic quayside.

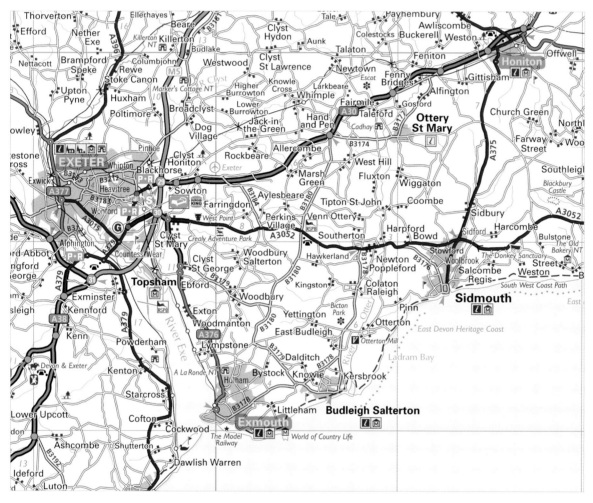

Dawlish Warren

The resort of Dawlish closes down in winter, but on the great sand spit that projects for 1½ miles (2.4km) into the Exe Estuary there is wildlife in profusion all year round. The area was used as a rabbit warren in the 18th century, hence the name. Today the 500 acres (200ha) of mudflats, dunes and saltmarshes is a major nature reserve where huge numbers of birds – grey plovers, dunlin, black-tailed godwits, curlews, Brent geese, sandpipers and more – congregate. The Warren is also noted for its plant life and its rare butterflies.

Dignified Budleigh Salterton derives its name from its medieval salt-panning, and its character from Victorian development

Budleigh Salterton

Budleigh Salterton developed as a Victorian resort along the same lines as Torquay and Sidmouth, though on a less grand scale. Today it has a detached, genteel air, less commercialised than its Torbay neighbours. The long gentle curve of the shingle beach runs from the mouth of the River Otter to the slopes of the wooded West Down. Budleigh has handsome Victorian villas, and several Regency period *cottage ornées*, mock-rustic buildings with surprising thatch crowning Gothic-style façades.

Exeter

Exeter was the Roman headquarters of the south-west, and the heart of the modern city lies within a surviving framework of its much-restored Roman walls. The focus of Exeter is the cathedral, an outstanding building within a splendid Close. The powerful 12th-century towers survive, and the interior is a feast of 13th-century Gothic design – overall a masterpiece of English architecture. The city's civic buildings complement the cathedral with their mix of period styles. The remodelling of

Tourist Information Centres

Budleigh Salterton: Fore Street (tel: 01395 445275)

Exeter: Civic Centre, Paris Street (tel: 01392 265700)

Exmouth: Alexandra Terrace (tel: 01935 222299)

Honiton: Lace Walk Car Park (tel: 01404 43716)

Ottery St Mary: 106 Broad Street (tel: 01404 813964)

Sidmouth: Ham Lane (tel: 01395 516441

The English Riviera

To be called 'The English Riviera' is giving more than a degree of latitude to publicity. But Torquay – or more precisely Torbay, of which Torquay is emphatically the focus – is a triumph of robust self-confidence. The originally modest 'Tor Quay' developed from being a Navy supply depot during the Napoleonic Wars to being a rest centre for officers and their families. Victorian fashion confirmed Torquay's future as a resort. Modern Torquay is perhaps too over-powering for some, but a healthy prosperity has saved it and its neighbour, Paignton, from becoming too brash. There are wide promenades, palm-fringed gardens and parks, and handsome 19th-century Italianate villas to take the edge off the more brutal modern buildings that have elbowed their way in. Torbay as a whole caters for all tastes in holidaymaking.

the bomb-damaged city centre has, in the main, been a happy one. The many attractions include the Historic Quayside, with its waterside paths, boat trips and Visitor Centre, the Royal Albert Memorial Museum and the underground passages.

Exmouth

Exmouth, at the broad, sandy mouth of the Exe Estuary, has an open, airy feel to its beaches and promenade. Above the seafront are dignified Georgian houses, while the eastern end of the town is a tight network of small streets around the harbour and dock area. Just outside the town is the National Trust's A La Ronde, a delightfully eccentric building, with interior feather friezes and shell gallery.

Honiton

Honiton, with its wide High Street, presents the face of a Georgian town, fires having destroyed the medieval original. Old coaching yards provide attractive adjuncts, and there is a lively pannier market twice a week. Honiton is famed for its elegant lace, a cottage industry that reached its zenith with the making of Queen Victoria's wedding veil, and the Allhallows Museum in High Street has excellent displays of lace making. The town has latterly become a centre for antiques and antiquarian books, with over 30 shops and regular auctions.

Ottery St Mary

Ottery St Mary's handsome church replicates, in a minor way, the great cathedral of Exeter. It is a stately focus for Ottery's attractive townscape, with its sloping square in the setting of Silver Street and Gold Street, the 18th-century Paternoster Ro, and Mill Street, leading to the River Otter. The poet Samuel Taylor Coleridge was born in Ottery amidst these evocative surroundings. The annual Tar Barrel Rolling event on 5 November is a popular attraction. To the north-west is Cadhay (occasionally open), a small Tudor manor house with a charming inner courtyard.

Sidmouth

Sidmouth is beautifully framed between high cliffs of red marl. The delightful esplanade is a mile (1.6km) long, and fishing boats are still launched from the beach. Sidmouth was a Regency resort of great style and the modern town retains the self-assurance and gentility of those days. The town has been carefully and imaginatively preserved. Handsome Victorian architecture has helped to maintain the image, expressed by the restrained, balconied hotels and the fine Georgian houses that line the seafront. A recurring motif of Sidmouth is the *cottage ornée*, an affectation of the Regency period. Sidmouth is the venue for a week-long International Folk Festival in early August each year.

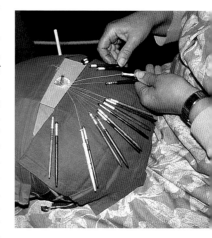

Delicate Honiton Lace is world famous and the craft once formed the town's main occupation. Today it is perpetuated by hobbyists, one of whom made the lace for a new jabot for the Speaker of the House of Commons

At the heart of the busy city centre, Exeter's Cathedral Close is a delight, with old houses, good restaurants and quality shops overlooking the spacious lawns around the magnificent cathedral

DORSET'S HERITAGE COAST

T he shores of Lyme Bay are a fascinating mix of fossil-bearing rocks, land-slipped cliffs and chalk headlands. To the east lies Bridport; further west is Lyme Regis, a famous resort of great character, and on the far western edge of the bay, just within the Devon border, is the charming little town of Beer, in the shelter of the most westerly chalk cliffs in England.

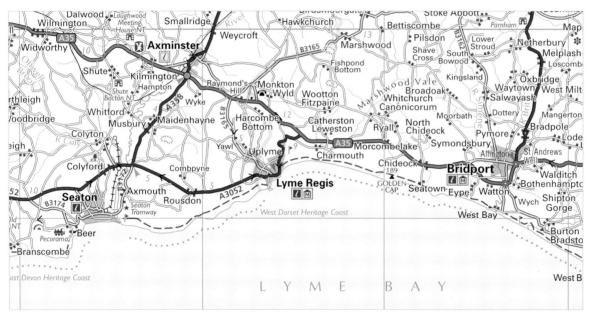

Beer's bright chalk cliffs are in sharp contrast with the red sandstone of its neighbours. Beer stone, quarried near by, has been much prized for building and monumental carving since Roman times

Axminster

Axminster was destroyed by fire during the Civil War and its oldest surviving houses are from the 18th and 19th centuries; they make a surprisingly serene townscape in spite of the busy flow of traffic on the main through road. The dignified Church of St Mary on its churchyard green dominates Trinity Square at the centre of the town. Axminster's fame rests on carpet-making. The industry began in 1755 in Silver Street, the narrow street running south from Trinity Square, but safety regulations introduced in the 1990s put an end to the popular factory tours.

Beer

The rather lip-smacking name of Beer, sheltered by the high chalk cliffs of Beer Head to the west, comes from the Anglo-Saxon word *beare*, meaning grove. Mosaic-walled cottages of flint and stone line the long ramble of Fore Street, down which a small stream tumbles through stone conduits. Common Lane rises from the seaward end of Fore Street past a terrace of delightful cottages, also faced with flint, but with brick trim. Beer beach is a wide apron of shingle upon which fishing boats with broad undercut sterns are hauled up by a capstan engine. The Jubilee Gardens are cut into the cliff face behind the beach. Close to the town are the Beer Quarry Caves, worked since Roman times, from which the distinctive local stone was taken for such eminent buildings as Exeter Cathedral.

Fossils

Fossils are the remnants of ancient animals and plants preserved within sediments that were subsequently transformed into rock, and the cliffs between Lyme Regis and Charmouth are well known for their fossils. These rocks are of the Jurassic period of 190 million years ago, and are composed of shale with alternate bands of limestone, laid down by the ancient sea that once covered most of England and Wales. Most of the fossils here are of ammonites – shell-dwelling creatures – and of primitive fish and marine reptiles. Some discoveries have been spectacular. A local woman, Mary Anning, became one of the most accomplished amateur collectors and was held in great regard by the leading palaeontologists of the day. She discovered a rare fossil of a winged lizard in 1828. Good collections of fossils are displayed in Lyme Regis at the museum in Bridge Street and at Dinosaurland in Coombe Street.

The Free Traders

A romantic image of smuggling has been especially associated with the West Country for generations. Proximity to France, coupled with the skills of West-Country seamen made this coast the ideal arena for 'free trade'. Smuggling flourished during the 18th and early 19th centuries as a reaction to punitive taxes on imported goods. It had a sheen of respectability because so many of the goods were luxury items, and the wealthy had no qualms about buying smuggled goods. Smuggling still goes on around these shores, but drug trafficking has cast a disturbing light on the romance of 'free trade'.

Colyton's unusual memorial commemorates local men who lost their lives in the ill-fated 'Pitchfork Rebellion' of 1685, when the Duke of Monmouth failed to sieze the throne

Bridport

Big, broad streets characterise Bridport, Hardy's 'Port Bredy' in his story *Fellow Townsmen*. It is a town with a sturdy tradition of making nets and rope – considered the best in England – that dates from at least the 11th century and continues to this day. The modern town tends to merge with suburbs and fast main roads, but the flavour of an older Bridport is still captured in side streets and alleyways. The local museum was updated in 2000.

Bridport Harbour, rewritten as West Bay by the hand of Victorian tourism, is a lively link that ties what is essentially a country town to the sea. More recently it has found fame as the location of the BBC series, 'Harbour Lights', and has an exhibition on the filming.

Colyton

Colyton, a few miles inland from Seaton, has busy sawmills, corn mills and a tannery, and is surrounded by modern housing. And yet it has one of the loveliest town centres in all of Devon and an outer hinterland of wooded hills, lush fields and wandering lanes. A sloping site adds to the individuality of the Market Place, where the façade of the 17th-century Church House strikes a satisfying note. Behind Church House stands the Church of St Andrew, the octagonal top storey of its crossing tower adding a Continental touch. The tower is crowned by a remarkably confident weathercock.

Lyme Regis

Stylish Lyme Regis has a genteel, subdued atmosphere even when its Marine Parade is crowded with people. Its best buildings are Georgian, such as those in Broad Street, although their handsome façades hide older houses. The great arm of Lyme's harbour-cum-breakwater, The Cobb, protects the town from the worst of the prevailing south-westerly winds, famously depicted framing the cloaked and forlorn figure of Meryl Streep as Sarah Woodruff in the film of John Fowles' *The French Lieutenant's Woman*. Jane Austen based part of *Persuasion* on Lyme Regis, having stayed in the town in 1803-4.

Lyme's early prosperity was built on world-wide trade that merged at times with lucrative smuggling. Both enterprises declined, but the town thrived on the early development of tourism, coupled with an influx of palaeontologists, attracted by Lyme's fossil sites in Black Ven Cliff.

The late 1990s saw the opening of Gun Cliff Walk, a ruggedly attractive new promenade, built to disguise the town's state-of-the-art resewerage works – which have also brought the local bathing waters up to EC standards. West of Lyme is The Undercliff, a green jungle of land-slipped woods; to the east is the shining summit of Golden Cap, towering above the sea.

Seaton

Seaton's seemingly endless pebble beach, backed by a rather featureless seafront, is well-framed between the slumped cliffs of The Undercliff National Nature Reserve to the east and Beer Head to the west. Old Seaton survives at the western end of the esplanade, where the narrow Fore Street winds down to Marine Place and to a refreshing open space above the sea. At the east end of the beach the River Axe flows quietly into the sea through the old harbour, and the enduringly popular Seaton Tramway operates open-topped and enclosed trams on a 3-mile (5km) route along the lovely Axe Valley to Colyton. Other attractions include a traditional cider-maker and the Sea Discover Centre, featuring the marine life of Lyme Bay.

A port since medieval times, Lyme Regis was one of the first towns along this coast to develop as a seaside resort

Tourist Information Centres

Axminster: The Old Court House, Church Street (seasonal), (tel: 01297 34386)
Bridport: 32 South Street (tel: 01308 24901)
Lyme Regis: Guildhall Cottage, Church Street (tel: 01297 442138)
Seaton: The Underfleet (tel: 01297 21660)

Seaton's electric tramway takes summer visitors to Colyton and back alongside the River Axe, with lots of wildlife to see along the way

GOLDEN BEACHES, GOLDEN VILLAGES

From the glorious golden stone of Abbotsbury to bleak grey Portland, from buckets and spades at Weymouth to Dorchester's Roman digs, this popular slice of south Dorset offers some colourful contrasts. There are surprises too: a unique swannery; a mysterious ancient giant; a castle that is not a castle, and the pebble beach to end all pebble beaches.

Abbotsbury

Abbotsbury is a lovely thatched, golden ironstone village in a valley of outstanding natural beauty. Its abbey is now a ruin and only the mighty 15th-century thatched Tithe Barn, housing a museum of agricultural and rural bygones, still stands tall.

By the sea, on a lagoon protected by Chesil Beach (see below), is the Abbotsbury Swannery, once a fresh food larder for the abbots, and now a unique visitor attraction. Swans have been kept here for 600 years and the setting is as tranquil and delightful as the birds are graceful. A flower-lined path alongside a stream leads to the lagoon where up to 600 swans gather, and there are walkways through the reedbed. On the edge of the village the Abbotsbury Sub-Tropical Gardens have evolved from an 18th-century walled garden into an award-winning collection of rare and exotic plants.

Abbotsbury has the only managed colonial herd of mute swans – over 600 of them – and they can be viewed at close quarters in their watery reserve behind Chesil Beach

Cerne Abbas

The picturesque village of Cerne Abbas hosts a glorious collection of architectural styles; from golden ironstone houses to colour-washed cottages, the old chequered flint and sandstone courthouse and the beamed and jettied Pitchmarket on Abbey Street. At the top of this street is a splendidly restored house, built around the 15th-century gateway of the old abbey. The adjacent Abbot's Porch and the Abbey Guest House are open to visitors.

Just outside the village is the viewing point for the famous Cerne Giant, a 180-ft (54.8m) tall chalk figure of a naked man with a large erect phallus, brandishing a 120-ft (36.6m) long club. The style of the figure suggests that the giant may be of Romano-British origin.

Tourist Information Centres

Dorchester: Unit 11, Antelope Walk
(tel: 01305 267992)
Portland: Portland Bill Lighthouse (seasonal)
(tel: 01305 861233)
Weymouth: The King's Statue, The Esplanade
(tel: 01305 785747)

Chesil Beach

In Old English 'chesil' means shingle, but this is no ordinary shingle beach. It comprises an 18-mile (28.8km) bank of pebbles up to 40ft (12.2m) high and 150–200yds (137–183m) wide, enclosing the Fleet Lagoon (where an oyster farm can be visited). The stones are naturally graded by powerful currents – swimming is not advised here – and decrease from cannonball-sized in the east to pea-sized in the west. The best view is from Portland.

Dorchester

The 'Casterbridge' of Thomas Hardy's novels is stamped with his signature: the statue at the top of the town; his study, reconstructed in the museum; St Peter's Church, which he helped to restore; Max Gate, the house he designed and occupied until his death in 1928, and any number of references along the High Street. But Dorchester is much more. The Dorset County Museum introduces the Roman town (*Durnovaria*), with excellent mosaics, and the Roman boundaries can be followed along traffic-free avenues to the remains of a Roman town house. The dark side of

The famous Cerne Giant is thought to be associated with fertility rites, endorsing the popular image of primitive man wooing his intended with an enormous club

Maiden Castle

Maiden Castle is not actually a castle at all, it is the finest earthworks (ie a fortification made of earth) in Britain. When built, largely in the 1st century BC, this hilltop retreat was fortified with ramparts and complex chicane-style entrances, easily defended against primitive attackers, though not against the technically advanced Roman legions, who in AD 43 slaughtered its inhabitants. All structures have long gone but its series of concentric rings, covering 115 acres (47ha), are still impressive. Try to view the hillfort in the early morning or early evening light, when the shadows accentuate the rings.

Historic and Literary Houses

Dorchester is ringed by a number of inviting houses. Athelhampton (5 miles/8km north-east) is probably the finest, a romantic 15th-century manor with a magnificent medieval hall. Thomas Hardy described 16th-century Wolfeton (1½ miles/ 2.4km north) as an 'ivied manor house flanked by battlemented towers'. Hardy's Cottage, his birthplace, is at Higher Bock-hampton (3 miles/ 4.8km north-east).

See Walk K page 61
The Mysterious Cerne Abbas Giant

See Walk L page 62
Dorset Heaths of Thomas Hardy

The award-winning Dorset County Museum in Dorchester is a must for anyone interested in the archaeology of the county

Dorchester's history is in its unsavoury judicial role. In the Old Crown Court the six Tolpuddle Martyrs were sentenced to deportation in 1834 for forming a trade union (court and cells are open to the public) and opposite, in what is now Judge Jeffrey's Restaurant, is where the infamous judge lodged while conducting the Bloody Assizes in 1685, meting out vicious retribution (74 deaths and 175 deportations) on the supporters of the unsuccessful bid for the throne by the Duke of Monmouth.

Portland

Portland, linked to the mainland only by a causeway, is famous for its stone, which was used in such diverse buildings as St Paul's Cathedral in London and the UN Building in New York. Some quarries are still working, others have been colonised by a profusion of wild flowers and butterflies, and one has become an imaginative sculpture park. Many areas are designated Sites of Special Scientific Interest and there are excellent opportunities for birdwatching, fossil-hunting, rock-climbing and walking. Down on the coast, the former Naval Air Station has become a world-class diving and watersports centre.

Weymouth

George III first popularised sea bathing at Weymouth in 1798 and he is honoured by a jolly statue on the Esplanade. Weymouth is a lively seaside resort with up-to-the-minute attractions and events, a long golden beach and a picturesque harbour busy with small fishing boats. Nothe Fort is now a Museum of Coastal Defence, while Brewer's Quay, a handsomely redeveloped Victorian brewery, houses shops, the Weymouth Museum, a multi-media Timewalk and other attractions. At the east end of the beach Weymouth Sea Life Park is within Lodmore Country Park.

Portland is a remarkable outcrop, and its famous stone has been used in some of Britain's most splendid buildings

FROM BOURNEMOUTH ROCK TO PURBECK STONE

The contrasting faces of the British seaside lie along this short stretch of coast; from Bournemouth's lively beaches and genteel gardens, to unspoiled Studland and the natural wild haven of Brownsea Island. Poole offers a maritime flavour, while inland the picturesque market towns of east Dorset and the Isle of Purbeck boast ancient churches and ruined castles.

Natural Beauty

Just west of Corfe Castle lies Lulworth Cove, a perfect circle of beach and one of southern England's most photographed spots. The cliff archway of adjacent Durdle Door is the most spectacular of the many sea- and wind-eroded rock formations to be found here.

The natural beauty of Poole Harbour and its islands is remarkable for a very different reason; over 100 million barrels of oil have been taken from here in recent years, making it the largest on-shore oilfield in Western Europe, and yet its exploitation has been rendered almost invisible by painstaking environmental management.

Miles of golden sands stretch around the bay at Bournemouth, now a thriving conference venue as well as an enduringly popular resort

Tourist Information Centres

Bournemouth:
Westover Road
(tel: 0906 802 0234)
Christchurch:
23 High Street
(tel: 01202 471780)
Poole: 4 High Street
(tel: 01202 253253)
Wareham: Holy Trinity Church, South Street
(tel: 01929 552740)
Wimborne Minster:
29 High Street,
(tel: 01202 886116)

Bournemouth

Popular since the early 19th century (Queen Victoria once recommended it to Disraeli), Bournemouth has shaken off its one-time image as a refuge for the elderly and is now a lively, year-round resort for all ages. It's natural features – 7 miles (11km) of glorious sands backed by steep 'chines' – remain the focus of the town, and beautiful gardens, illuminated by candles after dark, snake their way up the hillside. The town itself has excellent shopping and a huge variety of restaurants. The area around the pier has a fairground atmosphere in summer, with its merry-go-round, street performers and Friday night fireworks. Near by are the Oceanarium and the Waterfront Complex. The cultural counterpoint to all this is the excellent Russell-Cotes Art Gallery and Museum.

Christchurch

Christchurch takes its name from its priory, the longest parish church in England, and also one of the most impressive. Its Norman origins are clearly visible. Next to the priory are other reminders of the Conquest: the keep of the Norman castle and the 'Norman House', both in picturesque ruins.

From here, follow the shady Convent Walk beside the peaceful old mill stream to the Town Quay, a charming pastoral scene where lawns and gardens meet slow-flowing waters, dotted with small pleasure craft, ducks and swans. The Edwardian power station now houses the Museum of Electricity, with nostalgic exhibits and interactive experiments. Water-powered Place Mill has milling artefacts, arts and crafts, and the Red House Museum and Gardens can be found on Quay Road.

Corfe Castle

Corfe Castle is one of the most dramatic and picturesque spots in the whole south-west. Built high on a hill in 1080–1105, it dominated this region until it was slighted after the Civil War. Now it is a romantic ruin, offering marvellous views and dark distant memories – the tragic boy-king Edward (the Martyr) was murdered here in AD 978. The village below is an attractive collection of low stone houses, many of which date from the 16th to 18th centuries. There is a model village, a small museum in the tiny Town Hall and steam train rides on the reopened Swanage–Wareham Railway.

Remote and ruined now, Corfe Castle was historically an important stronghold, its hill-top site first fortified by King Alfred against the Danes

Kingston Lacey

This 17th-century mansion is owned by the National Trust and following major restoration its ornate interiors gleam brilliantly – the Spanish Room, in gilded leather with a gilded ceiling from a Venetian palace, is a highlight. The star attraction, however, is the art collection, which includes works by Van Dyck, Rubens, Titian, Lely, Lawrence and Jan Brueghel the Elder. There is a fine collection of Egyptian artefacts too. When you feel a surfeit of riches, take a breather in the grounds where Red Devon cattle graze.

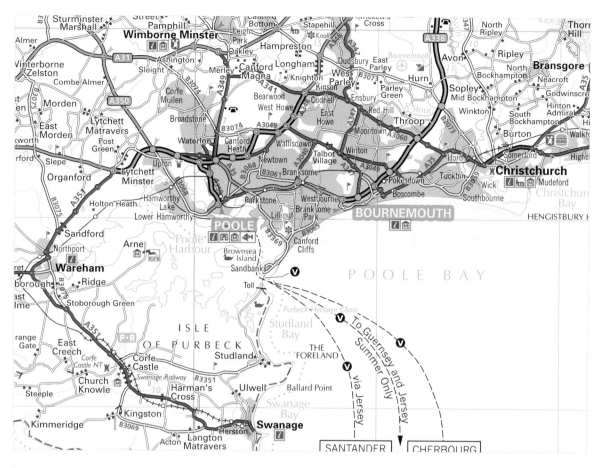

Compton Acres actually covers over nine acres (3.6ha), a colourful series of beautiful gardens with wonderful views over Poole Harbour and the Purbeck Hills

Poole

Poole Harbour is the second largest natural harbour in the world (after Sydney) and the jewel in its crown is Brownsea Island, a 500-acre (200ha) nature reserve, home to deer, rare red squirrel and waterfowl. Poole Quay, still a working harbour, is undergoing development that will provide a smart marina for the local fishing fleet and pleasure craft. The Waterfront Museum relates the town's colourful maritime history, while its adjunct, 15th-century Scaplen's Court, is also dedicated to local history. Poole Pottery offers an interesting factory tour and there is an Aquarium and Serpentarium. One of Europe's finest gardens is Compton Acres, where a number of gardens have been reproduced in colourful and magnificent detail. In 2001 their 80th anniversary was marked with two new gardens – the Sensory Sculpture Garden and the Deer Sanctuary, with a tree-top lookout.

Wareham

The Quay at Wareham features on countless calendars. Across the languorous River Frome, plied by pleasure craft, is the picture-perfect square, with its old granary house backed by the Anglo-Saxon church and priory of Lady St Mary. The church holds a stone coffin that is popularly supposed to be that of Edward the Martyr (see Corfe Castle opposite). St Martin's, at the north end of the High Street also dates from Saxon times and has an impressive memorial to T E Lawrence (of Arabia), who also features in the town's museum.

Wimborne Minster

Narrow Georgian streets and hidden courtyards distinguish this charming market town, and at its heart stands the sturdy and attractive Minster Church of St Cuthburga, founded in AD 705. Seek out its astronomical clock, its chained library and, on the outside, the colourful Quarter Jack figure which strikes the church bell every 15 minutes. Opposite the church is the excellent Priest's House Museum, portraying 400 years of East Dorset history.

CAVERNS AND CATHEDRALS; CHEESE AND WINE

T he Mendip Hills are a welcome contrast to the flatness of the Somerset Levels. The craggy valleys of Cheddar and Burrington Combe slice deeply into their smooth flanks and, on the lush, southern slopes, strawberries, apples and grapes flourish. To the south lies Wells, site of a magnificent cathedral. Further south again is Glastonbury, with its ruined abbey and the mysterious Glastonbury Tor, focus of both Christian and Arthurian legends.

Wookey Hole

Wookey Hole is a system of three underground chambers through which the River Axe flows into a lake from the heart of the Mendip Hills. There is strong evidence of Iron-Age, and possibly earlier Stone-Age occupation. The attractions of the Wookey Hole complex are delightfully bizarre. They include the essential guided tour of the floodlit caves along walkways and past fanciful silhouettes and colourful features. At the surface there is a Victorian papermill, a fairground exhibition with several rides from around the turn of the century, an old Penny Arcade and the Magical Mirror Maze.

Tourist Information Centres

Cheddar: The Gorge (seasonal) (tel: 01934 744071)
Glastonbury: The Tribunal, 9 High Street (tel: 01458 832954)
Sedgemoor Services: Somerset Visitor Centre, M5 South, near Axbridge (tel: 01934 750833)
Shepton Mallet: 70 High Street (tel: 01749 345258)
Taunton: Paul Street (tel: 01823 274785)
Wells: Town Hall, Market Place (tel: 01749 672552)

King John would never have seen the three-storey timber-framed house in Axbridge that bears his name – it was built around the year 1500 for a Tudor merchant of the town

Axbridge

Axbridge lies between the Mendips and the motorway. The Square, at the heart of the village, draws in the converging streets to a happy centre of medieval design. It is overlooked by the Church of St John the Baptist, and two ancient open wells lie beneath arches in the churchyard wall. The most striking building is King John's Hunting Lodge (National Trust) at the corner of High Street and The Square. Timber-framed and beautifully preserved, it now houses a good museum. The name is rather misleading, though – King John predated the building by 300 years, but it was certainly once an inn, coincidentally called the King's Head.

Cheddar

To give a name to a world-famous cheese is recognition enough for any place, but Cheddar is also noted for the spectacular scenery of the great gorge that slices into the flanks of the gentle Mendip Hills. The vast limestone bluffs that rise from the roadside are marble-white where the rock is exposed, but in places are draped with ivy and with precariously rooted trees. The showcaves of the lower gorge are an enduring tourist attraction, and these have been joined by other places to visit, including cheese-makers. There are several footpaths around and above the gorge and some spectacular views, notably from the top of Jacob's Ladder.

The Mendip Hills

The Mendips, rising to about 1,000ft (300m), were once islands in a vast prehistoric lake. The limestone flanks of the hills are pierced by great ravines – Cheddar Gorge, Ebbor Gorge, Burrington Combe – and are riddled with the serpentine cave systems which make these hills so popular with cavers. Villages such as Priddy stand at the heart of grassy sheep country, where Bronze-Age burial mounds and old lead workings, dating from Roman to Victorian times, lie amidst the lonely fields. Along the south-facing slopes of the Mendips, strawberries are grown and Mendip vineyards produce good English wines to match Somerset's famous cider.

Glastonbury

Christian symbolism vies with Arthurian legend and 'new age' culture in the shadow of the enigmatic Glastonbury Tor. Joseph of Arimathea is said to have brought the Holy Grail to Glastonbury, and from his staff is said to have sprung the original Glastonbury Thorn. The great abbey was founded by King Ine in AD 700. In 1191, after a destructive fire, the monks claimed to have discovered the bones of Arthur and Guinevere in the abbey grounds, thus boosting its fading appeal as a place of pilgrimage. Outstanding town buildings include the Elizabethan George and Pilgrim Hotel, the Tribunal, with its Somerset Rural Life Museum and the Peat Moors Centre. Traditional shops are interspersed with those giving off the smell of incense and the sounds of meditation music.

Shepton Mallet

Shepton Mallet's market place has lost some of its character, but retains a number of listed buildings, including the 15th-century Shambles, an open-sided market stall. From here streets and alleyways run to the River Sheppey. The market cross, with its three-stage pinnacle and arcaded base, is of 15th-century design, and was partly rebuilt in the 19th century. Wealth from the medieval wool industry paid for the splendid Church of SS Peter and Paul.

Street

Street and feet go together. The town's modern development came through the family of Cyrus Clark, which for generations dominated the footwear market in Britain. The family's strange mixture of austere Quakerism and generous paternalism has left Street with few pubs, but with an excellent library, swimming pools and a theatre among its 'improv-

ing' facilities. There is a shoe museum in High Street, and Clark's Village of factory outlet shops is a great attraction.

Wells

The glory of Wells is its magnificent cathedral and attendant ecclesiastical buildings – the merging of solid dignity with elegance in stone. The city, England's smallest, complements all this with unpretentious charm. The spacious Market Place has the style of a piazza, and gives access to the exhilarating expanse of the cathedral green through a narrow archway known as Penniless Porch. From the green, the splendour of the cathedral's west front is overwhelming. North of the cathedral is Vicar's Close, a glorious time capsule from the Middle Ages, though remodelled and restored in part. To the south the Bishop's Palace sits graciously within its moat.

Glastonbury Tor, rising out of the flat Somerset Levels, is redolent with the myths and legends of the Isle of Avalon and the Celtic Otherworld. For the less romantically inclined, there are wonderful views from its summit

See Walk P page 65
The Other Sides to Cheddar Gorge

St Andrew's Well, one of the springs that gave the little city of Wells its name, is in the shadow of the magnificent cathedral

CAMELOT COUNTRY

The border between Somerset and Dorset passes through a serene and beautiful landscape which is famous for its associations with the legendary King Arthur and his court of Camelot. It is a land of great houses such as Montacute, of splendid abbeys and churches at Sherborne and North Cadbury, and of villages of lovely cottages in honey-coloured stone from Ham Hill.

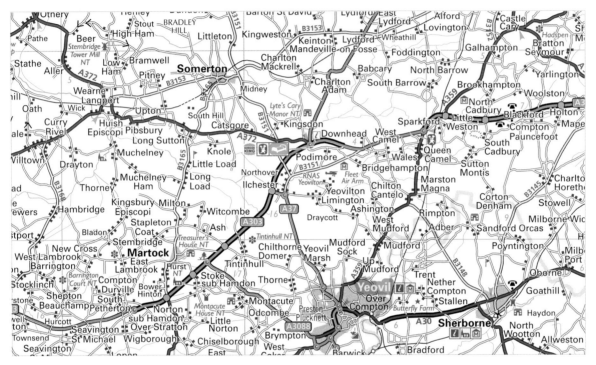

Golden Stone

Five miles (8km) to the west of Yeovil, above Montacute and Tintinhull, stands Ham Hill, site of a vast fortified settlement that rivals Cadbury Castle in size and that was used from Stone-Age times to the Roman period. Over the years the hill-top was farmed intensively and parts were used as rabbit warrens, but most significantly it was used for the quarrying of its building stone. The rock of Ham Hill was deposited 170 million years ago as sediments of shell and sand on the bed of a warm and shallow sea, subsequently compressed and cemented, with iron compounds seeping through the mix to give the golden hue that has made 'Hamstone' so aesthetically pleasing. See local examples in the villages of Stoke-sub-Hamden, Tintinhull and Montacute, including the splendid Montacute House.

The Cadburys

The Cadburys, North and South, are just over a mile (1.6 km) apart, and both are distinguished by great works. North Cadbury has its Church of St Michael the Archangel, an ambitious early 15th-century building of strong character, matched by the adjacent late Elizabethan house of Cadbury Court. South Cadbury has its more modest Church of St Thomas à Becket, but on the high hill above are the spectacular outlines of Cadbury Castle, a fortified prehistoric encampment of 18 acres (7ha). It is one of the largest of its kind in Britain and is claimed, inevitably, as the one true 'Camelot', the royal court of the legendary King Arthur. Today, the sheep-grazed hilltop is as green as felt. In places the surviving defensive banks rise to over 40ft (12.2m) from the external ditch.

Montacute

Montacute provides a veritable feast of fine buildings, displaying the glowing stone of Ham Hill at its best. The honey-coloured walls and tiled roofs are mellow with age and are mottled with lichen. The heart of the village is The Borough, a proper village square flanked by delightful houses. At one corner is the entrance to Montacute House (National Trust), one of the most grandly self-conscious Elizabethan buildings in England. Inside, are exquisite rooms that rise elegantly to the final flourish of the Long Gallery, 189ft (57.7m) long, which is hung with a National Gallery collection of portraits of the period.

Muchelney

The name Muchelney means 'Great Island', the site of this serene little community being on a raised area of land amidst watery levels. The Church of SS Peter and Paul, dominating the scene, has some startling features inside, not least the enchantingly overpainted wagon roof of the nave, upon which bosomy angels

Worn pathways up Ham Hill reveal the golden colour of the stone that has been much prized for building for many centuries, both in the surrounding villages and further afield

Tourist Information
Centres

Sherborne: 3 Tilton
Court, Digby Road
(tel: 01935 815341)
Somerton: The Parish
Rooms, Market Place
(tel: 01458 274070)
Yeovil: Petter's House,
Petter's Way
(tel: 01935 71279)

swirl amidst stars and billowing clouds. Across the road from the church is the National Trust's Priest's House, of medieval date and remarkably authentic inside. But Muchelney's greatest treasure is the Abbot's Lodging (English Heritage), a welcome survival amidst the ruins of Muchelney Abbey. Deceptively small from outside, the interior is breathtaking, full of golden light and with some glorious features.

Sherborne

Sherborne's main thoroughfare is called Cheap Street, though there is nothing undersold about this most self-confident of Dorset towns, where Georgian and Victorian buildings adhere to the medieval framework. Sherborne Abbey is a powerful building, and though it has a rather stolid exterior, the interior is splendid. It has all the dignity of a cathedral, and the exquisite fan-vaulting and extravagant decoration of the choir give density and richness to the constrained space. Sherborne has two castles – the ruined Norman castle east of the town and Sir Walter Raleigh's 16th-century extravagance near by, lavishly furnished and standing in beautiful grounds.

Somerton

Somerton's enduring appeal is the beauty of its Market Square and adjacent streets. The blurred greyness of Blue Lias stone enhances the buildings that line the Square, and at its heart is the market cross, octagonal and open-arched, with central tiers of shelves for produce. The inside angles of the pillars have little stone seats that are surprisingly comfortable.

From every angle good buildings catch the eye. The Church of St Michael, with an octagonal tower, fills the space to the north without overshadowing the Square. Broad Street leads from the Square and continues the theme of utterly charming buildings.

Yeovil

Yeovil has lost its old market town status and is now a thriving commercial and industrial centre, its traditional glove-making now diversified. Today its name is associated with the construction of helicopters. As elsewhere, modernisation has transformed the town, but there is interest still in the centre. Yeovil's Church of St John rather sternly occupies a central eminence between Princes Street and Silver Street. It is built of limestone that has weathered to give the exterior a satsifyingly rugged appearance, although dressings of Ham Hill stone have suffered from erosion.

High Street retains the style of a market place at its eastern end, where it merges with the pedestrianised Middle Street. Off High Street, to the south, is King George Street where handsome neo-Georgian buildings, now mainly finance houses, create a pleasingly classical enclave. Just south of the town centre is the Ninesprings Country Park, a green space extending to 40 acres (16ha).

Sherborne Abbey, a fine survivor from the important medieval monastery here, is the burial place of two Anglo-Saxon kings – Ethelbad and Ethelbert, brothers of Alfred the Great

World War I exhibits are just part of the story at the Fleet Air Arm Museum, which ranges from the earliest kites to supersonic modern jets

High Fliers

The modest tower of the pleasant little church at Yeovilton rises above the cluster of neighbouring houses. But Yeovilton's fame rises much higher than that, on the wings of the powerful aircraft of the adjoining Royal Naval Air Station. The station houses the Fleet Air Arm Museum where the development of Naval flying is detailed from the early days of the Royal Naval Air Service. There are over 40 aircraft on display, covering 80 years of naval flying, as well as exciting high-tech exhibits, including a flight simulator and the 'Ultimate Aircraft Carrier Experience' – all the sights, smells, sounds and activity of the flight deck of a carrier. Here, too, is the British prototype of *Concorde*, which visitors can climb aboard.

CHURCH AND HOME: BUILDINGS IN THE LANDSCAPE

LOCAL STONE

In the border country of Somerset and Dorset some of the finest building stone is found. The exquisite golden stone of Somerset's Ham Hill was transported across the county border to give such splendid buildings as Sherborne Abbey its mellow hue. Hamstone has been lavished on great Somerset houses too, as much as on the charming vernacular buildings of so many of the county's villages. In the immediate hinterland of Ham Hill are the Tudor and Jacobean piles of Montacute House, Tintinhull and the restored Barrington Court, the latter further enhanced by the 20th-century development of its gardens. All three are in the care of the National Trust and are open to the public.

In Cornwall the availability of durable granite has produced the solid four-square certainty of church tower and farmhouse alike, the roughness and earthy colour of the unadorned stone merging with the knuckly landscape of Dartmoor and the Atlantic coast of Cornwall. But in the non-granite country of Devon, cottages were often built of 'cob', unbaked mud that was remarkably durable. In Cornwall and Devon too, the use of less attractive slates and shales has resulted in darker, more sombre buildings that still merge satisfyingly with the landscape from which they emerged.

Granite is a rock that is often at its best when low to the ground, absorbed by the land-

Top: Egypt Cottage at Chulmleigh is of Devon cob and thatch; right: Forde Abbey, a superb example of an ecclesiastical conversion into a home

For many people, the West Country means the picture-postcard thatched cottages of Dorset, Somerset and Devon, the cobbled streets of the famous coastal villages of Clovelly and St Ives, and the elaborate façades of seaside hotels in Torquay and Ilfracombe. But memorable images apart, it is the building materials that characterise the different parts of a region, as represented by cottages and castles, churches and cathedrals. Above all else the best buildings appear to have grown from the very landscape that they adorn.

scape rather than set monumentally upon it. Yet types of Cornish granite have produced such great buildings as Lanhydrock, near Bodmin, and the magnificent Antony House on the banks of the River Lynher opposite Plymouth.

CHURCH ARCHITECTURE

An enduring motif of West-Country architecture is the local church, with its stately tower rising fortress-like from surrounding woods, or dominating the lower roof-line of numerous towns and villages. Somerset is particularly noted for its elegant church towers. Spires were few in Somerset; instead the tall, square tower, with its characteristic Somerset tracery and its elegant lace-like pinnacles and statue niches, big windows and ornamental string courses, has been the glory of the West Country for centuries. There are especially fine church buildings at Wells, Taunton, Glastonbury, Shepton Mallet, Huish Episcopi and Yeovil.

There was less church building during the 17th and 18th centuries. That period saw the development of nonconformist chapels and meeting places, and it was not until the 19th century that a new religious self-confidence produced such fine Regency churches as Teignmouth's St James's and the Norman-influenced St Paul's at Honiton. Large numbers of non-conformist churches were built throughout the West Country during the 19th century. They were simple preaching places, although neoclassical and Gothic themes emerged. In Cornwall, stern-faced Methodist chapels still dominate the rural landscape, their main façades seemingly always to face the unsmiling north as if to deny even the sun its elevated place.

CHANGING STYLES

The Romans left few traces of their presence west of Exeter, the Anglo-Saxons likewise. But Norman influence was substantial in churches and castles and there are numerous West-Country churches that have some element of Norman work that has survived the repeated restorations and extensions of the ensuing centuries.

It is the 15th and 16th centuries, however, that have bequeathed us fairly complete buildings. Rural buildings of the period were still vulnerable to structural erosion and decay from the impact of the heavy work that went on around them, but in Devon, good examples of larger farmhouses still exist. These include Sir Walter Raleigh's birthplace of Hayes Barton near Budleigh Salterton, constructed of cob and with a fine Devon thatch.

Good stone buildings of the period include the outstanding George Inn at Norton St Philip, between Bath and Frome. The George is pure medieval, its ground floor of stone with a fine entrance archway, the upper storeys timber-framed. In Glastonbury High Street is another famous Inn – The George and

Pilgrim – this time in three storeys of ornamented stone. A few yards further along is the 15th-century Gothic building known as The Tribunal.

The great buildings of the late 16th century are well represented in the West Country by beautiful houses such as Montacute and by town buildings such as The Guildhall at Exeter. Later developments of the Stuart period produced Dorset's Forde Abbey, an example of how buildings evolve from earlier forms. Forde lies on the site of a 12th-century Cistercian Abbey and parts of the abbey are incorporated into the 17th-century house. Tintinhull near Yeovil is another example of incorporation, the mainly 17th-century building having absorbed parts of a 16th-century farmhouse.

The George Inn at Norton St Philip is a fine medieval building

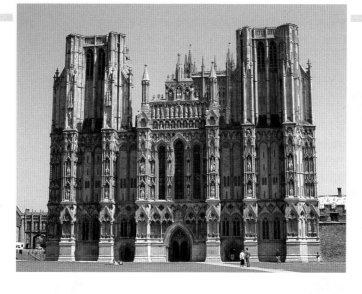

Above: the wonderful West Front of Wells Cathedral; above right: Montacute House has the lovely golden glow of Hamstone

THE LAST 200 YEARS

By the 18th century urban architecture was becoming increasingly sophisticated, as the burgeoning merchant class expressed its aspirations. Great country houses also reflected this. Devon's Saltram House, the county's finest country mansion, is an outstanding early Georgian building with fine interiors, the whole maintained by the National Trust. But it was urban building that became the focus for fashionable architecture. The legacy of the Georgian and Regency periods, so evident in our great cities and in such places as Bath, can be seen in most West Country towns of any size. Even as far west as Truro the stylish neo-classicism of entire terraces, such as those of Lemon Street, matched the sophistication of those of Bath, and the red-brick elegance of Taunton's Hammet Street and The Crescent match the crescents and terraces of Exeter.

During the late 18th century and well into the Victorian period the 'seaside' architecture peculiar to holiday resorts produced some outstanding buildings in towns such as Sid-

mouth, Ilfracombe and Torquay. Sidmouth still has some very fine Regency buildings, including the fascinating *cottage ornée*, a mock-rustic style incorporating Gothic façades topped with lavish thatch. At Ilfracombe, the use of polychromatic brickwork resulted in some outstanding Victorian Gothick buildings.

It was a stylishness soon to be overtaken by the bland and brutal convenience architecture of the 20th century, as technology and commercial enterprise ensured the triumph of function over style. Yet good modern architecture is still given breathing space, even in the featureless world of supermarkets and tower blocks. Award-winning buildings include Truro's Crown Court, designed by the same architects who were responsible for the Tate Gallery at St Ives, and in 1995 Sainsbury's superstore at Plymouth won an award for its bold design that features a white canopy made of overlapping sail-like armatures.

But it is in the surviving older buildings of Dorset, Somerset, Devon and Cornwall that the great legacy of good West-Country architecture is enshrined – the Hamstone villages, the thatched houses of quiet hamlets, and the lichened and mossy cottages of fishing villages. Above all, the marvellous churches and cathedrals and the great country houses of the west remain as priceless jewels within the landscape.

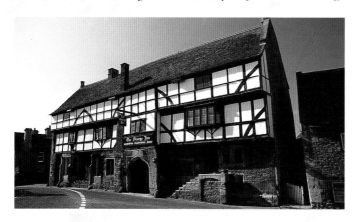

STANDING STONES AND A SOARING SPIRE

The great sarsen stones of Stonehenge tower 21ft (6.4m) high and weigh up to 50 tons; the majestic spire of Salisbury soars to over 400ft (121.9m) and is visible for many miles around. They were erected some 3,000 years apart, perhaps even to different deities, but one commonality is clear – both inspire awe and turn thoughts from worldly to spiritual matters.

Woodhenge

Woodhenge (English Heritage) is an even older circle than Stonehenge and, like its illustrious neighbour, is aligned to indicate where the sun would rise and set on the solstices. The wooden staves that made up the circular arrangements have long gone and their positions are marked by rather (continued opposite)

One of the best-known prehistoric monuments in the world, Stonehenge has managed to keep its secrets for 5,000 years

pied since the Iron Age, but by the early 13th century, friction between clerics and troops, and the parched and very uncomfortable windswept nature of the site, prompted a move. This was done quite literally, taking cathedral and castle stones down to New Sarum (Salisbury) for use in the new Cathedral Close. Substantial parts of the lower castle remain; elsewhere are only fragments, but the views and ambience alone make the trip worthwhile.

Amesbury

According to legend, Amesbury Abbey was founded in Saxon times by an uncle of King Arthur and it was here that Queen Guinevere retreated and died. The abbey was refounded by Henry II and became one of England's most important religious houses until its dissolution in 1539-40. Today all that remains of the abbey is the atmospheric low flint Church of St Mary.

Heale Garden

Charles II sheltered in Heale House after the Battle of Worcester in 1651, and a very restful spot it is too. The house is not open to the public but the charming gardens by the side of the peaceful River Avon evoke the quiet of a bygone age. Notable features include great pergola tunnels of apples and Japanese water gardens which criss-cross tiny streams.

Old Sarum

It is not easy to visualise today but this now deserted 56-acre (23ha) hilltop site was the forerunner of modern Salisbury – a town complete with a royal castle and cathedral built by the Normans. Old Sarum (English Heritage) had been occu-

Salisbury

At 404ft (123.1m) high the spire of Salisbury Cathedral is not only the tallest in England but is still the mighty landmark it was intended to be when erected in the 14th century. The cathedral is an architectural masterpiece, built in just 38 years (excluding the spire) during the 13th century, and is unique for its harmony. Although the interior may not quite live up to the promise of the superb exterior, it holds many fine monuments. The cathedral's fine cloisters, among the country's largest, lead to the the library, home to one of the four copies of Magna Carta, and to the very fine chapter house.

The Cathedral Close, originally designed to

Tourist Information Centres

Amesbury: Redworth House, Flower Lane (tel: 01980 622833)
Salisbury: Fish Row (tel: 01722 334956)

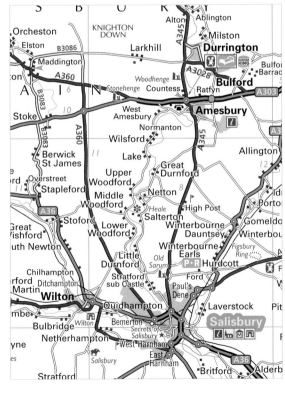

unflattering concrete posts. In the middle of these is what is presumed to be an altar stone. Near here the remains of a child with a deliberately fractured skull were found, leading to suppositions of human sacrifice. There are interpretive boards next to the site, but for more information visit the Devizes Museum.

Always overshadowed by its more famous neighbour, Woodhenge is nevertheless impressive. It is thought to date from the New Stone Age and was only discovered when aerial photography revealed its form

house the clerics, now forms a glorious precinct to the cathedral. Most of the houses have been altered over the centuries, so their appearance is now 16th to 18th century, and four of these are open to the public as museums. Mompesson House (National Trust), built in 1701, boasts superb plasterwork, a collection of glassware and a charming garden where tea can be taken. The award-winning Salisbury and South Wiltshire Museum, home of the Stonehenge Gallery and an archaeological collection of national importance, resides in the late 14th-century King's House while there is a military museum in the 13th-century Wardrobe.

A good introduction to the city can be found in the magnificent 13th-century Medieval Hall, where a large-screen presentation runs continuously. Other notable historic buildings include the Guildhall and the 13th-century Poultry Cross. Queen Elizabeth's Gardens, alongside the River Avon, enjoy a bucolic watermeadow setting and a classic view of the cathedral.

Stonehenge

Europe's most famous and most easily recognisable ancient site continues to impress and to intrigue. The origins of Stonehenge (English Heritage/National Trust) go back some 5,000 years to 3000 BC, when the first bank and ditch was constructed, possibly with a wooden building at its centre. A thousand years later the first stone circle was raised, but left unfinished. The present stone circle, c1500 BC, is possibly the remains of a temple and is famous for its trilithons, the large door-frame shaped stone arrangements, which are actually slotted together with mortice-and-tenon joints. These are arranged so that when the sun rises and sets on the solstices it shines straight through the circle along The Avenue on

to the Heel Stone. However, despite this solar alignment, evidence that Stonehenge was some sort of observatory or lunar calendar is still slight and the purpose of the design remains a mystery.

In 2000, access at the Summer Solstice was granted for the first time in 16 years and the event passed off peacefully, marking a new atmosphere of co-operation rather than confrontation. Plans to build a new visitor centre by 2006 are currently being developed.

Wilton

The pretty village of Wilton is famous for carpets and for Wilton House, home to the Earls of Pembroke and one of the great country houses of England. The present house (1649–52) was built by Inigo Jones and is notable for its art treasures and sumptuous interiors, including the Cube Room (30ft/9.1m long, wide and high) and the Double Cube Room. The latter is full of Van Dycks, and there are other Old Masters around the house. The focal point of the grounds is the Palladian Bridge, based on the Rialto Bridge.

In the village centre is a ruined Saxon church, and off handsome West Street is a rather incongruous mid-19th century Italianate basilica. The Royal Wilton Carpet Factory began weaving in the early 18th century, continuing an age-old local tradition. It remains on its original site, and offers factory tours and demonstrations of hand-weaving. Wilton's museum is in the courtyard, and some old factory buildings now form Wilton Shopping Village, with a variety of factory outlets in a pleasant riverside setting.

Salisbury's beautiful cathedral has provided both spiritual and artistic inspiration since it was built in the 13th century. This view was most famously painted by John Constable

The Royal Wilton Carpet Factory has been producing some of the finest quality carpets in the country for nearly three centuries. Its work can be seen in many of our greatest stately homes and most luxurious hotels

A TALE OF TWO CITIES

W hen John Betjeman referred to one of the two great western cities as 'the most beautiful, interesting and distinguished in England', the only surprise was that he was referring not to Bath but to Bristol. Bath can console itself with the fact that it is one of only three World Heritage Cities (alongside Rome and Florence), and is probably the finest 18th-century city in the world.

Man of Manners

Richard 'Beau' Nash (1674–1762) was first attracted to Bath as a gambler. Recognising its potential as a resort he organised balls and social functions on an opulent scale and opened the Pump Room to accommodate many of these events. He became the arbiter of fashion, laid down social rules and made the city a safer and cleaner place. He forbade the wearing of swords in the city and even smoking in certain public places (the latter being a particularly strong measure in those days). Bath became the most fashionable place in England and Nash, for his foresight, became an extremely wealthy man.

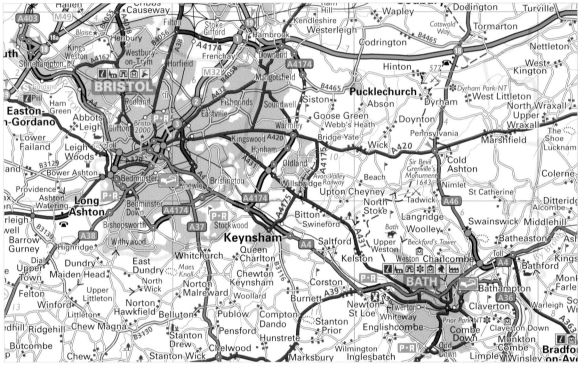

Bath Abbey, known for its wonderful fan-vaulting, was originally founded in the 9th century, but took its present form around 1500

Bath

Bath is a World Heritage Site, but its history and superb architecture have not set it in a timewarp – it is also a lively centre for the arts, with good restaurants and excellent shopping. It owes its importance to its hot springs, which are unique in Britain. The Romans built a great bathing complex here, and the site comprises the most impressive Roman remains in Britain, superbly preserved and presented. In 2002 the Bath Spa Project will again provide bathing in natural hot spring water, together with various therapies.

During the 18th century the city bloomed, made fashionable by Richard 'Beau' Nash and made beautiful by the two John Woods (father and son), working with the honey-coloured Bath Stone. One of the city's most famous landmarks is the 18th-century Pulteney Bridge, lined with tiny shops and dubbed 'Florence on Avon' for its Italianate appearance. A short walk due north leads to the Assembly Rooms, an architectural masterpiece, which, along with the Pump Room, was

the hub of 18th-century social life. The highly acclaimed and extensive Museum of Costume now resides in the basement. Close by, the Circus is a perfect appetiser for the Royal Crescent, the *tour de force* of John Wood the younger. Built in 1767, it is a majestic curved terrace of 30 houses, and Number One has been splendidly restored to show visitors how it would have looked back then. For another glimpse of 18th-century life, visit the Jane Austen Centre.

The Pump Room, directly above the Roman Baths, offers a taste of old Bath, both literally and metaphorically. Here you can drink the spa water, or take tea to the strains of the Pump Room Trio. Adjacent Bath Abbey is where, in AD 973, Edgar was crowned first king of all England. The present building was begun in the late 1490s and is famous for its fan-vaulting and monuments. A two-minute walk south takes you to Bath's oldest dwelling, Sally Lunn's House, built c1622 and now delightful tea rooms serving the delicious

The gentility of a previous age lingers on in the grand Pump Room, rebuilt in 1795. You can take tea or coffee – or some of the famous spa water that has drawn visitors to Bath for 2,000 years or so

Man of Iron

Isambard Kingdom Brunel (1806–59) was the greatest designer and wrought-iron architect of early Victorian England. Moving on from his triumphs with the Great Western Railway (which included the design of Bristol Temple Meads station), he built the famous transatlantic paddle steamer, the *Great Western*, launched from Bristol in 1837, then superseded this with the SS *Great Britain*. This was the first ever iron ocean-going propeller-driven ship and when launched was also the world's biggest ship. Brunel's final *pièce de résistance* was the Clifton Suspension Bridge, which, sadly, he did not live to see completed.

Tourist Information Centres

Bath: Abbey Chambers, Abbey Church Yard (tel: 01225 477101)
Bristol: The Annexe, Wildscreen Walk, Harbourside (tel: 0117 926 0767)

Sally Lunn Buns. Bath's many attractions, include the fascinating Building of Bath Exhibition, with spectacular models and full-size reconstructions.

Bristol

The city of Bristol celebrated the Millennium by spending £97 million on its harbourside area, an impressive redevelopment that combines up-to-the-minute attractions – science and nature discover centres, IMAX cinema – with trendy nightspots and restaurants and boat services that explore the historic waterways.

The history of the city is inextricably linked to the harbour. It was from here that John Cabot set sail in the 15th century on a voyage that resulted in the discovery of Newfoundland; from here that Brunel launched his famous ships; from here that countless pioneers set sail for the New World. Brunel's SS *Great Britain* is back at the Great Western Dock, restored and open to the public, beside the Maritime Heritage Centre and a replica of *The Matthew* in which Cabot made his voyage of discovery to Newfoundland. The Bristol Industrial Museum is on Princes Wharf.

A short walk away is Bristol's finest church, St Mary Redcliffe, a magnificent 14th-century building described by Elizabeth I as the 'the fairest parish church in England'. Historic harbourside King Street is picturesque and lively, featuring the outstanding 17th-century Landoger Trow inn, and the Theatre Royal, the oldest continuously working theatre in Britain, established in 1776 (ask to look inside).

Bristol Cathedral is a handsome uniform 'hall church', blending a 19th-century nave with early medieval work. Near by, off Park Street, The Georgian House, built 1787–91, is well worth a visit. Park Street is where you will find the excellent City Museum and Art Gallery,

and other attractions include the British Empire and Commonwealth Museum, housed in Brunel's historic railway station. The city is also a buzzing centre for nightlife, culture and artistic events and has interesting little shops along narrow lanes as well as the big modern shopping malls.

Chew Magna

Wool brought prosperity to this pretty red sandstone village in the Middle Ages and many of its fine buildings are a reminder of that period. Look for the Old School Room, formerly a church brewery, and the Old Bakehouse as well as the stone cottages and fine 18th-century mansions that line the High Street. The Church of St Andrews is part Norman and has a rare wooden monument to a knight.

Clifton

Clifton is a suburb of Bristol but, for sightseeing interest, merits a day in its own right. Foremost is the majestic Clifton Suspension Bridge, spanning the Avon Gorge, 702ft (214m) long, with the muddy Avon 245ft (74.7m) below. Alongside is Clifton Village, a delightful Georgian area. Near by, the gloriously landscaped Bristol Zoo showcases some 300 species of wildlife.

Dyrham

Dyrham is a pretty village with many 17th- and 18th-century stone houses and a fine 15th-century church. Dyrham Park is a beautiful William-and-Mary house (National Trust), built 1691–1710 and little altered over the centuries. Dyrham means deer park, and a herd of fallow deer grace the 263-acre (107ha) grounds.

Brunel's spectacular Clifton Suspension Bridge, some 245ft (74.7m) above the river, links the limestone cliffs of the Avon Gorge

See Walk Q page 66
Lansdown – A Civil War Battleground

In 1970 the rusting hulk of SS Great Britain was brought back from the Falkland Islands to the dry dock from which she was originally launched in 1843. Now restored, she is a proud reminder of Bristol's maritime heritage

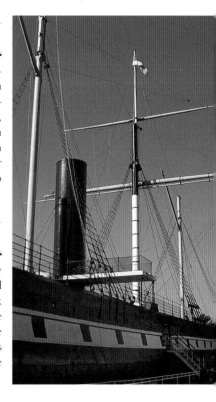

MYSTERIOUS SITES OF MARLBOROUGH COUNTRY

The rolling scenery around the Marlborough Downs, cut through by the ancient Ridgeway, is home to many strange shapes and sights – impenetrable Silbury Hill, the 60-ton sarsen stones of Avebury, a veritable herd of white horses cut into the chalk downland and Merlin's Mound. What do they all mean? Help may be at hand in Devizes Museum, and you can learn about the coming of the Iron Horse in modern-day Swindon.

White Horses

Six giant white chalk horses inhabit this area – the Marlborough Horse, carved by boys from the public school in 1804, the Alton Barnes Horse, cut in 1812, the Cherhill Horse of 1780, the Broad Town Horse of 1864, the Hackpen Horse, commemorating Queen Victoria's Diamond Jubilee in 1897 and the Devizes Millennium White Horse, cut in 1999. All were inspired by such ancient chalk figures as the Uffington Horse (see page 93). Wiltshire has two more white nags, the oldest and largest being the West-bury Horse (below), carved at Bratton Down in 1778 (on top of a much older figure); the other is near Pewsey.

Unlike its smaller neighbour, Stonehenge, the Avebury stone circle is completely accessible, forming an integral part of the village which it encircles and the surrounding pastures

Avebury

In 1633 the antiquary and author John Aubrey wrote to King Charles II recommending him to visit Avebury because '... (it) does as much exceed in greatness the renowned Stonehenge as a cathedral doeth a parish church'. These days Avebury, the largest stone circle in the world, is even more attractive, with an excellent National Trust interpretation centre.

Avebury comprises a total of 200 standing stones, which were arranged into circles and 'avenues', surrounded by huge circular earthworks, c2500–2200 BC. These patterns were destroyed over the ages and only partly restored in the 1930s, thanks largely to Alexander Keiller (of marmalade fame), who founded a museum in the village. Visit the museum before seeing the stones, as their layout is not easy to understand from ground level.

The Great Barn Rural Life Museum, in a huge 17th-century thatched barn, illustrates pre-war rural life in Wiltshire, and 16th-century Avebury Manor (National Trust) can also be visited.

Devizes

Devizes is the main market town of Wiltshire, and its large market place has a fine 19th-century market cross and fountain. The square is lined with 18th-century houses and is the location of both the Devizes Visitor Centre and the Town Hall. The adjacent Shambles has been a lively covered market since 1835, and at the north end of the market place is the imposing Victorian Wadworth's brewery; the stables are open to the public. In Long Street is the excellent Wiltshire Heritage Museum, which includes important finds from many of the county's famous sites, including Stonehenge, Woodhenge and West Kennet Long Barrow.

The Kennet and Avon Canal, with its colourful narrowboats, runs almost through the town centre, with a famous staircase of locks near by. A small museum here interprets the history of the canal and boat trips are available at weekends.

This Celtic carved head, on display in the Devizes Museum, is from the late Iron Age or early Roman period

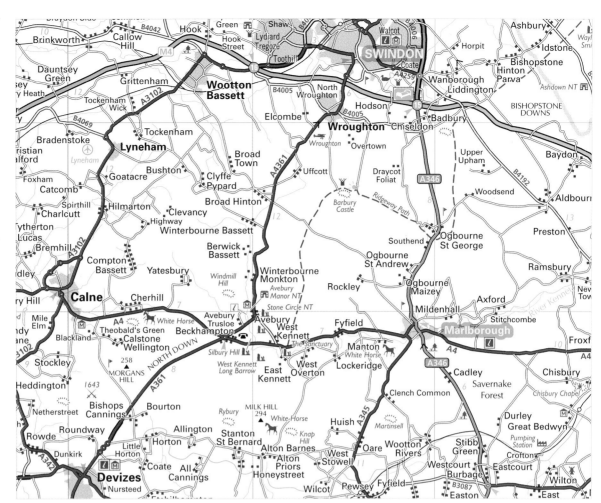

An Ancient Route

The Ridgeway is one of the oldest existing pathways in Europe. Evidence suggests that feet may have tramped along it for up to 5,000 years, and until around 200 years ago this broad track was used as a main highway for driving sheep and cattle. It runs from Ivinghoe Beacon (near Dunstable) to Overton Hill, (West Kennet) and the south-western section, a broad track which runs along the top of the chalk downland ridge, is particularly pleasant and has far-reaching views. You can cycle, ride a horse or travel the Ridgeway by Shank's Pony, but all motorised vehicles are prohibited.

Tourist Information Centres

Avebury: The Great Barn (seasonal) (tel: 01672 539425)
Devizes: Cromwell House, Market Place (tel: 01380 729408)
Marlborough: George Lane Car Park (tel: 01672 513989)
Swindon: 37 Regent Street (tel: 01793 530328/466454)

Marlborough

It is often claimed that Marlborough has the broadest High Street in England, possibly in Europe. Whether or not this is so, it is certainly one of the most handsome and individualistic streets in the country, with charming colonnaded and tile-hung houses and shops, splendid old inns, a classical-style Victorian Town Hall and a fine church at each end. One of the oldest houses is the Merchant's House, dating from 1656, which is being developed into a museum of 17th-century town life. Just beyond the south end of the High Street is the famous public school of Marlborough College. In the grounds (open to the public) is the College Chapel and The Mound, legendary burial place of Merlin.

Silbury Hill/West Kennet Long Barrow

Another mystery roughly contemporary with Avebury and Stonehenge is posed by the cone of Silbury Hill. This is the largest man-made mound in Europe, constructed in three definite stages c2800 BC. To put the monumental nature of this 130ft (40m) tall project into some context, it is estimated that the third stage alone took some 4 million man hours! Its purpose, however continues to elude – no clue, in fact nothing at all, has ever been found within. As this is a Site of Special Scientific Interest, visitors are requested not to climb the hill.

More straightforward is the West Kennet Long Barrow, south of the hill and reached by footpath from the road. One of Britain's largest neolithic burial tombs, it measures 330ft (100m) long by 75ft (22.9m) wide, was constructed c3000 BC and was in use for 1,000 years after that.

Swindon

Swindon is a thoroughly modern city which owes its importance to the Great Western Railway. From 1842 to 1948 jobs and prosperity came from the locomotive workshops. That heyday can be traced at STEAM – Museum of the Great Western Railway, which has some splendid old locomotives, a reconstructed station platform, lots of hands-on exhibits and nostalgic film footage.

There is more rail memorabilia on the outskirts of town, in the Swindon and Cricklade Railway, a preserved steam line. Swindon's Museum and Art Gallery, in the older part of the town, has a good collection of 20th-century art.

Swindon was one of the busiest railway towns in Britain. The age of steam is recalled in STEAM – Museum of the Great Western Railway

See Walk R page 67
Old Ways on the Wiltshire Downs

THE GLOUCESTER COTSWOLDS

While Cirencester is the self-styled 'Capital of the Cotswolds' and Cheltenham claims to be the 'Centre for the Cotswolds', it is Painswick, once the 'Queen of the Cotswolds', which conforms best to the popular idyllic image. Gloucester has one of England's great cathedrals and excellent museums; elsewhere are charming gardens, bird collections and castles to explore.

Tourist Information Centres

Cheltenham: 77 Promenade (tel: 01242 522878)
Cirencester: Corn Hall, Market Place (tel: 01285 654180)
Gloucester: 28 Southgate Street (tel: 01452 396572)
Painswick: The Library, Stroud Road (seasonal) (tel: 01452 813552)

The atmosphere of Regency Cheltenham is best appreciated along the elegant Promenade (below)
Right: a coin of Agrippa on display at the Corinium Museum in Cirencester

Cheltenham

Cheltenham began its transformation into Cheltenham Spa in 1738, with the discovery of Old Well (the famous Cheltenham Ladies College now occupies the site). In 1788 King George III came to take the waters, stayed for five weeks, and soon Cheltenham was Britain's most important spa. Other wells were discovered, the most famous being at Pittville, and the beautiful domed Pittville Pump Room, built in 1825–30, is still open to visitors. You can taste the salty alkaline water here.

At the heart of town lies the Promenade, dominated by a massive golden terrace and lined with elegant shops, statues, trees and flower beds. It encapsulates the genteel image and complements the superb 18th-century architecture of Britain's most complete Regency town.

The Cheltenham Art Gallery and Museum has a lively, varied local collection with outstanding Arts and Crafts exhibits.

Near by, in Clarence Road, Cheltenham's most famous son, Gustav Holst, was born in 1874; it is now the Holst Birthplace Museum. Cheltenham hosts a full programme of festivals and events, including the international music festival every July, and the famous National Hunt Festival at the racecourse every March.

Cirencester

Corinium, as the town was known by the Romans, was for a time second only in importance to *Londinium*, and the outline of an 8,000-seat Roman amphitheatre can still be seen to the west. All other Roman interest appears in the Corinium Museum, a highly acclaimed collection which includes some impressive mosaics.

The heart of modern Cirencester is the Market

Sudeley Castle

Enjoying a glorious Cotswolds setting, Sudeley Castle is an impressive sight. Originally built in the 15th century, it was slighted after the Civil War, leaving the romantic ruins of the banqueting house, and only rebuilt in the 19th century. The apartments are royally appointed and hung with Old Masters.

Sudeley was favoured by the Tudor monarchs, and became home to Katherine Parr, the only one of Henry VIII's wives to outlive him, when she married Lord Seymour.

Berkeley Castle

This compact classic fortress, complete with circular Norman keep and inner bailey, has been home to the famous Berkeley family for nearly 850 years and has two main claims to historical fame. In 1215 in the splendid Great Hall the Barons met before proceeding to Runnymede to force the Magna Carta upon King John, while in 1327, in the dungeon of its keep, King Edward II was horribly murdered. The other highlights of an entertaining guided castle tour are the picture gallery, the dining room, the medieval buttery and kitchens and the State Apartments.

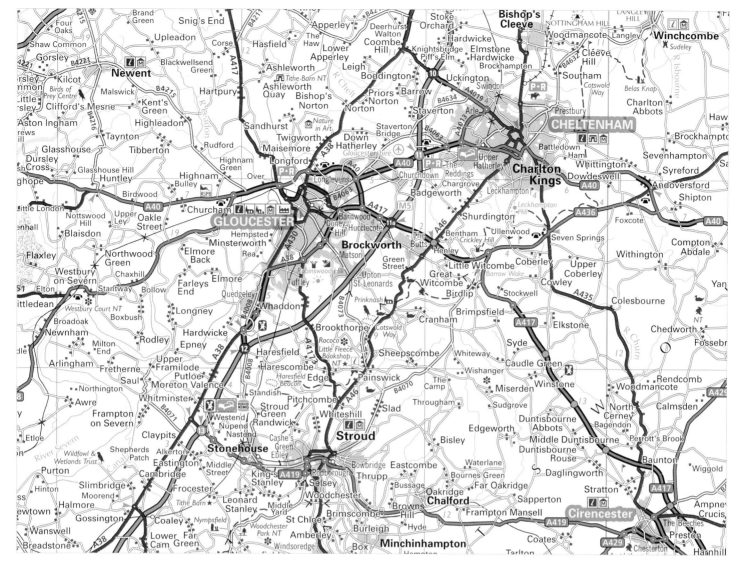

Slimbridge

Founded in 1946 by the renowned naturalist, Sir Peter Scott, the Slimbridge Wildfowl and Wetlands Trust hosts the world's largest collection of wildfowl, with over 180 different kinds of swan, geese and ducks. Many of the birds are very tame and delight children by feeding at close quarters. Serious 'twitchers' can be found in the hides with binoculars (available for hire), seeking out more elusive species. There is also a pink flamingo colony and other exotic varieties can be found in the Tropical House.

Place, an attractive medley of Cotswold-stone and Victorian buildings, watched over by the outstanding 15th-century church of St John Baptist. Adjacent are the Abbey Grounds, where the outline of the former Norman Abbey is marked out and a small part of the Roman city wall can be seen. Cirencester Park, famous for polo, makes for a pleasant stroll and other attractions include Brewery Arts, with craft workshops and exhibitions.

Gloucester

The glory of Gloucester is its magnificent cathedral, and the great medieval East Window, dating from c1352, is the largest example in Britain – best seen from the Choir, itself a masterpiece. Among many fine monuments, the tombs of Edward II and Robert of Normandy (son of William the Conqueror) are both remarkable. The charming College Court contains The House of The Tailor of Gloucester, now housing a Beatrix Potter exhibition and shop. At Westgate a range of Tudor houses contains the splendid Folk Museum.

Gloucester is the most inland port in Britain, important to canal trade for some 200 years. The docks have been developed as a tourist attraction, with the highly acclaimed National Waterways Museum as its centrepiece. Near by is the nostalgic Museum of Advertising and Packaging and the Soldiers of Gloucestershire Museum.

Painswick

Painswick is the quintessential Gloucestershire Cotswold village, a collection of old stone cottages around a web of narrow streets. The churchyard has 99 yew trees, trimmed into giant lollipops and tunnels, amid several 18th-century table-tombs. Close by, Painswick Rococo Garden is a restoration of a mid-18th century garden.

Prinknash

Set on a hillside, Prinknash (pronounced 'Prinnersh') Abbey will disappoint visitors in search of antiquity. Its controversial 1930s buildings (not open) find few admirers. Within its grounds, however, the Bird Park is charmingly informal, and in the famous pottery, you can watch the beautiful pieces being made.

See Walk S page 68
Uley Bury and Hetty Pegler's Tump

See Walk T page 69
Birdlip and the Cotswolds

The Wildfowl and Wetlands Trust Reserve at Slimbridge is home to the world's largest collection of exotic wildfowl

THE FOREST OF DEAN

The oak, beech, ash and birch trees of the 35sq-mile (90sq-km) Royal Forest of Dean are an echo of medieval England, when the area between the Severn and the Wye was a royal hunting preserve. But the trees hide evidence of 2,000 years of industry in iron and coal. Further south, the elegantly ridged estuary of the Severn opens the way to the Atlantic.

The shaded tranquillity of the ancient Forest of Dean is perfect for walking, enjoying a picnic or just quiet contemplation

The Queen of Forests

The Queen of Forests all that west of Severn lie, Her broad and bushy top Dean holdeth up so high

The 17th-century poet, Michael Drayton, was the first to praise the beauty of the Royal Forest of Dean and, despite the fact that it is now a commercial forest producing up to 85,000cu yds (65,000cu m) of timber each year, it retains its ancient, timeless atmosphere. The remains of coal-mining and iron-working show that the forest has always earned its keep.

Nearly half the forest is planted with broadleaved trees, and it has one of the largest areas of ancient oaks in Britain. It is the home of a wide range of wildlife, most notably pied flycatchers, which have taken advantage of a special nestbox scheme in the forest.

Coleford

Coleford, 'capital' of the Forest of Dean, holds an important place in the history of iron and steel. It was here in 1810 that David Mushet settled, and his son Robert invented self-hardening steel; Whitecliff Furnace, an early coke blast furnace, can still be seen in Newland Street. There is a railway museum in the old station.

Half a mile (0.8km) away on the Chepstow Road is Puzzle Wood, which contains open iron workings dating back to pre-Roman times, with a network of paths that wind maze-like through lovely woodland. Further down the same road are Clearwell Caves and the Hopewell Colliery Museum with underground tours led by miners.

Taking in wonderful views in all directions from Goodrich Castle, it is easy to see why the site was chosen as a strategic standpoint

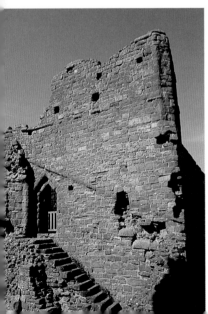

Goodrich Castle

This great red sandstone castle seems to grow naturally from the rocky bluff over-

looking the River Wye where, as recorded in the Domesday Book, Godric Mapplestone first built a fortress to guard an ancient river crossing. Most of what we see today dates from the early 14th century, when it was the principal residence of the Talbot family, Earls of Shrewsbury.

Lydney

Lydney is perhaps best known as the terminus of the Dean Forest Railway, which links with the main line between Birmingham and South Wales. The line runs between here and Norchard, but there are plans to extend it to Parkend. Just outside the town is Lydney Park, home of Lord Bledisloe, which has the remains of a Roman temple in the beautiful grounds.

Speech House

Standing in the centre of the forest near Cannop Pond, this house, dating from

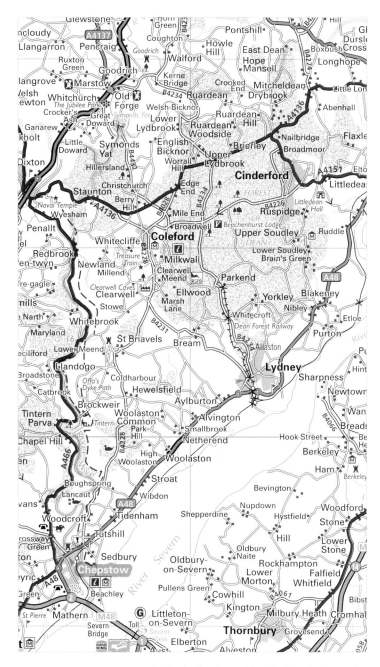

can witness charcoal being produced by the traditional method of open-air burning. A series of nature trails lead off from here, venturing deep into the forest.

The River Wye loops around the foot of the 473-ft (144.2-m) Yat Rock, famous for its wonderful views and its population of peregrine falcons

Symond's Yat

The Wye executes a great sweeping horse-shoe meander, cutting a wooded gorge around Huntsham Hill, on the edge of the Forest of Dean at this justly-famous view-point. Yat means 'gate' and the view from Yat Rock up or down river is one of the finest in Britain.

Symond's Yat has become famous in ornithological circles in recent years as the nesting place for peregrine falcons in the nearby limestone cliffs. Binoculars are provided for visitors to observe these powerful raptors swooping down from the rocks on to unfortunate passing pigeons.

Near by at Symonds Yat West is the Jubilee Park with its Silver Jubilee Maze, Museum of Mazes and Splendour of the Orient attraction.

Tintern Abbey, nestling in the Wye Valley, remains impressive, even in ruins

Tintern Abbey

One of Britain's most beautiful abbey ruins, Tintern, in its lovely setting in the wooded valley of the Wye, has attracted the attention of poets and painters over the centuries. Its stately roofless walls still rise gracefully from the valley, and the rose window in the east end is almost intact. The Abbey was founded by the Cistercians in 1131, and the white-robed monks were involved in the Forest of Dean's iron industry. Tintern Abbey was suppressed by Henry VIII in 1536.

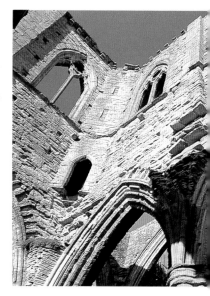

Tourist Information Centre

Coleford: High Street (tel: 01594 812388)

1680, is the site of the Verderer's Court for the Forest of Dean.

The Speech House picnic site is one of the places where you can join the circular Forest of Dean Sculpture Trail, a series of permanent sculptures by modern artists, strategically placed to blend harmoniously into the forest scene.

Soudley

Soudley is the site of the award-winning Dean Heritage Centre. Housed in an old mill, it features a water wheel, beam engine and a reconstructed forester's cottage, complete with Gloucester Old Spot pig. This is one of the few places in Britain where you

ZENNOR AND THE SPECTACULAR COAST PATH

Distance: 5½ miles (8.8km)
Total ascent: 800ft (244m)
Paths: mostly good but can be very muddy, particularly between Tregerthen and Wicca
Terrain: fields, farm tracks, coast path
Gradients: steep in places on the coast path
Refreshments: Tinners Arms and Old Chapel Café, Zennor
Park: car park, Zennor, on B3306 betweeen St Ives and St Just

8 Head back inland, rising slightly, to a stile. Follow the narrow path for 50yds (46m), to where it meets the road above a white house. Take the road back to Zennor and the car park.

1 Turn left out of the car park and head up the hill. Immediately after the church turn right by some railings and take the footpath over the fields, crossing several stiles, to Tremedda Farm.

2 Cross the farm track via two stiles, continue across open fields to the hamlet of Tregerthen and cross another track. Follow the narrow, muddy track through thickets until it opens out to fields which lead to Wicca Farm.

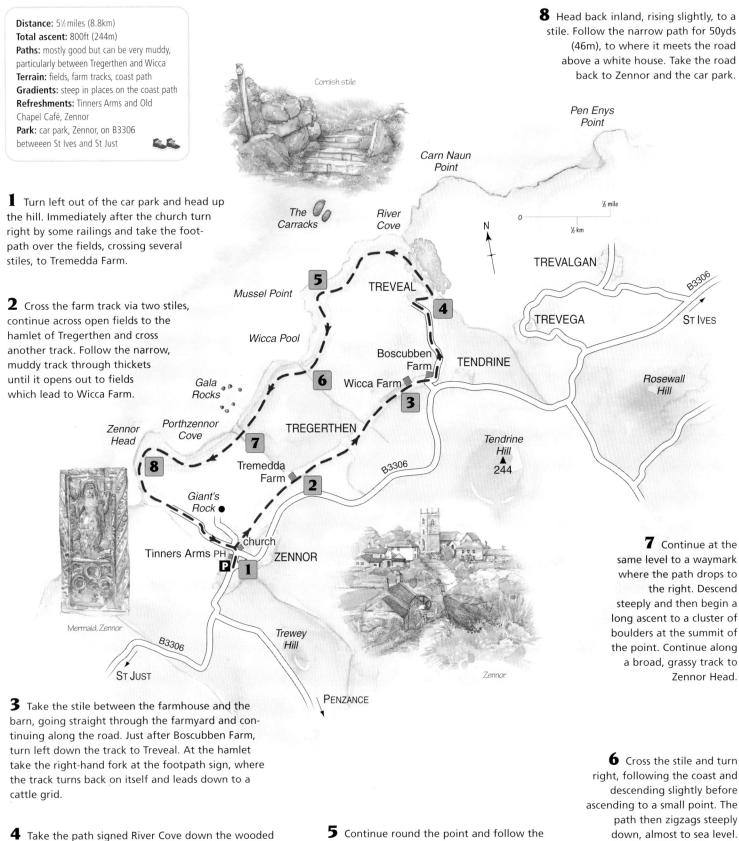

Cornish stile

The Carracks

River Cove

Pen Enys Point

Carn Naun Point

Mussel Point

TREVEAL

Wicca Pool

Boscubben Farm

TENDRINE

Gala Rocks

Wicca Farm

TREVALGAN

B3306

TREVEGA

ST IVES

Zennor Head

Porthzennor Cove

TREGERTHEN

Rosewall Hill

Tremedda Farm

B3306

Tendrine Hill
▲ 244

Giant's Rock ●

Tinners Arms PH

ZENNOR

church

Mermaid, Zennor

B3306

ST JUST

Trewey Hill

PENZANCE

Zennor

7 Continue at the same level to a waymark where the path drops to the right. Descend steeply and then begin a long ascent to a cluster of boulders at the summit of the point. Continue along a broad, grassy track to Zennor Head.

3 Take the stile between the farmhouse and the barn, going straight through the farmyard and continuing along the road. Just after Boscubben Farm, turn left down the track to Treveal. At the hamlet take the right-hand fork at the footpath sign, where the track turns back on itself and leads down to a cattle grid.

4 Take the path signed River Cove down the wooded valley to the stream, where the path starts to rise and then descends to the coast. Veer left and follow the coast path, which eventually rises steeply to some prominent rocks at the summit of Mussel Point.

5 Continue round the point and follow the path across the open, grassy hillside. After a prominent boulder on the right the path drops steeply into a small valley. Cross the stream on stepping stones to a stile.

6 Cross the stile and turn right, following the coast and descending slightly before ascending to a small point. The path then zigzags steeply down, almost to sea level. Continue along a flatter section for ½ mile (800m), then bear inland and uphill steeply, over one stream and on to another.

HELL'S MOUTH AND THE NORTH CORNWALL COAST

Distance: 5½ miles (8.8km)
Total ascent: 700ft (213m)
Paths: mostly good but can be muddy; short stretch of metalled road
Terrain: cliff top, open grassland
Gradients: two steep ascents on cliff path
Refreshments: café and Sand Sifters Hotel, Godrevy car park; Hell's Mouth café
Park: Godrevy National Trust car park, reached from the B3301, 2½ miles (4km) north of Hayle. Do not park adjacent to the café

1 Turn left out of the car park and walk up the road to the coast of St Ives Bay.

2 Follow the cliff-top road for ½ mile (800m), passing Godrevy Farm. St Ives is visible on the opposite side of the bay. Just before the toilets (seasonal only) on your right, bear left across open, springy turf to a stile.

9 Take the B3301 right, back past Hell's Mouth, up the hill to the North Cliff National Trust car park. Descend into the Red River valley with St Ives Bay ahead. At the stone bridge turn right and back to the car park.

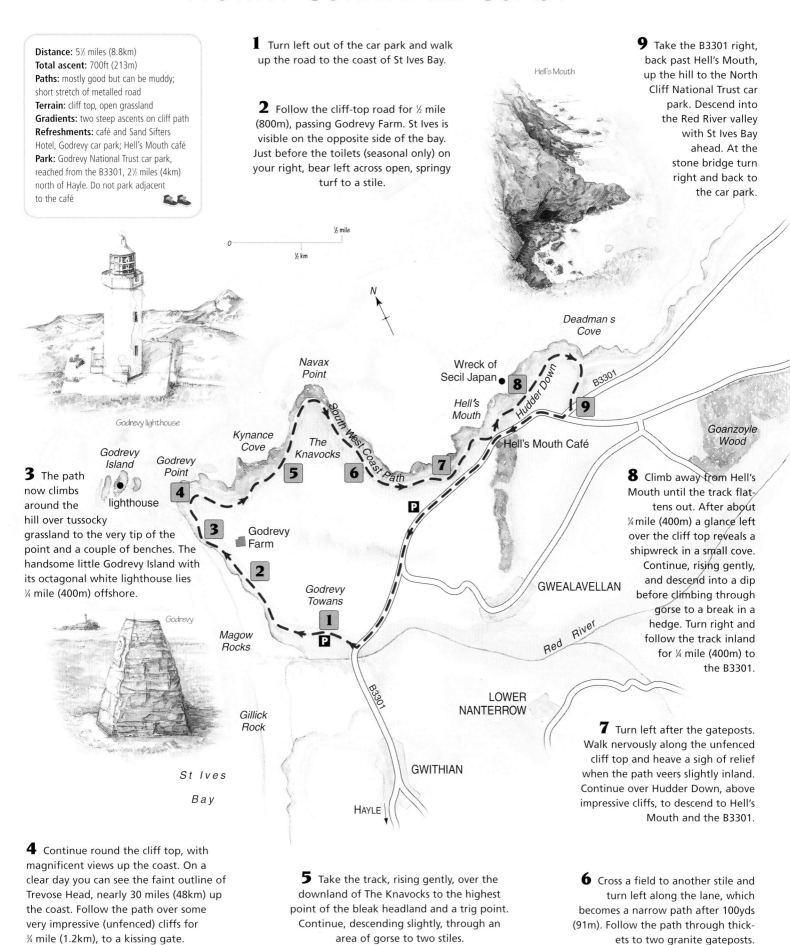

3 The path now climbs around the hill over tussocky grassland to the very tip of the point and a couple of benches. The handsome little Godrevy Island with its octagonal white lighthouse lies ¼ mile (400m) offshore.

8 Climb away from Hell's Mouth until the track flattens out. After about ¼ mile (400m) a glance left over the cliff top reveals a shipwreck in a small cove. Continue, rising gently, and descend into a dip before climbing through gorse to a break in a hedge. Turn right and follow the track inland for ¼ mile (400m) to the B3301.

7 Turn left after the gateposts. Walk nervously along the unfenced cliff top and heave a sigh of relief when the path veers slightly inland. Continue over Hudder Down, above impressive cliffs, to descend to Hell's Mouth and the B3301.

4 Continue round the cliff top, with magnificent views up the coast. On a clear day you can see the faint outline of Trevose Head, nearly 30 miles (48km) up the coast. Follow the path over some very impressive (unfenced) cliffs for ¾ mile (1.2km), to a kissing gate.

5 Take the track, rising gently, over the downland of The Knavocks to the highest point of the bleak headland and a trig point. Continue, descending slightly, through an area of gorse to two stiles.

6 Cross a field to another stile and turn left along the lane, which becomes a narrow path after 100yds (91m). Follow the path through thickets to two granite gateposts.

SMUGGLERS' HAUNTS ON THE HELFORD RIVER

Distance: 7 miles (11.3km)
Total ascent: 900ft (275m)
Paths: can be very muddy in places, particularly in winter
Terrain: fields, farm tracks, coast path
Gradients: undulating; several steep sections
Refreshments: Shipwright's, Helford
Park: by the church in St Anthony-in-Meneage, 8 miles (12.9km) from Helston

9 Opposite the church turn left, and after 100yds (91m) take the footpath on the right (signed Carne), which eventually descends through woods to the road beside Gillan Creek. Turn left and after 140yds (128m) turn left again for St Anthony.

8 Turn left and cross the road. After 15yds (14m), take the path on the right to some houses. Continue to the main road, turn right, then immediately left, downhill to Manaccan church.

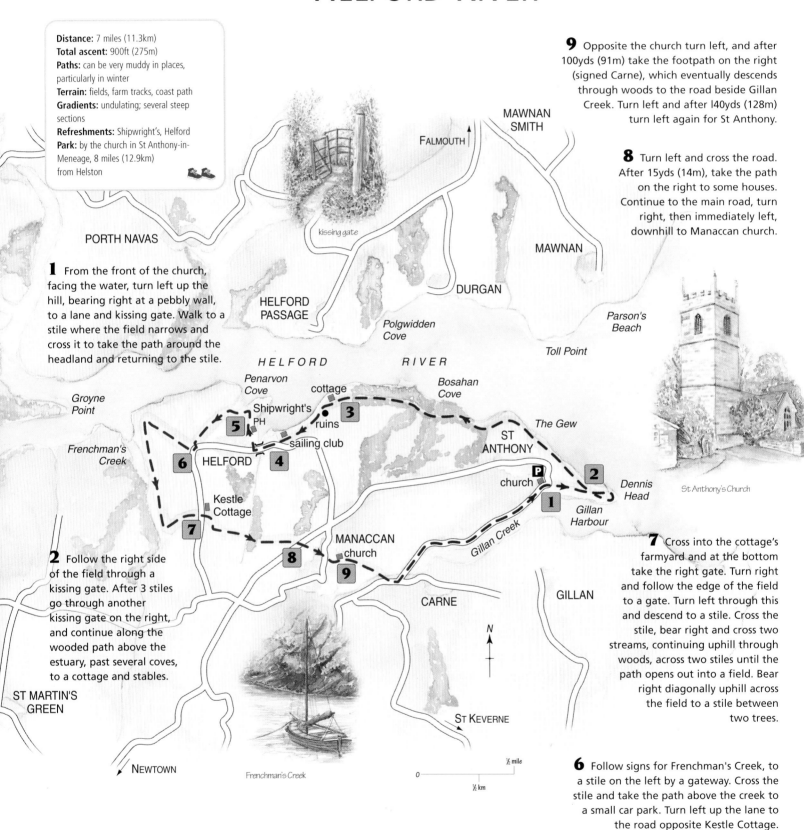

St Anthony's Church

1 From the front of the church, facing the water, turn left up the hill, bearing right at a pebbly wall, to a lane and kissing gate. Walk to a stile where the field narrows and cross it to take the path around the headland and returning to the stile.

2 Follow the right side of the field through a kissing gate. After 3 stiles go through another kissing gate on the right, and continue along the wooded path above the estuary, past several coves, to a cottage and stables.

7 Cross into the cottage's farmyard and at the bottom take the right gate. Turn right and follow the edge of the field to a gate. Turn left through this and descend to a stile. Cross the stile, bear right and cross two streams, continuing uphill through woods, across two stiles until the path opens out into a field. Bear right diagonally uphill across the field to a stile between two trees.

6 Follow signs for Frenchman's Creek, to a stile on the left by a gateway. Cross the stile and take the path above the creek to a small car park. Turn left up the lane to the road opposite Kestle Cottage.

3 Bear right between the ruins and the cottage and then left up a track. Fork downhill at the top of the track and turn left up some steps just before a white cottage. Continue past the sailing club and a kissing gate on the right and go through another one straight ahead.

4 Turn left, then immediately right, to follow the road down through the village to a footbridge. Cross this, turn right and continue to the Shipwright's pub. Go left up the hill out of the pub car park, ignoring the path on the right to the ferry, and after 100yds (91m), turn right at a footpath sign.

5 Take the footpath to Penarvon Cove. Cross the beach and take the track left and uphill, away from the cottages. Join the road and after another 120yds (110m) turn right at a cattle grid.

AROUND BOLT HEAD

1 From the boulders at the end of the car park, follow the coast path with the sea on your right for about ½ mile (800m) to where the track drops down and then cuts back inland to the floor of a steep valley.

2 Continue down the valley and over a footbridge spanning a stream. Ascend steeply along the path right, skirting the pinnacled ridge to seaward. After a stile, descend into a small valley, cross a footbridge and ascend straight to just before the ridge. Turn inland onto the plateau of The Warren.

3 Follow the clifftop for 1 mile (1.6km) to a wall and stile. At the next wall take the right-hand stile, signed for Bolt Head. Continue up over the open top of Bolt Head, bearing right to a wall and stile.

4 Descend rightwards via a small valley to the headland with its ruined lookout.

5 Return to the stile and continue downhill with the wall on your left. Turn left over a stile (signed Soar Mill Cove) and just before the next wall turn right (signed South Sands) down to a stile.

Distance: 7 miles (11.3km)
Total ascent: 700ft (213m)
Paths: cliff and field paths, farm tracks, short stretch of metalled road; mostly good but occasionally muddy
Terrain: cliff top, open grassland
Gradients: two steep ascents on cliff path
Refreshments: Port Light Hotel, Bolberry Down (limited winter opening)
Park: Bolberry Down car park, seaward of the Port Light Hotel and reached by following signs from the A381 at Malborough

8 Cross the road via two stiles and bear right, then left around the barn to take a path beside a bramble hedge for ¼ mile (400m) to a stile in the corner of the field. Cross this, turn left along the tree-lined Jacob's Lane for ½ mile (800m) to the road and follow this left past radio masts to the car park.

7 Follow the road to the white cottages, going straight on to where the Soar Mill road joins from the left. 100yds (91m) on, at Rew Cross, take the footpath which strikes left over fields to Southdown Farm.

6 Cross the stream and take the lane to a stone barn. Go through the gate, uphill for 50yds (46m) and right, through another gate, to a fingerpost. Turn left, up the valley to East Soar Farm, left through a gate, then through the farm gate to follow the farm track past the farmhouse and the nuclear bunker with its radio mast, to East Soar car park.

Map labels: Bolt Tail, Hope Cove, HOPE, GALMPTON, coastguard lookout, SW Coast Path, BOLBERRY, Slippery Point, Bolberry Down, Portlight Hotel, radio masts, KINGSBRIDGE, A381, Lantern Rock, Southdown Farm, MALBOROUGH, West Cliff, Soar Mill Cove, Rew Cross, SOAR, COLLATON, Lloyds Signal Station, REW, Steeple Cove, COMBE, BATSON, The Warren, bunker, East Soar Farm, radio mast, caravan park, SALCOMBE, Off Cove, North Sands, South Sands, Kingsbridge Estuary, ferry, Overbecks (NT Museum & Gardens), Starehole Bay, Bolt Head, Soar Mill Cove, SW Coast Path, gate and stile

AMONG THE TORS OF DARTMOOR

1 From the car park, cross the road and head up the wide grassy path to reach Haytor. Despite the forbidding face first reached, the tor can be easily climbed up a series of big steps at the back.

2 Walk past the rock mass, with it on your right, and pause. Ahead is an area of western Dartmoor, one of the most accessible, but beautiful, sections of the moor. In the distance, slightly left, is Hound Tor, with Greator Rocks to its right. Beyond Haytor Down, which spreads out in front of you, is the wooded valley of the River Bovey. Down and right (northeast) you will see the remains of Haytor Quarry. To continue the walk, aim for the quarry's perimeter fence and pick up the rough track just to the right.

3 After skirting the right hand edge of the quarry bear left to follow the clear granite tramway. Go past the quarry entrance and continue on the tramway as it bears right across a stone embankment to a T-junction. Turn left and follow the tramway to bear right at a fork. After a few paces take one of the many paths that head off right across open moorland towards Smallacombe Rocks.

7 The walk can be extended, in fine style, by heading onwards from Holwell Tor south across the moor to Saddle Tor, then turning left across the wide and low ridge back to Haytor.

6 From Holwell Tor take a direct line across the moor – there is a rough and indistict path – heading for Low Man, the cliff to the right of Haytor. From Haytor reverse the outward route back to the start.

5 Turn right along the tramway, passing a ruined building and the main quarry, then continuing round the back of the quarry, crossing a ruined bridge. Just over the bridge, head left up to the top of Holwell Tor.

4 There are excellent views of the surrounding moor from the rocks. Turning to face Haytor, lower and to the right you will see a quarry set in the back of Holwell Tor. Take the path from Smallacombe Rocks which heads just to the left of the quarry. This will take you back to the tramway.

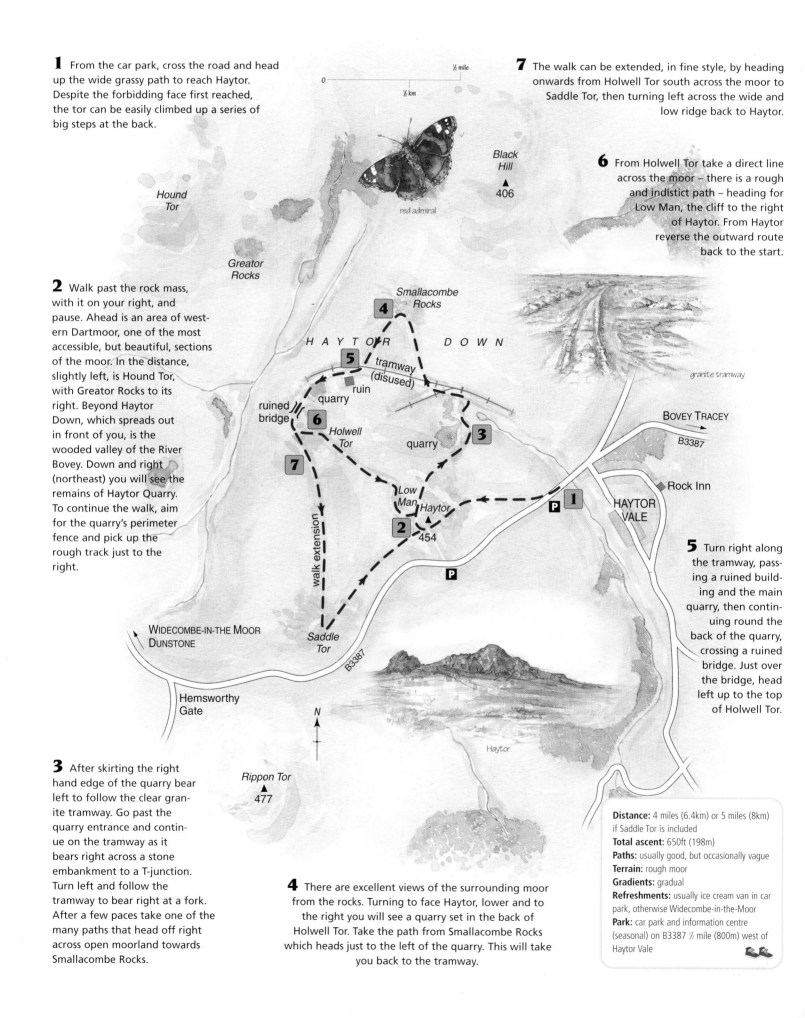

Black Hill ▲ 406

Hound Tor

Greator Rocks

red admiral

Smallacombe Rocks

4

H A Y T O R   D O W N

5 tramway (disused)

quarry   ruin

ruined bridge

6 Holwell Tor

3 quarry

7

Low Man   Haytor

2 454

walk extension

granite tramway

BOVEY TRACEY
B3387

Rock Inn

P   **1**

HAYTOR VALE

P

WIDECOMBE-IN-THE MOOR
DUNSTONE

Saddle Tor

B3387

Hemsworthy Gate

N ↑

Haytor

Rippon Tor ▲ 477

Distance: 4 miles (6.4km) or 5 miles (8km) if Saddle Tor is included
Total ascent: 650ft (198m)
Paths: usually good, but occasionally vague
Terrain: rough moor
Gradients: gradual
Refreshments: usually ice cream van in car park, otherwise Widecombe-in-the-Moor
Park: car park and information centre (seasonal) on B3387 ½ mile (800m) west of Haytor Vale

THE ROCKY COAST BEYOND WOOLACOMBE

1 From either car park turn left, following the South West Coast Path alongside the road to Mortehoe. It's possible to walk nearer to the sea in places but you must return to the road before the bend at the foot of the hill up to Mortehoe.

2 Follow the coast path signs to cut out the bend in the road and follow the road a short distance up the hill towards Mortehoe. About 300yds (273m) up the hill turn left. Follow the coast path signs for the next 3 miles (4.8km). The path keeps close to the coast all around Morte Point, down into a little valley below Mortehoe and another behind the beach at Rockham and up to Bull Point lighthouse.

3 At the entrance to the lighthouse compound turn right up the tarmac drive. However, it's worth continuing on the coast path to the seat on the hillock above the lighthouse for the view along the coast to Ilfracombe and returning to the drive. The drive ascends 1 mile (1.6km) to the edge of the village at Mortehoe.

4 Pass through the signed gateway at the end of the drive and take the second footpath signposted to the left, passing through a thicket alongside a house. Take the stile into the field, carrying straight on across the middle of the field and coming out by a stile onto a bend in a tarmac drive. Keep right, going up the drive past the golf course and from the bend onto a road at the top.

5 Turn right down the road towards Mortehoe and take the first field gateway on the left. Keep straight ahead with the bank on your right and cross a stile onto a drive in a caravan site. Turn left, following the drive to a footpath by a stream. Cross the stream at the bottom and go up to the junction with a footpath. Bear right along the path and take the first turning left. Keep straight ahead between the caravans.

6 At the end of the caravan site drive, find a path descending through the trees and crossing the stream at the bottom. Ascend to the path junction and turn right and over a stile by a National Trust sign. The path descends the valley side for nearly a mile (1.6km). Just before the bottom there is a small gate at a sharp bend in the path. Take the gate and follow the road straight down to the coast road. Turn left to return to the start.

Map labels:

Rockham Bay
Bull Point
lighthouse
3
Lee Bay
South West Coast Path
ILFRACOMBE
Rockham Bay
combe
4
combe
South West Coast Path
HIGHER WARCOMBE
Borough Valley
Morte Point
MORTEHOE
Ship Aground PH
golf course
5
caravan park
6
2
tourist information centre
war memorial, Woolacombe
ILFRACOMBE
Fortescue Arms PH
1
Red Barn PH B3343
B3343
WOOLACOMBE
Morte Bay
Woolacombe Sand
South West Coast Path
BRAUNTON
N
Woolacombe
0   ½ mile
½ km

Distance: 6 miles (9.7km)
Total ascent: 650ft (198m)
Paths: generally good; grass slippery when wet
Terrain: coastal grass and heathland, fields
Gradients: gradual and fairly short
Refreshments: Woolacombe
Park: either of two car parks by beach in Woolacombe village; can be busy in summer, but there is plenty of other parking

HIGH MOORS ABOVE THE RIVER EXE

1 From the lay-by walk along road towards Simonsbath for 350yds (319m). Turn right down drive signed to Mole's Chamber (follow blue waymarked signs all the way to Wood Barrow). Follow bridleway off the drive at point where it becomes private, and go through gate at bend after bridge. After next gate take smaller path straight ahead, keeping slightly right and following top of steep valley side, gradually descending to stream. Follow path through gate at Mole's Chamber.

6 Take gate signed to B3358 or detour 300yds (273m) for view from Chains Barrow and return. Follow line of posts all the way to bottom of field. Go through gate and follow bank on left down to road and back to the start.

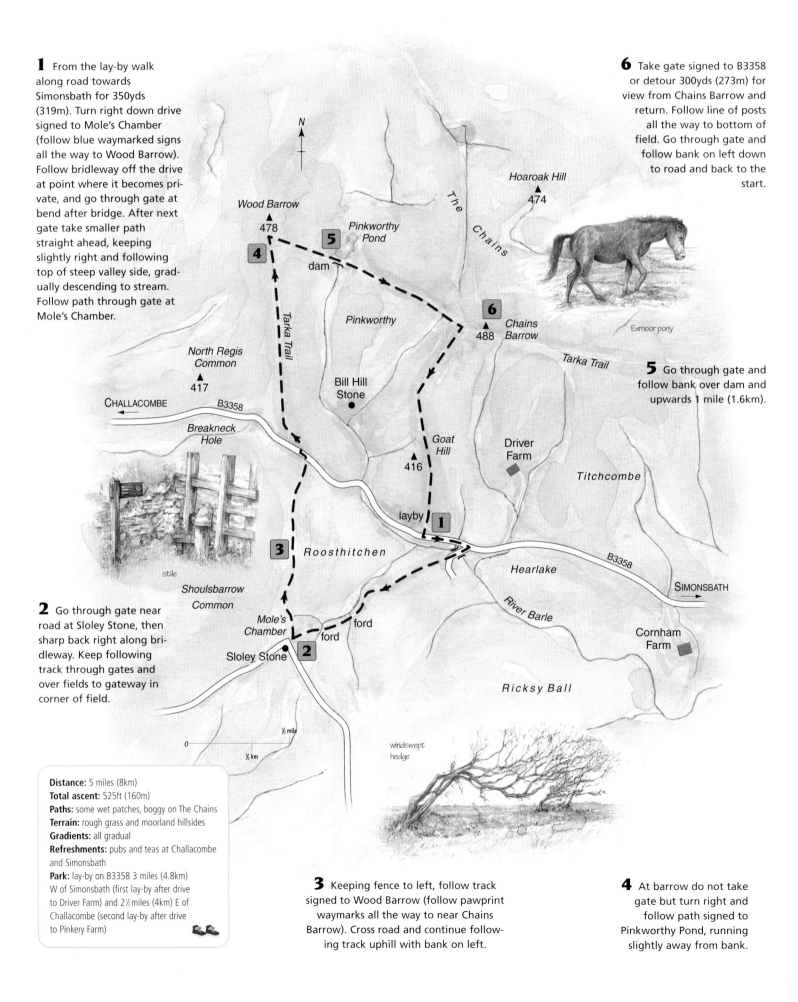

5 Go through gate and follow bank over dam and upwards 1 mile (1.6km).

2 Go through gate near road at Sloley Stone, then sharp back right along bridleway. Keep following track through gates and over fields to gateway in corner of field.

Distance: 5 miles (8km)
Total ascent: 525ft (160m)
Paths: some wet patches, boggy on The Chains
Terrain: rough grass and moorland hillsides
Gradients: all gradual
Refreshments: pubs and teas at Challacombe and Simonsbath
Park: lay-by on B3358 3 miles (4.8km) W of Simonsbath (first lay-by after drive to Driver Farm) and 2½ miles (4km) E of Challacombe (second lay-by after drive to Pinkery Farm)

3 Keeping fence to left, follow track signed to Wood Barrow (follow pawprint waymarks all the way to near Chains Barrow). Cross road and continue following track uphill with bank on left.

4 At barrow do not take gate but turn right and follow path signed to Pinkworthy Pond, running slightly away from bank.

IN SEARCH OF LORNA DOONE ON EXMOOR

1 Cross the road from the car park entrance and take the bridleway along the heath, signed to Broomstreet Farm.

2 Turn right up the drive past Yenworthy Lodge. Cross the road, take the stile and follow a yellow waymarked path down to Oare. Skirt through trees around a farm at Oare House then turn left onto a road, over a bridge and up to Oare church. Turn left, then take the gate to left of churchyard, signed to Larkbarrow. Follow the blue waymarks straight up over fields, keeping the field perimeter on your right.

3 At a bend leave the track and follow the Larkbarrow bridleway sign up over a field, bearing slightly right. Turn left through a gate and follow blue waymarks along the fence and banks for 1½ miles (2.4km) to a waymark at the end of the straight line of the bank. Cross the middle of the field, bearing slightly left to a gate in the fence.

Distance: 9 miles (14.5km)
Total ascent: 920ft (280m)
Paths: vary from wide tracks to open moor; boggy in patches
Terrain: valley, fields, moor and heath
Gradients: mostly easy with short steep parts
Refreshments: teas at Cloud Farm and Malmsmead, cold drinks at County Gate (all seasonal)
Park: National Park car park, toilets and visitor centre at County Gate, 7miles (11.3km) west of Porlock on A39

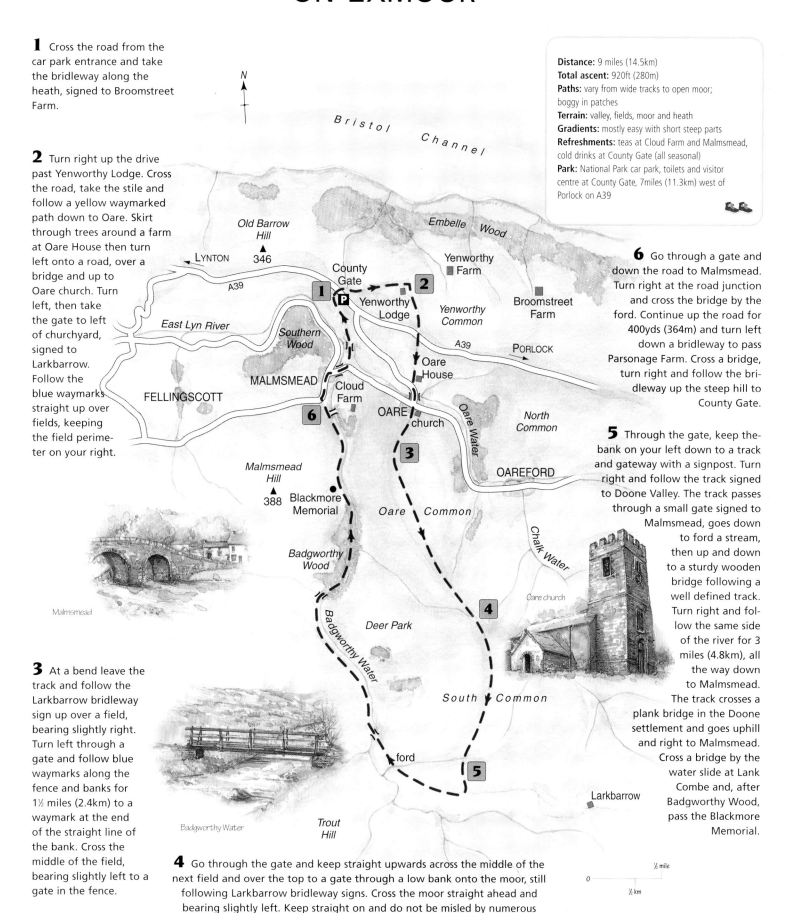

Malmsmead

Badgworthy Water

6 Go through a gate and down the road to Malmsmead. Turn right at the road junction and cross the bridge by the ford. Continue up the road for 400yds (364m) and turn left down a bridleway to pass Parsonage Farm. Cross a bridge, turn right and follow the bridleway up the steep hill to County Gate.

5 Through the gate, keep the bank on your left down to a track and gateway with a signpost. Turn right and follow the track signed to Doone Valley. The track passes through a small gate signed to Malmsmead, goes down to ford a stream, then up and down to a sturdy wooden bridge following a well defined track. Turn right and follow the same side of the river for 3 miles (4.8km), all the way down to Malmsmead. The track crosses a plank bridge in the Doone settlement and goes uphill and right to Malmsmead. Cross a bridge by the water slide at Lank Combe and, after Badgworthy Wood, pass the Blackmore Memorial.

4 Go through the gate and keep straight upwards across the middle of the next field and over the top to a gate through a low bank onto the moor, still following Larkbarrow bridleway signs. Cross the moor straight ahead and bearing slightly left. Keep straight on and do not be misled by numerous tracks. In ½ mile (800m) you should have rounded the head of a small combe and come to a gate in a bank with a bridleway sign.

SPECTACULAR VIEWS FROM THE QUANTOCK HILLS

Distance: 7 miles (11.3km)
Total ascent: 820ft (250m)
Paths: mostly good but muddy after rain; shallow stream to ford in Holford Combe
Terrain: mostly open heath or wooded valley
Gradients: gradual, but one short, steep downhill section
Refreshments: Plough Inn, Holford, and teas in village in season
Park: car park in old quarry by bowling green at Holford, on minor road between Holford village and Alfoxton Park

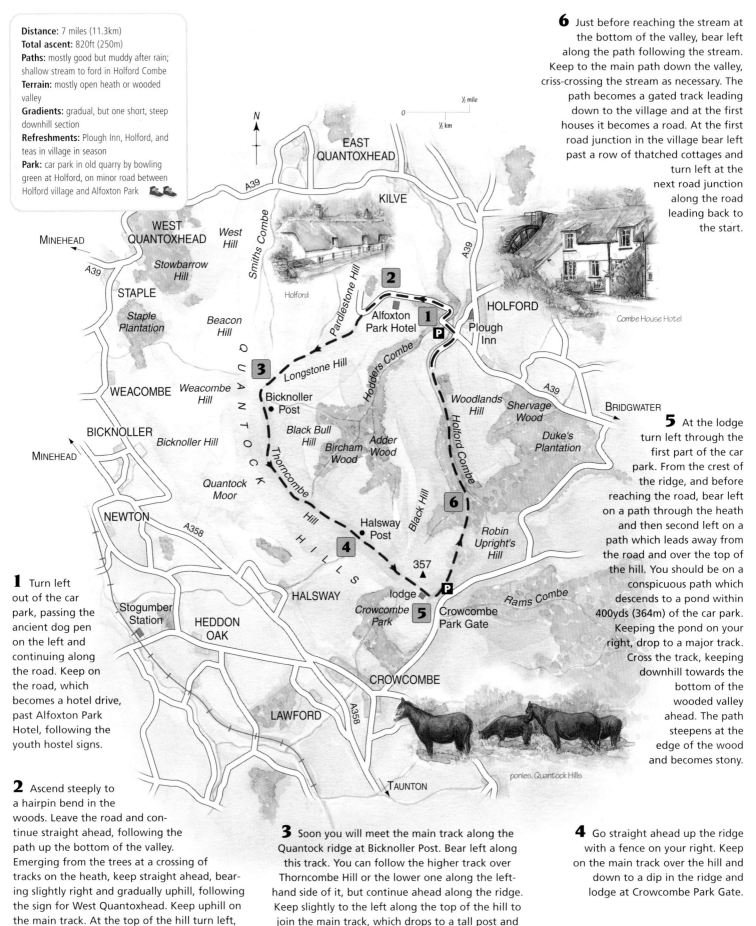

ponies, Quantock Hills

Combe House Hotel

6 Just before reaching the stream at the bottom of the valley, bear left along the path following the stream. Keep to the main path down the valley, criss-crossing the stream as necessary. The path becomes a gated track leading down to the village and at the first houses it becomes a road. At the first road junction in the village bear left past a row of thatched cottages and turn left at the next road junction along the road leading back to the start.

5 At the lodge turn left through the first part of the car park. From the crest of the ridge, and before reaching the road, bear left on a path through the heath and then second left on a path which leads away from the road and over the top of the hill. You should be on a conspicuous path which descends to a pond within 400yds (364m) of the car park. Keeping the pond on your right, drop to a major track. Cross the track, keeping downhill towards the bottom of the wooded valley ahead. The path steepens at the edge of the wood and becomes stony.

1 Turn left out of the car park, passing the ancient dog pen on the left and continuing along the road. Keep on the road, which becomes a hotel drive, past Alfoxton Park Hotel, following the youth hostel signs.

2 Ascend steeply to a hairpin bend in the woods. Leave the road and continue straight ahead, following the path up the bottom of the valley. Emerging from the trees at a crossing of tracks on the heath, keep straight ahead, bearing slightly right and gradually uphill, following the sign for West Quantoxhead. Keep uphill on the main track. At the top of the hill turn left, descending slightly.

3 Soon you will meet the main track along the Quantock ridge at Bicknoller Post. Bear left along this track. You can follow the higher track over Thorncombe Hill or the lower one along the left-hand side of it, but continue ahead along the ridge. Keep slightly to the left along the top of the hill to join the main track, which drops to a tall post and crossing of tracks at Halsway Post.

4 Go straight ahead up the ridge with a fence on your right. Keep on the main track over the hill and down to a dip in the ridge and lodge at Crowcombe Park Gate.

THE MYSTERIOUS CERNE ABBAS GIANT

1 In Cerne Abbas, make your way to the church, which stands in Abbey Street and walk along the street with the church to your right. To your left is an elegant row of timbered houses complete with overhangs.

2 Go past the village pond, to the right. Ahead now is beautiful Abbey Farm.

8 Cross the main road with care, bearing right and then left along the minor road towards the village, soon reaching the Kettle Bridge picnic site where there is alternative parking. Turn left (signed for the village centre), then follow the sign for the Pottery. Before crossing the bridge, turn right along a path with the river on your left. After about 200yds (182m) turn left over a footbridge and follow the path into the village.

7 Just beyond a white gate marked 'Private', go left along a field path, heading towards the modern barns, regaining the road and following it to its junction with the main road.

6 Turn left and follow the road, with great care, for 220yds (200m), then turn right along the road for Up Cerne. Follow this narrow, but quiet, road through beautiful Up Cerne, reaching the village 'square'. Continue uphill: there is a fine view of the Manor House from here.

5 Go through the gate and across the field beyond to reach another gate. Go through and maintain direction, passing several waymarkers to reach a gate. Cross the field beyond to reach a track, following it to a crossing of tracks. Turn left (signed for the main road) and follow the track (which becomes metalled) through Minterne Parva to the main road (A352).

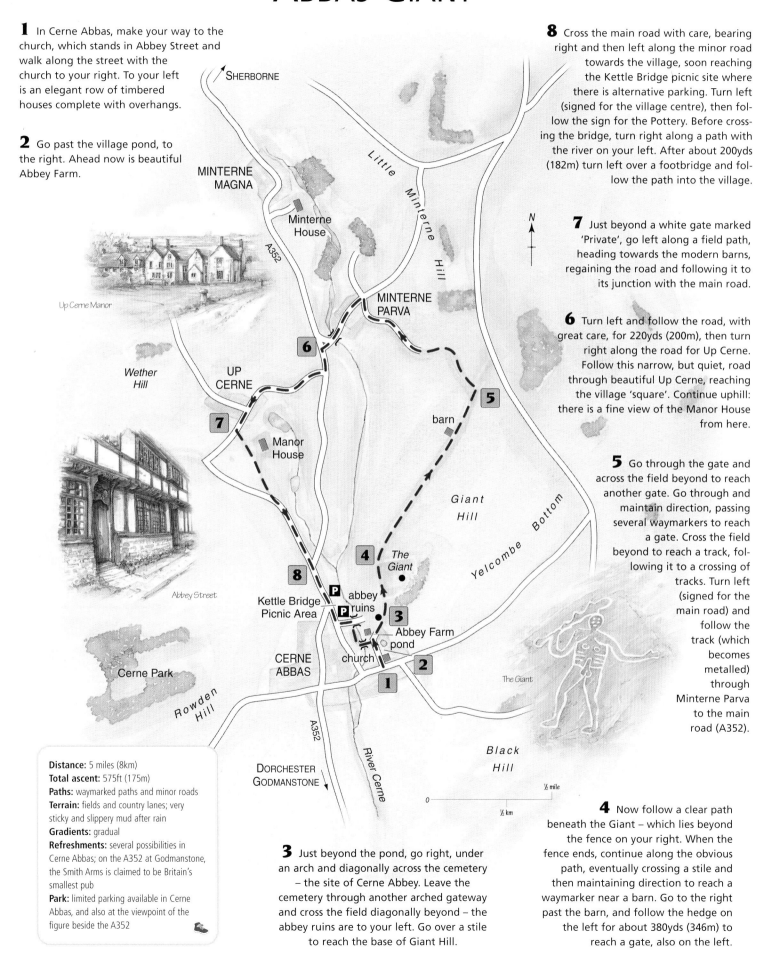

SHERBORNE

MINTERNE MAGNA

Minterne House

Little Minterne Hill

MINTERNE PARVA

Up Cerne Manor

Wether Hill

UP CERNE

N

6

7

Manor House

barn

5

Giant Hill

Yelcombe Bottom

4

The Giant

3

Abbey Street

Kettle Bridge Picnic Area

abbey ruins

Abbey Farm pond

church

8

1

2

The Giant

CERNE ABBAS

Cerne Park

Rowden Hill

A352

DORCHESTER GODMANSTONE

River Cerne

Black Hill

½ mile

½ km

0

Distance: 5 miles (8km)
Total ascent: 575ft (175m)
Paths: waymarked paths and minor roads
Terrain: fields and country lanes; very sticky and slippery mud after rain
Gradients: gradual
Refreshments: several possibilities in Cerne Abbas; on the A352 at Godmanstone, the Smith Arms is claimed to be Britain's smallest pub
Park: limited parking available in Cerne Abbas, and also at the viewpoint of the figure beside the A352

3 Just beyond the pond, go right, under an arch and diagonally across the cemetery – the site of Cerne Abbey. Leave the cemetery through another arched gateway and cross the field diagonally beyond – the abbey ruins are to your left. Go over a stile to reach the base of Giant Hill.

4 Now follow a clear path beneath the Giant – which lies beyond the fence on your right. When the fence ends, continue along the obvious path, eventually crossing a stile and then maintaining direction to reach a waymarker near a barn. Go to the right past the barn, and follow the hedge on the left for about 380yds (346m) to reach a gate, also on the left.

DORSET HEATHS OF THOMAS HARDY

Distance: 9 miles (14.5km)
Total ascent: 165ft (50m)
Paths: good but muddy in wet weather
Terrain: heathland, woodland, open roads and fields
Ascents: very few and gradual
Refreshments: Wise Man Inn, West Stafford (half way round the walk)
Park: Hardy's Cottage car park (National Trust), Higher Bockhampton, ½ mile from A35, NE of Dorchester

1 From the car park head for Hardy's Cottage, signed via a woodland path. From there take the path, signposted Puddletown, to a path junction. Continue to the next junction and turn right, continuing until the path descends steeply. The Rainbarrow is through a break in the hedge to the right.

8 Go through the farmyard and follow the footpath sign. Cross 3 fields, over stiles, through gates and past a house, turning left onto a farm track. Continue across a minor road, eventually turning left at a crossroads. The path forks right, then turns left and leads down to the car park.

2 Continue down the steep path, ignoring all other paths, until it turns left to the bottom of the hill. Take the small track through the bushes, ignoring the stile to the right, continuing over two stiles then left across the field. Cross the road to the track opposite.

7 Over a bridge turn right, following the waymarkers, through a kissing-gate, across a field and a bridge. Continue over another bridge, turn left and then right to Stinsford. Retrace your steps to the river and continue to Lower Bockhampton. Cross the bridge and turn left, signposted Thorncombe Wood.

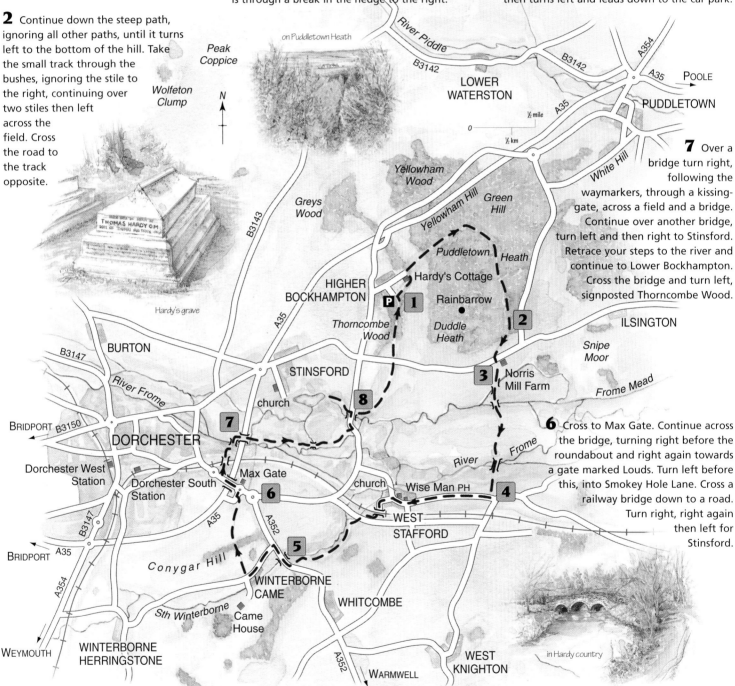

6 Cross to Max Gate. Continue across the bridge, turning right before the roundabout and right again towards a gate marked Louds. Turn left before this, into Smokey Hole Lane. Cross a railway bridge down to a road. Turn right, right again then left for Stinsford.

3 Continue along the farm track until a junction; bear left then right following the blue waymarkers. Follow this track across the field and cross the bridge over the river. Follow the blue waymarker through a gate and continue to the end of the track. Turn right at the gate, then go over the field to cross the wooden bridge and stile. Walk with the fence to the left, over another stile, across the field and through the gate to reach the end of the track.

4 Continue to the junction with the road, then turn right to West Stafford. Turn left at the church along Rectory Lane. Follow the blue waymarkers, under the railway bridge, across the road and over a stile. Continue through several gates until you reach a gate to the main road.

5 Turn right and then left through gates beside a lodge. Continue to the crossroads at Came and turn right towards Dorchester. At the top, where the road curves, go straight ahead. Cross the stile, following signs for Max Gate, exiting at a roundabout.

PURBECK'S GHOST VILLAGE

1 Turn right from the car park, towards Tyneham village. The town trail is short but interesting. Each of the buildings has a marker and a leaflet available from the church explains what they were. The church and schoolroom contain an exhibition of the village history.

7 Return to the path and, following the yellow markers, ascend Gad Cliff and proceed along the coastal path. Cross a stile and, at the sign pointing left to Tyneham, head downhill following the markers. This will return you to the car park.

2 From the water fountain in front of the church take the road to the right past a marker pointing to Flower's Barrow and Whiteway car park. Follow the yellow waymarkers, passing behind the church and going through a kissing gate, and continue uphill.

6 Continue over the wooden bridge and turn left up a stone track, going right at the yellow marker, up the steps to arrive at a cairn. From here take the track up Worbarrow Tout for a superb view over the bay and the switchback cliffs.

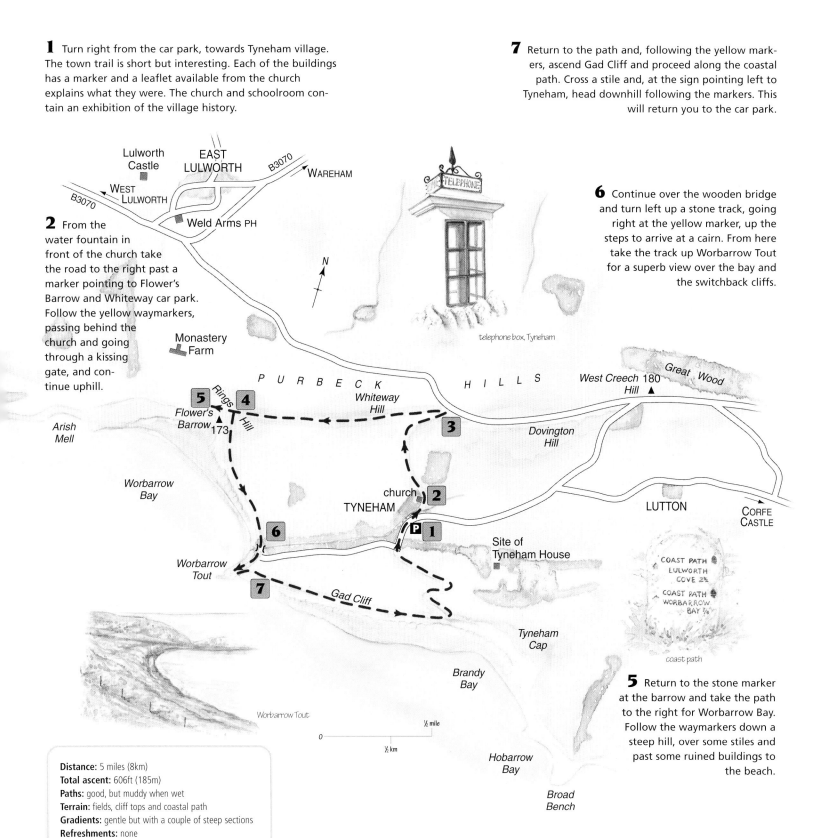

telephone box, Tyneham

coast path

Worbarrow Tout

Distance: 5 miles (8km)
Total ascent: 606ft (185m)
Paths: good, but muddy when wet
Terrain: fields, cliff tops and coastal path
Gradients: gentle but with a couple of steep sections
Refreshments: none
Park: car park at Tyneham village, in Lulworth Ranges, between Corfe Castle and West Lulworth
Note: this walk is on the Lulworth Army Ranges and access is strictly controlled. They are open most weekends and in holiday periods, but for up-to-date information, call the Range Office on 01929 462721 ext. 4819

5 Return to the stone marker at the barrow and take the path to the right for Worbarrow Bay. Follow the waymarkers down a steep hill, over some stiles and past some ruined buildings to the beach.

3 At the flagpole at the top take the path to the left, cross a stile and head uphill past a trig point. Continue on the path downhill, until the road curves to the right. Veer left onto a track at the yellow marker.

4 Continue along the track, over a stile, following yellow waymarkers. When you reach an area with picnic tables, you are in the middle of Flower's Barrow. A stone marker points the way to Lulworth Cove. Continue on this path to the outer rings of this prehistoric fortification for a superb view along the coast.

FROME'S MEDIEVAL HIGHLIGHTS

Distance: 4½ miles (7.2km)
Total ascent: 200ft (61m)
Paths: town streets and good paths
Terrain: town streets and fields
Gradients: gradual, though the ascent of Gentle Street belies its name
Refreshments: numerous opportunities in Frome
Park: car park beside the tourist information centre

1 From the courtyard of the tourist information centre, turn right, then right again, to the main street into town. To the left is the town museum. Turn right over the bridge, looking left to see the Blue House. Continue along Market Place, then turn left up Cheap Street.

2 At the top of the street turn right and go up the steps; left is the Via Crucis by the churchyard entrance. Continue up Gentle Street and, at the top, turn right along Christchurch Street West. First right is Bath Street, with Rook Lane Congregational Chapel to the left. Continue along Christchurch Street West, turning fourth right down Catherine Street. Where the road bears sharp left, continue down cobbled Catherine Hill.

3 Bear right with Catherine Hill, then left down Stony Street to return to Market Place and turn left along Cork Street. At the Coach House bear left into West End (unsigned). Turn right along Welshmill Lane. Bear left to go under the railway bridge and continue along Welshmill Lane, crossing the River Frome. Cross into Park Hill Drive, following it around to the right.

4 Take a footpath on the left, between Numbers 39 and 41, maintaining direction along Packsaddle Way for a few steps before turning left into Leys Lane. Continue to reach a gate for Selwood Lodge. Follow the drive beyond, but where it bears right, go left over a stile and follow the hedge on the right.

5 Go over a stile and follow the signed path over a stone stile and onto a road. Cross the stile opposite and head for a metal bridge. Cross this, reaching a lane soon after. Turn left for 100yds (91m) then turn left along a signed path across a field to a road.

6 Cross the road and the stile opposite. Cross the railway with care, go through a kissing gate and follow a path through a small copse to reach a metal stile. Cross and continue, with elegant Whatcombe Farm on your right. Go through a V-shaped stile and head for the pylon; Trinity Church is on the horizon. Follow the clear path with the sewage works on your left.

7 Go through another stile and continue with the river on your left, crossing another stile. Continue to reach the signed Riverside Walk. Follow this to reach a concrete road and a metal bridge. Cross the road and go under the bridge, following a sign for the town centre to reach Welshmill Bridge. Now cross the bridge and follow the left bank of the river, under the railway bridge back to the car park or reverse the outward journey to Cork Street and turn left at Market Place.

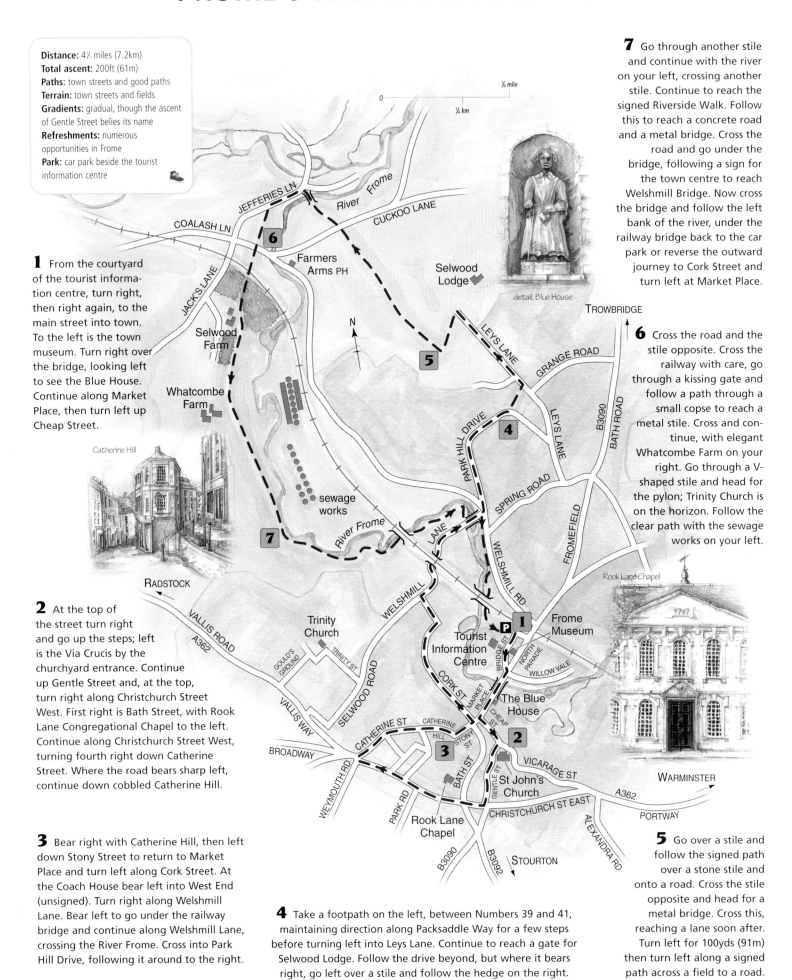

detail, Blue House

Catherine Hill

Rook Lane Chapel

THE OTHER SIDES TO CHEDDAR GORGE

1 From car park turn right towards the Gorge. Cross the bridge and take the next road on the right, keeping uphill. Just before the brow of the hill turn left up behind cottages. At the end of the lane follow the bridleway up to the left. Keep following the Gorge Walk waymarks along the edge of the gorge for 1¼ miles (2km). The path ascends to the top of a ridge and descends through woodland to the road at the head of the Gorge.

2 Cross the road and take the gate and track ahead into Black Rock reserve. Follow the main track up the bottom of the valley for ⅔ mile (1km). After the National Trust sign turn right over a wall and follow the waymarks up the bottom of the valley for another mile (1.6km).

6 Cross a stile from fields into a scrubby area. Bear left, then right, to pick up the Gorge Walk waymarks. Keep dowhill with the Gorge on your left. It is worth the detour down a steep flight of steps to a viewpoint. Returning, the path steepens to descend through woods to a track. Turn left down the track, then right and down the road through the Gorge to return to the start.

5 Turn right along the road and take the next turn to the left, down a farm drive. Keep right of Charterhouse and Piney Sleight Farms, then follow the yellow waymarks ahead across fields, keeping close to the walls on your right.

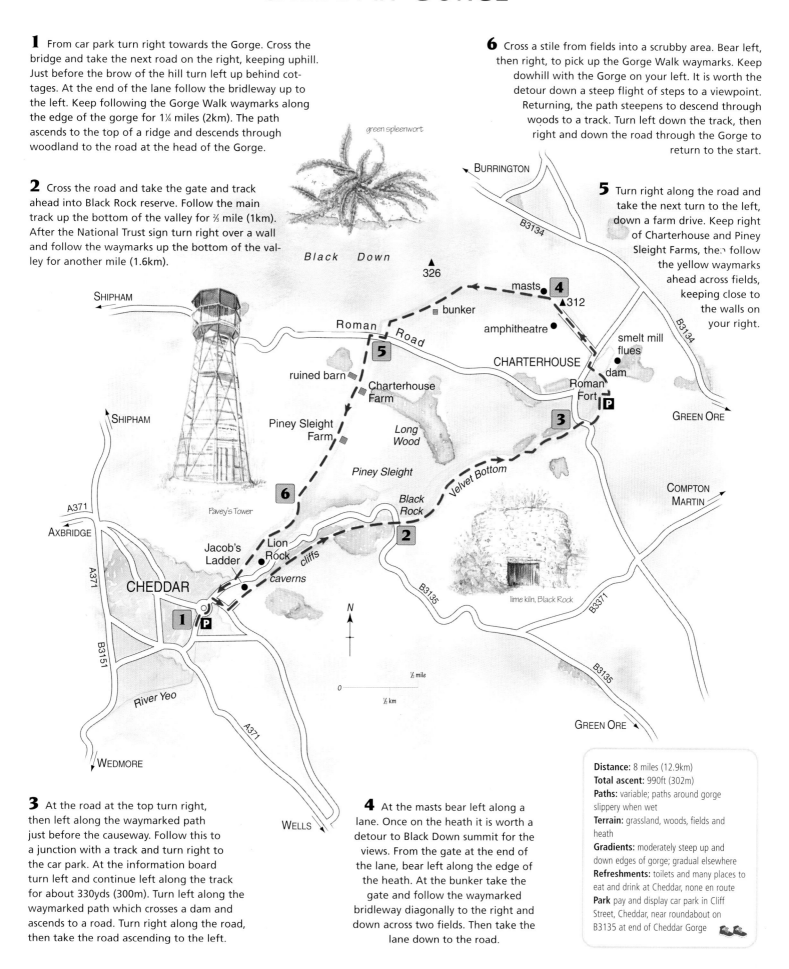

green spleenwort

lime kiln, Black Rock

Pavey's Tower

3 At the road at the top turn right, then left along the waymarked path just before the causeway. Follow this to a junction with a track and turn right to the car park. At the information board turn left and continue left along the track for about 330yds (300m). Turn left along the waymarked path which crosses a dam and ascends to a road. Turn right along the road, then take the road ascending to the left.

4 At the masts bear left along a lane. Once on the heath it is worth a detour to Black Down summit for the views. From the gate at the end of the lane, bear left along the edge of the heath. At the bunker take the gate and follow the waymarked bridleway diagonally to the right and down across two fields. Then take the lane down to the road.

Distance: 8 miles (12.9km)
Total ascent: 990ft (302m)
Paths: variable; paths around gorge slippery when wet
Terrain: grassland, woods, fields and heath
Gradients: moderately steep up and down edges of gorge; gradual elsewhere
Refreshments: toilets and many places to eat and drink at Cheddar, none en route
Park pay and display car park in Cliff Street, Cheddar, near roundabout on B3135 at end of Cheddar Gorge

LANSDOWN – A CIVIL WAR BATTLEGROUND

1 From lay-by cross road and follow well-waymarked Cotswold Way, joining private road to fire brigade building.

2 Turn right with Way just before brigade complex, then, soon, left along field path. Follow Way to trig point on Hanging Hill, seen over wall. Turn left over stile and step left to walk past trig point, continuing with hedge on right. Cross stile to reach golf course, bearing left to follow bridleway along left edge. Turn right, as signed, to follow Cotswold Way across course and then left along bridleway between wood on right, and course's northern edge, on left.

3 Leave course through gate, soon turning left off descending track, with Cotswold Way to stile. Walk parallel with fence on left, and follow it sharp left then on, across Little Down hill fort, exiting across section of ditch. Turn right and follow edge of hill, with race course starting stalls on left, to panorama dial at Prospect Stile.

8 Eventually, Cotswold Way joins from right. Carry on through gate and after 100yds (91m) go right, uphill to wall and Cotswold Way signpost. Go over stile and walk with wall on right to scarp edge where much of the Battle of Lansdown was fought, before bearing left to monument. Lay-by is 100yds (91m) further along track.

7 Continue past church, passing house on right, to Tynings Cottage (on left). Turn left just before cottage, climbing steep lane. Go over crest and descend to barn on right. Turn left up signed bridleway, maintaining direction where it narrows.

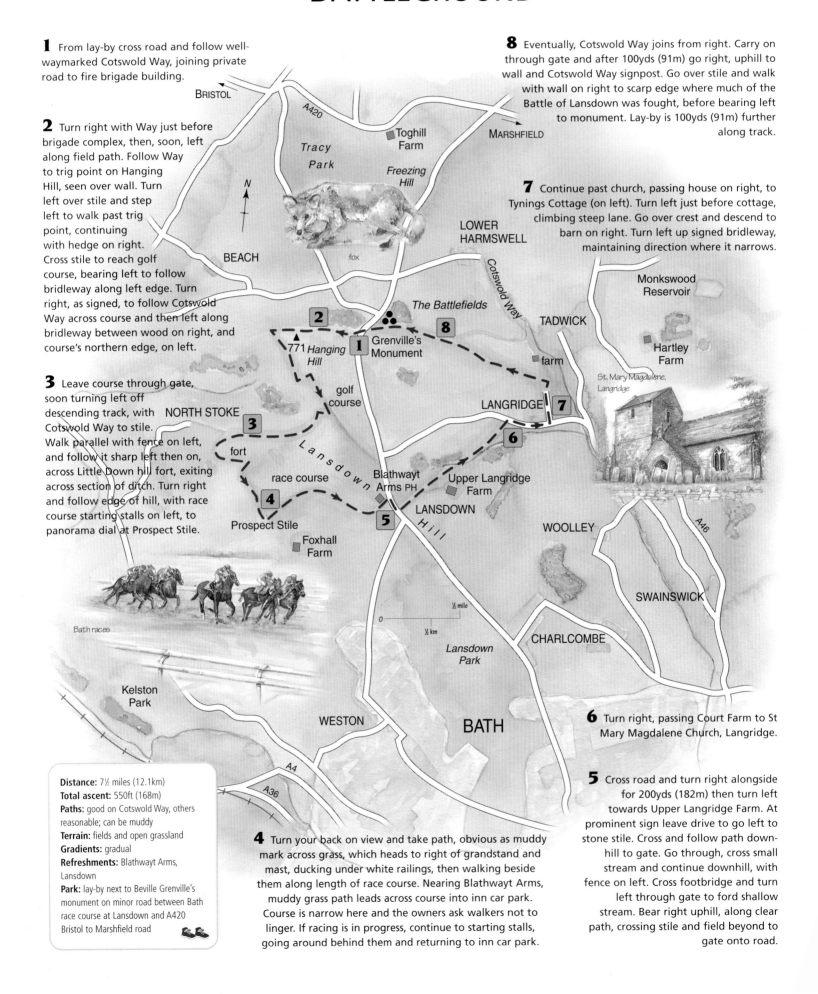

Bath races

6 Turn right, passing Court Farm to St Mary Magdalene Church, Langridge.

5 Cross road and turn right alongside for 200yds (182m) then turn left towards Upper Langridge Farm. At prominent sign leave drive to go left to stone stile. Cross and follow path downhill to gate. Go through, cross small stream and continue downhill, with fence on left. Cross footbridge and turn left through gate to ford shallow stream. Bear right uphill, along clear path, crossing stile and field beyond to gate onto road.

Distance: 7½ miles (12.1km)
Total ascent: 550ft (168m)
Paths: good on Cotswold Way, others reasonable; can be muddy
Terrain: fields and open grassland
Gradients: gradual
Refreshments: Blathwayt Arms, Lansdown
Park: lay-by next to Beville Grenville's monument on minor road between Bath race course at Lansdown and A420 Bristol to Marshfield road

4 Turn your back on view and take path, obvious as muddy mark across grass, which heads to right of grandstand and mast, ducking under white railings, then walking beside them along length of race course. Nearing Blathwayt Arms, muddy grass path leads across course into inn car park. Course is narrow here and the owners ask walkers not to linger. If racing is in progress, continue to starting stalls, going around behind them and returning to inn car park.

OLD WAYS ON THE WILTSHIRE DOWNS

1 From Alton Barnes church, go through the turnstile to follow the paved path towards Alton Priors church. Keep left of the tower, go through a kissing gate and turnstile and follow the road between houses. Cross over at the next road junction, follow the Ridgeway up to the next road and turn right. Turn left through a gate into Pewsey Downs National Nature Reserve, up the grassy track parallel to the road. Approaching a fence, bear left up to the summit of Walker's Hill.

> **Distance:** 8 miles (12.9km)
> **Total ascent:** 519ft (158m)
> **Paths:** mainly good; lower paths and towpath can be very wet
> **Terrain:** downland, linear earthwork, gentle farmland, canal towpath
> **Gradients:** one lengthy climb, though not steep
> **Refreshments:** Kings Arms, All Cannings; Barge Inn, Honey Street
> **Park:** on roadside by Alton Barnes church, in Vale of Pewsey between Devizes and Marlborough

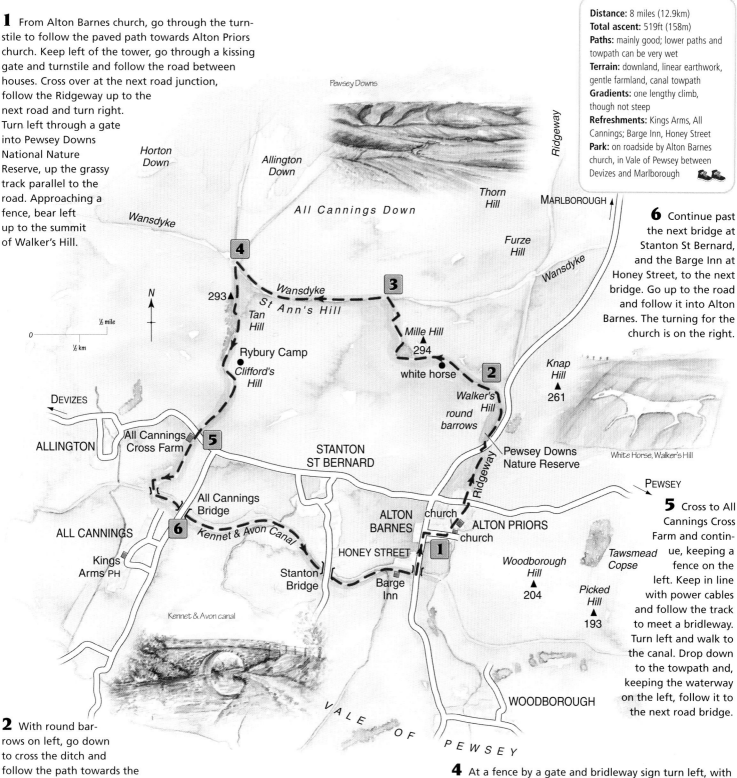

6 Continue past the next bridge at Stanton St Bernard, and the Barge Inn at Honey Street, to the next bridge. Go up to the road and follow it into Alton Barnes. The turning for the church is on the right.

White Horse, Walker's Hill

5 Cross to All Cannings Cross Farm and continue, keeping a fence on the left. Keep in line with power cables and follow the track to meet a bridleway. Turn left and walk to the canal. Drop down to the towpath and, keeping the waterway on the left, follow it to the next road bridge.

2 With round barrows on left, go down to cross the ditch and follow the path towards the White Horse. Continue above the chalk carving, through a gate and on to a fence on the right. Follow the fence, making for a gate round the far side of the woodland. Follow the track across open downland to a gate. Continue ahead with a fence on the right to the next gate. Go through it and, with a fence on the right, drop down the field to a gate and stile.

3 Turn left and follow the track down to the Wansdyke at the foot of the hill. Keep the ditch on the right and follow the linear earthwork in a westerly direction for about 1½ miles (2.4km).

4 At a fence by a gate and bridleway sign turn left, with the fence on the right and head south over Tan Hill. At the summit make for a stile in the field corner. Head down to the next stile and gate, then turn left and drop down to the field corner. Cross a stile and turn immediately right. Keep the fence on your right and follow the path to the next gate and stile. Don't cross it, but turn left and follow the path along the foot of the escarpment. Turn right at the fence corner and follow the path to a stile in the right-hand boundary; step over and join a path south through trees. Follow it to a grassy track running to the road.

ULEY BURY AND HETTY PEGLER'S TUMP

1 In Uley take the path to the right of the church; before the churchyard wall ends, bear right up a path which leads to a stile into a steeply rising grassy field.

2 Climb the slope, aiming diagonally left, up to a stile into the woods. Follow the path up through the woods to another stile. Cross the stile and bear left to walk around the ramparts of Uley Bury hill fort, a 1-mile (1.6km) circuit. Keep high up when you get to the second side of the fort.

3 After completing three sides of the circuit, keep ahead through the trees for 200yds (182m) to join the well-waymarked Cotswold Way below a lay-by on the B4066. Follow the Cotswold Way through Coaley Wood for 1 mile (1.6km) and on reaching a junction of path, bridleway and road end, take a sharp right, ascending to meet the B4066.

7 Descend on a path through the trees, and leave the wood in the valley bottom. Keep the wood edge close on your left for 1 mile (1.6km), descending over a stile to join a farm track to the road at Dingle Farm. Turn left here to view Owlpen Manor and church; turn right to return to Uley.

6 From the Rose and Crown turn right to pass the church. In 100yds (91m) turn right at a footpath sign to cross a field, a track and then a road. Cross the following field, descending half right into the trees.

5 After exploring inside and outside the chambered tomb, retrace your steps along the B4066 to where it meets the Cotswold Way and turn right along a side road, signposted Nympsfield. Take the first lane on your left and, in 300yds (273m), bear right into Nympsfield to find the Rose and Crown pub.

4 Turn right along the grass verge of the road. In ⅓ mile (535m), turn right off the road on a signposted track to Hetty Pegler's Tump, a green grassy mound lying by the edge of the wood.

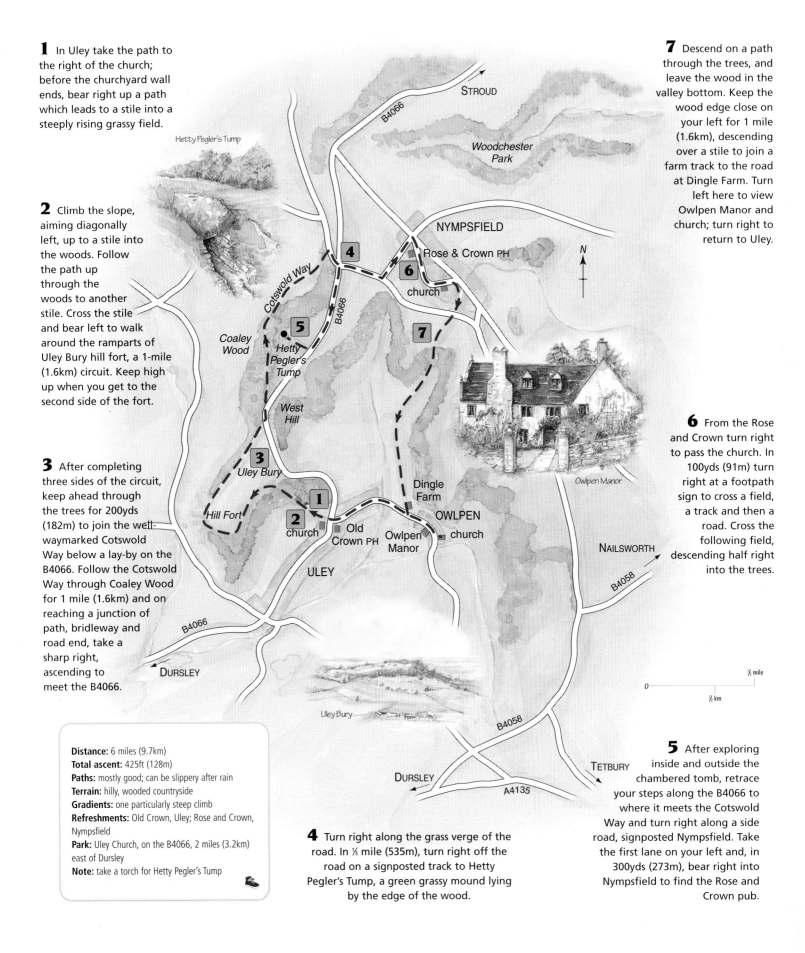

Distance: 6 miles (9.7km)
Total ascent: 425ft (128m)
Paths: mostly good; can be slippery after rain
Terrain: hilly, wooded countryside
Gradients: one particularly steep climb
Refreshments: Old Crown, Uley; Rose and Crown, Nympsfield
Park: Uley Church, on the B4066, 2 miles (3.2km) east of Dursley
Note: take a torch for Hetty Pegler's Tump

BIRDLIP AND THE COTSWOLDS

1 From the panorama board and memorial in the car park bear left along the Cotswold Way to a stile into beech woodland. There is a fine view to the right, but it is even better if the short detour is taken to The Peak. From here return to the Cotswold Way and follow it through the wood. After passing a high bank on the left a distinct path goes off left.

2 Turn left, bearing left at a fork to a gate. Follow the wall on the right across the field beyond to reach a road (the B4070). Cross the road, footbridge and waymarked stile and cross the field beyond to another stile (don't cross). Turn left along field edge to a stile on to the A417.

3 Cross with care and go over the stile opposite. Follow the hedge on the right to a waymarker post. Continue along the hedge on the right (beyond the gap), pass another waymarker and turn left in the corner to continue beside a hedge. Follow hedge sharp right along a wide track. After 30yds (27m) turn left, walking with a hedge on your right and turning left with it, then following a wall on the right to its end. Here step right, around the wall end, and turn left beside a hedge.

4 Follow the hedge to where it turns left and turn left along a broad, grassy swathe to a gate. Follow the lane beyond between houses to reach a road by the masts. Turn right and follow the road, but where it goes right, continue ahead, soon forking left along a metalled lane. Where the lane bears right at a mast and transformer, bear left along a track, following it downhill between deer fences to reach a road. Bear left for a few steps to the main road.

5 Cross and take the road opposite, following it past the golf club, to the right, and the National Star Centre, to the left. Between the two the Cotswold Way joins from the right. At the next crossroads go straight across, following the Cotswold Way. When the road descends, go left up steps and follow the Cotswold Way, crossing two stiles before descending into Short Wood. Stay close to the right edge, emerging close to a car park at Crickley Hill Country Park. Follow the Way through the car park, passing the visitor centre and interpretive panels. Follow the Way across the hill fort to reach a wall, turning left to walk with it.

6 Go through a gate, through the ramparts of the fort and a wood to reach the A417 by the Air Balloon Inn. Cross the road and follow the roadside path uphill. Bear right, away from the road, but where the Cotswold Way turns right, continue along the path to return to the start.

Distance: 7½ miles (12.1km)
Total ascent: 400ft (122m)
Paths: Waymarked section of the Cotswold Way on good paths, together with reasonable field paths
Terrain: fields and open grassland
Gradients: gradual
Refreshments: The Air Balloon Inn
Park: Barrow Wake viewpoint car park on A417 near the Air Balloon Inn

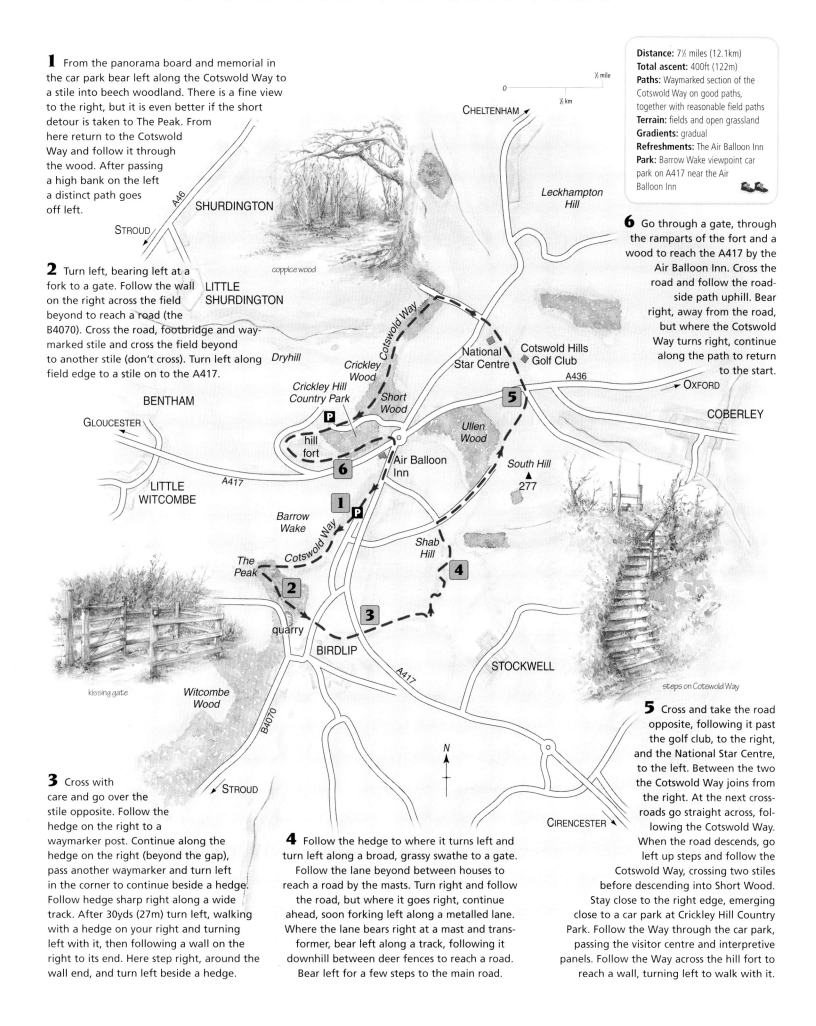

coppice wood

kissing gate

steps on Cotswold Way

CHELTENHAM

SHURDINGTON

STROUD

A46

LITTLE SHURDINGTON

Leckhampton Hill

National Star Centre

Cotswold Hills Golf Club

A436

OXFORD

COBERLEY

Dryhill

Crickley Wood

Crickley Hill Country Park

Short Wood

Ullen Wood

BENTHAM

GLOUCESTER

hill fort

Air Balloon Inn

South Hill
277

LITTLE WITCOMBE

A417

Barrow Wake

The Peak

Cotswold Way

Shab Hill

STOCKWELL

quarry

BIRDLIP

A417

CIRENCESTER

Witcombe Wood

B4070

STROUD

Cotswold Way

½ mile
0
½ km

N

SOUTHERN ENGLAND

THE CHARACTER OF SOUTHern England has been moulded by three main factors. Firstly, it is predominently lowland with a relatively gentle climate, its highest point being not mountains but ranges of rolling chalk downland. Secondly, it is Britain's nearest point to continental Europe and over the centuries routes to and from the Channel ports have been forged, first for trade and for the passage of Christian missionaries, archbishops, kings and ambassadors and later for recreational travellers. The third element is the pole position of London, the nation's centre of commerce and government. This is an exceptionally prosperous region, but, because 19th-century industrialisation focused on the Midlands and the North, it has remained free of big industrial towns. Expansion has instead been recent, and largely in the form of commerce and technology related developments.

Two of the region's biggest attractions are its landscape and its history. Thanks to over 60 years of green belt and other planning policies to protect the countryside, much of this landscape is remarkably unspoiled and tranquil. The Thames and most of the region's coastline have generally been spared the spread of obtrusive development. There are many pleasant seaside resorts, but long stretches of coastline are designated 'Heritage Coast', or have been acquired and conserved by the National Trust.

As for history, the great set pieces include prehistoric monuments such as the great Iron-Age fortress of Danebury in Hampshire, the extensive and well-preserved Roman villa at Fishbourne and Norman castles such as Rochester, Bodiam and, of course, Windsor. There is a wealth of stately homes, from the enormous Blenheim Palace in Oxfordshire to more modest but elegant country houses, all with landscaped grounds and gardens which, in the 18th and 19th centuries, made 'the English Garden' renowned throughout Europe. English Heritage and the National Trust have played leading roles in preserving these treasures, as have many private owners who have striven, often against financial odds, to maintain their family homes.

The region's treasures also include great historic cities like Winchester, Canterbury and Oxford, and countless country towns and villages where the conservation of attractive old buildings and townscapes has been reconciled with the demands of everyday living. Places like Southampton, Portsmouth, Brighton and the Medway Towns may have suffered from urban sprawl, but they too have their historic cores and have done much to preserve and promote their individual character. And often – outstandingly in Oxford, thanks to the patronage of university and colleges – excellent new buildings sit amicably alongside the medieval, the Jacobean and the Georgian, demonstrating that our architectural 'heritage' is still in the making – a dynamic rather than a static concept.

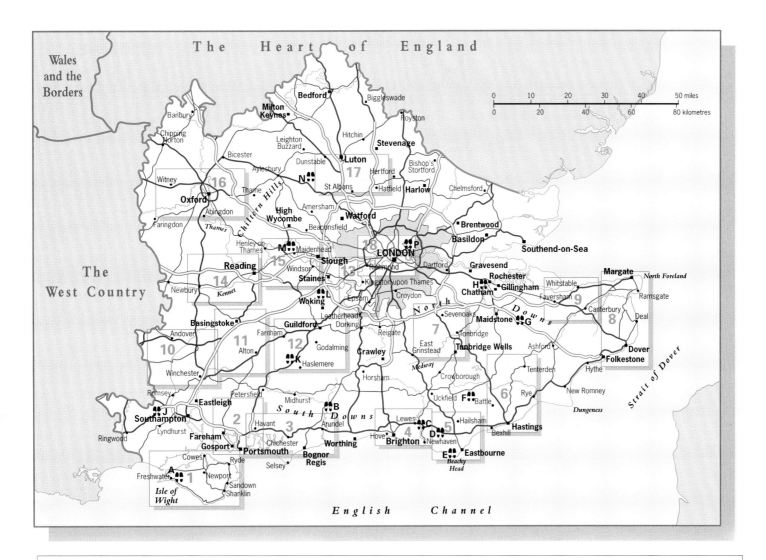

SECTION CONTENTS

FEATURES

WALKS

THE ISLE OF WIGHT

'Cowes you cannot milk; Freshwater you cannot drink; Needles you cannot thread'. The Isle of Wight can too easily be written off as quaint, old-fashioned and open to witicisms. But being an island has given it a certain tranquillity, which helps visitors to enjoy the fine views, unspoiled villages, and relaxed little towns that attracted Queen Victoria and Prince Albert.

Nunwell House at Brading is a lived-in, much-loved home with an interesting collection of family militaria. Concerts are occasionally held in the music room

Osborne House was Queen Victoria's favourite home, the place where she and her family probably came nearest to leading a normal life

Brading

Brading's past intertwines with that of the Oglander family, of nearby Nunwell House. Part Georgian, part Jacobean, the house was where Charles I spent his last night of freedom. There are fine gardens, channel views, and a museum of the Home Guard of World War II. To the west is the island's finest Roman villa, with mosaic floors, and Morton Manor, which has lovely gardens and a vineyard.

Carisbrooke

Standing on a spur of chalk downland, Carisbrooke Castle was for centuries the residence of the island's governor, and is Wight's only medieval castle. A perennial attraction are the donkeys which raise water from the well in the middle courtyard. The keep, gatehouse and curtain wall are 12th century, and the outer bastions were built in the 16th-century

Cowes

To many people Cowes means yachting – particularly Cowes Week, its international yachting festival. West Cowes became a place of consequence when Henry VIII built a fort there; this is now the headquarters of the Royal Yacht Squadron, and the focus of Cowes Week. Prince's Green on the waterside is a good viewpoint. East Cowes is the terminus of the car ferry from Southampton, and beyond it is Osborne House (see panel).

The Needles and Alum Bay

The line of chalk which runs through the island from east to west emerges in the west in the spectacular chalk stacks of The Needles. On the north side of the headland lies Alum Bay, famous for its coloured sands. Some of the many acres of the island owned by the National Trust are here, including Needles Old Battery, a Victorian defence, complete with guns, that sits 250ft (76m) above sea level, with views of the Needles, the lighthouse and the coastline.

Victoria and Osborne

Queen Victoria and Prince Albert bought the 1,000-acre (405ha) Osborne estate in 1845 as (to use the Queen's own words) 'a place of one's own, quiet and retired'. Prince Albert, who much admired Thomas Cubitt's Italianate London terraces, set about designing and building Osborne House (with Cubitt advising) in the style of an Italian villa, with terraced gardens overlooking Osborne Bay and the Solent. 'It is impossible', wrote Victoria, 'to imagine a prettier spot. We can walk anywhere without being followed or mobbed'. She could even swim from her private beach, conveyed into the water by a wheeled bathing machine, which English Heritage exhibits there today. The state and private apartments are largely untouched since Victoria's death and offer a fascinating insight into the lives of the royal family.

Tourist Information Centres

All telephone enquiries to 01983 313818

Personal callers:
Cowes: Fountain Quay
Newport: The Guildhall, High Street
Ryde: Western Esplanade
Sandown: 8 High Street
Shanklin: 67 High Street
Ventnor: 34 High Street (seasonal)
Yarmouth: The Quay

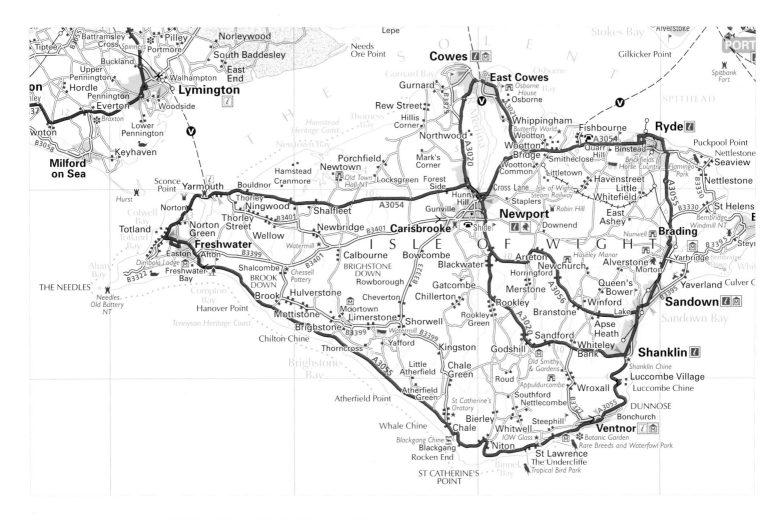

Tennyson and The Isle of Wight

As a young poet, Tennyson suffered from adverse criticism and meagre earnings, but in 1850 publication of his great poem 'In Memoriam' set the seal on his growing reputation, leading to his succeeding Wordsworth as Poet Laureate. To escape from the public eye, he rented Farringford at Freshwater, which he later purchased with the proceeds of his best-selling poem, 'Maud'. Here he entertained such eminent fellow-Victorians as Benjamin Jowett, Master of Balliol, and Sir James Knowles, editor of the *Contemporary Review*. Poems he wrote there include 'Maud' and 'Idylls of the King'. His granite monument stands on Tennyson Down.

Newport

The geographical and administrative centre of the island, Newport is a pleasant market town with Georgian and Jacobean buildings among those of later times. It centres on St James's Square, from which runs the high street with a fine pedimented Guildhall. Quays and warehouses on the River Medina are reminders that the 'port' in the name was a real one.

Sandown and Shanklin

These twin resorts on Sandown Bay are popular for family holidays, with beautiful sandy beaches and plenty of entertainments and attractions. Fine Victorian and Edwardian façades line the seafront, reflecting the days when the likes of Darwin, Lewis Carroll and Henry Longfellow were among the visitors. A pterodactyl-shaped building in Sandown houses Dinosaur Isle, with reconstructed dinosaurs, special effects and hands-on exhibits alongside the laboratories where experts study this aspect of the island's distant past.

Wroxall and Appuldurcombe

Hidden among the downs, Wroxall is an excellent centre for walks. Just west of the

village stands the still impressive shell of what was the island's grandest mansion, the 18th-century baroque Appuldurcombe House, its architect unknown.

Yarmouth

Yarmouth owes its importance to its harbour and a strategic position which led Henry VIII to build the castle. A short walk away is Fort Victoria, also designed to defend the Needles Channel, complete with a museum, planetarium, a marine aquarium and a country park.

The ferry is not the only connection between Yarmouth on the Isle of Wight and Lymington on the mainland – both are also popular yachting centres

See Walk A page 128 Coast to Coast on the Isle of Wight

HAMPSHIRE'S NAVAL HERITAGE

This is Navy country, with Portsmouth's great dockyard and Gosport's naval victualling and ordnance yards; the walls of Old Portsmouth and the great forts of the Napoleonic era on (and off) the coast; the Georgian houses for navy officers at Fareham and Alverstoke. Its impact extended up-country with hill-top signal stations that connected Portsmouth to the Admiralty.

Buildings of Defence

The Ministry of Defence, with some 500 listed buildings and ancient monuments, is one of Britain's biggest owners of historic buildings. Hampshire, with defence estates ranging from Aldershot's barrack blocks to the Palmerston Forts around Portsmouth, has probably the biggest share. But just as their historic and architectural importance was increasingly being recognised, many became surplus to MOD requirements. Hampshire's Historic Buildings Bureau has played a key role in finding appropriate, viable new uses – such as the development of Portsmouth's Naval Dockyard as a heritage attraction, and the conservation of Winchester's once-threatened Peninsular Barracks as very special luxury flats.

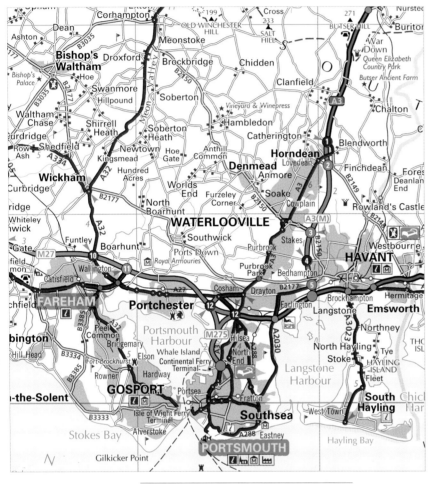

Bishop's Waltham Palace was at the heart of a powerful and profitable estate, run by the Bishops of Winchester

commute to the docks. Today's modern shopping centre is in West Street, which has probably been the salvation of its fine High Street, where many naval families lived.

Fareham was once a brick-producing centre, turning out the richly coloured 'Fareham Reds'. These fine 'sale-glazed' blue-grey bricks and the later 'whites' (which are actually yellow), together with mathematical tiles and Georgian features such as doorcases, windows and porches, all make for a harmonious townscape.

Gosport

Across the harbour mouth from Portsmouth, Gosport, too, has been dominated by the Navy, who built the Royal Clarence Victualling Yard in the 18th and 19th centuries to feed its sailors, and the Haslar Royal Naval Hospital to care for them. Barracks were built for the Marines, and an ordnance depot at Priddy's Hard, and ramparts were constructed. In the 19th century several monumental forts were built, part of a chain of 'Palmerston Forts' which guarded Portsmouth Harbour from a landward attack, should the threatened French invasion occur. The main attractions here are the Royal Navy Submarine Museum, with guided tours of HMS *Alliance*, and Explosion! at Priddy's Hard.

World War II bombs and post-war redevelopment have left only a fragment of the Georgian and Victorian town. Three buildings worth viewing are Holy Trinity Church with its landmark campanile, the splendid colonnaded ghost of the town's dead 1840s railway station and, to the west at Alverstoke, the gently curving, classical colonnaded Anglesea Crescent.

Bishop's Waltham

This was the medieval seat of the Bishops of Winchester, and the remains of their palace are still impressive. They include the great hall, kitchen, three-storey tower, and the moat which surrounded it all. English Heritage has furnished the ground floor of the dower house as a 19th-century farm-house. The first floor has an exhibition on Winchester's mighty bishops, one of whom laid out this charming little town.

Fareham

From the bypass or the M27, Fareham looks like a thoroughly modern commuter town for Portsmouth. In fact, Georgian naval officers also preferred to live here and

Tourist Information Centres

Fareham: Westbury Manor, West Street (tel: 01329 221342)
Gosport: 1 High Street (tel: 01705 522944)
Portsmouth: The Hard (tel: 01705 826722) 102 Commercial Road (tel: 01705 838382)
Southsea: Clarence Esplanade (seasonal) (tel: 01705 832464)

Queen Elizabeth Country Park

The London–Portsmouth road past Hampshire's windy Butser Hill has long been busy – in the stagecoach era a prodigious two coaches an hour passed Cannonball Corner. The present dual carriageway carries rather more traffic, considerably faster, but should not blind travellers to the very rewarding Queen Elizabeth Country Park which straddles the road. There is beech forest to the east with deer, a wildlife trail and waymarked walks, and open downland to the west, with a demonstration Iron-Age farm, bracing walks and wonderful views. An underpass links them, and there is an excellent park centre with exhibitions, audio-visual displays and a café.

Nelson's famous flagship of the Battle of Trafalgar (right) is an appropriate centrepiece of the historic ship collection in Portsmouth's naval dockyard. Top right, the sturdy grey walls of Portchester Castle

Hambledon

This pretty village is, as a granite monument opposite the Bat & Ball Inn at nearby Broadhalfpenny Down proclaims, traditionally the birthplace of the game of cricket. The Hambledon Cricket Club was founded in 1750, when the rules of the game were regularised, and in 1777 a Hambledon village team beat their All-England competitors.

Portchester

The face Portchester presents to the A27 belies its historic importance. Persist, follow Castle Street to its end, and you come to an unspoiled 18th-century village centre round a green. One fork leads past Portchester House to a shingle shore with views of Portsmouth Harbour; the other leads to the castle. This has a history going back nearly 2,000 years. The walls are those of a Roman fort, some 600ft (183m) square, and the most complete in Europe. Within, and rising above them, is a medieval castle and palace, used by Henry I when commuting to and from Normandy. An English Heritage exhibition tells the story. Also within the walls is a remarkably complete 12th-century church.

Portsmouth

Portsmouth is packed on to a little island, with sea or harbour on three sides, linked to the rest of Hampshire by four bridges and a causeway. For centuries it has been dominated by the navy, which has powerfully affected its social, economic and political life. Old Portsmouth clusters picturesquely round the original harbour and the Camber, guarded to seaward by Henry VIII's town walls; Portsea, north of the old town, developed in the 18th century; the Landport is the modern city's commercial heart; to the east is the elegant seaside resort of Southsea.

A five-year project leading up to the millennium saw a £350 million investment in the waterfront area, including the Millennium Promenade, a 4-mile (6.4km) trail around the most historic landmarks, and Gunwharf Quays, which incorporates heritage sites, entertainments and outlet shopping. The Historic Dockyard itself remains one of Britain's foremost attractions, containing three of the greatest ships ever built – HMS *Victory*, the 1860 iron-clad HMS *Warrior* and the Tudor warship, *Mary Rose*, salvaged after 400 years on the seabed. Georgian dockyard buildings contain the exciting Dockyard Apprentice Exhibition, Action Stations, and the Royal Naval Museum, and there are harbour cruises.

Southsea Castle, built by Henry VIII, is now open to the public, and nearby attractions include the D-Day Museum, containing the impressive Overlord Embroidery depicting the D-Day Landings, the Royal Marines Museum and a Sea Life Centre. In 19th-century Landport is Charles Dickens Birthplace Museum, and on Portsdown Hill Fort Nelson has artillery displays – and demonstrations!

CREEKS AND HARBOURS BELOW THE DOWNS

The countryside around Chichester is varied and interesting, with flat coastal land to the east culminating in a string of traditional seaside resorts, complete with piers and bandstands. To the south and west is a landscape broken by meandering rivers and the long, marshy arms of Chichester Harbour. Inland are the Downs, and the woodlands and villages of the Weald.

Tourist Information Centres

Arundel: 61 High Street (tel: 01903 882268)
Bognor Regis: Belmont Street (tel 01243 823140)
Chichester: 29a South Street (tel: 01243 775888)

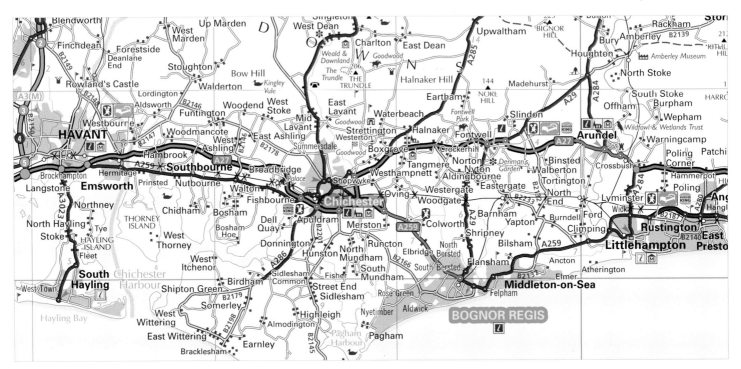

Amberley

A charming, tranquil village in the Arun Valley, Amberley has a history going back to medieval times and was the summer residence of the Bishops of Chichester. Amberley Wildbrooks are noted for their landscape and ecological qualities. Amberley Museum, imaginatively created from 36 acres (15ha) of depleted chalk pits, brings to life the industrial heritage of the area with craft workshops: a blacksmith, potter, printer and boat-builder; and a narrow-gauge railway and vintage buses.

Traditional crafts, including woodturning, can be seen at the Amberley Museum, set in a chalk pit beneath the downs

Arundel

This hilltop town rises dramatically out of the flood plain of the Arun with its silhouette of castle, parish church and Roman Catholic cathedral. From a distance it looks older than it is. The 11th-century castle was rebuilt in Georgian times in fashionable Gothic style and the cathedral is an 1890s celebration of the liberation of English catholicism by the Dukes of Norfolk. The Church of St Nicholas, dating from 1380, houses both Anglican and Roman Catholic worship under one roof. The town, largely Georgian and Victorian, is pleasing, with lots of antiques and other specialist shops, art galleries and the Arundel Museum and Heritage Centre. The Wildfowl and Wetlands Trust reserve here is a sanctuary for thousands of waterfowl, including some rare species.

Mighty Arundel Castle, seat of the Dukes of Norfolk, forms an impressive backdrop to the River Arun below. In spite of its historic importance, reflecting around 1,000 years of history, the castle is also very much a family home

The Weald and Downland Museum

Established in 1971 on the West Dean Estate near the village of Singleton, the Weald and Downland Museum is a collection of over 40 traditional, mostly timber-framed buildings from the Weald and Downland area – rescued and re-erected here when they faced destruction on their previous sites. They include a medieval farmhouse, 18th-century barns, a granary, a Tudor market hall, carpenter's and plumber's workshops, a blacksmith's forge and a village school. The watermill, still grinding flour, is a great attraction. The Weald and Downland is far from being a dead museum. Demonstrations of building crafts and hands-on displays make it all come vividly alive, and the buildings have been skilfully positioned to look as if they have always been here.

Developed over the last 50 years or so, Denmans Garden includes a delightful and colourful walled garden

Chichester

Chichester's glory is its cathedral, still dominating the surrounding flat coastal lands and, despite later changes, still recognisably 12th century. The town goes back much further – as its 'chester' suffix suggest, it was a Roman settlement. The four main streets, which meet at the 16th-century market cross, have many fine old buildings and the circular Walls Walk offers fine views. The lanes repay exploration, particularly to the south-east, where 18th-century Pallant House, a Queen Anne town house furnished in period style, is now an art gallery. In parkland to the north is the Chichester Festival Theatre and the smaller Minerva Theatre.

Denmans Garden

John Brookes, leading garden writer and designer, created this modern garden and his skilfully planned vistas provide colour, shape and texture all the year round. There are also rare species under glass, and the Georgian stables now house Brooks' studio and school of garden design. Nearby Slindon is a delightful village largely owned by the National Trust.

Emsworth

Emsworth is an old port at the head of one of the channels of Chichester Harbour. The original town (now bypassed) is an agreeable jumble of streets, lanes and alleys on a peninsula between two creeks. The large sea-filled basin to the south-west corner was created to power a tide mill.

Goodwood

'Glorious Goodwood' evokes visions of blue skies and fluffy clouds over the downs as crowds throng the famous racecourse. It has other attractions and is full of history. Trundle Hill was a major Neolithic encampment, and owes its name to a later wheel-shaped Iron-Age fort. The 18th-century Goodwood House, home of the Dukes of Richmond, endorses the importance of the horse hereabouts – the stables are as grand as the house. Both house and grounds are open to visitors.

Stansted Park

The present house here dates from the early 20th century, replacing a 17th-century house by Talman which was largely destroyed by fire. The grounds are the main attraction, with a long beech avenue, woodlands and fine gardens. There is also a theatre museum. Talman's buildings would seem to be fire-prone – he also designed Uppark to the north, which was all but destroyed in the same way in 1989, but has since been splendidly restored.

Chichester Cathedral's graceful spire, soaring to 277ft (84.5m), was rebuilt in the 19th century. Inside the cathedral are two great works of art – a dazzling modern tapestry by John Piper and a painting by Graham Sutherland

See Walk B page 129
A Wealth of Wildlife in the Arun Valley

Fishbourne

The Romans sailed their ships up Chichester Harbour's Fishbourne Channel in the first century AD, and Fishbourne Roman Palace – discovered only in 1960 and excavated by Professor Barry Cunliffe – is one of Britain's most important and splendid Roman sites. Built on a lavish scale, it was designed to show the conquered Britons just what Roman civilisation could achieve. After a fire, the remains were used in the building of the Roman settlement of *Noviomagus* – the original Chichester.

SUSSEX BY THE SEA

*I*t is easy to see why this part of Sussex has been popular for so long. The sea, setting a limit to the landscape, provides a destination and brings a stimulating whiff of salt to the air; the South Downs offer the traveller from London a sense of arriving in a brighter, cleaner and somehow freer world. And between hills and sea is Brighton – big, bustling and colourful.

Brighton

There is no mistaking the onion domes of Brighton Pavilion, a spectacular and decidedly unique building

Brighton has been called 'London by the sea', and there is a lot of London about it. Not just its racy reputation and hyperactive club scene, but also stuccoed terraces that might be in Belgravia and a sophistication that comes from having a commuting population of actors, lawyers, medical specialists and other professionals. It has a superb arts diary, with pre-West End theatre, art exhibitions and concerts. Its two universities and college of technology also add to the buzz of human activity.

The best-known architectural set piece is the Royal Pavilion, rebuilt by John Nash in Indian style between 1815 and 1822 for the Prince Regent. If its exotic skyline extends the imagination, some of the interiors are positively mind-boggling. Some of Brighton's liveliest areas are in humble streets behind the seafront – the maze of The Lanes has long been a tourist attraction, but the once run-down North Lanes area between the Pavilion and the station has developed a lively craft-and-café scene.

Other attractions include the marina, with moorings for 2,000 boats, overlooked by harbourside bars and restaurants, outlet shopping, leisure facilities and apartments. The 100-year-old Volks electric railway still runs along the seashore and there are two piers, though one of them, in spite of its Grade I listing, is in a sad state of dereliction. A 5,000-seat conference and exhibition centre draws the largest trade union and political party conferences.

Hove

The boundary between Hove and Brighton has long been obscure, even to locals, but this town does have a distinctive character. It is sedate rather than breezy, and stylish in a more reserved way. Its chief glory is its procession of early- and mid-19th century seafront terraces punctuated by squares and crescents. At Hove Park, high up above the seafront, stands a large Victorian pumping station where, in 1866, great steam-powered beam engines began pumping up water to send it down into the baths and basins of Brighton and Hove. In the late 1940s smaller but more powerful electric pumps took on the task, and in 1971 it was proposed to demolish the building and break up its engines for scrap. Happily, conservationist protests saved them, and the building became the British Engineerium, a temple to the age of steam and Britain's engineers – with one of the preserved beam engines 'in steam' from time to time.

Brighton beach, seen here from the end of the pier, still retains its traditional appeal on a bright sunny day

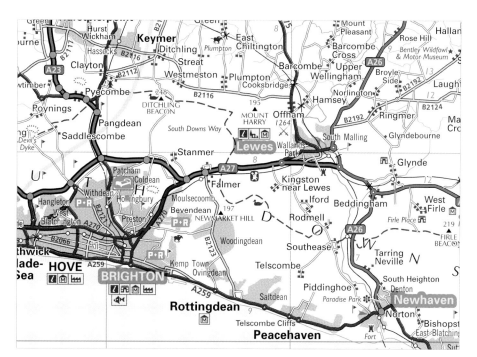

Tourist Information Centres

Brighton: 10 Bartholemew Square (tel: 0906 711 2255)
Hove: Town Hall, Church Road (tel 0906 711 2255)
Lewes: 187 High Street (tel: 01273 483448)

Climb to the top of Ditchling Beacon for panoramic views across the peaceful and lush Sussex countryside

Ditchling

This picture-postcard village has for many years attracted artists and craftsmen – notably sculptor and designer Eric Gill who made his home here in the 1920s. The 13th-century church, though somewhat over-restored, is still beautiful and there are some fine timber-framed houses. Half an hour's uphill walk to the south is the National Trust-owned Ditchling Beacon, at 813ft (247.7m) one of the high points of the Sussex Downs.

Glynde

Set at the foot of the downs, Glynde is a village rich in visual and other delights. It is full of typical Sussex cottages, and Glynde Place is a particularly fine Elizabethan manor house, built in 1579 from Sussex flint and stone from Caen in Normandy. It also has an unusual parish church, built in 1763 in Palladian style. On Mount Caburn to the west of the village is an Iron-Age hill fort, and a mile (1.6km) north is Glyndebourne Opera House, founded by John Christie in the 1930s and later enhanced by the completion of an award-winning auditorium by architect Sir Michael Hopkins.

Lewes

Castle-crowned, with a lovely curving high street full of idiosyncratic, mature old buildings, the county town of East Sussex

is one of those places that even the most enlightened town planning could never have achieved. Centuries of serendipitous development and adequate means have made it what it is. Access to stone from the ruins of the great Cluniac priory of St Pancras was a good start.

Off the high street run innumerable lanes and alleys, where houses are of warm brick, timber and sometimes the local speciality – mathematical tiles. While there are some fine timber-framed houses, most is Georgian. Despite its comfortable image, Lewes has traditionally been radical and nonconformist. Tom Paine, author of *Rights of Man* lived here, and in the more distant past of Mary's reign, this strongly Puritan town produced 17 Protestant martyrs, who are remembered each Guy Fawkes day with torch-lit processions and elaborate bonfires (see page 81).

Glynde Place, a lovely Elizabethan manor in a downland setting, is still occupied by descendants of the original owner

See Walk C page 130
Lewes – Birthplace of the English Parliament

CUSTOMS AND FESTIVALS

Traditional customs and festivals in southern England are many and varied. Some, like 'first footing' on New Year's Eve, pancakes on Shrove Tuesday, and bonfires and fireworks on Guy Fawkes Day, are nationwide, but sometimes may have peculiar local variants. Many go back to pagan times, though the early Christian church took them over. The variety of traditional festivals celebrated is, moreover, being interestingly extended and enriched as schools and communities respond to an increasingly multicultural population.

Thus primary school children in Kent or Oxfordshire are quite likely to know about Holi (when Hindus celebrate the end of winter), Id-ul-Fitr (the end of the Ramadan fast for Muslims), Vesak (when Buddhists leave gifts on the doorsteps of the poor), Shavuot (when Jews celebrate the first fruits of the harvest), or the Chinese New Year marked with fire-crackers and (as in London's Chinatown) dragon dancers. But in these two pages we look at some of the more traditional customs and festivals of the south and south-east.

THE FIRST QUARTER

One curious New Year custom is Queen's College, Oxford's Needle and Thread Gaudy (feast), when the college bursar presents each guest at table with a needle threaded with silk, and says: 'Take this and be thrifty'. Sound advice, no doubt, but all a bit of a joke, in arcane Oxford style. Needle and thread in Norman French is *aiguille* and *fil* – a pun on the college's 14th-century founder, Robert de Eglesfield.

Solemnity and fun are mixed in a different way in London in February, with the annual Clowns' Service at Holy Trinity Church, Dalston. Clowns attend in full costume and make-up and end with a prayer thanking God 'for causing me to share with others your precious gift of laughter'. It began relatively recently, in 1946, as a tribute to the great 19th-century clown Joseph Grimaldi.

In March people at Stockbridge in Hampshire elect jurors to the Courts Leet and Baron, which traditionally resolved disputes over the local commons. These now belong to the National Trust, but the revived ceremony is fun and provides a useful forum for discussion of local matters.

RITES OF SPRING

Easter and the period preceding it are rich in quaint and colourful customs, starting with Shrove Tuesday – traditionally associated with pancakes. This, it seems, is because pancake-making used up perishable foodstuffs before the 40 days of Lent. A well-known variant is the pancake race at Olney, Buckinghamshire. Contrary to general belief, dropping the pancake does not disqualify, though it may dull the appetite.

On Maundy Thursday the sovereign distributes Maundy Money – specially minted silver coins – at Westminster Abbey and varying cathedrals. In London Easter Sunday sees the Easter Parade in Battersea Park, followed on Easter Monday by the Harness Horse Parade in Regents Park. On Dunstable Down in Bedfordshire they roll oranges down the hill to waiting children.

May Day ceremonies are perhaps most spectacular in Oxford, where at 6am choristers climb the 144ft (44m) tower of Magdalen College to sing a Latin hymn to the (surprisingly large) assembled crowd. The tower's bells ring out, and a day of celebrations begins with morris dancing, punting parties and picnics. At Rye, Sussex, May Day is strangely celebrated by the throwing of hot pennies.

Towards the end of May at Rye, Sussex, the inauguration of the new mayor is strangely celebrated by the new incumbent throwing of hot pennies to children from the town hall. Along the coast, the Vicar of Hastings blesses the sea, presumably to

The country moves into the city when maypole dancers perform outside St Margaret's Church in London

enhance the catch (these days his pulpit is a lifeboat). Also in May, the charter trustees of High Wycombe, Buckinghamshire, choose a mayor, who is then weighed by the mayoress, out-going mayor and various others, the presiding weights-and-measures official pronouncing either 'Some more' (meaning 'You've put on weight since last year') or 'No more' (meaning 'You haven't').

SUMMER CELEBRATIONS

On a June Saturday in each leap year, Great Dunmow in Essex is the scene of the well-known Dunmow Flitch, a 900-year-old custom in which married couples seek to convince a local jury of 'six maids and six bachelors' that they have never been unfaithful nor had cross words. National celebrities dressed in wig and gown act as prosecuting and defending counsel; the prize for successful defendants is the flitch – a whole side of bacon.

On the second Wednesday in July the new Master of the Vintners' Company (a City of London livery company) processes from Vintners' Hall in Upper Thames Street to the Church of St James Garlickhithe, he and his entourage carrying nosegays against noxious fumes or infection, and preceded by their Wine Porter who sweeps a clean path with his broom. Later in the month the Vintners are concerned with Swan Upping on the Thames – the nicking of beaks of each swan to show whether it belongs to the Queen, the Vintners or the Dyers.

In August the Thames is the scene of the Doggett's Coat and Badge Race, when recently qualified Thames Watermen compete in a sculling race from London Bridge to Chelsea's Cadogan Pier. Thomas Doggett, an Irish actor-manager who died in 1721, inaugurated the

Top: Swan Upping on the River Thames; above: the best-known of all English traditions – morris dancing; Right: Pearly Kings and Queens are a long-established London tradition

race to show his support for George I and his new Hanoverian dynasty – the prizes being £5, a scarlet coat, breeches and shoes, and a huge silver badge.

WINTER CUSTOMS

The first day of October sees the Lord Chancellor processing from a service in Westminster Abbey to the House of Lords where he greets his guests and gives them 'Breakfast' (a recep-

tion for lawyers and others); and on the first Sunday London's Costermongers congregate for their service in St Martins-in-the-Fields, many of them kitted out in the dressy manner of 19th-century street traders, including 'Pearly Kings and Queens', their clothes studded

with innumerable pearl buttons.

Following Guy Fawkes' unsuccessful attempt to blow up King and Parliament in 1605, bonfires and fireworks in England are mostly not at the New Year but on 5 November. Nowhere is this festival so thoroughly celebrated as in Lewes, Sussex, where the memory of 17 Protestant martyrs in the reign of Queen Mary led to a (these days not serious) anti-Papist tradition. Lewes has a number of bonfire societies in different parts of the town, who dress up, go in procession, and burn effigies of currently-hated politicians and others on giant bonfires. In London, the second Saturday in November sees the City's new Lord Mayor ride in his state coach to be sworn in at the Royal Courts of Justice. The procession accompanying him consist of mobile floats on various aspects of a theme chosen by the incoming Lord Mayor.

On Christmas Day the Serpentine in Hyde Park is the scene of a swimming race for the Peter Pan Cup, originally presented in 1864 by Peter Pan's creator Sir James Barrie. The swimmers meet at 9am, and may need to break ice first.

DAILY EVENTS

Finally, some customs and ceremonies take place every day of the year. At the ancient Hospital of St Cross in Winchester, the first 32 people to arrive can claim, with no questions asked, a slice of bread (presented on a wooden platter) and a drink of ale from a horn cup. And each evening at the Tower of London the approaching Chief Yeoman Warder and his escort are challenged by a sentry, leading to the following exchange. 'Halt, who goes there?' 'The Keys'. 'Whose keys?' 'Queen Elizabeth's keys'. The sentry then presents arms, the Chief Warder removes his hat and proclaims, 'God preserve Queen Elizabeth', and the whole guard responds 'Amen!'

DOWNLAND VILLAGES AND A STATELY RESORT

A high, grass-covered stretch of the South Downs dominates this area, which is broken by the Cuckmere Valley, with flatter arable farmlands to its north. The stylish Victorian seaside resort of Eastbourne is to the east, with the Pevensey Levels beyond and the great chalk cliffs of Beachy Head and the Seven Sisters standing guard before the English Channel.

In summer people flock to peer over the edge of Beachy Head. The lighthouse below is dwarfed by the size of the sheer cliffs, but sends a powerful warning beam out to ships in the busiest stretch of water in the world

Alfriston

Where the little Cuckmere River breaks through the South Downs on its way to pebbly Cuckmere Haven stands the ancient village of Alfriston. Its heart is at the market cross, a triangular space where North Street and West Street converge into High Street, and inns and other old buildings line the thoroughfare. The village's second centre is a green called the Tye, which is near the river. Here stands the ancient and ample parish church of St Andrew's, known as 'the Cathedral of the South Downs'. Here also you will find the 14th-century Clergy House, the first building ever to be acquired by the National Trust. The South Downs Way drops down into the village before climbing again on the other side. Over the river

is Littlington (with a shady tea garden), and to the north is the Long Man of Wilmington, a huge figure cut in the chalk of Windover Hill.

Beachy Head and the Seven Sisters

Eastwards between Cuckmere Haven and Eastbourne runs a spectacular switchback of chalk cliffs, the Seven Sisters, culminating in Beachy Head. Derived from the Norman French, *beau chef* (beautiful headland), its name is tautological, but the views are spectacular. Over the years the National Trust has gradually acquired most of this coast and its hinterland, preserving it and restoring old farming patterns. As you walk the Sisters, each seems bigger and more exhausting than the last – but the views repay the exertion.

Eastbourne

After Brighton, the largest of Sussex's seaside resorts is Eastbourne, which developed very differently. The first entrepreneurial stirrings here were in the 18th century, but Eastbourne is a Victorian creation – well planned and generous in quality thanks to two dominant landowners, the 7th Duke of Devonshire and Carew Davis Gilbert. Compton Place, west of the town centre, was the Duke of Devonshire's seat. Eastbourne has a pier, spacious esplanades, stately seafront hotels, and four theatres. Its location is enviable, with sea to the east and downs to the west.

The town's origins are much earlier. A Roman boat was discovered here, and St Mary's Church, with its green sandstone tower, has some 13th-century interior features. Historic buildings in the town include the 16th-century Old Parsonage and the timber-framed Lamb Inn. The Redoubt, another feature of the area, is a Martello Tower built as part of the coastal defences against Napoleon.

Bloomsbury in Sussex

The Bloomsbury Group of the 1910s and '20s did not spend all their time in London WC2. Several of them had a foot in Sussex. The Monks House at Rodmell, part 16th century, was bought in 1919 by Leonard and Virginia Woolf as a country retreat. Now owned by the National Trust, it contains Woolf memorabilia and furniture painted by Vanessa and Clive Bell and Duncan Grant. These three lived at Charleston Farmhouse, off the A27 east of Lewes, where they were visited by (among others) Lytton Strachey and John Maynard Keynes. The house and garden, preserved and restored by a trust, are full of work by Grant and the Bells, and nearby Berwick Church has wall paintings by the trio.

Tourist Information Centres

Eastbourne: 3 Cornfield Road (tel 01323 411400)
Lower Dicker: Boship roundabout (A22) (tel: 01323 442667)

It is hard to believe, looking at Herstmonceux Castle today, that it was in ruins until its careful restoration in the 1930s

The South Downs Way

One of the Countryside Commission's National Trails, this is an 100-mile (161km) long-distance path running along the downs from Eastbourne to Winchester (see page 95). On rolling chalk downland, the path offers bracing walking and splendid views, and is generally dry underfoot. Few people walk it all in one go. There is easy access from a number of towns and railway stations, lateral bus services, and a network of cross paths, which, when combined with village car parks, mean that you can sample it a stretch at a time.

Herstmonceux

Herstmonceux Castle dates from the 14th century and was built in the fashionable brick of those times. According to Sir Nikolaus Pevsner, it shows the advent of all-round architectural symmetry in England three generations before the Renaissance. It was restored in the 1930s and a decade later became home to the Royal Greenwich Observatory, which had been forced out of London by atmospheric pollution. A new observatory complex was built here. In 1990 the observatory moved to Cambridge, and the complex became the Herstmonceux Science Centre, with lots of interactive displays and experiments. In Herstmonceux village, a mile (1.6km) north, the 12th-century All Saints Church has monuments to members of the Fiennes family, who were owners of the castle.

Pevensey

Straddling the old highway from Eastbourne to Hastings across the levels, Pevensey has seen plenty of history. The Romans landed here and built a huge ten-acre (4ha) fort, *Anderida*. William the Conqueror also landed here, and the Normans built a more compact stone castle within the Roman defences. Several centuries later the town joined the Cinque Ports federation. Pevensey was once on the coast (its final 'ey' indicates that it was an island between two creeks), but the river silted up and the sea receded, leaving it high and dry. The sea is now half a mile (0.8km) away at modern Pevensey Bay.

The little town is full of attractive old houses that speak eloquently of the past, including the Mint House, recalling the time when Pevensey had a royal mint, the Court House, which was the equivalent of a town hall when the town had its own corporation, and several old and very atmospheric inns.

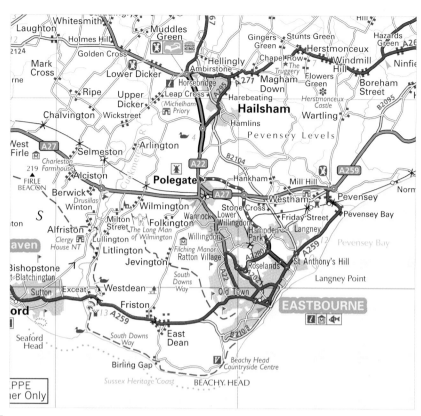

Westdean

Westdean is a tiny village hidden in a secluded valley among woodlands just north of the A259 at Exceat Bridge. The best way to discover it is on foot via a scenic footpath that starts at the car park at Seven Sisters Country Park. The path takes you sharply uphill through woodlands, then just as sharply down again by steps to the village. There are good walks from here through Friston Forest to Jevington, or by woodland and downland to Alfriston, passing Charleston Manor, part 13th century and with fine barns and dovecote. Pevsner calls it 'A perfect house in a perfect setting'.

See Walk D page 131
The South Downs of the Bloomsbury Set

See Walk E page 132
Up and Down on the Seven Sisters

Pevensey Castle, built by William the Conqueror close to his landing place, was never taken by force throughout its long history

THE COAST AND COUNTRYSIDE OF THE NORMAN CONQUEST

Here you will find three diverse kinds of country. The western sea coast has three contiguous but distinctive resorts – Hastings, St Leonards and Bexhill. The well-wooded hills behind them merge into the Kentish Weald. The flat marshlands round the ancient towns of Winchelsea and Rye extend inland along the River Rother and the Royal Military Canal to the Isle of Oxney.

Battle

It was here, and not 7 miles (11.2km) away at Hastings, that William the Conqueror defeated the Saxon King Harold and changed the course of English history. There was no town here then, only open land, but William built a church, an abbey soon followed, and the town grew up around it. Most of the battlefield is still open sheep pasture, which enhances the Abbey's setting, but the momentous battle is brought to life by an audio-tour and a video introduction. There is also a museum devoted to abbey life. Several other museums interpreting aspects of its history can be seen in the town.

Bexhill

Originally a fishing village, vestiges of which can be seen round the parish church, Bexhill was developed as a resort in the 1880s by the Earls de la Warr, who gave their name to the US state of Delaware as well as to the seafront De La Warr Pavilion. Designed by the leading modern movement architect Erich Mendelsohn, in Britain as a refugee from Naziism, its clean lines and pioneering use of concrete, steel and glass must have had quite an impact in 1934. Today it is an arts centre. Bexhill was the birthplace of British motor racing, remembered in the Motoring Heritage Centre, the Cooden Beach Heritage Gallery and the annual Festival of Motoring.

Hastings

Unlike most of its sister Cinque Ports, Hastings still gains a living from the sea. Fishing boats put out from the beach, where curious, tall

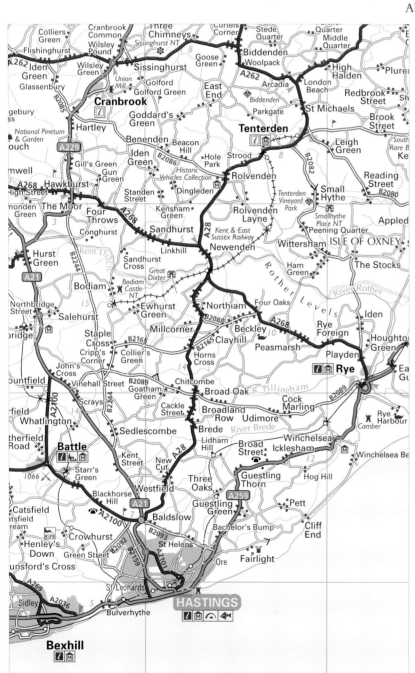

Many aspects of seafaring have been centred on Hastings, and are recalled today in its Fishermen's Museum and in Smugglers Adventure, a themed 'experience' in a labyrinth of caverns below West Hill. And fishing boats still pull up on the beach to unload their catch

wooden sheds, known as the net shops, are a distinctive landmark, and in their midst is the Fishermen's Museum housing the *Enterprise*, the last sailing lugger built in Hastings. This is at Hastings' eastern end, where the Old Town nestles picturesquely in the Bourne Valley under the shadow of Hastings Castle, which now houses the 1066 Story and St Mary in the Castle Arts Centre. Near by are St Clements Caves, where interactive displays take you into the world of smuggling. Two cliff railways make it wasy to explore this end of the town.

West of the Old Town – compulsive territory for exploring on foot – is the seaside resort and the town centre with lots of family attractions, including the peir which reopened in 2001. But beyond all this comes the still recognisably Georgian and Victorian Hastings, with marina and grand but faded architectural set pieces like Wellington and Warrior squares, interspersed with streets of terraced houses.

Here Hastings merges into St Leonards, the creation of a successful Georgian builder, James Burton, and his better-known architect son, Decimus. To promote their new watering place, they persuaded the young Princess Victoria and her mama to visit. St Leonards is a planned resort with style, with villas laid out round a landscaped quarry and its own centre, with a market and public buildings in classical stucco.

of the Edwardian literary establishment. Though much photographed and visited, Rye is still a busy working town, and also, once you get away from the honeypot tourist attractions, has many tranquil corners and hidden delights. Rye Heritage Centre is the ideal place to start.

The Old Grammar School building is among the varied architecture which lines the charming old streets of Rye

Tenterden

Tenterden, one of a whole series of characteristic Wealden towns and villages in this part of Kent, is full of white weatherboarding and warm, weathered brick and tile. It is dominated by St Mildred's Church, whose grey four-stage buttressed tower has been described as 'magnificent ...the finest of any parish church in Kent'. A hundred feet (30m) high, on a fine day it gives glimpses of the French coast. Station Road is where you will find the town museum and the Kent & East Sussex Railway, offering steam-hauled rides through the Rother Valley. The town grew rich on iron-founding and wool, and was a 'limb' of the Cinque Ports, with quays at Smallhythe, 2 miles (3.2km) to the south linking it to the sea. There the National Trust owns the 16th-century Smallhythe Place, once home of actress Ellen Terry and containing much theatrical memorabilia. The Tenterden Vineyard at Spots Farm has a rural museum and herb garden.

The ancient Strand Gate in Winchelsea hints at its former importance, which receded along with the sea during the 15th century

Rye

A walled town and port on the River Rother, Rye joined the Cinque Ports federation as an 'Antient Town', and it certainly deserves that title. Its twisting streets and lanes contain a wealth of old buildings – St Mary's Church, with golden 'quarter boys' who seldom fail to draw a crowd when they march out to strike the hour, the Mermaid Inn ('restored in 1420') in cobbled Mermaid Street, and the timber-framed houses of tranquil Church Square. The early 18th-century Lamb House in West Street was the home of author Henry James and a meeting place

Winchelsea

Like Rye, Winchelsea joined the Cinque Ports, but its character is very different from its bustling, prosperous neighbour. When 13th-century storms all but destroyed the original town, Edward I planned a new Winchelsea along the lines of the French *bastides*. But the sea receded, the harbour silted up, trade stagnated, buildings fell empty and the ambitious grid of streets was never completed. What remains, though, is a delightful and tranquil fragment.

CASTLES AND MANSIONS IN PEACEFUL SECLUSION

Motorists on the M25, M20 and A21 may well pass this country by, completely unaware of the tranquil landscapes and delightful country towns which are hidden away beyond the slip-roads. It is also an area which is rich in historic houses, not, for the most part, the classical 18th-century stately home, but medieval manor houses and great mansions of an earlier era.

Among the reminders of Sir Winston Churchill at Chartwell are paintings by him, his hats and uniforms, gifts from Stalin and Roosevelt and a garden wall that demonstrates another of his many talents

The romantic associations of Henry VIII's courtship of Anne Boleyn are enhanced by the 20th-century restoration of the enchanting moated Hever Castle

Chartwell

This was Sir Winston Churchill's home from 1922 to 1964. When he lost the 1945 election, Sir Winston considered selling Chartwell, but friends bought it and presented it to the National Trust, who allowed him to live there undisturbed for his lifetime. It is a Victorian house, remodelled in the 1920s, which is unremarkable, though superbly situated, and is full of reminders of the great statesman.

Edenbridge

Edenbridge is a sleepy little town tucked away in the Kentish Weald close to the Sussex border, away from main commuter routes. Its core lies around a narrow high street with half-timbered houses and the Crown Inn, whose sign spectacularly bridges the street. Mill buildings on the little River Eden indicate the town's role as an agricultural centre.

Hever

A fortified manor house rather than a serious fortress, Hever Castle stands romantically in its moat with what looks like a medieval village alongside. Built in the 13th century, it was the childhood home of Henry VIII's second wife, Anne Boleyn. The interior seems never to have been up to much until a rich American, William Waldorf Astor, bought Hever in 1903 and spent much time and money restoring and transforming it with the finest Edwardian craftsmanship, and filling it with furniture, tapestries and works of art. He also transformed the grounds, which include an Italian garden with statuary, a maze, topiary, a lake and a walled rose garden.

Ide Hill and Toys Hill

The wooded uplands of the Greensand Ridge, west of Sevenoaks and south of the M25, are marvellous walking country – thanks in no small measure to the National Trust's acquisition of 400 acres (162ha) at Toys Hill and neighbouring Ide Hill, with its village green, pubs and hill-top church. The Sevenoaks Society produces guides of exemplary clarity to many circular walks which bring you back to your parked car.

Ightham and Ightham Mote

Ightham is one of those Kentish villages which, despite its proximity to London, maintains a robustly independent existence. It is picturesque, with half-timbered

Sissinghurst Castle Gardens

Never a real castle, Sissinghurst was the mansion built by the son of a Tudor courtier. It had suffered several centuries of neglect when Vita Sackville-West and her husband Harold Nicolson bought it in 1930 and created, among the walls of ruined buildings, a unique and intimate series of gardens and landscapes – 'outdoor rooms', protected by the high brick walls, including the famous White Garden which has so influenced garden design. The surviving buildings which they made their home include the red-brick Tudor entrance range and four-storey Elizabethan Tower, with fine views and the book-lined study where Vita did her writing.

Tourist Information Centres

Clacket Lane Services (M25, between junctions 5 and 6): eastbound (tel: 01959 565063); **Sevenoaks:** Buckhurst Lane (tel: 01732 450305) **Tonbridge:** Tonbridge Castle, Castle Street (tel: 01732 770929) **Tunbridge Wells:** Old Fish Market, The Pantiles (tel: 01892 515675)

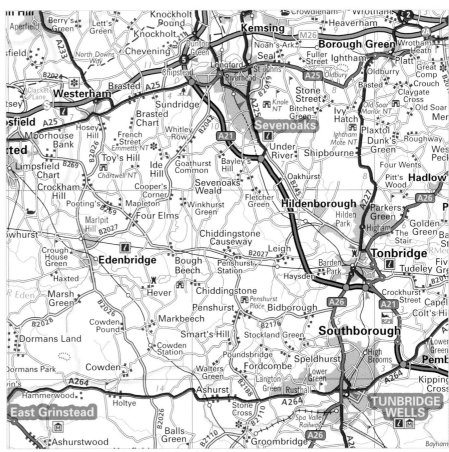

Leeds Castle

Leeds Castle, off the M20 just east of Maidstone, is a world and several centuries away from the roar of the motorway. Described by Lord Conway as 'the loveliest castle in the world', it stands on the site of the manor of the Saxon royal family. It, too, was a royal palace for three centuries, and it stands romantically silhouetted on two small islands in a lake, which is itself islanded in 500 acres (200ha) of tranquil gardens and landscaped parkland. It is Norman in origin and its oldest part is the Gloriette, on the smaller island, with rooms that include Henry VIII's fine banqueting hall. This is joined by a bridge to the main castle, battlemented Jacobean on Norman foundations. The grounds contain a vineyard, maze and grotto, as well as woodland and water gardens, where a variety of waterfowl, as well as peacocks, roam freely. The Culpeper Garden is full of old-fashioned flowers and herbs and you can visit the greenhouses. There is also a museum of medieval dog collars.

houses and inns, and a 12th- to 15th-century church with notable monuments. About 3 miles (4.8km) to the south lies Ightham Mote, a magical manor house, islanded in a moat, with fortified gateway, gardens, lakes, fountains and dovecote. C H Robinson, an American, having first seen it as a young man on a cycling tour, returned a rich man, bought and rescued it, then bequeathed it to the National Trust, who have steadily carried out its restoration.

Penshurst

Sir John de Pulteney, a rich London merchant who was four times Lord Mayor, began Penshurst Place in 1340. Although extended in Tudor and Elizabethan times, it is among the finest and most complete of medieval manor houses. Featuring a lofty Baron's Hall, it gives a vivid impression of how the rich and powerful would have lived. Not least of its delights is the way courtyards, galleries, walled gardens and house interconnect. It stands in, but not aloof from, the charming village of Penshurst.

Sevenoaks and Knole

Though a commuter town, Sevenoaks has retained its character and identity and is well worth a leisurely browse. But its glory is Knole, whose gates open out of the high street into its 1,000-acre (405ha) park. Traditionally said to have a courtyard for each month of the year, a staircase for each week and a room for each day, it is more a palace than a house. Begun in the mid-15th century by Thomas Bourchier, Archbishop of Canterbury, its scale was almost that of a little town, with brewhouse, bakehouse and other supporting facilities. Henry VIII confiscated and enlarged Knole, then in the 17th century it passed to the Sackville family who gave it some of its finest interior features.

Tunbridge Wells

Royal Tunbridge Wells' beginnings as a spa date from 1606, when Lord North discovered a medicinal spring while trying to find his way along muddy Kentish roads. Royal patronage followed, and Beau Nash came in 1735 to preside over the social life of the town as master of ceremonies. The heart of the original town is the Pantiles, a tree-lined promenade, paved with these curved roofing tiles and with tall 17th- and 18th-century houses. Here an interpretive display, 'A Day at the Wells', tells the story of the spa's development. Its appeal today rests on a combination of attractive old buildings and streets and, starting right in the centre of the town, the rising parkland of Tunbridge Wells Common.

Westerham

Only half a mile (0.8km) from the M25, but not directly accessible from it, Westerham is another world – a prosperous country town astride the old main road, with the Greensand Hills rising to the south. It has picturesque buildings and a triangular green with a statue of James Wolfe, victor of Quebec, who was born here. His home is now a Wolfe museum.

Royal patronage came to Tunbridge Wells in the shape of Queen Henrietta Maria, wife of Charles I, who arrived here in 1630 to recuperate after the birth of the future Charles II

HISTORIC PORTS OF THE GATEWAY TO ENGLAND

*E*ast Kent is England's front door to continental Europe and it was for thousands of years the obvious way in for invaders. It also witnessed the more peaceful passage of kings and queens, churchmen and ambassadors. The white cliffs of both Dover and Calais remind us that Britain and France were once joined – a link which the Channel Tunnel has now restored.

Deal

Deal, a fishing port and seaside resort, is a delightful jumble of narrow lanes, which make doglegs to divert the driving winds from the Channel. It is a 17th- to 19th-century townscape that, overall, amounts to more than the sum of its individual buildings. These include St Leonard's Church, which is part Norman, but with a cupola maintained by Trinity House as a landmark for shipping, the stately Royal Marine barracks towards Walmer, and three castles built by Henry VIII, namely Deal, Sandown and Walmer.

Fishing boats are a familiar sight in Deal, on the east coast of Kent

Dover

As impregnable as they look, Dover Castle's massive walls have presented a formidable face to our most vulnerable coastline since the 12th century

Modern Dover is a pleasant seaside town enlivened by the presence of Britain's busiest ferry port. Boat trips from De Bradelei Wharf explore the harbour, with views of visiting ships, the famous white cliffs and a townscape dominated by its

great fortress. And you can board the beautifully restored *Sorceress*, a 120-year-old 'gentleman's yacht' with royal connections.

Described by a medieval historian as 'the key to the kingdom', Dover has borne the brunt of onslaught by invading forces for more than 2,000 years. The castle dates back to 1066, but most of what we see today is 12th century. When Napoleon threatened, an elaborate set of fortifications were added – a network of tunnels that stretches back from the cliff face, where an additional tier of well-protected guns were installed above the shore-level batteries.

The tunnels were not needed against Napoleon, but came into their own during World War II, when, under constant artillery bombardment, they became known as 'Hellfire Corner'. Here the evacuation of 330,000 troops from Dunkirk was organised, and a tunnel extensions housed a Combined Services Headquarters for the defence of south-east England.

The Dover Museum has fascinating exhibits, notably its award-winning Bronze Age Boat Gallery housing the remains of a vessel that is about 3,600 years old. Loan items from the British Museum, and a recreated dwelling give a broad picture of life in Bronze-Age Britain. The town also has the remarkably well preserved Roman Painted House, a Transport Museum and the Women's Land Army Museum.

Folkestone

Eight miles (13km) south-west of Dover, beyond the great white cliffs and the downland behind them, lies this traditional seaside resort with a wide and sweeping promenade, turn-of-the-20th-century terraces and crescents and superb sea views. A zigzag path leads down to the town's newest attraction – a coastal park with wooded area, children's adventure playground and a 250-seat amphitheatre. A pededstrianised shopping area leads down to the harbour, with fresh seafood stands and a Russian submarine to visit.

The Cinque Ports

The Cinque Ports (pronounced 'Sink') were the forerunners of the Royal Navy. The name Cinque comes from the fact that there were originally five – Dover, Hastings, Hythe, New Romney and Sandwich – all prosperous Kent and Sussex ports that could provide the king with ships and men to defend the coast and fight sea battles. By 1278 they were supplying 57 ships, fully manned, for 15 days a year, in return for valuable privileges such as freedom from taxes and customs duties and the right to hold their own courts. The five were soon joined by two 'Antient Towns', Rye and Winchelsea, and by subsidiary ports known as 'limbs'. The Cinque Ports confederation still exists, but only as a focus for pageantry. Its ceremonial head is the Lord Warden, an office held by, among others, the Duke of Wellington, Sir Winston Churchill and Her Majesty, Queen Elizabeth the Queen Mother.

A modern yacht marina shares Ramsgate's harbour with fishing and cargo boats

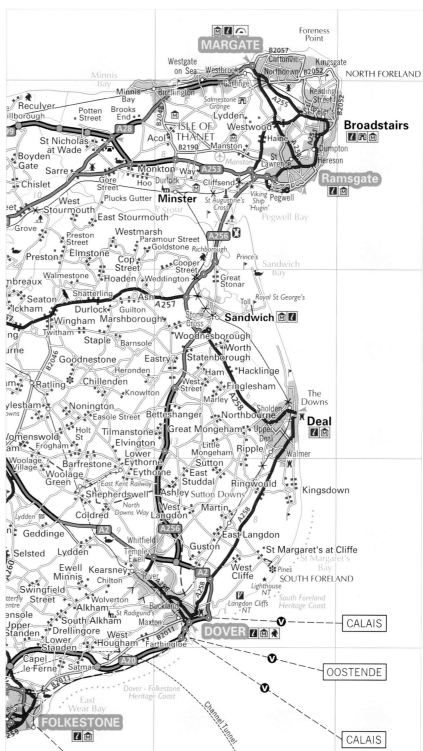

Sandwich

While old Deal is hidden among suburban sprawl, Sandwich has been preserved as a walled town in a largely green setting. This is a town perfect to walk in, whether on the ramparts or through the narrow twisting streets, with their overhanging timber-framed buildings. The Elizabethan Guildhall houses the town museum. In the 13th century Sandwich was England's chief port for wool exports, but in the 15th century the river silted up and that trade moved to Deal, leaving Sandwich tranquil and unspoiled.

The Thanet Resorts

The Isle of Thanet is no longer physically an island, and yet it retains a certain insular independence. Inland is a broad agricultural hinterland, while on its coastline is an almost unbroken string of seaside resorts. The biggest and brashest of these is Margate to the north, which has been not unfairly described as 'never smart but always jolly'.

Ramsgate, on Thanet's east coast, has more style, with its splendid Royal Harbour, Regency cliff-top terraces and bustling ferry port. The area is benefiting from a joint regeneration programme by the County Council, the District Council and the Civic Trust, who are conserving buildings and streetscape and encouraging new initiatives, such as the development of sailing facilities along the coast.

Broadstairs, which adjoins Ramsgate, is the archetypal Victorian seaside resort, with aspirations to become a place of consequence and style which have never quite been achieved. But Broadstairs is likeable, with a high street that charges downhill, then suddenly swerves left because of a cliff, below which lies the sheltered, popular beach of Viking Bay. Dickens was fond of Broadstairs, and in various houses in the town wrote all or part of *David Copperfield, Pickwick Papers* and *Nicholas Nickleby*.

Tourist Information Centres

Broadstairs: 6b High Street (tel: 01843 862242)
Deal: High Street (tel: 01304 369576)
Dover: Townwall Street (tel: 01304 205108)
Folkestone: Harbour Street (tel: 01303 258594)
Margate: 22 High Street (tel: 01843 220241)
Ramsgate: 17 Albert Court, York Street (tel: 01843 583333)
Sandwich: The Guildhall, Cattle Market (seasonal) (tel: 01304 613565)

KENTISH TOWNS AND A GREAT CATHEDRAL

Many tourists race through this part of Kent, completely missing out on its treasures — historic Canterbury, with its great cathedral and atmospheric old streets, delightful small towns and villages; and a countryside that is amazingly tranquil and beautiful. Among the downland and woodland are lovely old farms, manor houses, churches and pubs.

Tourist Information Centres

Canterbury: 34 St Margaret Street (tel: 01227 766567)
Faversham: Fleur de Lis Centre, 13 Preston Street (tel: 01795 534542)
Rochester: Eastgate Cottage, High Street (tel: 01634 843666)
Whitstable: 7 Oxford Street (tel: 01227 275482)

The last of Canterbury's fortified gatehouses sits astride St Peter's Street, with the river as a moat. There are cells in the towers, arms and armour in the guardroom and wonderful views from the battlements

Canterbury

The glory of Canterbury is its great cathedral which, together with St Augustine's Abbey and St Martin's Church forms a World Heritage Site. Whether viewed from the London approach, where each first glimpse of its magnificent west front surprises anew, or from the high ground of the university campus to the north, this cradle of English Christianity gains from being surrounded still by a huddle of domestic-scale buildings and streets with few modern intrusions. The city has not only strenuously defended old buildings and streetscape against inappropriate modern shopfronts and other changes, but achieved the sympathetic redevelopment of at least one jarring 1960s building. The cathedral, founded in the 8th century but destroyed by fire, was rebuilt by Archbishop Lanfranc in the 1070s. In 1178 it was the scene of Thomas à Becket's murder and his canonisation swelled the flow of pilgrims.

Exploring the city, with its traffic-free high street, walks on the medieval walls, and summer boat trips on the River Stour, is highly rewarding. The West Gate, one of the finest medieval fortified gatehouses in England, contains a museum and offers panoramic views of the city. A visit to the Canterbury Heritage Museum reveals the city's 2,000-year history, and the innovative underground Roman Museum is built around the remains of a Roman town house. At the end of 2000 the first of five 'Big Digs' got underway on the site of the Whitefriars redevelopment, an exciting project that will incorporate state-of-the-art exhibitions, displays of the latest finds and an aerial walkway around the site.

The Pilgrim's Way

The Pilgrim's Way can be traced as a track running along the ridge of the North Downs in Surrey and Kent, and in popular imagination was the route by which pilgrims to the tomb of Thomas à Becket arrived on foot in Canterbury. In reality it is something of a misnomer. As a dry, high-level route across the chalk uplands, it dates from prehistoric times and, though some pilgrims from London or Winchester used it, most of them probably followed the Roman Watling Street. Today's walkers following the Countryside Commission's waymarked North Downs Way towards Canterbury may well derive added pleasure from seeing themselves as modern pilgrims, particularly if they call in at the Chaucer Centre and the Canterbury Tales Visitor Attraction on arrival in the city.

Chilham

Set on the hillside above the Stour south-west of Canterbury, Chilham may be regarded as the perfect Kentish village, with its mellow brick and stone cottages

and their luxuriant, gardens, its church, rectory, pub and village square. As if all this were not perfection enough, through a gateway on one side of the square is the unexpected bonus of Chilham Castle. The building is Jacobean, with battlements for show

This is the picturesque scene at the heart of the village of Chilham, with the splendid castle close by

rather than defence, marking the status of its 17th-century owner, Master of the Rolls Sir Dudley Digges. Popularity has not spoiled Chilham, which seems to slow visitors down to its own tranquil pace.

Faversham

This market town has a port, a brewery and streets of quirky but comfortable old houses, and is well worth a visit. Faversham has no great architectural set piece, though it has nearly 500 listed buildings, including a Guildhall with Georgian upper storeys set on the open timber arches of the 16th-century original. A good starting point for any visit is the 15th-century Fleur de Lis Centre, which provides a lively outline of the town's history and attractions. At Iron Wharf sailing barges may still be seen, and the Chart Gunpowder Mills have been restored to show the early days of an explosives industry that periodically shattered the peace of the Swale marshes. At nearby Ospringe is the 16th-century Maison Dieu, founded in medieval times as a leper hospital.

Thomas Arden, sometime mayor of the town who lived at 80 Abbey Street, is the leading character in a 16th-century play, *Arden of Faversham*, which tells of his murder in 1551 by his wife and her lover. Every autumn there is a colourful Hop Festival in the town centre. Faversham has, like other small towns, needed ingenuity to conserve its past while still providing for modern life.

Whitstable

A Victorian seaside resort was grafted on to the existing fishing village after the railway arrived in 1830, but Whitstable's chief fame comes from its oyster beds. Oysters, mussels and a variety of fresh sea fish, are available at several establishments in the town – including the Royal Native Oyster Stores at Horsebridge and the Crab and Winkle on the harbour. This takes its name from the old railway line that linked the town with Canterbury, now the basis of a cycle route which opened in 1999. The town and seafront look smarter these days, thanks largely to a local improvement trust.

The Medway Towns

The best approach to Rochester is from the London direction by the A2 (the Roman Watling Street). On the approach to the bridge across the Medway, the four square stone keep of its Norman Castle looms ahead, guarding the river crossing, with the cathedral close behind. The Charles Dickens Centre celebrates the writer's many associations with the area, and two annual Dickens festivals are held here.

Chatham, further down river, once had a major naval dockyard, partly redeveloped to provide offices and housing, but the most historic part, begun under Henry VIII, and nobly redeveloped in Georgian times, has been conserved as a fascinating living museum.

See Walk H page 135
Historic Medway Towns

A working naval dockyard until 1984, Chatham's Historic Dockyard is now an 80-acre (32ha) museum with no less than 47 Scheduled Ancient Monuments and eight museum galleries, including one which offers the sights, sounds and smells of 18th-century wooden warship construction

THE NEW FOREST

THE LIVING AND WORKING FOREST

Occupying a large part of south-west Hampshire, the New Forest is both a major tourist attraction and a conservation area. A wide-ranging and detailed New Forest Heritage Area Management Strategy seeks to reconcile these conflicting functions, together with a third element – commercial timber production. Negotiations are underway to make the New Forest a national park, but the process is expected to be protracted because of the number of land-owners and other interested parties involved. A suggested park boundary has been drawn up, but so far has not met with universal approval.

If the forest becomes a fully fledged national park, it will be in the British rather than the international sense, because it encompasses not just beautiful scenery, flora and fauna, but towns and villages, and people who make a living from the land. The forest's 1,500 deer belong to the Crown and are managed by the Commission, but the 3,000 or so New Forest ponies belong to the Commoners – locals whose 11th-century predecessors secured grazing and other rights when the savage Forest Law deprived them of the right to hunt.

The 'capital' of the forest is Lyndhurst, seat of the Commission's local administration, of the ancient but still important Court of Verderers, and the New Forest District Council. A town of a few thousand people, it is idyllically set with great forestry 'inclosures' to north and south, and open heathlands to east and west, its church spire a

The name, it has been observed, is doubly misleading. The New Forest was 'new' only in 1097, when William the Conqueror declared it a royal hunting preserve, and 'forest' then meant not a large area of woodland, as we think of today, but an area of land reserved for hunting. Then, as now, trees occupied less space than the heathland and the often rather marshy fields, but today, though 130sq miles (336sq km) of New Forest are still 'preserved', it is for public enjoyment and for conservation as an ecological and landscape asset, rather than for a monarch's days out in the saddle.

Above: thatch amidst the forest at Swan Green; right: the famous and sturdy little New Forest ponies can be seen grazing any clearings between the woodland

distinctive landmark. The New Forest Museum and Visitor Centre adjoining the main car park at Lyndhurst provides both general tourist information and audio-visual and other displays on how the Forest came into existence, its way of life and its customs and traditions.

FOREST ATTRACTIONS

As well as the obvious attractions of the landscape and wildlife, the Forest has a number of places of interest to visit. The thrill of seeing native species in the wild is always an uncertainty, but visitors can be sure of seeing some of the animals at close hand at a number of attractions: New Forest Owl and Otter Sanctuary, at Longdown, houses Britain's largest native wildlife collection, including otter observation pools, wild boar, a walk-through deer enclosure and lots more, all in a lovely woodland setting; there is a Deer Sanctuary at Bolderwood (west of Lyndhurst), with a Reptiliary near by; the Owl Sanctuary at Crow, near Ringwood, dedicated to putting birds back into the wild, has over 100 spacious aviaries; New Forest Badger Watch at Ringwood provides a wonderful opportunity to view these delightful but elusive creatures both above and below ground. There is a hide and an observation set, and headphones provide an instructive commentary. You need to book about a month in advance to take part in an evening watch. The Long-

down Dairy Farm near Ashurst is a working farm which welcomes visitors.

The forest's days as a Norman hunting preserve are recalled at the Rufus Stone, commemorating the allegedly accidental shooting of the unpopular King William II (Rufus) while he was hunting.

A good way to appreciate the best of the woodland is on the magnificent Rhinefield and Bolderwood ornamental drives, and there are horse-drawn wagon rides as well as many waymarked woodland walks, all with skilfully sited car parks.

Of the Forest's half-dozen villages, Minstead is among the most visited, with its thatched cottages and largely 18th-century All Saints Church, notable for its three-decker pulpit, box pews and two galleries, one above the other. Furzey Gardens at Minstead consists of 8 acres (3ha) of flowering trees and shrubs. More famous are the Exbury Gardens, which are spectacularly colourful during the rhododendron season, and Spinners at Boldre, near Lymington is another lovely garden to visit. Burley in the south-east of the Forest, set amidst bracing open heathland, is a good centre for walkers. Castle Hill, 1¼ miles (2km) north, is an Iron-Age camp and one of the best vantage points to view the Forest.

In the south-east of the Forest stands Beaulieu Abbey, founded by King John for the Cistercians, but home of the Montagu family since 1538. Its battlemented Palace House was once the abbey's gatehouse, though its present appearance owes much to an 1870s 'restoration'. Understanding of the medieval remains is greatly helped by an exhibition about monastic life. Alongside the Abbey is the 3rd Lord Montagu's pride and joy, his splendid National Motor Museum, with 250 exhibits, including a fascinating range of cars, commercial vehicles and motorcycles. Another popular attraction is 'Wheels', described as 'a futuristic ride on space-age pods through 100 years of motoring', as well as a monorail and veteran bus rides.

Buckler's Hard, 2½ miles (4km) down the Beaulieu River, is a remnant of an early 18th-century plan to build Montagu Town, a port to rival Southampton. Two rows of attractive brick cottages were as far as the project got, but the little settlement was important for 80 years as a shipyard – Nelson's *Agamemnon* was built here, using 2,000 New Forest oaks. Buckler's Hard's Maritime Museum vividly evokes that era. On the next little river to the west stands Lymington, a lively yachting and ferry port and the New Forest's main market town. Its mellow streetscape and roof-scape, mixed with masts and the steeple of St Michael's Church, are as lively as the Saturday high-street market.

Exbury Gardens are a riot of colour during the rhododendron and azalea season in early summer

A City on the Forest Fringe

A large, modern city, port, and regional shopping and commercial centre, Southampton nonetheless has a long history. There was a Roman town on the east bank of the Itchen at Bitterne, and on the west bank the Saxons had a town called Hamwic. Despite World War II bombs and post-war development, a great deal from the past remains. South of the modern shopping centre, Above Bar is a surviving gateway of the medieval town, the fortified Bargate.

To right and left of Bargate run the impressive remains of the town walls with defensive towers, including the picturesquely named Catchcold Tower and Blue Anchor Postern. The Tudor House, a fine example of a rich merchant's town house of around 1500, is now a museum, its finest exhibit is arguably its handsome banqueting hall. Other medieval and Tudor buildings now house museums, including the Museum of Archaeology in God's House Tower on the old Town Quay, and the Maritime Museum, housed in the early 15th-century Wool House.

More recent history is celebrated in the Hall of Aviation, which tells the story of aviation – particularly flying boats and seaplanes – in and around the Solent. The name 'Supermarine' attaches not only to the *Spitfire*, first built in Southampton, but also to the racing seaplanes that took part in the Schneider Trophy races here in 1929 and 1931. The modern helicopter was also created in Southampton, and several are on show.

Southampton is very green, with a series of six parks right in the heart of the city, while to the north the 368 acres (149ha) of Southampton Common drive a green wedge between the adjacent suburbs. The waterfront is also a pleasant public amenity, with Mayflower Park looking out over the Test estuary between Town Quay and the Western Docks and the more recent development of Ocean Village focusing on the 'festival market' concept, with shops, bars and restaurants.

Lymington harbour is a delightful scene, popular with weekend sailors as well as Isle of Wight ferry passengers

See Walk J page 136
The New Forest – A Royal Hunting Ground

THE HEART OF HAMPSHIRE

Amidst glorious chalk downland, this area is far enough from London in one direction, and Southampton and Portsmouth in the other, to keep its independence and more sensible pace of life. It focuses chiefly on Winchester, the historic capital of Wessex; the famous trout waters of the Rivers Test and Itchen meander gently through the area.

Hillier Gardens and Arboretum

The Sir Harold Hillier Gardens and Arboretum, at Ampfield on the A31 between Winchester and Romsey, were begun by the famous nurseryman in 1953. Sir Harold gave the gardens in trust to Hampshire County Council in 1977. Now extending to 180 acres (73ha), they contain a unique collection of 42,000 plants and trees, including the British Isles' largest collection of hardy plants. Its sheer diversity ensures interest in all seasons – even winter has its subtle wonders, from fragrant witch hazels to beautiful bark. Guided tours are offered, and workshops take place regularly throughout the year.

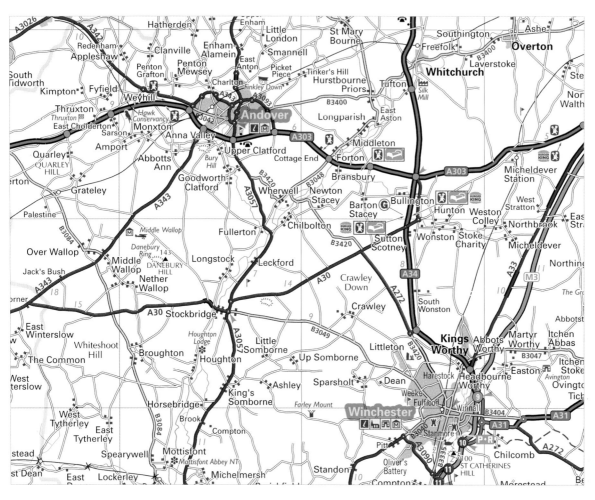

The Hillier Gardens and Arboretum comprise the largest collection of trees and shrubs of its kind in Britain, with plants from all over the world

Tourist Information Centres

Andover: Town Mill House, Bridge Street (tel: 01264 324320)
Romsey: 1 Latimer Street (tel: 01794 512987)
Winchester: Guildhall, The Broadway (tel: 01962 840500)

Andover

As one of the towns which expanded to take 'overspill' from London in the 1960s, the comfortable market town of Andover grew from a population of 10,000 to around 40,000, somewhat obscuring the fact that it has a history going back to Saxon times. The high street has attractive buildings, including the alluringly Grecian Town Hall of 1824. St Mary's Church, standing dramatically on a hill above the town, is one of Hampshire's best Victorian churches, the gift of a Winchester headmaster who retired to Andover, but died just before its completion in 1845. Andover's excellent Museum of the Iron Age has a good interpretive display on the Danebury hillfort.

Danebury and the Wallops

Danebury Hillfort is an impressive, oval-shaped 13-acre (5ha) Iron-Age fortress with three lines of ditches and ramparts, increasing in strength and height towards the centre; the innermost is 16ft (4.9m) high and a prodigious 60ft (18.2m) broad. It existed from the 6th century BC until around 100 BC, when even improved defences and an elaborately fortified eastern entrance did not prevent it from being overrun. Danebury Hill is south-west of Andover, near the picturesque village of Nether Wallop.

At Middle Wallop is the award-winning Museum of Army Flying, with its historic aircraft, including the largest collection of gliders in Europe.

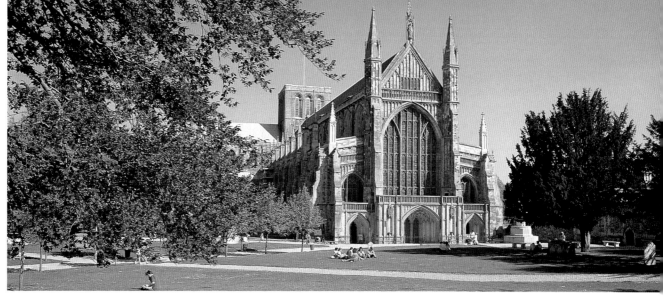

Romsey

Of all Hampshire's market towns, Romsey has one of the best townscapes. The town's chief glory is Romsey Abbey, which owes its survival to the 16th-century civic leaders. After the Dissolution, there was wholesale demolition of monastic buildings, but Romsey's representatives bought the abbey church and thus preserved it. Largely built in 1120–30 on the site of two earlier Saxon churches, it has, with its round Romanesque arches, an impressive simple grandeur. Of many old and beautiful houses in the town, the finest is King John's Hunting Lodge, a hall house of 1230. It is now a heritage centre, and provides town trails to guide your explorations. On the edge of the town, on the banks of the River Test, is Broadlands, an elegant Palladian mansion, once home to Lord Palmerston, but better known as the home of Lord Mountbatten until his untimely death. It is now occupied by his grandson, Lord Romsey, and is an interesting house to visit.

Mottisfont Abbey is a fine building, but it is mostly for the gardens of old-fashioned roses that visitors come here in the early summer

Headbourne Worthy

St Swithun's Church here is a Saxon church with one treasure which is regarded as internationally important – a Saxon rood, or representation of Christ on the cross, the Virgin and St John the Baptist. Religious fanatics damaged the figures, but it is still powerful. The church is delightfully situated, with a tributary of the River Itchen flowing round it.

Mottisfont

An Augustinian priory founded in 1201, Mottisfont Abbey was, at the Dissolution, handed to Lord Sandys who turned it into a house. It was remodelled and extended in Georgian times; the living rooms are in the nave of what was the priory church. The overall picture is harmonious and tranquil; a little river runs through the garden with its trees and lawns, and the well or 'font' which gave it its name. Come in the early summer for the magnificent display provided here by the National Collection of old-fashioned roses. In the house, the Whistler Room (which has *trompe l'oeil* decorations by Whistler) and the Cellarium have been restored.

Winchester

Winchester is probably less appreciated as a historic town than, say, York or Canterbury. Yet it was capital of England under Saxon Kings, joint capital for the Normans, with treasury and Domesday Book kept here. Its greatest glory is the cathedral, at 556ft (169.4m) the longest in Europe. It was begun by the Normans, but the magnificent nave is 13th to 14th century, in part the work of William de Wynford, master mason of Windsor Castle. Wynford was borrowed from the king by Winchester's most famous bishop, William of Wykeham, who founded Winchester College.

The cathedral does not provide many dramatic distant views. The drama is, on entering the Close through a narrow gate or lane, to find this immense building, set among green lawns with mature trees and a delicious mixture of domestic-scale architecture as its backdrop. This tranquil oasis connects with two other areas worth exploring: north is the High Street; south is a second walled precinct, that of Winchester College – one of England's oldest public school. Some of its oldest parts are again by de Wynford, with additions and alterations from the 15th century right up to the 19th and 20th, yet somehow it forms a harmonious whole.

In the Broadway is a statue of King Alfred, whose burial place was discovered in 1999 at Hyde Abbey. From here to the fortified West Gate runs the High Street, largely pedestrianised and showing that the city is alive and well and adapting with the times. Thanks to narrowings and projecting buildings, the High Street does not reveal itself all at once, and though its overall flavour is Georgian, it has a pleasing variety of styles, not to mention an excellent variety of shops.

Other delights include waterside walks in the Abbey Grounds, the 18th-century City Mill, Henry III's splendid medieval Great Hall of the Castle, and, to the south, the 12th-century Hospital of St Cross and the still peaceful water meadows beyond.

Winchester Cathedral is one of the most atmospheric places in the country. Ancient and impressive, it contains the bones of Saxon kings, a Norman font, superb carving and medieval wall paintings

It is a nice story, and an understandable one, but this round table has nothing to do with King Arthur. It is very old, however, and hangs in the Great Hall, the only remaining portion of William the Conqueror's first castle in Winchester

ANCIENT AND MODERN IN NORTH-EAST HAMPSHIRE

The broad, rolling expanses of the central Hampshire plain lie between the North Wessex Downs and those of East Hampshire. This is prosperous farming country, which is dotted with pretty villages and well-preserved market towns of a previous era. Amidst all this rural tranquillity, Basingstoke is a potent symbol of London's influence.

Just one of the architectural delights of Alresford's Broad Street, one of the most attractive main streets in the country

Alresford

This delightful place actually consists of Old Alresford and New Alresford, though 'Old' and 'New' are relative terms. New Alresford was 'new' in 1200, when Bishop de Lucy of Winchester laid it out as one of his planned new towns, alongside the existing village of Alresford to the north. He dammed the little River Arle, creating a 200-acre (81ha) reservoir with the aim of making the Itchen (which it joins downstream) navigable to Southampton. Old Alresford is tiny, with an 18th-century church and two substantial Georgian houses. The route from the north past watercress beds is a delight. Crossing de Lucy's dam, you come to New Alresford's Broad Street, a sumptuous Georgian townscape. A major attraction here is the restored steam railway known as 'The Watercress Line' from the days when this local harvest was its main cargo.

Alton

Traditionally a brewing centre, Alton dates back to Roman times, though the straight main thoroughfare is part of a much older route – a Bronze-Age track, later the Pilgrim's Way. The High Street is rich in 18th-century buildings. The oldest parts of the church of St Lawrence are Norman, with a second 15th-century nave and chancel alongside. The beautiful 17th-century pulpit was where Royalist colonel Richard Boles died, refusing to surrender though outnumbered and out-gunned by the Parliamentarians. Its main doorway still has their musket balls embedded in it.

Basingstoke

As the 21st century got underway, the oft-maligned town of Basingstoke was getting a much-needed facelift. Prior to the mid-1960s, it was a pleasant, small market town, until the demands of London overspill development largely flattened the old town centre and ringed it with vast housing and industrial estates. In spite of this, the town prospered, and peacemeal improvements were made over the intervening decades, notably the provision of the superb Anvil concert hall, the refurbishment of the Haymarket Theatre and the building of a leisure park.

During 2000 the opening of the excellent Milestones Museum provided the best reason yet for visiting the town, its labyrinthe of street scenes depicting Hampshire's history using state-of-the-art technology. The town's original museum, the Willis in the old Town Hall, is also very interesting, and determined explorers can find some attractive parts of the old town, including the Holy Ghost Chapel ruins near the station, St Michael's church and some attractive old almshouses at the 'top of town'. There is a pleasant footpath to Basing House (see opposite) along the course of the old Basingstoke Canal.

Jane Austen and Hampshire

Though readers of Jane Austen's *Persuasion* or *Northanger Abbey* may associate her with the fashionable world of Bath – and she did indeed live there for five years – she was born at Steventon in Hampshire. This village near Basingstoke is where she lived for her first 25 years and she died at Winchester, but in between she lived at two other Hampshire addresses – in Southampton and, more famously, at Chawton near Alton. She was at her most creative during the eight years (1809–17) she lived at Chawton, and her modest brick house is now a Jane Austen museum, providing many insights into her life and writings.

Jane Austen's house in Chawton is now a museum

Gilbert White and Selborne

The writings and reputation of Gilbert White have brought countless visitors to the little Hampshire village of Selborne for over two centuries. White was born there in 1720, went to Oxford and, after ordination, returned to serve as curate to neighbouring parishes. His passion for natural history led him to observe the area's flora and fauna in great detail, and in 1789 he published his *The Natural History and Antiquities of Selborne*. White's house, The Wakes, is now a museum devoted to him; it also has displays on two members of the Oates family – Captain Lawrence Oates, the Antarctic explorer, and Frank Oates, a widely travelled naturalist. White's garden has been restored to its 18th-century form, and the church has a memorial window featuring many species of birds he observed.

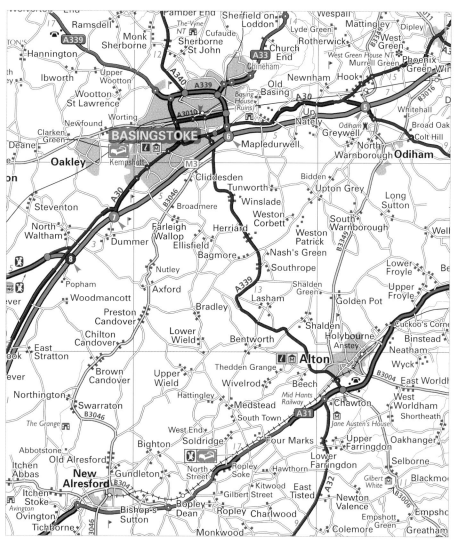

Gilbert White's house in Selborne is a must for naturalists everywhere

Northington Grange

William Wilkins, architect of The National Gallery, designed The Grange at Northington in 1809 for London banker Henry Drummond. Encasing an earlier house, he created a stunning Greek temple with a Parthenon-like portico supported by two rows of giant Doric columns. Its decay by the 1960s was such that its owner wished to demolish it. There was a national outcry and the Environment Secretary intervened. English Heritage rescued what is now a stabilised – but very dramatic – ruin.

Odiham

This is among the most attractive of Hampshire's small towns. Notable buildings include the church and The Priory, part Queen Anne, part Tudor; but the high street, lined with mellow brick Georgian houses and older timber-framed buildings, deserves exploration. It used to groan under the weight of through traffic, until it won its fight for a bypass. The Basingstoke Canal has been restored and boat trips are available in summer.

Old Basing

Here once stood England's largest private house, the palace of William Paulet, 1st Marquess of Winchester, and Lord Treasurer to three Tudor monarchs. In the Civil War, the house was defended by the Royalists but after a 2½-year siege fell to an assault led by Cromwell. What we see today includes Norman earthworks, the remains of Tudor kitchens, cellars, towers and a 300ft (91.4m) long tunnel. The Civil War defences were designed by Inigo Jones, who was here during the siege, and there is a recreated 17th-century garden.

The Vyne

A fascinating and harmonious mixture of periods and styles, the Vyne includes the original Tudor House, built in the early 1500s by William Sandys, courtier to Henry VIII. The classical portico was added in the 1650s for Chaloner Chute, barrister and Speaker of the House of Commons, while the dramatic classical staircase was installed in the 1770s by his grandson, John. Outside are peaceful gardens, a lake and woodland walks.

Tourist Information Centres

Alton: 7 Cross & Pillory Lane (tel: 01420 88448)
Basingstoke: Willis Museum, Old Town Hall, Market Place (tel: 01256 817618)

The mellow brick exterior of The Vyne does nothing to prepare visitors for the splendour of the Grand Staircase, just one fine feature of a particularly interesting house

SURREY TOWNS AND MILITARY HERITAGE

THE COUNTRYSIDE HERE INCLUDES wooded upland Surrey, with its prosperous market towns, a great sweep of chalk downland with a patchwork of woodland and villages beyond, and the open commons and heathlands around Hindhead. Historic Guildford is the main town, while to the north-west are the military towns of Aldershot and Farnborough.

Abinger Hammer

Few of those who pass Abinger Hammer's picturesque clockhouse, with its gilded weather vane and brightly painted figure of a sturdy blacksmith poised to strike the hour, realise that this pretty little village has an industrial past. Iron was worked here in Tudor times, and later the Tilling-bourne was dammed to power mechanical hammers. The village still has its working smithy. At Abinger Common to the south-west is Goddards, a country House by Sir Edwin Lutyens with gardens by Gertrude Jekyll, which is open by appointment.

A quaint rustic porch shelters St James's Well at Abinger

Leading up to the church are neat brick cottages in Church Lane, Farnham

Aldershot

Until the Crimean War Aldershot was a small village, but from 1854 onwards the Army developed it with a dreary grid of 'short-back-and-sides' architecture. Maturing trees and landscaping has softened this image, and though the main attractions are not architectural, the town has won Britain in Bloom awards. Britain's military heritage is celebrated here – outstandingly in the Aldershot Military Museum, the Airborne Forces Museum and the Red Church. The nearby bronze equestrian statue of the Duke of Wellington originally stood atop Constitution Arch at London's Hyde Park Corner.

Farnham

Part of this attractive town was originally laid out in the 12th century by the Bishop of Winchester, and the castle was the bishop's palace. In the early 18th century the town prospered as a corn market and hop-growing centre, and this financed the fine Georgian buildings which give it its character, particularly in Castle Street and West Street. The early 19th-century Maltings were saved from demolition by a local trust and now form a lively arts and community centre.

Guildford

For centuries a prosperous market town, sited where the River Wey breaks through the North Downs, Guildford today is testimony to the compromises that often need to be made between conserving the past and ensuring continued prosperity. Bulky, unsympathetic 1960s and '70s buildings and insensitive road building did violence to the townscape, and yet the town is very much alive, and there is much to see. Sightseeing 'musts' include the castle with 12th-century tower keep, and the Guildhall, with its superb 17th-century front, resembling the decorated poop of a

A Chieftain tank stands outside Aldershot Military Museum, which illustrates the daily life of the soldier over the last 140 years

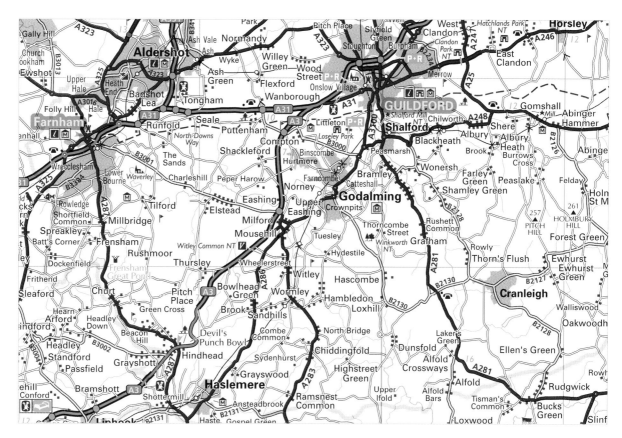

An ornate clock, on an arm stretching out from the 17th-century Guildhall, hangs out over Guildford's High Street. It is a famous landmark in a street that Dickens described as 'the most beautiful in the kingdom'

sailing ship. When exploring the attractive High Street, don't miss The Angel, the last survivor of a whole string of coaching inns along here, and the delightful Quarry Street which runs off it below the castle. Recent pedestrianisation of many streets and lanes off High Street makes exploration on foot a more enjoyable experience. By the riverside is the 1960s Yvonne Arnaud Theatre, and on Stag Hill to the west stands the imposing brick-built cathedral, also completed in the 1960s; to its north on a sloping site lies the University of Surrey campus, with some interesting hillside buildings. There are some attractive walks along the River Wey.

Haslemere

This was little more than a village until the railway came in 1859, but the Victorian commuter cottages fit well into the delicious wooded, hilly landscape. In the centre are some older buildings, notably the Town Hall, rebuilt in 1814 but looking much older, and the Haslemere Educational Museum, which has some rare collections and a delightful garden. One

big influence on the town was Arnold Dolmetsch, instrument maker and pioneer of early music, who made Haslemere his home. He set up workshops for making authentic instruments for the performance of early music, and established the annual music festival (July) which bears his name.

Hindhead

William Cobbett, reaching Hindhead in his *Rural Rides*, called it 'the most villainous spot that God ever made'. Today this certainly seems a severe judgement, but Cobbett's concern with agricultural potential – Hindhead is on heathland 850ft (259m) above sea level – and the fact that it was the haunt of highwaymen, were some justification. The later Victorians and Edwardians saw things differently – the air was pure, the landscape well-wooded and the views agreeable, and they built spacious brick and tile-hung houses among the pine trees. Notable residents included George Bernard Shaw, Sir Arthur Conan Doyle and Dr Marie Stopes, celebrated botanist and advocate of family planning.

Hindhead Commons, now owned by the National Trust, include the dramatic Devil's Punch Bowl, formed by springs cutting down and back from their sources, and Gibbet Hill, where three footpads were hanged after murdering a sailor.

Tourist Information Centres

Aldershot: 35–39 High Street (tel: 01252 320968)
Farnham: Council Offices, South Street (tel: 01252 715109)
Guildford: 14 Tunsgate (tel: 01483 444333)
Haslemere: 78 High Street (tel: 01428 645425)

See Walk K page 137
The Devil's Punch Bowl

PALACES AND GARDENS ON THE THAMES

The south-western suburbs of London which border the Thames are among its environmentally most favoured, with several large green open spaces – the parks of Richmond, Bushey and Hampton Court and the Royal Botanical Gardens at Kew. A string of historic houses and palaces lines the Thames, while Richmond is one of London's liveliest town centres.

One of the splendid vistas created at the 50-acre (20ha) Claremont Landscape Garden, which includes this lake with an island pavilion, a grotto and a turf amphitheatre

Claremont and Painshill

The A3 out of London is not the most beautiful of landscapes, but as it heads into Surrey it offers access to two outstanding 18th-century landscape gardens. Claremont is one of the earliest surviving examples of the English landscape art, and has been carefully restored by the National Trust. It dates from 1708, when architect Sir John Vanbrugh bought the site, which he thought 'romantick'. He later sold it to Thomas Pelham, Duke of Newcastle, who employed both Vanbrugh and William Kent. Kent provided a lake and grotto; Vanbrugh a striking hilltop Belvedere.

Painshill Park, 3 miles (4.8km) further along the A3, was created between 1738 and 1773 by The Hon Charles Hamilton, plantsman, painter and gifted designer, who transformed barren heathland into ornamental pleasure grounds of dramatic and often exotic beauty. Painshill is dominated by a meandering 14-acre (6ha) lake fed from the River Mole by a giant waterwheel. Other features include a grotto, Gothic-style temple, ruined abbey, Chinese bridge, castellated tower, Turkish tent and working vineyard. After 1948 the landscape sank into dereliction, but, during the 1980s and '90s the Painshill Park Trust peeled back the jungle to reveal and restore what Hamilton created.

Ham House, Marble Hill and Orleans House

Upstream from Richmond is a string of splendid 18th-century riverside buildings. First, on the north bank, is Marble Hill House, a magnificent Palladian villa built in the 1720s for Henrietta Howard, Countess of Suffolk, and set in 66 acres (27ha) of parkland. A few hundred yards upstream is Ham House, a large 17th-century house of exceptional interest, restored by the National Trust, together with its gardens. Finally, back across the river is the baroque Octagon Room of the Orleans House Gallery, built around 1720 by James Gibbs for William III's Secretary of State for Scotland; an adjoining wing is now an art gallery. A ferryman will row you swiftly and inexpensively from the Ham side to Marble Hill Park.

Hampton Court

Hampton Court Palace was not originally a royal palace, but built by Cardinal Wolsey,

RHS Garden Wisley

The Royal Horticultural Society's 250-acre (100ha) garden at Wisley contains a whole range of different habitats, and has much to delight and interest in different seasons. Its Alpine Meadow is carpeted with wild daffodils in spring; Battleston Hill is clothed in colourful rhododendrons in early summer; it has heathers and autumnal tints, glasshouses, trial grounds and model gardens. The garden is also a source of practical advice and the exemplar of best horticultural practice. Sunday opening is reserved for members of the Royal Horticultural Society. The tiny hamlet of Wisley is a charming survival, its centrepiece a tiny church dating from around 1250.

Ham House, one of the most complete 17th-century houses to have survived, has sumptuous interiors and fine works of art. The staircase is a suitably grand introduction to the state rooms on the first floor

Henry VIII's most powerful minister. Such a tangible display of power and wealth was not to the king's liking, and though Wolsey decided to give the palace to his monarch, his doom was already sealed. The great Tudor brick gatehouse dominates the main approach to the palace, and beyond the huge Base Court lies the Clock Court with its 16th-century astronomical clock and Henry VIII's Great Hall. Wren extended and remodelled the palace for William and Mary, adding the great East Front and the arcaded Fountain Court. Particular attractions include the Tudor kitchens, orangery, the Hampton Court vine and the maze.

Imposing shadows encroach across the lawns at the West Front entrance of Hampton Court Palace

Kew

Kew is synonymous with the Royal Botanic Gardens, 300 acres (121ha) of landscaped gardens devoted to the propagation, study and display of plant species. It all began with a small garden started in 1759 by Princess Augusta,

widowed daughter-in-law of George II. Botanically, Kew is a world leader; architecturally it contains some spectacular buildings, including Decimus Burton's Palm House and Temperate House, the Pagoda by William Chambers and the elegant Princess of Wales Conservatory. But Kew is not just the gardens. Kew Palace, which is sometimes known as the Dutch House, is the modest house of 1631 where George III and his family lived for a time. Kew Village is centred on its green, and has a Georgian parish church, old houses and a riverside path.

Kingston upon Thames

Saxon kings were crowned here, and this is where the Normans built the first Thames bridge above London Bridge. Today, though there are attractive old street, Kingston is primarily a busy shopping and commercial centre, where the 1980s John Lewis store is promenent, with sales floors piled up over the relief road.

New conservatories add an interesting roofscape to Kew Gardens and provide a counterpoint to the famous Palm House of 1848

Richmond upon Thames

Richmond combines a wealth of historic buildings and splendid Thames views with a bustling commercial centre and lively arts and restaurant scene. Architectural gems include its two greens and the adjacent lanes. Richmond Hill has 18th-century houses, a fine view upriver, and a fine riverside group by Richmond Bridge. Most of it is not as old as it looks, a 1980s neo-classical stage-set by architect Quinlan Terry, with functional modern offices behind it. The design is immensely popular, providing a dramatic backdrop to the lively riverside area. The Richmond Theatre on The Green is the best-preserved London theatre. Richmond Park, at 2,469 acres (1,000ha) is the largest of London's royal parks.

Tourist Information Centres

Kingston upon Thames: The Market House, Market Place (tel: 020 8547 5592)
Richmond upon Thames: Old Town Hall, Whittaker Avenue (tel: 020 8940 9125)
Twickenham: Civic Centre, 44 York Street (tel: 020 8891 7272)

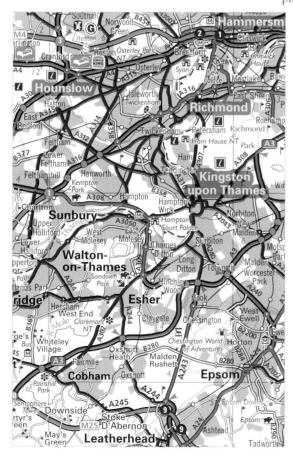

STEAM RAILWAYS

IN THE 1940s AND '50s, southern England was still criss-crossed by dozens of branch railway lines, mostly operated with steam-hauled trains. Typically built at the height of railway optimism in the late 19th century, they had for several decades been starved of money for either maintenance or modernisation, and were increasingly suffering from road transport competition.

Even before Dr Richard (later Lord) Beeching began wielding his notorious axe in 1963, many lines were struggling. But in those rationalising days there grew up a body of men and women who were unwilling to let these well-loved railways die. And, paradoxically, the fact that there had been no money available to modernise them added to their attraction.

THE FIGHT FOR SURVIVAL

The fight to save the branch lines was tough. From the nationalised railway's point of view, the sensible course was to take up track, which might be re-used or sold as scrap, and then to sell the land section by section for the best price obtainable. Buyers were there – property developers in towns and around stations; farmers in the open countryside, though the prices they were prepared to pay for overgrown cuttings and embankments were limited.

From the rail preservationists' point of view, piecemeal sales posed a dire threat. Even the smallest bite out of a proposed route prevented through running, and some ambitious plans had to be restricted to short stretches of line or sidings. Fortunately, this was not always the case. With surprisingly enthusiastic public backing and

some support from the local authorities, a number of preservation societies succeeded in securing viable routes, acquiring and restoring track, locomotives, rolling stock and buildings, and running respectable services.

Then a strange thing happened. As the realities of grimy, gritty, smoke-invaded commuting receded, so the steam railway as a tourist attraction gained romantic appeal. And it has a powerful appeal, not just to the retired railwaymen and the amateur (but knowledgeable) volunteer, but also to visitors who would not know a gland from a piston-rod.

KENT RAILWAYS

In south-east England, the preserved lines cluster most closely in the south coast counties of Kent and Sussex, and some have already celebrated their coming of age. The Sittingbourne and Kemsley Light Railway in 2000

Locomotive number 23 steams into action on the Kent and East Sussex Railway at Tenterden, a popular overnight stop-over location

celebrated its 31st year. Its 2ft 6in (0.76m) gauge line runs for about 1½ miles (2.4km) from its Sittingbourne Station (conveniently close to the main line) north alongside Milton Creek to Kemsley Down, overlooking the River Swale.

The line was built by the Edward Lloyd paper mill to transport materials from a dock on the Swale, and is leased from the company's successor. In addition to the three-mile (4.8km) return journey, there is a grassed picnic area, refreshment facilities, a small exhibits museum and a souvenir shop –

the kind of extras which most cash-strapped railway preservation groups need in order to survive. Like many others, the Sittingbourne and Kemsley operates mostly at weekends and bank holidays, when its dedicated volunteers are available to provide for the greater potential number of visitors.

On Kent's east coast is one of the best known of all steam rail-

ways, the 15 inch gauge 13½-mile (22km) Romney, Hythe and Dymchurch. Financed by railway enthusiast Captain J E P Howey in the late 1920s and built by Henry Greenly, it was threatened with closure after Howey's death, but saved by a consortium in 1972. It runs from Hythe, near Folkestone, along the coast to Dymchurch, St Mary's Bay, New Romney and Dungeness and operates an intensive daily service between Easter and the end of September, plus weekends in March and October.

The Kent and East Sussex Railway is, by contrast, full size and standard gauge. The first

Below, the brilliant livery of the Romney, Hyth and Dymchurch Railway

line to be built under the 1896 Light Railways Act, it opened in 1900, closed in 1961 and – as a result of the 'sheer dogged persistence and enthusiasm' of the preservationists – reopened in 1974, 20 years after British Rail ran its last passenger train. One of England's classic rural railways, with sharp curves, steep gradients and short trains calling at tiny country stations, it orig-

A gleaming locomotive of the Romney, Hythe and Dymchurch Railway leaves New Romney Station, headquarters of the world's smallest public railway. The line was developed by two enthusiasts in cooperation with Southern Railways

inally ran some 21 miles (33.8km) from Robertsbridge to Headcorn.

From just under 2 miles (3km) initially reopened, the line has now been extended to about 10.5 miles (17km), with trains running from Tenterden in Kent via Rolvenden and Wittersham Road through Northiam in East Sussex, and finally to Bodiam, depositing passengers just a short distance from the famous castle.

The popular Kent and East Sussex line also entices travellers with various specials – journeys which include a six-course meal, served in traditional style aboard the Wealden Pullman, the luxurious 1926 Pullman Bar Car 'Barbara' among them, and there are also pre-Christmas Santa Specials and packages combining dinner on the Pullman with an overnight stay in Tenterden's late Victorian Collina House Hotel.

STEAMING THROUGH SUSSEX

The Bluebell Railway and the Lavender Line are two preserved steam railways in Sussex. The Bluebell, saved for posterity in 1960, runs for some 9 miles (14km) from Sheffield Park Station, just off the A275 East Grinstead–Lewes road, via Horsted Keynes and West Hoathly Tunnel to Kingscote. Its name comes from the beautiful woodland en route that is a mass of bluebells in the spring. Not only does the Bluebell Line run a Pullman for Saturday dinner and Sunday lunch There is

A worker on the Bluebell line is dwarfed by a locomotive. Sheffield Park Station has a museum with the largest collection of locomotives and carriages in the region. At the start of the 21st century, the Bluebell Railway has been operating for 40 years

also a restaurant at Sheffield Park and a real-ale bar, the Bessemer Arms, named after the local resident who initially saved the line from closure.

The Lavender Line has nothing to do with flowers, but is named after the coal merchants A E Lavender & Sons, who operated out of the station yard. The railway began life in 1858 as part of the former Lewes–Uckfield Railway, but closed in 1969. It operates from the carefully restored station at Isfield, south of Uckfield.

HAMPSHIRE AND ISLE OF WIGHT TRACKS

The Mid Hants Railway runs for 10½ miles (16.9km) from the main line station at Alton through beautiful Hampshire countryside to Alresford, with intermediate stops at Medstead & Four Marks and Ropley. It is still known as 'the Watercress Line', from the days when Hampshire watercress growers would transport their harvest to London markets by rail. The line ceased operation in 1973, 108 years after it opened. It was saved by dedicated enthusiasts, and now runs at weekends in March and October, then most days between April and September, with an hourly frequency of trains.

On the Isle of Wight mainline services have shrunk from half a dozen lines, covering virtually every corner of the island in the late 1940s, to just one electrified line from Ryde to Sandown and Shanklin. But the days of steam are kept alive by the Isle of Wight Steam Railway running for 5 miles

(8km) from Havenstreet and linking with the main line at Smallbrook Junction.

Other steam railways in the south-east include the Colne Valley Railway, a restored stretch of Edwardian branch line at Castle Hedingham, Essex, and the Great Cockcrow miniature steam railway at Lyne near Chertsey, Surrey. Steam enthusiasts also head for the Great Western Society's Didcot Railway Centre in Oxfordshire and the North Woolwich Station Museum at Silvertown

Under pressure takes on a whole new meaning in the world of preserved steam railways, though these boiler pressure and speed gauges show a locomotive in repose.

in London Docklands. The Harpenden Railway Museum in Hertfordshire is a collection of railwayana assembled in their own garden by Geoff and Sue Woodward – it is open to the public on selected days.

Most of the railways featured here operate special themed attractions, including Santa Specials, Thomas the Tank Engine Weekends, Wartime Weekends and Vintage and Classic Vehicle and Bus events, with participants in full period costume.

VALLEYS OF THE THAMES AND KENNET

T wo features dominate this countryside – the Thames, meandering north-west to south-east towards Reading, and a belt of uplands crossing it diagonally: Chilterns to the north-east; Berkshire Down to the south-west. All converge at Goring Gap. Below the Downs the Kennet and Avon Canal drops gently down from Newbury to join the Thames at Reading.

The Kennet and Avon Canal

The Kennet and Avon Canal, built by the great engineer John Rennie, opened in 1810, linking the Thames to the Bristol Channel. It went the way of all canals, its prosperity killed off by the coming of the railway, and by the 1950s it was sliding into dereliction. Canal enthusiasts successfully fought against the plans close it, and mobilised a voluntary effort to help restore it. Parts of the canal had been in use for leisure purposes for some time, but in 1990, with the whole 57 miles (92km) again navigable, Her Majesty, the Queen formally reopened the canal at Devizes (see page 46). A Heritage Lottery Fund grant has now been secured to complete the restoration and make

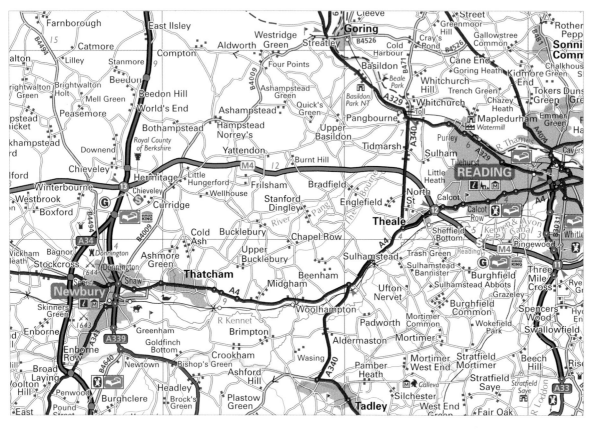

further improvements. As well as boating, and walking and cycling along its towpaths, the wildlife and industrial interest is immense. At Crofton the oldest working beam engine in the world is still doing its original job.

Tourist Information Centres

Newbury: The Wharf (tel: 01635 30267)
Reading: Town Hall, Blagrave Street (tel: 0118 956 6226)

Basildon Park

Basildon Park is the most splendid Georgian mansion in Berkshire. In golden bath stone, it is on a grand scale – the central building, with double-storey portico, Ionic columns and pediment, is flanked by twin two-storey pavilions. Inside, the focal point is the unusual Octagon Room, but all around is fine plasterwork, paintings and furniture. The garden and woodland walks are also delightful.

Goring and Streatley

Goring and Streatley face each other across the Thames, one in Oxfordshire, the other in Berkshire, linked by a bridge with lock and weirs. This is also a key link in the 85-mile (137-km) Ridgeway path from Avebury to Ivinghoe Beacon in Buckinghamshire. There is splendid walking in both directions and Goring is particular attractive, with a 12th-century church, a 17th-century vicarage and 18th-century almshouses.

Highclere Castle

Highclere Castle is actually a magnificent early Victorian mansion, designed by Sir Charles Barry (architect of the Houses of Parliament). It is a great square building, with towers and pinnacles, and the façades have a lovely golden glow. This is the home of the Earls of Carnarvon. The 5th Earl was famous as one of the discoverers of the tomb of Tutankhamun and the castle contains many of his Egyptian relics. There is also a horseracing exhibition, and the castle hosts special events, including concerts, craft fairs and country shows.

Stratfield Saye

Stratfield Saye was the gift of a grateful nation to Arthur Wellesley, 1st Duke of Wellington, victor of Waterloo and later Prime Minister. He chose it for its rich farmlands rather than for the house, which he later extended and remodelled, and its contents provide the main interest. They tell of the life and times of the great Duke and include his maps, weapons and personal effects. Wellington Country Park, 3 miles (4.8km) east, includes a National Dairy Museum tracing dairy farming's development from the time of Waterloo to the present day.

The Kennet and Avon Canal at West Mills, with the church of St Nicholas in the background, is a peaceful and attractive haven just a short walk from Newbury's busy town centre. Narrowboat trips to Kintbury are available in summer

Mapledurham

This small village, on the Oxfordshire side of the Thames beyond Reading's western sprawl, has traditionally been dominated by its manor house. Built in 1585 by Sir Richard Blount, Mapledurham House is one of England's largest Elizabethan houses. With its patterned brickwork, battlemented parapets and tall chimneys, it stands in riverside grounds – evoking literary connections with *Wind in the Willows* and *The Forsyte Saga*. A working 15th-century watermill here still produces flour.

Newbury

Newbury's controversial bypass has eased the apalling traffic congestion that once blighted the town, and its main shopping street, where signs of its long history peep out above the modern shopfronts, is now partially pedestrianised. The Kennet and Avon Canal cuts through the town, providing pleasant towpath walks and narrow-boat trips. The town's prosperity was originally founded on the cloth trade, which peaked in the 18th century, when both the turnpike road and the canal reached the town. Later, the railway detoured north, hitting the town's prosperity, but probably saving some attractive areas that may not have survived a 19th-century boom. These include the delightfully crooked 17th-century weavers' cottages and the 1626 Cloth Hall, which now houses the West Berkshire Museum.

Ruined Donnington Castle, on the edge of town, has twin-towered gatehouse and earth ramparts, featured prominently during the Civil War.

Reading

From the M4 or the railway, Reading appears to be a thoroughly modern town, prospering on computers, insurance and similar new industries. The town centre has been revitalised with one of Britain's finest shop-

A stretch of Roman wall lines a country lane at Silchester, historically very important and yet a very low-key site, which greatly adds to its atmosphere

pingt centres – The Oracle – which incorporates an attractive riverside area. But the town has a long history, with a 12th-century Cluniac abbey and a borough charter of 1542, but you have to search for visible signs of it. The lively Museum of Reading in the Town Hall is a good place to start. Reading University has a fascinating Museum of English Rural Life.

Silchester

The best-preserved Roman walls in Britain, almost 1½ miles (2.4km) round, defended the regional capital of *Calleva Atrebatum*, which was laid out by Hadrian. Settlement on the site goes back even further – a smaller pre-Roman ring of defences lies under the remains of the 3rd-century Roman town. Also within the site is an impressive and recently restored Roman amphitheatre.

Highclere Castle stands proud amidst lawns and wooded parkland

THE ROYAL COUNTY

The 'Royal' County of Berkshire has numerous connections with the crown – Windsor, royal residence from the 12th century right to the present day, the annual Royal Ascot race meeting and Henley Royal Regatta. At Runnymede in adjoining Surrey, the Magna Carta is traditionally held to have laid the foundation of English civil liberties; on Eton's playing fields Waterloo is (more questionably) said to have been won.

Burnham Beeches

In 1880 the City of London Corporation bought nearly 200 acres (80ha) of ancient commons and woodland in Buckinghamshire, between Burnham and Beaconsfield, including extensive beech woods with 300-year-old trees. The corporation still maintains them as a public open space.

Detail from Stanley Spencer's Christ Preaching at Cookham Regatta, *painted in 1954*

Ascot

Everyone has heard of Royal Ascot, but few realise it was Queen Anne who built the first racecourse there in 1711. It was revived by the Duke of Cumberland, who established a stud in nearby Windsor Great Park. Traditionally the sovereign opens Royal Ascot each June, driving round the course in an open carriage.

Cookham and Cliveden

Cookham is famous as the birthplace of artist Stanley Spencer, whose religious paintings include *Christ Preaching at Cookham Regatta*. A former Methodist chapel now houses the Stanley Spencer Gallery. The riverside, delicate cast-iron bridge, green and old houses all add to the charm of the village. Across the river is Cliveden, the great mansion designed by Sir Charles Barry in 1849 and made famous in the 1930s by Nancy, Lady Astor and her influential 'Cliveden Set'. Now owned by the National Trust, the house is let as a luxury hotel, but three rooms and the riverside grounds are open to visitors.

Eton

The little town of Eton, hemmed in tightly between the Thames and the riverside meadows, represents a small point of repose between the two great monuments of Windsor Castle and Eton College. Across Telford's fine Windsor Bridge (thankfully traffic-free) you enter a high street full of pleasingly idiosyncratic buildings, with a wealth of Georgian façades

and 19th-century shopfronts, many with old timber-framed structures behind them.

Eton College, founded in 1440 by Henry VI, starts at the north end. It was originally a religious community with a school for poor boys, but present-day pupils are not noticeably impoverished and have included 20 British prime ministers and countless other public figures. Notable buildings include the chapel, with its fan-vaulted roof and fine east window, and Lupton's Range with its twin-towered gatehouse leading to Cloister Court.

Henley-on-Thames

Henley is boating. It has two regattas, Henley Royal and the less well-known Town Regatta and the River and Rowing Museum in Mill Meadows. The best approach is across the bridge from Berkshire, where two 18th-century inns, the Angel and the Red Lion, frame the tower of St Mary's Church. Around the market place and Hart Street there are some pleasant streets to explore.

Windsor

Windsor Castle is England's largest, with 13 acres (5ha) inside its curtain wall, and it stands on a cliff above the Thames, dominating both river and town centre. William the Conqueror built the first castle here, but the earliest stone buildings we see today date from the 1160s. Not only a fortress, the castle has also been a royal residence for 900 years. The massive round keep is the heart of its defences, but transition from fortress to royal palace was celebrated in the late 18th and early 19th century by additions and remodelling in a romantic Gothick style by James Wyatt and

Varsity boat-race crews of the future perhaps: young pupils, dwarfed by their giant oars, prepare themselves for training at Eton College boatyard

This solitary swan appears oblivious to its surroundings on the tranquil River Thames at Henley

The Thames Path

At Goring Gap two of the Countryside Commission's 'national trails' (long-distance footpaths) cross: the 85-mile (136km) ancient track of the Ridgeway (see page 93), and the Thames Path. Starting at the river's source near Cirencester, it runs for 213 miles (340km) all the way to the Thames Barrier on the tideway below Greenwich. Much of the route is through a lush countryside of woods and waterside meadows, but it also passes many historic places – including Oxford, Windsor, Hampton Court, Westminster and the Tower of London. For centuries, travelling on the Thames was much easier than any overland route, and the river was the great royal thoroughfare and strategic highway of south-east England.

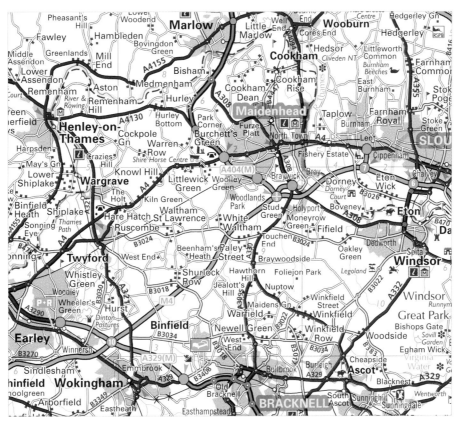

Tourist Information Centres

Henley-on-Thames: Town Hall, Market Place (tel: 01491 578034) **Windsor:** 24 High Street (tel: 01753 743900)

See Walk M page 139 Along the Bank of the Thames at Cookham

his nephew Jeffry Wyattville. After a disastrous fire that gutted many of the state apartments in 1992, architects were commissioned to design interiors in a style akin to theirs. Architecturally, the castle's prime glory must be the 15th- to 16th-century St George's Chapel, with its tall, slender columns and marvellous vaulted ceiling, an outstanding example of Perpendicular church architecture.

To the south and east of the castle lies the Home Park, in which stands the recently restored 17th-century Frogmore House, the least known of the royal residences, now furnished with contents reflecting the taste of former royal residents, including Queen Victoria's mother. South of the town is the immense, 4,800-acre (1944ha) Windsor Great Park, with the vista of its Long Walk stretching towards Virginia Water. It incorporates houses, woodlands, monuments, lakes and its own estate village. The Savill Garden and Valley Gardens are well worth a visit.

The town is utterly dominated by the castle, and this lends a particular atmosphere to the little streets that radiate out from its huge stone walls. There are many interesting old buildings, particularly in the cobbled streets of Guildhall Island – look for the curious Market Cross House, which slants precariously next door to the

more upright Guildhall. The Town and Crown Exhibition charts Windsor's history. Apart from its history, Windsor is a very stylish town, with excellent restaurants and shopping, notably in the Windsor Royal Station development, a pleasant concourse beneath the original Victorian arches and glass roof. The River Thames is another attraction, and boat trips run from the Promenade.

Old Windsor, beyond the Home Park, has a 13th-century flint church with shingled spire and agreeable riverside setting. To the south-east lie the historic Runnymede meadows where King John sealed Magna Carta in 1215.

The elegant grey stone towers of Windsor Castle provide the perfect backdrop to the calm River Thames flowing past. Within view of the grounds is Legoland, a veritable feast of fun for younger children

THAMES-SIDE TOWNS AND A GREAT SEAT OF LEARNING

Oxford, on the Thames (here called the Isis) and the River Cherwell, is a unique architectural treasure-house which can be no more than sampled in a brief visit. To its north lies Blenheim, a palace outshining any royal residence of its day, but built not for a king but for a victorious general. Around them, you will find pleasant countryside and delightful towns and villages.

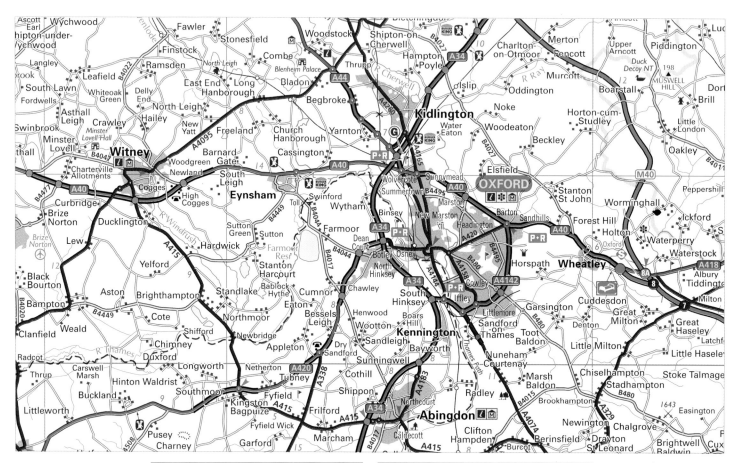

Abingdon

The abbey of Abingdon has all but disappeared, its impressive 15th-century Gateway and Long Gallery being the chief reminders of the religious house, founded in AD 675, in whose shadow the town began. It was once the county town of Berkshire, but it lost that distinction to Reading, and then boundary changes placed it in Oxfordshire. Its heart is the beautifully repaved market place, with its many splendid buildings; the most outstanding is the 17th-century County Hall. East St Helen's Street leads to St Helen's Church, with its splendid 13th-century steeple. Near the Thames bridge, Abingdon's Old Gaol of 1811 has been skilfully converted into an arts and sports centre, and there are lovely riverside walks.

Blenheim and Woodstock

As a token of the nation's gratitude for his victory over the French at Blenheim in 1704, Queen Anne presented John Churchill, 1st Duke of Marlborough, with the wherewithall to build Blenheim Palace, Britain's most magnificent stately home and a World Heritage Site. This vast baroque edifice, with its fantastic skyline, was the work of Sir John Vanbrugh, at that time better known as a dramatist than an architect, and it is indeed a dramatic *tour de force*. Blenheim's 2,000-acre (810ha) park was landscaped by 'Capability' Brown; it can be reached on foot from the little town of Woodstock, in itself charming. Note especially the market place with the Star and the Bear hotels, and 16th- and 17th-century houses in Park Street.

Rousham House

Rousham stands as a monument to the great 18th-century architect and garden designer, William Kent, who remodelled the house and, more importantly, the gardens for General James Dormer. The garden, in hanging woods above the Cherwell, is one of the earliest and least altered 'Picturesque' landscapes, with cascades, temples, ponds and statues, artfully contrived vistas and visual surprises.

This alabaster tomb and effigy in St Kenelm's Church, Minster Lovell, commemorates William, Lord Lovell (1397–1455), whose family gave their name to the village

The Vale of The White Horse

The Vale of the White Horse runs eastwards from near Swindon to follow the little River Ock down to meet the Thames at Abingdon. It is bounded on the north by the Berkshire Downs on which, cut in the chalk at Uffington, is the white horse which gives it its name. It was once thought that the horse was carved in AD 871 to celebrate King Alfred's victory over the Danes, but it is now considered to be at least 2,000 years old. On the hilltop above the horse is Uffington Castle, an Iron-Age fort covering 8 acres (3.25ha) and standing on the route of the ancient Ridgeway (now a long-distance footpath). About half a mile (0.8km) west along the track is Wayland's Smithy, a megalithic long barrow which has lost part of its earth mound, so its chambers are open to view. An excellent introduction to the Vale, its pretty villages and historic sites is provided by the Vale and Downland Centre in Wantage.

Minster Lovell

A romantic ruin by the peaceful River Windrush, Minster Lovell Hall was built in the 15th century by the 7th Lord Lovell and its handsome remains are now cared for by English Heritage. Note the medieval dovecot with nesting boxes.

Oxford

Oxford presents many different faces to the world, some of them delicious and memorable – distant views of its 'dreaming spires', close-ups of numerous college quadrangles, halls and chapels, looking down from Folly Bridge on punts full of lively undergraduates. Oxford is, of course, dominated by its university, though the town was large and prosperous in Saxon times, long before licensed teachers had begun to gather in halls and colleges. Having grown up thus, Oxford University remains a federation of self-governing colleges. There are university buildings, some of them historic and superb, such as the 16th-century Bodleian Library, the adjoining medieval Divinity School, and Wren's Sheldonian Theatre. But if a visitor in the High asks, 'Where's the university?', the answer must be, 'All round you'. There are about 40 colleges, some very ancient, others surprisingly modern.

Among the most spectacular colleges is Christ Church, with its huge Tom Quad and Tom Tower by Wren housing its massive bell, Great Tom; its chapel also serves as Oxford's cathedral. Riverside Magdalen (pronounced 'maudlin') also has a great bell tower, a sequence of quadrangles and a walled deer park. Merton is the oldest in foundation and perhaps the most medieval in atmosphere. Outstanding among the dozen or so 20th-century foundations is St Catherine's, which was designed by the great Danish architect Arne Jacobsen and recently extended.

You can visit some of the colleges at certain times, and Oxford has many excellent museums and galleries, including the Ashmolean Museum, which is the oldest museum in Britain, the Museum of Oxford and the high-tech Oxford Story where you are transported through the sights, sounds and smells of the past. Fresh-air attractions include the country's oldest botanic garden and the excellent walking tours led by the city's official guides.

Stanton St John

This attractive village lies a couple of miles from Oxford's north-east boundary, close to the edge of the remarkable Otmoor. This is a low-lying saucer-shaped basin, crossed by a Roman road, and is divided up by drainage dykes which inspired the chessboard landscape featured in Lewis Carroll's *Through the Looking Glass*. It was threatened by the M40 extension, but powerful protests got it diverted to loop round to the east. In the Church of St John the Baptist, the 13th-century chancel demands a long appreciative look.

Waterperry

Waterperry is known for its Horticultural Centre, comprising a college and 83 acres (34ha) of gardens and nurseries, most open to the public, beside the River Thame. Waterperry House is classical 18th and 19th century with a 17th-century wing. St Mary's Church is small and charming, with Saxon and Norman parts remaining.

Tourist Information Centres

Abingdon: 25 Bridge Street (tel: 01235 522711)
Faringdon: 7a Market Place (tel: 01367 242191)
Oxford: The Old School, Gloucester Green (tel: 01865 726871)
Wantage: Vale and Downland Centre, 19 Church Street (tel: 01235 760176)
Woodstock: Oxfordshire Museum, Part Street (tel: 01993 811038)

The Ceremony of Degrees adds colour and a historic sense of occasion to the streets of Oxford

NEW TOWNS, OLD PALACES

This is where Ebenezer Howard's dream of garden cities for overcrowded Londoners first took shape, most extensively at Welwyn. Yet just across the railway from its twin new town, Hatfield, is the great Jacobean palace of Hatfield House. Just as close to modern Luton, the mansion of Luton Hoo provides a showcase for an outstanding, historic art collection.

Tourist Information Centres

Hertford: 10 Market Place (tel: 01992 584322)
Luton: The Bus Station, Bute Street (tel: 01582 401579)
St Albans: Town Hall, Market Place (tel: 01727 864511)

Literary and political giants were among the guests of novelist and statesman Sir Edward Bulwer Lytton at Knebworth in its 19th-century heyday

George Bernard Shaw lived in this charming house at Ayot St Lawrence from 1906 until his death in 1950

Ayot St Lawrence

A pleasant if unexciting village among wooded hills north-west of Welwyn Garden City, Ayot St Lawrence has two points of distinction. Its churches (one 14th century and in ruins, the other 18th century with Greek portico and colonnades) and the fact that George Bernard Shaw came to live here at the age of 50 and remained until his death 44 years later. His house, Shaw's Corner, (National Trust) is undistinguished, but the downstairs rooms remain as they were during his lifetime, and in the garden is the summerhouse where he did much of his writing.

Hatfield

The original town of Hatfield grew up round the gateway to the palace of the Bishops of Ely. Its remains are to be found in the grounds of Hatfield House, home of the Marquesses of Salisbury and among the most spectacular Jacobean houses in England. It was built by Robert Cecil, 1st Earl of Salisbury, James I's chief minister, and has been the Cecil family's home ever since. Elizabeth I spent much of her girlhood here, and appointed William Cecil, Lord Burghley, as her chief minister.

The old town has some fine Georgian houses and inns, including the Eight Bells which Dickens knew and featured in *Oliver Twist*. In contrast is the new town, mostly across the railway to the west, which was designated a new town in 1948 and developed in tandem with the existing Welwyn Garden City.

Luton

This Bedfordshire town is most widely known for its football team and Vauxhall car factory, but it also has London's fourth (and independent) international airport, a very new university and, just to the south, Luton Hoo. Though only just over a mile (1.6km) from the town's suburban southern edge, this great house in its 'Capability' Brown landscape is another world. The

Knebworth

Knebworth House has been the home of the Lytton family since 1490, but the high Gothick exterior we see today is a Victorian transformation carried out by the novelist and statesman Sir Edward Bulwer-Lytton. Behind this façade, the original Tudor great hall turned Jacobean banqueting hall remains. The gardens were laid out by Lutyens (who also designed part of St Martin's Church) and include a herb garden by Gertrude Jekyll. The house stands in a 200-acre (80ha) country park.

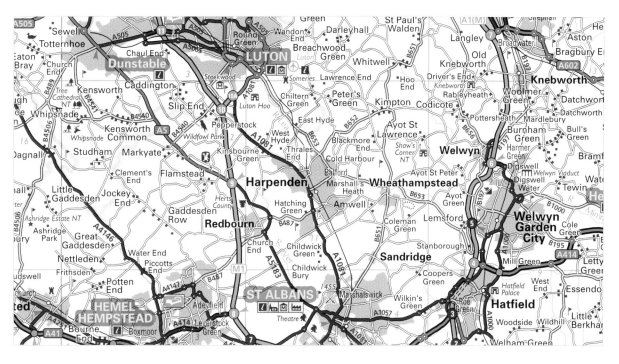

Whipsnade Wild Animal Park

Opened by the Zoological Society of London in 1931 on a spacious site on the edge of the downs south of Dunstable, Whipsnade was a pioneer of the more humane and enlightened treatment of zoo animals. Its 600 acres (243ha) allow it to provide the space for animals to roam in natural breeding groups in a large open environment – hence its considerable success in the captive breeding of rare and endangered species. You can explore the park on foot, by car or on the free Trailbreaker Roadtrain, which lets you hop on and off at various points and enables you to concentrate on the animals, not the road. There is also the Great Whipsnade Railway and many other attractions and special events.

mansion itself, restyled in the 20th century by Ritz Hotel architects Mewès and Davis, provides a sumptuous setting for a unique collection of works of art, acquired by diamond merchant Sir Julius Wernher and his son Harold. They include Gobelin tapestries, Dutch and Italian masters, ceramics, Fabergé jewellery, and mementoes of the Russian imperial family.

St Albans

St Albans is a historic place, with a great cathedral standing high above the River Ver. The medieval street pattern is discernable and some medieval buildings remain. The Fighting Cocks Inn and Kingsbury Watermill are worth visiting. Below the town, across the Ver, is a blissfully green and open landscape in which are the extensive remains of the Roman city of *Verulamium,* with the excellent Roman Museum housing excavated finds, mosaics and recreated Roman rooms. The Roman Theatre, unique in having a stage, is the only one in Britain that is open to the public. Both the cathedral and town take their name from Alban, a Roman who in the 3rd-century became Britain's first Christian martyr.

The Museum of St Albans has various collections and reconstructed workshops, and the town boasts an Organ Museum, which includes great theatre organs and other instruments. In early summer a visit to the Gardens of the Rose at Chiswell Green is a must. Here over 30,000 colourful and fragrant plants are on display

Welwyn Garden City

This was, after Letchworth, the flagship of Ebenezer Howard's Garden City Movement, which aimed to create an attractive, healthy living and working environment as an alternative to the crowded, unhealthy conditions in London. It provided houses with gardens, industry which was separate but within easy reach and access to countryside. Building started in 1919 and the original garden city neighbourhoods have a distinctive style and maturity. Welwyn expanded greatly as a post-war new town. Stevenage to the north, another 1940s new town, was built round an existing settlement following similar principles.

'Capability' Brown designed a fitting landscape to surround magnificent Luton Hoo. The house contains the finest private collection of art treasures in Britain

LONDON

IT IS IMPOSSIBLE TO SUM UP London in a few pages, such is the diversity of this most vibrant of cities. Instead, these pages concentrate on a small selection of its many features – some familiar to residents and visitors alike, but others perhaps a little surprising. Think of London and we usually think of ceremony and tradition, entertainment and business. These pages touch on a few of these topics in an attempt to show the contrasting faces of modern London.

Today's London is a sprawling metropolis, teeming with energy and seemingly swallowing up all in its path, stretching from Surrey to Kent and Essex and receiving around 16 million visitors annually – over twice its own population. But, despite its traffic, crowds and somewhat eccentric public transport system, London can be a charming and subtle place. Cosmopolitan London shows the rich diversity of cultures and traditions which have become an integral part of the capital's life over the decades, with different communities stamping their own character on various parts of the city. Then follows the traditions and ceremonies familiar to millions around the world, from the State Opening of Parliament to the Promenade Concerts, and from Trooping the Colour to the Lord Mayor's Show – traditions which give London its unique character.

That London is a progressive city is shown in its buildings, ancient and modern, from the familiar dome of St Paul's Cathedral to the spectacular and controversial Canary Wharf development. The capital also has its genteel side, reflected in its profusion of green spaces – its great parks, heaths, commons and elegant squares, each offering its own particular respite from the bustle of the city. Then there is the Thames itself, spanned by some 30 diverse bridges, including the awesome Tower Bridge and the elegant arches of Westminster Bridge. We end our brief tour with a trip out of town to the surrounding historic houses, royal palaces and gardens further afield.

The familiar sight of Buckingham Palace, at the end of The Mall

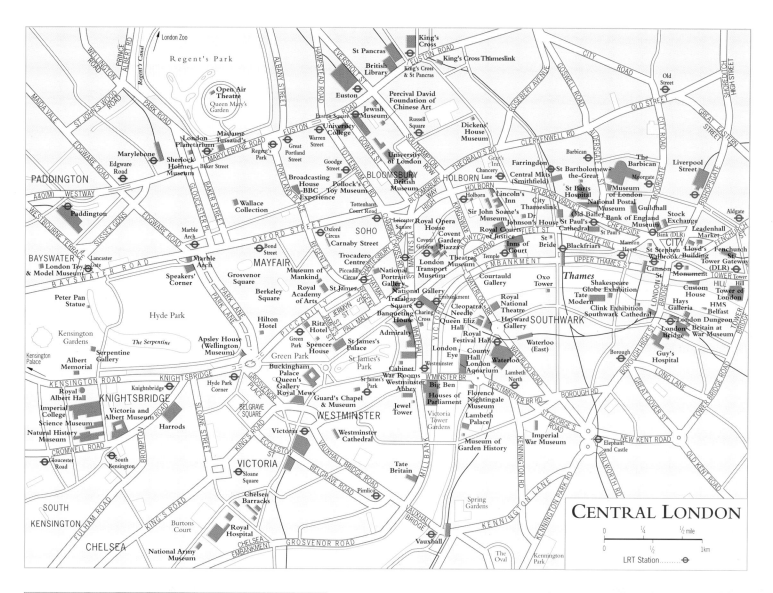

CENTRAL LONDON

0   ¼   ½ mile

0   ½   1km

LRT Station.........⊖

Right: detail from the historic Cutty Sark, once the fastest clipper, moored at Greenwich; below: the bright lights of the Empire, Leicester Square, in the heart of the West End; below right: the famous Downing Street residence of the Prime Minister; overleaf: the Tudor Pond Garden at Hampton Court Palace

One landmark which is familiar to millions around the world as a symbol of London is the clock tower of the Houses of Parliament, mistakenly called Big Ben. This name does, in fact, belong to the grand bell within, whose dulcet tones can be heard throughout the heart of town at every hour

COSMOPOLITAN LONDON

London at the end of the 20th century is cosmopolitan in a way that would have amazed Londoners in the late 1940s. The crowds in the streets were then uniformly white-skinned, with any black or Asian face standing out as the rare exception. Foreign restaurants did exist, at least in the centre, and there were even a few Chinese and Indian, but they were regarded as wildly exotic. Most Londoners were still wedded to a meat-and-two-veg, nice-cup-of-tea approach to mealtimes. And in spite of the enthusiasm in the 18th and 19th century for things oriental (often misinformed, as it happened), the capital's architecture showed little of outside influences.

Today's London is intensely cosmopolitan and multicultural. Travel by bus or ride the underground in the capital and you will be surrounded by a buzz of foreign tongues and a group of fellow passengers who reflect many different cultures. Many will be tourists, but the others are today's Londoners.

ETHNIC VILLAGES

A cultural mix is not altogether new to London. Spitalfields, barely ten minutes' walk from the Bank of England, is these days the home or workplace for several thousand Bangladeshis – the shops and colourful street market in Brick Lane might almost be in Dacca or Calcutta, were it not for the climate. Yet Spitalfields has been an immigrant quarter for three centuries. First came French Huguenots, fleeing religious persecution, then in the 1880s, similarly impelled, Jews came from eastern Europe. The Bangladeshis, arriving in the 1970s, were just the latest wave of incomers seeking shelter and a better life. A direct reflection of the development of this area can be seen in the plain 18th-century building on the corner of Brick Lane and Fournier Street – it was built as a Huguenot chapel, became a synagogue, and is now the local mosque.

One of the longer-established communities is London's Chinatown, which was originally established in Limehouse in the 1890s, after several hundred Chinese seamen from ships in West India Docks decided to stay. Those who were ships' cooks opened restaurants. After the heavy bombing of the docks during World War II, this community mostly moved to Soho, and by the 1970s the area round Gerrard Street had become Chinatown, with not only Chinese restaurants but Chinese accountants, supermarkets, bookmakers and the like. Other 'ethnic villages' in London have included Little Italy, established in the 19th century in Clerkenwell, the strong and colourful Caribbean community in Brixton, Greek Cypriots in Kentish Town and Turkish Cypriots around New Cross.

EASTERN ARCHITECTURE

In London's buildings expressions of ethnic diversity are as yet rare. Places of worship are one field in which new, consciously exotic buildings are springing up - notably mosques and temples. Best known are perhaps the Central London Mosque at Hanover Gate, Regent's Park, by Frederick Gibberd & Partners, its gilded dome and high minaret fitting in well with the sequence of Regency terraces, itself rather exotic in places, and Casson &

Eastern splendour has been brought to Neasden with the Mandir Mahotsav Temple; below, Muslem ladies take a stroll in Regents Park

Exotic ingredients are readily available in the shops and supermarkets of London's Chinatown

Conder's Ismaili Centre, a beautifully made building skilfully integrated into the South Kensington townscape for a discriminating client, the Aga Khan. Both by British architects, these buildings may be called 'modified Islamic' in style.

In 1995 a magnificent new Hindu temple, Shri Swaminarayan Mandir, was completed in Neasden. Its assembly hall, with capacity for 2,500 people, is the largest in Europe. It was developed by and for the local Hindu community and, says Madhu Patel of Rako Design and Build, is faithful to a thousand-year tradition of design in timber and stone. London will certainly see more such architectural expressions of ethnic diversity; the challenge will be to combine these traditions agreeably with traditional London townscape.

THE FOOD OF THE NATIONS

The choice of restaurants in central London is enormous, with areas such as Soho and adjoining Covent Garden long established as melting pots of different nationalities.

France is represented by such establishments as Chez Gerard in Charlotte Street, Fitzrovia ('the best steak-frites this side of Paris'), Mon Plaisir, Monmouth Street (50 years in Covent Garden and noted for its pre-theatre fixed-price menus) and Grill St Quentin (Breton oysters and lobsters) in Brompton Road.

Italian restaurants are more numerous. Among the oldest is Bertorelli's which, after years of catering for a regular clientele in Charlotte Street, was successfully transplanted to Floral Street, just behind Covent Garden Opera House, where it has

taken on a new lease of life. Its dominant flavour is of Tuscany. The family-run Spaghetti House chain still provides good, honest Italian food and wine at the tall, thin stack of restaurant floors in Goodge Street where it started 40 years ago

Other European gastronomy is represented by, among others, the the Swiss Centre in Leicester Square, the Gay Hussar (Hungarian) in Soho and Belgo Centraal in Earlham Street WC2, for all things Belgian – including the beer.

Spanish and Latin American eating places, including tapas bars, have multiplied in recent years. Cafe Pacifico in Covent Garden has the noise, bustle and fiery flavours of a Mexican cantina, while the Gaucho Grill in Swallow Street offers Argentinian beef prepared 'in the refined style of barbecue cooking known as assado'. Salsa! offers Latin food, music and dance in Charing Cross Road and you can sample Hispanic American specialities at Havana in Fulham Road and Hanover Square.

Eastern Mediterranean and Middle East cuisine find expression in countless kebab houses and tavernas. Among the more stylish are Halepi (Cypriot) near Hyde Park, Pasha (Moroccan) in Gloucester Road, South Kensington and the Maroush chain (Lebanese). The oldest Indian restaurant in London is Veeraswamy in Regent Street, which is good but expensive. The Punjab in Neal Street specialises in dishes from that region, Mandeer in Hanway Place offers excellent vegetarian Indian dishes in an exotic subterranean environment, while Drummond Street near Euston Station has several Indian restaurants and food stores.

For Chinese food, the whole area from Shaftesbury Avenue through Chinatown to Leicester Square is thronged with eating places, including the long-established Gallery Rendezvous in Beak Street and the more recent Ming in Greek Street. There is a floating Chinese restaurant at Glengall Bridge in the Isle of Dogs. Thai restaurants have also multiplied – try the Blue Elephant on Fulham Broadway, or one of Jim Thompson's chain of Oriental establishments, which incorporate bar, restaurant and bazaar.

The Notting Hill Carnival is surely Britain's most colourful annual event, with a cheerfully noisy procession and constant party atmosphere

POMP AND CIRCUMSTANCE

Londonhas many odd and colourful ceremonies. Some are public, others private; some vouchsafe passers-by a glimpse of worthy-looking persons in bizarre old-fashioned costume, processing through the public street in the course of honouring some ancient tradition. Often the origins and purpose seem obscure; these are traditions kept alive when the reasons for them have long disappeared. But these quaint and colourful ceremonies can be savoured simply because they are quaint and colourful. Parliament, the Monarchy, Armed Forces, Law and the City of London are the main focuses of traditional ceremony.

The 'Beefeaters' of the Tower are a daily attraction; the Lord Mayor's Show, led by his fairytale golden coach, takes place once a year in November

ROYAL TRADITIONS

Ceremonial relations between Crown and Parliament reflect the struggle of the elected House of Commons in the 17th century to assert its independence from the Stuart kings. Thus, when the Queen opens each new session of Parliament, it is not in the House of Commons – no sovereign has been admitted here since the Civil War and subsequent execution of Charles I – but in the House of Lords.

The State Opening of Parliament usually takes place in late October or early November and begins with a coach carrying the imperial state crown to Parliament, followed some 20 minutes later by the Queen in the splendid Irish state coach. From Buckingham Palace they drive down the Mall, through Horseguards Arch into Whitehall and thus to Parliament. As the Queen enters the Lords, guns in Hyde Park fire a salute; as she takes her seat on the throne, the Lord Great Chamberlain (a hereditary royal official) raises his wand to summon the Commons. But when Black Rod, a House of Lords official, arrives at the Commons

chamber, something odd happens. The Sergeant at Arms, a Commons official, slams the door in his face. This recalls Charles I's attempt to arrest five MPs in 1642, one of the events which led to the Civil War. However, eventually Black Rod gets to delivers his message, and MPs follow the Speaker of the House of Commons to the Lords to hear the Queen's Speech. In a curious way, this is proof of Parliament's triumph, because the speech is written not by the Queen, but by government ministers and it sets out their policies and legislative programme for the new parliamentary session.

Earlier that day another historic ceremony is performed. The Queen's bodyguard of Yeomen of the Guard, in their picturesque red and black uniforms, search the cellars beneath of the Palace of Westminster for gunpowder – recalling the attempt on 5 November 1605 to blow up King James I and Parliament.

The most colourful of the public royal ceremonies is the annual Trooping the Colour which celebrates the sovereign's official birthday, usually on the second Saturday of June. The parade's original purpose was to show the men of a particular regiment their 'colour' of flag so

that they would recognise it as a rallying point in battle. In today's ceremony, the Queen, dressed in the uniform of the Foot Guards she is reviewing, goes with an escort of Household Cavalry to Horseguards and inspects the parade; there is then a march past, and finally the Queen leads her Foot Guards back to Buckingham Palace. Until 1987, the Queen rode on horseback; now she rides in a carriage.

Beating the Retreat is another display of military precision involving the marching and drilling bands of the Household Division in their colourful uniforms. It takes place on Horseguards Parade in late May or early June and involves mounted bands, trumpeters, massed marching bands and pipes and drums. The name has nothing to do with defeat in battle – it goes back to the ancient custom of signalling or 'beating' the retreat of sunlight at nightfall.

For those who miss these annual parades, the Changing of

the Guard is a colourful daily ceremony which takes place at four royal palaces in London. Most impressive is that at Buckingham Palace, with one detachment of Foot Guards, in their scarlet tunics and tall bearskin helmets, taking over from another the duty of guarding the Queen's residence. Similar ceremonies also takes place at the Horse Guards in Whitehall, St James's Palace, and the Tower of London.

CIVIC DIGNITORIES

Over the years London's local authorities have often been reorganised to suit new conditions, but the oldest, the City of London Corporation, which administers only the 'Square Mile' – the tiny area containing London's financial centre – has retained its independence. It combines an efficient (though arguably undemocratic) administration with the pomp and pageantry of 800 years of proud municipal independence.

Its figurehead is the Lord Mayor, elected each year in an unbroken 800-year tradition by the liverymen of the City livery companies, or guilds. When the reigning Lord Mayor and Sheriffs arrive at Guildhall in their traditional robes of office, the Keeper of Guildhall presents them with nosegays of garden flowers. This tradition goes back to the days when they were believed to give protection not only against the evil smells of London streets, but against the diseases harboured there.

The election of the Lord Mayor takes place around Michaelmas Day (29 September), followed in November by the Lord Mayor's Procession (or Lord Mayor's Show). This dates back to Magna Carta in 1215 when King John, under pressure from his barons, sought support from the City in return for giving it a new charter allowing annual elections. His proviso was that each new Lord Mayor

Trooping the Colour, with the Queen's guardsmen resplendent in their ceremonial uniforms, takes place in June to mark the sovereign's official birthday

CEREMONY IN MUSIC

A different kind of Pomp and Circumstance exists in Elgar's five marches of that name, redolent of the imperial pride of the Edwardian era. At least one (Number 1), features each year at the festive Last Night of The Proms (the Henry Wood Promenade Concerts) at the Royal Albert Hall. Sung lustily by the Prom audience with the words of 'Land of Hope and Glory', it typifies the way in which Londoners enjoy celebrating the past without necessarily taking too seriously the attitudes that lie behind such traditions.

The imposing Royal Albert Hall

took an oath of allegiance before the king or his justices, and so, on a Saturday each November, the new Lord Mayor of London goes in procession to the Royal Courts of Justice in the Strand to swear loyalty to the crown.

The processional route is along Cheapside, Ludgate Hill and Fleet Street to the Strand. The Lord Mayor's gilded coach, built in 1757 and looking for all the world as if it has come straight out of a fairy tale, has actually come straight out of the Museum of London, harnessed to six magnificent Shire horses; he is attended by a personal bodyguard of pikemen in armour and musketeers from

England's oldest regiment, the Honourable Artillery Company. A huge retinue of mobile floats or tableaux make up the procession, and illustrate various aspects of a theme chosen by the new Lord Mayor for his year of office.

Another highlight of the City calendar is the Lord Mayor's Banquet, held on the Monday following the Show, and the most important in a series of banquets and feasts which each Lord Mayor must enjoy or endure during his year of office. The new Lord Mayor and Sheriffs give this banquet in honour of the outgoing Lord Mayor, and invite some 700 VIPs, the most important of them welcomed with fanfares by splendidly costumed trumpeters. The evening is normally the occasion for a major speech by the Prime Minister.

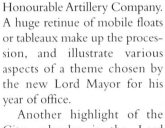

The Ceremony of the Keys at the Tower of London has taken place at 10pm every night for centuries

LONDON BUILDINGS, OLD AND NEW

London's architectural riches range from great set-pieces like the Palace of Westminster and Wren's two great waterside 'hospitals', or retirement homes (for old soldiers at Chelsea and old sailors at Greenwich) through to smaller, more hidden gems like the Blewcoat School in Caxton Street, Westminster, and the more out of the way City churches.

London has its grand sequences, like The Mall, with Nash's stuccoed, columned sweep of Carlton House Terrace, his great processional route from Regents Park along Portland Place and Regent Street, and Pall Mall with its procession of Italianate 19th-century gentlemen's clubs. But the capital generally eschews grand gestures. Its townscape tends to be both more reticent and more anarchic.

THE HEART OF THE CAPITAL

Perhaps the place to start is at Charing Cross in the heart of London, and the hotel which fronts the station (Decimus Burton, 1834) is worth more than a glance. Trafalgar Square has two fine classical buildings. The first, St Martin-in-the-Fields Church (Gibbs, 1726), has a magnificent temple-like portico and steeple. The other is the National Gallery (Wilkins, 1838), with its controversial but extremely likeable 1991 Sainsbury Wing, designed by American architect Robert Venturi after criticism by Prince Charles scotched the original plan.

Whitehall is full of architectural delights, outstandingly the Banqueting House (Inigo Jones), which, in the early 17th century, was shockingly modern. There is also the Horse Guards (1760), the ceremonial gateway to the parade ground and park beyond, and Richmond Terrace. A 1960s scheme for a new government precinct would have swept away this and the famous New Scotland Yard, but by 1970 the tide of conservation was running strongly enough to stop it. William Whitfield's attractive Department of Heath building, alongside Richmond Terrace, shows how modern infill can have strength and character, yet exist in sympathy with its surroundings.

More MPs' offices on the Parliament Square corner await

completion of a new station for the Jubilee Line. The architects of the 11 new stations on the line's extension have a brief to bring light and spaciousness into the underworld. The Houses of Parliament and Westminster Abbey are, of course, the great architectural events of this square, but the Queen Elizabeth II Conference Centre (1986) demonstrates how large modern buildings can sit happily in a historic townscape.

Other notable buildings hereabouts include Westminster Cathedral (Bentley, 1903); and Channel 4's television studios and headquarters in Horseferry Road (Rogers, 1994).

THE CITY AND DOCKLANDS

The City of London has rather different planning policies from neighbouring Westminster, most of which is now a conservation area. The City has its historic jewels – Wren's St Paul's Cathedral, his 'wedding cake' St Bride's and a string of other churches, built after the Great Fire of 1666. The tranquil and beautiful Inns of Court are here, along with such monuments to commerce as the Bank of England, Royal Exchange, Custom House and the Mansion House and Guildhall. Just over the City boundary is that great riverside fortress, the Tower of London.

Because it is a money-making machine, the City has looked favourably on new developments designed to give

Top: St Paul's Cathedral is an impressive sight amidst the towering modern office blocks of the City

Above: Westminster Cathedral and St Pancras Station both reflect the flamboyance of the 19th century

its money-makers the accommodation they want, resulting in many large, dull or ugly buildings, some bold and beautiful ones, and a striking new City skyline. Notable new buildings include Rogers' 1986 Lloyds building in steel and glass, with a lofty atrium looking down on its underwriting room. Another is the stylishly upgraded Liverpool Street Station (British Rail architects) with the huge Broadgate office development (Arup Associates, Skidmore Owings Merrill). And there is the 1950s-1980s Barbican development, combining accommodation with entertainment venues and restaurants (Chamberlin Powell & Bon).

These days the Square Mile has a rival in its near neighbour to the east – London's renascent Docklands. Here is the capital's most spectacular and controversial group of buildings, Canary Wharf. Conceived as a sort of Wall Street-on-Thames, this £4billion development extends more than half a mile (1km) across the Isle of Dogs, and includes London's tallest tower by American architect Cesar Pelli. It has its own shopping centre and waterside restaurants, with a mixture of architectural styles that are often pastiche. Canary Wharf is best approached by the elevated Docklands Light Railway, but do get out and walk all round it!

AROUND THE CENTRE

On the north-central fringe of central London are four buildings of particular merit – the British Museum (1847, Smirke), University College's original Gower Street group (Wilkins, 1829), St Pancras Station and the new British Library. St Pancras's spectacular and recently restored High Victorian hotel front (1874, G G Scott) faces Barlow's great 1868 train shed, being adapted for trains from the planned Channel Tunnel fast rail link (completion expected 2007); the Library next door, designed by Colin St John Wilson, is clad in red brick to match the station.

The 'museums area' of South Kensington also merits a good, long look. Here is the expression of Queen Victoria's and (especially) Prince Albert's belief in the nation's intellectual and cultural advancement, and stylistically reflects that age. Impressively self-confident buildings in brick, terracotta and stone line spacious boulevards. They include the Victoria and Albert, Natural History and Science Museums; Imperial College tower and the Royal Albert Hall. There are plans to enhance the overall area ('Albertopolis') for the Millennium by submerging the road

in front of the Royal Albert Hall and creating a piazza between it and the Albert Memorial.

Everything on the South Bank is now dwarfed by the London Eye. The two most notable buildings of the cultural complex here are the Royal Festival Hall (Robert Matthew, Leslie Martin, 1951) and the Royal National Theatre (Denys Lasdun, 1975). Wide-ranging plans currently on the drawing board include refurbishment of the existing buildings, the building of another concert hall, the creation of public squares, the provision of shops and cafés in the area, the expansion of the Jubilee Gardens to stretch from County Hall to Hungerford Bridge, and improved access in the form of new footbridges,

tramways and even cable cars. The conversion of the Bankside Power Station into the impressive Tate Modern art gallery has proved a powerful magnet.

Just downstream you see the thatched roof of the replica Globe Theatre, part of an international Shakespeare centre close to the site of the original Globe. Further along this very walkable historic riverside are Southwark Cathedral, London Bridge City, where lofty Hay's Galleria rises from a former dock basin, and (below Tower Bridge) Butler's Wharf, an area of 19th-century warehouses, recycled into flats, restaurants and design studios – an eminently suitable location for the Design Museum.

THE GREEN LUNGS OF LONDON

CENTRAL LONDON PARKS

Centuries ago these parks were mostly royal hunting forests outside the confines of a much smaller capital. Central London has now engulfed many of them, and the oldest is St James's Park, with its neat lawns, colourful flower beds and shrubberies around a lovely lake. It is hard to imagine this as marshland, as it was until it was drained to provide Henry VIII with a bowling alley, tiltyard and deer nursery. Charles II redesigned it, and by the late 17th century it was already home to many species of wading birds, including two pelicans given to the king by the Russian ambassador. The variety and profusion of birdlife around the lake is one of its attractions; another is the splendid roofscape seen from the bridge.

St James's Park forms the first link in a great green chain, leading past Buckingham Palace into Green Park, then into the wide expanses of Hyde Park and Kensington Gardens. Lush and restful Green Park is the smallest Royal Park, while

Above, sweeping lawns beside the Serpentine in Hyde Park bring a taste of the countryside into central London; left: the ornate gates which lead into Green Park

Cities, and the people in them, need to breathe, and one feature of London that appeals to visitors and residents alike is the number and richness of green spaces. A recent survey carried out for the Royal Parks Agency showed that in that particular year its parks attracted some 30 million visitors, which put them collectively above such national tourist attractions as St Paul's Cathedral (2.6 million) and the Tower of London (2.4 million). Other research among visitors from abroad shows that they are drawn to London by the relaxed, civilised image created by its parks – particularly the Royal Parks.

Hyde Park is the largest of those in central London – quite exhilarating amidst this densely built-up area. Deer-hunting ceased here in the 1750s, and the deer have long gone, but people still ride horses along a sandy track called Rotten Row. The name is a corruption of *Route du Roi* (the king's road), because it is on the line of the road which led to Kensington Palace. Just north of Rotten Row is The Serpentine, which, with the Long Water, forms a long curving lake. In the park's north-east corner are Marble Arch and Speakers' Corner, where various soap-box orators, from anarchists to evangelists to flat-earthers, traditionally harangue passers-by.

Across the Broad Water lie Kensington Gardens, originally the gardens of Kensington Palace and now effectively a westward extension of Hyde Park, though it is more intimate and sedate. Features include the Albert Memorial (currently under restoration), the Round Pond, Broad and Flower Walks, the Sunken Garden and the Orangery. Don't miss the intricately carved Elfin Oak, Frampton's statue of J M Barrie's eternally youthful hero, Peter Pan, and (near Lancaster Gate) the recently restored Italian Water Gardens with their fountains and ornate statuary.

Regent's Park formed part of an inspired 19th-century property development scheme, a collaboration between architect John Nash and the Prince Regent. It was originally to be the grounds of a new palace, which was never built, and consists of landscaped, wooded parkland with a lake; villas lie hidden within it, and the park is ringed by a sequence of grand stucco terraces. It is a magical combination of landscape and water, with a well-preserved architectural backdrop. Other features include the delightful Queen Mary's Rose Garden and the open-air theatre's summer season. On the northern boundary of the park are London Zoo and the Regent's Canal. The adjacent Primrose Hill, once part of the same hunting forest, retains a more rural atmosphere and where it rises to 207ft (63m) there are panoramic views over London.

FURTHER AFIELD

The outer Royal Parks include three huge open spaces near the Thames in west London, all associated with former royal palaces. Richmond Park still has ancient oak trees, a large herd of deer and lots of other wildlife. From Robin Hood Gate a pedestrian link connects with another huge belt of parkland – Wimbledon Common, with its lake and windmill, and adjoining Putney Heath. Bushy Park and Hampton Court Park lie west and north of Hampton Court Palace and are somewhat similar to Richmond's landscaped parkland, except that

Hampton Court's gardens have a more urbane, cultivated character, with formal vistas, a canal lined with lime trees, statuary and the famous maze.

Greenwich Park, too, was a royal hunting park, walled in from adjoining Blackheath. Today it forms part of a unique sequence, which starts on the Thames waterside with Sir Christopher Wren's Royal Naval College. It then moves through the National Maritime Museum's grounds, along the twin colonnades flanking Inigo Jones's superb Queen's House and into the park, which contains Wren's charming hill-top Old Observatory, standing at zero degrees longitude. The sequence continues along a broad chestnut-lined avenue to the windswept, kite-flying Blackheath and terminates at the spire of All Saint's Church in Blackheath Village.

HEATHS, COMMONS AND SQUARES

London's unique inheritance of Royal Parks constitutes only the crème de la crème of its green open spaces, but there are many other appealing tracts of land.

Hampstead Heath, Kenwood and Parliament Hill to the north are famous for their wonderful views (Guy Fawkes' compatriots intended to watch the result of their conspiracy to blow up Parliament from here). Epping Forest, a huge green wedge stretching from Wanstead out into Essex, is real countryside on London's doorstep, and on the eastern edge are Lee Valley Park and Thames Chase, the latter a new forest, planted by the Countryside Commission.

Clapham, Tooting, Streatham, Wandsworth and Barnes all have their commons, and London also has a number of big municipal parks, providing relief from urban sprawl and a refuge for wildlife. The Grand Union and Regent Canals, forming an arc of waterways with towpaths round north inner London, offer tranquil walking and are an important part of a network of ecological corridors.

There remain many parts of London which are not so fortunate in having a green open space in their vicinity, and their

saving grace is the London square. These railing-enclosed gardens with mature trees are sometimes open to the public, sometimes the private reserve of the residents, but are always a green lung among busy streets. There are over 600 squares in Greater London, with a huge diversity of character. They range from such fashionable and architecturally magnificent ensembles as Belgrave and Eaton Squares to unnumbered squares, crescents, and circuses with soft green centres all over London. These – like the parks – bring delight and refreshment to Londoners and visitors alike.

Below, colourful flower beds in St James's Park; below left: the Regents Canal is a peaceful backwater in north London; Bottom: Richmond Hill looks down over the Thames

CROSSING THE THAMES

Floodlit Tower Bridge is a spectacular sight against the night sky of the capital

CENTRAL LONDON BRIDGES

When it comes to bridges in London, most people tend to think first of Tower Bridge, London Bridge and Westminster Bridge. Tower Bridge – until 1991 the lowest bridge on the Thames – reflects the Victorian obsession with Gothic architecture. A glass-covered walkway, 142ft (43m) above the water, links the two towers and gives panoramic views along the river. The opening mechanism was electrified in 1976, but the original hydraulic machinery is now the centrepiece of a museum, which uses state-of-the-art effects to tell the story of the bridge in a dramatic and exciting way. Recent surveys suggest that the bridge is suffering from heavy traffic; its life may be prolonged by providing a replacement tunnel a little downstream and restricting Tower Bridge's use to pedestrians, cyclists and perhaps buses.

The next bridge upstream is London Bridge, the oldest and

The River Thames was once London's greatest thoroughfare – by far the easiest means of travelling in and out of the capital in the days of horses and carriages, rough, muddy tracks, footpads and highwaymen. But the great river always needed to be crossed, and there have been bridges over the Thames for about 1,000 years. Today there are about 30 of them within Greater London – for road, rail and pedestrians – not to mention the tunnels or the towering Queen Elizabeth II suspension bridge downstream, which doubles up with the twin Dartford Tunnels to carry the M25 across the river.

most famous, which has its origins in a wooden bridge built to connect Roman *Londinium* via the Kent section of Watling Street to the Roman ports of *Dubris* (Dover) and *Rutupiae* (Richborough). It was broken or burnt down several times until, in 1176, Peter de Colechurch erected the first stone bridge, with a chapel on it dedicated to St Thomas à Becket. Soon after, houses were built alongside its roadway, and the gruesome custom developed of displaying the impaled heads of executed rebels and

traitors on the bridge.

De Colechurch's bridge was not well designed. It had many narrow arches, and their piers obstructed the river's flow and made navigation hazardous. But it saw service until the 18th century, when the houses were removed and a wider central channel was created. In 1801 Thomas Telford designed a new and revolutionary single-span iron bridge, but it was too innovative for the powers-that-be. They built instead a five-arched stone bridge, by the Scottish engineer, John Rennie, and

built by his more famous son who was knighted upon its completion in 1831. That bridge was bought and transported, stone by stone, to the USA, where it now stands incongruously in the Arizona desert. The latest incarnation of London Bridge is a three-span construction, opened in 1972.

Next come Southwark Bridge and Blackfriars road and railway bridges before we reach Waterloo Bridge, which opened in 1942, replacing Rennie's much admired stone bridge of 1817. Hungerford (or Charing Cross) railway bridge, with a well-used pedestrian way, connects Charing Cross to the South Bank arts complex. Dating from 1864, the rail bridge replaced Brunel's suspension bridge, but used its brick piers; the chains were recycled into his Clifton Suspension Bridge in Bristol.

Westminster Bridge, alongside the Houses of Parliament, was the second bridge to be

built in what is now central London. The present structure, was completed in 1862, but it replaced an earlier bridge, which opened in 1750. That was the bridge on which Wordsworth wrote his famous sonnet ('Earth has not anything to show more fair...'), but it later suffered - like others - from the notorious scouring action of strong Thames tides.

The idea of a second crossing at Westminster provoked strong opposition from vested interests – the Thames Watermen had to be bought off with £25,000 compensation; the Archbishop of Canterbury, owner of the horse ferry at Lambeth, collected £21,000 – considerable amounts in those days. Later, in 1862, Lambeth Bridge was completed, right where the Archbishop's ferry used to be – on its east side stands Lambeth Palace, the Archbishop's official residence; its western approach, Horseferry Road, is a lasting reminder of the ferry. The present bridge was built in 1932.

Upstream again are Vauxhall Bridge, Grosvenor railway bridge (carrying the lines out of Victoria) and Chelsea Bridge, a handsome suspension bridge. On the other side of Battersea Park is perhaps the most attractive of them all, Albert Bridge. Opened in 1873, it was designed by R M Ordish and may be described as a 'semi-suspension' bridge – the diagonal stays radiating so picturesquely from the towers to support the deck are rigid; the light suspension chains take only the weight of the stays.

Eighteen London bridges lie upstream of this, starting with Battersea (designed by Sir Joseph Bazalgette, who built the Victoria Embankment). They include the monumental Hammersmith Bridge with its rather Empire-style towers and the suspension footbridge at Teddington Weir, ending with Hampton Court Bridge, of which only one side (Hampton Court) is in London; the other

is in Surrey.

Tunnels under the river are numerous, and include several carrying Underground lines. Within London there are also three road tunnels: Rotherhithe, with bends definitely for horse-drawn rather than motor vehicles, and the two Blackwall Tunnels. Also downstream of Tower bridge are two pedestrian tunnels, the one at Woolwich, providing an alternative to the free Woolwich Ferry, the other at Greenwich, connecting the Cutty Sark Gardens to Island Gardens on the Isle of Dogs, the present terminus of the Docklands Light Railway (DLR). Another tunnel at this point will soon extend the line of the DLR to Greenwich, Deptford and Lewisham.

Two contrasting bridges across the Thames are the sturdy Lambeth Bridge, built in the 1930s, and the beautiful Albert Bridge, looking like a delicate metal cobweb across the water

Just upstream of the Woolwich ferry and foot tunnel is something which is neither a bridge nor a tunnel, but is an important link between the north and south banks of the river. The Thames Barrier is a vital part of a £480million flood defence scheme for London, which was completed in 1984. The Barrier has four enormous curving steel gates, each 200ft (61m) long, shaped like barrels sliced longways and

The river near Westminster Bridge is busy with tourist boats, cruising the historic artery of the city

each weighing 3,200 tonnes. These fit into concrete sills on the river bed and only rise if winds and the North Sea surge threaten to cause flooding in the capital. On the south bank immediately downstream is the visitors' centre, with landscaped viewing esplanades, a café, and an exhibition.

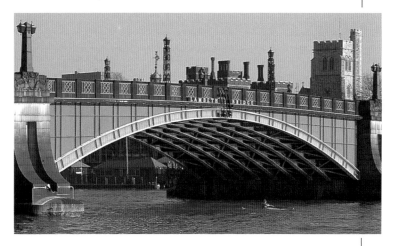

OFF-CENTRE LONDON

GREENWICH AND THE SOUTH-EAST

On a nice day, you cannot beat the boat trip to Greenwich from the city, but travel to Greenwich by the Docklands Light Railway and you will alight at Island Gardens on the opposite side of the river. From here you can enjoy the finest view of the great architectural ensemble of the Royal Naval College and National Maritime Museum, before continuing on foot through a tunnel beneath the Thames. As well as the museum, there is a historic ship collection which includes the *Cutty Sark* Clipper Ship and *Gipsy Moth IV*, Sir Francis Chichester's round-the-world yacht. The restored Queen's House is also open, as is the Old Royal Observatory, standing at zero degrees longitude in Greenwich Park. The Millennium Dome remains a landmark on the Greenwich waterfront, but its future is uncertain and negotiations for its sale are expected to extend well into the first decade of the

Most visitors to London look at a few famous tourist attractions, perhaps take a bus tour round the centre, and think they have seen what the city has to offer. To do this is to miss out on some real treats, because 'off-centre London' has interesting and attractive places that are well worth visiting. Here we explore some of the more notable of them – moving clockwise, we start at about the four o'clock position at one of the best known of London's outer limits.

21st century.

Woolwich, to the east, has the imposing Royal Artillery Barracks and Academy on the common, and the Museum of Artillery, housed in the Rotunda, by John Nash. Also at Woolwich is the Thames Barrier Visitor Centre, while at nearby Eltham are impressive ruins of a medieval royal palace.

To the south, near Bromley, are Chislehurst Caves, a mysterious labyrinth hewn out of the chalk over a period of 8,000 years. During World War II the caves became a huge air-raid shelter which even had its own church. North-west again, Dulwich has a historic 'village' centre, the impressive 19th-century Dulwich College and the Dulwich Picture Gallery, with many old masters.

ALONG THE THAMES

Richmond combines historic buildings and splendid Thames views with a bustling commer-

Syon House, left, and magnificent Hampton Court Palace, below

cial centre and lively arts and restaurant scene. Architectural set-pieces include its two greens, with delightful old lanes, and Richmond Hill, with 18th-century houses and fine views.

Kew, downstream, is best known for the Royal Botanic Gardens, 300 acres (122ha) of landscaped gardens, with some spectacular buildings. Seventeenth-century Kew Palace is the most modest but charming of royal residences, and Kew Village is charming too. In nearby Brentford is the Kew Bridge Steam Museum, a Victorian pumping station with enormous beam engines and London's only steam railway.

Upstream from Richmond are a string of splendid 18th-century buildings – Marble Hill House, a magnificent Palladian villa of the 1720s set in lovely parkland; Ham House, a large 17th-century house of exceptional interest; the early 18th-century Orleans House Octagon, its adjoining wing now an art gallery. A ferryman will row you from the Ham side to Marble Hill Park.

Further upstream is Hampton Court Palace, built by Cardinal Wolsey, Henry VIII's most powerful minister, who gave the palace to his monarch. His great gatehouse in Tudor brick dominates the main approach, and beyond the huge Base Court lies the Clock Court with its 16th-century astronomical clock and Great Hall. Later monarchs all left their mark here, notably the work carried out by Wren for William and Mary, with the arcaded Fountain Court and great East Front, looking out over the formal gardens and lovely parkland.

Downriver, the riverside is studded with attractions – Horace Walpole's 'Gothick castle' at Strawberry Hill, Syon House with its Adam interiors

Ham House is a superb riverside mansion which was built in 1610

and spacious park, Old Chiswick with its 18th-century Chiswick Mall, and Fulham Palace in Bishop's Park. Chelsea, known for its King's Road boutiques and cafés, also has Wren's Chelsea Hospital (home to the famous pensioners), a maze of streets leading to the river and the 320-year-old Physic Garden, a pioneer botanical garden.

Further north are two notable historic houses – Lord Burlington's Chiswick House, an essay in Palladian style, and Osterley Park, built in the 16th century by Sir Thomas Gresham, merchant, Lord Mayor of London and founder of the Royal Exchange, and later splendidly remodelled in classical style.

AROUND NORTH LONDON

Harrow-on-the-Hill is noted for 400-year-old Harrow School. To the east, at Colindale, is the Royal Air Force Museum, with 70 aircraft and other exhibits, including flight simulators and the incredible 'Battle of Britain Experience'.

Hampstead's Fenton House was built in the late 17th century; it accommodates a collection of musical instruments, and often resounds to the sound of harpsichords or virginals. Keats House is now a museum devoted to the famous poet, and the house once occupied by Sigmund Freud contains his

Greenwich is the centre of London's maritime heritage, with the superb Royal Naval College and museum and a collection of historic vessels down on the river

collection of antiquities and displays relating to his work, while Kenwood, in lovely wooded grounds, contains fine art collections. Highgate has the unusual and surprisingly popular attraction of its impressive cemetery, housing the remains of many luminaries, such as George Eliot, Michael Faraday and Karl Marx.

See Walk P page 141
In London's East End

SPORTING MUSEUMS

Sports fans are spoilt for choice, with the MCC Museum at Lords Cricket Ground in St John's Wood, the Lawn Tennis Museum at the All England Club in Wimbledon, or the

popular Wembley Stadium Tour.

COAST TO COAST ON THE ISLE OF WIGHT

1 From The Square in Yarmouth head towards the church and walk along St James Street to cross the A3054 into Mill Road. At the sharp left bend, follow the arrowed path ahead (signed Freshwater) towards the old tide mill. Ignore the footpath left, walk beside the mudflats and turn right along the old railway. Remain on this path for 1½ miles (2.4km) to the causeway at Freshwater.

2 Turn left, away from the river, and follow the lane to the B3399. Turn left and cross almost immediately into Manor Road. In a few paces bear left (Freshwater Way) and gently ascend across grassland towards Afton Down. Go straight at a junction beside the golf course, soon to follow the gravel track right to the clubhouse. Go through the gate, pass in front of the building and walk down the access track, keeping left, to the A3055. Turn right, downhill, into Freshwater Bay.

3 Walk past the car park and turn right into Coastguard Lane, opposite the Albion Tavern. Keep ahead at the end, along a path skirting the edge of marsh and eventually reaching a road. Turn right, then, just before the river bridge, turn left into Afton Marshes Nature Reserve.

Distance: 6 miles (9.7km)
Total ascent: 240ft (73m)
Paths: good; very wet and boggy after rain
Terrain: marsh, open grassland, woodland
Gradients: one gentle climb
Refreshments: tearooms and Albion Tavern, Freshwater Bay; Red Lion, Freshwater; various pubs and tearooms, Yarmouth
Park: car park by A3054, near Lymington to Yarmouth ferry terminal, or leave your car at Lymington Pier and take the ferry to Yarmouth

6 Climb the stile to the right of the metal gate, pass through a copse to a stile and bear left, uphill, along the field edge. Enter the field on your left and keep to the path along the right-hand edge to a stile on the edge of woodland. Soon drop down through the wood to a track and turn left, following it to the A3054. Turn right along the pavement, back into Yarmouth.

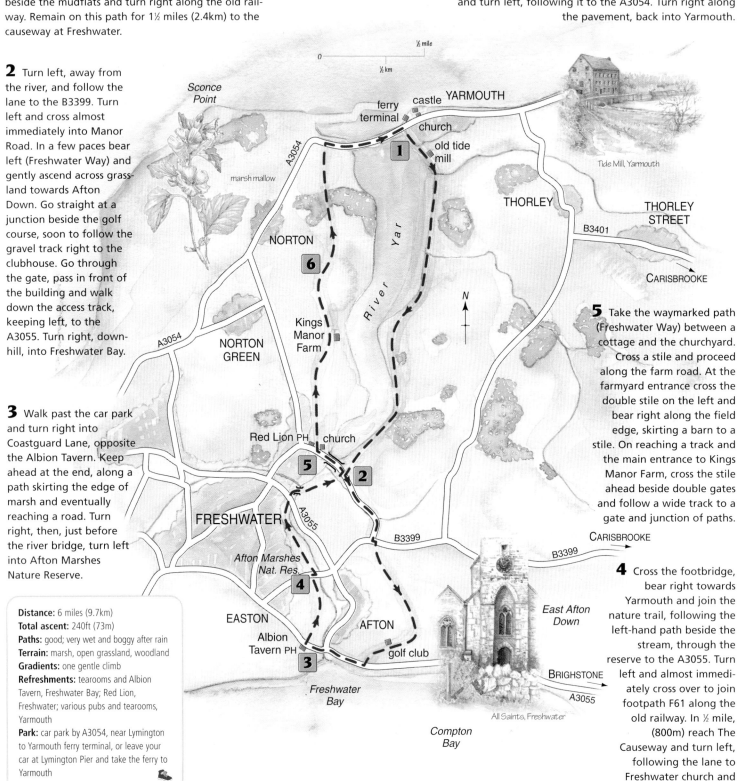

Tide Mill, Yarmouth

All Saints, Freshwater

5 Take the waymarked path (Freshwater Way) between a cottage and the churchyard. Cross a stile and proceed along the farm road. At the farmyard entrance cross the double stile on the left and bear right along the field edge, skirting a barn to a stile. On reaching a track and the main entrance to Kings Manor Farm, cross the stile ahead beside double gates and follow a wide track to a gate and junction of paths.

4 Cross the footbridge, bear right towards Yarmouth and join the nature trail, following the left-hand path beside the stream, through the reserve to the A3055. Turn left and almost immediately cross over to join footpath F61 along the old railway. In ½ mile, (800m) reach The Causeway and turn left, following the lane to Freshwater church and the Red Lion.

A WEALTH OF WILDLIFE IN THE ARUN VALLEY

1 From the car park turn right across the bridge and over the stile (Wey-South Path) immediately right. Walk along the river bank, pass through a gate and bear right on reaching a track. Bear sharp left beyond Limekiln house and follow the track through farm buildings, ignoring the path right by metal barns. At a fork bear right and descend past Hayles Barn.

2 Turn left along the field edge to a gate in the corner. Turn right following Wey-South Path marker to go through a gate and across a bridge on the left. Turn right beside the ditch and soon cross the wooden bridge into Amberley Wild Brooks. Keep to the path, heading south through marshland, over a stile to open pasture and on to another stile, joining the track to Amberley village. Turn right at the lane then right again at the T-junction towards the church. Drop down to pass Rock Cottage and follow the track beneath the walls of Amberley Castle.

3 Bear right at a gate and follow the path to the railway line. Cross via stiles and remain on the path towards Bury Church. Climb a stile and bear left to cross a bridge over a dyke. Keep ahead, cross a further bridge and water meadow to join the raised path beside the River Arun. Turn left and follow the river bank, bearing left to a gate beyond the footbridge over the river. Now on the South Downs Way (SDW), soon follow the fenced path right to reach the B2139.

6 Turn left and continue to a T-junction at Greatham. Turn left and follow the road for just over ½ mile (800m) back to the car park.

5 Turn left, then right in 50yds (46m) to join narrow Rackham Street. Walk through Rackham, passing the lane to Amberley and soon taking the path left by houses to a gate. Pass a house and skirt woodland to a junction of paths by a footbridge. Bear right along the edge of woodland, ignore the path on your right and keep left, eventually passing through woods to a metalled lane.

4 Turn right and, shortly, cross the road, soon to reach a metalled lane. Turn left with SDW marker and gradually ascend the South Downs. Keep right at the junction, pass High Down house, then bear left up a steep stony track to a gate. Continue ascending on SDW, then at the crossing of bridleways at the top of Rackham Hill, turn left and descend on a winding path through woods to the B2139.

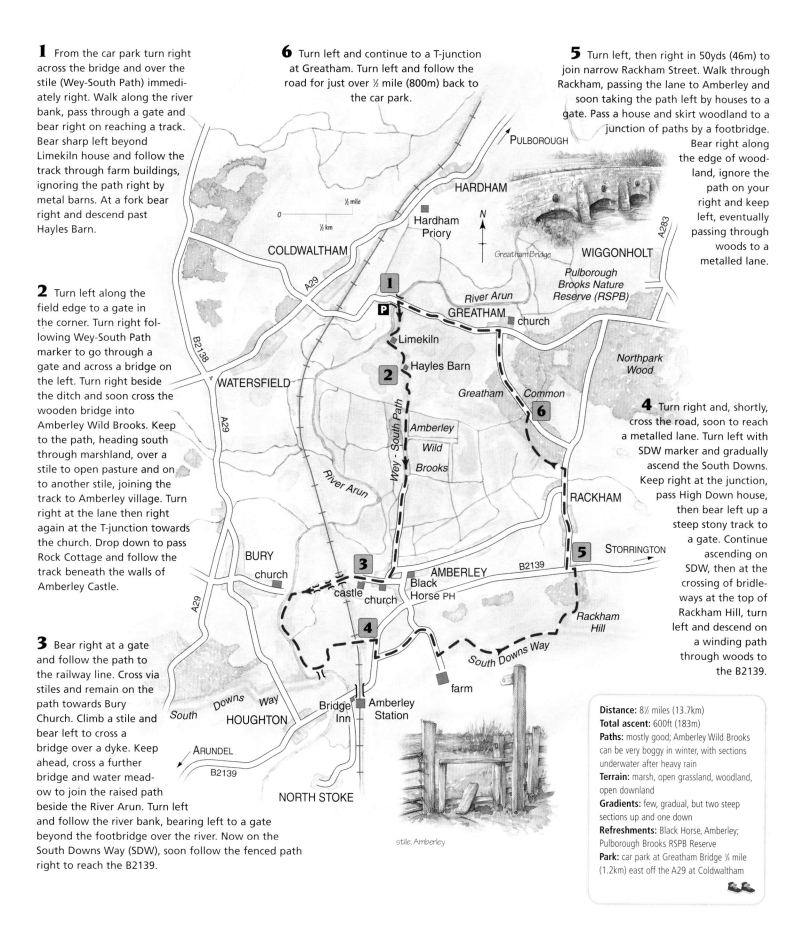

stile, Amberley

Distance: 8½ miles (13.7km)
Total ascent: 600ft (183m)
Paths: mostly good; Amberley Wild Brooks can be very boggy in winter, with sections underwater after heavy rain
Terrain: marsh, open grassland, woodland, open downland
Gradients: few, gradual, but two steep sections up and one down
Refreshments: Black Horse, Amberley; Pulborough Brooks RSPB Reserve
Park: car park at Greatham Bridge ¾ mile (1.2km) east off the A29 at Coldwaltham

LEWES – BIRTHPLACE OF THE ENGLISH PARLIAMENT

1 With your back to Lewes railway station, turn left. Turn first left into Mountfield Road and almost immediately right into narrow path. Continue to end of path and turn right alongside playing fields. Bear right by brick lock-up workshops through to priory ruins. Follow grass path with ruins on right to tennis club on left.

> **Distance:** 7 miles (11.3km)
> **Total ascent:** 100ft (30m)
> **Paths:** good, mostly paved; some muddy sections
> **Terrain:** town streets and riverside
> **Gradients:** moderate
> **Refreshments:** wide choice
> **Park:** car park at railway station
>
>

8 At T-junction, retrace steps back to end of precinct, turn left into Friars Walk which becomes Lansdown Place. Turn left at the crossroads into Station Road and back to station.

2 Leave priory grounds, turn right at Priory Cottage on corner into Cockshut Road and follow this under low-arched bridge to Southover High Street. Turn left. Anne of Cleves House is a little way along on right. Retrace steps back along Southover High Street with Southover parish church on right, to King's Head and turn left.

7 At top, turn left. Cross road almost immediately into Fisher Street. Continue to end and turn left into High Street. Walk past war memorial, down to pedestrian precinct. Continue over river into Cliffe High Street.

3 At corner of Eastport Lane (right) is entrance to Southover Grange gardens. Explore gardens but return to this point. On leaving gardens, turn right. Walk past 16th-century Southover Grange, continue up steep, cobbled Keere Street to 15th-century bookshop at top. Turn right into High Street. Follow High Street to Castlegate on left and walk to castle.

6 At end of field, cross stile next to five-bar gate, turn left along woodland path. At converted barn (on right) keep left, continue through council estate, past school and after bollards, fork left to narrow path. Follow it over railway bridge to The Pells. Return to Abinger Place and go left after church into Lancaster Street and right up Sun Street.

4 Turn left up through 14th-century Barbican arch, continue past 300-year-old bowling green to Battle of Lewes memorial plaque on left under trees. Go down steps (on right, if facing plaque), down Castle Banks, and cross road into Abinger Place. Continue to end. Fork left at church (St John sub Castro), down to The Pells, an L-shaped canal.

5 Continue along path (canal on left) to white, railed bridge. Turn left just before bridge, and walk along river path. Ignore first rail bridge and at third stile, just past a small concrete building, turn left. Cross another stile, walk under railway bridge into meadow, with stream on left.

Map labels: OFFHAM, LANDPORT RD, STANSFIELD RD, NEWTON RD, OFFHAM ROAD, school, A275, River Ouse, playing field, Pell's Pool, The Pells, BROOK ST, PELHAM TERR, church, LANCASTER ST, TORONTO TERR, Elephant and Castle PH, WHITE HILL, SUN ST, WEST ST, Memorial Plaque, Barbican Gate, castle, CASTLE BANKS, PRECINCTS, HIGH STREET, FISHER ST, MARKET STREET, EASTGATE ST, EASTGATE ST, CLIFFE HIGH ST, MALLING ST, UCKFIELD, Lewes Castle, War Memorial, Lansdown Arms PH, FRIARS WALK, LANSDOWN PL, STATION RD, SOUTHOVER RD, GARDENS ST, station, MOUNTFIELD ROAD, HAM LANE, playing fields, EASTBOURNE, NEWHAVEN, SOUTH ST, Southover Grange, gdns, GRANGE RD, Anne of Cleves House, EASTPORT LN, PRIORY ST, Kings Head PH, church, SOUTHOVER HIGH ST, COCKSHUT RD, BRIGHTON, priory ruins, Priory Cottage, Lewes Tennis Club, Keere Street, Anne of Cleves House, N, ½ mile, ½ km, 0

THE SOUTH DOWNS OF THE BLOOMSBURY SET

1 From the main street walk past the Cricketers Arms to the end of the village and take the walled path signposted to the church. Continue past the church to a field where you turn right. Walk past a silage pit and at a T-junction turn left onto a farm track.

2 With a barn on your right, turn left into a tree-lined path. Continue up the hill, past a house, to meet a pebbled track. At crossroads, turn right towards Firle Beacon, about 4 miles (6.4km) away. At the end of this path, take the far left track with wonderful views over to Alfriston and the Cuckmere Valley, up to a ridge on the South Downs Way.

7 Continue past barn on right and brick and hung-tile cottages on left, until fork in the road. Turn left and take road back to Berwick's main street.

6 Climb stile and go straight on along the edge of a field (signposted for Berwick). Go through a break in the hedge on the right and turn left into next field. Continue along the edge of it, turning left at the end and walking alongside a hedge, then turn right, following path between two fields which leads to a farm track. Bear left.

5 Cross this road and follow the path between two houses. Take the first track on left down to Alciston. At the church turn right up public footpath to the porch door. Climb over stile on left and walk alongside flint wall on right to another stile.

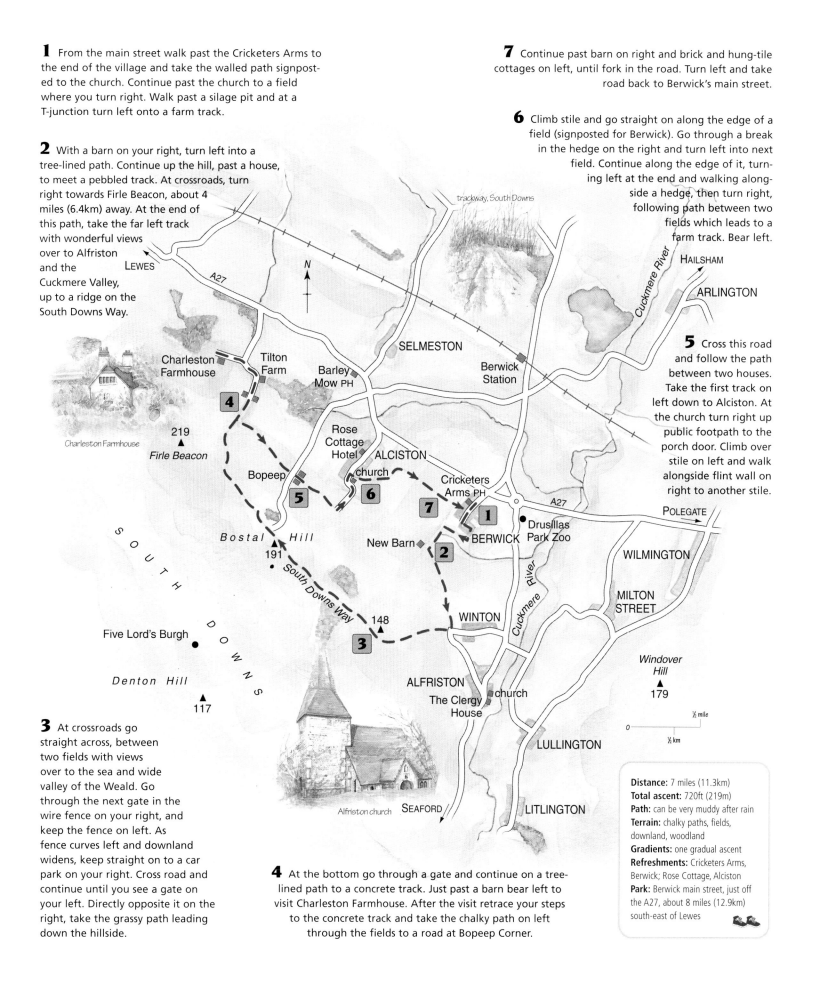

3 At crossroads go straight across, between two fields with views over to the sea and wide valley of the Weald. Go through the next gate in the wire fence on your right, and keep the fence on left. As fence curves left and downland widens, keep straight on to a car park on your right. Cross road and continue until you see a gate on your left. Directly opposite it on the right, take the grassy path leading down the hillside.

4 At the bottom go through a gate and continue on a tree-lined path to a concrete track. Just past a barn bear left to visit Charleston Farmhouse. After the visit retrace your steps to the concrete track and take the chalky path on left through the fields to a road at Bopeep Corner.

Distance: 7 miles (11.3km)
Total ascent: 720ft (219m)
Path: can be very muddy after rain
Terrain: chalky paths, fields, downland, woodland
Gradients: one gradual ascent
Refreshments: Cricketers Arms, Berwick; Rose Cottage, Alciston
Park: Berwick main street, just off the A27, about 8 miles (12.9km) south-east of Lewes

UP AND DOWN ON THE SEVEN SISTERS

2 Take the road on the right of the pond, signposted Friston and Jevington, and continue on into Friston Forest. Follow the ride between the trees until it curves left. Do not follow this, but take the wide fork straight ahead and continue until this meets a narrow track.

1 From the car park cross the road, and with the visitor centre on your left, walk up the grassy hill, on the South Downs Way, to a flint wall at the top. Climb over the wall, turn slightly to the right and take the Friston Forest Forestry Commision signpost. The path soon leads steeply to steps down to Westdean Pond.

Distance: 7 miles (11.3km)
Total ascent: 250ft (76m)
Path: wide forest rides; good field paths
Terrain: forest, fields, downland
Gradients: some steep sections on Seven Sisters
Refreshments: Seven Sisters Restaurant and Tea Rooms, Exceat
Park: car park at Exceat, on A259 opposite Seven Sisters Country Park Visitor Centre

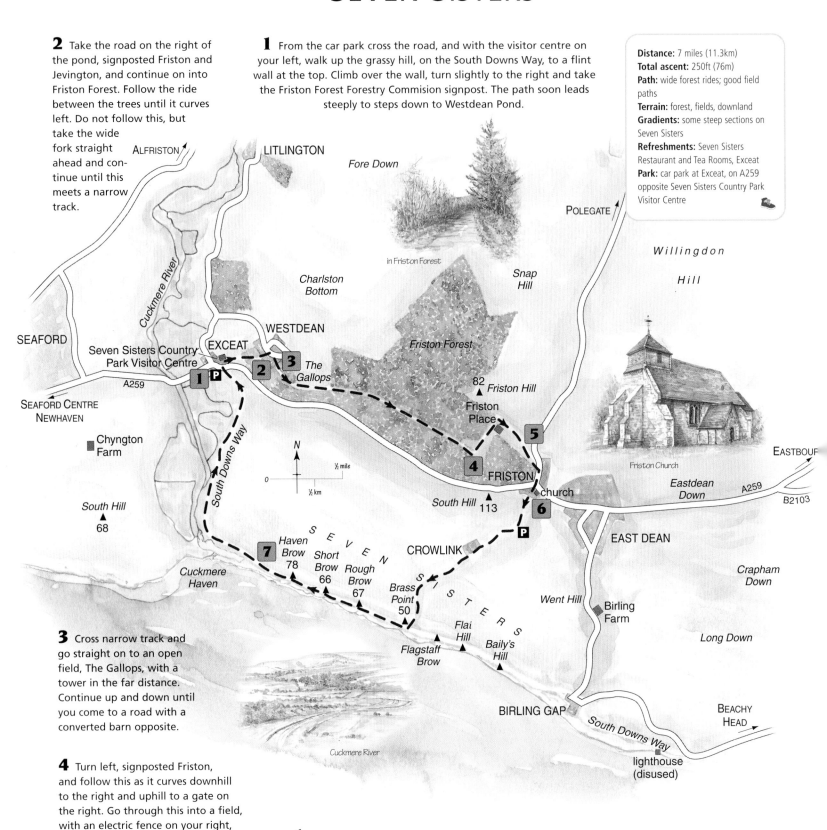

in Friston Forest

Friston Church

3 Cross narrow track and go straight on to an open field, The Gallops, with a tower in the far distance. Continue up and down until you come to a road with a converted barn opposite.

4 Turn left, signposted Friston, and follow this as it curves downhill to the right and uphill to a gate on the right. Go through this into a field, with an electric fence on your right, and walk to the gate at the far end.

5 Walk diagonally across the next field. Climb over the stile at the end, up some steps onto a minor road which leads to the A259 at Friston church and pond. Cross the road.

6 Follow the no-through road next to the church, past the National Trust car park, and down the tarmac path to the hamlet of Crowlink. Walk through a gate to a grassy path and follow this until the Downs open up. Bear right up the hillside to tackle Brass Point l60ft (49m), Rough Brow 216ft (66m), Short Brow, 2l4ft (65m), and the last Sister before Cuckmere Haven, Haven Brow (also, the highest at 253ft/77m).

7 At a signpost follow the South Downs Way down to Cuckmere Haven, with a wire fence on your left. Turn right along a concrete path which leads back alongside the river to Exceat car park.

THE FOLLIES AT BRIGHTLING

1 From crossroads follow Willingford Lane (signed Burwash Weald) with Obelisk on left. Pass Barn Farm right and take bridleway left along concrete track. At junction, just beyond cottage, turn left over a stile and follow left-hand edge of field to another stile.

2 Bear half-right downhill to bridge and stile. Head straight uphill, then down to stile and descend to cross bridge. Climb steps and stile, then head uphill to gate and turn right at junction, following hedge to stile. Proceed to stile on edge of woodland, turning left at fingerpost on path parallel with woodland. Shortly, turn right at junction.

3 Cross forest track and descend through gorse. Ignore path on left and continue down sunken bridleway to cross stream. Follow path left to track and turn sharp left on bridleway, passing two posts. Ascend for ¼ mile (400m), past two houses.

4 Follow lane uphill. Disregard first footpath left and take second arrowed path, beyond two houses. Go through gate, pass right of pond to fingerpost by hedge ahead. Keep straight on path towards Sugar Loaf. Cross double stile and bear half-left to gap in hedge near end of houses.

8 Ignore arrowed path right through trees and keep to ha-ha. Proceed at end through small copse and large gate into field. Turn left along field edge to gate and follow path signed The Sugar Loaf through woodland to forest drive. Bear right and keep right by Forestry Commission board to lane. Turn right, then left at junction (signed Burwash), and follow lane back to start.

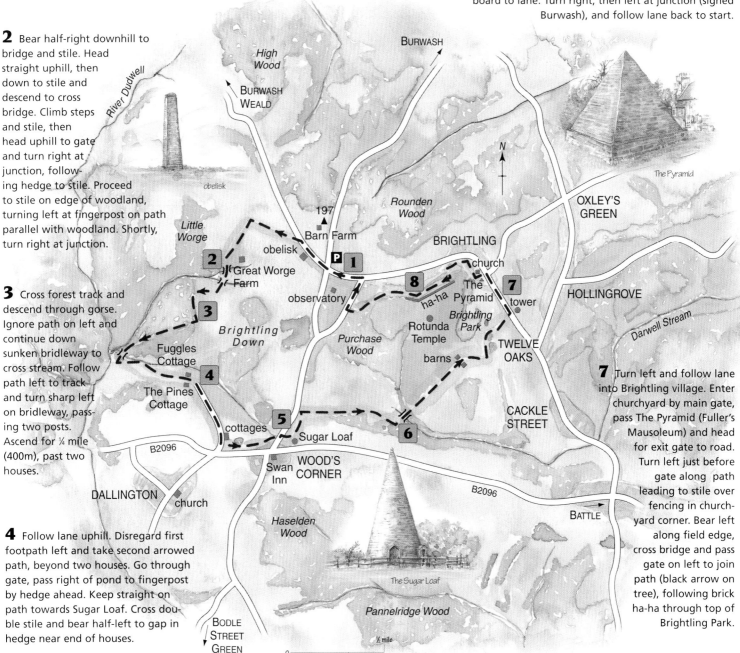

7 Turn left and follow lane into Brightling village. Enter churchyard by main gate, pass The Pyramid (Fuller's Mausoleum) and head for exit gate to road. Turn left just before gate along path leading to stile over fencing in churchyard corner. Bear left along field edge, cross bridge and pass gate on left to join path (black arrow on tree), following brick ha-ha through top of Brightling Park.

6 Descend into wood, cross bridge and pass through gate into Brightling Park. Proceed through gate ahead and follow path through edge of woodland to gate. Keep left along field edge (The Temple clearly visible to left – no access), eventually reaching gate by barns. Turn right on track and keep left at junction to follow track to lane. Turn right to view The Tower.

Distance: 6 miles (9.7km)
Total ascent: 650ft (198m)
Paths: good; muddy after rain
Terrain: fields, woodland, open parkland
Gradients: gradual
Refreshments: Swan Inn, Wood's Corner
Park: on verge near Fuller's Obelisk and Observatory on Brightling Down, between Wood's Corner and Burwash, 1 mile (1.6km) north of B2096 at Wood's Corner

5 Turn left along road to entrance to salvage yard. To view Sugar Loaf, enter yard (yellow arrow), pass gates to first yard and follow markers uphill along fenced path to gate. Return to yard entrance and follow white arrows on right into Purchase Wood. Ignore path to Brightling, left, and keep ahead on path (signed The Tower), eventually merging with gravel track. ½ mile (800m) into woodland look for arrowed post left for The Tower.

FOLLOWING THE PILGRIMS THROUGH KENT

1 From the street opposite the manor house walk up the road by the house. Turn right where the path forks. You will pass a converted oast house. Follow the byway sign. At the electricity sub-station, go right and up to the Pilgrims' Way.

6 Cross Broad Street then go up steps following North Downs Way signs, over a stile, then down steps into a wood. At the T-junction, turn left then right and go through a metal barrier. Coming out onto open land, turn left and go through three gates and follow the path across fields and through trees back down to Hollingbourne.

5 Go up a steep hill, then down and over two stiles. Follow North Downs Way as it bends, left then right near the farm, then go over two more stiles and through the wood. In a field follow the path to the top corner and go over a stile then right to the road.

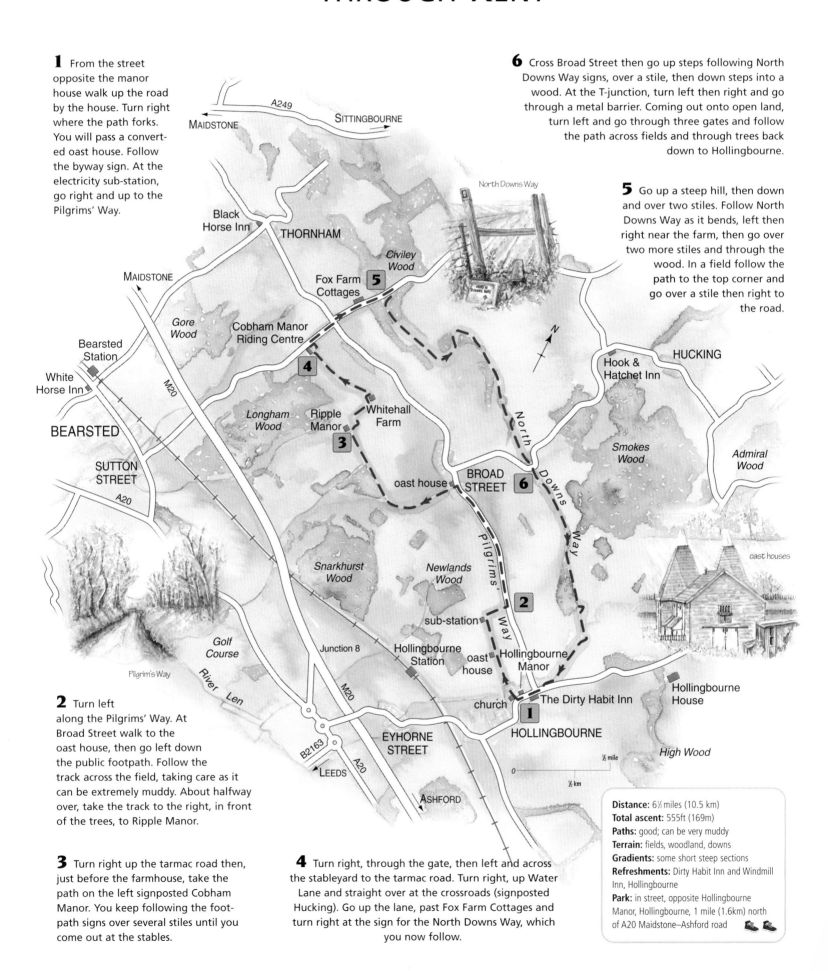

2 Turn left along the Pilgrims' Way. At Broad Street walk to the oast house, then go left down the public footpath. Follow the track across the field, taking care as it can be extremely muddy. About halfway over, take the track to the right, in front of the trees, to Ripple Manor.

3 Turn right up the tarmac road then, just before the farmhouse, take the path on the left signposted Cobham Manor. You keep following the footpath signs over several stiles until you come out at the stables.

4 Turn right, through the gate, then left and across the stableyard to the tarmac road. Turn right, up Water Lane and straight over at the crossroads (signposted Hucking). Go up the lane, past Fox Farm Cottages and turn right at the sign for the North Downs Way, which you now follow.

Distance: 6½ miles (10.5 km)
Total ascent: 555ft (169m)
Paths: good; can be very muddy
Terrain: fields, woodland, downs
Gradients: some short steep sections
Refreshments: Dirty Habit Inn and Windmill Inn, Hollingbourne
Park: in street, opposite Hollingbourne Manor, Hollingbourne, 1 mile (1.6km) north of A20 Maidstone–Ashford road

HISTORIC MEDWAY TOWNS

Distance: 5½ miles (8.8km)
Total ascent: 100ft (30m)
Paths: good
Terrain: city streets
Gradients: gentle
Refreshments: available throughout
Park: Rochester Station

1 From Rochester Station turn left, go under the rail bridge and walk right, down to the main road. Turn left along Medway Street, follow the road round, then turn left again up Dock Road, signposted to Historic Dockyard.

2 Keep walking up this busy road. Go straight on at the roundabout, then left into the Historic Dockyard. After exploring the dockyard come out and turn left. Go over the roundabout, then past the Medway Tunnel. Cross the road at the next roundabout and walk up to the submarine Ocelot.

3 Follow the road back into town. At the clock, cross over to the Pentagon Shopping Centre. Turn right up a pedestrianised street, then go right along a quiet part of Chatham High Street. Keep going straight ahead, back to Rochester Station.

4 Pass the station, walk up to the main road, cross over and walk down the pedestrianised High Street. Just after Eastgate House turn left, up Crow Lane. Cross over at Restoration House and follow the sign for Centenary Walk, which leads over a small park.

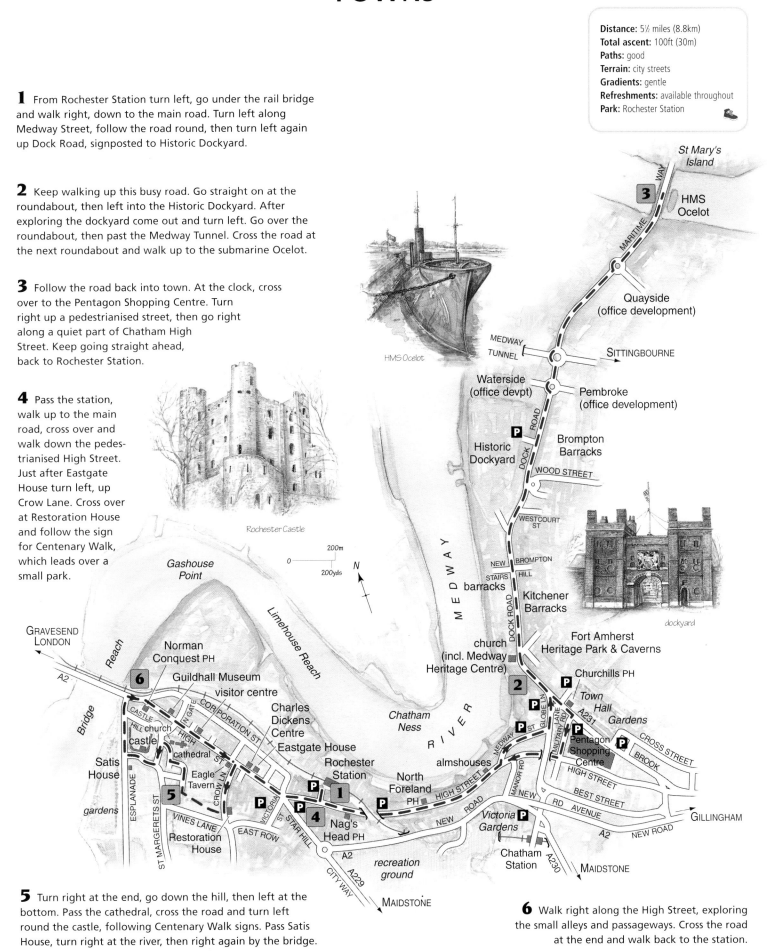

HMS Ocelot

Rochester Castle

dockyard

5 Turn right at the end, go down the hill, then left at the bottom. Pass the cathedral, cross the road and turn left round the castle, following Centenary Walk signs. Pass Satis House, turn right at the river, then right again by the bridge.

6 Walk right along the High Street, exploring the small alleys and passageways. Cross the road at the end and walk back to the station.

THE NEW FOREST –
A ROYAL HUNTING GROUND

1 With Rufus Stone opposite, turn right and walk along to Sir Walter Tyrrell Inn. Veer left at 'Except for Access' sign and cross turf, keeping to right-hand half of open grassy area. Cross several little streams and make for obvious gap in trees. Negotiate shallow ford here and follow indistinct path ahead. Cross winter ford and simple water meadow bridge spanning gully. Keep left when path forks just beyond bridge and follow it through trees to join concrete track leading to Long Beech Caravan Park. Pass several barriers to reach water tower.

2 Pass concrete track immediately beyond tower and continue for about 50yds (46m) to barrier. Veer right here and make for some wooden posts. Follow path between bracken and gorse bushes and head for corner of King's Garn Gutter Inclosure. Continue on path, keeping inclosure boundary fence on right. Avoid gate in fence and look for Janesmoor Pond up ahead. Make for next corner of inclosure and turn right.

3 Follow path down between inclosures descending gently into glade. Head for track, avoid gates on left and right and go straight on over track to wood. Cross over stream (King's Garn Gutter) and follow path through trees to emerge on edge of golf course. Keep to track beside greens and fairways and when it peters out, continue over grass, keeping tight to woodland on left. Walk behind two greens before heading out across open ground, dotted with gorse bushes and fringed by woodland on left, towards car park on far side.

4 Cricket ground is to right between trees. Cross grass, keeping building on right, and continue along wooded edge of golf course. Curve left to another green on right, and join clear track running up slope to left. Walk across car park and continue to road. Turn left and head for Brook. Follow road through village, pass The Bell Inn and The Green Dragon and avoid footpath just beyond on left.

5 Pass Canterton Lodge and veer right into Canterton Lane. Follow road over several streams and note large white house up on left bank. Continue ahead when lane becomes stony underfoot and pass bridleway on right. On left now is Bignell Wood. Follow track as it swings right to Greys Farm.

6 Pass between wooden posts and veer left off track, following path to gap in trees ahead. On reaching clearing immediately beyond them, turn right at junction by manhole cover and follow path across stream, up gentle slope and back to car park.

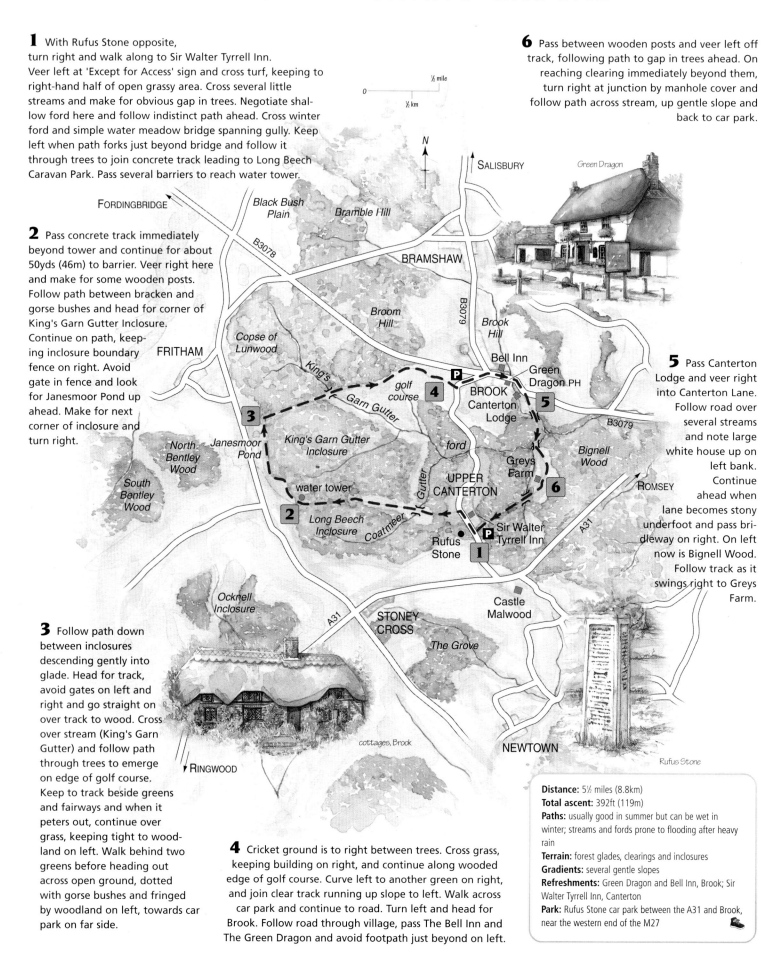

cottages, Brook

Green Dragon

Rufus Stone

Distance: 5½ miles (8.8km)
Total ascent: 392ft (119m)
Paths: usually good in summer but can be wet in winter; streams and fords prone to flooding after heavy rain
Terrain: forest glades, clearings and inclosures
Gradients: several gentle slopes
Refreshments: Green Dragon and Bell Inn, Brook; Sir Walter Tyrrell Inn, Canterton
Park: Rufus Stone car park between the A31 and Brook, near the western end of the M27

THE DEVIL'S PUNCH BOWL

1 From car park follow track to left of café, heading away from A3. Keep left at path junction, walking to crossing of tracks by mast. Turn right towards height barrier and immediately bear right down steep path to Highcombe Bottom. Keep left on merging with track. Leave woodland and take next path right, downhill to cross stream.

2 Pass youth hostel and turn left beyond gate. Pass Gnome Cottage and go straight ahead at bend to gate (by cattle grid). Cross open heath, ignoring tracks left and right before taking left path at fork (animal pens in field on right). Go through gate (by cattle grid) and continue to path junction by lane.

3 Turn right up steps, pass through Upper Highfield Farm, and pass tennis court to stile by gate. Follow concrete track down to silage storage area. Cross stile on left and ascend to cross A3. Bear left down to stile and descend through trees to another stile and driveway by house. Keep left, then, at crossing of tracks, turn right, around lake, to Blackhanger Farm driveway.

4 Bear right, cross stream and stile on left. Skirt house and garden to stile in field corner and pass through copse. Follow telegraph poles across next field to gate. At waymarker post bear right and follow track to Begley Farm. Go through gate on left and keep to right-hand edge of field to lane.

8 Walk down lane (eventually metalled) and take path (Greensand Way) right, just before post box. Disregard all paths left and right, cross edge of open heath and descend, going straight ahead at crossing of paths then forking left, steeply uphill. Keep right at house, keeping to track back to A3 and start.

7 Take second path right (ahead) for ⅔ mile (1km). Descend to crossing of trails and turn right. Cross next main path and descend steeply into wooded valley. Keep ahead at crossing of bridleways, cross stream then, just past gate on left, take unmarked path left. Ascend steeply to wide trackway by house and turn left.

6 Walk south from trig point, pass car park and take path ahead. Shortly, at crossing of paths, turn left and descend to staggered crossing of paths. Take second path right and gently climb, forking left at marker post to gate. Go round gate and shortly reach junction of five ways.

5 Turn left, then just before Boundless Farm (300yds/273m), take footpath right into Boundless Copse. Keep ahead, soon forking left, steeply uphill through coniferous trees and clearing. Continue ahead as paths cross and ascend steeply to waymarker post (Greensand Way) at top and summit of Gibbet Hill.

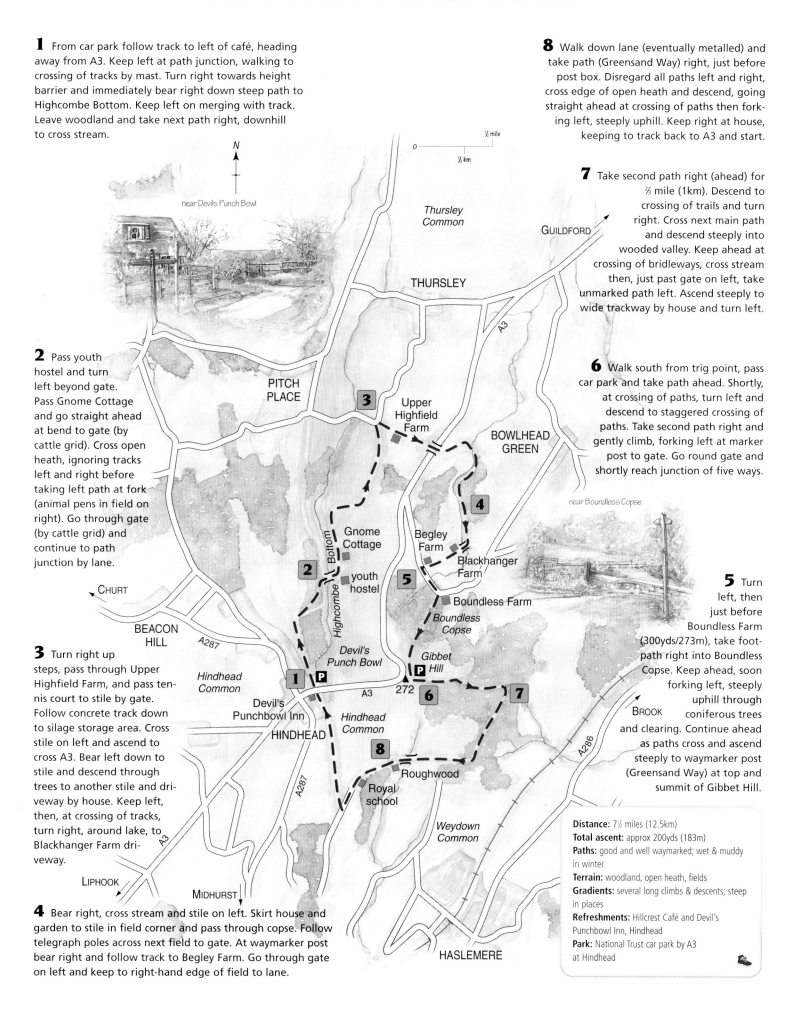

near Devils Punch Bowl

near Boundless Copse

Distance: 7½ miles (12.5km)
Total ascent: approx 200yds (183m)
Paths: good and well waymarked; wet & muddy in winter
Terrain: woodland, open heath, fields
Gradients: several long climbs & descents; steep in places
Refreshments: Hillcrest Café and Devil's Punchbowl Inn, Hindhead
Park: National Trust car park by A3 at Hindhead

CHOBHAM COMMON –
LAST OF THE SURREY HEATHS

Distance: 7 miles (11.3km)
Total ascent: 245ft (75m)
Paths: mostly good; can become waterlogged after heavy rain
Terrain: heath, common, woodland, fields, several stretches of road
Gradients: gentle
Refreshments: Four Horseshoes and Cricketers Inn, Burrowhill
Park: Longcross car park, just off the B386, western end of Longcross village

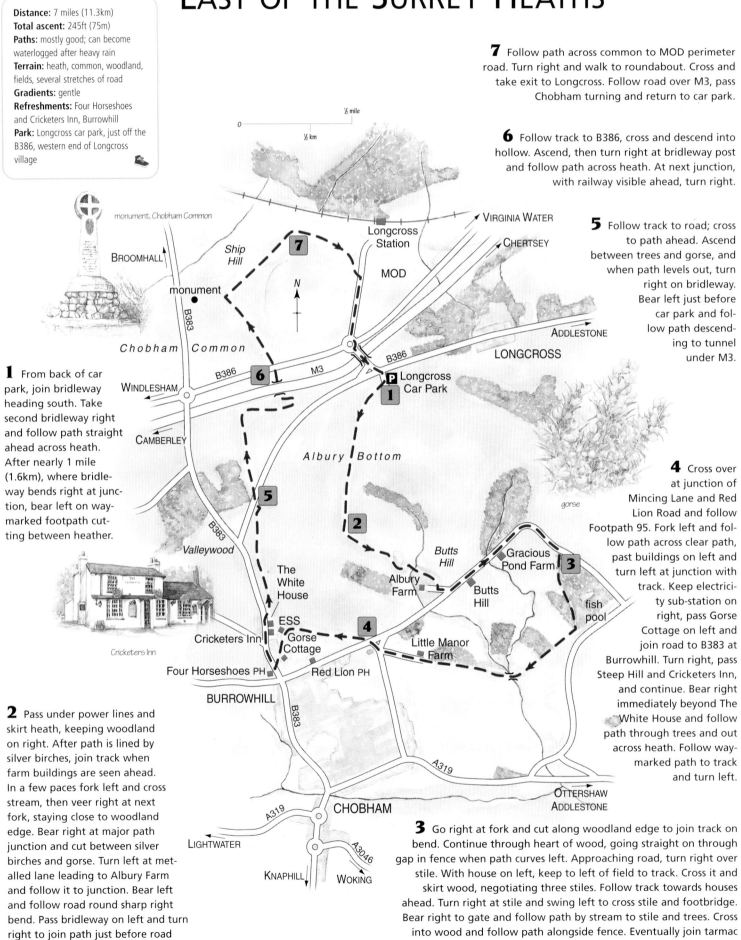

monument, Chobham Common

Cricketers Inn

7 Follow path across common to MOD perimeter road. Turn right and walk to roundabout. Cross and take exit to Longcross. Follow road over M3, pass Chobham turning and return to car park.

6 Follow track to B386, cross and descend into hollow. Ascend, then turn right at bridleway post and follow path across heath. At next junction, with railway visible ahead, turn right.

5 Follow track to road; cross to path ahead. Ascend between trees and gorse, and when path levels out, turn right on bridleway. Bear left just before car park and follow path descending to tunnel under M3.

4 Cross over at junction of Mincing Lane and Red Lion Road and follow Footpath 95. Fork left and follow path across clear path, past buildings on left and turn left at junction with track. Keep electricity sub-station on right, pass Gorse Cottage on left and join road to B383 at Burrowhill. Turn right, pass Steep Hill and Cricketers Inn, and continue. Bear right immediately beyond The White House and follow path through trees and out across heath. Follow waymarked path to track and turn left.

1 From back of car park, join bridleway heading south. Take second bridleway right and follow path straight ahead across heath. After nearly 1 mile (1.6km), where bridleway bends right at junction, bear left on waymarked footpath cutting between heather.

2 Pass under power lines and skirt heath, keeping woodland on right. After path is lined by silver birches, join track when farm buildings are seen ahead. In a few paces fork left and cross stream, then veer right at next fork, staying close to woodland edge. Bear right at major path junction and cut between silver birches and gorse. Turn left at metalled lane leading to Albury Farm and follow it to junction. Bear left and follow road round sharp right bend. Pass bridleway on left and turn right to join path just before road curves left.

3 Go right at fork and cut along woodland edge to join track on bend. Continue through heart of wood, going straight on through gap in fence when path curves left. Approaching road, turn right over stile. With house on left, keep to left of field to track. Cross it and skirt wood, negotiating three stiles. Follow track towards houses ahead. Turn right at stile and swing left to cross stile and footbridge. Bear right to gate and follow path by stream to stile and trees. Cross into wood and follow path alongside fence. Eventually join tarmac drive straight ahead to road and turn right.

Along the Bank of the Thames at Cookham

Distance: 8 miles (12.9km)
Total ascent: 316ft (96m)
Paths: mostly good; can get very wet and muddy
Terrain: riverbank, meadow, escarpment, woodland, fields
Gradients: one short steep section
Refreshments: various in Cookham; The Jolly Farmer at Cookham Dean
Park: Cookham Moor car park, west of Cookham

1 From car park walk across grass towards village. Ignore kissing gate left and follow Cookham High Street to junction with A4094. Turn left towards Wooburn and Bourne End, past Tarry Stone. Turn left through churchyard towards riverbank.

7 Keep left of September Grange and follow path to field corner. Turn right past golf course sign, keeping fence and hedge on right. Cross fairways, aim left of corrugated barns and make for railway bridge ahead. Cross it and turn right to follow grassy path by fence and hedge. Join track and follow it to road. Turn left by drive to 'Fiveways' and follow path to kissing gate. Bear right and return to Cookham Moor car park, crossing footbridge over Fleet Ditch just before it.

2 At Thames Path turn left, passing through two gates by sailing club. Continue upstream, crossing Marsh Meadow to kissing gate leading to Cock Marsh. Follow path by river, veering left under railway bridge.

3 With line of villas right, follow path back to riverbank. Pass through kissing gate and veer away from river at Ferry Cottage. Turn left at concrete drive and head towards Winter Hill. Follow track across field to pond. Pass through kissing gate to junction and turn right. Head diagonally up to gate and stile, then join road.

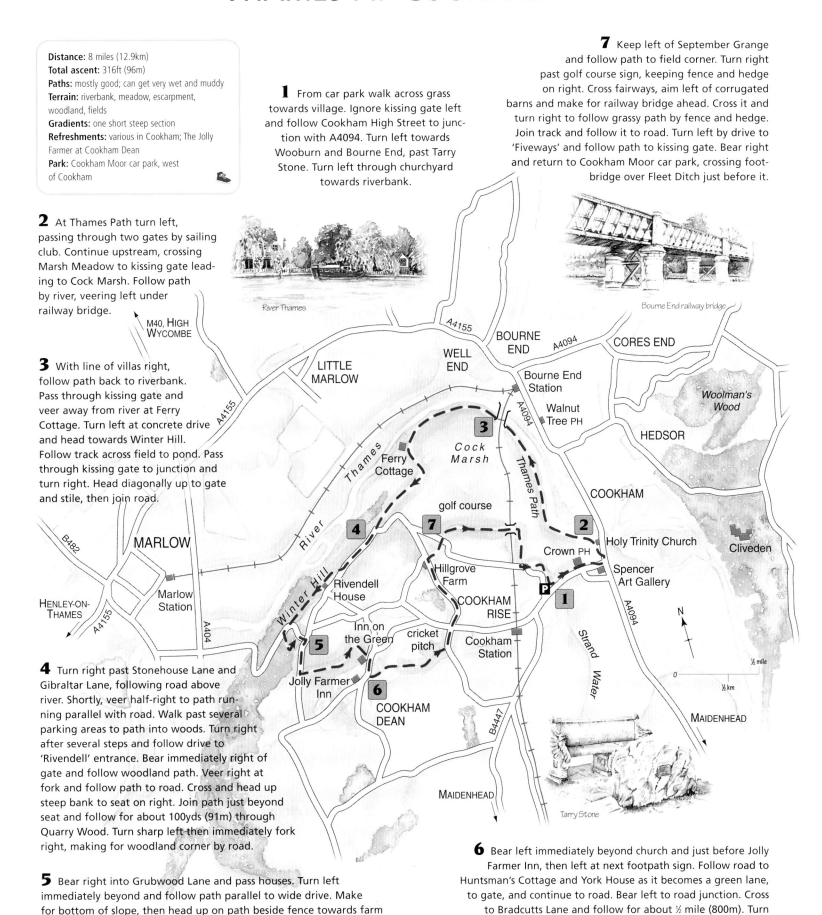

River Thames

Bourne End railway bridge

4 Turn right past Stonehouse Lane and Gibraltar Lane, following road above river. Shortly, veer half-right to path running parallel with road. Walk past several parking areas to path into woods. Turn right after several steps and follow drive to 'Rivendell' entrance. Bear immediately right of gate and follow woodland path. Veer right at fork and follow path to road. Cross and head up steep bank to seat on right. Join path just beyond seat and follow for about 100yds (91m) through Quarry Wood. Turn sharp left then immediately fork right, making for woodland corner by road.

5 Bear right into Grubwood Lane and pass houses. Turn left immediately beyond and follow path parallel to wide drive. Make for bottom of slope, then head up on path beside fence towards farm buildings. In field corner join woodland path to left. At green at Cookham Dean follow lane to war memorial. Turn right into Church Road.

6 Bear left immediately beyond church and just before Jolly Farmer Inn, then left at next footpath sign. Follow road to Huntsman's Cottage and York House as it becomes a green lane, to gate, and continue to road. Bear left to road junction. Cross to Bradcutts Lane and follow for about ½ mile (800m). Turn right at Hillgrove Farm and follow path to right, over concrete stile. Fork left to lane and cross over to footpath opposite.

HISTORIC ROUTES ACROSS THE CHILTERNS

1 From centre of village, facing Greyhound Inn, go right, up road for 300yds (273m), past footpath and sports ground on left, to bridleway on left, by Greenings Farm. Follow this gently uphill for 500yds (455m), ignoring path off left, to footpath on right. Cross stile and take this as it dog-legs up through golf course to sign visible in front of woodland at top of course.

2 Go through fence gap, cross over track and enter woodland through kissing gate. Go through woodland, turning right to join Ridgeway National Trail, continuing down to edge of wood to view Nature Reserve interpretative panel. Retrace steps 30yds (27m) and follow Ridgeway National Trail up to left. Follow this through woods, emerging at gate in open grassland above remains of Pitstone Quarry on left.

3 Follow Ridgeway path onto ridge then straight ahead across road, aiming for right side of Steps Hill ahead. As bowl of Incombe Hole cuts in from left, traverse its edge to Steps Hill and follow track to gap in fence in far corner, ignoring gate and stile on right. Follow national trail signs through woods, then descending to road. Take care here as this was once an army range and signs warn against touching unidentified objects.

> **Distance:** 7½ miles (12.1km)
> **Total ascent:** 1,100ft (335m)
> **Paths:** good; can be muddy
> **Terrain:** farmland, downland and woodland
> **Gradients:** moderate, two steeper sections
> **Refreshments:** two pubs and a shop in Aldbury
> **Park:** in the centre of Aldbury, by the pond

7 As path levels out, take right fork above cottage, then bear left into clearing by Bridgewater monument. Facing front of monument turn left and leave clearing on descending track to right of cottages. Descend quite steeply down sunken lane, staying right at any junctions, to emerge in village. Turn right on metalled road to return to village centre.

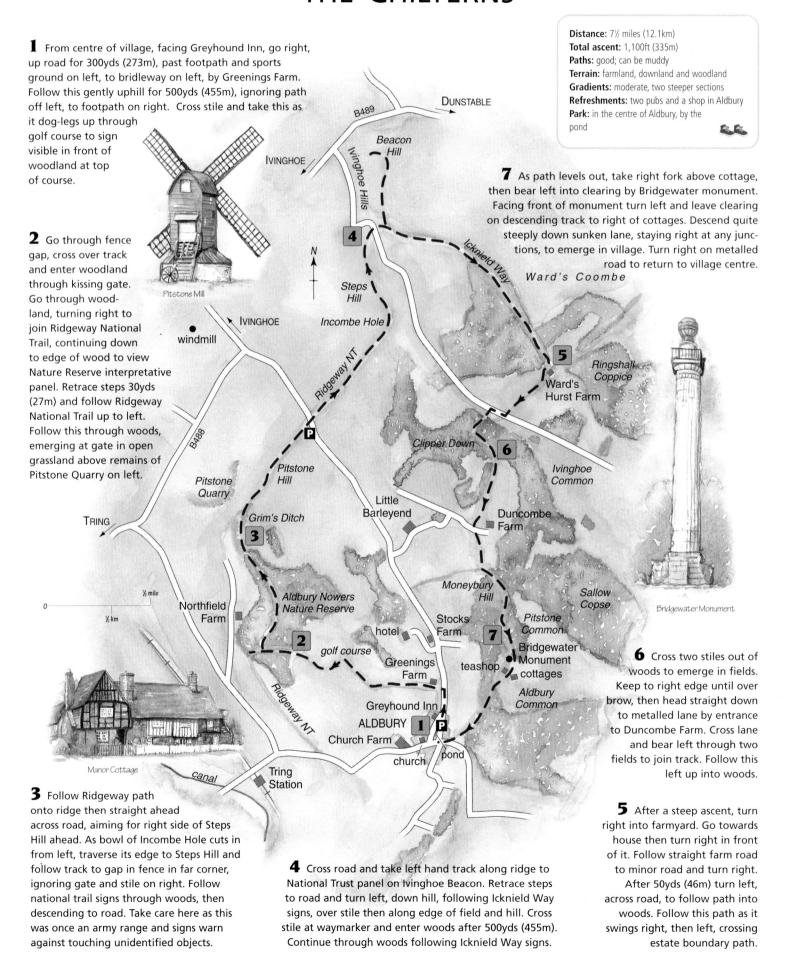

Pitstone Mill

Manor Cottage

Bridgewater Monument

4 Cross road and take left hand track along ridge to National Trust panel on Ivinghoe Beacon. Retrace steps to road and turn left, down hill, following Icknield Way signs, over stile then along edge of field and hill. Cross stile at waymarker and enter woods after 500yds (455m). Continue through woods following Icknield Way signs.

6 Cross two stiles out of woods to emerge in fields. Keep to right edge until over brow, then head straight down to metalled lane by entrance to Duncombe Farm. Cross lane and bear left through two fields to join track. Follow this left up into woods.

5 After a steep ascent, turn right into farmyard. Go towards house then turn right in front of it. Follow straight farm road to minor road and turn right. After 50yds (46m) turn left, across road, to follow path into woods. Follow this path as it swings right, then left, crossing estate boundary path.

IN LONDON'S EAST END

1 From the Tower Thistle Hotel, by Tower Bridge, turn right and walk up St Katherine's Way. Cross the road and take the right fork which is Mansell Street. Go under the subway and take exit 14 marked Middlesex Street (Petticoat Lane).

6 Turn left and follow the signs for the Thames Path and Riverside Pubs. Follow the Thames Path signs all the way, taking the riverside links off left wherever possible. Not all are continuous and you'll need to return to the road on occasions. When you reach St Katherine's Dock, follow the signs through the dock and come out on the other side at Tower Bridge.

5 Turn right and follow pedestrian signs to Canary Wharf. At Ontario Way, on your left, is a spiral staircase at the corner of a new building. Go up the stairs and walk above the road to Westferry Circus. Walk down to Riverside Pier and Canary Wharf, then turn back, go down the steps again and back to Westferry Station.

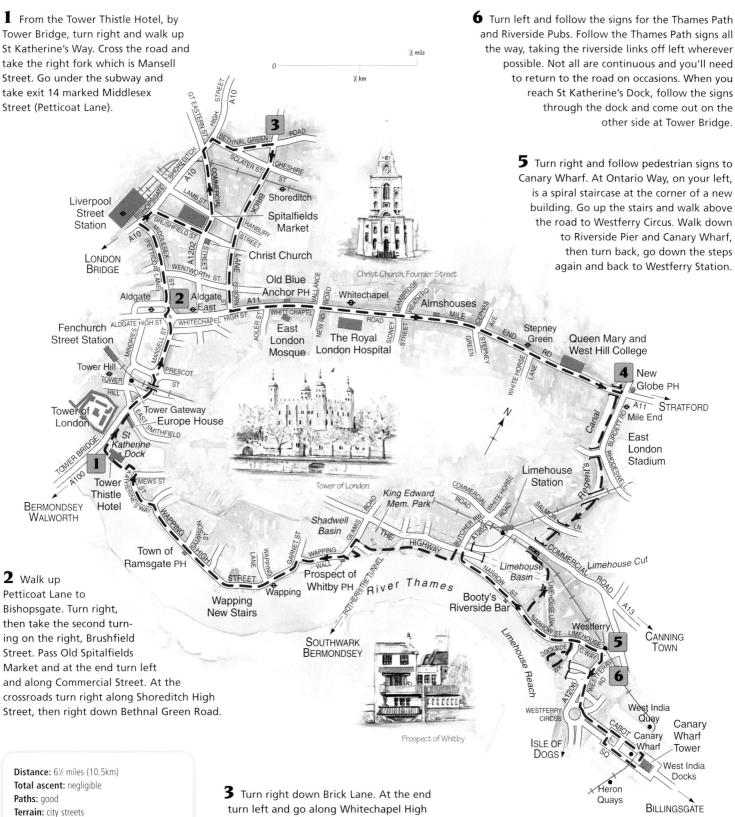

Christ Church, Fournier Street

Prospect of Whitby

Tower of London

Distance: 6½ miles (10.5km)
Total ascent: negligible
Paths: good
Terrain: city streets
Gradients: some flights of stairs
Refreshments: pubs, cafés and restaurants all along route
Park: NCP St Katherine's Way car park, next to Tower Thistle Hotel, by Tower Bridge

2 Walk up Petticoat Lane to Bishopsgate. Turn right, then take the second turning on the right, Brushfield Street. Pass Old Spitalfields Market and at the end turn left and along Commercial Street. At the crossroads turn right along Shoreditch High Street, then right down Bethnal Green Road.

3 Turn right down Brick Lane. At the end turn left and go along Whitechapel High Street, which eventually becomes Mile End Road. Keep walking ahead until you reach the bridge over the Regent's Canal. Go over the bridge and immediately turn left. Take the steps down to the canal and walk down to the left.

4 Walk down to Limehouse Basin, under the Docklands Light Railway, then turn left. Go over a bridge, through a play area then turn left at the converted wharves and walk along Barleycorn Way and Limehouse Causeway to Westferry Station.

THE HEART OF ENGLAND

THIS LARGE AREA COVERS TWO essentially disparate regions linked together only by latitude. East Anglia, which includes Norfolk, Suffolk, Cambridgeshire and Essex, has always been purely rural, its character governed by predominantly flat fertile land and the 'bracing' proximity of the North Sea. The character of Central England, which here includes Northamptonshire, Staffordshire, Derbyshire, Nottinghamshire, Lincolnshire and the counties clustering about Birmingham and the Black Country, is entirely different. Here the course of English history has made much more of an impact on the landscape.

In the centuries after the Norman Conquest, the counties of central England were the stage for the great events, the battles and upheavals that gave England its political identity – Bosworth Field, which brought the Tudor dynasty to the throne, and decisive confrontations between Roundheads and Royalists in the Civil War. It was also the heartland of the Industrial Revolution, which, despite the great 17th-century engineering feats of fen drainage, largely passed East Anglia by. In East Anglia, even now, there is little industry. The market towns are still redolent of country life and villages are just as likely to support a shop specialising in agricultural machinery as they are a greengrocer. For its seclusion alone the east of England, all too often ignored by visitors (with the exception of Cambridge), is worth visiting, but also for its distinctive character, its churches and great houses and its undiscovered countryside.

Middle England, too, has its surprises. Its great cities and towns are usually lively, if lacking in allure, and their industrial heritage has endowed them with some fascinating working museums, notably the Black Country Museum at Dudley. There is plenty of railway nostalgia, and restored canals have become attractive leisure facilities which link town and city centres with the most rural landscapes. Between the built-up areas are green belts of charming countryside, which harbour innumerable delights. There are mighty castles, as at Warwick, Kenilworth and Rockingham; Belvoir Castle is more 19th-century fantasy than a castle in the accepted sense, but is a magnificent treasure-house of works of art. There are the great estates of the Dukeries and one of the great Elizabethan palaces – Burghley House. It is barely stretching the truth to say that both areas are in some measure awaiting discovery.

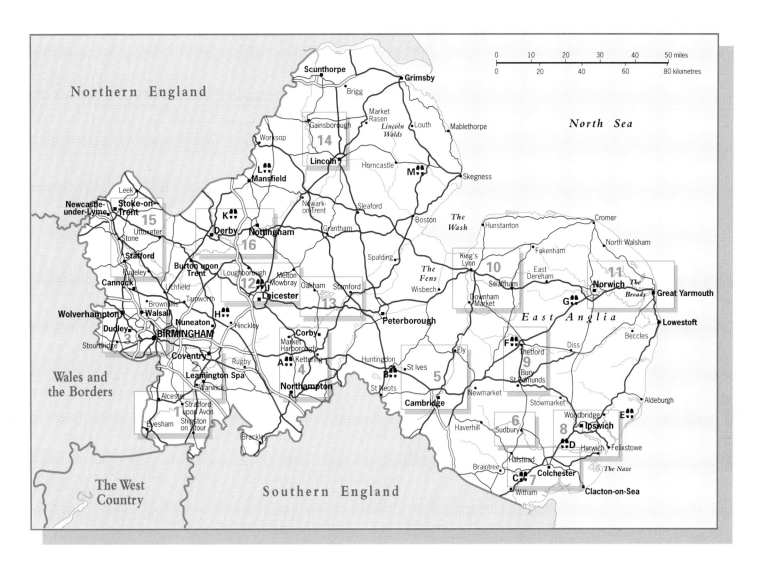

STRATFORD AND THE VALE OF EVESHAM

*B*etween the Cotswold escarpment and the Malvern Hills, the Vale of Evesham bristles with fruit trees and asparagus. Just to its north is what has become known as 'Shakespeare country', which is probably as unfair to the area as it is to the man. As well as the Shakespeare connections, there are lovely old villages, a fine mansion and two of the country's loveliest gardens.

Everyone's idea of the perfect English cottage – though considerably larger than most – this house at Shottery was the home of Anne Hathaway before her marriage to William Shakespeare. It now shows many aspects of 16th-century domestic life

Hidcote, one of the most delightful gardens in the country, was created out of nothing by Major Lawrence Johnston in the early part of the 20th century

Alcester

This small town has two stately homes – Ragley Hall and Coughton Court. The first, a 17th-century Palladian house set in 400 acres (162ha) of parkland, has remarkable baroque plasterwork by James Gibbs and *The Temptation*, a mural added between 1968 and 1982. In 1409 Coughton Court became the property of the Catholic Throckmorton family, who were thoroughly entangled in a plot in 1583, but only indirectly involved in the more famous 'Gunpowder Plot' of 1605. Protestant rioters destroyed the east wing in 1688, but there remains plenty to see, including the Tudor gatehouse, a fine collection of portraits and lovely gardens.

Charlecote Park

According to legend, the young William Shakespeare was caught poaching deer in the grounds of this Elizabethan mansion by Sir Thomas Lucy, who was to become the model for Justice Shallow in *The Merry Wives of Windsor*. True or not, the house is set in parkland which is still filled with deer and Jacob sheep. The grounds were later landscaped by 'Capability' Brown. The house, built in 1558, was much altered and

enlarged in the 19th century, but some of the original buildings, including the gatehouse, stables and brewhouse, remain unaltered. The house contains a collection of ceramics, lacquerware and furniture, much of it from the collection of William Beckford, the wealthy 18th-century eccentric, traveller and writer.

Evesham

Famous for the battle of 1265 in which Simon de Montfort was defeated by royal forces, this pleasant market town used to have an important Benedictine abbey. All that remains today is the bell tower, which was built in 1539 and considered to be the last piece of important monastic construction in the country. The lovely River Avon, which flows through the town, is busy with pleasure boats.

Hidcote Manor Garden

One of the finest gardens in the country, Hidcote, close to Mickleton and Chipping Campden, is the result of decades of painstaking nurturing. It consists of a series of small gardens, each with its own character and style, separated by walls and hedges. The gardens are famous for rare shrubs, trees, herbaceous borders and 'old' roses. The modest house (not open to the public) is a mere backdrop to the artistry of the gardens, and, in summer, to productions of period dramas which take place in the open air.

Ilmington

This charming village is Cotswold in flavour, lying at the northern extremity of this magical area. It can best be appreciated by strolling about its streets of pretty cottages and pubs. The Norman church is notable for the wooden furnishings, carved and installed in the 1930s by the craftsman

The Royal Shakespeare Company

This world-famous company was founded in 1879 in Stratford-upon-Avon, with the opening of the Shakespeare Memorial Theatre. That theatre was destroyed by fire in 1926, and the current home of the Royal Shakespeare Company (RSC) was built in 1932, around the shell of the original. The RSC has spread its horizons far and wide since then, gaining a theatre in London (the Aldwych) in 1960, and a studio theatre (the Warehouse) in 1977. Both were re-housed in the newly built Barbican in 1982.

The company has expanded within Stratford too, opening a studio theatre, The Other Place, in 1974, and a third theatre, the Swan, in 1986. With all this, as well as tours around the world, the RSC consistently manages to present the works of Shakespeare, as well as those of Shakespeare's contemporaries, and modern works. Among the RSC's artistic directors have been Sir Anthony Quayle, Sir Peter Hall and Trevor Nunn.

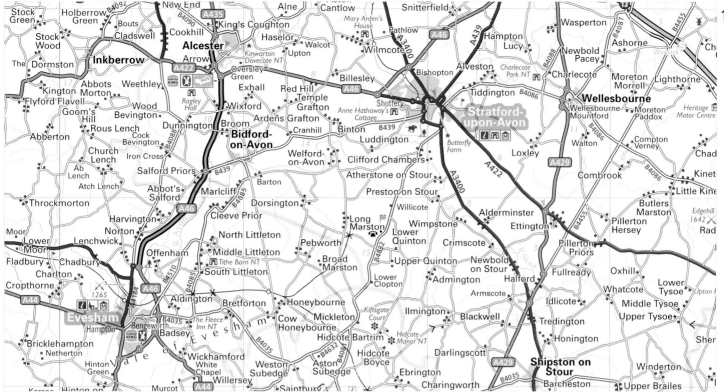

The River Stour meanders through the verdant Cotswolds countryside just outside Shipston-on-Stour

Robert Thompson, the 'mouseman', whose trademark was the little carved mouse that is to be found on each of his pieces of work.

Kiftsgate Court Garden

A near neighbour of the more famous Hidcote (above), the gardens of Kiftsgate surround a house of golden Cotswold stone with classical features. The site is dramatic, with a series of gardens tumbling down a steep Cotswold slope, giving panoramic views over the Vale of Evesham and the Malvern Hills beyond. Each area of the garden has its own character and its own plant specialities, and a network of paths links them together, beneath a cliff covered with pine trees. Kiftsgate is especially noted for its roses.

Shipston-on-Stour

Once an important centre of the wool trade, this small and bustling market town has considerable character, due in part to the interesting variety of houses that date back as far as the 17th century. Its former importance was largely derived from its position on an important coaching route; later it was a beneficiary of a 19th-century endeavour to link Stratford and Moreton by railway. Shipston-on-Stour is an attractive town for ambling and browsing around (a town trail leaflet is available from some of the local shops) and there are also delightful riverside walks.

Stratford-upon-Avon

This town owes almost everything of its modern prosperity to one man – William Shakespeare, considered by many to be the greatest among all playwrights, who was born here in 1564. In truth, although the town has some attractive features, and although the lure of Shakespeare is apparently irresistible, Stratford has lost its soul to the tourism on which it thrives.

Shakespeare's birthplace is in the town, as are Hall's Croft, where his daughter lived, and New Place where you can see the foundations and garden of his last residence. Ann Hathaway's Cottage and Mary Arden's House are just outside the town. More classically theatrical is the backstage tour of the Royal Shakespeare Theatre, with costumes, props, recordings and special displays.

Stratford also has attractions unrelated to Shakespeare, including a butterfly farm and Teddy Bear Museum. The best time to visit Stratford is in the evening, when a stroll along the river can be followed by a visit to one of the RSC theatres. Just to the south of the town is the excellent Shire Horse Centre, popular with families.

Wellesbourne

This is a small and scattered village with a working watermill on the River Dene. The mill, which is open to the public, produces stoneground flour, and there are also demonstrations of other old crafts, such as chair bodging and hurdle making.

Stratford's distinctive Shakespeare Centre is a good place to start a tour of the bard's home town

ANCIENT CASTLES AND A MODERN CATHEDRAL

Amidst the Warwickshire countryside are one or two pleasant surprises, including two of the finest castles in the country – one a romantic ruin, the other hardly changed in hundreds of years. Coventry, another place often overlooked as 'industrial', also has a wonderful modern cathedral and Roman remains. Perhaps most unexpected in this area are the pretty villages.

Berkswell

This little village has an imposing Norman church with an unusual Elizabethan porch, its upper part designed as a Priest's room, complete with stove. The Norman crypt is one of the finest in England and may have been the burial place of St Milred, Saxon Bishop of Worcester. Tucked away in a residential area is an old windmill. Something of a curiosity in this part of the world, it is in good condition and is regularly open to the public. Nearby Temple Balsall, founded by the Knights Templar, has some 17th-century almshouses and the 13th-century church and Olde Hall.

Berkswell's clergy were fortunate indeed, having this charming half-timbered (heated) room over the porch of their church, above

Less fortunate was Lady Godiva, below, remembered for riding naked through Coventry, rather than for the reason behind the gesture

Coventry

This industrial city, which surpassed Birmingham in importance until the 18th century, is forever associated with Lady Godiva who rode naked through the city in protest at the heavy taxes imposed by her Saxon husband, Earl Leofric.

Lady Godiva, or at least a statue of her, still presides over the city centre, and nearby are a number of places of interest, including Holy Trinity Church, Whitefriars Carmelite Friary, the Toy Museum in Whitefriars Gate and the 14th-century St Mary Guildhall. But Coventry is best known for its cathedrals. The medieval parish church became a cathedral in 1918, but the blitz on Coventry in 1940 left only the spire and part of the walls. After the war it was decided to build a new cathedral alongside and linked to the ruins. This ancient/modern combination has the

rare distinction among modern buildings of enjoying the general public's approval.

One of the most interesting places to visit is the Museum of British Road Transport, close to the city centre, which contains over 400 vehicles. Among these are the great British marques of cars, motorcycles and buses. There is also an impressive model collection and a reconstruction of the blitz. Air transport is represented at the Midland Air Museum at Coventry Airport in Baginton.

Also in Baginton is Lunt Roman Fort, a reconstruction, based on archaeological evidence, of a Roman fort as it would have been in AD 64, just after the Roman invasion. Re-enactments of Roman military manoeuvres take place here and an audio-cassette tour is available.

Hampton Lucy

This is one of the prettiest villages in Warwickshire and is noted for its church of St Peter *ad Vicula* (in Chains). The list of rectors goes back to 1279, but the present building is much more recent. In the 1820s a bequest endowed funds for the embellishment of the old church, but it was

Coventry Cathedral is a happy blend of ancient and modern, and both elements are supremely impressive in their own way

Tourist Information Centres

Coventry: Bayley Lane (tel: 024 7622 7264)
Kenilworth: The Library, 11 Smalley Place (tel: 01926 852595)
Royal Leamington Spa: Royal Pump Room, The Parade (tel: 01926 742762)
Warwick: The Court House, Jury Street (tel: 01926 492212)

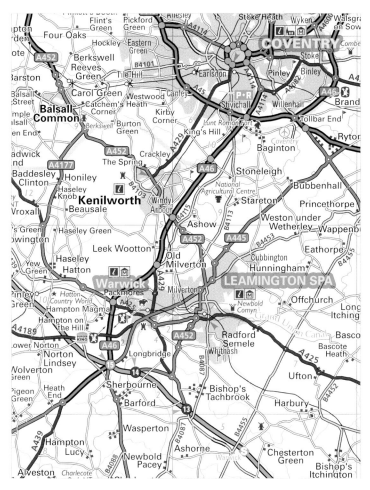

exudes something of the elegance of that period, with Regency terraces and crescents. More hints of its genteel past can be found in the pump room, in Jephson Gardens, laid out in the early 19th century, the Old Town Hall, the Assembly Rooms and in Landsdowne Crescent and Circus. There are a few oddities too, including the Mill Bridge and the Elephant Wash, where travelling circus proprietors brought their animals to be scrubbed.

Warwick

This small town is of great historical importance, noted above all for its magnificent castle, which is in a miraculous state of preservation. Set atop a grassy embankment, with huge towers, ramparts and crenellated walls, it is every child's vision of a medieval castle. Until 1978, when it was sold to Madame Tussauds, it was the seat of the Earls of Warwick.

The ensuing changes (waxwork tableaux, complete with sound effects) are difficult to ignore, as are the crowds, but the castle's aspect and grounds remain extremely impressive.

A short walk brings you to the town centre, an attractive mix of Georgian and medieval architecture. Here you will find the Oken's House and Doll Museum, the church of St Mary, with its glorious Beauchamp Chapel, the well-preserved almshouses of the Lord Leycester Hospital near the city's Westgate, the Warwickshire Museum in the 17th-century market hall and the medieval buildings of Mill Street.

Ufton Fields

There is a fascinating nature reserve on the site of an old limestone quarry here, protecting some of the more vulnerable species of British flora and fauna. According to the season you can see cowslips and orchids, butterflies, dragonflies, grass snakes and toads, all in a natural setting.

Warwick Castle, towering above the River Avon, was never far removed from the power struggles and the decisive events of past centuries, some of which are recreated in a special high-tech exhibition

decided to erect a new one instead. The first architect was Thomas Rickman, but later additions were made by Sir Gilbert Scott and the result is considered an architectural gem.

Kenilworth

Although it is Warwick that tends to receive all the plaudits, the castle at Kenilworth should not be missed. Despite being severely damaged during the Civil War, the red sandstone castle is in a reasonable state of preservation and is highly evocative of the Middle Ages. The nearby re-opened Stoneleigh Abbey displays architectural styles spanning 600 years.

Leicester's building and the Lobby of Kenilworth Castle look over the smooth lawns of the Inner Court

Royal Leamington Spa

Once a fashionable spa town whose zenith was reached during the late 18th and early 19th centuries, Royal Leamington Spa still

ENGLAND'S INDUSTRIAL HEARTLAND

There is no reason these days to be put off by the word 'industrial'. The major cities and towns of central England have to some extent dusted off their coal-associated reputations and are capitalising on their rich industrial heritage. Birmingham is not alone in become a lively centre of culture and entertainment. The surrounding countryside also has its own allure.

Birmingham still has an extensive canal network, and areas like the Gas Street basin, above, are preserved as a reminder of the days when the city depended on them for transporting goods

Selly Manor, below, is one of two medieval houses re-erected in Bournville and now forming a museum

Birmingham

Britain's second largest city is sometimes thought of as an industrial centre with little to offer the visitor. While it is not a city of obvious charm, there is a lot to seek out, and it is a vibrant cultural centre, with exceptionally good nightlife.

The city centres on Victoria Square and Chamberlain Square, which are dominated by the Council House, the Town Hall of 1834 and the excellent City Museum and Art Gallery, which houses an excellent collection of Pre-Raphaelite art. The main shopping area runs along New Street to the City Plaza and the Bull Ring, although the Jewellery Quarter and the wholesale clothing markets are also a magnet to shoppers. The award-winning waterfront complex at Brindleyplace is full of bustling bars and restaurants.

Birmingham's industrial heritage can be explored along its immense canal system or by visiting the New Discover Centre at Millennium Point. Other attractions include the Barber Institute of Fine Arts, the Birmingham Railway Museum, with steam train rides, and the National Sealife Centre. Transport is also on display at the National Motorcycle Museum at Bickenhill, with over 650 machines; in contrast are the Birmingham Botanical Gardens and Cannon Hill Park, both at Edgbaston.

Bournville

The most interesting of Birmingham's many suburban towns is a place better known around the world for its chocolate. Bournville is the home of Cadbury's, and owes its very existence to the Quaker Cadbury family who planned the village in 1879 to provide decent working and living conditions for their employees. The main attraction is Cadbury World, attached to the factory, where an exhibition, complete with sounds and smells, relates the history and manufacture of chocolate. Here visitors can sample the product and buy it at reduced prices.

Selly Manor consists of two half-timbered houses which were moved the mile from Bournbrook to Bournville by George Cadbury. Restored and opened to the public, they contain one of the finest displays of crafted furniture in the country.

Clent Hills

This stretch of windswept upland is a wonderful area for walking and offers the finest views in the area. At the summit, just over 1,000ft (305m) high, are four large stones, a curious folly created by landscape gardener and minor poet William Shenstone, who lived 2 miles (3.2km) away at Halesowen. To the north-east of Clent is the small 13th-century chapel marking the site of the martyrdom of St Kenelm, the Mercian prince who was buried at Winchcombe in Gloucestershire and whose shrine became one of the most important medieval places of pilgrimage.

Dudley

Dudley is dominated by castle ruins which look out across seven counties. Part of the castle is Norman, and there is an audio-visual display and visitor centre. Within the 40 acres (16ha) of grounds is Dudley's

The City of Birmingham Orchestra

Birmingham has had its orchestra only since 1920, when it was founded by a group of citizens led by Neville Chamberlain. It was the first to receive a municipal grant and its opening concert was conducted by Sir Edward Elgar in the Town Hall. The orchestra soon became internationally respected, but although the principal conductor in 1925, Sir Adrian Boult, was promised a new concert hall, it was not until 1991 that the Symphony Hall finally materialised. Sir Simon Rattle did much to bring international renown to the orchestra, which now performs here more than 50 times a year. The current Principal Conductor is Sakari Oramo, and under his stewardship the orchestra tours extensively all over the world and makes regular recordings.

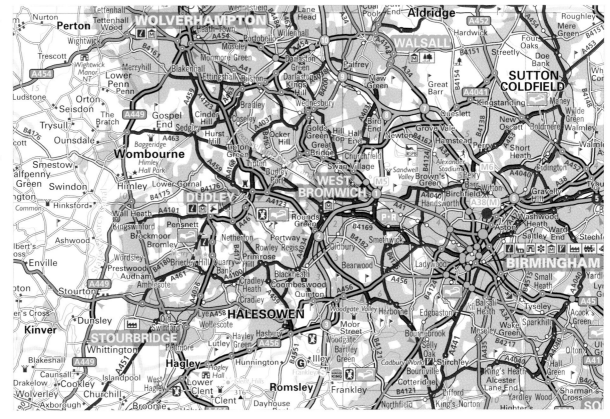

well-known zoo, which houses one of Britain's largest collections of animals. The Dudley Museum and Art Gallery is also worth a visit, and hosts excellent temporary exhibitions.

A mile from the town centre is the award-winning Black Country Museum, a recreation of an industrial village, with shops and a pub, cottages and a chapel. Chain making demonstrations take place in an authentic workshop, and there is a canal dock with narrowboats and trips into the Dudley Tunnel. Visitors can also go underground in an 1850s mine. Near by is Himley Hall Park, landscaped by 'Capability' Brown, and the Wren's Nest Nature Reserve, widely known for the fossils found here – many of which can now be seen in Dudley's museum.

The hardware store at the Black Country Museum is one of the most evocative places on the site – there is usually at least one visitor who remembers using the items on display

Kinver Edge

This upland area of sandstone heath and woodland is all that remain of a huge forest that once extended across this area. There are remains of an Iron-Age fort in the north, from where there are fine views, but of greatest interest are the old rock dwellings which were occupied as recently as the 1960s by besom broom makers. Now rather bare, their former occupants made real homes out of them with the addition of bricks and windows.

Stourbridge

Close to Birmingham, Stourbridge is noted for the production of crystal and glass, although it was iron production that originally put Stourbridge on the map – the first steam locomotive to run on rails in America was built here. Visits can be arranged to various glass factories, whilst the Broadfield House Glass Museum at Kingswinford provides a historical background. The Stuart Crystal and Red House Glass Cone Museum features a 100-ft (30.5-m) high glass cone that was built in 1790.

Wolverhampton

Although not a town that could be described as aesthetically pleasing, Wolverhampton is not entirely devoid of interest. It has an enterprising Museum and Art Gallery, which reopened in 2001 following refurbishment, and two interesting houses. Moseley Old Hall, with 17th-century formal gardens, is the Elizabethan house in which Charles II hid after the Battle of Worcester. Wightwick Manor is a 19th-century building in Pre-Raphaelite style. Near by is Cannock Chase, the largest area of unspoilt countryside in the county.

Historic King Edward VI Grammar School at Stourbridge has some finely detailed stonework

CHURCHES, CROSSES AND RESILIENT TOWNS

Northamptonshire is one of those counties that seems both familiar and remote, not far from everything and yet curiously amorphous. In fact, it is filled with places of interest, including some delightful villages that are very close to the Cotswolds in character, and some particularly fine houses and estates, all reflections of the area's location at the heart of English history.

Tourist Information Centres

Corby: Festival Hall, George Street (tel: 01536 407507)
Kettering: The Coach House, Sheep Street (tel: 01536 410266)
Northampton: Mr Grant's House, St Giles Square (tel: 01604 622677)
Wellingborough: Wellingborough Library, Pebble Lane (tel: 01933 276412)

Kirby Hall is a beautiful Elizabethan manor house, set in extensive gardens that were among the finest in England in their 17th-century heyday

Corby

The growth of the steel industry transformed Corby from a village to a large town, but the closure of the steelworks in 1980 had an appalling impact, from which the town is still recovering. Its centre is mostly rather depressing but there are incipient efforts to improve matters. Corby has a pleasant location at the edge of Rockingham Forest, where there are lovely walks at Stoke Wood and Stoke Albany. Rockingham Castle is near by, impressively overlooking Rockingham village. The town is also well located for Kirby Hall, Deene Park and King's Wood, a nature reserve of ancient woodland.

Holdenby House

Built by Queen Elizabeth I's Lord Chancellor, Sir Christopher Hatton in the late 16th century, Holdenby was then the largest house in England. Subsequently it became the prison of Charles I, where he was kept under guard for five months after his defeat in the Civil War. Today you can visit Rosemary Verey's Elizabethan Garden and the 17th-century farmstead, which houses rare breeds of animals. There is also a falconry centre and armoury.

Kelmarsh

Designed by James Gibbs, Kelmarsh Hall was built in the 1720s and is one of the finest and most unspoilt stately homes in the county, one of only two surviving houses by this talented architect. The south lodge gates, designed in the late 18th century, were made only in the 1960s upon the discovery of the original plans.

Kettering

This town, whose growth has depended upon leather and the quarrying of ironstone, though visually undistinguished, is not without interest. The Alfred East Art Gallery is named after the Royal Academician who bequeathed many of his paintings to the town. Close by is the Manor House Museum, with exhibits ranging from a mummified cat to a car built in Kettering at the turn of the century. Wicksteed Leisure Park is a giant playground founded by the industrialist and philanthropist Charles Wicksteed in 1920. It has over 50 rides, many original.

Lamport

The family home of the Isham baronets between 1560 and 1976, Lamport Hall is essentially Palladian in style and contains a fine art collection. It is set in spacious grounds, complete with alpine garden. A 19th-century Isham is thought to have been the first to import garden gnomes into Britain, from Germany.

Northampton

This is a classic case of a town with a considerable heritage that has suffered, first in a fire (which destroyed most of the medieval buildings) and then at the heavy hands of redevelopment. Despite this, the

Naseby

The Battle of Naseby in 1645 is considered to be the most important engagement of the English Civil War, and perhaps the most crucial for modern Britain. The Royalist forces of Charles I had, until that point, been holding their own, but at Naseby they were beaten decisively by Cromwell's New Army, thus securing the future of Parliamentary democracy. The battlefield, 14 miles (22.5km) north of Northampton, is marked with a monument at the point where Cromwell's army gathered to face the Royalists on Dust Hill. At Purlieu Farm is the Naseby Battle and Farm Museum, with a miniature reconstruction of the battle (and taped commentary) and an exhibition of the military paraphernalia of the era.

The memorial overlooking the site of the Battle of Naseby, just outside Northampton

Eleanor Crosses

When Queen Eleanor, the wife of Edward I, died in Lincoln in 1290, her body was carried to London for burial. At each stopping place on the journey a stone cross was erected, of which two remain, at Geddington and Hardingstone. The Hardingstone cross is incomplete, but dramatically sited at the top of the London Road outside Northampton, whilst the cross at Geddington is less time worn and is picturesquely located in the centre of a charming village.

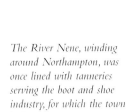

The River Nene, winding around Northampton, was once lined with tanneries serving the boot and shoe industry, for which the town is famous

city centre is not without interest. The central market square, one of the largest in Britain, is surrounded by some handsome houses, including Welsh House, which escaped the fire. Near by is the Guildhall, a Gothic extravaganza decorated with events from Northampton's history. All Saints Church is considered to be the finest 17th-century church outside London, and Northampton has several other religious masterpieces: St Peter's, probably the finest Norman church in the county, and the Church of the Holy Sepulchre, the largest and best preserved of only four round churches in Britain. The Central Museum and Art Gallery specialises in footwear, a long-established local industry.

Triangular Lodge

This is close to being a folly, but it is no idle fancy, for it was built by Sir Thomas Tresham in 1593 for serious reasons. It is a stone manifestation of his Catholicism, an affirmation of his beliefs which were not diminished by his imprisonment for 13 years, charged with being a papist. The building takes its name from the fact that everything about it is triangular; its is constructed according to a factor of three.

Wellingborough

Like Northampton, Wellingborough too had a fire, in 1738, which destroyed much of its medieval heart, but it has escaped some of the worst of modern development. A 15th-century thatched ironstone barn has been restored and there are two handsome old inns in the centre. The Heritage Centre, next to a park that was once the swannery of Crowland Abbey, is dedicated to local history, and also serves light refreshments. The Walks is a relaxing area of promenades, shaded by trees, along the River Nene.

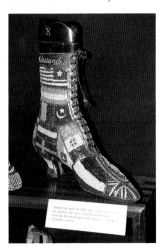

A fascinating array of footwear throughout the ages – considered to be the finest collection of its kind in the world – is on display at Northampton's Central Museum and Art Gallery

See Walk A page 182
Around the Civil War Battlefield at Naseby

CAMBRIDGE AND THE FENLANDS

Outside and beyond Cambridge there is a world that is largely unknown to the majority of visitors. This is a pity, for though the county is not blessed with a dramatic landscape, there are plenty of gems to discover in fen and fold. Where hills rise out of the flat land there is usually something special built upon them, most notably at Ely, and the fens have a singular wildness.

Ely

Ely, an island of upland in a sea of fenland, was an outpost of Saxon resistance to the Norman invaders who built a cathedral here to celebrate their eventual victory, complementing the abbey that had stood here since AD 673. The cathedral remains the highlight of a visit to Ely, although the city is also home to some of the finest remaining medieval architecture in the country. Work began on the cathedral in 1081 and, among the many additions made over the centuries, perhaps the most impressive are the 14th-century Octagon, an engineering miracle, and the Lady Chapel, with its wonderful stonework.

Among many fine buildings in Ely, Prior Crauden's Chapel and Cromwell House (where Oliver Cromwell lived for many years) are especially interesting, and there are plenty more along the High Street and down on the banks of the Ouse. There are two museums – the Ely Museum and, in the cathedral, the Stained Glass Museum, with examples covering the 14th century to the present day, from all parts of Britain.

There are lovely walks beside the wide River Ouse in Ely, one of which leads to the magnificent cathedral

King's College Chapel in Cambridge is a masterpiece of Gothic architecture and its fan vaulting is among the finest in Europe

Anglesey Abbey

In the village of Lode, east of Cambridge, Anglesey Abbey is part of a former Augustinian foundation that dates back to 1135. After the dispersal of the monks there were a number of owners, including Thomas Hobson who was the inspiration for the notion of 'Hobson's choice', meaning no choice at all. The house contains a marvellously eclectic collection of art and artefact that was part of Lord Fairhaven's collection. In the grounds, which belong to the National Trust, 18th-century Lode Watermill is still grinding corn.

Cambridge

Retaining the atmosphere of a rural market town, Cambridge is nevertheless dominated by its university, which grew up along the banks of the River Cam, west of one of the principal shopping areas.

It is possible to visit several of the colleges, although they are subject to restricted opening hours. The most celebrated, because of its chapel, is King's College, though most of its original 15th-century college buildings now house the university administration offices. The chapel is a marvel, however, and certainly inspires the soul to leap to the rafters. The largest of the colleges is Trinity and its Great Court is surrounded by a magnificent collection of Tudor architecture, including the splendid Wren Library.

St John's College has a replica of Venice's Bridge of Sighs, while the university's oldest building is the School of Pythagoras, dating from 1200. Magdalene College has on display the diary of the distinguished former student, Samuel Pepys; the Old Court of Corpus Christi College is where Marlowe wrote *Tamburlaine* and Queen's College boasts a galleried Cloister Court and half-timbered President's Lodge. On Trumpington Street is the Fitzwilliam Museum which contains a giddy array of exhibits from many of the great civilisations, including European, Chinese and Korean porcelain and paintings from all the great European masters.

The Backs are the water meadows along the Cam, facing the rear of the colleges – a delightful place for strolling and punting, especially in spring or autumn.

Hemingford Grey

This is one of the county's most attractive villages, with some fine houses in the area of the High Street, and the church of St James charmingly located by the river.

Tourist Information Centres

Cambridge: Wheeler Street (tel: 01223 322640)
Ely: Oliver Cromwell's House, 29 St Mary's Street (tel: 01353 662062)
Huntingdon: The Library, Princes Street (tel: 01480 388588)

Duxford

Duxford is the home of a branch of the Imperial War Museum, housed at an airfield which was an important Spitfire base during the Battle of Britain – events of those days have been simulated in the Operations Room. There are over 180 historic aircraft here, as well as midget submarines, armoured fighting vehicles and other large exhibits. Duxford Aviation Society's collection of civil aircraft includes the prototype *Concorde 001*, and there is an exhibition on the US 8th Air Force. Major flying displays are held in summer and pleasure flights are available on summer weekends, or visitors can keep their feet almost on the ground in a flight simulator.

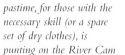

A favourite summer pastime, for those with the necessary skill (or a spare set of dry clothes), is punting on the River Cam in Cambridge

The Manor House was built in 1150 and is thought to be the oldest continuously inhabited house in the country. Substantial parts of the original Norman house remain, and the garden has been filled with roses and topiary chess pieces.

Madingley

A few miles to the west of Cambridge, Madingley is close to the huge American War Cemetery at Coton, over 30 acres (12ha) donated by the university, where rows of white marble crosses commemorate the 3,812 Americans who lost their lives while stationed in Britain during World War II. A long Portland stone wall is inscribed with the names of over 5,000 of those whose graves are unknown.

The 16th-century Hall, now part of the University, is where Edward VII stayed as an undergraduate.

Wandlebury

The Gog Magog Hills, just south-east of Cambridge, are named after the legendary giants, images of whom were supposed to have been carved into them. The Iron-Age fort crowning the hills was probably built in the 4th century BC and abandoned in the 1st century AD, when the Romans arrived. A wooded area, with lovely walks, includes a section of Roman road.

Wicken Fen

Near the village of Soham, Wicken Fen is over 750 acres (304ha) of undrained fenland. Owned by the National Trust, it gives a splendid insight into how East Anglia would have been before the 17th century. One of the most important 'wetland' reserves in Western Europe, it is also possible to visit a Fenman's cottage and the only complete Fenland windpump. Comprising reed and sedge, an open mere and areas of alder and buckthorn, a nature trail affords the ideal opportunity for discovering the fens.

See Walk B page 183
The Huntingdon Home of Oliver Cromwell

The wetlands of the Fens have been drained for agriculture since Romans times, making Wicken Fen a rare untouched survivor

WATERWAYS OF CENTRAL ENGLAND

Before the proliferation of the canal system in the late 18th and 19th centuries, the movement of freight across large distances had been a practical impossibility, effectively limited to something like 12 miles (19.3km) by both the cost and the poor state of roads. The only exceptions were those areas lucky enough to be on one of the larger rivers like the Severn and, in the eastern part of the country, the Ouse.

Attempts to find a way of improving on river navigation date back at least to the days of the Romans who constructed artificial waterways near Lincoln and Cambridge.

From the 12th century onwards the idea was resurrected and small scale navigation allowed the passage of narrow barges here and there. The first pound locks in Britain were introduced in 1566 (having already been in existence in Holland for 200 years), after which the domestication of rivers, such as the Great Ouse, became much easier and their development and use increased throughout the 17th century. These projects were not generally government financed, but were instead in the form of investment by merchants, who were driven by the expectation of eventually being able to make a profit.

THE CANAL AGE

Large-scale construction was nonetheless surprisingly slow to get off the ground considering that most of the technical problems had already been overcome in the 17th century; the first long-distance canal was built only in the 1730s, in Ulster, running between Newry

and the Upper Bann. However, it was really with the construction of the Bridgewater Canal, designed by James Brindley, that canals began to proliferate all over the country. Brindley gained his ideas through his experience as a millwright in

Whole families would once live and work on the narrowboats which are so popular today for holidays

Leek, Staffordshire – the Bridgewater and The Trent and Mersey were his two greatest achievements.

The success of these canals encouraged the formation of joint stock companies to build others. Whilst this certainly led to a flurry of activity, it also created problems. These companies built their canals as they saw fit and according to local conditions. The lack of coordination meant that some canals were open to just about any size of craft, whilst others were restricted to narrow boats only. Nonetheless, it became clear that canals were at least of great use locally and construction continued until the 1830s, at which point nearly every town of any importance was within striking distance of a stretch of navigable water.

Central England and East Anglia were two of the areas where waterways were particularly important. The Midlands were at the heart of the Industrial Revolution and there are still 130 miles (209.1km) of navigable canal in Birmingham and the Black Country alone. With Wolverhampton and Cannock to the north and Stourbridge to the south, in its great days this area had 212 working locks, with 550 factory side basins, forming the greatest concentration of industrial canals in the country. In its heyday canal transport carried eight million tons a year, and even as late as the 1950s a million tons a year were still being transported on the waterways.

The Grand Union Canal, 300 miles (482.8km) long and as important as its name suggests, links London with Birmingham and, had it not been for the outbreak of World War II, might have seen wide boats of 66 tons pushing along its waters.

A spur breaks away from the Grand Union near Daventry in Northamptonshire and runs for 66 miles (106.3km) to link up with the River Trent. This in

turn is linked to the Fossdyke near Lincoln and to the Wash, also served by the River Nene which is itself linked to the Grand Union via Northampton and Wellingborough.

DECLINE AND REBIRTH

Ironically, it was this very comprehensiveness of the canal system that led to the canal's downfall. Waterways were used to transport the coal that powered the steam locomotives on the railways, which were new, much faster and more efficient. Canals were gradually abandoned, and in some cases drained in order to become railbeds. With one or two major exceptions, commercial traffic has all but died and canals have assumed a new role as leisure amenities. And not only on the water – the old tow paths make excellent walk and cycle ways and many tourist offices produce routes and trails to follow.

In Norfolk the greatest nav-

Top: Birmingham's Gas Street Basin is part of a canal-side redevelopment; above: the traditional dress of the boatmen, c1900–1910

igation is that based on the Great Ouse, one of Britain's greatest rivers. It was first made navigable from the sea upstream to Bedford in the 17th century, when the surrounding land was drained by the Dutchman, Cornelius Vermuyden, creating new waterways. But its commercial usefulness had vanished by the late 19th century, and by the turn of the century much of it lay derelict. Today, after many vicissitudes, it has been reopened through the enthusiasm of the Great Ouse Restoration Society.

Colourful craft on the Shropshire Union Canal near Colemere

MEDIEVAL TOWNS AND VILLAGES

These lands on either side of the Stour really do look as if time has passed them by. Lavenham, Sudbury and Clare are full of wonderful old half-timbered houses and, though in 'deep Suffolk', their rich churches and fine houses show they were once leading centres of trade, and castle remains at Clare and Castle Hedingham are evidence of former strategic importance.

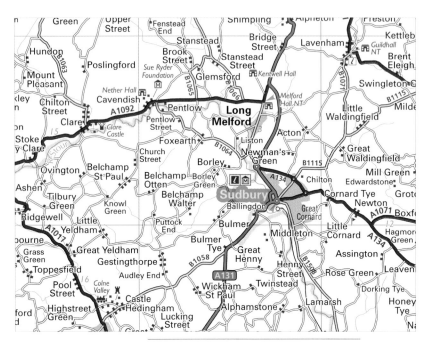

The Belchamps

Belchamp Otton, Belchamp St Paul and Belchamp Walter are three small Essex villages which, along with the picturesquely named Foxearth, Gestingthorpe and Little Yeldham, lie in a quiet, rolling area of countryside between Sudbury and Haverhill, south and west of the Stour which is the county boundary. Walter is the most attractive of them, with 18th-century Hall, 15th-century church, and fields running down to the Belchamp Brook. 'Belchamp' sounds like a Norman-French description of those fields, but apparently has an earlier, Anglo-Saxon meaning: house with 'roof made of beams'.

This ornate and descriptive town sign leaves visitors in no doubt about which town they are about to enter

Castle Hedingham

One cannot but feel that the de Veres, to whom the Conqueror gave Hedingham in 1066 or soon after, had a sound sense of priorities. Within two years they had planted a vineyard, but it was 50 years before they got round to building the castle – a square Norman keep with two 100ft (30.5m) corner towers still standing – which commanded the trade route along the Colne Valley a short distance to the west. The church is largely Tudor, within a fine west tower and hammerbeam roof; the triangular open space to its east was the site of the medieval market.

Cavendish

Although such perfection can sometimes seem eerie, a village like this nonetheless exerts a certain fascination. Thatched cottages cluster in the shadow of an ancient church, and there are several pubs, a vineyard and the Sue Ryder Foundation Museum with memorabilia illustrating the reason for its existence.

Clare and Stoke-by-Clare

Clare was once an important town, as shown by the remains here of the first Austin Friars priory in England, its Norman castle mound, with an impressive fragment of what must have been a massive keep, and its fine, largely 14th-century

Preserving Suffolk

Not all preservationists are backward-looking, as proved by the Suffolk Preservation Society, based at the delightful 14th-century Little Hall in Lavenham. Founded in 1929, the society works to conserve the quality of the countryside and buildings of Suffolk, while ensuring that necessary new development is sympathetic and environmentally sustainable. The Society also tries to set a practical example. In the 1970s it turned property developer and used a gift of a piece of land at Wetherden to show how new houses could fit into an existing village. Its sister organisation, the Suffolk Building Preservation Trust, restored the attractive Pakenham Watermill which is open to visitors, grinds corn and sells the flour.

The Square in Castle Hedingham has some fine examples of ancient colour-washed buildings

church. Clare is still recognisably a town, rather than a village, its harmonious townscape a feast for the eye, with buildings of substance that reflect its former commercial status. Note especially the pargeted 15th-century Ancient House adjoining the spacious churchyard.

The Tudor Rose brick maze was added in the mid-1980s at Kentwell Hall, where the owners specialise in taking visitors back to its 15th-century origins

Kentwell Hall

A fine Tudor house just to the north of Long Melford, Kentwell is the home of J Patrick Phillips QC and his family, and has a very 'lived in' feel to it. The Phillipses have been undertaking a phased restoration project for both house, gardens and farm and have won several awards for their re-creations of Tudor domestic life on selected weekends in summer. There are also 1940s re-creations on several summer weekends. House and grounds are open Easter to October.

Lavenham

Lavenham prospered on the wool trade in the 14th and 15th centuries, leaving a legacy of fine medieval buildings. The Wool Hall, pictured here, is among the most impressive

Even from the main road Lavenham looks old and interesting, but you need to stop and explore on foot. It is emphatically not a village, but a town which grew rich on wool and in Henry VIII's reign was reckoned to be the 14th wealthiest town in England. Standing in the hilltop market place, you are surrounded by signs of that past wealth – the beautiful, timber-framed, 15th-century Corpus Christi Guildhall, built for one of the town's four medieval guilds (now National Trust), and Little Hall, also timber-framed and appropriately headquarters of the lively and impressive Suffolk Preservation Society (SPS).

Round the corner in Barn Street is another fine timber-framed building, Molet House, then down Shilling Street, past a row of higgledy-piggledy but well-preserved weavers' cottages, comes yet another, Shilling Old Grange. And so it goes on. The SPS has published an excellent illustrated walk from the market place to the church and back, with drawings of the Tudor and later buildings, including the magnificent church of SS Peter and Paul, on the eastern edge of the village.

Long Melford

Living up to its name, this village is strung out along a main street of about a mile (1.6km). Melford means 'ford by the mill' – that mill being mentioned in the Domesday Book. At the south end of the main street stands the 18th-century Melford Place, followed by the 15th-century Cadges's House and a whole procession of timber-framed and Georgian houses, until you come to delicious Melford Green, with the late 15th-century Holy Trinity Church, which Pevsner called 'one of the most moving parish churches of England, large, proud and noble.' It, too, is long, with a splendid nave and clerestory.

Among other buildings round the green are the 16th-century Trinity Hospital and, from the same century, Melford Hall, turreted and mullioned in warm red brick. Queen Elizabeth I was a guest here in 1578 and, on the outside at least, the house is little altered since that time. It has an Elizabethan Long Gallery, a dramatic Georgian staircase, a Regency library and a Victorian bedroom, and there is a pretty two-storey Tudor pavilion, possibly a guardhouse, in the garden.

Sudbury

A prosperous market town above the River Stour, Sudbury has its focus round St Peter's Church, a large church expressing the confidence and solidity of a rich wool town. Market Hill descends towards the bridge past a statue of the artist Thomas Gainsborough, who was born at 46 Gainsborough Street, a handsome early-18th century house, where, perhaps, his artistic achievement was stimulated by such a beautiful environment.

Tourist Information Centres

Lavenham: Lady Street (seasonal) (tel: 01787 248207)
Sudbury: Town Hall, Market Hill (tel: 01787 881320)

Gainsborough's House in Sudbury has more of the artist's work than any other gallery. It is displayed here in his birthplace amongst furniture of the period

ROMANS AND OYSTERS

Colchester was an important town even before the Roman invasion, mostly because it stood on a good, defensible hill above the Colne. This is just one of a series of rivers that divide up the country behind the coast and keep the land in something of a timewarp. Further inland you find gentle countryside, dotted with attractive, bustling market towns and villages.

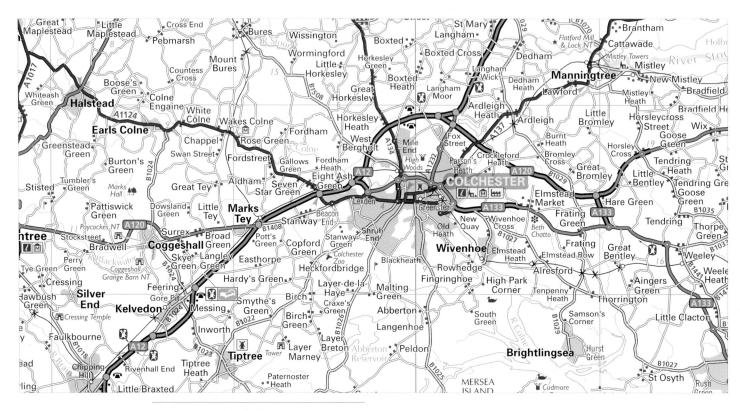

Brightlingsea

The estuary of the River Colne at Brightlingsea is popular with sailors, who have lots of creeks to explore upstream

A quiet little port and seaside resort islanded among marshes near the mouth of the River Colne, Brightlingsea may look faded and forgotten; but from time to time it comes unexpectedly awake as a port, as in 1984 during the coal strike and in 1995 with spirited demonstrations against live calf exports. It is, however, a town with enduring appeal for all who love the sea, boats and boatyards. Brightlingsea joined the Cinque Ports as a 'limb' or 'member' of Sandwich, to which it traditionally pays ten silver shillings each July, in a ceremony held in the belfry of All Saints Church.

Coggeshall

Coggeshall Grange Barn (National Trust) was originally part of a Cistercian monastery. Dating from 1140, it is the oldest surviving timber-framed barn in Europe, and exhibits a small collection of farm carts and waggons. In nearby West Street, Paycockes is a wealthy wool merchant's house, built around 1500 by John Paycocke. The front is close-timbered with five oriel windows, while the interior has fine panelling, wood carving and, in the Great Hall, a magnificent ceiling. There is also a display of Coggeshall lace. The attractive village has had its tranquillity restored by a bypass.

Tourist Information Centre

Colchester: 1 Queen Street (tel: 01206 282920)

Colchester

Standing four-square on its hill-top site, Britain's 'oldest recorded town' is packed with history. It was the Romans' first *colonia* after they invaded Britain in AD 43. Before they took it, it was already important as *Camulodunum*, the capital from which Cunobelin (Shakespeare's Cymbeline) ruled the whole of south-east Britain. In her last fling of defiance, Boudicca, Queen of the Iceni, sacked the city in AD 60, then the Romans rebuilt it in the 2nd century and the street pattern of the present town centre still shows their layout.

Prizing open the shells in preparation for the annual Colchester Oyster Feast

In its north-east corner, over the Roman temple, the Normans built a huge castle, but only its keep – the largest in Europe – remains. It houses the Colchester and Essex Museum, with good Roman exhibits. Other attractions include The Minories Art Gallery, housed in two Georgian houses in the High Street, and the Social History Museum, in the redundant All Saints Church. Redevelopment in the town centre has been generally sympathetic. The old Dutch Quarter, stretching from the High Street down to the River Colne, is worth exploring.

Colchester is traditionally renowned for its oysters, and still holds an annual oyster feast. Bourne Mill, a 16th-century fishing lodge converted into a cornmill, stands by a 4-acre (1.6ha) mill pond south of the centre. Three miles (4.6km) west of the town is one of England's finest zoos, with over 200 types of animal and amusements, while to the east at Elmstead are the Beth Chatto Gardens, created from a wasteland over the last 30 years or so and featuring a dry, a shade and a wetland garden.

Colchester Castle, built by the Normans on the site of a magnificent Roman temple, is now a museum with some of the finest archaeological collections in the country

A little more than 30 years ago, the Beth Chatto Gardens were just a patch of wasteland. Today there are three distinct areas, each with their own types of plants – over 1,000 species in all

Halstead

One of those East Anglian market towns strung out along a main thoroughfare, Halstead gains visually from the steep descent of its bustling high street down to the River Colne. Here stands the handsome white weatherboarded silk mill built by Courtaulds in 1826. Higher up are a windmill and St Andrew's Church, with tombs of the Bourchiers, including Robert who fought with the Black Prince at Crécy. Some 2½ miles (4km) south-east is Gosfield Hall, with a fine Tudor gallery.

Layer Marney Tower

The Marney family were already in this part of Essex by the 12th century, but it was in 1520 that Lord Marney built his superb Layer Marney Tower. The tallest Tudor gatehouse in the country, and among the finest, it affords expansive views over the Essex countryside. The adjacent church, in the same mellow Tudor brickwork, contains Marney effigy tombs going back to 1414. The farm has a medieval barn, rare breeds of farm animals and deer.

Manningtree and Mistley

On the Essex bank of the Stour as it widens into its estuary, Manningtree was once an important port, but it is now a tranquil waterside village. Downstream, Mistley is the spa that never was – planned by Richard Rigby of Mistley Hall, whose fortune came from the South Sea Bubble. He became Paymaster General and poured his money into the spa at Mistley, even employing Robert Adam to design a new church, but when it was discovered that he had been embezzling the Forces' pay, work on Mistley ceased. What is left is a green waterside with tall maltings buildings, gracious Georgian façades and swans. The twin towers of a demolished Mistley church have been kept as shipping landmarks.

In spite of the fact that Sir Henry Marney's planned mansion at Layer Marney was never completed, its eight-storey gatehouse is one of the great buildings of the 16th century

See Walk C page 184
Village Ways in
Coggeshall

IPSWICH AND CONSTABLE COUNTRY

*S*uffolk is a delightfully rural county, forever associated with the painter John Constable, who immortalised many local scenes which remain unchanged to this day. The area he made famous extends into Essex. This county's recently acquired reputation for wide-boy excess is unfair on its rural reaches, which are as unspoilt as you could wish for.

Constable Country

The artist John Constable was born in East Bergholt, Suffolk, in 1776 and went to school across the Stour at Dedham in Essex. He wandered the fields and lanes of Dedham Vale, and later recreated what he saw in some of his best-known paintings. Flatford Mill, owned by his father, now serves as a field studies centre; Dedham Church with its pinnacled tower still stands in a landscape which, thanks to the National Trust and the planners, is remarkably unchanged. From Dedham there is a pleasant walk along the Stour to Flatford Mill where you can have tea by the riverside.

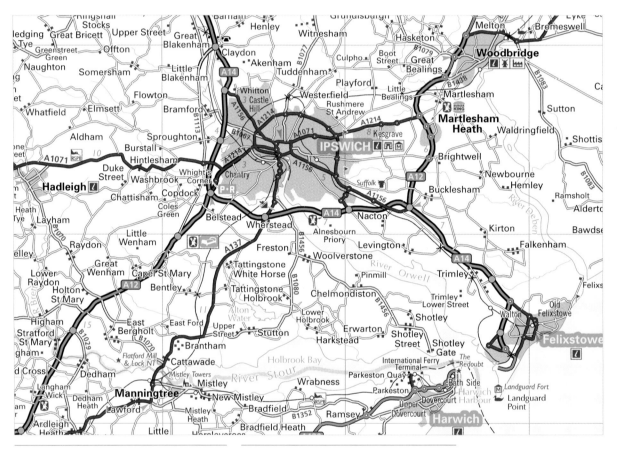

The splendid church at Dedham is further distinguished by the fact that it was painted by Constable

Dedham

This handsome country town has a number of fine buildings and a particularly impressive church, built by wealthy cloth merchants in the late 15th century. If the church tower, completed in 1520, seems familiar it is because it has featured in paintings by Constable, who was born just over the border in Suffolk, but who went to school here.

The village has other artistic associations – Sir Alfred Munnings lived at Castle House, which remains as he would have known it. There is an interesting toy museum at the Arts and Crafts Centre in the old Congregational Church. From Dedham it is possible to walk (or drive) the 2 miles (3.2km) to Flatford Mill, owned by Constable's father and subject of one of the artist's most famous scenes.

Erwarton

Legend states that the heart of Ann Boleyn is buried in the church of St Mary, in the handsome family vault of her uncle, Philip Calthorpe. Close to the church is the Calthorpe family home, Erwarton Hall, with its red-brick gatehouse, decorated in a distinctively Jacobean style.

Felixstowe

Suffolk's main port, situated on a peninsula across the Orwell estuary from Harwich, is also an Edwardian seaside resort that still radiates a calm gentility. The beach is stony and in typical east coast style, segmented by breakwaters, and behind it are avenues of sedate villas which once housed fashionable holiday-makers.

A particularly local architectural feature is the decorative plasterwork, or pargeting, which can be seen on the exterior walls of many buildings. This fine example is on the Ancient House in Ipswich

Harwich and the Redoubt

The principal passenger port for Essex has one or two oddities. The 17th-century treadmill crane preserved on the quay is probably the only one extant in the world and was originally used to service Royal Navy ships. Port life is commemorated in the Port of Harwich Maritime Museum, which is housed in the old Low Lighthouse and is devoted to the Navy, shipping and the lifeboat service. The old High Lighthouse contains a wireless museum. Harwich is also the perhaps unlikely home of one of Britain's oldest cinemas, the Electric Palace of 1911, which is still working.

The Redoubt on Tower Hill is a practically impregnable round fort with 18 rooms, built in 1808 as a defence against a possible Napoleonic invasion. Undergoing restoration by the Harwich Society, it contains three small museums and ten guns can be seen on the battlements.

Its great days have, for the time being at least, gone, but it is a pleasant resort in which to take a restful stroll along the prom, or through the countryside beyond. There is a nature reserve at Landguard Point and close to it an 18th-century fort, whilst beyond Old Felixstowe is a pair of 19th-century Martello Towers

Hadleigh

This is a rather beautiful Suffolk town, with a medieval bridge over the River Brett and an unusually long main street that is positively crammed with delightful buildings, many washed in those curiously fruity colours beloved of the region. St Mary's church, with an interesting spire, stands close to Deanery Tower, a 15th-century gatehouse of some splendour. Hadleigh's most famous building is the Guildhall, which remains little altered since its construction in 1438.

Ipswich

An ancient town, founded in the 6th century, Ipswich became a prosperous inland port because of its location on the estuary of the Orwell. It was one of the first towns to be granted a charter and in the Middle Ages became a great trading centre, exporting East Anglian wool.

First impressions of the pedestrianised city centre are unpromising, but closer inspection reveals quite a lot of interest. Christchurch Mansion is a wonderful Tudor House with period furnished rooms and an art gallery, which is set in parkland and yet close to the heart of the town. Wolsey's Gateway was to be the portal of a college (never completed) in the town of his birth. In the vicinity of the new Buttermarket there is an extensive sprinkling of ornate medieval houses, most famously the Ancient House, with its added 17th-century pargeting – a decorative form of exterior plaster work.

Ipswich's Victorian expansion is manifest in the Old Custom House at the Wet Dock and in the Town Hall and Corn Exchange in the main square. Students of modern architecture will find much to enjoy, including Contship House at the Wet Dock and Willis Corroon, by Sir Norman Foster. There are a number of museums – the Wolsey Art Gallery, the Transport Museum and the Ipswich

Museum, with replicas of the treasure found in the Saxon burial at Sutton Hoo. Tours of the Tolly Cobbold Brewery and the Wet Dock can be arranged.

Levington

This pretty Suffolk village overlooks the wider reaches of the River Orwell and has a charming little 12th-century red brick church, conveniently located next to the pub. The church interior is delightfully rural and contains some unusual 17th-century Jacobean panelling around the chancel and a medieval font, complete with decoration which neither Puritan nor Victorian saw fit to despoil.

Woodbridge

This delightful town on the River Dene does not need to make a conscious effort to look good for visitors. Not only pretty and unspoilt, Woodbridge derives enormous charm from the fact that it goes about its business with unselfconscious zeal. There are handsome buildings to admire, especially on Market Hill, and on the quayside is the Woodbridge Tide Mill, rather Dutch in style, with a red gabled roof and brilliant white clapboard flanks. St Mary's church is charmingly located amid a fan of gardens, and close by is the local museum. Not far away, and located in the Shire Hall, is the Suffolk Horse Museum.

Christchurch Mansion in Ipswich is particularly noted for its art collection, which includes a good number of works by Constable and Gainsborough

Tourist Information Centres
Ipswich: St Stephen's Church, St Stephen's Lane (tel: 01473 258070
Felixstowe: Felixstowe Leisure Centre, Sea Front (tel: 01394 276770)
Harwich: Essex County Council, Iconfield Park, Parkeston (tel: 01255 506139
Woodbridge: Station Buildings (tel: 01394 382240)

See walk D page 185 Constable's Suffolk Landscapes

ANCIENT SITES AND COUNTRY TOWNS

*W*here Suffolk meets Norfolk we find a great deal of variation and an indeterminate landscape which tends to produce the occasional curiosity. The route north from Bury St Edmunds is dominated by the vastness of Thetford Forest, contrasting with the small, mellow towns. In Ickworth House, the area has one of the great eccentricities of English architecture.

Bury St Edmunds

A very attractive rural town of 33,000 souls, Bury St Edmunds, attractively situated on the Rivers Lark and Linnet, claims to be the birthplace of Magna Carta, and is replete with 18th-century architecture. St Edmund was the last Saxon king of East Anglia who, when asked to renounce his Christian faith by the Danes, refused and was then promptly executed. His martyrdom here meant that Bury Abbey became an important medieval place of pilgrimage. The abbey was, of course, dissolved by Henry VIII in the 16th century, but what remains, set in a wonderful garden, has some romantic charm, and the remaining Abbey Gate on Angel Hill is particularly impressive.

Though in ruins, the former importance and wealth of the abbey at Bury St Edmunds is clearly apparent

The largely 16th-century St Edmundsbury became a cathedral in 1914. The latest building project, due to be completed in 2004, includes a Gothic-style lantern tower bringing the height to 150 feet (45m) The nearby St Mary's Church contains the tomb of Mary Tudor, sister of Henry VIII. The Moyses Hall Museum of local history and natural history is housed in one of the few Norman houses to survive in the country and is the oldest secular building in the region.

Of special interest here is the Manor House Museum which specialises in clocks and contrives to have all those that can strike doing so in unison at midday. One of the main employers in the town is the Greene King brewery, and tours can be arranged by contacting the brewery in advance.

The Church of St Edmundsbury in Bury St Edmunds was elevated to cathedral status in 1914

Euston Hall

Overlooking a lake, and home to the Dukes of Grafton, Euston Hall was built in the 1660s by the Earl of Arlington, Secretary of State to Charles II. It subsequently came into the possession of Dukes of Grafton when Lord Arlington's daughter, Isabella, married a son of the king, Henry Fitzroy, who became the 1st Duke of Grafton. It contains a splendid art collection, including a number of portraits of Charles II (and Charles I) as well as works by Stubbs, Van Dyck and others.

Thetford Forest and Grimes Graves

In the 1920s, in an attempt to control the erosion of the Breckland, 80,000 acres (32,400ha) of woodland were planted, creating Britain's largest lowland pine forest and a scene more reminiscent of Scandinavia than of England. Under the auspices of the Forestry Commission, it has become an important source of timber as well as providing a habitat for wildlife, notably the treasured red squirrel. The area is now threaded by pleasant forest walks and provided with amenities of all types.

It is also the site of the ancient Grimes Graves, something of a misnomer, since these are nothing to do with burial chambers. Grimes Graves are, in fact, flint mines dug by Neolithic people between about 3000 BC and 1900 BC. Some 360 of these mines have been discovered here, consisting of shafts and underground galleries which present a memorable picture of the remarkable level of industry attained by people at this early stage of our civilisation. It is possible to descend by a series of ladders to the bottom of one of these shafts to see how flint was extracted with antler picks and wooden levers to be made into axes and cutting tools.

Ickworth House

This extraordinary confection, now in the possession of the National Trust, was built by Frederick Hervey, the 4th Earl of Bristol and Bishop of Derry. It is in that eccentric vein that was the hallmark of aristocratic architecture of the late 18th century and, though unfinished, it is one of Britain's great curiosities. The most pronounced feature is the huge rotunda, inspired by the Pantheon in Rome, among other places. Set in parkland landscaped by 'Capability' Brown, the house contains a magnificent collection of silver and paintings, including works by Gainsborough and Titian. Near the entrance to the park is Horringer Crafts where demonstrations of traditional craftwork are given.

Thetford

In the heart of Breckland, an area that was once sparsely populated heathland, Thetford is a small, historic town. It was the birthplace of the great 18th-century philosopher, Thomas Paine, whose seminal work, *The Rights of Man*, was published in 1791. The place where he was born is in White Hart Street, close to the 15th-century Ancient House Museum, which is devoted to Paine and the history of the area. During the 11th century Thetford was the seat of the Bishops of East Anglia, and the ruined Cluniac priory is on the outskirts of the town.

Just outside Thetford is the village of Elveden, burial place of the last Sikh Maharajah, Duleep Singh, who died in 1893. Having expropriated his Punjab state, the British Government lured him to England and presented him with a 17,000-acre (6,885ha) estate.

West Stow

Close to West Stow village is the West Stow Country Park and Anglo-Saxon Village, a 125-acre (51ha) country park that is a magnet for migrating birds as well as human visitors. The recreated Anglo-Saxon vil-lage has been built on the site of excavations made between 1965 and 1972 of a settlement dated AD 420–650. Six buildings have been reconstructed, using the same techniques, tools and materials that would have been used in the original village. There is a visitor centre containing objects and displays telling the story of the settlement and the people who lived there.

Woolpit

A few miles to the south-east of Bury St Edmunds, Woolpit, close to some unspoilt woodland, is the home of the Woolpit Bygones Museum which depicts traditional daily life in a Suffolk village. There are demonstrations of brick-making, an industry that thrived here during the 19th century – indeed ochre bricks from here were used in the construction of part of the Capitol in Washington DC. The church ceiling is seemingly supported by an array of delicately carved angels.

Two arms, each the size of a substantial country house, curve away from the central Rotunda of Ickworth

Tourist Information Centres

Bury St Edmunds: 6 Angel Hill (tel: 01284 764667)
Newmarket: Palace House, Palace Street (tel: 01638 667200)
Stowmarket: Wilkes Way (tel: 01449 676800)

See Walk F page 187 Grimes Graves and Brooding Breckland

West Stow Hall is an interesting building of brick and timber, set in delightful gardens

A SECLUDED CORNER OF EAST ANGLIA

There is perhaps nowhere as truly rural in Britain as this part of East Anglia. Not quite as flat as might be expected, although in places very flat indeed, this area abounds in interest. There are charming market towns and exquisite village churches with extraordinary carvings; great houses and ruined castles; few people and quiet roads. It all adds to the delight.

Sandringham

Norfolk's royal house was built in the late 19th century for the then Prince and Princess of Wales, later Edward VII and Queen Alexandra. The house is open in summer, except when the royal family is in residence, and most of the rooms they use are on show. The house contains some marvellous collections of firearms, jade and crystal. It is set in 60 acres (24ha) of informally landscaped grounds, within which is the Sandringham Museum, displaying royal memorabilia, from family photographs to vintage Daimlers. The nearby Wolferton Station Museum is housed in the former Royal Retiring Rooms of the station, built at the same time as Sandringham House and used by all British monarchs since Queen Victoria. Exhibits include furniture from royal trains and Queen Victoria's travelling bed.

Twenty five monks once lived in great state at Castle Acre Priory, and the remains are still impressive more than 450 years after the building was abandoned

Castle Rising was built, probably by the Norman Earl of Arundel, to protect the one-time port, but the sea receded long ago

Castle Acre

Situated on a steep slope overlooking the River Nar, the village of Castle Acre was once important because of its closeness to the pilgrim shrine at Walsingham. Its Cluniac priory was founded in 1090 by the son-in-law of William the Conqueror, William de Warenne. Although incomplete, it forms a series of extensive ruins, including a monastic herb garden and the great west front, with its sublimely beautiful Romanesque design. The charming little Saxon church of All Saints has scarcely been altered.

Remains of the old castle earthworks are considerable, whilst the 13th-century Bailey Gate, at the edge of the town, is the only part of the medieval town to survive.

Castle Rising

Here you will find the 12th-century keep of a ruined Norman motte and bailey castle, but one which has retained much of its original decoration, including fine vaulted

ceilings. Queen Isabella was confined here for 30 years from 1327 for her role in the murder of Edward II. In the village itself, which has a medieval atmosphere, is a row of handsome 17th-century almshouses, as well as a market cross.

Cockley Cley

A settlement of the Iceni tribe of the 1st century AD has been reconstructed here, on what is thought to be the actual site of the original village. It dates from the time of Queen Boudicca, who led the Iceni revolt against the Romans. Beautifully sited in the Breckland, close to the River Gadder, there is also a nature trail, a museum in an Elizabethan cottage and a Saxon church, which is thought to be the oldest in the country.

King's Lynn

A truly delightful, bustling and well cared for town, King's Lynn was once England's greatest inland port, with many fine, ancient buildings. The old town is an integral part of an agricultural area, the sort where the bank is filled with farmers in wellington boots. The marvellous church

Tourist Information Centres

King's Lynn: The Custom House, Purfleet Quay (tel: 01553 763044)
Wisbech: District Library, Ely Place (tel: 01945 583263)

Oxburgh Hall

Built in 1482 by the Bedingfield family, this is a beautiful house with a water-filled moat and Tudor gatehouse. The gatehouse is particularly admirable in that it is completely original, unrestored by over-zealous Victorians. The rooms within show the changes in style and comfort that evolved from the Tudor to Victorian periods. The chapel is noted for its altarpiece, whilst the formal gardens, which date from the 19th century, include an ornate knot garden in the French style.

of St Margaret is 12th century and overlooks the Saturday market and the early 15th-century Trinity Guildhall. King and Queen streets are lined with old merchants' houses, and St George's Guildhall is the largest surviving medieval guildhall in the country. The Tuesday Market is also surrounded by interesting buildings.

There are many other delights to savour – the Custom House by the River Ouse, the Red Mount Chapel, Greyfriars Tower Gardens, the charming St Nicholas Chapel and the Jacobean Greenland Fisheries Building – and a number of museums, and you can watch the production of Caithness crystal on the Hardwick Industrial Estate.

The Massinghams

Little Massingham is a scattered village with a pretty church standing alone and containing memorials to the Mordaunt family who were eminent in the area for some 300 years. However, it is Great Massingham that is the more impressive – a village of pretty houses built around a huge green (one of the largest in the county) and pond. The church has an unusually complete 13th-century porch.

Swaffham

A busy market town with a huge market place, centred on a classical 18th-century market cross topped with the little statue of Ceres, Roman goddess of harvests. A fashionable focal point during the 18th century, the square is lined with handsome houses from the period, including Montpelier House where Lady Nelson once stayed. The town sign features the 'Pedlar of Swaffham' who, it is said, went to London in a suicidal frame of mind, but was dissuaded from jumping into the Thames by a man who related a dream of finding treasure in a remote garden. The Pedlar recognised that garden as his own and went home to discover two pots of gold.

Discoveries of an environmental nature are on offer at the EcoTech Discovery Centre, which includes a huge wind turbine with a viewing platform.

The streets of Swaffham have a pleasing mixture of styles that have their roots in the town's medieval prosperity

Around Medieval Norwich

This is an area of almost surreal contrasts. From the noble medieval streets of Norwich it is not very far to the saucy postcard world of the Norfolk resorts. Between them come a whole host of sleepy villages, the waterways of the Norfolk Broads and an astonishing variety of little churches with round towers and thatched roofs.

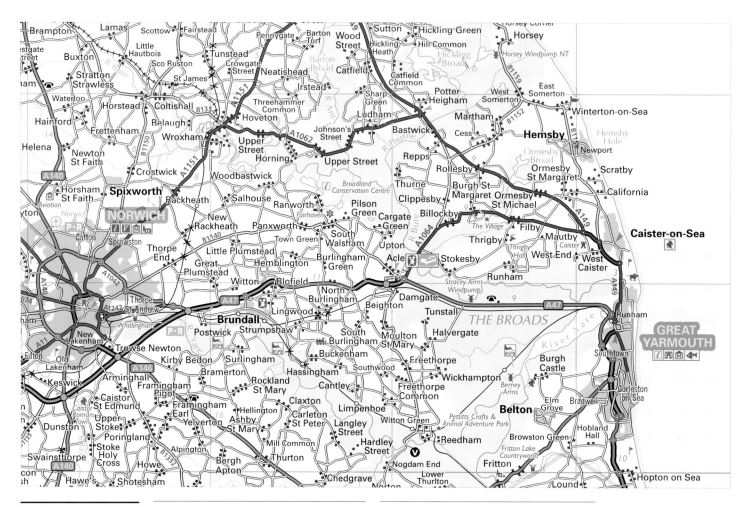

Tourist Information Centres

Great Yarmouth: The Town Hall, Hall Quay (tel: 01493 846347) **Norwich:** Millennium Library (tel: 01603 666071, subject to change)

Burgh Castle

Burgh Castle, or *Gariannonum*, is a well-preserved Roman fort that formed part of the so-called Saxon Shore. It is in a secluded situation, close to the junction of the Rivers Waveney and Yare.

Caister-on-Sea

Caister is an ancient Roman port and fishing village that has become a popular resort. The picturesque ruin of Caister Castle, built in the mid-15th century, now houses an excellent car museum. Near by is Caister Hall, of similar date. The foundations of a Roman construction have been discovered on the edge of town and are open to the public.

Fritton

This village is noted for its exceptionally interesting church, mostly Norman, but with a Saxon apse which may have been the original wayside chapel. Fritton Lake is the largest in England outside the Lake District, and at Fritton Lake Countryworld there is a falconry centre and stables with Shire and Suffolk Punch horses.

Great Yarmouth

An important seaside resort that is also a port, Great Yarmouth has a considerable history, its former herring industry now replaced with offshore gas and oil. The Victorian seafront promenade is still evocative of the traditional English resort, complete

Fairhaven Garden Trust

This area of woodland and water garden, extending to 174 acres (70ha), takes in the private Inner Broad and a bird sanctuary. The gardens, particularly good for primulas and rhododendrons, were laid out by the late Lord Fairhaven and include the 900-year-old King Oak.

Bure Valley Railway

This narrow-gauge railway runs steam and diesel trains across 9 miles (14.5km) of attractive Broadland between Aylsham and the Broads 'capital' of Wroxham, with three intermediate stops at Coltishall, Brampton and Buxton. Among the locomotives are two half-scale replicas of ZB class tender engines which were built for narrow-gauge railways in India, where the full-scale versions are still operating. Carrying 115,000 passengers a year, the construction of the railway was an initiative of the local district council, making use of an existing standard-gauge railbed. Steam driving courses are available, aimed both at the absolute beginner and more advanced levels.

with pier, the Maritime Museum, the marina and the Kingdom of the Sea. A Norfolk Nelson Museum, to be located on South Quay, is planned. There is also a plethora of amusement arcades, rock shops and fast food places.

Parts of the old town centre remain and there are several stretches of medieval wall, as well as a number of the 'rows', narrow alleys linking the port with the river. In the market place is St Nicholas' Church, with the widest nave in the country, and near by is the charming early 18th-century Hospital for Decayed Fishermen. Among Great Yarmouth's museums are the Elizabethan House, which tells the story of English domestic life, and the Tolhouse Museum, housed in the old courthouse, which is devoted to the history of the town.

Horsey and Horsey Mere

Horsey is an attractively desolate expanse of dune and strand. A little way inland, standing between a narrow, undulating country lane and a Broad staith, is Horsey windpump, acquired and restored by the National Trust in 1948.

Just beyond it stretches brackish Horsey Mere, part of a 2,000-acre (810ha) Site of Special Scientific Interest, where osprey and marsh harriers may flourish in comparative peace and where there are walks through the marshy landscape.

Norwich

Once an important *entrepôt* for the medieval weaving industry and one of the most prosperous centres outside London, Norwich went into decline for some time, although the establishment of a university and, in recent years, more industry, has made it prosperous once again. Those years of comparative isolation have contributed to what is probably the best-preserved medieval city in Britain.

Most notable perhaps is the cathedral, with the second highest spire in the country and a 13th-century cloister which is the only two-level example left in the country. Whilst the exterior is impressive, especially when viewed from the east, it is

the airy interior that is of most interest, containing some excellent examples of medieval workmanship and artistry – look for the frescoes in the treasury and the carved misericords in the presbytery.

South-west of the cathedral, in the town centre, are the remains of the 12th-century castle, now housing a museum of local history, which underwent major refurbishment in 2000, and a fine collection of paintings, with special emphasis on the Norwich School of Painters.

Linked to the castle is the Royal Norfolk Regimental Museum. Elsewhere in the centre there are a large number of delightful corners, particularly in the picturesque area of Elm Hill, and several medieval halls. The Bridewell Museum is concerned with local industries, whilst the Mustard Shop tells the story of Coleman's Mustard, still made here. The Sainsbury Centre for Visual Arts, situated on the university campus, includes works by Picasso, Bacon and Moore.

West Somerton

Sitting in the shadow of rows of sleek modern windmills, West Somerton's charming little church, with its round Norman tower built between 1000 and 1300, contains some fine wall paintings dating back to 1377. The 15th-century pulpit has some tiny heads carved on it, whilst in the graveyard is the tomb of Robert Hales, the 'Norfolk Giant', who grew to 7ft 8in (2.3m) and was exhibited all over England and the United States along with his sister, a mere 7ft (2.1m) tall.

Picturesque Pulls Ferry, on the River Wensum at Norwich

The Broads

Where the Rivers Ant, Bure, Thurne, Waveney and Yare widen into small lakes they become the Norfolk Broads. Long considered to be natural lakes, the Broads are, in fact, the result of peat extraction, creating pits that were filled with water following rising sea levels in the 13th and 14th centuries. The Broads are now protected as one of the most important wetland areas in Europe and are a haven for bird, plant and insect life.

Horsey Mere is an important breeding ground for marshland plants and animals

The Bure Valley Railway, linking Wroxham and Aylsham, is the longest miniature railway to be built in Britain since the 1920s. Trains run on most days between Easter and the end of September

RARE BREEDS AND TRADITIONAL CROPS

Despite the Industrial Revolution and the proliferation of the great towns and cities that have become closely associated with the Midlands, England remains an essentially rural country. Gone, however, are the smallholdings that are still a significant feature of France and Italy; and gone, for the most part, are the meadows filled with orchids and other wild flowers that until recently seemed to fill summer horizons. England is one of the most advanced and efficient farming economies in the world, but has become so, it would seem, at the expense of a human dimension that has always seemed attractive to the romantically-inclined outsider.

The truth is that such changes have actually been taking place for centuries and resistance to them is not something new. Often it was not through the publication of letters in newspapers, but by riots and violence. The most famous example of this is the early 19th century Luddite movement which is supposed to have been named after a Leicestershire worker, Ned Ludd, who destroyed his machinery in anger.

CHANGING THE LANDSCAPE

Even as far back as the 17th century, the drainage scheme in the Norfolk fens instigated by the Duke of Bedford met with fierce opposition from local farmers who had previously made use of the marshes to rear geese, which were driven in their thousands as far away as London. Before the construc-

Below: not quite the prairies, but certainly the new face of farming, near Chelmsford; right: a Cotswold ewe, of the breed that brought so much wealth to the Cotswolds in medieval times; below right: rare breeds can be seen at Stratford's Shire Horse Centre

tion of the network of drainage ditches, the landscape of Norfolk had been essentially marshy with rivers flowing aimlessly and with fickle unpredictability across it, ideal for geese but hopeless for crops.

Yet, even the construction of drainage ditches proved inadequate for the successful leaching of the fields, particularly of the peaty, black soil which tended to subside. Thus a way had to be found to pump the water from field to ditch and then from ditch to main channel. The windpump made its entry to enhance the popular vision of the Fenlands.

In the case of the Fens, a farming landscape has been created deliberately and although the sails of the windpumps no longer turn, modern pumps have taken their place. A flat landscape of hedgeless fields and farmsteads surrounded by dense, tall hedges as protection against the wind, seems to have become permanent.

Norfolk and Leicestershire have both made several contributions to the changing aspect of English agriculture. The Norfolk Four Course Rotation is the foundation of modern farming. It is based on the principal of ploughing in compost instead of manure in sequence – roots, barley, seeds and wheat – which is said to bring the best out of the soil. Leicestershire's contribution was the development of modern sheep farming.

THE COTSWOLD BREED

SELECTIVE BREEDING

There are some forty breeds of sheep still in existence in Britain, far more than in any other country in the world. Wool, after all, was the key to English prosperity in the Middle Ages, most notably in the Cotswolds and East Anglia. Yet, the breeds that provided the wool are no longer used and incredibly have come close to extinction. One reason for this is cross breeding, which is not

entirely a modern phenomenon. The man behind this was Robert Bakewell, a farmer born in 1725 in the hamlet of Dishley, near Loughborough. Before inheriting the family farm, Bakewell travelled extensively in England and the continent. By the time he started farming his own land, he had learnt the science of selective breeding, but instead of selecting the best from other herds he concentrated on inbreeding. He used his ideas for cattle rearing but his greatest successes came with sheep, the result of a programme based on the Leicester breed, which were similar to the old Lincoln and Cotswold sheep that had been the foundation of the medieval wool trade. The result was that he was able to produce early maturing sheep for the butcher. His Leicesters, and his ideas, made a vital contributions to sheep farming throughout the world.

Similarly, the Lincoln Long Wool breed was found all over the Midlands until it was later crossed with the ubiquitous Merino. Other local breeds of sheep have been less successful and are hardly used — the Staffordshire Ryeland and the Norfolk Horn, although this latter is the ancestor of the Suffolk which is still sometimes crossed for fat lamb. Most of these local breeds of sheep, however, have disappeared from commercial farms.

A field of buttercups and sheep near North Nibley; right: a traditional landscape, seen from above, near Winchcombe in Gloucestershire; below right: the Berney Arms Windpump in Norfolk, accessible by boat or rail, was used in draining the marshland and grinding clinker for cement

The same is true of cattle, though once again breeds from Lincolnshire and Suffolk have been important in producing modern strains. Sometimes the demise of a breed may be put down to vainglory – a strange case is that of the Lincolnshire Shorthorn which was too often bred for its show qualities at the expense of its advantages as a producer.

As for pigs, local breeds such as the Essex Saddleback have lost out to fashion, leap-frogged by the popularity of the leaner Scandinavian varieties.

A certain monotony therefore grazes the landscape of our farms. But the developments that have led to this state of affairs are the fruition of centuries of striving as much as to the technocratic notions of our own time.

If the meadow flowers have gone, they have been replaced by the dazzle of yellow rape and the milky blue of flax; and no doubt the world will in due course regard them as much a part of the traditional rural panorama as were once upon a time poppies and cowslips.

RURAL PEACE AND RAILWAY HISTORY

L eicestershire is one of the 'shires', a word that epitomises Englishness and unchanging traditions. But don't expect it to be all country folk eating Stilton cheese and Melton Mowbray pork pies – amidst the timeless countryside there is a strong industrial heritage, including the preserved Great Central Railway at Loughborough, and the Grand Union Canal at Leicester.

Modern and forward-looking it may be, but Leicester still has many pleasant backwaters and attractive old streets, such as Castle View, to explore

Tourist Information Centres

Leicester: 7–9 Every Street, Town Hall Square (tel: 0116 299 8888)
Loughborough: Town Hall, Market Place (tel: 01509 218113)
Melton Mowbray: Windsor House, Windsor Street (tel: 01664 480992)

Anstey

A large scattered village with some attractive houses, Anstey is often considered the home of the Luddite movement (workers against mechanisation in the Industrial Revolution), which was named after Ned Ludd, an Anstey man. On the road from Leicester, beside the modern bridge, look for the five-arch stone packhorse bridge which is thought to date back to the early 16th century.

Bradgate Park, the largest country park in the county, is a mixture of heathland, woodland and rock outcrops. At its highest point is the well-known Leicestershire landmark, a folly called the 'Old John Tower'. The estate was owned by the Grey family, who attained their zenith when

Lady Jane Grey was proclaimed Queen of England in 1553 after the death of her cousin Edward VI. The euphoria was short lived – Jane was deposed after just nine days and beheaded the following year. The house has since fallen into ruin, but there is enough left to evoke its splendid past.

Burrough Hill

From this Iron-Age hill fort at 700ft (213.4m) there are wonderful all-round views. The high earthen ramparts here indicate that this must have been a particularly important fort, and so effective were its defences that it appears to have been in continuous use from the Bronze Age to the last years of the Roman occupation. It is also the start and finishing point of the Leicestershire Round, a 100-mile (161km) path through the best of Leicestershire.

Leicester

The county town of Leicestershire suffered from war damage and industrial decline, but has forged ahead in more recent times thanks to the presence of its multi-cultural immigrant population. The latest testament to progress was the opening here, in 2001, of the exciting National Space Centre.

The past is by no means forgotten, though, with a positive glut of museums and historic places. In the High Street is the Roman Jewry Wall (the largest of its kind in Britain), the Roman baths and the museum which has some impressive Roman mosaics and painting. The Newarke Houses Museum, in 16th-century buildings, is devoted to county history, and others include the Leicestershire Museum and Art Gallery, the Royal Leicestershire Regiment Museum and the Museum of Technology, housed in the Abbey Pumping Station.

Leicester's early history can be further explored in its old churches, including the partly Saxon St Nicholas' and the cathedral of St Martin. The area around the church

The Great Central Railway

In 1899 the line between Nottingham and London, formerly used for coal haulage, opened to passenger traffic. It was one of the later railway companies to come into being, and the last major line to open in this area, but in some ways it was too late. It was never able to compete seriously with the car, and by 1966 several sections of the line were closed. The M1 motorway actually covers part of the old line south of Leicester. Since 1969, however, enthusiasts have succeeded in reopening the section between Loughborough and Leicester and several stations along the way have been restored, notably 1940s Quorn and Edwardian Rothley. Reconstruction events, complete with actors in costume, vintage cars

and buses bring to life the days when the railway was the heart of the community. Period and themed galas reflect more than 100 years of the Great Central Railway.

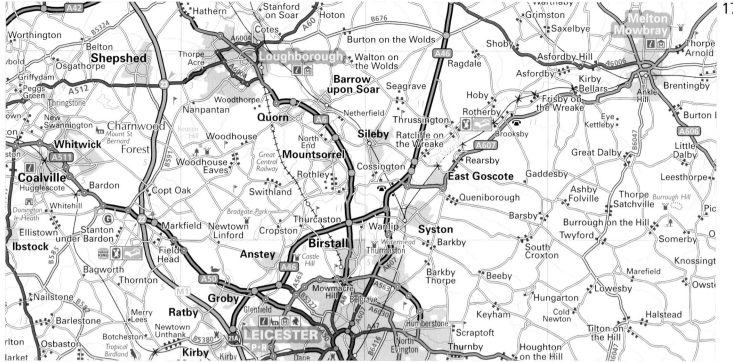

Fort and Fossils

North-west of Leicester are 30 square miles (77.6sq km) of heathland with some of the oldest crags and rock formations in the country. The area is known throughout the world for its fossils, some of which date back 700 million years and are the oldest evidence of anything more complex than seaweed. From the high points like Bardon Hill (912ft/278m), near Coalville, and Beacon Hill (818ft/249m), near Woodhouse Eaves, there are tremendous views.

Although Beacon Hill has not been excavated, there is evidence to show that it has been of interest to man since the early Bronze Age, and there is a line of defensive earthworks. The hill is also important geologically. The obtruding layered rocks are layers of volcanic ash formed on the seabed, each representing a different eruption around 700 million years ago.

of St Mary de Castro is the site of the old castle, but the only evidence that remains is in the Great Hall, which became part of the 17th-century Courthouse, and the Turret Gate. The nearby Trinity Hospital almshouses date from 1331.

One of the joys of a visit to Leicester is the chance to sample one of the city's famous Indian restaurants, many of which are to be found along Belgrave Road.

Loughborough

This Victorian town is perhaps best known for the sportsmen produced by its university, but it is also associated with the casting of bells, and a visit to the John Taylor Bellfoundry Museum is highly recommended. These workshops produced the carillon for Washington Cathedral in the United States and a 53-bell carillon for Canberra in Australia. In Queen's Park is the unmistakable 151ft (46m) Carillon Tower, a memorial to local men who were killed during World War I. It has a 47-bell carillon, with recitals during the summer, and there is also a War Memorial Museum.

Melton Mowbray

In England Melton Mowbray is commonly associated with pork pies, and indeed they have been made here for at least 150 years, partly at least because the area was important for the raising of pigs. A Melton pork pie is distinguished by the fact that it is baked without hoops or moulds for support. They are still produced in the town by Dickinson and Morris.

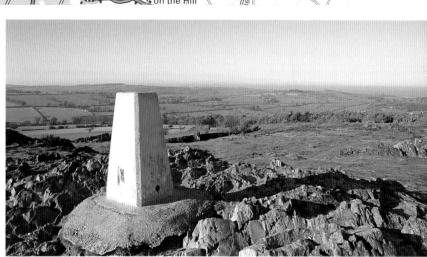

Melton is responsible for the expression 'painting the town red', after the antics of an exuberant Marquis of Waterford, one of the hunting fraternity that regularly descended on Melton, who did just that in 1837. Visitors should seek out St Mary's medieval church, with its soaring tower and fine Perpendicular clerestory, and the Melton Carnegie Museum (closed for refurbishment until spring 2002), which is devoted to local history, particularly to the production of pork pies and Stilton cheese.

Mountsorrel

There are good views from here over the River Soar, which forms part of the Grand Union Canal, and the part of the village on the canal is very pretty. The domed market cross dates back to 1793, and just off the main street is Stonehurst Family Farm, a working farm museum with forge, tractor rides and motor museum.

Beacon Hill, near Woodhouse Eaves, has far-reaching views over Charnwood Forest

See Walk J page 190
A Woodland Walk in Charnwood Forest

Loughborough's Bellfoundry Museum is housed in part of the largest working bell foundry in the world

ENGLAND'S SMALLEST COUNTY

*I*f Leicestershire can be seen as the heart of the 'shires', then Rutland is even more so, especially since it was reinstated as England's smallest county in 1997. Small it may be, but there is a surprising amount to see. Even so, we venture just across the border into Lincolnshire to visit the delightful town of Stamford and magnificent Burghley House.

Rutland Reinstated

Only 17 miles (27.3km) wide, with an area of 150 square miles (388.5sq km), England's smallest county has the motto '*multum in parvo*', or 'much from little'. As an entity it has 1,000 years of history. In Saxon times it was a royal estate, the dower of the Queens of England. As an historic county, however, 'Roteland', its name probably taken from the redness of its ironstone, goes back to the time of King John.

Because of its size Rutland fought against becoming part of Leicestershire in the 1960s and won, for which victory a special beer, 'Rutland Victory Ale' was brewed. That victory was short-lived, though, and subsequently they were overcome at the second attempt in 1974. However, the county of Rutland was never forgotten, and in April 1997 Rutland reclaimed its crown as Britain's smallest county.

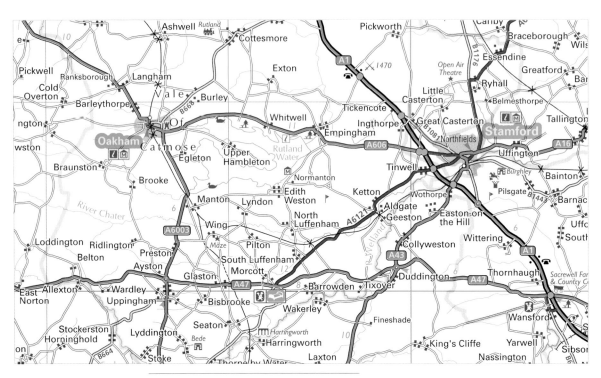

Tourist Information Centres

Oakham: Flore's House, 34 High Street (tel: 01572 724329)
Stamford: The Arts Centre, 27 Mary Street (tel: 01780 755611)

Barnsdale Garden

This is the BBC Gardeners' World garden, created by the TV programme's much-loved presenter Geoff Hamilton, who died in 1996. Occupying the 8-acre (3.2ha) garden of his Victorian farmhouse at Exton, the gardens took shape, often on the air for the benefit of viewers, from 1984 onwards. They comprise a large number of different themed areas, including the First Time Garden, Ornamental Kitchen Garden, Town Garden, Japanese, Rose and Herb gardens, woodland walk, and many more. There is also a plant nursery with around 1,500 varieties for sale.

Burghley House

Just outside Stamford, Burghley House is a marvellous late Elizabethan mansion, built between 1565 and 1587 and surrounded by parkland. The house itself was rather fancifully designed with the help of William Cecil, whose descendants still live here, and who, in his political life as adviser to Elizabeth I, was better known

Burghley House, right, is the ultimate expression of Elizabethan ostentation, its roofline a riot of pinnacles, cupolas and chimneys

for his caution and sobriety. The interior was considerably altered by later generations, especially by the 5th Lord Burghley, whose tour of Italy in the 17th century prompted the remarkable array of classical murals on the walls of the State Rooms. Burghley also houses a noted collection of 17th-century Italian paintings, as well as furniture and porcelain. The grounds are the venue for internationally famous horse trials and other events.

Belvoir Castle

Looking for all the world like a fairy-tale medieval castle, with a plethora of turrets and towers, Belvoir's current manifestation is actually of the 19th-century. There has been a castle on the site since the 11th century though. During the many political upheavals of the Middle Ages, it changed master many times, finally coming into the hands of the Dukes of Rutland. It was destroyed during the Civil War, and subsequently rebuilt, but the 5th Duchess decided that something more grand was required. Finished in 1830, Belvoir (pronounced 'Beever') is still the home of the Dukes of Rutland. Inside are many lavishly decorated rooms with works by Poussin, Reynolds and Holbein.

The horseshoes which adorn the walls of Oakham Castle are of the ceremonial kind – gilded, decorated and inscribed

Cottesmore

Home to the famous hunt, which dates back to the early 18th century, Cottesmore is also associated with the iron horse. The Rutland Railway Museum has over 30 locomotives, many of which are in working order, and one of the largest collections of goods rolling stock in the country. The village church has a chapel dedicated to the RAF and American Air Force personnel stationed here during World War II.

Lyddington

Strung prettily along the Gretton Road and village green are Lyddington's array of 17th- and 18th-century houses, and there is a 13th-century market cross. The church, in Perpendicular style, was probably built at the same time as Bede House, forming a fine range of 15th-century buildings which were originally intended to serve as a residence for the bishops of Lincoln. The hall, with its 16th-century wooden ceiling, is particularly attractive.

Oakham

A small market town of stone terraces and Georgian villas, Rutland's county town has an attractive market place with a striking octagonal butter cross and stocks. Just off the square is a Norman fortified manor house known as Oakham Castle. Its interior walls are adorned with horseshoes; the earliest, which are 15th century, could stem from the ancient custom that all noblemen visiting Oakham were compelled by the lords of the manor, the de Ferrers, to present them with a shoe. Near the market place is Oakham School, a late 16th-century foundation. The 13th-century All Saints Church is near to the school and contains some fine medieval carving. The Rutland County Museum is housed in the former Riding School of the Rutland Fencible Cavalry.

Rutland Water

Much of the Vale of Catmose is now under water – Rutland Water. One of the largest man-made lakes in Europe, this reservoir was created in the 1970s and, though controversial at the time, it has become an accepted part of the landscape. On its banks, like a docked ship, is Normanton Church, now a museum.

Stamford

This winsome town of ancient limestone buildings and narrow, sometimes cobbled streets, was once famous for its Stamford cloth and later became an important inland port. Stamford is one of those towns that is a delight to enjoy on foot.

There are some distinct places of interest. Brownes Hospital is a charming set of almshouses complete with chapel and 15th-century stained glass. St Martin's Church contains the extravagant Burghley tombs, including that of William Cecil, adviser to Elizabeth I.

In Stamford Museum there are exhibits devoted to the strange lives of the tiny 'General' Tom Thumb and, at the other extreme, the 53-stone (742lb/337kg) Daniel Lambert. By appointment, the Melbourn Brothers' All Saints Brewery, with mash tuns, fermenting vessels and a steam engine, gives visitors an insight into 19th-century brewing techniques.

Wing

This village has a surviving medieval circular turf maze, some 40ft (12.2m) in diameter, the exact origins of which are unclear. One theory is that it provided a form of penance for sinners who would crawl along its low passages on their hands and knees to shake off the devil, who cannot follow around curves. It may also have been associated with religious observances of pagan origin.

Overlooked by the 18th-century Normanton Church, Rutland Water is now a popular watersports centre

Welland Viaduct

This magnificent feat of Victorian engineering was built in 1876–8 to carry the Midland Railway line across the Welland Valley. It is one of the most spectacular viaducts left in Britain, with 82 arches looping across the vale for over three-quarters of a mile (1.2km). In celebration of the completed work '...a grand banquet was given by Messrs. Lorden and Holmes... in a large shed, tastefully decorated, near to Seaton Railway Station'.

LINCOLNSHIRE'S CROWNING GLORY

*L*incoln and its surrounding area is fascinating, and local people quite rightly point out that it tends to be overlooked. Clearly this is a shame, for Lincoln possesses one of the great cathedrals of the world, an impressive castle and narrow cobbled streets of ancient buildings. All of this stands on a high ridge above the flat Lincolnshire plain – a magical sight from afar.

Coates

Almost alone on the landscape, hidden among some trees, is the little church of St Edith's at Coates-by-Stow. An unspoilt little church, with an interior which has been barely touched since the Middle Ages, the Norman font, Elizabethan brasses, early pews and, above all, the 15th-century rood screen, are charmingly evocative of Lincolnshire's rural past.

Doddington

Close to Lincoln, this little village is noted above all for Doddington Hall, an Elizabethan house built for Thomas Taylor at the end of the 16th century by the architect of Longleat, Robert Smythson. Although the Hall has a Georgian interior, its exterior has hardly changed at all, and the formal gardens are among the finest in the county.

Not far from the village of Doddington is the Lincolnshire Road Transport Museum which houses a display of an eclectic assortment of vehicles and early transport paraphernalia.

The elegant dining room of Doddington Hall, a house which has never been sold and has passed by marriage through a number of families to its present owners, the Jarvises

Looking for all the world like any other canal in the country, it is hard to believe that the Fossdyke Navigation was constructed nearly 2,000 years ago by the Romans

Fossdyke Navigation

The Romans were quick to notice the strategic advantage of the place that was to become Lincoln, and this became the headquarters of the 9th Legion. The Romans were also responsible for the construction of the Fossdyke, which stretches for 11 miles (17.7km) between Torksey, on the Trent, and Brayford Pool, just outside Lincoln. Over 1,800 years old, this is the oldest working canal in England. Brayford Pool is in part responsible for Lincoln's name which is derived from *Lindis Colonia*, meaning the 'colony by the water'.

Gainsborough

A pretty town on the River Trent, spanned by a bridge built in 1791, Gainsborough boasts the only Georgian parish church in Lincolnshire, although its 90ft (27.4m) spire is Perpendicular. The most handsome building in the town is the Old Hall, parts of which date back to at least 1484, when Richard III stayed here. When in later years its owners, the Hickmans, built a new house, the Old Hall was put to various uses, including as a theatre, an inn and a Congregational chapel, until it was saved for posterity in 1952. It is one of the country's best-preserved manor houses – the Great Hall is magnificent. Gainsborough can also boast a fine building from the industrial age, the Britannia Works of 1850, formerly occupied by the firm of Marshalls, which manufactured steam engines and tractors.

The Delphs

The Delphs is an area of fenland to the southeast of Lincoln, where isolated farms sit on a flat, hedgeless landscape. This kind of featureless country is an acquired taste but it is not without interest. The Witham Valley, on the edge of this area of fen, was an important monastic area and there are several interesting churches in the area, notably at Nocton and Kirkstead. Of the villages, two are of specialised interest. Metheringham was the site of an important bomber airfield during World War II and photographs and memorabilia can be seen at the Metheringham Airfield Visitor Centre. Good leaflets available locally offer a tour around a selection of interesting farm buildings in the area. At Timberland the old pumping station, built in 1839 to drain 2,500 acres of the surrounding fenland, is open to visitors.

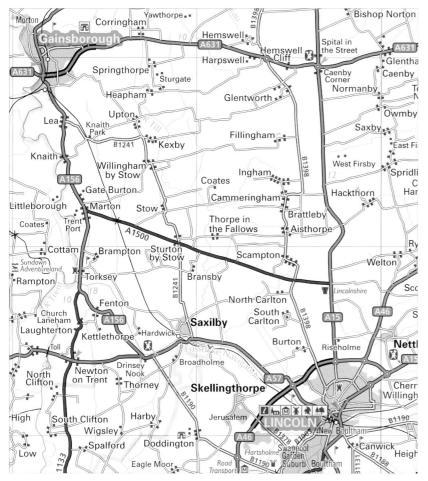

Lincoln

Tourist Information Centre

Lincoln: 9 Castle Square (tel: 01522 873213)

Rising high above the gentle Lincolnshire wolds from the north bank of the River Witham, the ancient city of Lincoln is dominated by its magnificent cathedral, with a beautiful Romanesque west front, kaleidoscopic Bishop's Eye window and handsome cloister. It is the third largest medieval cathedral in the country, after St Paul's and York Minster, and towers majestically over the city and the surrounding countryside. It was begun in the 11th century, but most of the original is buried within later additions and alterations. Its famous Library contains many treasures, including the best preserved of the four existing copies of Magna Carta, and first editions of *Paradise Lost, Don Quixote* and part of Spenser's *Faerie Queen*.

Many of Lincoln's other attractions are concentrated around the cathedral. The castle dates back to Norman times and substantial parts of it remain. There are many charming houses, medieval and Georgian, in the cathedral precincts and particularly along the well-named Steep Hill, which leads down to the High Street and the Norman vaulted High Bridge, still carrying timber-framed buildings. At the end of Bailgate is the Newport Arch, the only Roman arch in Britain still in everyday use; the 20ft (6.1m) Mint Wall is also Roman, all that remains of the Basilica.

Greyfriars is a beautiful 13th-century building and the oldest Franciscan church in the country. It is used as an exhibition centre with displays from the county's extensive historical collections. The Museum of Lincolnshire Life illustrates the social history of the county, and behind the museum is a working windmill, built in 1798, that still produces flour.

Torksey

At the meeting point of the Trent and the Fossdyke, Torksey was a medieval town of some importance, with three churches, a monastery, a nunnery and a castle. One church remains, St Peter's, with an early English nave, as well as a fragment of the Elizabethan castle, destroyed during the Civil War, which stands forlornly on the banks of the Trent.

The beautiful, triple-towered Lincoln Cathedral towers magnificently over the ancient townscape below, much of which follows its original medieval plan

NEW TOWNS AND OLD TOWNS

Like many countries with long histories, Britain has had to adapt over the centuries to rapidly changing circumstances. Much that was taken for granted in the past has become redundant. Towns that were once prosperous have fallen on hard times as their once-famous products have become superfluous. New towns and communities have been planned and built, and their merits, or otherwise, continue to be debated.

Historically, with the exception of resort towns like Leamington Spa, towns have tended to grow organically. There was a moment of foundation in the sense that a family or a tribe settled at a particular place which sometimes attracted others as time passed. Industries in turn grew according to need. The 20th century in Britain has seen the development of the 'new town', not a result of serendipity but of philosophy.

VISIONS OF UTOPIA

Although visions of Utopia have been expressed in England since the Elizabethan era, to a large extent the ideas behind 'new' towns have been based on post-Victorian philanthropic reactions to urban poverty. The functions of towns were rationalised and organised, sorted and graded and then new ones were designed and laid out. Public buildings, entertainments and shops were to be in the centre, around this would be residential areas, and then, at the perimeter, the factories. From this grew the 'garden' towns of the early 20th century.

After World War II, the New Towns Act of 1946 promoted the construction of new towns, the first generation including Corby and the second including Peterborough and Milton Keynes. Such towns were less genteel than their garden predecessors and made much more use of strictly modern materials and designs and also made provision for traffic. Their express aim was to remove the poor from the slums of big cities, particularly London, to provide them with a more congenial and more humane environment. At the same time, it was hoped that they would divert potentially harmful pressure

The Point at Milton Keynes, above, an adventurous town quite unlike anywhere else, contrasts sharply with Lincoln's medieval townscape

away from green belt areas.

In many ways the new towns appear to have been a surprising success, at least economically, and indeed there is a still a lobby for the construction of more. Yet curiously, there is still a tendency to sneer at them. The principal accusation levelled is that they are 'soulless', an accusation that carries some weight when it is borne in mind that although it has been reasonably easy to attract business and employees to Milton Keynes, for example, it has proved a great deal harder to get

their bosses to buy homes for their families there.

The attraction of the leafy suburbs of old fashioned cities or the traditional village green with pub is still very strong. In the case of Milton Keynes, founded in 1967, the business argument has been won – with a population in excess of 150,000, it has become the 13th-largest district in the country. The challenge now is to find other reasons for people to move there. Television campaigns emphasise the mix of old and new, whilst its proximity to Cambridge, Oxford and Stratford is cited as an advantage for the tourist.

IN EASY REACH

These days, perhaps, such arguments are almost superfluous. Milton Keynes, and others of the new towns, seem to be able to weather economic stagnation better than many of the older towns. One reason is location. The sites for the new towns were deliberately chosen with their relative position in mind and Milton Keynes is rated as being the best centre for distribution in the whole country. The older towns are, of course, stuck with their location and have to choose industries that suit them, not the other way

around – although, should rail transport ever make a comeback, it could well be to the advantage of some of Britain's historic towns.

A good general location results in a town that will attract a broad range of companies. Milton Keynes was chosen by Coca Cola some 25 years ago and since then at least another 3,000 businesses have followed, bringing with them over 65,000 jobs.

If, however, the accent appears to be purely on financial gain, that is not an entirely accurate impression. Another advantage to 'newness' is that heritage legislation, for the time being at least, is meaningless. Experiments can be made, thereford, and not just visual ones. The National Energy Foundation, for example, resides in Milton Keynes and as a result of the lessons learned in energy conservation there in the last 30 years, other towns are following its example. Soulless some of the new towns may be, but they are certainly not artless.

Ancient and modern can be found all over Britain, and there are splendid examples of both – top right: a medieval building in Lincoln; middle right: the magnificent façade of Lincoln Cathedral; bottom right and below: glass palaces in Milton Keynes

THE POTTERIES

This area of the Midlands is often overlooked by visitors, probably because of a misplaced idea of what the industrial 'potteries' are really like. It is not all motorway and Alton Towers. There is some attractive countryside, threaded with canals, some wonderful historic houses and an industrial heritage that is well worth exploring, particularly in Stoke-on-Trent.

Stomach-churning rides such as the corkscrew rollercoaster are the main attraction at Alton Towers

Alton Towers

England's answer to Disneyland has over 125 different attractions and rides of varying degrees of terror, but it is not all a 'white-knuckle' experience. There are gentler rides for younger children, cinema shows and sedate swan boats on the lake, as well as items that celebrate home-grown fictional characters like Peter Rabbit. Among all these attractions it is easy to overlook the fact that the grounds were originally landscaped by 'Capability' Brown for the 15th Earl of Shrewsbury's great Gothic mansion, built in 1809 and now in ruins.

At the heart of Abbots Bromley is a scene unchanged for centuries, with the late-16th century Goat's Head Hotel overlooking the old Buttercross

Abbots Bromley

This attractive Staffordshire village is well known for its annual Horn Dance which takes place in early September. One theory on its obscure origins is that the dance celebrates the establishment of ancient hunting rights, another that it is derived from an ancient fertility rite. During the day the dance is performed at various places.

Cheddleton

Cheddleton is situated where the Caldon Canal runs parallel with River Churnet. It was once important for the grinding of flint, used in the production of slip for the pottery industry. Its twin mills, with their picturesque water wheels, were last worked commercially in 1963, although they continue to turn through the dedication of volunteers. Also in Cheddleton is the Churnet Valley Railway, which offers a programme of special events and steam train rides.

The Shugborough Estate

The family home of the Earls of Lichfield, Shugborough House, now owned by the National Trust, dates back to 1693. It is beautifully furnished, but even more fascinating are the servants' quarters, with laundry, kitchens, brewhouse and coach-house, all staffed by costumed guides who show what domestic life was like around 100 years ago. Within the estate is a Georgian farm with an agricultural museum, working corn mill and rare breeds centre.

Stafford

The county town of Staffordshire has few of its medieval buildings, but among those that have survived the Ancient High House, built in 1595 on Greengate Street, is the tallest half-timbered town house in England. It houses period room settings reflecting the history of the house. The Stafford Art Gallery and Craft Shop blends contemporary craftwork and changing art exhibitions, while the William Salt Library contains an important collection of books and drawings. Outside the town the exten-

Caldon Canal

The Caldon Canal runs for 17½ miles (28km) from the main line of the Trent and Mersey Canal at Etruria, near Stoke, to Froghall and passes through 17 locks. Completed in 1778, its main purpose was the carriage of limestone and horse-drawn tramways were built to link Froghall with the quarries. The Caldon was never officially closed down and indeed remained partly navigable until the 1960s. A canal of contrasts, it passes through some exquisite countryside. Parts of it, however, became impassable and it was only constant pressure from the Caldon Canal Society, and the work of volunteers, that finally led to its reopening in 1974.

Tourist Information Centres

Stafford: The Ancient High House, Greengate Street (tel: 01785 619136)
Stoke-on-Trent: Potteries Shopping Centre, Quadrant Road (tel: 01782 236000)

The skill and artistry of the potter is demonstrated for visitors to Spode, the oldest manufacturing ceramic factory on its original site

The displays at the Wedgwood Visitor Centre include a comprehensive collection of the works of Josiah Wedgwood from 1750 onwards. The traditional skills of the potter are also demonstrated, and there is, of course, the opportunity to buy

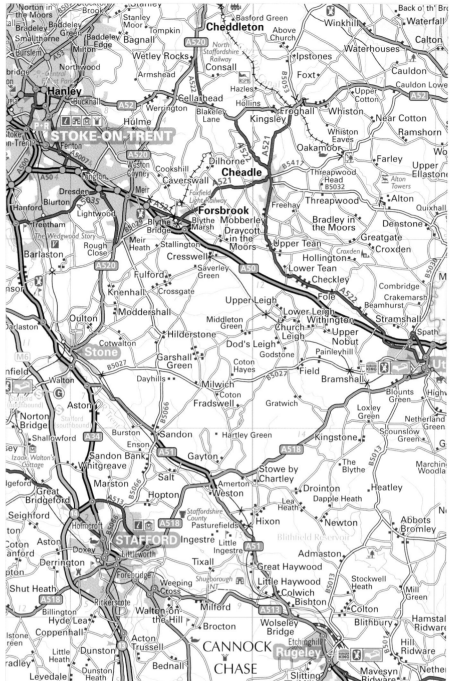

Cannock Chase

Officially designated an Area of Outstanding Natural Beauty, Cannock Chase is 20,000 acres (8,100ha) of heath and woodland. Once a Norman hunting ground, it still has fallow and red deer, which thrive in an environment that varies from oak and birch woodland to heather and gorse, and tracts of bracken. Vantage points, such as the Hednesford Hills, and Castle Hill and Iron-Age hill fort, offer excellent views across the Chase and the countryside of the Trent Valley. Near Broadhurst is a surprising and poignant place – a German military cemetery where 5,000 German servicemen who died in Britain are buried. The Marquis Drive Visitor Centre provides detailed information and trail guides for walkers.

Once a royal hunting preserve, Cannock Chase is an extensive area of heathland, woods and little valleys. Fallow deer still roam here – descendants of the fortunate survivors of past times

sive remains of Stafford Castle are brought to life through video, model reconstructions and hands-on equipment.

Stoke-on-Trent

Stoke-on-Trent, famous for its potteries, consists of the six towns of Burslem, Fenton, Hanley, Longton, Stoke and Tunstall which were formally confederated in 1910. Stoke gives its visitors a real experience of Britain's industrial heritage through working museums and walks along canals and abandoned railway lines.

The heart of the modern town is Hanley, the largest of the old towns, where the Potteries Museum and Art Gallery houses one of the most magnificent collections of china and pottery in the world. In Long-ton the Gladstone Pottery Museum is, housed in a working 19th-century pottery. Many of the famous china producers, including Royal Doulton, Coalport, Wedgwood and Spode, offer tours. Just to the north at Smallthorne is Ford Green Hall, a 1624 timber-framed yeoman farmer's house showing what life was like before the Industrial Revolution.

Weston Park

Weston Park, the family home of the Earls of Bradford, was built in 1671 and is one of the finest examples of its kind. Set in over 1,000 acres (405ha) of landscaped park, the house contains a superb collection of art. Within the grounds are a miniature railway, adventure playground and gardens.

NOTTINGHAM AND DERBY

Tourist Information Centres

Derby: Assembly Rooms, Market Place (tel: 01332 255802) **Nottingham:** 1–4 Smithy Row (tel: 0115 915 5330) **Nottingham (West Bridgford):** County Hall, Loughborough Road (tel: 0115 977 3558)

The mention of Nottingham brings Robin Hood to mind, or perhaps D H Lawrence, who was born near by. The Merry Men would not find much that is familiar today, and even Lawrence would notice a great many changes, but though Sherwood Forest has largely disappeared, this area has lots of beautiful countryside, historic cities and unusual attractions.

Castle Donington

This village is noted for its racetrack and the Donington Collection, the largest assembly of single-seater racing cars in the world. Many of the cars have been raced by the world's greatest drivers – Juan Fangio, Tazio Nuvolari, Stirling Moss and Ayrton Senna. There are over 130 exhibits in five halls portraying the history of motor sport.

Some of the world's fastest cars can be seen at the Donington Collection

Denby

A name associated with pottery, although the modern pottery works are in fact some way from the village, closer to Ripley. Denby ware has been produced since 1809, based on local clay, the exceptional smoothness of which produces a flawless glaze when fired. Tours of the works are available. There is also a museum and a shop which sells slightly imperfect items as well as those of the highest quality.

Derby's Industrial Museum is housed in an early-18th century silk mill and the adjacent flour mill. Rolls Royce feature prominently among the displays, along with mining, quarrying and railway exhibits

Derby

Derby became a city only in 1977. Its growth began with the construction of silk mills, then came porcelain manufacture; but its essentially genteel character only changed with the coming of the railways, when Midland Railways established their headquarters here, and the motor car in the form of the Rolls Royce factory.

Much of the city centre has been rebuilt, not very kindly, but older Derby is well preserved in Friar's Gate and St Mary's Gate, with its County Hall dating back to 1660. There are fine houses in the Wardwick, as well as the church of St Werburgh where Samuel Johnson was married. The cathedral has a magnificent 16th-century west tower, but its character is derived essentially from the clean lines of 18th-century architecture. The city also has several museums – Derby Museum and Art Gallery, the Royal Crown Derby Visitor Centre devoted to the history of porcelain production, Derby Industrial Museum in the Silk Mill and Pickford's House Museum of social history.

Eastwood

The author D H Lawrence was born here in 1885 in a small terraced house at 8a Victoria Street, which is now a museum. The Lawrence family subsequently moved to 28 Garden Road, renamed 'Sons and Lovers House', since it featured in the novel. It can be visited by appointment.

Elvaston

Formerly the home of the Earls of Harrington, Elvaston Castle is now a country park and a working museum. The formal gardens were laid out in the 1830s for the 4th Earl, as a gesture of love for his wife, and are especially notable for their topiary and evergreen bushes. The estate museum illustrates life on a great estate during the early 20th century.

The Trent and Mersey Canal

Much of this canal runs through Staffordshire, linking the River Trent near Derby with the Mersey at Runcorn, and is therefore largely rural. It was the most ambitious undertaking of the engineer James Brindley, who died in 1772 – a canal of enormous contrasts, varying in width to accommodate the largest commercial barges in some places and with room only for narrowboats in others. It was started in 1766, but such were the difficulties in construction that the 93 miles (149.6km) were completed only in 1777. Known as the Grand Trunk Canal, which reflected the hope that it would lead to the construction of feeder canals, it was a commercial success, many observers holding the opinion that its existence was entirely responsible for the growth of the Potteries. Regular commercial use came to an end only in the 1960s.

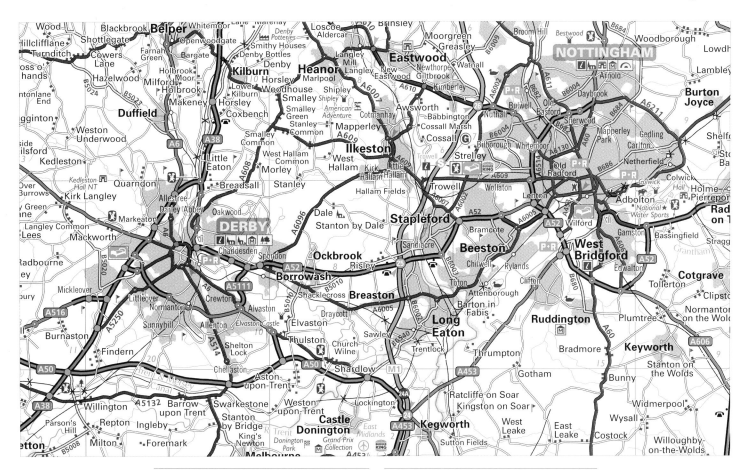

Robin Hood

The archetypal English folk hero was first mentioned in 1377 in William Langland's *Piers Plowman*. According to legend he was a 12th-century gentleman robber who used his skill with the longbow to poach the land of Sherwood Forest in Nottingham and to rob the rich in order to help the poor. His driving ethos was one of English resistance to the Norman monarchy. Quests to substantiate these stories have failed, and what clues there are hint at a Yorkshire yeoman, nothing like the Robin Hood of legend. As for Maid Marian, Friar Tuck, and so on, they appear to derive from a variety of sources, and when all is said and done, Robin would seem to be a fabrication – an all-purpose English hero.

Holme Pierrepont

This village is noted for two establishments – Holme Pierrepont Hall and the Holme Pierrepont Country Park and National Watersports Centre. The latter offers facilities for, and tuition in all kinds of watersports and there is a nature reserve. The Hall dates from the 16th century. It contains period furnishings and in one of the bedrooms the ceiling has been removed to show the roof construction.

Ilkeston

A hill-top industrial town with fine views, Ilkeston's main attractions are the Erewash Museum, with displays of lace making and other crafts, and the American Adventure theme park with rides such as The Missile rollercoaster and Europe's tallest skycoaster.

Kedleston Hall

The finest Georgian house in Derbyshire was the work of three major architects, including Robert Adam, who also designed the park. The house belonged to the Curzon family, whose most eminent member was Viceroy of India from 1898 to 1905 and about whom there is a display inside the house.

Nottingham

For centuries an important town, reaching its zenith with lace production in the 19th century, Nottinghamshire's capital has an imposing centre. The huge Old Market Square and surrounding streets have stately 19th and early-20th century buildings from its industrial heyday.

In a sense, the town is dominated by its historic castle, but in truth only the 13th-century gatehouse, sections of medieval wall and moat remain. Mostly it is a 17th-century Italianate palace, built by the Duke of Newcastle and now housing the Castle Museum, with a fine collection of British paintings, silver and ceramics. There are many other museums – Brewhouse Yard, the Lace Centre, the Costume and Textiles Museum – as well as a contender for the title of Britain's oldest pub, The Trip to Jerusalem. Wollaton Hall, a 16th-century mansion 3 miles (4.8km) outside the city, houses the Natural History Museum. As for Robin Hood, he and his lawless cohorts have been resurrected at the high-tech Tales of Robin Hood.

Nottingham lace is exquisite, and the town's Lace Centre is full of examples of this delicate craft. On Thursdays in summer there are lace-making demonstrations

See Walk K page 191
D H Lawrence's Nottinghamshire

AROUND THE CIVIL WAR BATTLEFIELD OF NASEBY

1 From the car park, walk into Naseby village to All Saints' Church and the Fitzgerald Arms. Follow the road signposted Sibbertoft, leaving the village and heading downhill. Turn right and follow a minor road, rising over a busy main road, crossing over Mill Hill and several gentle humps.

2 On the left is a stone monument, overlooking the countryside; an information board sketches out the salient points of the battle. You are now standing in Parliament's front line, facing the King's men on Dust Hill opposite.

3 Continue along the minor road, rising over Dust Hill, so that you can turn around and see things from the Royalists' point of view. When a road junction is reached, Sibbertoft is signposted to the left.

4 A bridleway is signposted at a gateway just to the left of the junction. If the fields have just been ploughed, then note that the signpost points exactly to the crucial gap in a hedge giving access to the next field. At that point, a gateway can be seen leading onto the next road. Turn left to walk into Sibbertoft.

5 To continue the walk, turn left without actually entering Sibbertoft, then left again following the signpost for Naseby. When this road suddenly bends left, walk straight on along another signposted bridleway, and turn right to follow a track past a brick building. The track runs alongside hedgerows bounding fields, so it twists left and right as it proceeds. When a junction of tracks is reached, turn right.

6 The track loses its firm surface and can be muddy. When a gate is reached on the left, go through it, then head off to the right to find a small gate leading into a woodland. There is a muddy track through the wood. When the track leaves the wood, it rises to a quiet minor road.

7 Turn left to follow the road back towards Naseby where the spire of All Saints' Church can be seen. There is a dip in the road, then later it rises over the main road and back into the village. Naseby Obelisk is in sight from the car park, and is easily visited by anyone wanting a short extension to the walk.

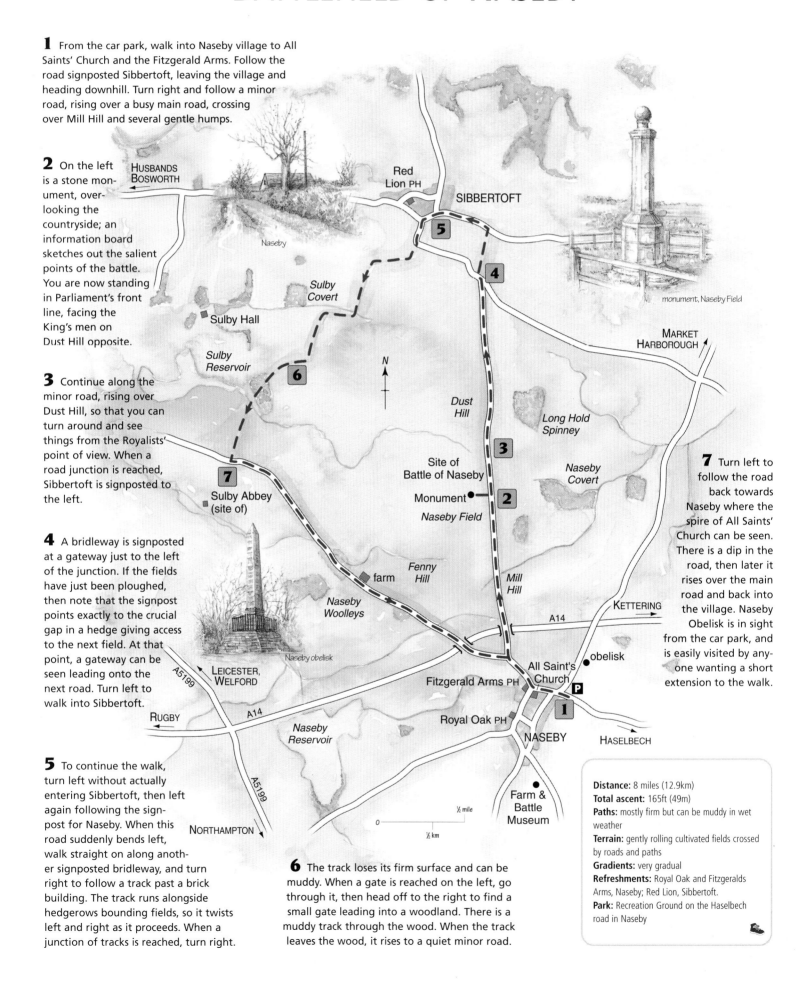

monument, Naseby Field

Naseby obelisk

Distance: 8 miles (12.9km)
Total ascent: 165ft (49m)
Paths: mostly firm but can be muddy in wet weather
Terrain: gently rolling cultivated fields crossed by roads and paths
Gradients: very gradual
Refreshments: Royal Oak and Fitzgeralds Arms, Naseby; Red Lion, Sibbertoft.
Park: Recreation Ground on the Haselbech road in Naseby

THE HUNTINGDON HOME OF OLIVER CROMWELL

2 Go straight on at the traffic lights. When the road bends to the right, turn left along a footpath to Mill Common. Go diagonally left to a road and turn right, past Castle Hill, under the A14 and over a brook to join the Ouse Valley Way in Port Holme Meadow.

3 Walk straight across to a footbridge at Godmanchester Lock. Having crossed, turn left to reach Chinese Bridge. Cross into Godmanchester, leaving the Ouse Valley Way. Cross the B1043 to Cambridge Street then left into Chadley Lane to St Mary's Church.

1 From Princess Street, follow Literary Walk to High Street and turn left to All Saints' Church, the Falcon Tavern and the Cromwell Museum. Continue past the church and turn left into George Street.

Distance: 8 miles (12.9km)
Total ascent: negligible
Paths: good, but very muddy after rain; flooding possible in winter
Terrain: meadows, riverside, some streets
Gradients: none
Refreshments: good choice in Huntingdon and Godmanchester; pubs at Hemingford Abbots and Houghton
Park: car park in Malthouse Close off Princess Street, opposite bus station

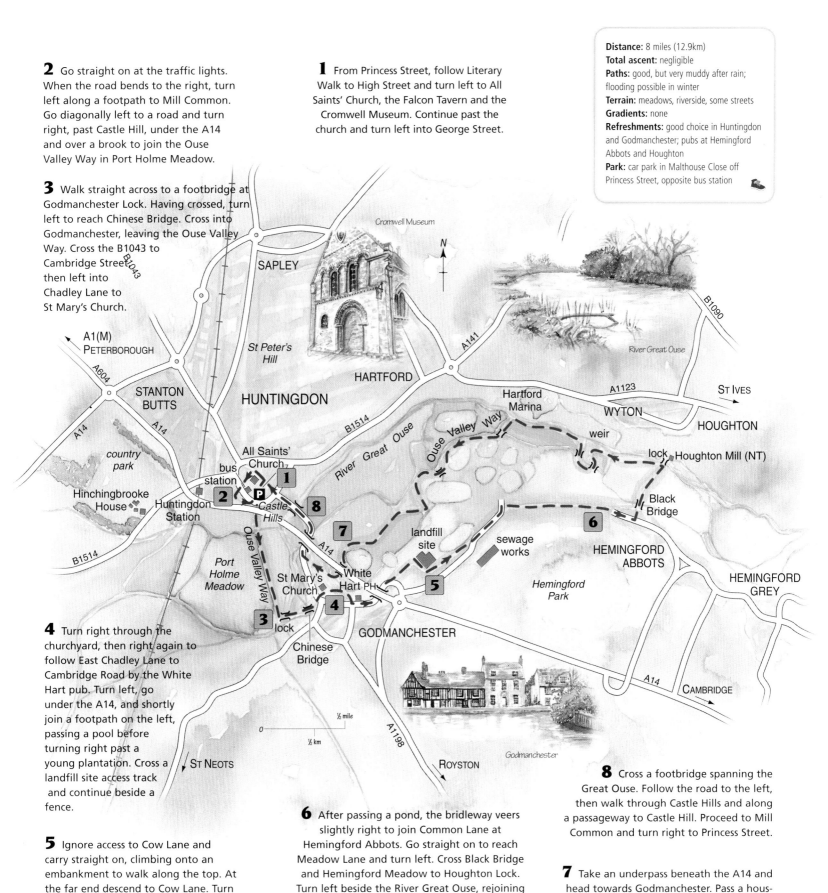

4 Turn right through the churchyard, then right again to follow East Chadley Lane to Cambridge Road by the White Hart pub. Turn left, go under the A14, and shortly join a footpath on the left, passing a pool before turning right past a young plantation. Cross a landfill site access track and continue beside a fence.

5 Ignore access to Cow Lane and carry straight on, climbing onto an embankment to walk along the top. At the far end descend to Cow Lane. Turn left, then join the second path on the right, a bridleway running beside a dismantled railway across a common.

6 After passing a pond, the bridleway veers slightly right to join Common Lane at Hemingford Abbots. Go straight on to reach Meadow Lane and turn left. Cross Black Bridge and Hemingford Meadow to Houghton Lock. Turn left beside the River Great Ouse, rejoining the Ouse Valley Way. Just follow the frequent waymarks now as the route explores the river, a tributary and flooded gravel pits.

8 Cross a footbridge spanning the Great Ouse. Follow the road to the left, then walk through Castle Hills and along a passageway to Castle Hill. Proceed to Mill Common and turn right to Princess Street.

7 Take an underpass beneath the A14 and head towards Godmanchester. Pass a housing estate to intercept a footpath/cycleway and turn right to the B1043. Turn right towards Huntingdon, crossing at the lights.

VILLAGE WAYS IN COGGESHALL

1 Leave the car park by the clock tower. Cross the road diagonally and turn left into Church Street. Continue to Woolpack Inn and church on the left. Cross road opposite the end of the church and take marked Essex Way path on the right.

2 Continue past the school into the recreation ground to the left-hand corner and turn left into East Street. Follow a footpath then cross over and take the Essex Way to right at the end of houses. Follow hedge to a stile and continue by fence following Essex Way towards farmyard.

3 Turn right and pass a mill on the left, through the farmyard with abbey ruins on right. Continue past the chapel to T-junction (Grange Barn opposite). Turn right down the hill. Beyond a bridge, turn left then shortly left again into West Street. (Paycocke's is on left). Cross over, taking the path by an old school.

Distance: 8½ miles (13.7km)
Total ascent: 100ft (30m)
Paths: good, some can be very muddy after rain
Terrain: pavements, fields, woodland tracks
Gradients: few, very gradual
Refreshments: numerous in village; Compasses, Pattiswick; teashop, Marks Hall
Park: public car park, Stoneham Street, Coggeshall

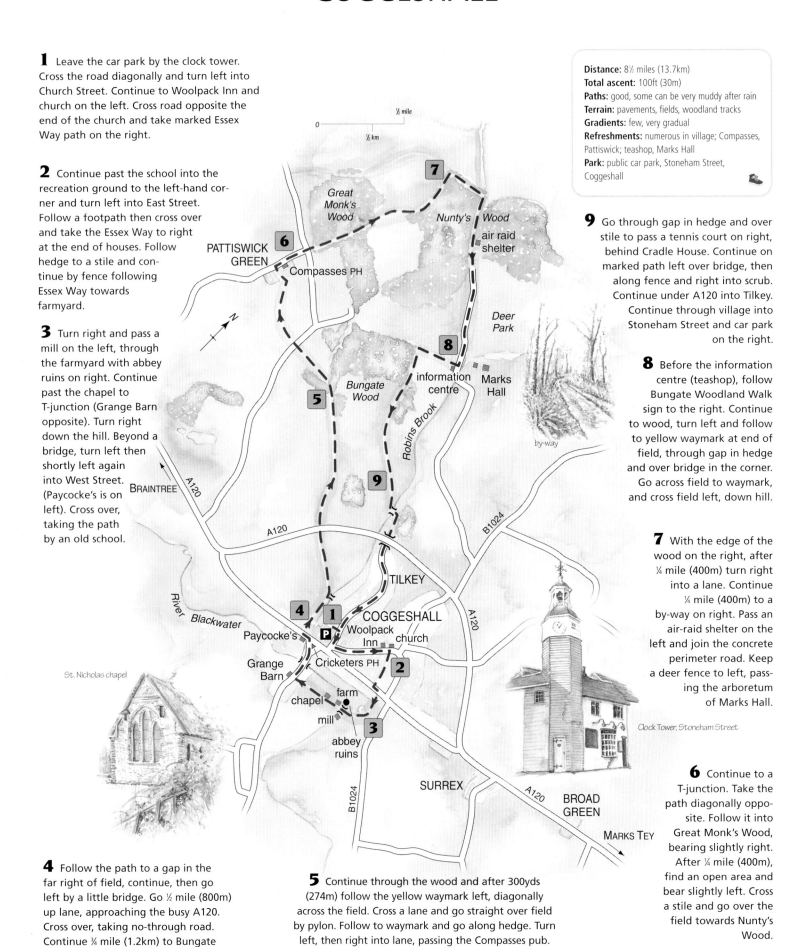

by-way

St. Nicholas chapel

Clock Tower, Stoneham Street

9 Go through gap in hedge and over stile to pass a tennis court on right, behind Cradle House. Continue on marked path left over bridge, then along fence and right into scrub. Continue under A120 into Tilkey. Continue through village into Stoneham Street and car park on the right.

8 Before the information centre (teashop), follow Bungate Woodland Walk sign to the right. Continue to wood, turn left and follow to yellow waymark at end of field, through gap in hedge and over bridge in the corner. Go across field to waymark, and cross field left, down hill.

7 With the edge of the wood on the right, after ¼ mile (400m) turn right into a lane. Continue ¼ mile (400m) to a by-way on right. Pass an air-raid shelter on the left and join the concrete perimeter road. Keep a deer fence to left, passing the arboretum of Marks Hall.

6 Continue to a T-junction. Take the path diagonally opposite. Follow it into Great Monk's Wood, bearing slightly right. After ¼ mile (400m), find an open area and bear slightly left. Cross a stile and go over the field towards Nunty's Wood.

4 Follow the path to a gap in the far right of field, continue, then go left by a little bridge. Go ½ mile (800m) up lane, approaching the busy A120. Cross over, taking no-through road. Continue ¾ mile (1.2km) to Bungate Wood.

5 Continue through the wood and after 300yds (274m) follow the yellow waymark left, diagonally across the field. Cross a lane and go straight over field by pylon. Follow to waymark and go along hedge. Turn left, then right into lane, passing the Compasses pub.

CONSTABLE'S SUFFOLK LANDSCAPES

1 Turn left out of the car park and up to T-junction. The church and old grammar school are opposite. Turn left and where the road bends sharp right, take the path signed Flatford, diagonally to the left. Keep right at the farm.

2 Follow the path and take the river route to Flatford, over a small dyke then across a field to the river. Keep right of the bridge and continue alongside the river. Turn left over a stile before the bridge at Flatford. Go over the river and past Bridge Cottage (teashop). Turn right, past Flatford Mill and Willy Lott's Cottage.

3 Follow a yellow waymark forward at Flatford Mill then left at the car park and take the public footpath to the right. At a double finger post take the Stour Valley path left. Cross the stile and keep by the fence, to the right side of a pylon, to a stile. Continue, crossing over two more stiles.

4 Continue to a double stile. Go straight over the field and continue by a hedge. Go over a stile then take the lane on left. Continue uphill about 600yds (546m) to road and turn left. After 40yds (36m) take the very narrow public footpath to left.

8 After 75yds (68m) take right fork, signed to Dedham. Follow a narrow path to a gate and cross a field with the river to left. Follow the path across a field to a road. Turn left, over the bridge, past the mill and back to the car park on the left.

7 Retrace your steps to the war memorial opposite the church. Take the no-through road right. After 300yds (273m) take a footpath to right, signed private road. Continue down the track, past a cottage, keeping left, then right to a bridge. Go over bridge.

6 Turn left at the crossroads and follow the road for ¾ mile (1.2km) to the church, turning right. Continue past the Constable birthplace plaque on the fence to the right. Turn left at the no-through road by a shop to see his studio, on the left.

5 Proceed to an open field and go straight over to a waymark. Go through the wood, past houses to a gate. Cross over the lane, through a field and over a stile. Continue to the left of next field, towards a farm. Go down the hill and turn right into a lane, then up hill to East Bergholt.

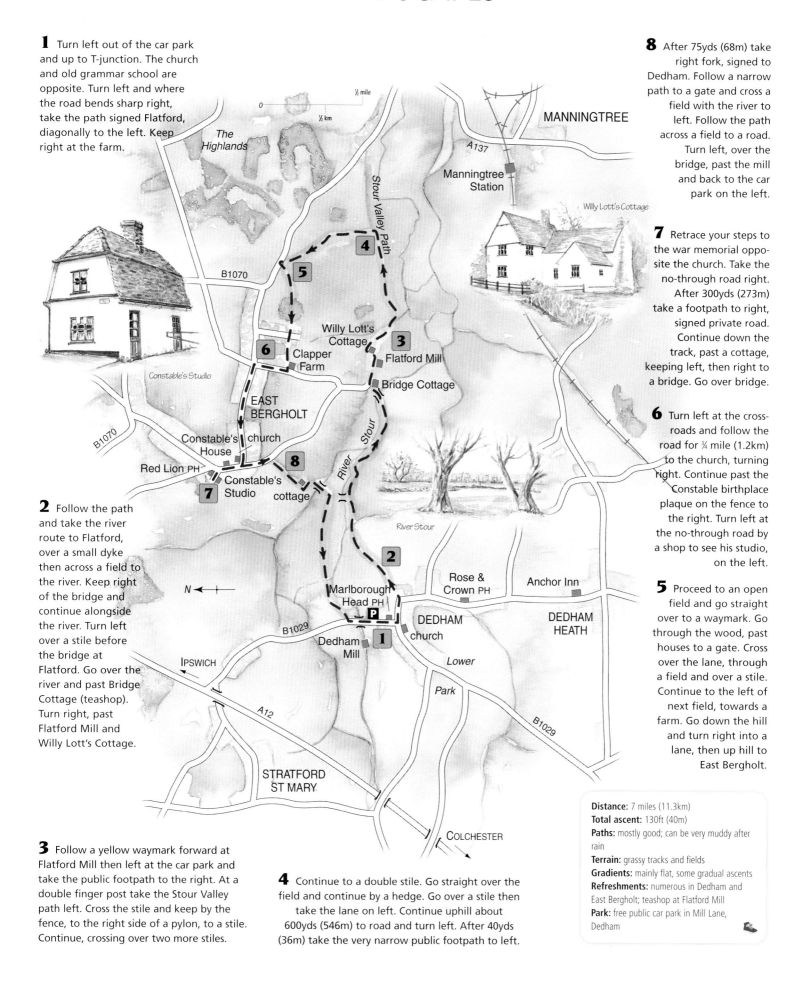

Distance: 7 miles (11.3km)
Total ascent: 130ft (40m)
Paths: mostly good; can be very muddy after rain
Terrain: grassy tracks and fields
Gradients: mainly flat, some gradual ascents
Refreshments: numerous in Dedham and East Bergholt; teashop at Flatford Mill
Park: free public car park in Mill Lane, Dedham

ATOMIC SECRETS OF ORFORD NESS

1 From Orford Quay take the National Trust ferry to Orford Ness jetty. The Red Trail leads off up the road for ½ mile (800m) to a T-junction. Immediately on your right is the Old Telephone Exchange display building.

2 Leaving the display, turn right to pass the NT offices and workshops. In ½ mile (800m) bear right across a Bailey bridge over Stony Ditch. Bear immediately left, aiming for the lighthouse, to reach the Bomb Ballistic Building (display).

6 From Lab 1 return to the Black Beacon, and bear left to reach the Bailey bridge and the road back to the jetty.

5 The Blue Trail leaves the Red Trail at the Black Beacon and heads out south-west along the shingle for ⅓ mile (535m) to reach Lab 1 where non-fissile experiments were carried out on Britain's first nuclear weaponry.

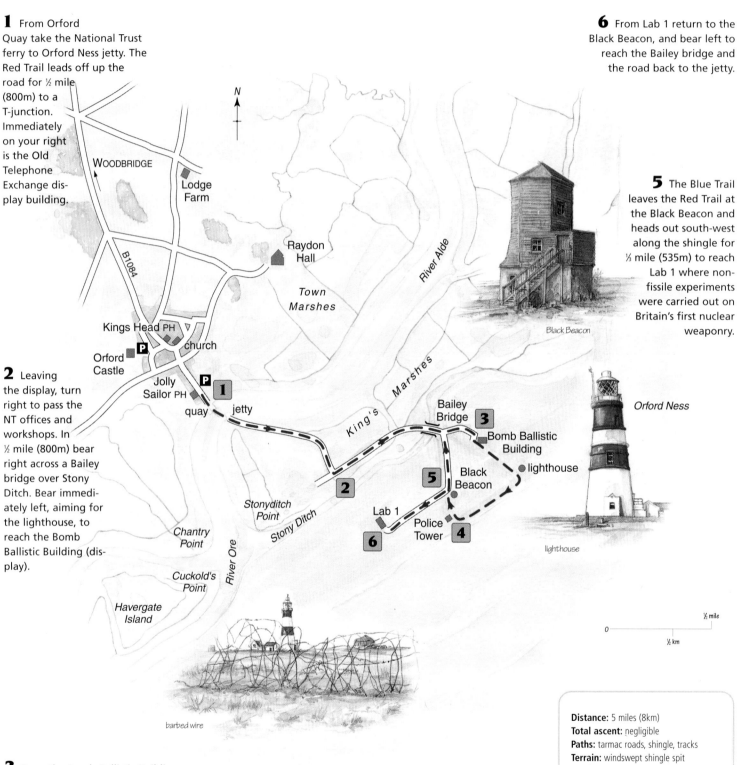

Black Beacon

Orford Ness

lighthouse

barbed wire

3 From the Bomb Ballistic Building, walk forward along the clear path through the shingle ridges to reach the lighthouse. Turn right and follow the path across the shingle and parallel with the shore, to the skeletal-looking Police Tower.

4 At the Police Tower turn right and walk inland to arrive at the Black Beacon (displays and upper-storey viewpoint over the entire shingle spit and surrounding countryside).

Distance: 5 miles (8km)
Total ascent: negligible
Paths: tarmac roads, shingle, tracks
Terrain: windswept shingle spit
Gradients: none
Refreshments: Jolly Sailor, Orford Quay
Park: Orford Quay
Note: passenger ferry from Orford Quay every 20 minutes, Thu, Fri, Sat, Easter–end Oct. To visit in winter, tel: 01394 450900. This is National Trust land and an entrance fee is payable

GRIMES GRAVES AND BROODING BRECKLAND

1 Turn left out of the Forestry Commission office car park. Cross an iron bridge over the Little Ouse river, then up the metalled road and over the level crossing. Continue along the road for about 1½ miles (2.4km), passing a house on your right along the way.

2 Turn left along the main road, keeping to the wide verge. After about 300yds (275m), just before the 'Hidden dip' road sign, take a wide grassy track to the left. Carry straight on to the fence with a 'sheep grazing' sign. The track goes right, then immediately left by the fence, so that the grazing area is on your left.

3 Keep on the path until you reach the entrance to Grimes Graves. Turn right up the metalled road until you reach a gate by a house. Go through the gate and walk left along the wide verge.

Distance: 6½ miles (10.5km)
Total Ascent: 100ft (30m)
Paths: good; grassy tracks, metalled roads
Terrain: forest and heathland
Gradients: mainly flat, some gradual ascents
Refreshments: shop in Santon Downham
Park: Forestry Commission car park in Santon Downham, off B1107 between Brandon and Thetford

8 Take the second left track, signposted 'conservation ride', and walk along with the railway line on your right. After 600yds (546m), go under the railway bridge and turn left. Continue to the road, then turn right over the iron bridge and return to the car park.

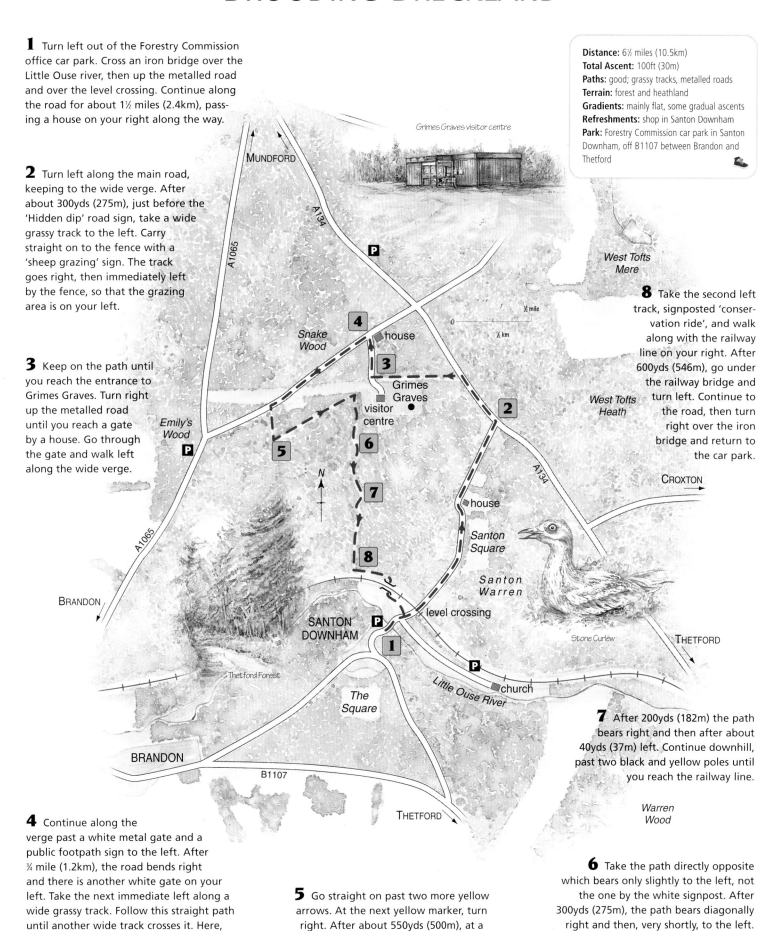

Grimes Graves visitor centre

West Tofts Mere

West Tofts Heath

CROXTON

Stone Curlew

THETFORD

7 After 200yds (182m) the path bears right and then after about 40yds (37m) left. Continue downhill, past two black and yellow poles until you reach the railway line.

Warren Wood

4 Continue along the verge past a white metal gate and a public footpath sign to the left. After ¾ mile (1.2km), the road bends right and there is another white gate on your left. Take the next immediate left along a wide grassy track. Follow this straight path until another wide track crosses it. Here, turn left to follow a yellow arrow waymark.

5 Go straight on past two more yellow arrows. At the next yellow marker, turn right. After about 550yds (500m), at a clearing, five paths converge.

6 Take the path directly opposite which bears only slightly to the left, not the one by the white signpost. After 300yds (275m), the path bears diagonally right and then, very shortly, to the left. Continue, following the yellow signs.

HETHEL AIRFIELD AND NORFOLK'S AMERICAN CONNECTION

1 From lane by Hethel church continue to T-junction and turn right. Turn left to view air-raid shelters. Retrace steps to lane and T-junction.

2 Cross stile by gate on left and go diagonally across field towards left of White Cottage. Cross stile near pond in front of cottage, then bear left towards Hethel Thorn. Cross stile in corner then walk diagonally across field to stile in corner by trees. Walk with field left and trees right to track.

3 Turn right and follow track past farm buildings to lane. Turn right and, after 150yds (137m), take footpath left. Cross stile and continue through woods. At gate path crosses ditch to right. Cross another ditch and follow right-hand ditch past small pond to corner of wood.

Distance: 7 miles (11.3m)
Total ascent: 120ft (37m)
Paths: mostly good; can be muddy; some roads
Terrain: farmland and villages
Gradients: mainly flat; some gentle ascents
Refreshments: Bird in Hand, Wreningham
Park: on verge just past Hethel church, ¾ mile (1.2km) from B1113 at Bracon Ash

½ mile

0

½ km

White Cottage, Hethel

EAST CARLETON

N

US war memorial

moat house

ruins of air raid shelters

old airfield

farm **3**

Hethel Thorn

Old Entertainment Hall

Lotus Car Works

Brunel House

2

white cottage church

Bracon Hall **4**

B1113

NORWICH

10 **1**

Church Farm

HETHEL

church

5

BRACON ASH

WYMONDHAM

Corporation Farmhouse

old school

4 At gate turn right along edge of field, with ditch and hedge left. Turn left at road down to church on right. Cross churchyard left of church, to stile. Cross field diagonally right to stile, then over another field to telephone box.

B1135

6

farm buildings

10 Walk along track with Brunel House on left as it bears right and becomes grassy. Cross double stile into field with pond. Old Entertainment Hall is through hedge on left. Pass through gateway to track. Bear left, go through gate, turn left and walk past Church Farm. Pass through two gates and turn right to Hethel church.

Hethel Bridge

B1113

9 WRENINGHAM

church

Bird in Hand PH **7**

ruined cottage

8

TOPROW

9 Walk along road for 400yds (364m), then take footpath on right towards farm buildings. Keep left of farm and go through gap in hedge to road. Turn left and take next right into Potash Lane, signposted East Carleton. End of old runway is to left. Turn right at Brunel House.

Wreningham church

FLORDON

BUNWELL

5 Turn right on B1113. After 75yds (68m), turn right into Poorhouse Lane. At end bear left between hedges. At fields, bear left and continue left of ditch and hedge towards farm buildings. Cross lane to stile and path.

6 Continue by field edge to footbridge. Cross to next field and stile ahead. Cross to road, turn left then right, over stile to path under B1113. Continue with fence on left for 400yds (364m) to cottage. Bear right over footbridge.

7 Turn right, then immediately left with hedge and ditch left. Follow to road and cross to lane past Bird in Hand to Wreningham church. Take path opposite, along field edge to end. Turn right towards wood.

8 Don't cross stile, but turn right and after 60yds (55m) turn left over bridge. Take path to road and turn right. Where road bends right, take footpath left. After 50yds (46m) bear left over stile and bridge. Go right again, keeping ditch and hedge on right, to kissing-gate. Pass through and turn left on road.

THE BATTLE OF BOSWORTH FIELD

1 From the car park entrance, turn right to cross the canal bridge; go down the steps (right) and follow the Ashby Canal footpath, straight ahead.

8 Just before the visitor centre, turn right and take the path signed to the Marsh and Sutton Cheney Wharf. This leads across the field, through the woods and along the canal to the car park.

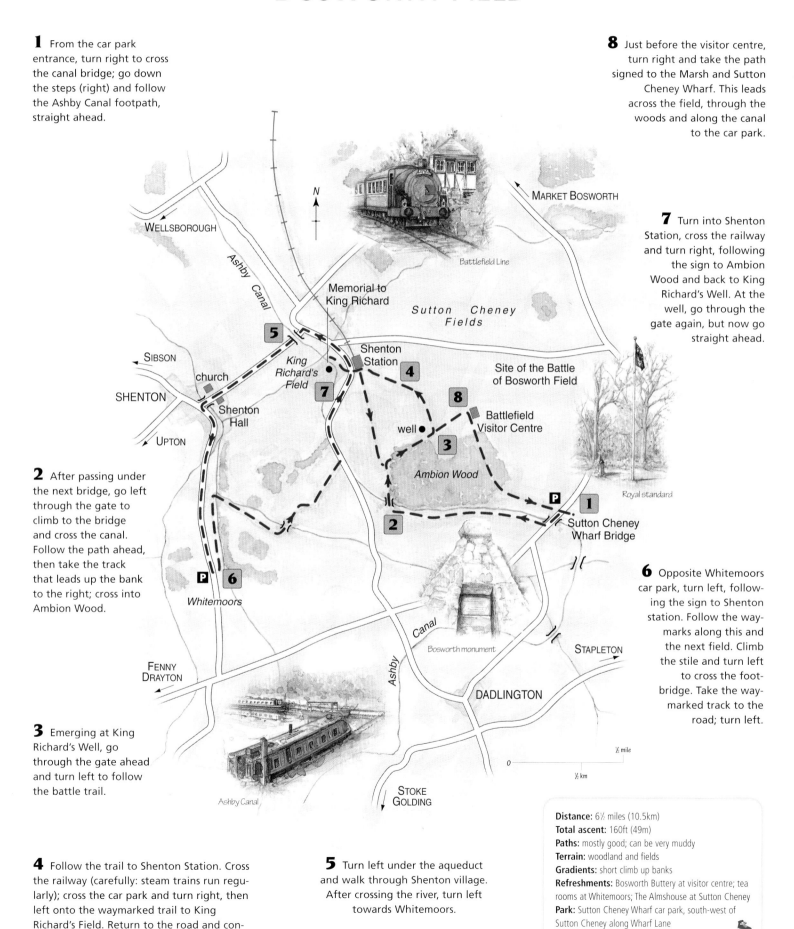

7 Turn into Shenton Station, cross the railway and turn right, following the sign to Ambion Wood and back to King Richard's Well. At the well, go through the gate again, but now go straight ahead.

2 After passing under the next bridge, go left through the gate to climb to the bridge and cross the canal. Follow the path ahead, then take the track that leads up the bank to the right; cross into Ambion Wood.

6 Opposite Whitemoors car park, turn left, following the sign to Shenton station. Follow the waymarks along this and the next field. Climb the stile and turn left to cross the footbridge. Take the waymarked track to the road; turn left.

3 Emerging at King Richard's Well, go through the gate ahead and turn left to follow the battle trail.

4 Follow the trail to Shenton Station. Cross the railway (carefully: steam trains run regularly); cross the car park and turn right, then left onto the waymarked trail to King Richard's Field. Return to the road and continue towards Shenton.

5 Turn left under the aqueduct and walk through Shenton village. After crossing the river, turn left towards Whitemoors.

Distance: 6½ miles (10.5km)
Total ascent: 160ft (49m)
Paths: mostly good; can be very muddy
Terrain: woodland and fields
Gradients: short climb up banks
Refreshments: Bosworth Buttery at visitor centre; tea rooms at Whitemoors; The Almshouse at Sutton Cheney
Park: Sutton Cheney Wharf car park, south-west of Sutton Cheney along Wharf Lane

A WOODLAND WALK IN CHARNWOOD FOREST

Distance: 5 miles (8km)
Total ascent: 655ft (200m)
Paths: firm paths on Beacon Hill but can be muddy around Broombriggs
Terrain: woodland, heathland, fields and farmland
Gradients: gradual
Refreshments: a variety of pubs and restaurants at Woodhouse Eaves
Park: Broombriggs car park on B591 Beacon Road above Woodhouse Eaves

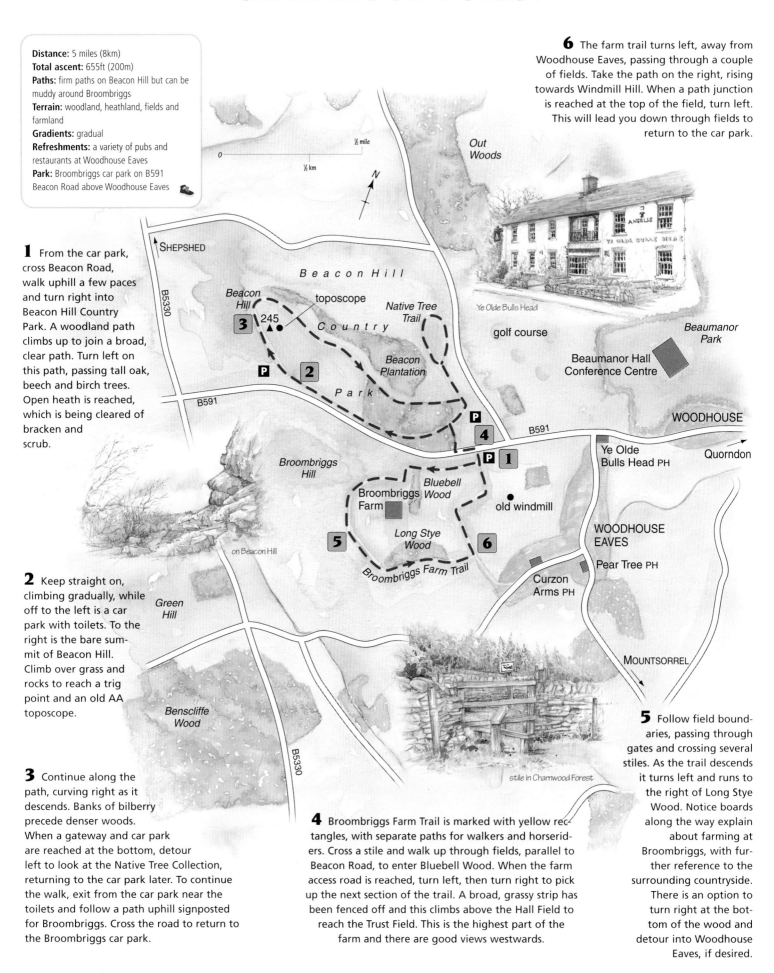

6 The farm trail turns left, away from Woodhouse Eaves, passing through a couple of fields. Take the path on the right, rising towards Windmill Hill. When a path junction is reached at the top of the field, turn left. This will lead you down through fields to return to the car park.

1 From the car park, cross Beacon Road, walk uphill a few paces and turn right into Beacon Hill Country Park. A woodland path climbs up to join a broad, clear path. Turn left on this path, passing tall oak, beech and birch trees. Open heath is reached, which is being cleared of bracken and scrub.

2 Keep straight on, climbing gradually, while off to the left is a car park with toilets. To the right is the bare summit of Beacon Hill. Climb over grass and rocks to reach a trig point and an old AA toposcope.

3 Continue along the path, curving right as it descends. Banks of bilberry precede denser woods. When a gateway and car park are reached at the bottom, detour left to look at the Native Tree Collection, returning to the car park later. To continue the walk, exit from the car park near the toilets and follow a path uphill signposted for Broombriggs. Cross the road to return to the Broombriggs car park.

4 Broombriggs Farm Trail is marked with yellow rectangles, with separate paths for walkers and horseriders. Cross a stile and walk up through fields, parallel to Beacon Road, to enter Bluebell Wood. When the farm access road is reached, turn left, then turn right to pick up the next section of the trail. A broad, grassy strip has been fenced off and this climbs above the Hall Field to reach the Trust Field. This is the highest part of the farm and there are good views westwards.

5 Follow field boundaries, passing through gates and crossing several stiles. As the trail descends it turns left and runs to the right of Long Stye Wood. Notice boards along the way explain about farming at Broombriggs, with further reference to the surrounding countryside. There is an option to turn right at the bottom of the wood and detour into Woodhouse Eaves, if desired.

stile in Charnwood Forest

DH LAWRENCE'S NOTTINGHAMSHIRE

1 From Durban House turn left up Mansfield Road, then left into Princes Street. Take the first right along Victoria Street.

2 Turn left onto Nottingham Road. Opposite the war memorial turn left up Walker Street and follow it round. Take the third right onto Lynncroft. At the end turn left onto Dovecote Road and continue into Moorgreen.

3 At the Horse & Groom pub turn right, then first left up New Road.

4 Follow New Road (tarmacked) for about 1¼ miles (2km) before turning left at the public footpath sign to Hucknall, Annesley and Underwood. The track swings left, running parallel with the M1, passing a sign for the footbridge over the motorway. Eventually it leads you into the woods. At the next junction turn right to continue alongside the motorway.

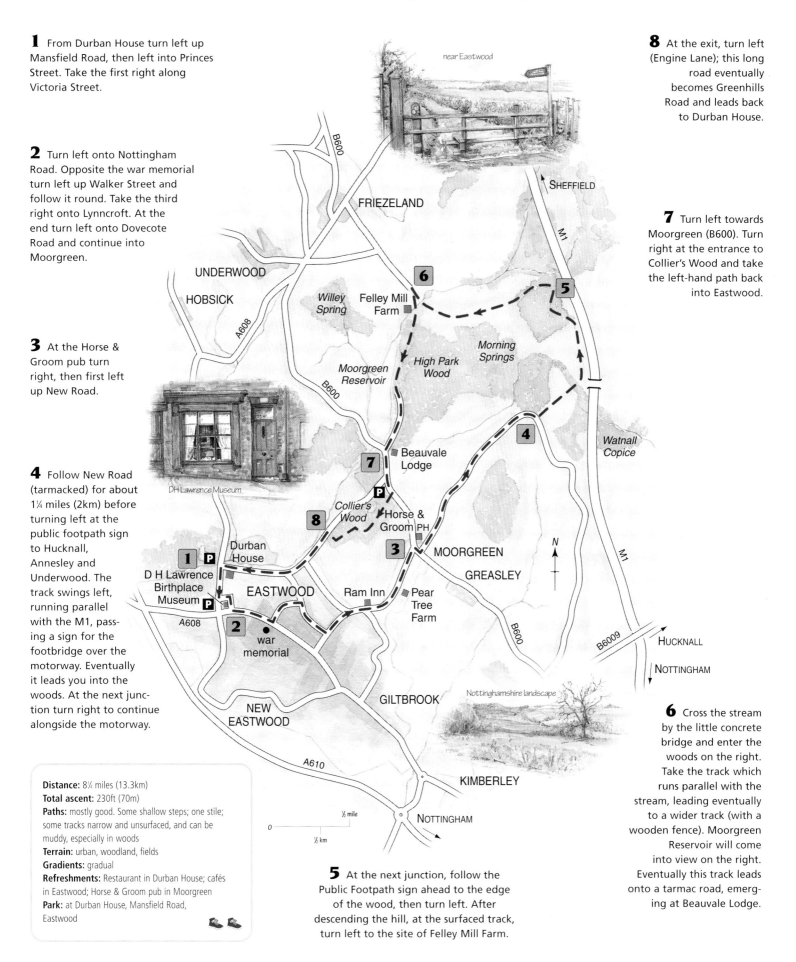

near Eastwood

DH Lawrence Museum

D H Lawrence Birthplace Museum

8 At the exit, turn left (Engine Lane); this long road eventually becomes Greenhills Road and leads back to Durban House.

7 Turn left towards Moorgreen (B600). Turn right at the entrance to Collier's Wood and take the left-hand path back into Eastwood.

6 Cross the stream by the little concrete bridge and enter the woods on the right. Take the track which runs parallel with the stream, leading eventually to a wider track (with a wooden fence). Moorgreen Reservoir will come into view on the right. Eventually this track leads onto a tarmac road, emerging at Beauvale Lodge.

Nottinghamshire landscape

Distance: 8¼ miles (13.3km)
Total ascent: 230ft (70m)
Paths: mostly good. Some shallow steps; one stile; some tracks narrow and unsurfaced, and can be muddy, especially in woods
Terrain: urban, woodland, fields
Gradients: gradual
Refreshments: Restaurant in Durban House; cafés in Eastwood; Horse & Groom pub in Moorgreen
Park: at Durban House, Mansfield Road, Eastwood

5 At the next junction, follow the Public Footpath sign ahead to the edge of the wood, then turn left. After descending the hill, at the surfaced track, turn left to the site of Felley Mill Farm.

LAND OF LEGEND, LAIR OF OUTLAWS

1 From the visitor centre café, follow the waymarked path to Major Oak (not the path which goes through the complex and out the other side).

2 Go around the oak, following the path signed 'Visitor Centre 20 minutes', but turn almost immediately left onto the minor track.

3 After about 1 mile (1.6km), at a barrier and crossroads, turn left (before the Public Bridleway signs) on to a wide, straight route of red shingle. The path reaches the A6075 and swings right. Keep on the red path alongside the main road until it emerges on to it and you can cross safely. Take the tarmac path through the woods on the opposite side.

4 Beyond Archway House, cross the River Maun. Go under the railway bridge and turn right before the second bridge. Pass under another railway bridge (with signalbox) and follow this path to the end for a view of King John's Palace.

8 Leave the church by the Church Street gate (with steps, right). Continue up Church Street, out of the village. A footpath leads back to the visitor centre from the Sherwood Forest Country Park sign on the left.

7 Walk through the housing estate and along Sixth Avenue. Follow the road round to the left and turn right into Fourth Avenue. At the end, turn left and continue to the traffic lights; cross to St Mary's Church.

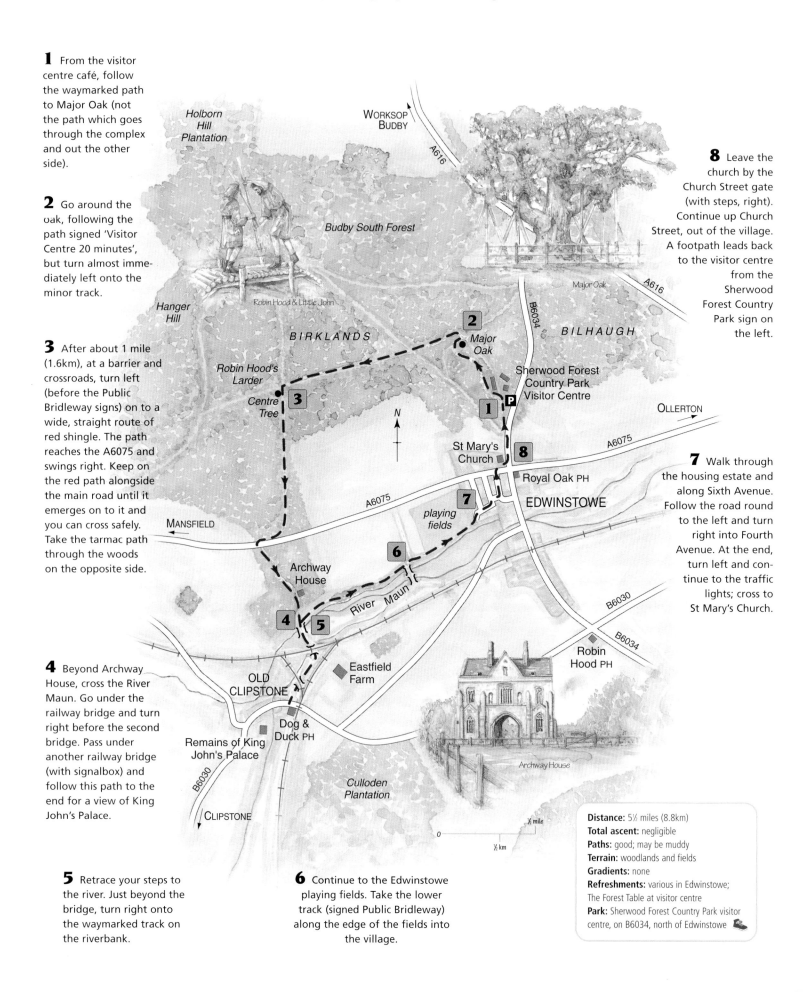

5 Retrace your steps to the river. Just beyond the bridge, turn right onto the waymarked track on the riverbank.

6 Continue to the Edwinstowe playing fields. Take the lower track (signed Public Bridleway) along the edge of the fields into the village.

Distance: 5½ miles (8.8km)
Total ascent: negligible
Paths: good; may be muddy
Terrain: woodlands and fields
Gradients: none
Refreshments: various in Edwinstowe; The Forest Table at visitor centre
Park: Sherwood Forest Country Park visitor centre, on B6034, north of Edwinstowe

THE EDGE OF THE WOLDS

Distance: 5 miles (8km)
Total Ascent: 170ft (52m)
Paths: mostly unsurfaced; can be very waterlogged and muddy
Terrain: woodland, grassland, fields, village streets
Gradients: gradual
Refreshments: none
Park: Snipe Dales Country Park car park, west of Lusby on B1195

1 Follow Forest Trail (green fir tree symbol) and Snipe Dales Round (red square symbol) signs to right of main noticeboard at bottom of car park. Route emerges from trees at flight of steps. Continue downhill to footbridge across stream with pond to left. Cross bridge and follow Snipe Dales Round right along hardcore path, now also part of Bolingbroke Way (signposted).

2 After about ½ mile (800m), path reaches another pond. Follow Bolingbroke Way right, skirting pond and crossing stile. Turn immediately right up around edge of field. At top, turn left to follow field boundary to end of field. Climb stile and carry on alongside Winceby Beck (left) to minor road.

3 Cross into Furze Hill Nature Reserve, almost directly opposite. Once over stile, cross footbridge, 50yds (46m) away. Climb up field, over three stiles to gravel drive. Follow this left towards Hagworthingham. After about 80yds (75m) drive meets road with red brick cottages straight ahead.

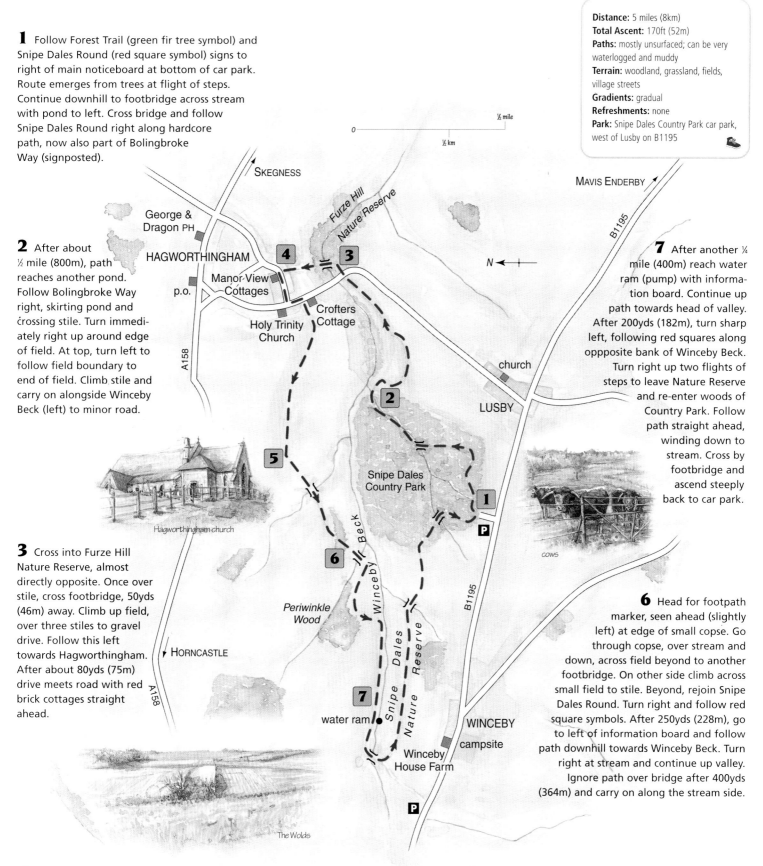

7 After another ¼ mile (400m) reach water ram (pump) with information board. Continue up path towards head of valley. After 200yds (182m), turn sharp left, following red squares along opposite bank of Winceby Beck. Turn right up two flights of steps to leave Nature Reserve and re-enter woods of Country Park. Follow path straight ahead, winding down to stream. Cross by footbridge and ascend steeply back to car park.

6 Head for footpath marker, seen ahead (slightly left) at edge of small copse. Go through copse, over stream and down, across field beyond to another footbridge. On other side climb across small field to stile. Beyond, rejoin Snipe Dales Round. Turn right and follow red square symbols. After 250yds (228m), go to left of information board and follow path downhill towards Winceby Beck. Turn right at stream and continue up valley. Ignore path over bridge after 400yds (364m) and carry on along the stream side.

4 Turn left and follow road through edge of village to road back to Lusby. Turn left and head out of village for 100yds (91m), where stile leads to footpath to right of Crofters Cottage. Follow narrow, green belt between two houses to another stile, then go straight ahead across several fields.

5 Path heads down after third field turning, first sharply right, then left, before entering an open field. Cross footbridge at far edge of field and continue straight ahead to stile. Cross this and another stile, heading straight ahead then bearing left to top of rise in field.

WALES & THE BORDERS

O F ALL PARTS OF BRITAIN, THE
last western outpost of Wales has always maintained its fierce historical independence and individuality. Nowhere else in Britain is the ancient Celtic mother tongue so vigorously defended and promoted, and nowhere else retains its spirit of separateness and that almost indefinable feeling of longing and nostalgia known in Welsh as *hiraeth*. It is communicated through the fierce nationalism of its people, and in the elements of earth, water, fire and air (*daear, dwr, tan* and *awyr*) in its landscape. The land of Wales includes some of the oldest rocks on earth and the highest ground south of the Scottish border.

But Wales is much more than mountains and sheep. It has a coastline which, because it is the first part of Britain to receive the balmy influence of the Gulf Stream, can at times seem positively Mediterranean. Crystal clear Welsh water has played an important part in the creation of the spectacular landscapes of Snowdonia, the Cambrian Mountains and the Brecon Beacons. And it is still in demand today, filling the many reservoirs of mid and south Wales which slake the thirst of a large part of industrial Britain, just as the blue slate from Snowdonia's hills roofed the Empire a century ago.

Today, about half the population of Wales live in the industrial towns and cities like Cardiff, Swansea, Newport and Wrexham which circle its mountainous interior. And although the traditional industrial base in the South Wales valleys of coal mining and steel making has long gone, the Welsh people still manage to exert a disproportionate influence on the world through its famous choral music, its brass bands and its fervent love of sport, particularly Rugby football. But perhaps the true spirit of Wales can only be found in its sparsely-populated interior, on the hill farms where Welsh is still the first language and where the people are still close to the land and the elements which made the country what it is today.

Although the principality of Wales officially became part of the Union as long ago as 1536, any visitor passing through the Marches – as the beautiful border country with England is still known – can have no doubt that they are entering a proudly different country. But despite that long and at times bloody history of conflict between nations, the visitor is assured that the true Welsh *croeso* (welcome) will be as warm as ever.

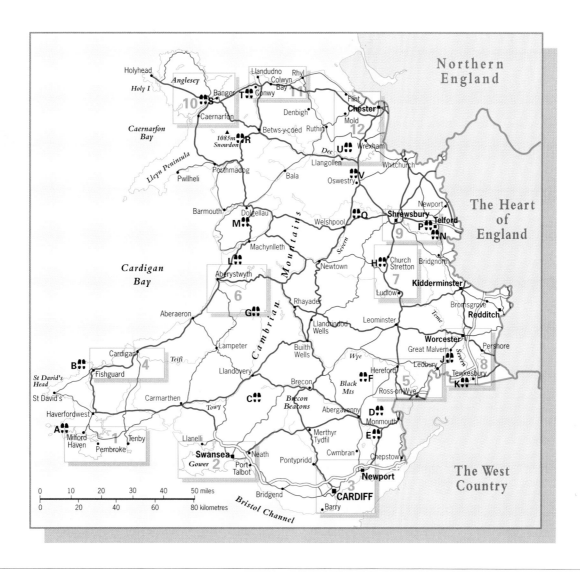

SECTION CONTENTS

FEATURES

WALKS

LITTLE ENGLAND BEYOND WALES

Giraldus Cambrensis, the 12th-century Welsh cleric and scholar who was born at Manorbier Castle, described Pembrokeshire as 'the most beautiful part of Wales.' The thousands who flock to the resorts on the lovely craggy coastline of Wales's most westerly county, seem to agree. This area has history, wildlife, wonderful scenery and a coastline that is all National Park.

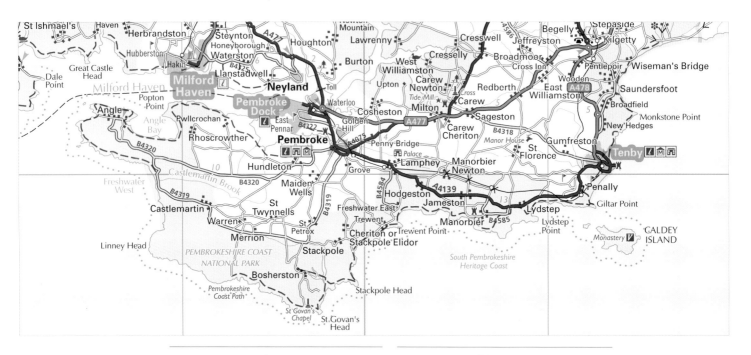

Bosherston

The Norman church of St Michael's at Bosherston has a fine medieval cross in the churchyard, but this picturesque village is most famous for its lily ponds. These were formed by the Stackpole Estate in three narrow limestone valleys in the late 18th and early 19th centuries, and are now nationally important examples of calcareous marl lakes, protected as a National Nature Reserve. They are reached by raised causeways, which take the path across the water. South-east of Bosherston is a wonderful secluded beach at Barafundle Bay, which is well worth the walk.

Bosherston's lakes make an entrancing picture in late spring and early summer when the white water lilies are in bloom

Caldey Island

Regular boat trips from Tenby take visitors to Caldey Island, the only Pembrokeshire island which is permanently occupied. The inhabitants are the monks of the modern Cistercian priory, who make sweet-smelling perfume here. There are also the remains of a 12th-century Benedictine monastery, and the ancient priory church contains a stone with inscriptions in Latin and 5th-century Ogham script.

Carew Castle

This 13th-century castle standing on the Carew estuary was modified with mullioned and oriel windows in Tudor times, giving it the appearance of a romantic ruined country house. Now owned by the Pembrokeshire Coast National Park Authority, it is the scene of regular 'living history' events. Downstream is the restored Carew tidal cornmill, also owned by the Park and open to the public. Carew Cross is a highly decorated 11th-century royal memorial near the castle entrance.

Tourist Information Centres:

Milford Haven: 94 Charles Street (tel: 01646 690866)
Pembroke: The Commons Road (tel: 01646 622388)
Tenby: The Croft (tel: 01834 842402)

Birds of Dyfed

One of the great joys of walking the 186-mile (299.3-km) Pembroke-shire Coast Path National Trail, which runs from St Dogmael's to Amroth, is the variety of birdlife. The steep cliffs and sea stacks, such as those found around Govan's Head and Castlemartin, are home to the rare red-beaked chough, surely the most acrobatic of the crow family, as well as kittiwake, guillemot and razorbill, the plump, penguin-like emblem of the National Park. Comical puffins and the rare Manx shearwaters nest in burrows on the islands of Skomer, a National Nature Reserve, and Skokholm, while Grassholm, an RSPB Reserve, is the site of the largest gannetry in England and Wales.

Manorbier

Giraldus Cambrensis, born here around 1146, described Manorbier as 'the most delectable spot in Wales.' The mighty walls of Manorbier Castle have been compared to the great crusader castles of the Middle East, and its grey walls dominate the delightful sandy beach from its low headland overlooking the bay. The parish church of St James, entered down crypt-like steps, contains a memorial to a member of the de Barri family, of whom Giraldus was a member.

Pembroke

The ancient county town of Pembroke lies on a low ridge of limestone, where the impressive castle was built in the late 11th century. The circular vaulted keep is 75ft (22.9m) high with walls 7ft (2.1m) thick, and a subterranean cavern known as the Wogan leads out to the harbour. Henry VII was born in the castle in 1457.

Pembroke has a pleasing High Street with some Tudor façades, and retains parts of its original town wall and water defences, including the attractive Mill Pond to the north. Pembroke Dock is a creation of the 19th century where about 240 men-of-war were built, and was an important flying-boat base during World War II.

St Govan's Chapel

This is one of the real gems of the Pembrokeshire Coast. Approached by a steep flight of steps down through the cliffs near Bosherston, this tiny 13th-century chapel is only accessible when firing is not taking place on the nearby Castlemartin military ranges.

West along the Coast Path are the Huntsman's Leap, a giddy gash in the cliffs, the equally spectacular Elegug Stacks, two massive pillars of limestone standing out from the cliffs, and the huge natural arch known as the Green Bridge of Wales.

Saundersfoot

This is a small town whose popularity as a holiday resort is strangely due to its development as a harbour to export high quality anthracite in the early 19th century. Today its golden beaches and fine little harbour reflect nothing of its industrial past, and it has become one of the most popular resorts on this coast.

Tenby

The largest town (pop. 5,000) within the National Park, Tenby retains its medieval charm and character despite the annual influx of thousands of tourists.

The sailboat-dotted harbour and narrow, winding streets between what remains of the medieval town walls give Tenby the air of a Cornish resort. Notable Tudor buildings are the Merchant's House and Plantagenet House on Quay Hill, both now in the care of the National Trust.

There is a very good town museum, incorporating part of Tenby Castle, built to defend the natural harbour in the 13th century. The parish church of St Mary, also 13th century, is one of the largest and most splendid in Wales, and contrasts with the tiny fishermen's chapel of St Julian, which overlooks the Harbour Sands.

Tudor alterations have not detracted from Carew Castle's sturdy Norman character. Beside the water Carew Mill is one of only three restored tide mills in Britain

See Walk A page 224
Dale – A Pembroke-shire Peninsula

Tenby's history as a thriving port is illustrated in the National Trust's 15th-century Tudor Merchant's House on Quay Hill

SWANSEA AND THE GOWER

Between the industrial towns of Swansea Bay and the great sweep of Carmarthen Bay are startling contrasts. The long finger of the Gower Peninsula pokes out into the Bristol Channel like a delightful cameo of the best of the English West Country, while on either side the industry-ravaged towns of the valleys are slowly recovering from generations of dereliction and decay.

Mumbles Head, at the western extremity of Swansea Bay, shelters the popular resort of The Mumbles

The Gower Peninsular

'Golden Gower' is often dubbed the 'lung' of Swansea, but this 15-mile by 8-mile (24km by 12.9km) peninsula is really a place apart from the rest of South Wales. It is also a place of great scenic beauty and contrast. Gower's south coast is more akin to south-western Dyfed, with superb beetling cliffs of limestone where many ships have foundered on the rocks, which terminate at weird Worm's Head. The northern coast consists of broad sand and mud flats leading down to the Burry Inlet, while the interior is pastoral and scattered with pretty villages.

Aberdulais

The River Neath emerges from its lovely valley here in a series of beautiful waterfalls. The recently excavated ironworks and the carefully restored sections of the Neath and Tennant Canal make this small village on the outskirts of Neath of great interest to the industrial archaeologist. Two miles (3.2km) north of the village is the Penscynor Wildlife Park.

Aberdulais Falls are more than just a spectacular natural phenomenon – they have also been a source of power to local industry for over 300 years, most recently for a hydro-electric scheme, which is open to visitors from Easter to October

Mumbles

The southernmost headland of Swansea Bay is known as The Mumbles, and there are fine views from the summit of Mumbles Head. The modern resort of Mumbles owes its existence to the first and one of the longest-running railway passenger services in the world, opened in 1807 between here and Swansea, using horses as the motive power. The railway closed in 1960.

Mumbles has now swallowed up the fishing village of Oystermouth, whose All Saints Church has bells from Santiago Cathedral. The ruins of 13th-century Oystermouth Castle are on a small hill overlooking the bay.

Neath

Guarding the entrance to the narrow Vale of Neath, this busy market and industrial town boasts the remains of a 12th-century Benedictine abbey and a Norman castle. Nearby Briton Ferry, with its small dockyard, is now part of the borough and is overshadowed by the massive viaduct which carries the M4 motorway round the South Wales coast.

(map of the Gower Peninsula, Swansea and Port Talbot area)

Tourist Information Centre

Swansea:
Plymouth Street
(tel: 01792 468321)

Oxwich

Situated at the western end of the sweeping sands of Oxwich Bay, this charming little village, with its Devon-like thatched and whitewashed cottages, has been important since a castle was built here by the Norman de la Mare family. Their tombs can still be seen in the lovely church of St Illtyd, which stands deep in woodland at the edge of the bay, some way from the village. Oxwich Burrows is an important National Nature Reserve.

Port Talbot

Famous for its massive steelworks on Margam Burrows, Port Talbot is a relatively modern creation, owing its existence to the plentiful supplies of coal from the Welsh valleys and to its easy access to the sea. In contrast to the industrial landscape to seaward, Margam Country Park, covering 850 acres (344ha) is in the grounds of Margam Castle, home of the Talbot family which gave the town its name, and includes abbey ruins, the orangery gardens, a fine herd of deer, a sculpture trail and children's attractions.

Reynoldston

At the very centre of Gower, Reynoldston stands on the west flank of the central Cefn Bryn ridge, on which visitors can enjoy fine walks with views across the entire peninsula. One to the north will take you to Arthur's Stone, or Maen Ceti, an unusually large Neolithic chambered tomb consisting of ten uprights and a massive, 30-ton capstone.

Rhossili

Rhossili stands at the southern end of the superb beach of Rhossili Bay, one of the finest stretches of flat sand in Wales. The church contains a memorial to Edgar Evans who went with Scott to the South Pole. The village is backed by the open downland of Rhossili Down, a veritable treasurehouse of prehistory which rises to The Beacon at 632ft (192.6m). The bracing downs contain 14 Bronze-Age burial mounds and at Sweyne's Howes, just north of the Beacon, are a pair of Neolithic burial chambers. Rhossili Downs are very popular with the hang-gliding fraternity, and are now owned by the National Trust.

The westernmost extremity of Gower is the spectacular headland of Worm's Head, which takes its name from the Old English *orme* meaning dragon or serpent. The long ridge of the Inner Head is joined to the conical Outer Head by a treacherous route across slippery rocks which should only be attempted by the sure-footed, and then only at low tide (more information is available from the National Trust Visitor Centre at Rhossili).

Swansea

Many of the finest prehistoric remains from the caves and burial mounds of Gower are to be found in the Royal Institution of South Wales in Swansea, which was made a city, Wales' second largest, in 1969. There is also a Maritime and Industrial Museum, echoing Swansea's industrial past, and The Guildhall is worth a visit if only to admire the magnificent Empire Murals of artist Frank Brangwyn. The dockland areas have been extensively redeveloped as a leisure centre and marina.

Sunrise over Swansea docks demonstrates how industrial areas can have their own particular beauty

CARDIFF AND THE COASTAL PLAIN

The great city of Cardiff, capital of Wales, dominates the mouth of the Severn and the famous valleys of South Wales, which lead up to the mountains beyond. It is the natural focal point of the coastal plain, important as the gateway to Wales ever since the Romans and Normans built their fortifications at places like Caerleon, Cardiff and Caerphilly.

The Chapel

A feature of almost every Welsh village is the nonconformist chapel, and these stern, functional buildings, usually well over 100 years old, are still the focal point in many. Following the advent of Methodism in the second quarter of the 18th century and the Calvinist preaching of John Wesley, the Welsh people turned almost exclusively against the Anglican Church. By 1851 a survey showed that there were nearly 3,000 dissenting chapels in Wales, compared with just over 1,000 Anglican churches. From the chapels came the wonderful Welsh male voice choirs and strongly nonconformist Liberal politicians like David Lloyd George.

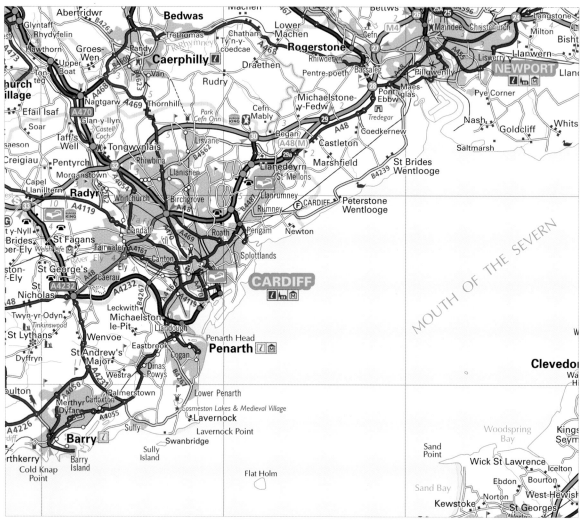

Barry

Barry was once one of the biggest ports in the world, established specifically to serve the nearby coalfield. Its development as a holiday resort for the mining towns coincided with the development of its dockyards in the 19th century, and the population exploded.

Today holidaymakers flock to the enormous amusement park, the beaches at Whitmore Bay and the Porthkerry Country Park. The Welsh Hawking Centre is another popular attraction, which has over 2,000 birds of prey.

Caerleon

Home of the 2nd Augustan Legion for 300 years, the Roman fort of *Isca Silurum*, as Caerleon was known, was one of their most important fortresses in Wales, and is the most complete survivor. Most impressive is the great amphitheatre built around AD 80, which could seat 6,000 people – the most complete excavated Roman amphitheatre in Britain. Other remains include barracks blocks and cook-houses, and there is a very good small museum by the church, which stands in the middle of the 50-acre (20ha) complex.

Tourist Information Centres

Barry Island: The Triangle, The Promenade (tel: 01446 747171)
Caerleon: High Street (tel: 01633 422656)
Caerphilly: Lower Twyn Square (tel: 029 2088 0011)
Cardiff: 16 Wood Street (tel: 029 2022 7281)
Newport: Newport Museum & Art Gallery, John Frost Square (tel: 01633 842962)
Penarth: The Esplanade, Penarth Pier (tel: 029 2070 8849)

Caerphilly

Best known for its white, crumbly cheese, Caerphilly also boasts one of the largest and best-preserved castles in Britain, second only in size to Windsor. The site incorporates magnificent remains of its original water defences and most of the inner, middle and outer walls. The castle was started by Richard de Clare, Earl of Gloucester and Hereford, in 1268 to defend his lands against the Welsh. This it did until the Civil War, when exposives used by besieging Parliamentary forces gave the south-east tower its precarious lean.

Caerphilly Castle, built over a period of 58 years in the 13th and 14th centuries, has massive land and water defences, and its very own leaning tower

Cardiff

Cardiff has only been the capital of Wales since 1955, but is now a truly international city of culture and commerce, and, since 1998, the seat of the Welsh Assembly. The city grew mainly due to the efforts of successive Marquesses of Bute, who were also responsible for restoring the castle. During the 1898 restorations the walls of an extensive Roman fort were discovered and restored, and its history had to be rewritten. The remains of the handsome circular Norman keep stand beside the ornate 19th-century Gothick living quarters.

Elsewhere this is a thriving modern city, its centre the first to be planned after World War II. Buildings of note include the splendid City Hall and Law Courts, the National Museum of Wales in Cathays Park, the University College and the Welsh Assembly building on the redeveloped Cardiff Bay. Cardiff Arms Park is the Welsh 'home' of rugby football, and the splendid Millennium Stadium hosts national and international games as well as concerts.

North of the city centre is the leafy suburb of Llandaff, where the city's cathedral, Bishop's House and Deanery are dominated by Joseph Epstein's soaring central arch depicting Christ in Majesty.

Penarth

Just 2 miles (3.2km) from Cardiff, this is a popular seaside resort which came to prominence in Victorian times. The old

This splendid clock tower is part of the Victorian reconstruction of Cardiff Castle, a collaboration between the 3rd Marquess of Bute and the architect William Burges

harbour retains its charm, although sailing and water-skiing are now the most common activities. The Turner House Art Gallery, part of the National Museum of Wales, is one of the best in the country, containing works by Turner, Cox and Cotman. Further south along the coast, beyond Lower Penarth, is Lavernock and the Cosmeston Lake Country Park and Medieval Village.

St Fagans

This small village of thatched cottages is most famous for the Welsh National Folk Museum, housed in the grounds of St Fagans Castle, an Elizabethan manor house which is also open to the public. Within the 100-acre site, about 20 different types of traditional Welsh buildings have been reconstructed, ranging from a Unitarian chapel to cottages, farmhouses, a smithy, a tannery and a working woollen mill. A museum at the entrance houses agricultural and costume collections.

Newport

Newport is a busy industrial town, standing where the River Usk flows into the Bristol Channel. There is a good museum and art gallery, and St Woolos Cathedral has Norman arches and a medieval tower. Near by is the fine 18th-century mansion of Tredegar House, its grounds now a country park.

Marble figures, standing sentinel over the interior of City Hall, hint at the historic importance of Cardiff, the capital city of Wales only since 1955, but a prominent seaport since Roman times

CARDIGAN BAY

The heather-clad heights of the Preseli Hills look down across a neatly hedged landscape to the blue waters of Cardigan Bay. This delectable corner of Dyfed is something of a backwater on the normal tourist trail, and is all the more delightful because of it. The ancient market towns of Cardigan and Newcastle Emlyn remain charmingly unspoilt.

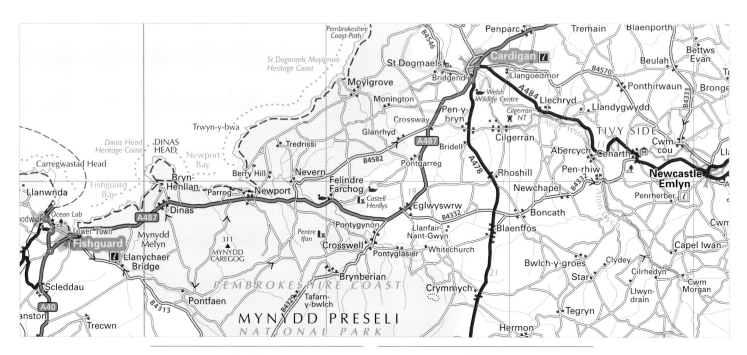

Tourist Information Centres

Cardigan: Theatr Mwldan, Bath House Road (tel: 01239 613230)
Fishguard: The Town Hall, The Square (tel: 01348 873484)
Fishguard Harbour: Ocean Lab, The Parrog, Goodwick (tel: 01348 874737)

Cardigan

Coracles, the ancient handmade small Welsh craft, can still be seen plying for salmon and sea trout on the River Teifi at Cardigan. In medieval days before the harbour silted up, this was an important seaport, giving its name to the whole sweep of Cardigan Bay. There are few reminders of its former glory, but chief among them are the remains of the Norman castle, overlooking the 17th-century, six-arched bridge over the Teifi.

A weekly market is still held beneath the arches of the 19th-century Guildhall. Just off the modern resort of Gwbert-on-Sea is Cardigan Island, which is now a nature reserve.

Castell Henllys

Near Felindre Farchog, this is an award-winning reconstruction of an Iron-Age village, owned and run by the Pembrokeshire Coast National Park Authority. It is an imaginative and exciting project which enables visitors to step inside a heather-thatched dwelling and experience just how people lived 2,000 years ago.

Cilgerran

Romantic Cilgerran Castle, perched high on a crag overlooking the River Teifi, makes a splendid backdrop to the annual coracle 'regatta' where local fishermen compete against each other in various contests of skill. The pretty village of Cilgerran is dominated by the early 13th-century castle. It was built by William Marshall, Earl of Pembroke, shortly after he captured this strategic site, on a promontory between the Teifi and the Plysgog, from the Welsh. The gatehouse and the two great circular towers are the most impressive remaining features.

Fishguard

The old fishing village of Fishguard in the picturesque bay between Carregwastad Point and Dinas Head was the scene of the pathetic conclusion of the last invasion of Britain, by a drunken rabble of Frenchmen, in 1797. They were, apparently, frightened off by the sight of a group of local women in Welsh traditional costume, the headgear of which is somewhat reminiscent of soldiers' helmets.

The Pembrokeshire Coast Path, seen here at Cemaes Head, with Cardigan Island in the background, gives access to the magnificent coastal scenery of south-west Wales

The Pembrokeshire Coast Path

Officially opened in 1970, the Pembrokeshire Coast Path has its northern terminus at St Dogmaels. It runs its roller-coaster route for 186 miles (299.3km) around the rugged coastline of Pembrokeshire, with only a slight hiatus at Milford Haven, to Amroth, beyond Tenby.

It was surveyed by the distinguished local naturalist Ronald Lockley in the early 1950s, so it is appropriate that among its greatest attractions are the wildlife that the walker can see along the way, from the wheeling seabird colonies on the cliffs to the glorious carpet of wildflowers, especially in early summer.

The Old or Lower Town is particularly attractive, while the Upper Town has a fine Square, complete with Market Hall. Nearby Goodwick is the terminus for ferries crossing the Irish Sea to Rosslare. A few miles to the east is the lovely village of Dinas Cross, sheltering behind the great 500ft (152.4m) cliffs of Dinas Head, from where basking seals can often be seen.

Mynydd Preseli

Famous as the source of the Stonehenge bluestones which were somehow transported to far-off Wiltshire by Neolithic man, the Preseli Hills include the highest point of the Pembrokeshire Coast National Park, reaching 1,759ft (536m) at Foel Cwm Cerwyn.

The views from these rugged summits of Ordovician rock are truly panoramic, extending as far south as Dunkery Beacon on Exmoor and to Cadair Idris in Snowdonia to the north. Sometimes even the Wicklow Mountains of Ireland are visible across the Irish Sea.

Nevern

A firm candidate for the title of most beautiful village in Wales, Nevern's cottages are set on a slope overlooking the River Nyfer, which is crossed by a medieval bridge. Nevern is famous for its wonderful, intricately carved Celtic cross of St Brynach, which dates from around AD 1000 and stands over 12ft (3.6m) high in the churchyard. There are other carved stones near by, and the churchyard also has a famous 'bleeding' yew which secretes blood-red sap. The church of St Brynach is of cruciform construction with a low battlemented tower, and dates mainly from the 15th century.

Newcastle Emlyn

This bustling little market town on the Teifi gets its name from the castle, which was 'new' in the 15th century – its builders wanted to distinguish it from the older Cilgerran Castle downstream. The town was the site of the first printing press in Wales, set up in 1718, and was also a centre of the 'Rebecca Riots' of the mid-19th century, in which men dressed as women were protesting against road tolls.

Pentre Ifan

Probably the best known and most photographed prehistoric monument in Wales, and certainly one of the finest megalithic monuments in Britain, this Neolithic chambered long barrow occupies a spectacular site on the northern slopes of the Preseli Hills. Originally covered by earth and stones, the massive capstone, thought to weigh about 17 tons, is still delicately balanced on the three pointed uprights that have supported it for 5,000 years.

St Dogmaels

St Dogmael, a descendant of Ceredig, after whom Ceredigion was named, founded a hermitage here in the 6th century. The Benedictine abbey was founded by Robert Fitz-Martin in 1115, but the remaining ruins mainly date from the 14th to 16th centuries. Among the most important remains that can be seen in the adjoining 19th-century parish church is the Sagranus Stone, a 7ft (2.1m) high pillar inscribed in both Latin and Ogham lettering, which helped scholars to decipher this mysterious, Dark-Ages script.

Just beyond the village are the beautiful and extensive Poppit Sands, which lead up to the wild cliffscape of Cemaes Head.

Excavated in the 1930s, Pentre Ifan burial chamber is the remaining part of a vanished long barrow

The impressive ruins of St Dogmaels Abbey still evoke the atmosphere of medieval times

CIDER COUNTRY AND THE WYE VALLEY

The meandering River Wye coils down through green pastureland as it makes its way south from the cathedral city of Hereford to the Forest of Dean. This is prime agricultural land, where the dusty red soil matches the sandstone of the rocks and the hides of the famous Hereford cattle, whose white faces are now to be found all over the world.

The church at Abbey Dore, sadly neglected after the Dissolution, was reconstructed during the 17th century by master craftsman John Abel. His work includes a superb oak screen

Abbey Dore

This quiet village lies at the heart of the apple orchards at the southern end of the long valley of the River Dore, on the eastern shoulder of the Black Mountains. The valley is known as the Golden Valley, though it is a vision of pink blossom in the spring. Abbey Dore takes its name from the fact that its magnificent parish church was once part of a Cistercian abbey, founded in 1147.

Dorstone

On a ridge overlooking the Golden Valley, Arthur's Stone is a prehistoric tomb dating from c2000 BC

Richard de Brito, one of the knights who murdered Thomas à Becket, founded the church here at the northern end of the Golden Valley. When it was restored, his tomb was opened and a chalice which was found inside is now on display.

Not far to the north, near Pen-y-Moor Farm, is the Neolithic chambered long barrow known as Arthur's Stone – one of many alleged burial sites of that legendary monarch. It has nine uprights and a massive capstone which weighs about 25 tons. The ruined passageway still survives.

Hereford

The small Norman cathedral of Hereford, with its great forest of pink sandstone columns lining the nave, is one of the finest in England. The massive central tower of around 1325 adds distinction to every view of the building, which underwent extensive restoration after the collapse of the 14th-century west tower in 1786.

One of the cathedral's greatest treasures, saved for the nation by public outcry and subscription, is the *Mappa Mundi*, drawn on vellum around 1290, making it one of the earliest maps of the world in existence. The cathedral's famous chained library, containing 1,500 books, is the largest in the world.

Formerly the Saxon capital of West Mercia, Hereford reflects its place in history, and its fascinating Art Gallery and Museum in Broad Street has many exhibits from its ancient past. High Town is the nucleus of Old Hereford, while the River Wye, with its 15th-century bridge, just upstream from the cathedral, is a constant artery.

Hereford Cathedral has a magnificent chained library containing some 1,500 volumes, each attached to its bookcase with an individual chain

Kilpeck Church

Kilpeck is a tiny hamlet 8 miles (12.9km) south-west of Hereford, usually overlooked by travellers on the A465. But it is worth stopping for a while to visit the tiny 12th-century parish church, which contains some of the finest examples of Romanesque carvings in Britain. The richness of the carvings, especially around the south doorway, is overpowering, with mythical beasts, warriors, angels and devils competing for space. Near by are the remains of Kilpeck Castle and the 6-acre (2ha) site of a deserted medieval village.

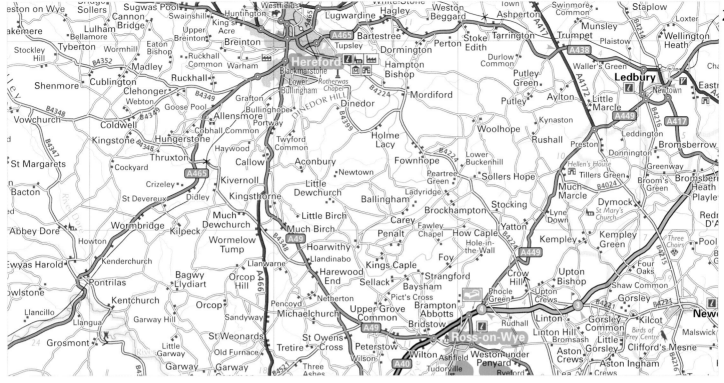

Hereford Cattle

One of the finest sights in British agriculture is that of a curly, white-faced Hereford bull being led to receive the prized winner's rosette in the superb setting of the Three Counties Show at Malvern.

Renowned for their fine lean beef, hardiness and early maturity, the red and white Hereford cattle have transported the name of their county of origin around the world. Their distinctive white faces can often be seen in Western films, and their hardiness makes them suitable for conditions ranging from the Arctic to the Equator.

Major improvements to the breed were made by the local Tompkins family in the 18th century, and it was not until the 19th century that the red and white colour that we know so well predominated.

Ledbury

Historic Ledbury, with its leaning, half-timbered cottages and narrow winding alleyways, is for many people the quintessential small English market town. Gathered around the soaring, detached Georgian spire of the mainly early 14th-century parish church of St Michael and All Angels, Ledbury continues in its role as the commercial centre for the surrounding Herefordshire villages.

John Masefield was born here, and Ledbury has long been a favourite place for poets and painters, from Wordsworth to the Brownings. The October Hiring Fair no longer hires farm labourers, but continues as a festival. Near by is Eastnor Castle, a magnificent Georgian pile in a fairytale setting, with Italianate and Gothick interiors which have been splendidly restored. The grounds include a deer park, nature trails, an arboretum and a lake.

Much Marcle

The centre of the Herefordshire cider country, Much Marcle is the place where local farmer Henry Weston set up one of the first specialist cider-making factories in the 19th century. However, local farmers have been selling surplus supplies of the clear, strong, golden beverage since the 17th century.

Much Marcle's church dates mainly from the 13th century and contains a fine collection of carved effigies, one of which, dating from about 1350, is sculpted from a solid block of local oak.

Pembridge

Pembridge is a compact village of ancient timber-framed houses, and its 600-year-old parish church of St Mary recalls the days when Welsh raids across Offa's Dyke were frequent. The detached timber-framed belfry tower – one of seven in Herefordshire – was used as a place of refuge for villagers in times of trouble, like the pele towers of Northumberland. Arrows could be shot from the embrasures, or slits in the stone base of the tower.

Ross-on-Wye

Another fine little Herefordshire market town, Ross-on-Wye stands on a bluff overlooking a sweeping meander of the River Wye, with marvellous views across to the Welsh hills to the west.

At the top of the hill in Ross, just beyond the half-timbered and arcaded 17th-century Market Hall is the elegant 14th-century spire of the parish church of St Mary. There are splendid views of the Wye Valley from The Prospect, near the churchyard, and many reminders of John Kyrle, the local philanthropist made famous as Alexander Pope's Man of Ross.

Ross is now one of the main tourist centres for exploring the Wye Valley and Symond's Yat, but it retains its peaceful market town atmosphere with good shops and a lively community spirit. ·

Tourist Information Centres

Hereford: 1 King Street (tel: 01432 268430)
Ledbury: 3 The Homend (tel: 01531 636147)
Ross-on-Wye: Swan House, Edde Cross Street (tel: 01989 562768)

Local benefactor, John Kyrle, was born in this house in Ross-on-Wye. His many good works included the restoration of the church, providing the town with a public water supply and laying out the Prospect Gardens

THE WELSH MARCHES – A FRONTIER LAND

A glance at Sheet 137 of the Ordnance Survey's 1:50,000 Landranger series, covering Ludlow and Wenlock Edge and the western edge of Shropshire, shows a landscape shaped by conflict and war. Here in the heart of the troubled borderland of the Welsh Marches, many examples of defensive structures are still visible. Ludlow's great red sandstone keep, built by Roger Montgomery, Earl of Shrewsbury, in the 11th century to repel Welsh raiders, was succeeded by many smaller 'motte and bailey' castles, such as those scattered along Offa's Dyke. A classic example can be found at New Radnor. Later, the fortified manors of Stokesay Castle, Bromfield, and Richard's Castle tell of more settled times, while the manors of Wilderhope and Croft Castle show the gradual trend away from defence towards the country houses found in more peaceful areas.

EARLY TIMES

In prehistoric times, the slopes of every major hill formed their own frontier with everything below, and settlers fortified their summits with banks, ditches and palisades, within which they enjoyed the best possible coigns of vantage. One of the most striking features of the above-mentioned map is the number of these 'Forts,' 'Camps' and 'Earthworks' – over 20 of them – marked in the Gothic typeface which the OS uses, rather imprecisely, to indicate a 'Non-Roman antiquity.'

The better-known examples include Croft Ambrey, south-west of Ludlow, where hundreds of regularly placed huts have been traced; and Caer Caradoc, overlooking the Church Stretton valley, where Caractacus is alleged to have made his last stand against the Romans. But there are many other lesser-known examples. Some, like Burfa Camp, Bury Ditches and Bagbury, are now hidden under blanket forestry plantations, but many others command the same sweeping views over the countryside which first attracted their builders over 2,000 years ago.

Radio-carbon dating shows that most British hillforts were built between 750 and 500 BC,

Magnificent views for miles around can be enjoyed from high up on Croft Ambrey Iron-Age hillfort – it is said that 14 counties are visible

though many were still in use up to the Roman invasion in the first century AD. The name 'hillfort' can be misleading, although many must have had a defensive purpose. But the idea that they were all the last outposts of the native Britons who fled there in the face of the invading Romans is one which is no longer in favour with modern archaeologists. Some believe that hillforts were the spiritual or religious centres of the Iron Age, and temples have been found in some of them. But there is no doubt that many others were settlements which were perhaps used only in the summer to watch over grazing stock, or as administrative or market centres.

AFTER THE ROMANS

Winding up from south to north through the western side of the said map is the ancient earthwork known as Offa's Dyke – now followed by the 177-mile (285km) Offa's Dyke Path, which opened in 1971. Built in the last quarter of the 8th century by King Offa of Mercia to mark the western edge of his kingdom and to control Welsh incursions, Offa's Dyke is the longest continuous earthwork in Britain, and links the Severn and Dee Estuaries.

There can be little doubt from its method of construction that Offa's Dyke was primarily defensive in nature, and there is some evidence that it may once have had a permanently manned stockade along its crest. It was said to have been instigated by Offa in AD 782, but the first reference to this monumental earthwork is not recorded until 100 years later, when Bishop Asser notes that Offa ordered the dyke to be built between Wales and Mercia 'from sea to sea'.

Following the decline of Mercia, the usually bickering Welsh princes united under

When Harlech Castle was built it had a sheer drop to the sea on one side. Though the sea has receded, it still has one of the most impressive situations of all Edward I's Welsh castles. The defence of its walls during the Wars of the Roses inspired the stirring song 'Men of Harlech'.

Llywelyn was eventually defeated by Edward in 1282, and to confirm his conquest, he built a series of massive fortresses throughout Wales. These castles, such as Conwy, Caernarfon, Harlech and Beaumaris, were at the forefront of medieval military architecture and even today stand as impressive ruins.

By 1472, in an attempt as much to subdue the powerful Marcher Lords as the still warring Welsh, Edward IV set up a Lord President and Council of the Marches, who were to supervise the affairs of Wales and the border for the next two centuries. The Council usually sat at Ludlow or Shrewsbury Castles, but Welsh opposition was not finally stamped out until the defeat of Owain Glyndwr, another great hero of Welsh nationalism, in 1410.

AFTER THE TUDORS

It was not until the reign of Henry VIII that the boundary between England and Wales was finally settled, and today's visitor can still hear strong echoes of the troubled history of the Welsh Marches. One of the most impressive is Roger Montgomery's still-formidable red sandstone castle towering above the River Teme at Ludlow. Started in 1085 during the first wave of castle-building, in its chequered history it has been the prison for Edward IV's sons – 'the Princes in the Tower' – and the place where Arthur, elder brother of Henry VIII, died. On a more cultural note, it was the scene in 1634 of the first production of John Milton's masque, *Comus*, and is still the regular venue for open-air Shakespearean productions.

Monmouth, with its rare portcullised gatehouse over the River Monnow, still boasts the ruins of its 11th-century castle, where Henry V was born in 1387. Chepstow's great Norman castle still dominates the town's medieval streets, and across the border at Goodrich an almost perfectly preserved 13th-century castle still frowns down over the River Wye. At Rhuddlan, near Rhyl on the coast of north Wales, Edward I is said to have made his famous sacrificial move to win over the Welsh by proclaiming his infant son as the first Prince of Wales, later presenting him to his people at Caernarfon in 1284.

See Walk V page 243
Border Lines – on Offa's Dyke

Chepstow Castle, in a commanding position high above the River Wye, is the first recorded Norman stone castle and was used as a base for advances into Wales

Gruffydd ap Llywelyn and began serious incursions across the Dyke into England. These were eventually thwarted by Harold, who was later to become the short-lived King of England, in a vicious campaign of retaliation in 1063.

NORMAN BARONS AND WELSH PRINCES

The next chapter in the trouble-torn history of the Marches begins with the Norman conquest of 1066. William set about subduing his new nation by making grants of land to favoured 'Marcher' barons, who ruled by right of conquest and claimed special rights, not subject to the usual restraint of the law. It was these autocratic barons who built the string of earth mounds and wooden forts known as 'motte and bailey' castles, such as that still visible at New Radnor. The word 'Marches' has the same origin as 'mark', meaning a boundary.

The great stone castles of the Marches, such as Ludlow, Monmouth, Chepstow, Rhuddlan and Shrewsbury, came later, as the English overlords tried to stamp their authority over an unwilling populace. A double, and sometimes triple, line of castles were erected along the border, such as Grosmont, Skenfrith and White Castles in Monmouthshire.

But the Welsh princes like Gruffydd, now known as Llywelyn the Last, were still unwilling to bow under the English yoke, and after he evaded taking the oath of loyalty to Edward I, he was soon in open conflict with the king's army, commanded by Roger de Mortimer, Earl of Shrewsbury. Mortimer was just one of the immensely powerful Marcher Lords. Others included Roger de Lacy of Ludlow and Robert de Say of Clun.

ABERYSTWYTH AND THE VALE OF RHEIDOL

*A*berystwyth looks out on to the broad expanse of Cardigan Bay and has as its backdrop the mountains of Central Wales. These rise to 2,467ft (752m) at Plynlimon Fawr, the great mountain mass which gives rise to the mighty border rivers of the Severn and the Wye and to the Rheidol, which dashes down over wild waterfalls at Devil's Bridge to enter the Irish Sea at Aberystwyth.

Borrow's Wild Wales

When George Borrow, Norfolk-born linguist and traveller, reached Devil's Bridge in his classic travelogue *Wild Wales* (published in 1862), he was harangued by the natives who were terrified by his appearance and could not understand his earnest though bombastic attempts at the Welsh language.

Wild Wales remains one of the most entertaining and amusing of the early guidebooks to Wales, and Borrow's description of Plynlimon Fawr, where he symbolically drinks in turn from the sources of the Rheidol, Severn and Wye, 'all three ...contained within the compass of a mile', sees him at his descriptive best.

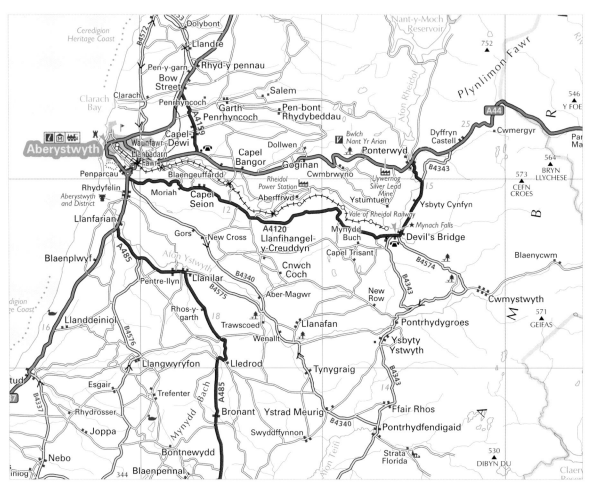

Aberystwyth

This pleasant seaside town has a good claim to be the Oxbridge of Wales. 'The college by the sea' – University College of Wales – occupies a splendid position in a former hotel on the sea front near the pier; the rest of the campus is on the hills behind at Penglais, where the National Library of Wales houses some of the great literary treasures of the Principality.

The largest resort on Cardigan Bay, Aberystwyth combines seaside attractions with a history that goes back to the Iron Age. The hillfort of Pen Dinas overlooks The Bar to the south of the town, and the ruins of one of many castles built in Wales by Edward I is perched on a headland just south of the pier. There is a small harbour and a beach of shingle and sand.

A Victorian funicular railway operates on Constitution Hill at the north end of the promenade, and the views from the 430ft (131m) summit extend to Snowdonia in the north and the Preseli Hills to the south.

Devil's Bridge

Three bridges, built on top of one another in a sequence covering seven centuries, make this dramatic wooded gorge of the River Mynach one of the great scenic highlights of Wales. The first (lowest) bridge was built in the 12th century by the monks of nearby Strata Florida Abbey, and

Tourist Information Centre

Aberystwyth: Lisburn House, Terrace Road (tel: 01970 612125)

The massive dam of the Craig Goch reservoir holds back the waters which flood the Elan Valley

Three bridges, the first dating from the 12th century, sit one on top of the other across the gorge at Devil's Bridge, high above the whirlpool known as the Devil's Punchbowl. Near by the River Mynach plunges down the gorge, forming a spectacular waterfall

was succeeded by another stone bridge and lastly by a modern steel structure. The Mynach meets the Rheidol here in a series of spectacular waterfalls, the highest of which is about 300ft (91.4m) high.

Plynlimon Fawr

One of the three great mountains of Wales, Plynlimon Fawr (2,467ft/752m) lacks the imposing appearance of Snowdon and Cadair Idris only because it rises from almost uniformly high ground. But as the source of the Rivers Severn, Wye and Rheidol, its significance as a physical feature cannot be denied. Its boggy and mainly featureless slopes show signs of previous industry in the remains of lead and silver mines, and the easiest approach to the undistinguished summit is from Eisteddfa Gurig Farm on the A44 between Ponterwyd and Llangurig.

Strata Florida Abbey

Now reduced to romantic, though sparse, ruins, the Abbey was once one of the major cultural centres of Wales and governed a large part of mid Wales. The community of Cistercian monks, founded by Prince Rhys ap Gruffydd in 1184, administered huge sheep ranches over the surrounding Cambrian Mountains. All that remains now is a soaring western doorway, some foundations laid out in the grass, and some lovely medieval floor tiles.

Near by in the upper reaches of the River Teifi near Tregaron is the Tregaron Bog (*Cors-goch Glan Teifi*) National Nature Reserve, the largest peat bog in Wales, which covers some 1,900 acres (770ha).

There is a nature trail along which visitors can spot such wetland rarities as the golden plover and the curlew.

Vale of Rheidol Railway

Running for 12 sylvan miles (19.3km) through the valley of the Rheidol between Aberystwyth and Devil's Bridge, the Vale of Rheidol Railway was the last narrow-gauge steam railway owned by British Rail before privatisation in 1989.

Originally opened in 1902 to carry lead ore to the coast from the mines in the mountains, the railway is now exclusively used for tourist passenger traffic. It is a popular and attractive way to reach the honeypots of the waterfalls of Mynach and Devil's Bridge from Aberystwyth and the coastal resorts of Cardigan Bay.

The Welsh Lake District

The insatiable thirst of the booming industrial cities of the West Midlands in the late 19th and early 20th centuries turned the attentions of the water engineers to the isolated, steep-sided valleys of the River Elan and its tributaries in mid-Wales.

Its clean, unpolluted water and the comparative ease of providing gravity-fed pipelines to the Midlands made it an ideal choice, and the Craig Goch, Penygarreg, Garreg-ddu, Caban-coch and finally the Caerwen Reservoirs followed. They now supply Birmingham and district with 75 million gallons of Welsh water every day. The sheer scale of the engineering and the imposing architecture of the dams make a visit worthwhile.

Though little remains of Strata Florida Abbey, its former role at the centre of an enormous estate can be discerned in such remnants as these decorated floor tiles

See Walk G page 230 Abbey in the Wilderness

The success of the Vale of Rheidol Railway was assured by its route between a major holiday resort and a popular tourist attraction, with wonderful scenery along the way

SHROPSHIRE'S HILL COUNTRY

S hropshire's 'blue remembered hills' are dominated by the north-east/south-west ridges of the Stiperstones, the Long Mynd, Caer Caradoc, Wenlock Edge and the Clee Hills to the east. It is a surprisingly wild part of the Midlands, where heather-covered hills rise dramatically from steep-sided valleys and where fortified houses tell of a troubled past.

Legends of the hills

Myths and legends abound in the isolated hill country of Shropshire, where tales of mysterious happenings have been retold over the generations. Perhaps the earliest is the legend of the giant Ippikin, who can be recalled by chanting his name near his rock on Wenlock Edge. The Devil himself is supposed to be sitting on the highest point of The Stiperstones, still known as The Devil's Chair, when the frequent clouds and mists envelop the quartzite summit.

Another giant, known as Wild Edric – a Saxon lord who was deprived of his lands by the Normans – is supposed to be imprisoned in the lead mines below The Stiperstones, while Caer Caradoc, the fort-topped hill opposite Church Stretton, is alleged to be the site of Caractacus's last stand against the Romans.

Tourist Information Centre

Ludlow: Castle Street (tel: 01584 875053)

This tractor seat at the Acton Scott Working Farm and Museum is a far cry from today's padded seats in temperature controlled cabs, but is a fine example of the combination of the attractive and the functional

Acton Scott

Acton Scott Working Farm and Museum near Little Stretton is a marvellous place for both children and adults to experience farming in the Shropshire hills before the days of tractors and combine harvesters. Shire horses are used for most of the heavy work, such as ploughing and the pulling of carts, and there is a varied range of demonstrations in a lovely setting, transporting the visitor back to when craftsmen created the countryside.

Church Stretton

Capital of Shropshire's hill country, Church Stretton nestles at the eastern end of the Carding Mill Valley, one of the most beautiful of the approaches to the Long Mynd, which dominates the town. Cheerful tearooms and a range of other shops are a feature of this pleasant little village, which was granted its market charter by King John in 1214. The parish church features an unusual blocked-up Corpse Door on its north side.

The Clee Hills

At 1,791ft (546m), Brown Clee Hill near Abdon is the highest point in Shropshire, with Titterstone Clee Hill at 1,749ft

Stokesay Castle, right, is a wonderfully preserved example of a 13th-century manor house. Its features include a timber-framed Jacobean gatehouse and the Great Hall, reached via an outside staircase

Wilderhope Manor

Tucked away in a fold of the hills beyond Wenlock Edge is Wilderhope Manor, a beautifully gabled Tudor manor house which is now surely one of the most romantic youth hostels in Britain. Built in 1586 by the Smallman family, it was the home of Major Thomas Smallman, who escaped a party of raiding Roundheads during the Civil War by leaping off Wenlock Edge on his horse. He landed in a crab-apple tree, which broke his fall and saved his life.

The Stiperstones, left, a seemingly innocuous rocky summit, has become the focus of local legend – both above and below the ground

(533m) a close second. These bleak hills of Carboniferous limestone, later covered by volcanic basalts, have been extensively exploited by man over the centuries. There are many remains of coal mines on Brown Clee, and iron ore, copper and limestone have also been extracted. Even today, black basalt is still extracted for roadstone from Titterstone Clee Hill, where a massive quarry blights the hillside.

The highest points of the hills were settled by Iron-Age people, who built a series of hill-forts – at Abdon Burf, Clee Burf, Nordy Bank and on the quarry-ravaged Titterstone Clee, the largest fort of all.

Craven Arms

Craven Arms, a bustling little market town on the busy A49 Shrewsbury to Ludlow road, takes its name from its Georgian coaching inn. It is famous for its autumn sheep sales, when farmers from the surrounding hills come to buy and sell their livestock, including the local brown-faced Clun Forest breed.

The Long Mynd

This 10-mile (16.1km) whaleback is the most massive physical feature in Shropshire, although its summit at Pole Bank (1,693ft/516m) is not the county's highest point. Crossed by the prehistoric track known as The Portway, the Long Mynd is the most southerly grouse moor in England, with plentiful heather on the broad plateau. It is split by coombs and steep-sided valleys, especially on the eastern side of the ridge. The most famous of these is the Carding Mill Valley, which runs west from Church Stretton, and is now owned by the National Trust. There is a gliding club at Asterton, and among the plentiful wildlife on the Long Mynd are red grouse, buzzards and wheatears, with ring ouzels and dippers in the batches.

Ludlow

One of Britain's best-preserved medieval towns, Ludlow has a wealth of the black and white, half-timbered box-framed houses which are such a feature of Shropshire. Perhaps the most famous of these is the much-photographed 17th-century Feathers Hotel in The Bull Ring, where

bulls were baited in the Middle Ages. But Ludlow is dominated by the massive red sandstone castle, built by Roger Montgomery, Earl of Shrewsbury, shortly after the Conquest to repel Welsh incursions. The castle has been the home of kings and princes ever since, and today plays host to regular Shakespearean performances in its ancient courtyard.

Stokesay Castle

This perfect and romantic example of a 13th-century fortified manor house stands frozen in time at the end of a lane, just off the A49. Its North Tower is uniquely topped with a half-timbered construction, the earliest part of the house, begun about 1240. It has a massive polygonal South Tower of 1291 and an Elizabethan gatehouse, and was the home of the Say and Ludlow families, before passing to the Cravens (of Craven Arms) and the Baldwyns from nearby Diddlebury.

Wenlock Edge

Wenlock Edge is a well-wooded 10-mile (16.1km) escarpment of Silurian limestone to the south of Much Wenlock, bounded in the north-west by Hope Dale and in the south-east by Corve Dale.

Now owned by the National Trust, the Edge is a fine viewpoint for the Shropshire Hills, with Caer Caradoc and the Long Mynd across Ape Dale, and The Wrekin to the north.

Ludlow's most famous building is the 17th-century Feathers Hotel, a superb example of the black and white, box-framed architecture of the area

See Walk H page 231
Over the Long Mynd

WORCESTER AND THE MALVERN HILLS

The mighty River Severn is the silver thread which binds together these lush fields, bordered by the whaleback spine of the Malvern Hills to the west and Bredon Hill and the Cotswolds to the east. The cathedral of Worcester, the abbey of Tewkesbury and the priory of Malvern dominate their streets, while in the villages, many half-timbered houses still survive.

The Malverns

This impressive miniature mountain range has long had the ability to inspire. From the medieval author of *The Vision of Piers Plowman* to that most supremely English of composers, Edward Elgar, born in their shadow at Lower Broadheath, the Malverns have exerted their influence. They were historically important and the Herefordshire Beacon is the site of an impressive Iron-Age hillfort.

The Malverns stand between upland and lowland Britain, and the views from their 5-mile (8km) ridge are stunning. Formed from Precambrian rocks, their name echoes their frontier role, coming from the Welsh, *Moel Bryn* or 'bald hill.'

Sunrise over the Malvern Hills, as seen from the high point of the Worcestershire Beacon

Great and Little Comberton

Of the Bredon Hill villages, the Combertons are among the most attractive. Great Comberton lies on the northern slopes of the hill, clustered around the Norman Church of St Michael. Little Comberton, despite its name, is bigger and busier, and boasts a good medieval church and early-18th century manor house, complete with dovecote and 16th-century barn.

Great Malvern

The hillside town of Great Malvern was a spa in the mid-19th century, although it had been attracting people who believed in the curative powers of its pure spring water since the 17th century. With its great rambling houses and steeply climbing streets, the town retains an air of faded gentility. The 15th-century priory is famous for its outstanding medieval glass, tiles and choir stalls, perhaps the most complete in the country.

Its neighbours of Malvern Wells, where the composer Edward Elgar is buried, and Little Malvern, which climbs up the hills to the pass of Wynds Point, contain many villas built at the height of its health spa

heyday. The annual Three Counties Show, on one of the best showgrounds in the country, is held near Malvern Wells.

Pershore

Pershore is in the heart of Worcestershire's orchard country, and is renowned for the delicious Pershore plums. The parish church is the only remaining part of the abbey. The magnificent lantern tower, built in about 1330, was the central tower of the abbey, which John Betjeman claimed must have been finer than Worcester Cathedral.

Tewkesbury

The view of the magnificent Norman tower of Tewkesbury Abbey, peeping over the black and white half-timbered buildings of Mill Street from the Abbey Mills, is one of the most famous sights in the Midlands. Dominated by the massive Norman abbey, Tewkesbury has a strategic position at the confluence of the Rivers Severn and Avon. A crucial battle in the Wars of the Roses was fought in the water meadows near here in 1471.

Bredon Hill

In summertime on Bredon The bells they sound so clear The Worcestershire poet A E Houseman could have heard the bells of ten churches from Bredon Hill, and this prominent Jurassic limestone outlier of the Cotswolds dominates many of the views east of the Severn Plain. Its 958ft (292m) summit was pushed to over 1,000ft (304.8m) by the addition of a summerhouse by a Mr Parsons of Kemerton in the early 19th century.

Tourist Information Centres

Malvern: 21 Church Street (tel: 01684 892289)
Pershore: 19 High Street (tel: 01386 554262)
Tewkesbury: 64 Barton Street (tel: 01684 295027)
Worcester: The Guildhall, High Street (tel: 01905 726311/722480)

Saxon Church and Chapel

The isolated little priory church of St Mary at Deerhurst is one of the earliest surviving Saxon churches in England, originally built in the 7th century. Look for the tiny, triangular-headed windows, the superb font and the animal heads in the porch.

The nearby Saxon Chapel was only discovered in 1885 when repairs were being carried out to a medieval farmhouse. Its Saxon antecedents were proved by the discovery of the so-called Odda's Stone, now in the Ashmolean Museum, Oxford.

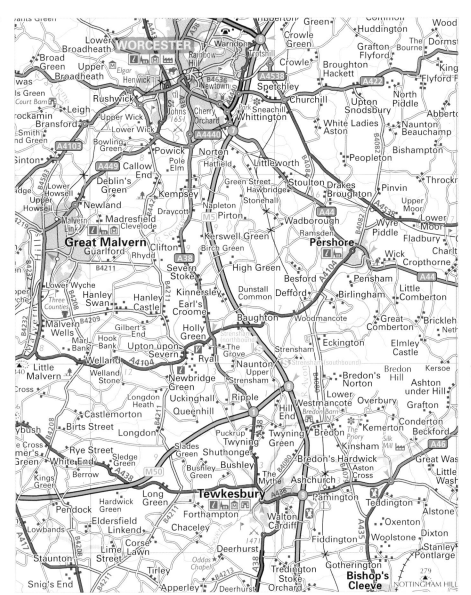

Upton upon Severn

The soaring iron bridge over the Severn here is a well-known landmark, as is the sandstone church tower, topped by an eight-sided cupola, locally known as 'The Pepperpot.' This is now a heritage centre which tells the story of the town, including an account of the Civil War battle of Upton Bridge.

Worcester

Watched over by the soaring spires of the 14th-century tower of the cathedral, Worcestershire's Severnside cricket ground is surely one of the most beautiful in the country. The city is rich in ancient buildings, such as The Guildhall and the Tudor House Museum, interesting in itself, but also housing a fascinating museum of local life. The Commandery is a splendid 15th-century timber-framed building which was the headquarters of Charles II's army during the Battle of Worcester in 1651. Now England's only Civil War Centre, it has spectacular audio-visual displays, including the trial of Charles I. The world's largest collection of Worcester's famous porcelain is displayed at the Dyson Perrins Museum in Severn Street, next door to the Royal Worcester factory.

Luckless King John is buried in the cathedral, and there is an effigy of him in the chancel. Henry VIII's elder brother, Prince Arthur, is also buried here. The cathedral was started in the 11th century, and the crypt is a fine example of Norman architecture. The Chapter House and Cloisters, dating from the 12th century, are reminders of the cathedral's monastic past.

Just 3 miles (4.8km) west of Worcester, at Lower Broadheath, is the cottage in which Sir Edward Elgar, the composer, was born in 1857. It is now a museum of his life, with musical scores, photographs and personal possessions.

Tewkesbury's Royal Hop Pole Hotel, upon which this plaque is fixed, is just one of the town's many fine old buildings and was mentioned in Dickens' Pickwick Papers

AT THE HOP POLE, Tewkesbury

They stopped to dine upon which occasion there was more Bottled Ale, with some more Madeira and some Port besides and here the Case Bottle was replenished for the fourth time. Under the influence of these combined stimulants Mr. Pickwick & Mr. Ben Allen fell fast asleep for thirty miles while Bob & Mr. Weller sang duets in the dickey.

PICKWICK PAPERS, Chap. 50.

See Walk K page 233
Tewkesbury and Odda's Chapel

See Walk J page 232
On Elgar's Malverns

King Charles's House in Worcester is where the king took refuge after his defeat in the nearby battle

SHREWSBURY AND IRONBRIDGE

The River Severn and the Roman Watling Street, still followed by the modern A5, are the main arteries of this corner of Shropshire, both watched over by The Wrekin. Shrewsbury is one of the most pleasant English towns; Telford is one of the most modern, but it includes the 'suburb' of Ironbridge, where the Industrial Revolution first sparked into life.

In the 18th century the course of worldwide industrial progress took a massive leap forward in this once peaceful valley of the River Severn. The first iron bridge in the world still stands as an impressive and beautiful monument to those times

Atcham and Attingham Park

The pretty little village of Atcham has two fine bridges over the Severn, one classical, built in 1771, and a more modern road bridge. The Palladian mansion of Attingham Park, built in 1785 by Lord Berwick to designs by John Nash, is now owned by the National Trust. The grounds, landscaped by Humphry Repton, have a fine herd of deer and afford sweeping views towards The Wrekin.

Buildwas Abbey

Overshadowed now by the massive cooling towers of the Buildwas Power Station, the noble remains of this 12th-century abbey were once one of the most important in Shropshire. Founded in 1135 as a Savignac monastery, it was later merged into the Cistercian order, but was razed by Thomas Cromwell. The Norman arches are among the finest in Britain.

Coalbrookdale and Ironbridge

Generally held to be the birthplace of the Industrial Revolution, it was here in 1709 that Abraham Darby first used coke to fire an iron furnace. The incredible, lace-like iron bridge, the first in the world, which spans the Severn here, was built by Darby's son in 1777 and gave the town both its fame and its name.

Now these twin settlements are the home of the award-winning Ironbridge Gorge Museum complex covering 6sq miles (15.5sq km). You will need a full day to explore the various sites, which include the original hearths used by the Darby family in their revolutionary methods of smelting, the houses where their workers lived and the incredible inclined plane which took materials down from the Shropshire Canal to a wharf on the Severn. The main attraction is the Blists Hill Open-Air Museum, a recreated town of the 1890s covering 42 acres (17ha), where visitors can really step back in time and experience how people lived and worked. Two miles (3.2km) downstream at Coalport there is a museum on the site of the original Coalport China Works.

Much Wenlock

Shropshire's 'magpie' villages reach their black-and-white crescendo at Much Wenlock, a pretty settlement at the northern end of Wenlock Edge. Among the half-timbered gems are The Goal, Raynald's Mansion and the Guildhall, built on sturdy wooden pillars. The little town was granted its market charter in 1468, but by then its splendid priory, founded in the 7th century by King Merewald of Mercia, was already ancient. It was later converted to a Cluniac priory by Roger of Montgomery. The Early English tracery work in the chapter house wall is particularly fine.

Shrewsbury

Shrewsbury stands on an enormous loop of the River Severn, which is crossed by two splendid bridges – the English and the

The Wrekin

'All friends around the Wrekin' is still a favourite Shropshire toast, and this modest 1,335ft (407m) summit, which is such a prominent feature for travellers on the M65 motorway, exerts a powerful influence on the surrounding countryside.

There are many legends associated with this isolated hill, which is crowned by a hillfort of the Iron-Age Cornovii people. The best known is that of a malevolent Welsh giant, who had a grudge against the people of Shrewsbury and was on his way to drop a great load of earth to dam the Severn and flood the town. Getting weary from his load, he stopped to ask a cobbler carrying a sack of boots and shoes for repair how far it was to Shrewsbury. The quick-thinking cobbler said he had worn out his sack of boots just walking from the town. The giant groaned and dumped his load of earth where he stood, forming the Wrekin.

Tourist Information
Centres

Ironbridge: The
Wharfage (tel: 01952
432166)
Much Wenlock: The
Museum, High Street
(tel: 01952 727679)
Shrewsbury: The Music
Hall, The Square
(tel: 01743 281200)
Telford: The Telford
Centre, Management
Suite (tel: 01952 238008)

Welsh – reflecting its role as a border town. It is full of romantic old half-timbered houses, leaning together as if whispering secrets in intriguingly-named streets such as Grope Lane, Frankwell and Butcher Row. There is an equal wealth of fine Georgian buildings, notably the town's library, art gallery and museum which are housed in the 17th-century buildings of Shrewsbury's famous public school. Circular St Chad's Church, also dating from the 17th century, is topped by a dome and overlooks the River Severn.

Much of the rich red sandstone for the town's buildings came from the Quarry, now the centrepiece of the beautiful park gardens known as The Dingle. It was created by one of Britain's best-known gardeners – the late Percy Thrower. Shrewsbury Castle, which stands above the railway station, was severely restored by Thomas Telford when he was appointed surveyor of public works for the county in 1788. It was from here that Henry IV conquered the Welsh rebels in 1403 at the Battle of Shrewsbury, fought 3 miles (4.8km) north of the town.

Telford

One of the latest of Britain's post-war new towns, Telford takes its name from Thomas Telford, county surveyor from 1788 and famed for his pioneering work on canals, aqueducts, bridges and turnpike roads.

The town was built in the early 1970s on land which had been scarred by 19th-century industrialisation, to house overspill populations from Birmingham and the Black Country. Today it is bisected by the M54 motorway and watched over by the conical hill of The Wrekin.

Wroxeter

The Roman columns at the gate to the church of St Andrew in the small village of Wroxeter give a small clue to the historical importance of the place. The tribal home of the Cornovii was taken over by the Romans and made their provincial capital of *Vironconium Cornoviorum*, headquarters of the XIV Legion in their campaign against the Ordovices of North Wales.

Partly discovered and protected by Thomas Telford, the most impressive remaining feature of the Roman town is the enormous wall which formed part of the entrance to the baths, the foundations of which can be seen. There is a good museum which explains the significance of this remarkably well-preserved site.

The restored Norman castle at Shrewsbury, above, now houses the Shropshire Regimental Museum, where, among the uniforms, weapons and medals is a lock of Napoleon's hair

Detail from the Market House in Shrewsbury, far left

See Walk N page 236
Valley of the Industrial Revolution

See Walk P page 237
Panorama from the Wrekin

Both Sides of the Menai Strait

The Menai Strait, between the castle-crowned towns of Beaumaris and Caernarfon, has always made ancient Anglesey a place set apart from the rest of Wales. Its dolmen-scattered interior is fringed by a beautiful coastline of steep cliffs and sandy bays. Over on the mainland, the narrow coastal plain rears up to the Llanberis Pass and the cloud-capped foothills of Snowdonia.

Prehistoric Anglesey

The distinguished archaeologist, Jacquetta Hawkes commented that there was no better place than Anglesey to combine a seaside holiday with painless archaeology. Certainly, this small, ancient island, known to the Romans as *Mona* and to the Welsh as *Ynys Môn* is a treasurehouse of prehistoric remains, and the fabled home of the mysterious priesthood known as the Druids, who caused the conqueror of Britain, Julius Caesar, so much anguish.

Among the most impressive sites are the Neolithic chambered barrows of Barclodiad y Gawres near Llangwfan and Bryncelli Ddu near Llanddaniel Fab, both unequalled outside Ireland, along with the various 'dolmens' at Lligwy, near Amlwch and Trefignath, just south of Holyhead. These are now known to be the exposed remains of other Neolithic tombs and barrows.

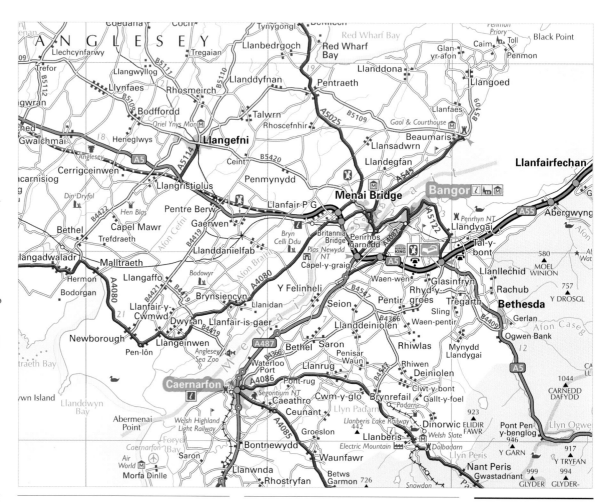

Bangor

Bangor is a university and cathedral city which boasts the oldest bishopric in Britain. Bangor is part of the collegiate system of the University of Wales, founded in 1893. Old Bangor is a delightful maze of streets leading down to the sea, and on Ffordd Gwynedd is an art gallery and museum of Welsh antiquities.

Three miles (4.8km) east is the splendid Penrhyn Castle, which has all the appearance of an authentic Norman fortress, with a cavernous great hall and enormous stone staircase, but it was actually built in the early 19th century as a sumptuous family home. There is an industrial railway museum in the stables.

Beaumaris

One of the most beautiful of Edward I's castles, moated Beaumaris Castle was built in the late 13th century to guard the approaches to the Menai Straits. The concentric walls with their circular towers were never completed to their full height, and the castle never saw military action. The Great Hall and chapel in the central tower are particularly memorable. The town itself is interesting, with such attractions as the former Gaol and Courthouse, where visitors can see the treadmill, grim cells and 19th-century courtroom. The Museum of Childhood has nine rooms of exhibits which reflect 150 years of dolls, toys, games and other related items.

Tourist Information Centres

Bangor: Town Hall, Deiniol Road (tel: 01248 352786)

Caernarfon: Oriel Pendeitsh, Castle Street (tel: 01286 672232)

Holyhead: Penrhos Beach Road (tel: 01407 762622)

Llanberis: 416 High Street (tel: 01286 870765)

Llanfair P G: Station Site (tel: 01248 713177)

Caernarfon

Dominated by the most imposing and complete of Edward I's castles, with its banded walls and angled towers on the sea front, Caernarfon does have deliberate echoes of Constantine's city. The castle was built over 44 years and completed to its present unequalled magnificence in 1327. The old town is still ringed by the almost intact town walls built on the order of Edward I, and the even earlier foundations of the Roman fort of *Segontium* can still be seen on the eastern edge of the town.

Holyhead

Holyhead Mountain (719ft/219 m) is one of the best viewpoints in Anglesey, taking in the distant coast of Ireland to the west, the Isle of Man to the north, and the jagged peaks of Snowdonia to the south-east. Nearer to hand are a wealth of prehistoric remains and the rocky little island of South Stack, with its gleaming white lighthouse serving as a beacon to the Ireland-bound ferries which scuttle in and out of this busy port. Holyhead is the biggest town on Anglesey, and its 13th-century church of St Cybi is built on the site of a Roman fort.

Llanberis

Slate predominates in this grey little town at the foot of the Llanberis Pass, and just across the waters of Llyn Padarn are the terraced shelves of the Dinorwig Slate Quarry, in its time one of the biggest in the world. It is now the location of a slate-mining museum and a spectacular underground hydro-electric scheme, also

LLANFAIR PG

This small, otherwise undistinguished village has traded on its name (the full version, that is) to become quite a tourist attraction. Few visitors can resist turning their cameras on the famous railway sign of: Llanfairpwllgwyngyll-gogerychwyrndrobwyll-llantysiliogogogoch. Llanfair PG's other, and perhaps most abiding claim to fame is that the first UK branch of the Women's Institute was founded here in 1915.

Curlews, godwits, sandpipers and oystercatchers are among the birds that find refuge at the Newborough Warren National Nature Reserve

open to visitors.

Today, Llanberis is a popular tourist centre and the starting point of two of the easiest ways to the summit of Snowdon. One is the Llanberis Path, which winds up the southern slopes, and the other is the famous Snowdon Mountain Railway, operating since 1896. Between the lakes of Llyn Padarn and Llyn Peris is the circular 13th-century keep of Dolbadarn Castle, a rarity in that it was built by Welsh princes before the English conquest.

Menai Bridge

Two feats of civil engineering dominate this Victorian town, which grew up as a result of them. Thomas Telford's graceful suspension bridge of 1826 originally took mail coaches across the Menai Strait. Today, the busy A5 crosses the Britannia Bridge, originally a tubular structure constructed by Stephenson in 1850 to carry the railway, but substantially rebuilt in 1970 to carry both road and rail traffic.

Newborough Warren

A National Nature Reserve covering 1,500 acres (608ha) of shifting sand dunes and forest plantations, Newborough Warren has waymarked nature trails enabling visitors to enjoy the famous birdlife of the reserve.

Plas Newydd

Plas Newydd, now in the care of the National Trust, was designed by James Wyatt for the Marquess of Anglesey in the late 18th century, and contains a military museum with a collection of uniforms and relics of the Battle of Waterloo, where the 1st Marquess lost his leg. There are magnificent views across the Menai Strait to Snowdonia from the park, which also contains two fine prehistoric dolmens.

Edward I built a total of 17 castles in Wales, but Caernarfon was the most ambitious, intended to be not only a fortress, but also the seat of government and the monarch's official residence

See Walk S page 240
Groves and Graves in Anglesey

Thomas Telford's suspension bridge, 100ft (30.5m) above the Menai Strait, was the longest single span in the world when it was built

THE NATIONAL PARKS OF WALES

The three National Parks of Wales – Snowdonia, the Brecon Beacons and the Pembrokeshire Coast – could hardly offer greater scenic contrasts. From the jagged volcanic peaks of Snowdonia, which includes the highest British ground south of Scotland, to the sweeping sandstone escarpments of the Brecon Beacons and the dramatic cliffs and bays of the Pembrokeshire Coast, the variety is breathtaking. In their tightly controlled protected areas, they encapsulate the very best of the unspoilt landscapes in the Principality.

A proposal for a fourth Welsh national park in the Cambrian Mountains of mid-Wales, centred on Plynlimon and the source of the Rivers Severn and Wye, was thwarted as a result of local opposition, mainly from farmers and landowners, in the mid 1970s.

SNOWDONIA

Snowdonia, at 827sq miles (2,142sq km), is the second largest national park in Britain after the Lake District, and was the first of the three to be designated (in 1951). Outdoor campaigners such as Sir Clough Williams Ellis, who built the Italianate fantasy village of Portmeirion, had long pressed for the proper protection of this unique landscape.

It was medieval English sailors crossing the Irish Sea who gave Snowdon and Snowdonia its name – the wild, rocky landscape beyond Anglesey always seemed to be brushed with snow. To the Welsh, though, this mountainous region had always been known as *Eryri,* the 'abode of eagles', and it was the place where their leaders, from the legendary Arthur through to the historical figures of Llywelyn the Great and Owain Glyndwr, traditionally sought refuge from the invading English.

There is still an indefinable air of nostalgia and 'Welshness' in these sometimes savage hills, where Welsh speakers are still in the majority.

The physical shape of the national park is best described as a large diamond split into three by valleys which run north-east to south-west. These deep gashes neatly separate the main mountain groups of Snowdon, the Glynders and Carneddau in the north; the rugged Rhinogs and Arenig in the centre; Cadair Idris and the Arans to the south. Most visitors gravitate to the area around Snowdon, which at 3,560ft (1,085m) is a natural magnet to the peak-bagger. There are several well-established routes to the summit, some of which have had to be extensively restored because of overuse. If the climb is too much, there is always the rack-and-pinion railway which winds up from Llanberis to the summit, where there is a café.

Slate and forestry have been the traditional industries in Snowdonia, but tourism is now as important in the slate-built villages of Llanberis, Capel Curig, Betws-y-Coed and Blaenau Ffestiniog.

THE BRECON BEACONS

The Brecon Beacons National Park, straddling the borders of Powys, Dyfed, Gwent and Mid Glamorgan, takes its name from, and is centred on the triple peaks of the Beacons themselves, which dominate the lush valley of the River Usk. These Old Red Sandstone mountains, the highest of which is Pen-y-Fan at 2,907ft (886m), stand like a petrified wave about to break over the ancient county town of Brecon, where the Romans had a fort at Y Gaer. The ascent of Pen-y-Fan is most easily achieved from the Storey Arms on the A470; the climb is rewarded with spectacular views.

There is much more to the 522sq mile (1,352sq km) park, established in 1957, than the Beacons. Two other distinct mountain masses make up the area, both of which confusingly carry the name 'Black'. The Black Mountains (plural) are a range of sandstone hills running north–south between Hay-on-Wye and Abergavenny. Offa's Dyke, the 8th-century bound-

ary embankment and ditch which separated England and Wales, runs along its crest and makes a fine walk. The Black Mountain (singular) is a wilder, less-visited area to the west of the A406 Sennybridge to Ystradgynlais road. It is centred on the sweeping crest of Carmarthen Van, at 2,631 ft (802 m) the highest point in the Black Mountain, which has the mysterious little glacial lake of Llyn y Fan Fach at its feet. Further west, near the boundary of the national park, remote Carreg Cennen Castle has one of the most spectacular situations of any castle in Wales.

There is another, altogether different landscape which dominates the south of the park. The area of Carboniferous rocks which stretches across the southern boundary has created a landscape of tumbling waterfalls, huge caves and potholes and beautiful woodlands which are a major attraction to visitors, and is easily accessible from the valleys of South Wales. A pleasant way to view the scenery is on the Brecon Mountain Railway from Pant Station, north of Merthyr Tydfil.

The Mellte and Hepste valleys, between Ystradfellte and Pont-neddfechan, are the centre of the Beacons caving country. Dan-yr-Ogof Showcaves system, north of Abercraf, has the largest chamber in any British showcave and in Bone Cave evidence was found of human occupation 3,000 years ago. The caves are now part of a tourist complex with a number of attractions.

THE PEMBROKESHIRE COAST

This area of Dyfed is sometimes known as 'Little England beyond Wales' and the popularity of resorts such as Tenby and St David's is undeniable. But the epithet has its basis in history,

since a string of castles were erected by the Norman invaders, along a line from Newgale in the west to Amroth in the east, to subdue the native Welsh. The line – known by the Norse word *landsker* meaning frontier – can still be traced through the area's placenames. South of the line, there is a predominance of places with anglicised names and English is still the most common language, but north of the *landsker*, Welsh is more commonly spoken and it is Welsh placenames that abound.

The Pembrokeshire Coast National Park – at 225sq miles (583sq km) one of the smallest of Britain's national parks – is the only one which is largely coastal, and it is not difficult to understand why. Its main glory is its superb 230-mile (370-km) coastline, which is followed for most of its way by the Pembrokeshire Coast Path, a wonderful rollercoaster of a walk with rugged cliffs, secluded sandy bays and the ever-changing seascapes.

The 170 miles (274km) of the Pembrokeshire Coast Path also offer a crash-course in geology, for the route shows at a glance the story of the forma-

tion of the earth from the earliest pre-Cambrian rocks around the tiny cathedral city of St David's to the Ordovician volcanic structure that underpins the the northern area.

The only real uplands in this mainly coastal park are the Preseli Hills in the north, a self-contained moorland block of Ordovician rocks rising to 1,759 ft (536m) at Foel Cwm Cerwym south of Bryberian. The Preseli Hills are famous as the source of the bluestones which were somehow transported to far-off Wiltshire for the inner circle of Stonehenge.

Wild and remote it may be, but the reality of Black Mountain is far removed from the image of its name

The main attraction of Pembrokeshire will always be its coastline, and there are few more invigorating walking experiences in Britain than to stride along these cliffs in early spring, on a carpet of wild flowers, accompanied by the cries of the seabirds and the salty tang of the sea.

St David's Head separates the rocky coastline to the north from the sands of the aptly named Whitesand Bay to the south

THE NORTH WALES RESORTS

One of the most pleasant and refined of the North Wales coastal resorts, Llandudno shelters between the great twin limestone headlands of the Great Orme and Little Orme, west of Colwyn Bay. Further east, the candy floss and kiss-me-quick attractions of Rhyl and Prestatyn beckon. To the west lies Conwy, guarded by its splendid medieval castle, one of the finest in Wales.

The combination of its mighty castle, its largely intact town walls and three fine bridges over the river give Conwy one of the most splendid townscapes in the country

Amidst all the grandeur of Conwy's massive and ancient walls is Britain's smallest house, 6ft (1.8m) wide by 10ft (3m) high

Abergele

This ancient market town is now also a busy resort, with the caravan-besieged suburb of Pensarn on the coast at the centre of 5 miles (8km) of sand and shingle beaches. A short distance down the A55 is the famous 'white marble' and lavishly ornate church at Bodelwyddan, its shining white limestone spire a landmark for miles.

Bodnant Garden

One of the finest gardens in the world, Bodnant consists of 80 acres of formal terraces, a pinetum and a wild garden, all laid out in 1875. It shelters in the valley of the River Hiraethlyn, a tributary of the Conwy. Bodnant is especially famous for its rhododendrons, azaleas and camellias, and for its magnificent laburnum arch.

Colwyn Bay

A charming traditional Victorian resort, Colwyn Bay has some fine architecture and a wonderful promenade, unfortunately shared by the parallel railway line. Colwyn stretches round its east-facing bay from Old Colwyn to Rhos-on-Sea. Among the attractions are the Eirias Park Dinosaur World and the interesting Welsh Mountain Zoo, which has a fine collection of mountain birds of prey. A little way south on the A470 is Felin Isaf, a working flour mill on the River Conwy.

Conwy

The eight drum towers of Edward I's superb 13th-century castle dominate this pleasant little town at the mouth of the River Conwy. The massive 15ft (4.6m) thick castle walls are matched by the virtually complete town walls with gates and their barbicans still intact.

Three bridges span the river beside the castle – a modern road bridge, Stephenson's tubular railway bridge of 1848 and Thomas Telford's suspension bridge of 1826, which has 'medieval' towers to match those of the castle. This bridge is now in the care of the National Trust.

Another National Trust property in Conwy is the fascinating 14th-century Aberconwy House, the only medieval merchant's house to survive in this once-thriving seaport. It now contains a heritage centre telling the story of the town. Visitors, though only a few at a time, can also see Britain's smallest house (verified by the Guinness Book of Records), which is just 6ft (1.8m) wide by 10ft (3m) high.

Edward I's Castles

The 35-year reign of Edward I saw an unprecedented period of castle-building in North Wales, of which Conwy and Rhuddlan are just two. Most of these superb examples of medieval military architecture were supervised by Master James of St George, the outstanding military engineer of his day. But the craftsmen who built them were nearly all conscripted from English counties by the King. All the major castles – Flint, Rhuddlan, Conwy, Caernarfon, Beaumaris, Criccieth and Harlech – were built so that they could be supplied from the sea, because of the threat to land-borne supplies by the constantly warring Welsh princes.

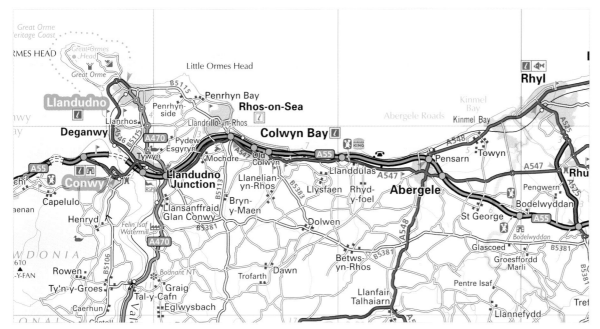

**Tourist Information
Centres**

Colwyn Bay: Imperial
Buildings, Station Square,
Princes Drive (tel: 01492
530478)
Conwy: Conwy Castle
Visitor Centre, Castle
Street (tel: 01492
592248)
Llandudno: 1–2 Chapel
Street (tel: 01492
876413)
Rhyl: Rhyl Children's
Village, West Parade
(tel: 01745 355068)
Prestatyn: Offa's Dyke
Centre, Central Beach
(tel: 01745 889092)

Llandudno

A century ago, Llandudno was just a sleepy
little fishing village, but today it is the
largest resort on this coast and is justly
popular with holidaymakers. The architect
of this transformation was the Liver-
pudlian surveyor, Owen Williams, who laid
out the sweeping Promenade, the Marine
Drive and the spacious streets. Modern
Llandudno includes a conference centre
and many good shops. The Mostyn Art
Gallery and the Doll Museum are well
worth a visit.

Dominating the town is the great lime-
stone bulk of the Great Orme, which can
be reached by Victorian tramway, by cabin
lift or by cable car. Whichever route you
take, the views from the 676ft (206m)
summit are stunning.

Rhuddlan Castle

*High above the River
Conwy, with wonderful
views, Bodnant Garden has
five terraces of Italian style
gardens as well as a
sheltered woodland valley, a
rock garden and the famous
laburnum walk. There is
also an open-air stage*

Rhuddlan Castle, guarding the mouth of
the River Clwyd and the coastal route into
North Wales, is a good example of how a
castle develops over the centuries. Just to
the south-east are the earthworks of a
much earlier motte-and-bailey castle, built
in 1073 in the first phase of the English
invasion. The present castle dates back to
the 13th century, its massive West Gate-
house being particularly impressive, and
was one of the first to be built in the con-
centric style. The River Clwyd was
re-channelled by the castle builders to
enable it to be supplied from the sea
2½ miles (4km) away.

The castle is also historically important
– the Statute of Rhuddlan was signed here
in 1284, confirming Edward I's sovereignty
over Wales. The castle was badly damaged
by Parliamentary forces in 1646.

*Even though its ancient
towers and walls are
crumbling, Rhuddlan Castle
still towers majestically over
the River Clwyd*

Rhyl

Rhyl was developed into a successful
resort in Victorian days. 'Sunny Rhyl' now
offers the holidaymaker all the entertain-
ments that a modern seaside town should.
The latest attraction is the multi-million
pound Sun Centre, which provides year-
round amusements, recreation and
protection from the unpredictable Welsh
weather. The sandy beach seems to go on
for ever when the tide is out.

See Walk T page 241
Lost Civilisations on Tal
y Fan

CHESTER AND THE RIVER DEE

*I*nland from its estuary, the River Dee passes through the beautiful cathedral city of Chester, then loops around Wrexham to the south-east before reaching the eisteddfod town of Llangollen. The first hills of Wales rise up to the north, and snaking up between the Llantysilio and Cyrn-y-Brain ranges is the hairpin Horseshoe Pass, with its fine views over the Vale of Clwyd.

Chester

County town of Cheshire, and famous for its fine red sandstone cathedral and two-storey galleried medieval shops known as

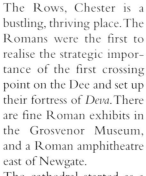

The Rows, Chester is a bustling, thriving place. The Romans were the first to realise the strategic importance of the first crossing point on the Dee and set up their fortress of *Deva*. There are fine Roman exhibits in the Grosvenor Museum, and a Roman amphitheatre east of Newgate.

The cathedral started as a Benedictine abbey, but what can be seen today is mainly restored 14th-century work. It is especially noted for its unusual Early English rectangular chapter house.

A fine way to explore Chester is to take the 2-mile (3.2km) walk around its city walls, some parts of which are the Roman original, but which are embellished by mainly medieval towers and gates. King Charles's Tower is so named because Charles I is said to have watched the defeat of his forces at the Battle of Rowton Moor

In Chester's Bridge Street, the black and white façade of The Rows hides one of the most pleasant shopping precincts in the country

from here in 1645. Chester's Heritage Centre, Visitor Centre and the Grosvenor Museum offer an excellent introduction to the city. Chester Zoo is the largest in the country and one of the finest in Europe, with 5,500 animals in 110 acres (45ha) of enclosures and landscaped gardens.

Flint

Once the county town for this part of Wales, Flint has always occupied a strategic position on the western shore of the Dee Estuary. Flint Castle was the first of Edward I's chain of castles to control the Welsh, built between 1277 and 1284 at the huge cost (in those days) of £7,000. Richard II surrendered to Henry Bolingbroke at Flint Castle in 1399.

Llangollen

Llangollen, sheltered in its green vale, is famous as the annual venue, since 1947, for the International Musical Eisteddfod. During that summertime festival of song and dance, the streets of this pretty Dee-side town are colourful with folk costumes and music from all over the world.

But Llangollen has other attractions, including the 14th-century bridge over the Dee – one of the 'Wonders of Wales' – and Plas Newydd, a stunning black and white, timber-framed house on the edge of the town which was the home of the hospitable 'Ladies of Llangollen' in the 18th century.

Mold

Mold is a busy little market town which was once the 'capital' of the old county of Flintshire. The splendid parish church of St Mary, with its 16th-century aisled nave and magnificent 18th-century tower, dominates the lovely High Street and, indeed, the whole of the Alun Valley. Look out for the unusual art deco flooring in the War Memorial chapel.

Offa's Dyke Path

The Offa's Dyke long-distance footpath winds under the limestone terraces of Eglwyseg Mountain and across the moorland of Cyrn-y-Brain on one of the last stages of its 177-mile (285km) journey from Chepstow on the Severn Estuary to Prestatyn on the North Wales coast.

The creation of the path, which follows fairly faithfully the line of King Offa of Mercia's defensive western boundary of his kingdom, was the brainchild of the Offa's Dyke Association and the Ramblers' Association. Years of patient campaigning came to fruition in July 1971, when the path was officially opened by Lord Hunt at Knighton.

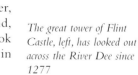

The great tower of Flint Castle, left, has looked out across the River Dee since 1277

Tourist Information
Centres

Chester: Town Hall,
Northgate Street
(tel: 01244 402111)
Llangollen: Town Hall,
Castle Street (tel: 01978
860828)
Wrexham: Lambpit
Street (tel: 01978
292015)

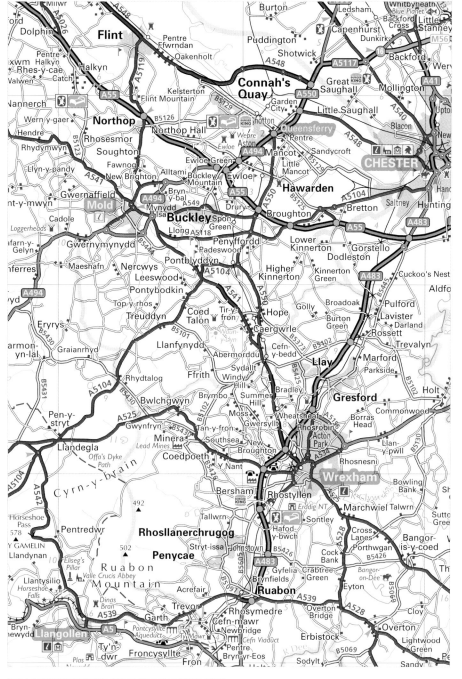

*The flavour of a real
country town can be
sampled in Mold, which still
has its cattle market – an
increasingly rare event in
other parts of the county*

The Horseshoe Pass

Motorists using the precipitous 1,299ft (396m) Horseshoe Pass between Llangollen and Ruthin in the Vale of Clwyd get an intimate view of the Llangollen Hills. Passing Eliseg's Pillar, a 9th-century monument to a Welsh prince, and the lovely ruins of Valle Crucis Abbey, the A542 heads towards Pentredwr with tremendous views of the sweeping limestone escarpments of the Eglwyseg Rocks to the north, where the northern summit is known somewhat prophetically as World's End (1,614ft/492m). These terraced hills of white limestone scars and scree are said to take their alternative name of Church Rocks from the abbey in the valley below.

From Pentredwr, the road climbs relentlessly between Llantysilio and the Cyrn-y-Brain Mountains, with a bird's-eye view of the Vale of Clwyd below, before dropping down to the valley.

Pontcysyllte Aqueduct

This 'canal in the clouds' was one of the wonders of Britain when it was built by Thomas Telford as a revolutionary solution to the question of how he could carry the Ellesmere Canal across the valley of the River Dee. The aqueduct takes the canal on 19 arches in an iron trough more than 1,000ft (305m) long, 120ft (37m) above the valley of the Dee. Technology may have come a long way, but this is still a breathtaking piece of engineering.

Valle Crucis Abbey

The name of this romantic, tree-framed ruin, one of the most beautiful in Wales, is 'the Vale of the Cross' and is thought to come from the nearby Eliseg's Pillar, on the hill to the north. Founded in 1202, this Cistercian house fits perfectly the monks' vow to 'glory in their poverty.' The slender, Early English windows of the western end are particularly beautiful.

Wrexham

Although the collieries and steelworks on which Wrexham prospered are largely things of the past, this bustling town is still the largest in North Wales. The church of St Giles is the chief architectural attraction, with its elegant 135ft (41m) steeple, dating from the 14th century. A copy of the church tower was built on the campus of Yale University in the 1920s in memory of Elihu Yale, the Pilgrim Father buried in the churchyard here, who gave his name to the distinguished American university.

See Walk U page 242
Eastern Moorlands

DALE – A PEMBROKE PENINSULA

1 From the National Trust car park return to the road and go left where the road bends right towards Dale. Turn left to follow a concrete track which bears left to a stile beside a gate. Cross this, turn right and take another stile to reach the coast path.

2 Go left to walk with the sea on your right (leaving the islands of Skokholm and Skomer behind you). Follow the coast path to the road as it approaches St Ann's Head.

3 Go right along the road to pass the old High Lighthouse on your right, then turn left through a gate and turn right immediately to take a signposted path towards the Low Lighthouse. Turn sharply left, as signposted, to follow the coast path towards Mill Bay, still walking with the sea on your right.

4 Descend steps to cross a footbridge and climb up the other side. Continue with the sea on your right around West Blockhouse Point (with it's three transit marks – navigational aids). Follow the coast path around Watwick Point (where there is a single transit mark), cross a footbridge above Castle Beach and climb to join a road on Dale Point.

5 Turn left to follow the road downhill into Dale. Ignore a turning on your left and reach the Griffin Inn. Take a footpath on your left immediately after the pub and just before a boathouse. This leads to a road. Cross this and go ahead over a stile beside a gate and turn right to cross a stone stile and reach another road.

7 Turn left with the signposted coast path to walk with the sea on your right. After crossing a series of stiles, take a kissing gate and look out for the stile beside a gate on your left, which you used on your outward journey. Turn left, inland, to cross this and retrace your steps to the car park.

6 Go left along the road to pass St James' Church on your left. When the road turns left, leave it by going straight ahead on a track which passes Dale Castle on your right. When this track bends left, take the signposted footpath ahead to Westdale Bay.

Map labels:

HAVERFORDWEST

B4327

Dale Fort

St James' Church

Dale Roads

Westdale Bay

Dale Castle

one way

DALE

Dale Boat House
Griffin Inn

cemetery

iron age fort

Keeper's Lodge

one way

PO

Great Castle Head

Blue Anchor Wood

Hayguard Hay Farm

Point Farm

Dale Fort Field Centre

Hayguard Hay Wood

Point House

Castle Beach

Dale Point

Broomhill Farm

Castlebeach Wood

Castlebeach Bay

Maryborough Farm

pond

Moorlands Cottage

Watwick Point
transit mark

Short Point

P 1

DALE PENINSULA

KETE

Watwick Bay

2

N

Pembrokeshire Coast Path

Frenchman's Bay

West Blockhouse Point

Pembrokeshire Coast Path

transit marks

cottages

4 Henry Tudor's Landing, 1485

3

High Lighthouse

Mill Bay

cottages

Low Lighthouse

St Ann's Head

St Ann's Head

transit marks

Site of Sea Empress Wreck

½ mile

0

½ km

Distance: 7½ miles (12.1km)
Total ascent: 300ft (91m)
Paths: good; some road walking
Terrain: clifftops, pastureland
Gradients: two short, steep, stepped sections
Refreshments: Griffin Inn, Dale
Park: National Trust car park, Kete, on minor road to St Ann's Head from Dale

STRUMBLE HEAD, SITE OF A FRENCH INVASION

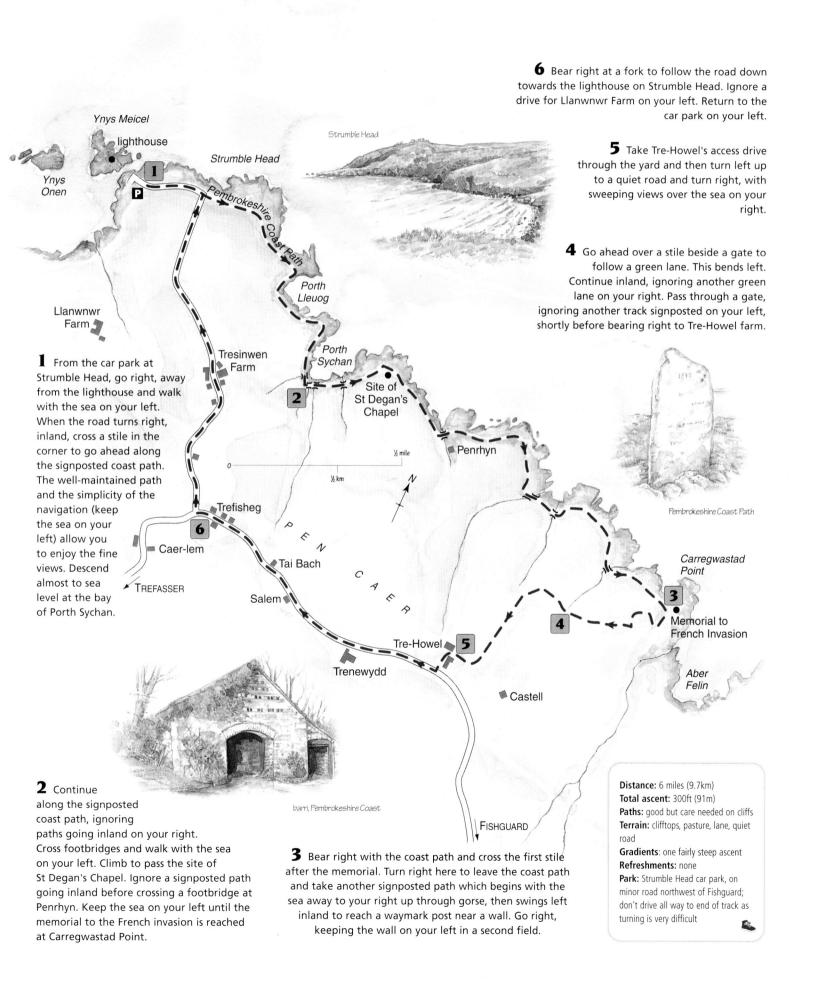

6 Bear right at a fork to follow the road down towards the lighthouse on Strumble Head. Ignore a drive for Llanwnwr Farm on your left. Return to the car park on your left.

5 Take Tre-Howel's access drive through the yard and then turn left up to a quiet road and turn right, with sweeping views over the sea on your right.

4 Go ahead over a stile beside a gate to follow a green lane. This bends left. Continue inland, ignoring another green lane on your right. Pass through a gate, ignoring another track signposted on your left, shortly before bearing right to Tre-Howel farm.

Strumble Head

Ynys Meicel
lighthouse
Ynys Onen
Strumble Head
Pembrokeshire Coast Path
Porth Lleuog
Llanwnwr Farm
Tresinwen Farm
Porth Sychan
Site of St Degan's Chapel
Penrhyn
1
2
½ mile
0
½ km
N
Trefisheg
6
Caer-lem
TREFASSER
Tai Bach
Salem
P E N   C A E R
Tre-Howel **5**
4
Carregwastad Point
3
Memorial to French Invasion
Aber Felin
Trenewydd
Castell
FISHGUARD

Pembrokeshire Coast Path

1 From the car park at Strumble Head, go right, away from the lighthouse and walk with the sea on your left. When the road turns right, inland, cross a stile in the corner to go ahead along the signposted coast path. The well-maintained path and the simplicity of the navigation (keep the sea on your left) allow you to enjoy the fine views. Descend almost to sea level at the bay of Porth Sychan.

2 Continue along the signposted coast path, ignoring paths going inland on your right. Cross footbridges and walk with the sea on your left. Climb to pass the site of St Degan's Chapel. Ignore a signposted path going inland before crossing a footbridge at Penrhyn. Keep the sea on your left until the memorial to the French invasion is reached at Carregwastad Point.

barn, Pembrokeshire Coast

3 Bear right with the coast path and cross the first stile after the memorial. Turn right here to leave the coast path and take another signposted path which begins with the sea away to your right up through gorse, then swings left inland to reach a waymark post near a wall. Go right, keeping the wall on your left in a second field.

Distance: 6 miles (9.7km)
Total ascent: 300ft (91m)
Paths: good but care needed on cliffs
Terrain: clifftops, pasture, lane, quiet road
Gradients: one fairly steep ascent
Refreshments: none
Park: Strumble Head car park, on minor road northwest of Fishguard; don't drive all way to end of track as turning is very difficult

A FAIRY LAKE AND THE BLACK MOUNTAIN

1 From the car park at Blaenau, follow the stony reservoir supply track by the Sawdde stream up to the shores of Llyn y Fan Fach, taking the right fork just before the reservoir.

6 Turn left on a path descending above the north banks of the stream. The path comes down the sides of Bryn Mawr, towards a bridge conveying the outward track across the stream. It then swings right to avoid some squat cliffs. Look out for a little path on the left which makes the final descent to the car park at Blaenau.

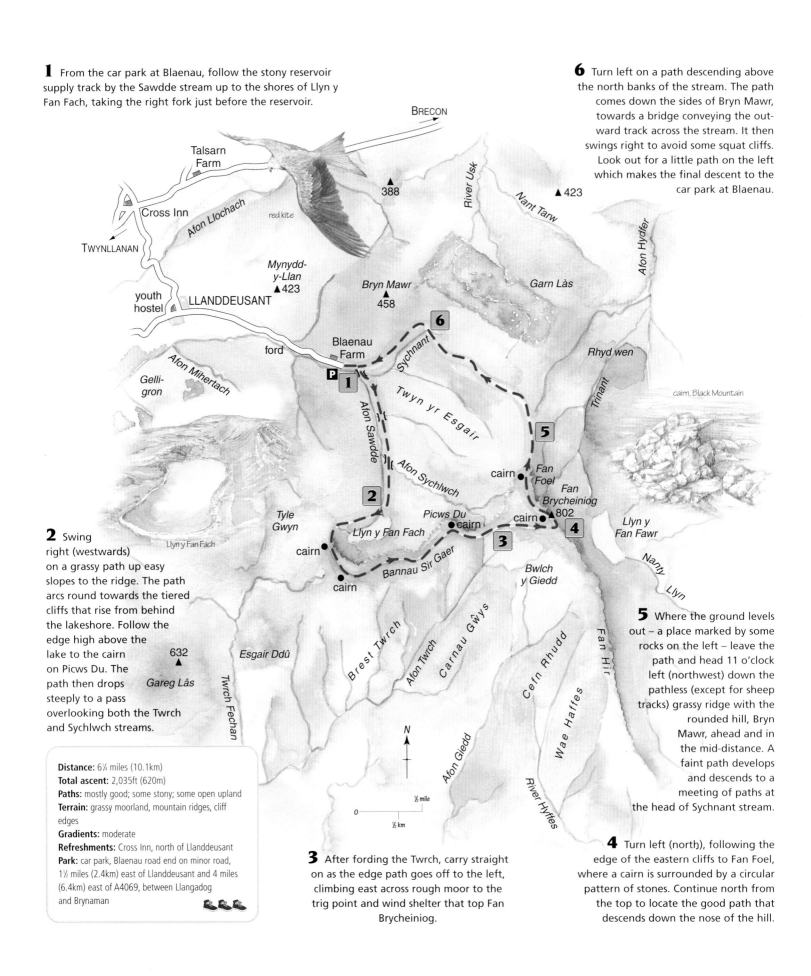

caim, Black Mountain

2 Swing right (westwards) on a grassy path up easy slopes to the ridge. The path arcs round towards the tiered cliffs that rise from behind the lakeshore. Follow the edge high above the lake to the cairn on Picws Du. The path then drops steeply to a pass overlooking both the Twrch and Sychlwch streams.

Distance: 6¼ miles (10.1km)
Total ascent: 2,035ft (620m)
Paths: mostly good; some stony; some open upland
Terrain: grassy moorland, mountain ridges, cliff edges
Gradients: moderate
Refreshments: Cross Inn, north of Llanddeusant
Park: car park, Blaenau road end on minor road, 1½ miles (2.4km) east of Llanddeusant and 4 miles (6.4km) east of A4069, between Llangadog and Brynaman

3 After fording the Twrch, carry straight on as the edge path goes off to the left, climbing east across rough moor to the trig point and wind shelter that top Fan Brycheiniog.

5 Where the ground levels out – a place marked by some rocks on the left – leave the path and head 11 o'clock left (northwest) down the pathless (except for sheep tracks) grassy ridge with the rounded hill, Bryn Mawr, ahead and in the mid-distance. A faint path develops and descends to a meeting of paths at the head of Sychnant stream.

4 Turn left (north), following the edge of the eastern cliffs to Fan Foel, where a cairn is surrounded by a circular pattern of stones. Continue north from the top to locate the good path that descends down the nose of the hill.

MONMOUTHSHIRE'S WHITE CASTLE

1 From the Hostry Inn turn right down the lane. In 300yds (275m), on a left bend, keep ahead to St Teilo's Church.

2 Walk down the stone steps from the west end of the graveyard and take the signed footpath between a wire fence and the churchyard wall. Go through a kissing gate and over a field to the B4233. Across the road is the moated site of Hen Cwrt, the Old Court.

3 Turn left along the B4233. In 90yds (82m) turn right over a stile, and follow Offa's Dyke Path signs across five fields to a farm track at Great Treadam. Turn left to the road, and right for 150yds (137m), to turn right into a lane.

4 Follow the lane northwards for ¾ mile (1.2km) to a road by a large white house. Keep forward for 250yds (229m) to White Castle.

8 Don't cross this stile, but follow the fence uphill to the lane. Turn right and walk for 1 mile (1.6km) to the B4233. Turn right and, in 350yds (320m), follow a footpath sign on the left across the fields to Llantilio Crossenny church. Return from here to the Hostry Inn.

7 From the saddle of ground at the top of the slope aim ahead across a field to a stile in a post-and-wire fence. Follow yellow arrows and Three Castles Walk signs across the next field, then over a stile and round to the right, to reach a stile in the corner of a fence.

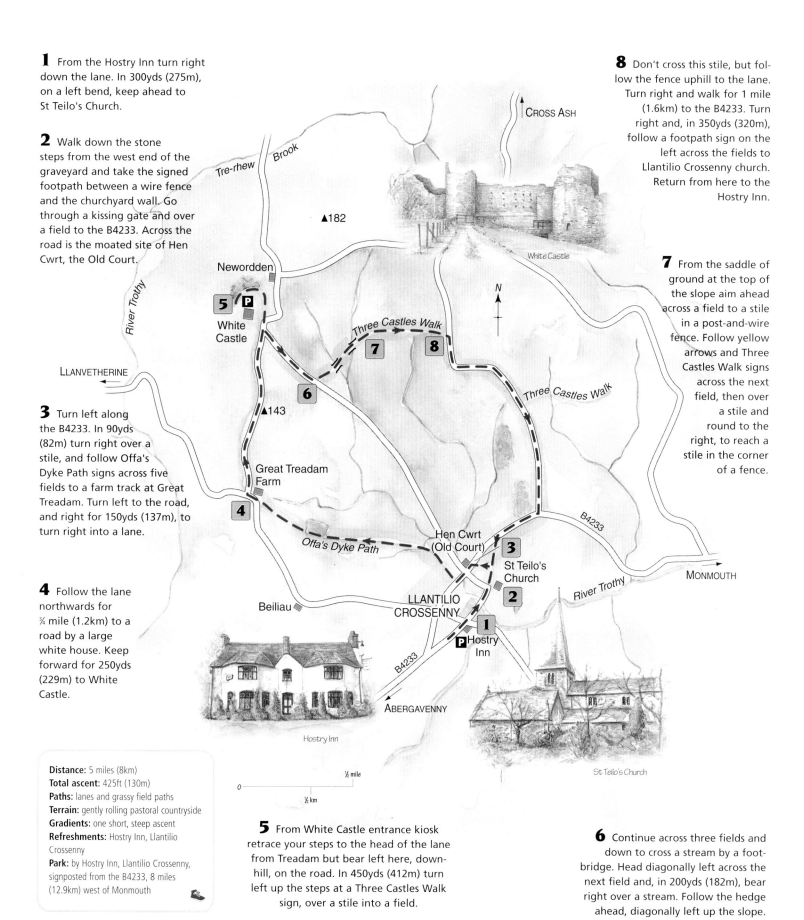

Distance: 5 miles (8km)
Total ascent: 425ft (130m)
Paths: lanes and grassy field paths
Terrain: gently rolling pastoral countryside
Gradients: one short, steep ascent
Refreshments: Hostry Inn, Llantilio Crossenny
Park: by Hostry Inn, Llantilio Crossenny, signposted from the B4233, 8 miles (12.9km) west of Monmouth

5 From White Castle entrance kiosk retrace your steps to the head of the lane from Treadam but bear left here, downhill, on the road. In 450yds (412m) turn left up the steps at a Three Castles Walk sign, over a stile into a field.

6 Continue across three fields and down to cross a stream by a footbridge. Head diagonally left across the next field and, in 200yds (182m), bear right over a stream. Follow the hedge ahead, diagonally left up the slope.

Hostry Inn

St Teilo's Church

RAGLAN'S CIVIL WAR FORTRESS

Distance: 5 miles (8km)
Total ascent: 250ft (76m)
Paths: good; can be muddy after rain
Terrain: fields, enclosed bridleway
Gradients: few ascents and very gradual
Refreshments: various in Raglan
Park: Castle Street, Raglan or by Raglan Castle

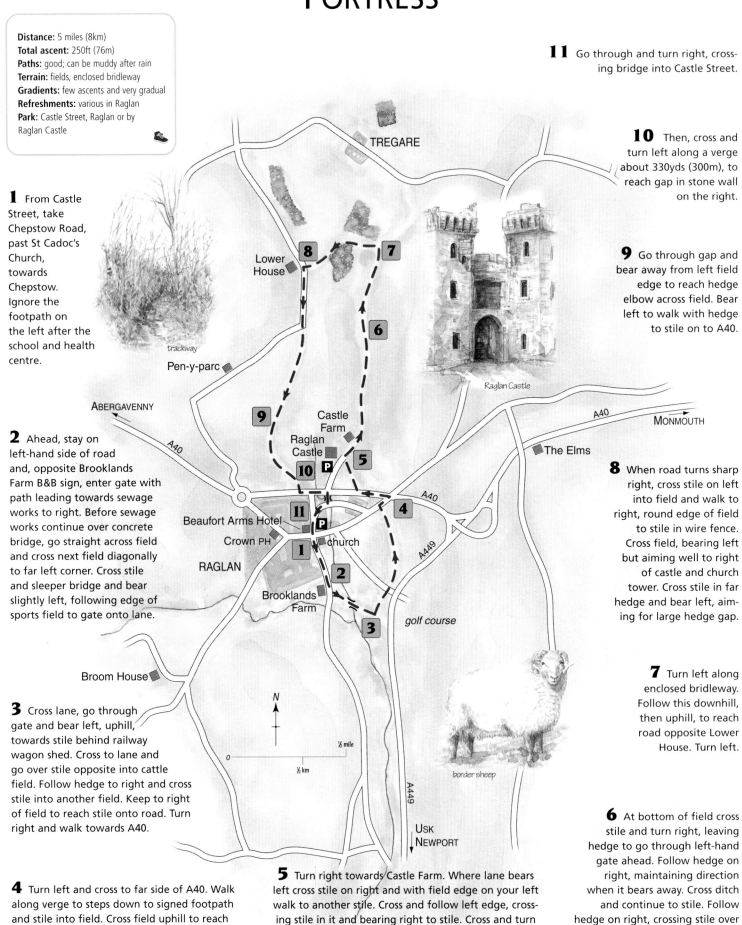

Raglan Castle

trackway

Pen-y-parc

TREGARE

Lower House

ABERGAVENNY

A40

MONMOUTH

The Elms

Castle Farm

Raglan Castle

A40

Beaufort Arms Hotel

Crown PH

RAGLAN

church

Brooklands Farm

golf course

A449

Broom House

N

½ mile

½ km

border sheep

A449

USK
NEWPORT

1 From Castle Street, take Chepstow Road, past St Cadoc's Church, towards Chepstow. Ignore the footpath on the left after the school and health centre.

2 Ahead, stay on left-hand side of road and, opposite Brooklands Farm B&B sign, enter gate with path leading towards sewage works to right. Before sewage works continue over concrete bridge, go straight across field and cross next field diagonally to far left corner. Cross stile and sleeper bridge and bear slightly left, following edge of sports field to gate onto lane.

3 Cross lane, go through gate and bear left, uphill, towards stile behind railway wagon shed. Cross to lane and go over stile opposite into cattle field. Follow hedge to right and cross stile into another field. Keep to right of field to reach stile onto road. Turn right and walk towards A40.

4 Turn left and cross to far side of A40. Walk along verge to steps down to signed footpath and stile into field. Cross field uphill to reach gate onto lane leading to Raglan Castle car park.

5 Turn right towards Castle Farm. Where lane bears left cross stile on right and with field edge on your left walk to another stile. Cross and follow left edge, crossing stile in it and bearing right to stile. Cross and turn left through gate. Cross track, go over stile and turn half-right across field beyond, passing small hillock.

11 Go through and turn right, crossing bridge into Castle Street.

10 Then, cross and turn left along a verge about 330yds (300m), to reach gap in stone wall on the right.

9 Go through gap and bear away from left field edge to reach hedge elbow across field. Bear left to walk with hedge to stile on to A40.

8 When road turns sharp right, cross stile on left into field and walk to right, round edge of field to stile in wire fence. Cross field, bearing left but aiming well to right of castle and church tower. Cross stile in far hedge and bear left, aiming for large hedge gap.

7 Turn left along enclosed bridleway. Follow this downhill, then uphill, to reach road opposite Lower House. Turn left.

6 At bottom of field cross stile and turn right, leaving hedge to go through left-hand gate ahead. Follow hedge on right, maintaining direction when it bears away. Cross ditch and continue to stile. Follow hedge on right, crossing stile over it and turn left uphill. Where field widens, turn left to cross stile.

A WALK IN THE BLACK MOUNTAINS

1 Take the lane between the chapel and the telephone box, climbing the hill. After 800 yards (730m), by a sign to the youth hostel, go right through a gate, down the track, over the river and up to a second gate.

6 When the path reaches the lane, turn left down the hill, go over a ford and pass The Monastery back to the village.

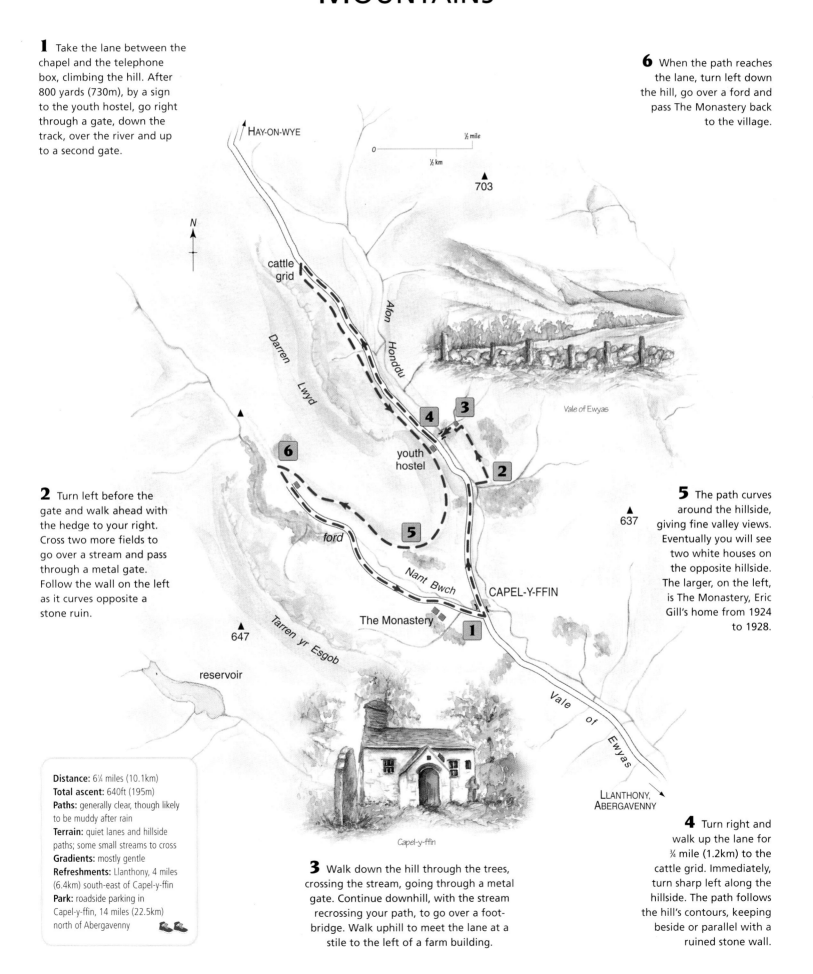

2 Turn left before the gate and walk ahead with the hedge to your right. Cross two more fields to go over a stream and pass through a metal gate. Follow the wall on the left as it curves opposite a stone ruin.

5 The path curves around the hillside, giving fine valley views. Eventually you will see two white houses on the opposite hillside. The larger, on the left, is The Monastery, Eric Gill's home from 1924 to 1928.

Distance: 6¼ miles (10.1km)
Total ascent: 640ft (195m)
Paths: generally clear, though likely to be muddy after rain
Terrain: quiet lanes and hillside paths; some small streams to cross
Gradients: mostly gentle
Refreshments: Llanthony, 4 miles (6.4km) south-east of Capel-y-ffin
Park: roadside parking in Capel-y-ffin, 14 miles (22.5km) north of Abergavenny

Capel-y-ffin

3 Walk down the hill through the trees, crossing the stream, going through a metal gate. Continue downhill, with the stream recrossing your path, to go over a footbridge. Walk uphill to meet the lane at a stile to the left of a farm building.

4 Turn right and walk up the lane for ¾ mile (1.2km) to the cattle grid. Immediately, turn sharp left along the hillside. The path follows the hill's contours, keeping beside or parallel with a ruined stone wall.

ABBEY IN THE WILDERNESS

1 From lay-by at south end of village, continue south along road towards Tregaron, going gently uphill to stile and ancient wooden foot-path sign on left.

2 Cross stile and follow track beyond towards caravans. Go on to cara-van site road and bear left, between vans. As road bears right, bear left past last caravan to stile in corner.

10 At farm lane bear left to road. Turn left, crossing hump-backed bridge and passing road, on left, for Strata Florida, to return to start.

9 As road turns sharp left, go right past tele-phone box and, soon, cross waymarked stile on left. Cross footbridge and bear left towards way-marked stile by gate. The path now follows Afon Teifi (left) all the way to Pontrhydfendigaid, with occasional waymarkers, stiles and gates.

> **Distance:** 5½ miles (8.8km)
> **Total ascent:** 500 ft (152m)
> **Paths:** mainly obvious paths and lanes
> **Terrain:** fields, country lanes and forestry
> **Gradients:** gradual
> **Refreshments:** Red Lion and Black Lion, Pontrhydfendigaid
> **Park:** along main street or in lay-by at southern entrance to village, Pontrhydfendigaid

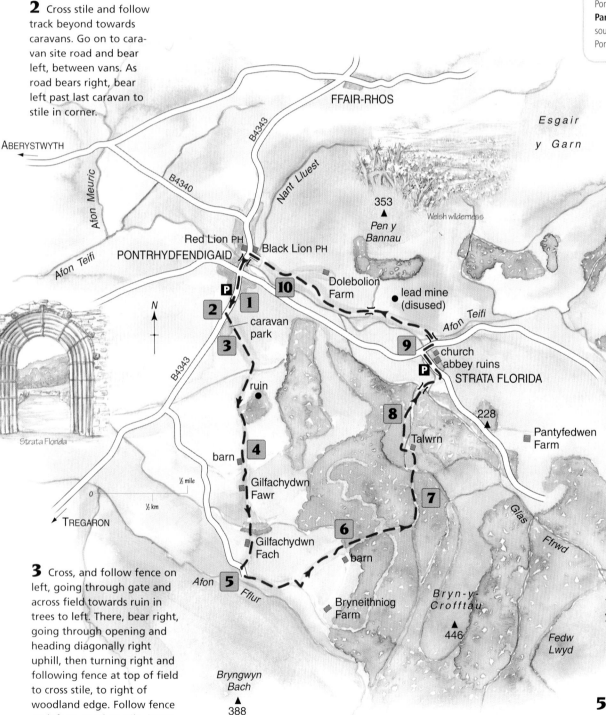

Strata Florida

tile, Strata Florida

8 An occasionally indistinct path follows stream down, crossing it once, to foot-bridge. Cross and follow stream bank to gate. Keep ahead along road beyond. Strata Florida car park is to left, ruins and church to right.

7 Follow track to gate and continue along lane beyond to ruin (Talwrn). Go left along ruin's top, near wall, to follow another lane to end. Go through gate and turn right, following stream. Soon bear left to gate, bearing right beyond to regain stream.

6 Follow bridleway through forest to forestry road. After 50 yds (46m), as it goes sharp right between trees, bear left along another bridleway. Follow to path coming down from right. Bear left with waymarker.

5 Turn left. When road ends, go through gate and follow lane beyond. As farm comes into view about ¼ mile (400m) ahead, take lane coming in from left, following it uphill. Approaching barn, go through gate on left and turn right along fence to gate into forest.

3 Cross, and follow fence on left, going through gate and across field towards ruin in trees to left. There, bear right, going through opening and heading diagonally right uphill, then turning right and following fence at top of field to cross stile, to right of woodland edge. Follow fence on left to another stile, ignor-ing gate, then go diagonally right across field to reach gate in top right corner. Go through and turn left immediately through another gate. Go diago-nally right towards barn.

4 Go through gate beside barn and along farm lane oppo-site. Beyond first farm, lane degenerates to track, but remains obvious. Beyond farmyard keep to left of hut and take lower, right-hand track into trees. Ford stream, go through gate and follow track uphill to second farm. Go through gate and ahead along farm lane to road.

OVER THE LONG MYND

1 From the car park leave town by walking along the Shrewsbury Road. Turn left into a road signposted for Carding Mill Valley and golf course. Fork right up a winding road at Trevor Hill, eventually turning left to reach the golf course and clubhouse.

2 Go through the gate to the right of the clubhouse marked 'Public Footpath to the Hills'. Turn right and walk alongside beeches, then turn left and follow marker posts up a valley and across the golf course. The path runs around the head of a valley and passes a shelter, then climbs a rise before heading off to the left. Keep following the marker posts, passing a black hut, until you overlook the Carding Mill Valley.

3 Go through a gate at the top of the golf course, bear right and follow a path gently uphill, around Haddon Hill. Use the most well-trodden path. Cross two boggy patches and step over a tiny stream a little further on. The path descends slightly and crosses a wider, fast flowing stream before continuing to contour round the hillside. After stepping over another stream, turn left uphill on a faint path to intercept a wide track.

4 Turn left and rise along the broad track over extensive heather moorlands. Ignore other paths, keeping to the broad track. At one junction there is a view down Carding Mill Valley to Church Stretton. Keep straight on, rising gently to reach a complex junction. Simply step to the right to follow a narrow track uphill.

Distance: 8¾ miles (14.1km)
Total ascent: 1,150ft (350m)
Paths: mostly clear and firm, some boggy areas and some parts muddy when wet
Terrain: extensive heather moorlands buttressed by steep hill slopes
Gradients: fairly steep early on but much gentler ascent to the top
Refreshments: various in Church Stretton; Ragleth Inn and Mynd House Hotel at Little Stretton
Park: car parks on Easthope Road in the middle of Church Stretton

7 Turn right along the lane, then left and left again in Little Stretton. Note All Saints Church at the crossroads, with the Ragleth Inn opposite. Follow the road as it passes through fields to return to Church Stretton.

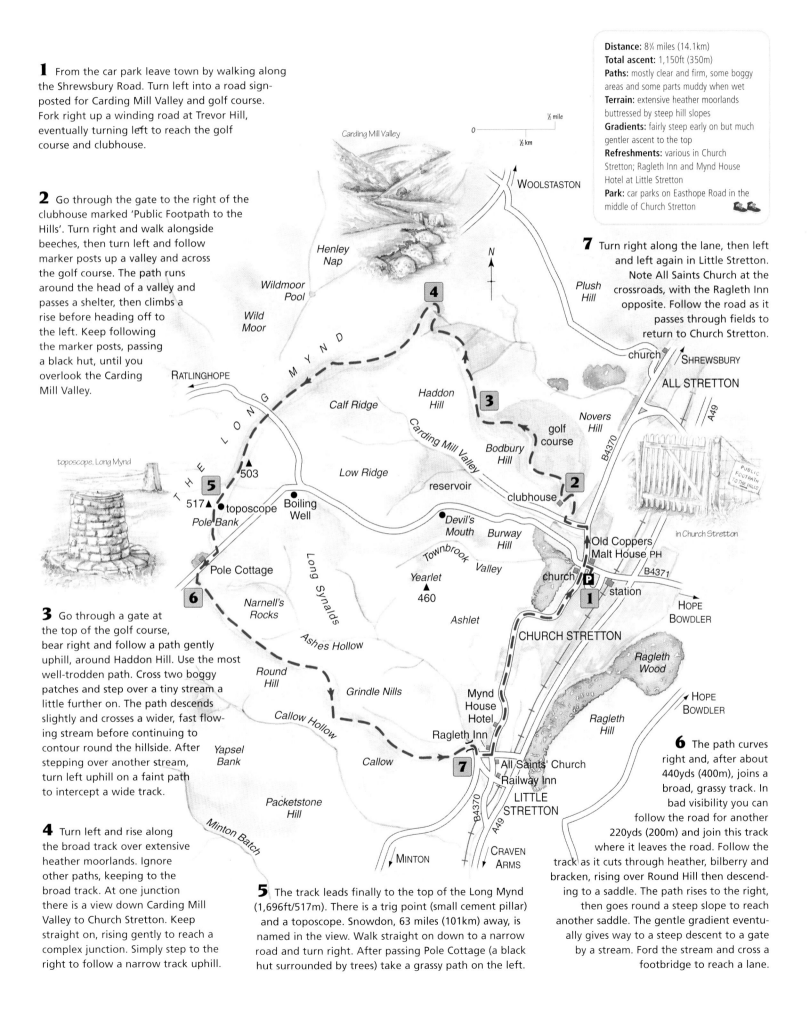

toposcope, Long Mynd

Carding Mill Valley

½ mile
0
½ km

WOOLSTASTON

N

Henley Nap

Wildmoor Pool

Wild Moor

RATLINGHOPE

THE LONG MYND

Calf Ridge

Haddon Hill

Plush Hill

SHREWSBURY

church

ALL STRETTON

A49

4

3

Novers Hill

golf course

B4370

503

5

Low Ridge

Bodbury Hill

517 ▲ toposcope
Pole Bank

Boiling Well

reservoir

clubhouse

2

Devil's Mouth

Burway Hill

PUBLIC FOOTPATH TO THE HILLS

in Church Stretton

Pole Cottage

Long Synalds

Townbrook Valley

Yearlet ▲ 460

Old Coppers Malt House PH

B4371

6

Narnell's Rocks

Ashlet

church

P

1

station

HOPE BOWDLER

Ashes Hollow

Round Hill

Grindle Nills

Mynd House Hotel

CHURCH STRETTON

Ragleth Wood

Callow Hollow

Ragleth Inn

Ragleth Hill

HOPE BOWDLER

Yapsel Bank

Callow

7

All Saints' Church

Railway Inn

LITTLE STRETTON

Packetstone Hill

Minton Batch

MINTON

B4370

A49

CRAVEN ARMS

5 The track leads finally to the top of the Long Mynd (1,696ft/517m). There is a trig point (small cement pillar) and a toposcope. Snowdon, 63 miles (101km) away, is named in the view. Walk straight on down to a narrow road and turn right. After passing Pole Cottage (a black hut surrounded by trees) take a grassy path on the left.

3 continued...

6 The path curves right and, after about 440yds (400m), joins a broad, grassy track. In bad visibility you can follow the road for another 220yds (200m) and join this track where it leaves the road. Follow the track as it cuts through heather, bilberry and bracken, rising over Round Hill then descending to a saddle. The path rises to the right, then goes round a steep slope to reach another saddle. The gentle gradient eventually gives way to a steep descent to a gate by a stream. Ford the stream and cross a footbridge to reach a lane.

ON ELGAR'S MALVERNS

1 From the car park go through the red gates towards the pool's entrance, but bear right to walk beside the building. Bear left around the back of the pool, then turn right across the footbridge over the pond. Follow the path through Priory Park, bearing left in front of the theatres building to reach a prominent lamp. Here, turn right to leave the park, bearing left, then right up a lane.

2 When the lane reaches Grange Road, turn left to a T-junction with Abbey Road.

3 Turn right along Abbey Road, passing the Abbey Hotel and going through the arch of the Abbey Gatehouse. Opposite the post office, bear left up the steps and turn right along Worcester Road. Just after The Unicorn, turn left up St Ann's Road. Go up the rising road, keeping straight ahead through the trees to reach a 'Turning Place Only' sign on the right. Here turn sharply back right on a path which rises through trees and rhododendrons.

4 Ignore a crossing path, continuing to join a wider path (from left) and following it to Ivy Scar Rocks, the largest Malvern rock outcrop. Immediately beyond the outcrop, bear left up a steep, narrow path, zigzagging through gorse, broom and bracken.

5 At a T-junction with a wider path (Lady Howard de Walden Drive), turn right, soon reaching a seat. Turn left up a steep, but obvious, grassy path. Bear right at a junction, continuing to the top of North Hill with its splendid views.

6 Go downhill towards Table Hill ahead, bearing left at the col between the peaks and following a grassy path down to rejoin de Walden Drive. Turn right and follow the track towards Worcestershire Beacon, prominent ahead. At a panorama dial, bear right off the path for a steep short-cut to the summit.

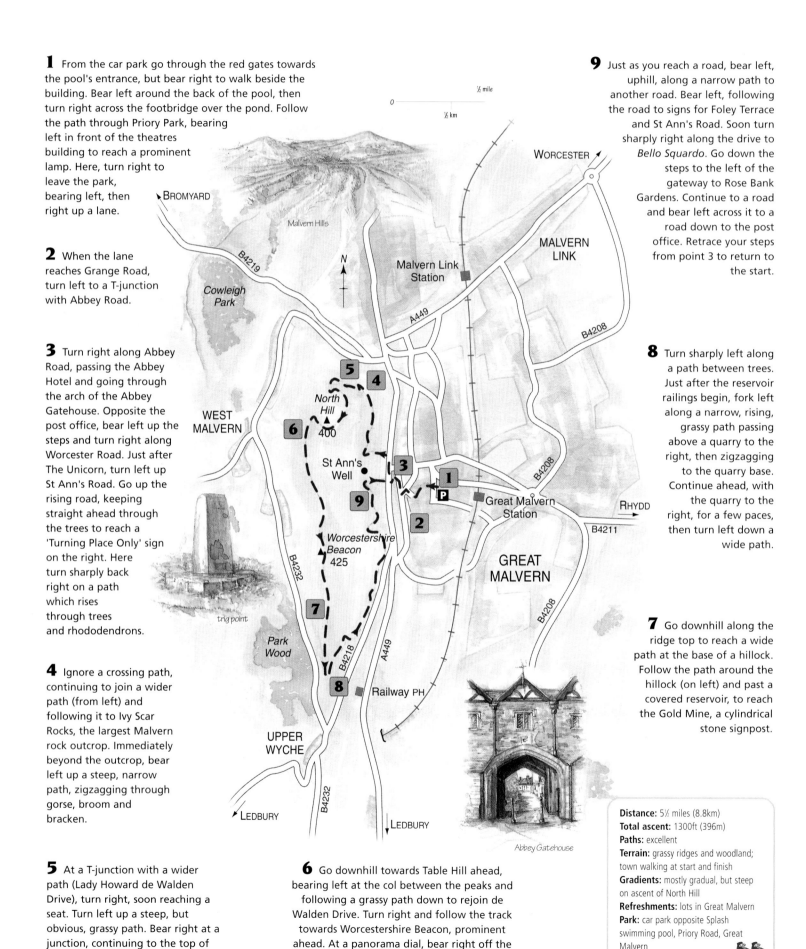

Abbey Gatehouse

9 Just as you reach a road, bear left, uphill, along a narrow path to another road. Bear left, following the road to signs for Foley Terrace and St Ann's Road. Soon turn sharply right along the drive to *Bello Squardo*. Go down the steps to the left of the gateway to Rose Bank Gardens. Continue to a road and bear left across it to a road down to the post office. Retrace your steps from point 3 to return to the start.

8 Turn sharply left along a path between trees. Just after the reservoir railings begin, fork left along a narrow, rising, grassy path passing above a quarry to the right, then zigzagging to the quarry base. Continue ahead, with the quarry to the right, for a few paces, then turn left down a wide path.

7 Go downhill along the ridge top to reach a wide path at the base of a hillock. Follow the path around the hillock (on left) and past a covered reservoir, to reach the Gold Mine, a cylindrical stone signpost.

Distance: 5½ miles (8.8km)
Total ascent: 1300ft (396m)
Paths: excellent
Terrain: grassy ridges and woodland; town walking at start and finish
Gradients: mostly gradual, but steep on ascent of North Hill
Refreshments: lots in Great Malvern
Park: car park opposite Splash swimming pool, Priory Road, Great Malvern

TEWKESBURY AND ODDA'S CHAPEL

1 From the Abbey Lawns car park go through the gate, along the north of the abbey and leave by the main gateway, turning left. Pass the long-stay car park then turn right along Lower Lode Lane. Go left at the Battle Trail sign (crossed swords).

2 Go over a stile to the right and follow the hedge to a plinth commemorating the battle. Turn right along the lane, through the golf club gates and along the drive, veering left along the signed footpath, and following further waymarks to reach a stile.

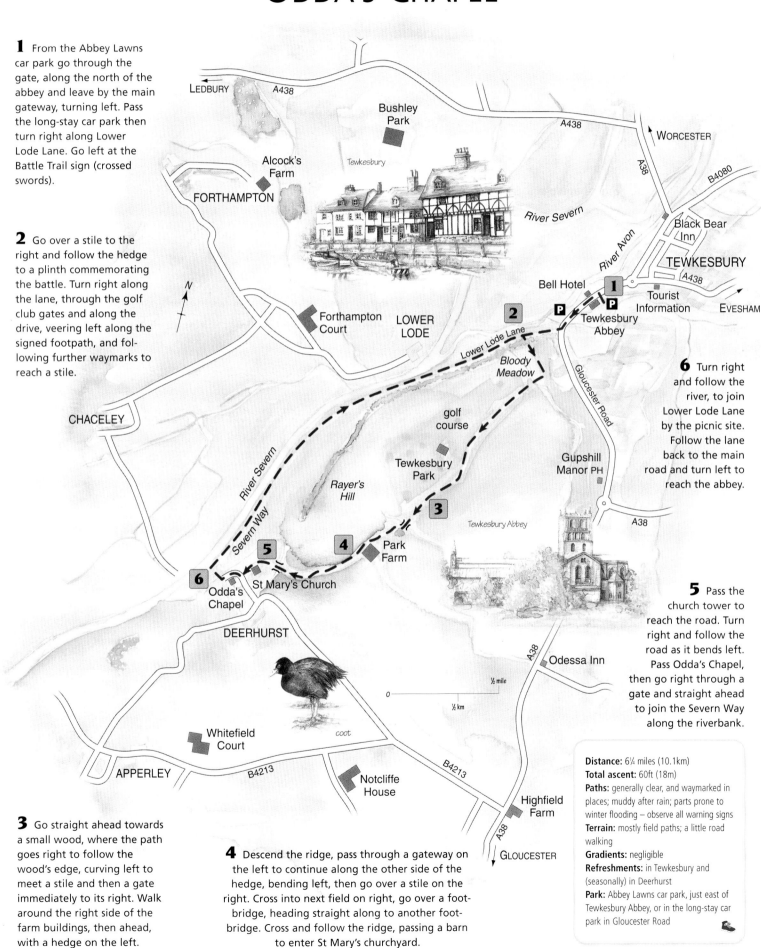

6 Turn right and follow the river, to join Lower Lode Lane by the picnic site. Follow the lane back to the main road and turn left to reach the abbey.

5 Pass the church tower to reach the road. Turn right and follow the road as it bends left. Pass Odda's Chapel, then go right through a gate and straight ahead to join the Severn Way along the riverbank.

3 Go straight ahead towards a small wood, where the path goes right to follow the wood's edge, curving left to meet a stile and then a gate immediately to its right. Walk around the right side of the farm buildings, then ahead, with a hedge on the left.

4 Descend the ridge, pass through a gateway on the left to continue along the other side of the hedge, bending left, then go over a stile on the right. Cross into next field on right, go over a footbridge, heading straight along to another footbridge. Cross and follow the ridge, passing a barn to enter St Mary's churchyard.

Distance: 6¼ miles (10.1km)
Total ascent: 60ft (18m)
Paths: generally clear, and waymarked in places; muddy after rain; parts prone to winter flooding – observe all warning signs
Terrain: mostly field paths; a little road walking
Gradients: negligible
Refreshments: in Tewkesbury and (seasonally) in Deerhurst
Park: Abbey Lawns car park, just east of Tewkesbury Abbey, or in the long-stay car park in Gloucester Road

SARN HELEN – THE ROMAN HIGHWAY THROUGH WALES

1 Start at the Wildfowler Inn in Tre'r-ddôl. On the village street, face the pub, go right, past the garage, shop and café, to join the A487. Turn right towards Machynlleth, and, after passing the last house, turn right through a wooden gate into a forestry plantation. Climb with an attractive, narrow, path.

2 Bear left when the path forks. Ignore paths descending from your right. Go ahead across clear-felled hillside. The path becomes a firm track before reaching a lane. Go right uphill, passing a number of houses and, eventually, farm buildings at Cefngweiriog.

3 Reach the junction with Sarn Helen, coming as a track through a gate on your left. Turn right to walk along this quiet lane. Follow this section of Sarn Helen for over 1 mile (1.6km), ignoring a lane descending on your right. Cross a bridge over the Afon Clettwr and climb towards Gwar-cwm-uchaf farm. Turn left before you reach it, onto a rising track and ignore all branching paths.

4 At a T-junction turn right along a walled track, admiring the view over the Dyfi Estuary away to your right. Shortly before returning to the lane which forms the route of Sarn Helen, notice the remains of the prehistoric burial chamber known as Bedd Taliesin on your left. Go through a gate to turn right along Sarn Helen, with fine views towards Aberdyfi over the stone wall on your left.

5 Back at Gwar-cwm-uchaf, go past the farmhouse then turn left through a gate and follow a path along the top edge of a sloping pasture. Keep on along the remains of a green lane. After passing a small group of trees, go forward to pass through a gate then proceed first by a stream and then beside a line of tree stumps. Keep on in the same direction along a hedged section and then along a rutted path.

6 Enter woodland at a bridleway waymark post and soon turn sharp right to descend a rough path which zigzags steeply down between oak trees. Go ahead through a gate into a plantation of conifers.

7 Take a gate ahead to descend on a tree-lined hollow way towards Tre'r-ddôl. Emerge on the road, with a chapel on your left, and turn right across a bridge over the Afon Clettwr to return to the start.

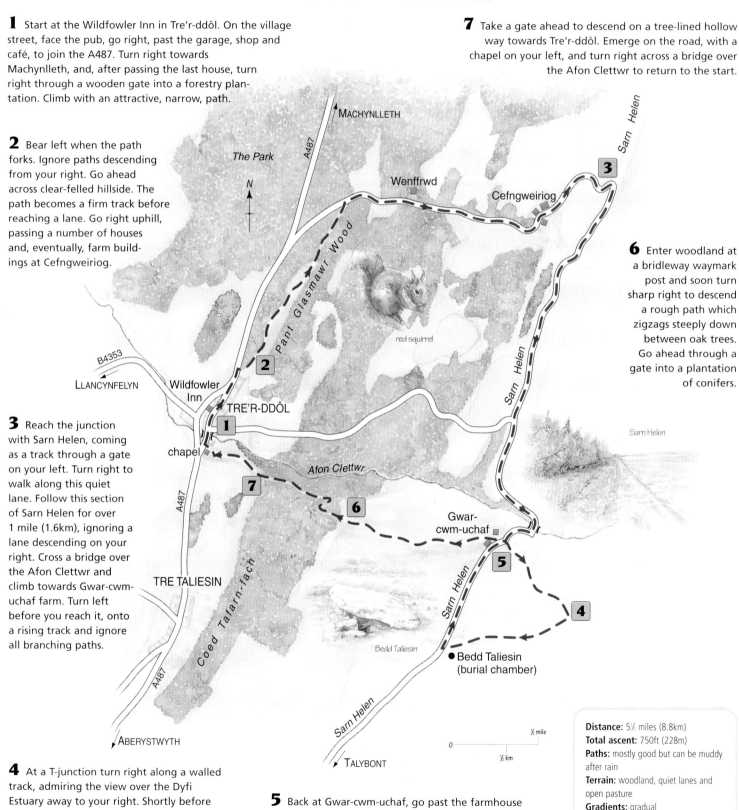

MACHYNLLETH

The Park

A487

N

Wenffrwd

Cefngweiriog

Sarn Helen

3

6

red squirrel

Sarn Helen

Pant Glasmawr Wood

B4353

LLANCYNFELYN

Wildfowler Inn

TRE'R-DDÔL

2

1

chapel

A487

7

Afon Clettwr

6

Sarn Helen

Gwar-cwm-uchaf

5

4

Coed Tafarn-fach

TRE TALIESIN

A487

Bedd Taliesin

Bedd Taliesin (burial chamber)

ABERYSTWYTH

Sarn Helen

TALYBONT

½ mile

0

½ km

Distance: 5½ miles (8.8km)
Total ascent: 750ft (228m)
Paths: mostly good but can be muddy after rain
Terrain: woodland, quiet lanes and open pasture
Gradients: gradual
Refreshments: Wildfowler Inn, Tre'r-ddôl
Park: considerate roadside parking in Tre'r-ddôl, just off the A487 between Aberystwyth and Machynlleth, 2 miles (3.2km) north of Tal-y-bont

CADAIR IDRIS –
THE MOUNTAIN NATURE
RESERVE

Distance: 5½ miles (8.8km)
Total Ascent: 2,950ft (899m)
Paths: good; some rough; stream crossing difficult after heavy rain
Terrain: rocky, mountainous
Gradients: steep; occasionally very steep
Refreshments: none
Park: Minffordd car park at junction of A487 and B4405

1 Walk to the back of the car park, where a well-signed path leaves through a gate. Follow a raised causeway to a kissing gate and visitor centre. Follow the path over a bridge to a gate into the nature reserve.

2 Follow the steep, mostly stepped path up through the woods, with the stream to your right.

3 Go through a gate to reach more open country, continuing to climb to a point where the plantation on your right swings away and the path runs very close to the stream. Note the path down to the water here. Take it to study the stream crossing. The stream must be crossed on the return route. In dry weather it can be crossed easily. **If not, you should reverse the route from Pen-y-gadair, rather than complete the circuit.**

4 Return to, and continue along, the path. High up to the right a ladder stile over a fence can be seen, the diagonal path descending to the stream is the return route. The outward path now takes you into Cwm Cau.

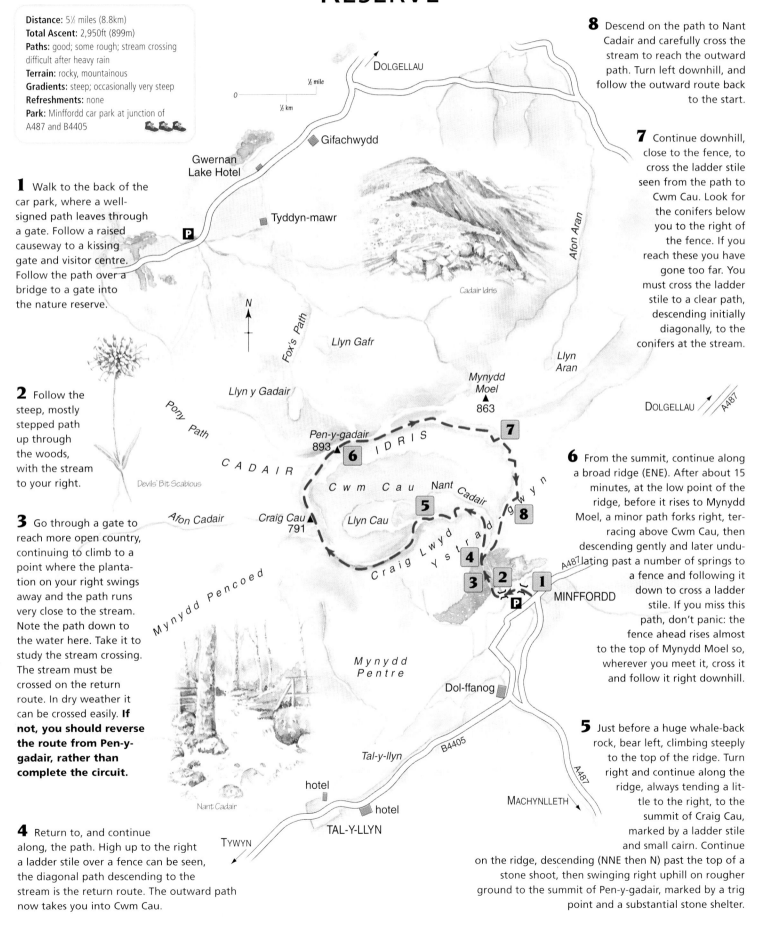

8 Descend on the path to Nant Cadair and carefully cross the stream to reach the outward path. Turn left downhill, and follow the outward route back to the start.

7 Continue downhill, close to the fence, to cross the ladder stile seen from the path to Cwm Cau. Look for the conifers below you to the right of the fence. If you reach these you have gone too far. You must cross the ladder stile to a clear path, descending initially diagonally, to the conifers at the stream.

6 From the summit, continue along a broad ridge (ENE). After about 15 minutes, at the low point of the ridge, before it rises to Mynydd Moel, a minor path forks right, terracing above Cwm Cau, then descending gently and later undulating past a number of springs to a fence and following it down to cross a ladder stile. If you miss this path, don't panic: the fence ahead rises almost to the top of Mynydd Moel so, wherever you meet it, cross it and follow it right downhill.

5 Just before a huge whale-back rock, bear left, climbing steeply to the top of the ridge. Turn right and continue along the ridge, always tending a little to the right, to the summit of Craig Cau, marked by a ladder stile and small cairn. Continue on the ridge, descending (NNE then N) past the top of a stone shoot, then swinging right uphill on rougher ground to the summit of Pen-y-gadair, marked by a trig point and a substantial stone shelter.

VALLEY OF THE INDUSTRIAL REVOLUTION

Distance: 5½ miles (8.8km)
Total ascent: 300ft (91m)
Paths: mostly good; riverside tracks are unsurfaced and can be muddy; steps
Terrain: roads and pavements, unsurfaced river track
Gradients: steep climb to top of ridge
Refreshments: several cafés and pubs in Ironbridge
Park: in long-stay car park beyond roundabout from visitor centre

7 Facing the museum gates, turn left, following the road under the railway bridge. Immediately after the bridge turn left into Coach Road. At the end (now Station Road) turn left to return to the visitor centre.

6 At the end of the road (now Hodge Bower) turn right, then after 50yds (46m) bear left past the cottages. At the White Horse pub turn left, continuing to the top of the hill before descending down Church Road. At the end of the road cross over to the Museum of Iron.

1 From the visitor centre turn right, towards the Iron Bridge. Go under the bridge and keep ahead on the riverside path to the end, then climb the steps and turn right.

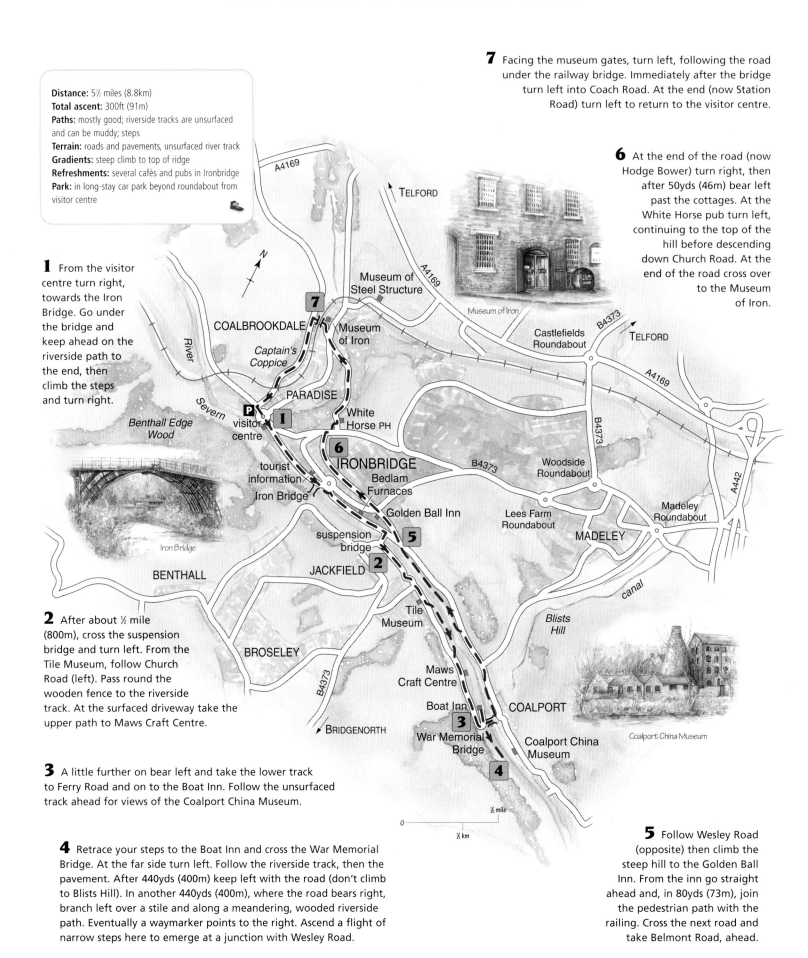

2 After about ½ mile (800m), cross the suspension bridge and turn left. From the Tile Museum, follow Church Road (left). Pass round the wooden fence to the riverside track. At the surfaced driveway take the upper path to Maws Craft Centre.

3 A little further on bear left and take the lower track to Ferry Road and on to the Boat Inn. Follow the unsurfaced track ahead for views of the Coalport China Museum.

4 Retrace your steps to the Boat Inn and cross the War Memorial Bridge. At the far side turn left. Follow the riverside track, then the pavement. After 440yds (400m) keep left with the road (don't climb to Blists Hill). In another 440yds (400m), where the road bears right, branch left over a stile and along a meandering, wooded riverside path. Eventually a waymarker points to the right. Ascend a flight of narrow steps here to emerge at a junction with Wesley Road.

5 Follow Wesley Road (opposite) then climb the steep hill to the Golden Ball Inn. From the inn go straight ahead and, in 80yds (73m), join the pedestrian path with the railing. Cross the next road and take Belmont Road, ahead.

PANORAMA FROM THE WREKIN

Distance: 5 miles (8km)
Total ascent: 820ft (250m)
Paths: good, but muddy in places after rain
Terrain: roads, woodland, fields and steep ridge
Gradients: gentle, except for final very steep climb to the summit
Refreshments: Huntsman pub, Little Wenlock
Park: lay-by at Forest Glen, on minor road between Wellington and Little Wenlock, near a reservoir

8 Continue across the summit ridge, soon descending through Heaven Gate and Hell Gate, and following a broad track as it curves past a semi-derelict cottage. After a little more descent, another bend, and a final fling with the woodland, the track ends directly opposite the start point.

7 Here, by a prominent yew tree, turn right and climb very steeply, finally breaking free of the tree cover as you approach a conspicuous rocky outcrop. The summit of the Wrekin rises just a short distance further on, and, on a clear day, is a good place to linger. A nearby toposcope identifies distant hills and features.

1 Walk to the nearby road junction and turn right, heading for Little Wenlock. Continue (with care as there is no footway) until the road makes a pronounced bend to the right, where you leave it by branching left onto a shady green lane.

2 The green lane rises through trees to a track junction close to a group of ruined buildings. Beyond, the track – an old route to the hamlet of Huntington – descends gently, but you must leave it only a few strides after the ruined buildings by turning right onto an initially indistinct path into a narrow belt of woodland.

3 The path meanders through the woodland but eventually reaches a more direct, and slightly raised, path parallel with the woodland edge.

4 Leave the woodland at a stile and cross the field to another stile, before a short stretch of farm track leads you out to a road. Turn right and go down the road until, just before it bends sharply right, you can leave it at a stile on the left, to enter more light woodland.

5 A woodland path guides you down to a farm track. Cross this to a stile opposite, leading to open pasture. Turn left along the field edge and, after crossing an intermediate stile, continue up the field to another stile, beyond which is a broad forest track.

6 Turn left and follow the track for about ½ mile (800m) along the wooded base of the Wrekin until, just as it begins to descend, the track forks. Here, branch right into trees onto a path that also descends, as it rounds the south-western edge of the hill. Continue with the track to an obvious path junction.

Map labels: SHREWSBURY, B5061, A5, Junction 7, M54, WOLVERHAMPTON, trackway, the Wrekin, ASTON, UPPINGTON, toposcope, the Wrekin, reservoir, Wrekin Course, quarry (disused), Short Wood, firing range, derelict cottage, Willowmoor Farm, ruined buildings, LAWLEY, Hell Gate, Heaven Gate, The Wrekin 407, Wenlock Wood, HUNTINGTON, golf course, Little Hill, Wrekin Farm, scout camp, Huntsman PH, Horsehay R/bt, A5223, LITTLE WENLOCK, GARMSTON, B4380, WSBURY, Jiggers R/bt, LEIGHTON, Devil's Dingle, the Wrekin, Holbrook Coppice, A4169, MUCH WENLOCK, B4380, ½ mile, ½ km, N

BREIDDEN HILLS – THE GATEWAY TO WALES

1 From car park, walk up lane directly opposite Breidden Hotel. Ignore footpath left and follow lane towards Middleton Quarry. Fork right at junction, soon turning left on path uphill through gorse and bracken. Keep climbing through all path junctions to ridge at the top. Turn right on wide track to Middletown Hill.

2 Walk along ridge to summit then down to saddle. Descend left to lane and turn right. Pass Belleisle Farm and carry on to track on left, taking you past another farm, into pastureland. Maintain direction through first field, then follow left-hand hedge to woods. Cross stream and follow waymarked bridleway rising through woods. It crosses a flinty forestry road then continues to climb up to Rodneys Pillar, taking two left forks along the way. Beyond stile in fence, path traverses open hillside to another stile preceding steep climb to Rodney's Pillar.

3 From the summit, head along ridge (south-west) to edge of wood, then turn sharp left to double-back down hillside and through sparse woodland to open area.

7 At signpost by fence corner, near lower edge of wood, turn right. Two routes meet up by stile at edge of wood. Turn sharp left if you have just descended from higher route. Another stile leads to field. Turn left along its edge, past pig enclosure to farm track. Turn right to road, a little way out of Middletown, and follow it left, back into village.

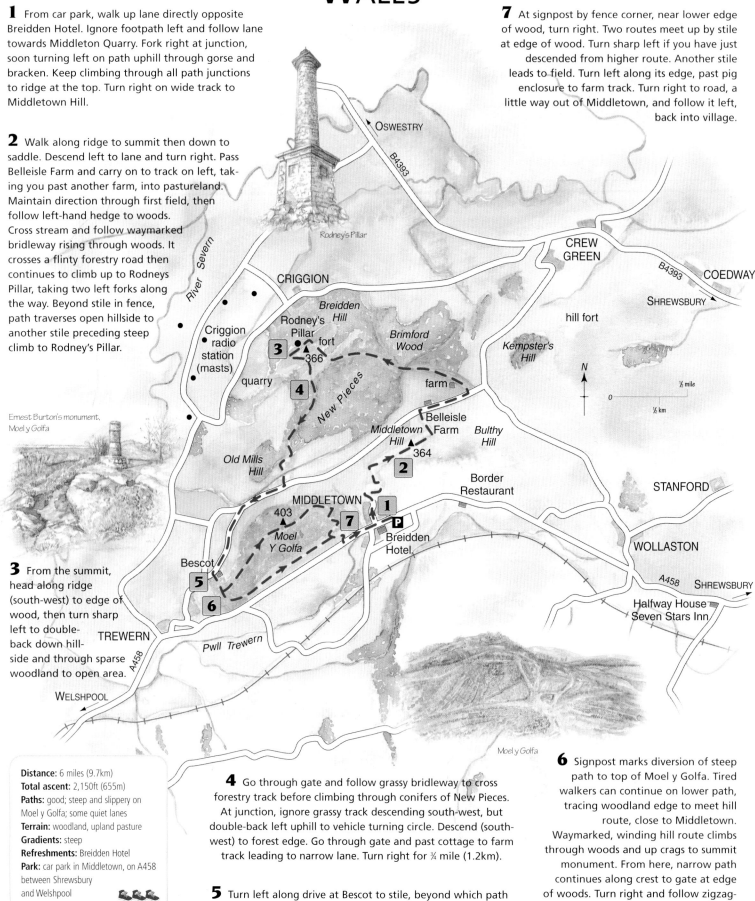

Rodney's Pillar

Ernest Burton's monument, Moel y Golfa

Moel y Golfa

Distance: 6 miles (9.7km)
Total ascent: 2,150ft (655m)
Paths: good; steep and slippery on Moel y Golfa; some quiet lanes
Terrain: woodland, upland pasture
Gradients: steep
Refreshments: Breidden Hotel
Park: car park in Middletown, on A458 between Shrewsbury and Welshpool

4 Go through gate and follow grassy bridleway to cross forestry track before climbing through conifers of New Pieces. At junction, ignore grassy track descending south-west, but double-back left uphill to vehicle turning circle. Descend (south-west) to forest edge. Go through gate and past cottage to farm track leading to narrow lane. Turn right for ¾ mile (1.2km).

5 Turn left along drive at Bescot to stile, beyond which path traverses afforested western slopes of Moel y Golfa.

6 Signpost marks diversion of steep path to top of Moel y Golfa. Tired walkers can continue on lower path, tracing woodland edge to meet hill route, close to Middletown. Waymarked, winding hill route climbs through woods and up crags to summit monument. From here, narrow path continues along crest to gate at edge of woods. Turn right and follow zigzagging path down towards Middletown.

WATKIN PATH AND THE HEART OF SNOWDONIA

1 From car park follow road towards Beddgelert for 50yds (46m), then cross to reach signed path. Cross cattle grid and follow tarmac lane away from main road, with river on right and woodland on left.

2 Leave tarmac lane at footpath sign, bearing left through gate on rough track, with wall on left and rhododendrons on right. Go ahead through gate and follow track curving right to reach kissing-gate, shortly after obvious incline up and down hillside.

3 Kissing-gate allows access to Snowdon National Nature Reserve. Within reserve track runs close to river. Cross bridge of massive sleepers over river and continue past ruined copper mines, and tall cypress tree looking distinctly out of place. Ahead now is bulky flat-topped rock outcrop of Gladstone Rock.

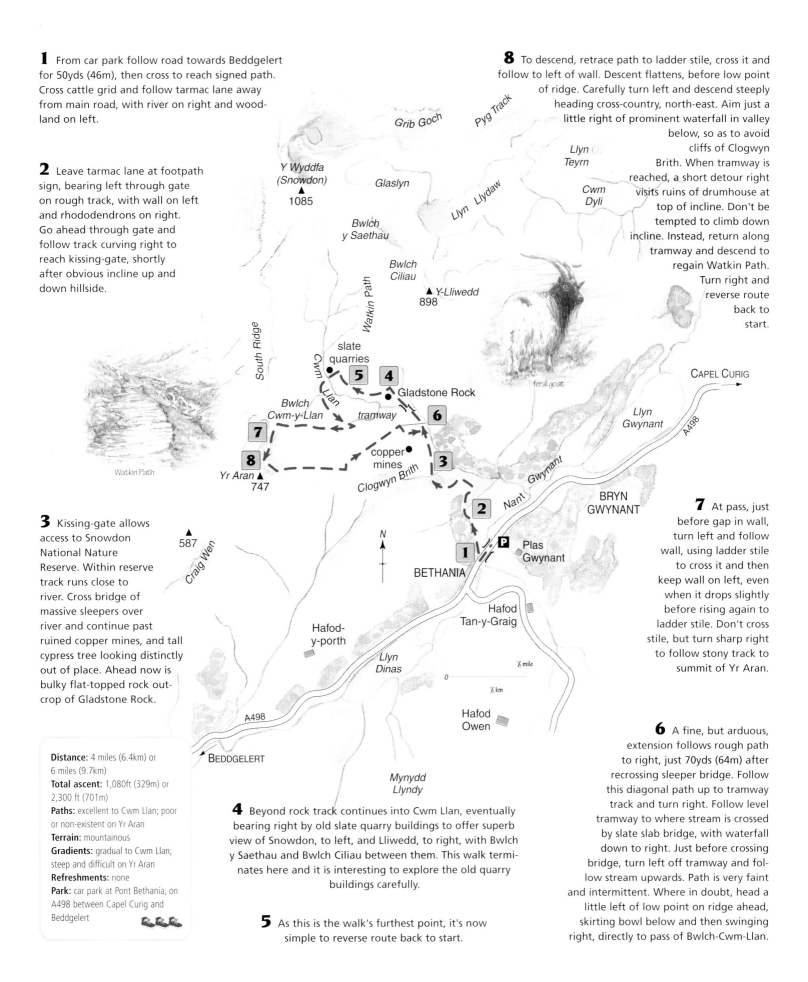

8 To descend, retrace path to ladder stile, cross it and follow to left of wall. Descent flattens, before low point of ridge. Carefully turn left and descend steeply heading cross-country, north-east. Aim just a little right of prominent waterfall in valley below, so as to avoid cliffs of Clogwyn Brith. When tramway is reached, a short detour right visits ruins of drumhouse at top of incline. Don't be tempted to climb down incline. Instead, return along tramway and descend to regain Watkin Path. Turn right and reverse route back to start.

7 At pass, just before gap in wall, turn left and follow wall, using ladder stile to cross it and then keep wall on left, even when it drops slightly before rising again to ladder stile. Don't cross stile, but turn sharp right to follow stony track to summit of Yr Aran.

6 A fine, but arduous, extension follows rough path to right, just 70yds (64m) after recrossing sleeper bridge. Follow this diagonal path up to tramway track and turn right. Follow level tramway to where stream is crossed by slate slab bridge, with waterfall down to right. Just before crossing bridge, turn left off tramway and follow stream upwards. Path is very faint and intermittent. Where in doubt, head a little left of low point on ridge ahead, skirting bowl below and then swinging right, directly to pass of Bwlch-Cwm-Llan.

4 Beyond rock track continues into Cwm Llan, eventually bearing right by old slate quarry buildings to offer superb view of Snowdon, to left, and Lliwedd, to right, with Bwlch y Saethau and Bwlch Ciliau between them. This walk terminates here and it is interesting to explore the old quarry buildings carefully.

5 As this is the walk's furthest point, it's now simple to reverse route back to start.

Distance: 4 miles (6.4km) or 6 miles (9.7km)
Total ascent: 1,080ft (329m) or 2,300 ft (701m)
Paths: excellent to Cwm Llan; poor or non-existent on Yr Aran
Terrain: mountainous
Gradients: gradual to Cwm Llan; steep and difficult on Yr Aran
Refreshments: none
Park: car park at Pont Bethania, on A498 between Capel Curig and Beddgelert

Map labels: Grib Goch, Pyg Track, Y Wyddfa (Snowdon) 1085, Glaslyn, Llyn Llydaw, Llyn Teyrn, Cwm Dyli, Bwlch y Saethau, Bwlch Ciliau, Watkin Path, Y-Lliwedd 898, South Ridge, Cwm Llan, slate quarries, Gladstone Rock, feral goat, CAPEL CURIG, Bwlch Cwm-y-Llan, tramway, Llyn Gwynant, A498, copper mines, Clogwyn Brith, Nant Gwynant, BRYN GWYNANT, Yr Aran 747, 587, Craig Wen, Watkin Path, BETHANIA, Plas Gwynant, Hafod Tan-y-Graig, Hafod-y-porth, Llyn Dinas, Hafod Owen, BEDDGELERT, Mynydd Llyndy, ½ mile, ½ km

GROVES AND GRAVES IN ANGLESEY

Distance: 8¼ miles (13.3km)
Total ascent: 280ft (85m)
Paths: mostly clear tracks and field paths; often muddy
Terrain: undulating farmland, with some woodland
Gradients: slight
Refreshments: Plas Coch or Brynsiencyn
Park: at the end of the Moel-y-don peninsula, south of the A4080

8 At the gate, go across the field to a waymarker, then turn right towards the cottage and chapel. Immediately before the cottage, go left through its grounds to the road. Turn left, cross the main road and follow the road signed Moel-y-don for a mile (1.6km) back to the car.

7 50yds (46m) beyond the gate turn right along a track. After the second stile, go right of a brick building, then diagonally left towards a rhododendron thicket, going right of it to a stile into woodland. Follow the track through the wood, keeping the wall to your left.

1 Walk up the road away from the Strait. Turn left by the post box, along the lane bending left by Bron Menai cottage and right at the T-junction, to reach a farm. Just before the pond, turn left along the track, going left where it swings to join another.

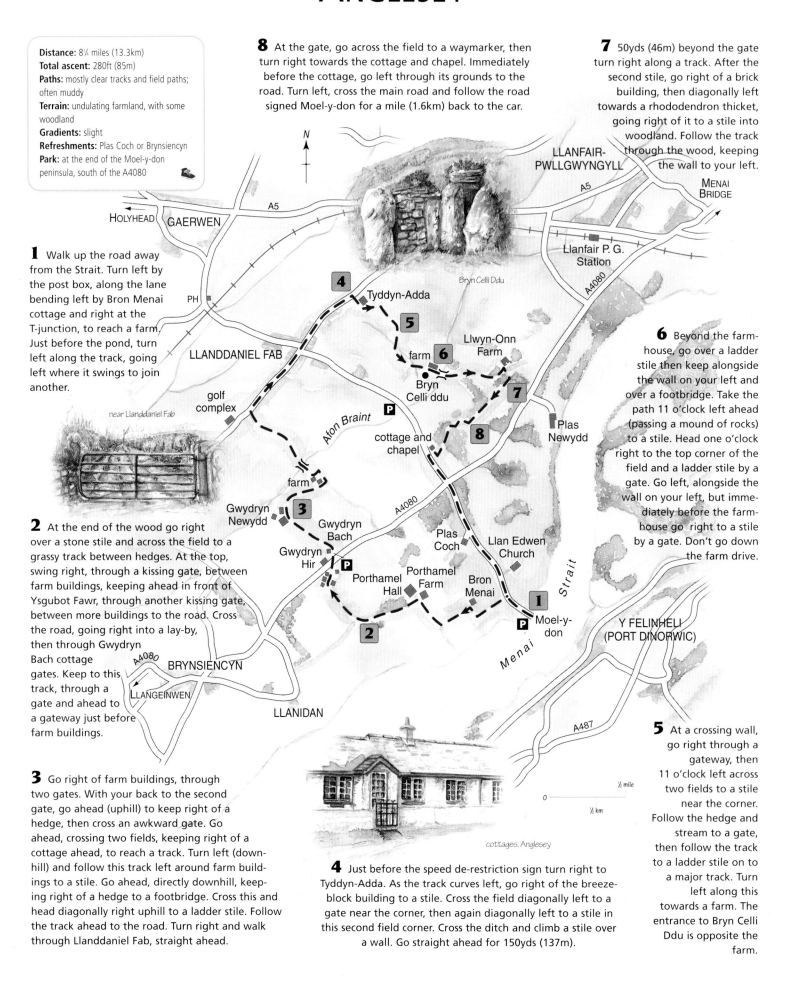

near Llanddaniel Fab

Bryn Celli Ddu

cottages, Anglesey

2 At the end of the wood go right over a stone stile and across the field to a grassy track between hedges. At the top, swing right, through a kissing gate, between farm buildings, keeping ahead in front of Ysgubot Fawr, through another kissing gate, between more buildings to the road. Cross the road, going right into a lay-by, then through Gwydryn Bach cottage gates. Keep to this track, through a gate and ahead to a gateway just before farm buildings.

6 Beyond the farmhouse, go over a ladder stile then keep alongside the wall on your left and over a footbridge. Take the path 11 o'clock left ahead (passing a mound of rocks) to a stile. Head one o'clock right to the top corner of the field and a ladder stile by a gate. Go left, alongside the wall on your left, but immediately before the farmhouse go right to a stile by a gate. Don't go down the farm drive.

3 Go right of farm buildings, through two gates. With your back to the second gate, go ahead (uphill) to keep right of a hedge, then cross an awkward gate. Go ahead, crossing two fields, keeping right of a cottage ahead, to reach a track. Turn left (downhill) and follow this track left around farm buildings to a stile. Go ahead, directly downhill, keeping right of a hedge to a footbridge. Cross this and head diagonally right uphill to a ladder stile. Follow the track ahead to the road. Turn right and walk through Llanddaniel Fab, straight ahead.

4 Just before the speed de-restriction sign turn right to Tyddyn-Adda. As the track curves left, go right of the breeze-block building to a stile. Cross the field diagonally left to a gate near the corner, then again diagonally left to a stile in this second field corner. Cross the ditch and climb a stile over a wall. Go straight ahead for 150yds (137m).

5 At a crossing wall, go right through a gateway, then 11 o'clock left across two fields to a stile near the corner. Follow the hedge and stream to a gate, then follow the track to a ladder stile on to a major track. Turn left along this towards a farm. The entrance to Bryn Celli Ddu is opposite the farm.

LOST CIVILISATIONS ON TAL Y FAN

Distance: 9½ miles (15.3km)
Total ascent: 1,725ft (526m)
Paths: mainly grassy and clear, but confusing in poor visibility
Terrain: mountain upland, hill pastures and rocky outcrops
Gradients: moderate
Refreshments: nothing near by; many places in Conwy.
Park: on roadside at the top of Sychnant Pass, the old hill road between Conwy and Penmaenmawr

9 Retrace your outward journey for ½ mile (800m), then continue ahead on a good track descending to turn left onto a gravel track. Follow this to a car park and turn left again onto the road back to the start.

8 Pass around the hill fort and bear left to walk beside a collapsed wall, heading for Craig Celynin. A terraced track passes round the western side of Craig Celynin. From its north-western edge, cut across hill pasture to a wall gap in a corner. Through this, turn right, beside a wall, and follow it until you meet your outward route on the slopes of Cefn Maen Amor.

1 From the parking area, cross the road and go up to a gate. Beyond this, a track curves around the northern end of a broad ridge.

2 After 200yds (182m) take an obvious track turning sharply right onto higher ground and, at next waymarker, bear left on a green track. In 300yds (273m), at power lines, branch right and head across heather moorland to a wall and ladder stile.

3 Beyond the stile, descend a little (signposted North Wales Path) across the western slopes of Maen Esgob, and turn left above the white farmhouse through a pronounced pass between low hills (ignore a nearby waymark). Following a stony track, pass a small lake, and continue over the col on a grassy path to reach a substantial wall on your left.

4 Turn right and continue on a grassy track for 1 mile (1.6km) with the wall on your left and later veer right on the track across the flanks of Cefn Maen Amor. The track ascends to a massive standing stone below quarries. Go past this and, when the track forks, keep right, over the col.

7 This eventually leads to a ladder stile by a gate and continues above a wall. Follow this track to the hill fort of Caer Bach.

6 Go down an obvious waymarked track with ladder stiles until you meet a lane near Cae Coch Farm. Turn left and, in 100yds (91m), branch left. In another 100yds (91m), turn left over a ladder stile and ascend towards the farm. In 50yds (45m), turn right to follow a track with a wall on your right.

5 Keep ahead, and in ¼ mile (400m), pass a ruin. The track continues across the northern slopes of Tal y Fan before turning and climbing south to a col between Tal y Fan and Foel Lwyd, where it meets a wall. Cross the ladder stile; the summit of Tal y Fan lies a few minutes up to the left. Return to the col.

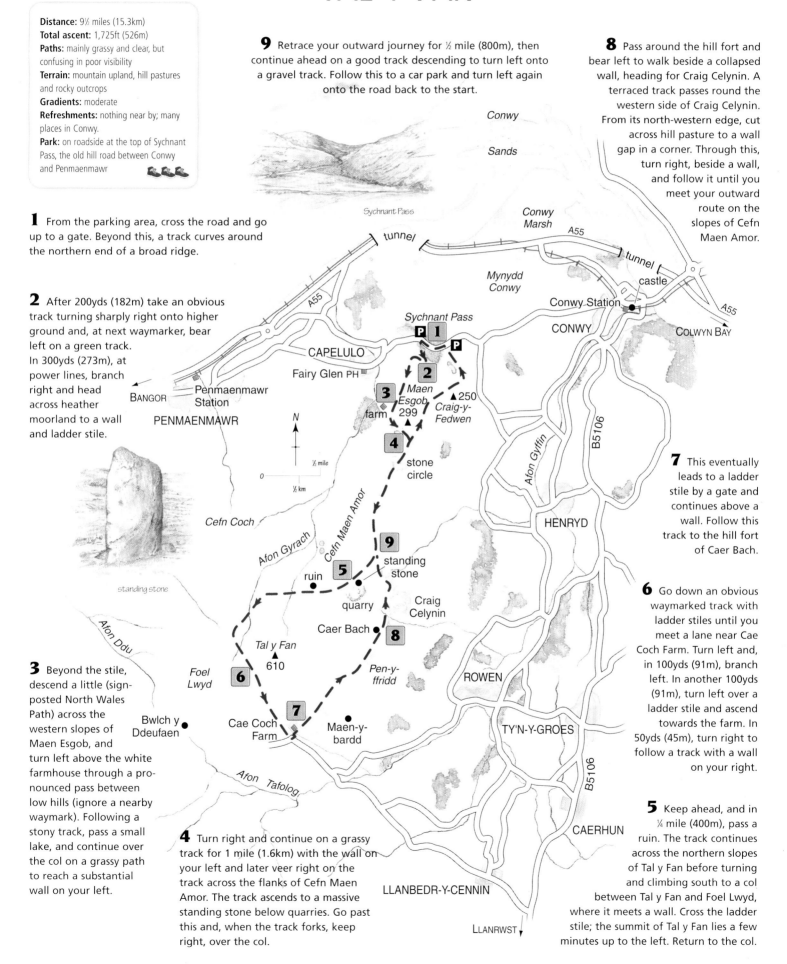

EASTERN MOORLANDS

1 Leave the car park at its top corner by crossing a stile and turning left along the road. Cross the road and in a few strides turn right onto a signposted track, which curves right and rises onto heather moorland.

2 A number of tracks soon branch from the main track. Keep to the highest, and after ¼ mile (400m) go on past an isolated tree. A second isolated tree stands near a path junction, where the most prominent track turns right and descends. Ignore this, and go forward on a narrow and boggy path through heather.

3 At a waymark post, keep forward into a rising gully, beyond which you emerge onto the open top of Ruabon Mountain. Go forward, descending easily in a south-easterly direction towards a clump of trees at Mountain Lodge, about ¾ mile (1.2km) away.

8 Take an obvious path through a dip, and continue on the other side to join a good path parallel with a plantation boundary. Later, join the outward route just a few minutes from the start.

7 Beyond the plantation boundary, there is a steady haul on a narrow path across the heather moor, crossing the high point, veering right and descending to a waymark post at a path junction. Bear left and descend to another track. Turn right for 50yds (46m) passing a small pond, and then go left on a faint green path to pass around a circular bell pit after 100yds (91m).

6 Enter the plantation and follow the path with a stream on your right, to reach a clearing after ½ mile (800m). Cross the clearing to take the path on the right (now with a stream on your left). Shortly, at a fork, veer right uphill on a rocky path to the top of the plantation, ignoring the path from the left crossing the stream.

5 A few minutes further on leave the road for a bridleway on the right, going forward through a metal gate and along a delightful green track that soon rises to the left above a stream. As you near Newtown Mountain Plantation, watch for a path branching right, down to the stream, and taking you into the plantation.

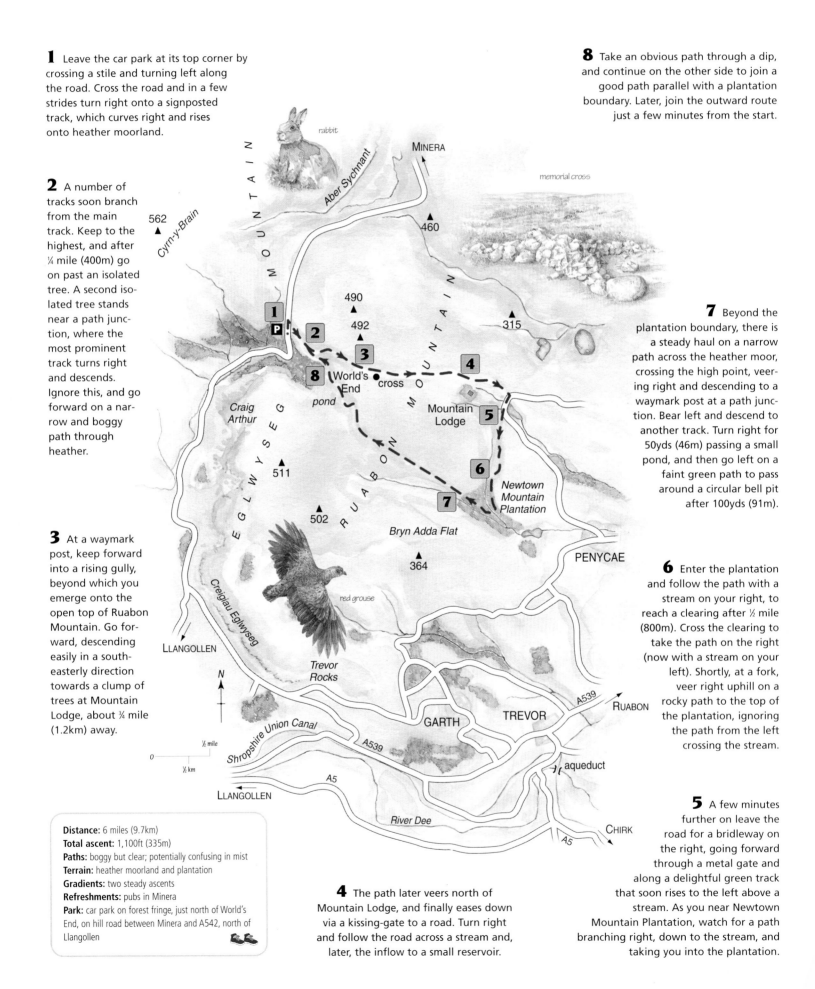

Distance: 6 miles (9.7km)
Total ascent: 1,100ft (335m)
Paths: boggy but clear; potentially confusing in mist
Terrain: heather moorland and plantation
Gradients: two steady ascents
Refreshments: pubs in Minera
Park: car park on forest fringe, just north of World's End, on hill road between Minera and A542, north of Llangollen

4 The path later veers north of Mountain Lodge, and finally eases down via a kissing-gate to a road. Turn right and follow the road across a stream and, later, the inflow to a small reservoir.

BORDER LINES – ON OFFA'S DYKE

1 Across the road from the Chirk Bank post office follow the canal towpath back towards Chirk, crossing the aqueduct to a tunnel at the end of it. A footpath now climbs to the Glyn Ceiriog road.

2 Turn left down the road for 100yds (91m) to a house named Pen-y-Waen, then follow a waymarked footpath on the right, across the cutting of the old Glyn Valley Tramway. Walk through woodland, returning to the road just short of Pont-Faen (bridge).

3 Cross the bridge and turn right along the lane. After 150yds (137m), near a telephone box, go over a stile into fields. The path follows the south banks of the Ceiriog. Take the left fork on entering Woodland Trust land and climb through Pentre Wood to a country lane. turn right and follow the lane for 300yds (274m) to The Old School.

4 Go down the enclosed track to the left of The Old School. Take the second of two signposted paths, heading across the sloping fields of Bron y Garth, crossing an enclosed farm track en route. Ascend across the next field and pass through a gate. In the next field follow a fence up on the right then cross a stile. On nearing some woods on the right, the path gets rather marshy, but the difficulties are short-lived. Past the woods, aim for the whitewashed cottage directly ahead.

5 Turn left, uphill by the cottage on a path that now keeps the earthworks of Offa's Dyke to the right. Beyond a narrow tarmac road the path drops into a wooded ravine, crossing the stream via a footbridge before climbing out on some steps.

6 Shortly after the ravine, the path comes to an enclosed track. Turn left along this to meet another lane next to Mount Wood. Turn left along the lane, which descends past two farms. At a sharp right-hand bend, leave the road for a field path tracing a hedge northeastwards and pass through a gate. Continue north-east across another field to emerge at the roadside by The Pentre.

7 Cross the road to another cross-field path, heading for a gap in a hedge then veering right to the bottom right hand corner of the next field, crossing a stile into the lane. Follow the lane down to the bridge.

8 Cross the bridge and follow a path tracing the northern banks of the River Ceiriog, going beneath the arches of the aqueduct and the viaduct. On climbing to the road, turn right, then climb past the Bridge Inn back to the post office.

Distance: 5¼ miles (9.2km)
Total ascent: 900ft (274m)
Paths: waymarked but faint; field paths muddy after rain
Terrain: fields, country lanes, woodland and canal towpath
Gradients: gradual
Refreshments: hot take-away snacks at Chirk Bank Post Office and the Bridge Inn
Park: by Chirk Bank Post Office, in Chirk Bank, on English side of border near Chirk, between Oswestry and Llangollen

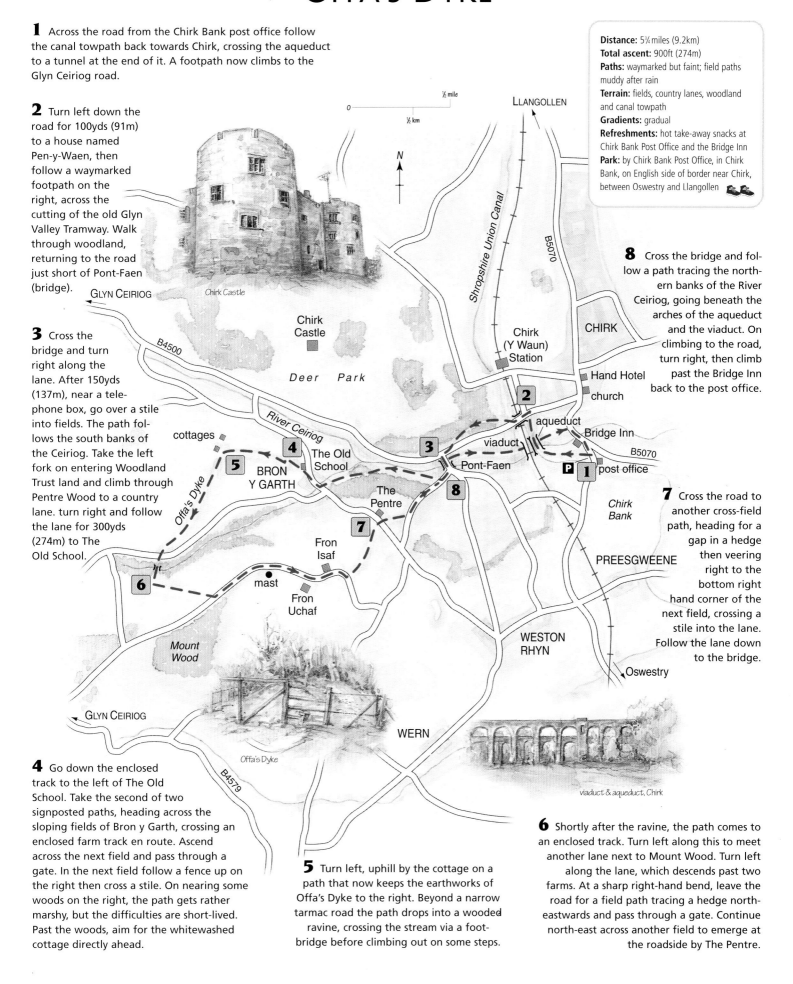

Chirk Castle

viaduct & aqueduct, Chirk

Offa's Dyke

NORTHERN ENGLAND

THE NORTH OF ENGLAND IS often referred to as a single entity, but it is by no means a homogenous region. Topographically, culturally and historically there are great differences – the barren emptiness of the Cumbrian fells is totally different from that of the rolling hills of Northumberland; the west coast has golden sands and a mild climate, while the east is famous for its rugged cliffs and bracing weather; there is gentle pastoral scenery in the limestone Dales, in contrast with the dramatic mountains of the Lake District.

The Industrial Revolution changed the face of the North of England more than any other part of the country, with great conurbations developing around the coalfields and the ports. Though these areas may not immediately suggest themselves as tourist attractions, many have been revitalised in recent years and have much to offer – proud museums to their industrial heritage, imaginative new uses for redundant sites, lively arts and entertainments and superb sporting venues. Even shopping attains new heights at Gateshead's MetroCentre, at Meadowhall in Sheffield and at Manchester's Trafford Centre.

Even in the north's great cities, you are never far from peaceful landscapes, pretty villages and stunning scenery, and in spite of the conurbations of Tyneside, South and West Yorkshire, Manchester and Merseyside, this is one of the most sparsely populated parts of the country. This sense of isolation, combined with the constant struggle against a hostile landscape and inclement weather and a history of aggressive neighbours, has created a common spirit of independence and self-reliance in the north, which is as obvious in the Dalesman as it is in the Cumbrian. Famed for their taciturnity, their sense of humour and their apparent refusal to compromise, the people of the north also pride themselves on their hospitality – visitors are warmly welcomed and, in all probability, fed to bursting point.

Whether travelling by train on the scenic Settle to Carlisle or Pickering to Grosmont lines, by car along narrow roads that climb and twist before reaching some breathtaking summit, or on foot along the Pennine and Cleveland Ways, the Lyke Wake Walk or the Three Peaks, the natural beauty of the landscape is enhanced by its history. Bronze-Age stone circles on remote mountains or moorlands; Roman roads, walls and forts; medieval abbeys in lush valleys and castles presiding over the hills and rivers; higgledy-piggledy cottages in small fishing villages and splendidly grand crescents in fashionable Victorian and Edwardian seaside resorts.

Modern times have brought the excitement of theme parks at Morecambe, Southport and Lightwater Valley near Ripon, equally matched by the famous Pleasure Beach in Britain's premier resort, Blackpool.

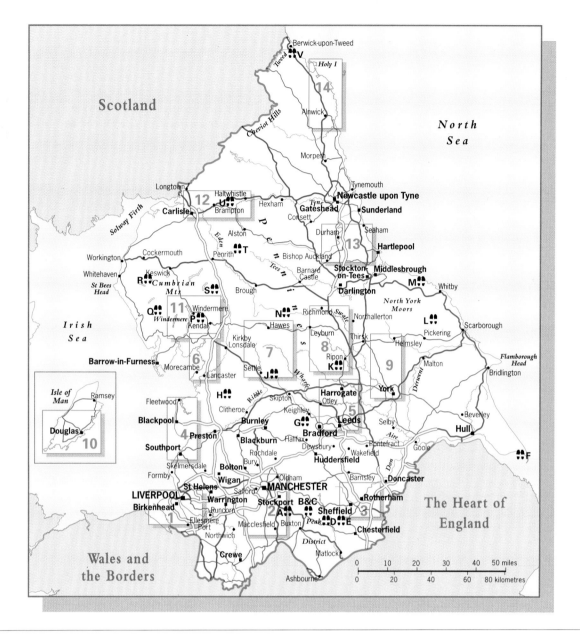

AROUND THE RIVER MERSEY

The Beatles have hijacked Liverpool's more recent history – long after the world's most famous group split up, they attract ever more visitors to the city. But Liverpool has a long and fascinating history as one of the world's great ports, and the revitalisation of once-derelict dockland areas is helping to bring that history alive once again.

Birkenhead

Only the width of the River Mersey separates Liverpool and Birkenhead, just a hamlet until the ship-building boom of the 19th century. The town contains the oldest building on Merseyside – Birkenhead Priory, where interpretative displays describe the daily routine of the monks. They were granted a charter by King Edward III in 1150 to run the first ferry across the river. Don't miss the view across the river from the adjacent tower, all that remains of St Mary's Church.

HMS Plymouth *and HMS* Onyx *are moored in the waters of the River Mersey at Birkenhead*

At East Float Dock are two vessels – the frigate HMS *Plymouth* and submarine HMS *Onyx* – that played important roles in the Falklands conflict, as well as the restored German submarine U534. This is one of the waterfront attractions that, along with the tram and transport museum and Woodside Visitor Centre, comprise what is known as the 'Birkenhead Packet'.

The famous waterfront scene in Liverpool, with the twin-towered Liver Building in the background, watching over the historic docks

Vintage trams now carry visitors between the museum and the ferry. Birkenhead's other main attraction is the Williamson Art Gallery, which is renowned for its collection of English watercolours and works by the Liverpool school of artists.

Croxteth Hall and Country Park

On the outskirts of Liverpool, near the junction of the M57 and A580, this fine historic mansion and its 500-acre (203ha) park was once the home of the Earls of Sefton. The rooms of the hall are now a wonderful re-creation of its Edwardian heyday, furnished in style and populated by figures in appropriate garb. Outside, visitors can step back a little further in time in the Victorian walled garden and visit the collection of rare breeds of farm animals. Other attractions include a miniature railway and an adventure playground, and there is a full programme of special events.

Liverpool

Liverpool, a city with two cathedrals, gazes out across the River Mersey to the sea, as it has done for centuries. In its long history as a port Liverpool has unloaded cargoes such as tobacco, cotton and cane sugar from across the Atlantic. Until the practice was outlawed in 1807, many of those same ships would continue on to West Africa, taking wretched human cargoes back to the Americas to be sold into slavery.

Albert Dock, built in 1846 to accommodate sailing ships, proved too shallow for steamships and by the end of the 19th century it had become largely obsolete. Comprising the largest collection of Grade I listed buildings in the country, Albert Dock has been sensitively restored in recent years to become the city's recreational centrepiece. Around the dock are a fascinating array of attractions, including the award-winning Merseyside Maritime Museum, the HM Customs and Excise National Museum, the northern outpost

Port Sunlight

A short ferry ride across the River Mersey from Liverpool lies the Wirral peninsula. Late in the 19th century Lord Leverhulme built a 'model' village for the workers at his soap factory. Port Sunlight (named after the company's most famous brand of soap) offered tree-lined roads, open spaces and good housing – a fine example of social engineering at a time when not all employers gave much thought to their employees' well-being. A heritage centre tells how the garden village, now a conservation area, was planned (a total of 30 architects were employed) and built, and you can explore it by following the village trail. Visitors are also welcome at the splendid Lady Lever Art Gallery, dedicated by Lord Leverhulme to his wife, and built to house his extensive collection of art treasures. These include a world-famous collection of pre-Raphaelite paintings and Wedgwood.

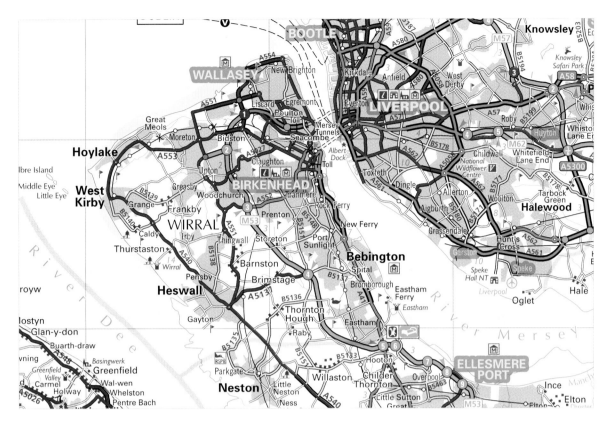

Tourist Information
Centres

Birkenhead: Woodside
Visitors Centre,
Woodside Ferry Terminal
(tel: 0151 647 6780)
Liverpool: Queen
Square (tel: 0906 6806
886)

Ferry Across the Mersey

Celebrated in song, film and folklore, the ferry from Liverpool to Birkenhead has acquired almost legendary status. The first ferry across the Mersey was operated by the monks of Birkenhead Priory as early as the 12th century, when Liverpool itself was a mere village. The ferries now run from Liverpool's Pier Head, where splendid Victorian buildings create a skyline that is as readily identifiable as Manhattan's. There is no better way to view the city's waterfront and architectural heritage.

of the Tate Gallery and the Museum of Liverpool Life. There is also a wide range of speciality shops and places to eat.

Albert Dock's greatest attraction is The Beatles Story. More than 30 years after they broke up, The Beatles are a bigger tourist attraction than ever, and The Beatles Story (open 'eight days a week'...) tells the remarkable story of the four local lads who conquered the world with their music. The Cavern Club, which became synonymous with the Liverpool sound in the 1960s, still stands on Mathew Street at the heart of the 'Cavern Quarter'. The current club is a reconstruction of the original, which closed in 1973. A few miles away in Allerton, the National Trust has restored Paul McCartney's former family home, 20 Forthlin Road – a 1950s terraced house where The Beatles met and wrote many of their early songs.

Liverpool Football Club has supporters all over the world and they will be drawn to Anfield, not just for fixtures but also for the club's visitor centre and museum.

Prescot

On a road map, Prescot seems to be lost amidst a network of motorway and road junctions to the east of Liverpool, but it is well worth a visit, particularly if you are interested in horology. In an attractive 18th-century town house in Church

Street you will find the Museum of Clock and Watch Making, which illustrates the main industry of the area. It includes a reconstruction of part of a traditional watchmaker's workshop and displays of the equipment used to make the intricate parts of clock and watch movements.

Just to the north of the town is Knowsley Safari Park, with a 5-mile (8km) drive through reserves containing lions, tigers, elephants, rhinos, monkeys and many other animals. Children will also enjoy the pets' corner, the reptile house and the amusement park.

Speke

Speke Hall seems to shrug off its uninspiring surroundings, and it is remarkable that this delightful and unpretentious house, with parts dating from as early as 1490, has survived at all. Built around a courtyard, and enclosed by a dry moat, this 'black and white' house is one of the most richly timbered houses in England; the vast Tudor Great Hall is particularly impressive. There is also some fine plasterwork, and the kitchen and servants' hall offers fascinating glimpses into domestic life below stairs in days gone by. There is a 16th-century priest hole, where persecuted Catholics could be hidden when danger threatened, examples of William Morris wallpaper and Mortlake tapestries.

Just one of the many lovely timepieces which are on display at the Museum of Clock and Watch Making at Prescot

MANCHESTER

*M*anchester has a reputation for its damp climate, but this was a positive asset – cotton brought prosperity to the city, and it is easier to spin in a damp atmosphere. Great names of the Industrial Revolution – Arkwright, Hargreaves, Crompton – made the mass production of cloth possible, and a network of canals and railways set the seal on the city's lasting importance.

Dunham Massey Hall was built in an E shape, a popular tribute the monarch in Elizabethan times

Tatton Park forms England's most complete historic estate, centring on a splendid Georgian mansion

Dunham Massey Hall

This beautiful country house is set in parkland and gardens near Altrincham. It contains fine 18th-century furniture and magnificent silverware, and no less than 30 rooms of the house are on show, including a fully equipped kitchen, butler's pantry and laundry. The formal landscaping was the handiwork, 300 years ago, of George Booth, 2nd Earl of Warrington. The gardens have been restored by the National Trust, and include an 18th-century orangery and a well-house, which once supplied the Hall with fresh water.

Manchester

There is quite a buzz to this cosmopolitan city today, with a huge variety of restaurants and nightclubs. The colourful Chinatown district (the second largest in Britain) is announced by the Imperial Chinese Archway, which overlooks the pavilions of the Chinese Garden.

In building on its industrial heritage – two centuries at the forefront of cotton manufacture – the city now attracts more than one and a half million visitors each year. The legacy of handsome Victorian buildings is much in evidence.

Manchester boasts a clutch of exceptionally good museums, particularly the

Museum of Science and Industry, the Museum of Transport and the Gallery of English Costume. There is also a museum dedicated to Emmeline Pankhurst and the Women's Suffrage Movement, and the Pump House People's History Museum, which records the day to day struggles of ordinary working people through the ages. The city is know throughout the world for sporting excellence. Host to the Commonwealth Games in 2002, it boasts the best cycling facilities in Britain at the Velodrome, while at Old Trafford, visitors can revel in the footballing glory surrounding the world's richest soccer club. The Manchester United museum and megastore is open all week, not just on match days.

Nearby Salford was immortalised by the artist L S Lowry and the largest collection of his unique works are now displayed in the spectacular Lowry arts complex next to the Salford Quays waterfront development. Salford is also home to the Lancashire Mining Museum, and a few miles further west, the Trafford Centre is the largest purpose-built shopping and entertainment destination in the northwest of England. East of the centre of the old town of Ashton under Lyne is the Museum of the Manchester Regiment and the Portland Basin Museum, an industrial and social history museum located at the junction of three canals.

Quarry Bank Mill

Founded in 1784 by Samuel Greg, Quarry Bank Mill at Styal was one of the very first factories to use water power to drive its textile machinery. It is now fully restored as a working museum of the cotton industry. The centrepiece is England's biggest working waterwheel (weighing 50 tons and 24ft/7.3m high) that transforms the quiet waters of the River Bollin into a powerful driving force. The museum tells the story of the industry and emphasises the contrasting lives of the Greg family, the mill's workforce and the children who helped to tend the machines.

Jodrell Bank

A name synonymous with the study of distant stars and galaxies, Jodrell Bank brings the interplanetary world down to earth in its award-winning Science Centre, which stands at the foot of one of the largest fully steerable radio telescopes in the world – the famous Lovell telescope. As well as its exhibitions on space, astronomy and satellites, it has 'hands-on' exhibits and shows every half-hour in the largest planetarium outside London. More down to earth, literally, is the Environmental Discovery Centre and the 35-acre (14ha) arboretum, with over 2,000 species of trees and shrubs.

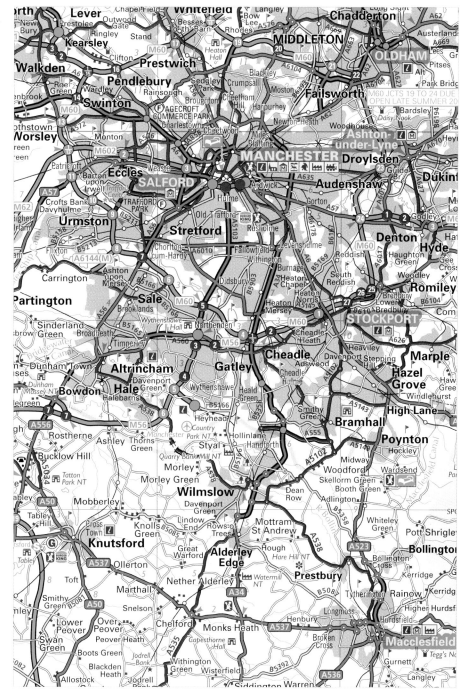

Tourist Information
Centres

Bury: Derby Hall,
Market Street (tel: 0161
253 5111)
Knutsford: Council
Offices, Toft Road (tel: ·
01565 632611/632210)
Manchester: Town Hall
Extension, Lloyd Street
(tel: 0161 234 3157/8)

Urban Heritage

Designated as Britain's first Urban Heritage Park, the Castlefield area of Manchester has been transformed into a major recreational amenity for locals and visitors alike. The original castle, dating from the Roman occupation, made way, during the late 18th century, for the building of the country's first modern canal. The Bridgewater Canal helped to transform Manchester into a major industrial city, exemplified by the wharves and warehouses that line the canal.

Castlefield gradually slipped into dereliction, a decline halted in recent years by a massive restoration scheme. Now there are festivals, carnivals and exhibitions throughout the year to supplement permanent attractions such as the Museum of Science and Industry.

Saddleworth Moor

Just a few minutes' drive from industrial Oldham brings you to one of the wildest landscapes in the North. Saddleworth Moor extends mile after lonely mile – perfect for those hardy walkers who want to swap the din of the town for the bubbling call of the curlew. The Saddleworth district incorporates a number of intriguing little gritstone villages, former centres of woollen industries, where traditions such as rush-bearing and morris dancing are very much alive. Uppermill is the home of the Saddleworth Museum and Art Gallery, in an old mill building by the Huddersfield Narrow Canal. Displays include a reconstruction of an 18th-century weaver's cottage and working machinery from a woollen mill.

An old drawing illustrates work in a cotton mill in the late 18th and early 19th centuries. The industry is now depicted at the restored Quarry Bank Mill at Styal

Tatton Park

At the end of a long, tree-lined drive, Tatton Park is a great country estate and one of the National Trust's most popular properties. It has Japanese gardens, a 2,000-acre (809ha) deer park, orangery, outdoor and sailing centre based around Tatton Mere, adventure playground and a 1930s working farm, echoing to the rumble of vintage machinery. The rooms of the Old Hall offer a glimpse into various periods from the Middle Ages to the 1950s. The mansion is Georgian, and is a storehouse of fine furniture, paintings and family treasures.

See Walk A page 280
The Goyt Valley

STEEL CITY ON THE FRINGE OF THE PEAK

Now the fourth largest city in the country, Sheffield rose to prominence during the 19th century to become the steel capital of the world. The legend 'Made in Sheffield', engraved on tools and cutlery, has long been a byword for quality. Yet industrial Sheffield lies on the fringe of the Peak National Park, very close to some of the finest scenery in the north.

Abbeydale Industrial Hamlet

This open-air museum, in a leafy waterside suburb of Sheffield, occupies one of the oldest industrial sites around the city. In its workshops, some dating back to the 18th century, agricultural tools were made. The motive power came from the waters of the River Sheaf, diverted over a huge water-wheel, which is still in working order. Today visitors can see the forges, water-driven forge hammers, grindstones and the only surviving crucible steel furnace in the world. Some of the workshops are occupied once again by craftsmen, carrying on Sheffield's tradition of working in metal. Visitors can also look round the Victorian manager's house and a workman's cottage.

Conisbrough

The 12th-century castle at Conisbrough, towering over beside the River Don, has recently undergone intensive restoration, and visitors to the new heritage centre will discover much about the castle's history. The keep, still standing to its original height of 90ft (27.4m), was probably built by Hamelin Plantagenet, the bastard half-brother of Henry II. Readers of Sir Walter Scott's books will probably recognise Conisbrough Castle from his novel, *Ivanhoe*.

Rotherham

North-east of Sheffield, at the meeting of the Rivers Rother and Don, is Rotherham – much the older of the two communities, with an entry for its church in the Domesday Book. Earlier relics, from Roman times, can be seen at the Clifton Park Museum, a mansion house of 1783. Heavy industry put Rotherham on the map – the cannons that decided the outcome of the Battle of Trafalgar were made here. In the cavernous former Templeborough Steelworks is Magna, Britain's first science adventure centre.

Rother Valley Country Park

Sheffield is reckoned to be one of the 'greenest' cities in Europe, with more than 50 public parks and gardens. Indeed, more than a third of the city falls within the borders of the Peak National Park. The 750 acre (304ha) Rother Valley Country Park has excellent facilities for water sports, such as sailing, wind-surfing and canoeing (equipment can be hired). Less energetic visitors can enjoy peaceful woodland walks, and visit the craft centre. A visitor centre has been created in the restored 17th-century Bedgreave Mill.

Sheffield

Sheffield is trying very hard to shake off its rather dour image; today the city is being revitalised as a centre for leisure activities, conferences and sporting excellence. The Don Valley International Stadium emphasises Sheffield's ambition to be the sporting capital of the north. This 25,000-capacity, all-seater stadium, built to international standards, is the country's top athletics venue along with the nearby

Sheffield Ski Village

The largest artificial ski resort in Europe occupies a splendid setting, looking over the City of Sheffield and the Peak District beyond. Eight ski runs cater for all levels of skill – nursery runs for the novice and testing descents and moguls for the more experienced. All the other elements of a ski resort are here too, including a café, a restaurant and a fitness suite. Everything, indeed, except the likelihood of snow.

Conisbrough Castle, with its unique design – circular with six buttresses – soars beside the River Don, with wonderful views across the surrounding industrial landscape

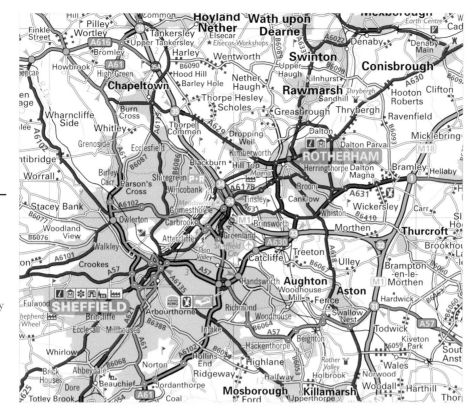

Tourist Information Centres

Rotherham: Central Library, Walker Place (tel: 01709 823611)
Sheffield: corner of Tudor Square and Surrey Street (tel: 0114 221 1900)

This Sheffield Simplex 50hp SSK, dating from 1920, is just one of the many exhibits at the lively and fascinating Kelham Island Industrial Museum

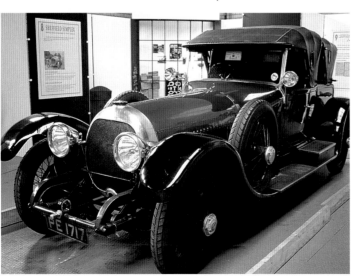
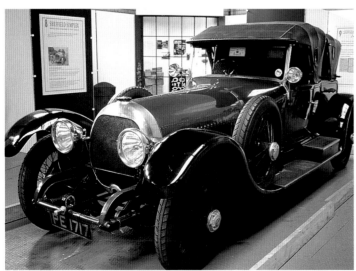

Sheffield Arena. It also hosts other events such as rugby league games and rock concerts. In the city centre, the Ponds Forge International Sports Centre boasts Olympic standard swimming facilities. Sheffield is not only known for athletics – the 'Blades' and the 'Owls' continue to ensure soccer rivalry, and snooker fans have become familiar with the Crucible Theatre through televised championships.

This diversification does not consign Sheffield's steel-making to the history books and the heritage industries. The city is still a hive of industry. In fact, more steel and cutlery is made today than ever before, though production is streamlined and hi-tech. At the lively Kelham Island Industrial Museum, on Alma Street, visitors can trace the history of Sheffield's industrial development over the last 400 years, with displays of working machinery and some of the products that have made Sheffield famous, particularly iron, steel and silverware. One curiosity is a pen-knife with no fewer than 365 retractable blades! The massive and mighty River Don steam engine – the largest in the world – once powered a steel-rolling mill and it can still be seen 'in steam'. Skilled cutlers, using traditional methods, can be seen at work in the 'Little Mesters' workshops.

Sheffield's Supertram system is an enviable public transport system that is quiet, quick and comfortable. The trams offer the most convenient way to get to both the Don Valley Stadium and the Meadowhall Shopping Centre. This huge complex has risen, phoenix-like, from the ashes of the industrial wasteland that was one of the city's largest steel-works. It attracts over half a million shoppers each week to its wide range of shops, from the multiples to specialist outlets, a huge choice of places to eat and even an 11-screen cinema.

The Kelham Island Industrial Museum in Sheffield contains the largest working steam engine in the world

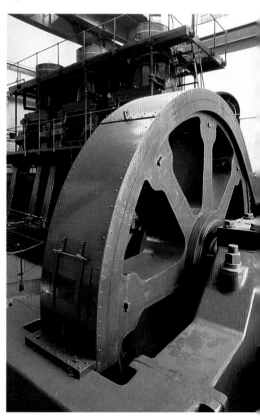

THE PEAK DISTRICT

The Peak District stands at the crossroads of Britain – a beautiful link between the hard, uncompromising landscapes of the north and the lush greenness of the lowland south. As the southernmost extremity of the Pennine Chain, the Peak is the last knobbly vertebra in the backbone of England, and the first real hill country to be met by the traveller from the south and east. The change is quite sudden, as reflected by an early 18th-century traveller leaving Ashbourne to enter the Peak. 'At the summit of the hill,' he reflected, 'it was a top coat colder'.

The landscape changes too, as you climb on to the limestone plateau in the south and centre, which is known as the White Peak. Gone are the neatly hedged fields of the Midlands, replaced by tumble-down drystone walls spreading up hill and down dale, seemingly oblivious to the swelling contours.

WILD FLOWERS OF THE PEAK

To the botanist, the Peak represents the best of both worlds. Here can be found southern types, like the nettle-leaved bellflower, at their northern limit and northern types, like the cloudberry, at their southernmost extent. But to see the delicate white flowers of the cloudberry, the visitor has to travel north, leaving the limestone of the White Peak behind. Enclosing the limestone plateau to the north, east and west is a mantle of bleak and sometimes forbidding, peat-covered moorland known, in contrast, as the Dark Peak. This is the home of hardy species such as the cloudberry which, as its name suggests, is frequently to be found in the clouds, and of the blue or mountain hare, which changes the colour of its coat to match the winter snows.

The cloudberry survives on the high moors where many plants would fail

THE ROCKS BENEATH

The predominant rock in the Dark Peak is millstone grit, a coarse sandstone which takes its name from the fact that it was once much in demand for mill and grindstones. Abandoned millstone quarries can be found beneath many gritstone edges, with piles of finished but now unwanted stones. The Peak National Park, which encompasses 555 sq miles (1,437.4sq km) and was the first in Britain to be set up, in 1951, took the millstone symbol as its boundary marker and logo.

Both limestone and gritstone were laid down under tropical seas during the Carboniferous period, about 330 million years ago; if you look carefully at a limestone wall or gatepost, you may be able to see the remains of the sea lilies and shells which created the rock. The grit was laid down later over the limestone under deltaic conditions not unlike those found in the Mississippi or Nile today.

EARLY SETTLERS

The Peak District, like any upland region, is the creation of its underlying geology, and the high and dry plateaux of the Peak were particularly attractive to the first settlers who made their way across the land bridge from Europe. The remoteness of the region has resulted in the survival of a surprising number of remains of these first hunter-gatherers, including perhaps the most spectacular – the stone circles of Arbor Low, near Youlgreave and the Nine Ladies on Stanton Moors. Almost every hilltop in the Peak seems to be marked by a burial mound or barrow, most dating from the Bronze Age and known by the local name of 'low.' Complete

Bronze-Age landscapes, including huts, stone circles, fields and barrows, have been identified on the moorlands to the east.

The Iron Age saw the construction of a number of apparently defensive hillforts, such as Mam Tor, commanding the upper Hope Valley near Castleton, and Fin Cop above Monsal Dale. Whether these defensive positions were ever the last resort of native Brigantians against the invading Romans will probably never be known, but the Imperial legions' chief interest in the Peak was in its abundant supplies of lead ore.

WEALTH FROM THE LAND

The Romans were the first to exploit the mineral wealth of the Peak District, and mining and quarrying has been a major local source of employment ever since. In the 18th and 19th centuries, lead production was a major source of Peak District wealth and over 10,000 miners were at work in the limestone area. Evidence of their passing can still be seen in White Peak meadows, where over 50,000 shafts have been identified.

The wealth won from lead and from the wool of their sheep gave landowners like the Dukes of Devonshire and Rutland the confidence to build their magnificent houses of Chatsworth and Haddon Hall, both near Bakewell and superb

The Nine Ladies Stone Circle is evidence of the early occupation of Stanton Moor, amidst lovely countryside above the River Derwent

Mock Beggars Hall, above, is a natural rock formation, while Bakewell Pudding, bottom right, was an accidental creation

but contrasting examples of the English country house.

Haddon Hall, the older and more intimate of the two, was abandoned for 200 years and therefore not significantly 'improved' since the late Middle Ages. It stands on a prominent bluff overlooking the River Wyel. Just over the hill in the Derwent Valley is Chatsworth, the palatial, Palladian-style seat of the Dukes of Devonshire, largely rebuilt in the 17th century and now a treasurehouse of works of art. It stands in extensive parkland.

A much earlier seat of power in the Peak is the romantic ruin of Peveril Castle, high above the tiny township of Castleton in the Hope Valley. It was built by William Peveril shortly after the Conquest as the administrative centre for the Royal Forest of the Peak – a hunting preserve for medieval kings and princes.

MOST VISITED NATIONAL PARK

Today, Castleton is a popular centre for the millions of visitors who throng to Britain's most-visited national park, many coming to visit the four famous caverns. Treak Cliff and the Blue John Cavern and Mine are where the rare semi-precious stone, Blue John, is found. Peak Cavern is the most spectacular, while Speedwell's flooded passages are explored by boat.

Matlock and Matlock Bath have family attractions such as Gulliver's Kingdom, the Heights of Abraham, with its cable cars, caverns, maze and water gardens, and its illuminations. Matlock Bath is also home to Temple Mine and the Peak District Mining Museum.

The 'capital' of the Peak is Bakewell, famous for the Pudding (never known as a 'tart' here). The friendly little town is the natural centre and has the biggest local livestock and street market every Monday.

Most of today's 22 million annual visitors come from the surrounding towns and cities. Half the population of England live within day-trip distance of this precious island of unspoilt scenery. To them, the Peak District is a vital lung and breathing space – right on their doorstep.

See Walk B page 281
Wonders of the Peak at Castleton

See Walk C page 282
A Walk in the Dark Peak

See Walk D page 283
Eyam – Village of the Damned

See Walk E page 284
Packhorse Trails Across the Peak

LANCASHIRE'S HOLIDAY PLAYGROUND

The resorts of Lancashire are where the North of England has traditionally gone on holiday; whole mill-towns would once decamp here during 'Wakes Week'. Despite the lure of foreign climes, Blackpool and Lytham St Annes still attract millions, and yet away from the resorts much of the coastline is unspoilt, with sandy beaches where yours may be the only footprints.

Blackpool's famous tower looks down over the Golden Mile – part of a promenade that runs for 7 miles (11.3km) along the sands. The long established Pleasure Beach has kept right up to date with the most terrifying rides, below

Blackpool

A late starter as a resort, Blackpool soon made up for lost time. In the 1840s it was just a village, but the arrival of a railway branch-line provided the impetus for creating a major resort along this strand of sandy beach. Ever since then the town's main concern has been to find more and more ways of entertaining visitors, who number more than 15 million per year. It was in Blackpool, for example, that the first sticks of seaside rock were made, their success assured by having 'Blackpool' written all the way through.

Brash, brazen and bustling, Blackpool wears its heart on its sleeve; there is nothing subtle about the attractions of the Pleasure Beach and the celebrated Golden Mile. It is noted, as Stanley Holloway used to sing, 'for fresh air and fun', and those who want their pleasures to involve 'white knuckles' will not be disappointed. When the sky turns leaden there are as many amusements under cover, including the

attractions at the base of the famous tower and the fascinating Sea Life Centre. Here visitors can view marine life at close quarters, including a walk through the largest shark display in Europe.

In autumn, when most other resorts are putting up the shutters, Blackpool gears up for a major influx of visitors. The famous illuminations, along 7 miles (11.3km) of sea-front, bring a touch of Las Vegas to the country's biggest holiday resort.

Lytham St Annes

At Lytham St Annes you get two resorts in one. Until 1923 Lytham and neighbouring St Annes were two distinct communities. Lytham, mentioned as a port in the Domesday book, is kept at arm's length from the shore by the expanse of the Green. Here you will see the town's most distinctive landmark – a beautifully restored windmill dating back to 1805; at one time there were many such mills on

Blackpool Tower

There can be few better-known landmarks in the country than Blackpool Tower. The town's soaring ambitions as a holiday resort were confirmed by the building, in 1894, of a convincing 519ft (158.2m) replica of the Eiffel Tower in Paris. But Blackpool's version is more than just a tower. It rises out of a building which is large enough to accommodate the famous circus and the vast Tower Ballroom, with its mighty Wurlitzer organ. There are lifts to the top of the tower, from where there are magnificent views over the resort and miles of coastline.

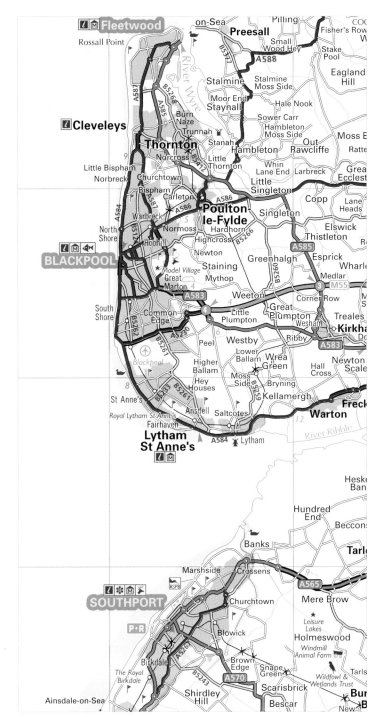

Martin Mere

This Wildlife and Wetlands Trust Centre near Ormskirk was established in 1976 and has birds from all over the world, including ducks, geese, swans and flamingos which can be observed from hides overlooking the floodwaters.

In winter the bird population is swelled by the arrival of huge numbers of pink-footed geese (up to one tenth of the world population) and migrating Whooper and Bewick's swans which can be viewed at close quarters from the many hides or watched from the comfort of the heated Raines Observatory.

The centre also has the exciting Wetland Adventure for children, which is in the form of an exciting expedition through simulated wetland, via a swaying bridge, to a pond maze.

Southport

In the early 19th century, the place where Southport now stands was nothing but sand dunes. A passion for sea-bathing prompted a local man, Duke Sutton, to build the South Port Hotel at the best beach. Though he ended his days in a debtors' prison, he inspired the town's creation and his hotel gave it a name. By 1860 this was the largest seaside resort in the north, when Blackpool was just being developed. Lord Street is the main thoroughfare: wide, elegant and lined with fine Victorian buildings, their elaborate canopies extending over the pavement.

Tourist Information Centres

Blackpool: Visitor Centre, 1 Clifton Street (tel: 01253 478222) Pleasure Beach, 525 Ocean Boulevard, South Promenade (seasonal) (tel: 01253 403223)
Fleetwood: Ferry Office, Ferry Dock, The Esplanade (tel: 01253 773953)
Lytham St Annes: The Square (tel: 0906 680 0033)
Southport: 112 Lord Street (tel: 01704 533333)

Many of the birds and waterfowl which are protected at the Martin Mere Wildfowl and Wetlands Trust can be viewed at very close quarters

the flatlands of the Fylde peninsular.

St Annes was a Victorian creation, built on sand dunes by entrepreneurs who took note of the prevailing fashion for sea-bathing. They created a health resort that would be a little more elegant than some of its more boisterous neighbours; the resort's name was found in the chapel, which is dedicated to St Anne.

One rainy-day attraction here is the delightful Toy and Teddy Bear Museum on Clifton Drive North, an award-winning collection which includes a mini motor museum and a series of tableaux featuring teddy bears in scenes such as 'bears at the seaside' and the inevitable picnic.

LEEDS AND BRADFORD

Brick-built Leeds and stone-built Bradford are the closest of neighbours. Once vital cogs in the engine room of the Industrial Revolution, these twin cities are being revitalised to meet the expectations of the 21st century. Harrogate, to the north, is content to offer echoes of a more leisurely age, and in between are some delightful villages in surprisingly rural settings.

Tourist Information Centres

Bradford: National Museum of Photography, Film and Television, Pictureville (tel: 01274 753678)
Harrogate: Royal Baths Assembly Rooms, Crescent Road (tel: 01423 527300)
Knaresborough: 35 Market Place (seasonal) (tel: 01423 866886)
Leeds: 19 Wellington Street (tel: 0113 242 5242)
Otley: Council Offices, 8 Boroughgate (tel: 0113 2477 7076)

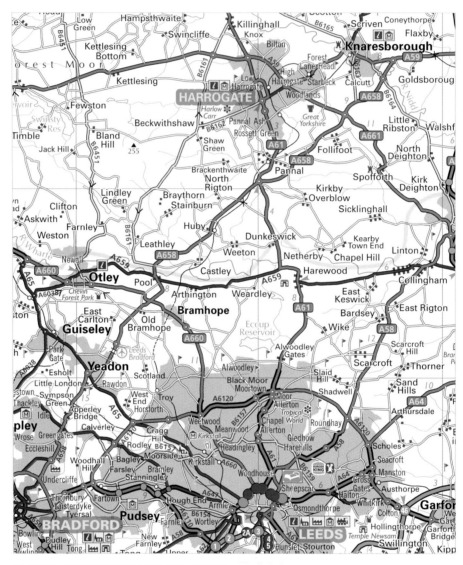

Harewood House

Halfway between Leeds and Harrogate lies one of Yorkshire's finest and stateliest homes. Harewood House was designed by John Carr and Robert Adam, and the 1,000 acres (405ha) of parkland was created by that doyen of landscaping, 'Capability' Brown. The house contains many treasures, including an unrivalled collection of 18th-century furniture made especially for Harewood by Thomas Chippendale, who was born in Otley.

Harewood House stages a variety of exhibitions and events, and the bird garden brings visitors face to face with rare and exotic species from around the world.

Bradford

Cosmopolitan Bradford is a bustling city with fine Victorian architecture. The Wool Exchange, textile mills and the warehouse district are evocative reminders of a time when Bradford was the woollen capital of the world. The story is vividly told at the Industrial and Horses at Work Museum, in a former spinning mill in Eccleshill, which includes working machinery, horse-drawn rides, textile workers' cottages and the mill-owner's house to visit.

The National Museum of Photography, Film and Television portrays the history and future of the media using special effects, interactive devices and a massive IMAX cinema screen. The Colour Museum is a revealing exploration of colour technology and the Life Force Millennium Faith Experience challenges the way we look at the world.

Harrogate

The discovery of spring waters – and their restorative powers – transformed Harrogate from a sleepy village into a bustling spa town. By the 16th century it was well-

Kirkstall

On the outskirts of Leeds, on the banks of the River Aire, is Kirkstall Abbey, founded in 1152 and one of the finest monastic sites in the country. After the Dissolution of the Monasteries, the building fared better than many and still stands substantially to its full height. Near by is the Abbey House Museum, a major folk museum with full-size Victorian shops, workshops and cottages.

The magnificent domed glass roof of the Corn Exchange in Leeds once threw light on market dealings below; today a variety of designer shops are housed here, with occasional crafts fairs and exhibitions

The Music Room at Harewood House is a stunning example of 18th-century interior design, with a carpet that reflects the fine plasterwork of the ceiling and furniture and works of art that were chosen to create a unified overall effect

Temple Newsam House

This fine house, dubbed 'The Hampton Court of the North' and dating from the 16th and 17th centuries, was the birthplace of Lord Darnley. Just 4 miles (6.4km) from Leeds city centre, the house enjoys views over parkland designed by 'Capability' Brown. The walled gardens are a riot of colour in the rhododendron season, while the house itself boasts a fine collection of Chippendale furniture and Leeds pottery.

known as an inland resort, where well-heeled visitors would socialise and 'take the waters'. In more recent times Harrogate has successfully reinvented itself as a venue for conventions and trade shows. The old Royal Pump Room, now a museum, still stands in the town centre, and adventurous visitors can still taste the water. The Valley Gardens are near by; further out are the impressive Harlow Carr Botanical Gardens.

Knaresborough

This idiosyncratic and historic little town has a castle which gazes down into the steep gorge of the River Nidd, a cobbled market place which boasts the oldest chemist's shop in the country and a Petrifying Well that turns to 'stone' any objects hung in its flow. Near by is the cave in which Old Mother Shipton lived 500 years ago and foretold the future. Some of her prophesies strike resonant chords. Could these four lines perhaps refer to the M25 and the Internet?...

> *'Carriages without horses shall go,*
> *and accidents fill the world with woe.*
> *Around the world thoughts shall fly*
> *in the twinkling of an eye...'*

Leeds

Its reputation built on the textile and tailoring trades, Leeds is rapidly changing to meet new challenges. Smoke-blackened mills are giving way to new developments

overlooking the River Aire and the Leeds–Liverpool Canal, creating riverside walks and, at Granary Wharf, a labyrinth of speciality shops. Other buildings, such as the splendid, domed Corn Exchange, have a new lease of life, filled with shops, and the city's arcades have been restored to their original Victorian splendour.

Bobbins and shuttles still fly at Armley Mills Industrial Museum, evoking memories of its heyday and showing all the stages of production, from sheep to clothing. Along the waterfront from Tetley's Brewery Wharf development you'll find the superb Royal Armouries – a purpose-built museum displaying over 8,000 exhibits from 3,000 years of conflict.

Otley

John Wesley, on a preaching visit in 1759, found 'such noise, hurry, drunkenness, rioting and confusion I know not when I have met with before'. It is hard to believe he was speaking of Otley, a delightful little market town straddling the River Wharfe. This was the birthplace, in 1718, of cabinet maker Thomas Chippendale. The artist, J M W Turner, was a regular visitor to Farnley Hall, as guest of the Horton-Fawkes family (whose most notorious relative was Guy Fawkes), and the landscapes of the Yorkshire Dales provided inspiration for many of Turner's paintings.

Tetley's Brewery Wharf brings to life the history of the English pub, with reconstructions of ale-houses of the past (and future), all staffed by actors

THE ABBEYS OF THE NORTH

EARLY CHRISTIANITY

St Paulinus (d. AD 644) was the first successful Christian missionary in the north, converting King Edwin, who made him Archbishop of York. Paulinus preached, baptised and encouraged the setting up of churches throughout the north, but when his patron was killed in battle, he returned to Kent and the north reverted to paganism.

The second wave of missionaries came from the Irish, rather than Roman tradition, and were spearheaded by St Columba (AD 521–97), who founded the monastery on Iona. His monks established churches throughout the north and one of them, St Aidan (d. AD 651), became the first Bishop of Lindisfarne (Holy Island), off the coast of Northumberland. The clash between the Celtic and Roman monasticism was finally resolved at the great Synod of Whitby, held at Whitby Abbey on the North Yorkshire coast, where it was decided to adopt Roman, Papal observances.

The most famous chronicler of these events was the Venerable Bede (AD 673–735), whose reputation has stood longer than the great abbey at Jarrow, where he lived and died. Bede was born into a Saxon family who sent him, at the age of seven, to be brought up as a monk at Wearmouth Abbey; he soon moved on to Jarrow where he spent the rest of his life. He learnt Latin, Greek and Hebrew and wrote treatises on theology, natural phenomena and orthography, but his most famous work was his *Ecclesiastical History of the English People*. Full of vividly told anecdotes, the work is also scholarly and accurate. Its extraordinary qualities were

From the very earliest days of Christianity, the remoteness and wildness of the northern English landscape attracted hermits and monastic communities alike, offering opportunities for retreat from the civilised world and the adoption of a life of self-sufficiency and poverty. It is ironic then that the success of these establishments resulted not only in the building of some of the finest and richest abbeys in the kingdom, but also in a transformation of their surroundings. The Cistercian brotherhood, in particular, by a combination of sheer hard work and technical expertise, turned unproductive land into fertile, well-drained fields which supported vast numbers of sheep. Though their grandiose abbeys are now reduced to ruins, the achievement of these medieval pioneers lives on in the oases of lush pasture which they created in the midst of moorland and fells.

The dedication stone of St Paul's Church in Jarrow, which contains the chapel where Bede worshipped. The church is now at the heart of the Bede's World exhibition, which tells of the former monastery here and of the life of the great chronicler

immediately recognised and it has remained the standard textbook on the early English Church for over 1,200 years.

CISTERCIAN PIONEERS

It was the Cistercians who left the greatest legacy of monastic architecture. The oldest foundation, Rievaulx, was, as its name suggests, established by French

monks from Clairvaux, where the abbot, St Bernard (1091–1153), was one of the most influential of all medieval Christians. Rievaulx was founded in 1131 and by the end of the century there were said to be over 140 monks and 500 lay brothers living there. Its evocative ruins are set in a wooded valley in the Hambleton Hills of North Yorkshire. They are best seen from the vantage point of Rievaulx Terrace, which, with its Tuscan and Ionic Temples, was built specifically for that purpose in the mid-18th century.

On an even grander scale are the ruins of Fountains Abbey, founded a year after Rievaulx,

but reconstructed in the second half of the century after a disastrous fire. Built on a site once described as 'fit more for the dens of wild beasts than for the uses of man', the abbey became the wealthiest Cistercian house in England, a pre-eminence which is still evident from the sheer size of the remaining buildings and the rich beauty of their setting. Approached through the delightful water gardens of Studley Royal, the sight is breathtaking.

Between Rievaulx and Fountains are the ruins of Byland Abbey, founded in 1134, which boasts the longest Cistercian church in England. Its daughter house, Jervaulx, was, according to tradition, founded by a group of monks from Byland who lost their way on the banks of the River Yore and were guided to safety by a vision of the Virgin and Child, who declared 'Ye are late of Byland but now of Yorevale'.

The distinctive red sandstone remains of Furness Abbey in Cumbria, which was founded in 1123 but taken over by the Cistercians in 1147, testify to the fact that it came second only to Fountains in terms of wealth, owning extensive properties in northern England and the Isle of Man. In terms of size, it belittled even Fountains, having a dormitory twice as long.

The Cistercians were not the only monks to settle in this area. Two 12th-century Augustinian foundations were preserved to a degree. Brinkburn Priory, despite its pretty setting by the River Coquet, was always impoverished, but its church survived the Reformation because it served the parish; it was completely restored in the 19th century and is regarded as Northumberland's finest example of early Gothic architecture.

The remains of Rievaulx Abbey are still substantial, showing its former importance and prosperity. The nave, which dates back to 1135, is the earliest large Cistercian nave in Britain and the choir is a notable example of 13th-century work

THE DISSOLUTION

Picturesque and tranquil though their ruins may be now, the great abbeys were once at the centre of religious, social and commercial life. This might have continued, had Henry VIII not divorced Katherine of Aragon so that he could marry Ann Boleyn. Because the Pope refused to approve of the arrangement, Henry VIII made himself Supreme Head of the Church in England, and the Dissolution of the Monasteries began in 1536, with around 800 monasteries suppressed. In the south of England there was little resistance, but in the north up to 40,000 men rallied to join the Pilgrimage of Grace, a peaceful protest which soon became an armed revolt, with finance, and even physical support, from the monks of Byland, Furness, Rievaulx and Whitby. With typical guile, Henry VIII persuaded the rebels to disband by promising that the monasteries would be saved, but then reneged and exacted a terrible revenge on all who had taken part. Monks were among the leaders whom he had executed, and every religious house was forcibly disbanded, its wealth seized and its lands sold.

Newburgh Priory in North Yorkshire lives on only because it was incorporated into the mansion built by Henry VIII's chaplain; the house boasts possession of the tomb of that other destroyer of churches, Oliver Cromwell. The most unusual of all, however, is Mount Grace Priory, founded in 1398, the best-preserved Carthusian charterhouse in England. Living in individual two-storey cells, each with its own garden, the Carthusians lived the life of hermits within the Priory precincts, reviving the Irish ideal which had inspired the very first monastic foundations in the area.

Fountains Abbey is the largest monastic ruin in Britain and is in a wonderful setting, surrounded by landscaped gardens. These were created in the 18th century and include water gardens, ornamental temples, follies and magnificent views

AROUND MORECAMBE BAY

A mild climate and seemingly endless sands have made Morecambe Bay popular with generations of holiday-makers, who enjoy the genteel pleasures of its seaside towns. In sharp contrast are the bleaker beauties of the surrounding hills, the Lake District, visible to the north across the bay, and the Pennines to the east, with their tumult of moors and stormy skies.

Carnforth

Once a busy steel-working town, Carnforth has unlikely romantic associations. Its station, at the junction of railway lines linking the scenic Settle to Carlisle, the West Cumbria and the main London to Glasgow routes, was the setting for the classic 1940s film, *Brief Encounter*, starring Celia Johnson and Trevor Howard. There are splendid views across Morecambe Bay from Warton Crag, a hill remarkable for its limestone pavements and cliffs, which is now a nature reserve; park in Warton Crag Quarry and walk along the trails, one of which is suitable for wheelchairs.

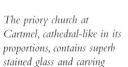

The ruins of the 14th-century Old Rectory at Warton suggest that it was like a small medieval manor house, built of stone, with the remains of the hall, buttery, kitchen and chambers still visible. The village of Warton has other historic links, including the ancestors of George Washington, in whose honour the Stars and Stripes are flown from the church tower on Independence Day.

In the 19th century Warton was a favoured holiday destination of Mrs Gaskell, the novelist, who wrote part of her *Life of Charlotte Brontë* at Lindeth Tower.

Grange-over-Sands

Taking its name from the grange or granary once built here by the Augustinian monks of Cartmel Priory, the town became a popular holiday resort in the 19th century. Sheltered by the Lakeland fells, its mild climate has made it a gardener's paradise: Grange is renowned for its ornamental gardens, and the Lakeland Rose Show is held each July at nearby Cark-in-Cartmel. Holker Hall is close by, a charming house which dates from the 16th century and contains a delightful mix of fine furniture and woodcarving, alongside family photographs and personal possessions. There are formal and woodland gardens, a 120-acre (49ha) deer park and the Lakeland Motor Museum.

The beautiful 12th-century monastic church of Cartmel Priory at Cartmel, 3 miles (4.8km) from Grange, is one of only a handful to have survived the Reformation and should not be missed. Among its treasures is a first edition of Spenser's *Faerie Queene*. At Lindale-in-Cartmel, 2 miles (3.2km) north of Grange, there is an unusual iron monument to John Wilkinson, the 18th-century forgemaster, who grew up in the area and cast the pieces for the world's first iron bridge at Ironbridge in Shropshire.

Lancaster

The county town of Lancashire, Lancaster goes back to Roman times, when a fort (*castrum*) was built to guard the crossing over the River Lune of the road from Chester to Hadrian's Wall. A medieval castle, which is owned by the Queen as 'Duke of Lancaster', still dominates the city today. Since the 18th century the castle has housed the county courts and prison; the notorious Pendle witches, convicted and

Leighton Moss Reserve

The Royal Society for the Protection of Birds has turned this man-made fen, which was drained in about 1920, into a birdwatcher's paradise. Open water, reed beds, marshes and woodland offer a variety of habitats to attract abundant birdlife, which can be observed from a network of footpaths and hides. Escorted wildlife events, such as otter and deer watches, allow visitors to see some of the other rare inhabitants of the reserve.

The 16th-century Holker Hall, in Cark-in-Cartmel, is set within lovely formal and woodland gardens.

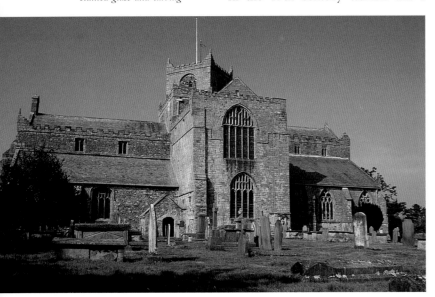

The priory church at Cartmel, cathedral-like in its proportions, contains superb stained glass and carving

Lancaster's Shire Hall, located within the castle walls, reflects the importance of the county town in the 18th century, when it was the chief port for trade with America

Forest of Bowland

The Forest of Bowland is one of the most dramatic natural features of the Lancashire landscape. A vast plateau of rolling hills and moors rising to over 1,800ft (550m) above sea level, it is dissected by deep valleys, such as the Trough of Bowland, once notorious as the haunt of smugglers from Yorkshire, and highwaymen. Drive from Quernmore, near Lancaster, to Dursop Bridge, 12 miles (19.3km) to the southeast, to get a taste of this lonely, rugged hill country. Better still, discover its waterfalls, sweeping views and wildlife on foot. For leaflets and information about guided walks contact Lancaster Tourist Information Centre.

hanged in 1612, were also held there while awaiting trial.

Exploring the network of streets below the castle offers more pleasant reminders of Lancaster's wealth in Georgian times. The Old Town Hall in the Market Square houses the excellent City Museum, which illustrates aspects of local life from the neolithic age all the way up to the present day. It is also home to the Museum of the King's Own Royal Regiment; the Judges' Lodgings on Castle Hill houses the Gillow Furniture Museum and a Museum of Childhood. A Maritime Museum, occupying the former Custom House on St George's Quay, tells the fascinating story of Lancaster's trading past and the fishing communities of Morecambe Bay. For panoramic views of the city and beyond, head for the Ashton Memorial in Williamson Park, a folly built in 1909.

Leighton Hall

Three miles (4.8km) north of Carnforth, set against a dramatic backdrop of Lakeland fells, is Leighton Hall, an Adam-style house with a splendid neo-Gothic façade. A fortified manor was first built on this site in 1246, but during the 1715 rebellion it was sacked and burnt by Government troops. Rebuilt in 1763 by George Townley, it then passed into the hands of the Gillow family, whose cabinet-making business, based in Lancaster, is well represented throughout the house. A replica of a Maryland mansion, built in the 1870s and containing 1,200 antique fittings, is just one of its many treasures.

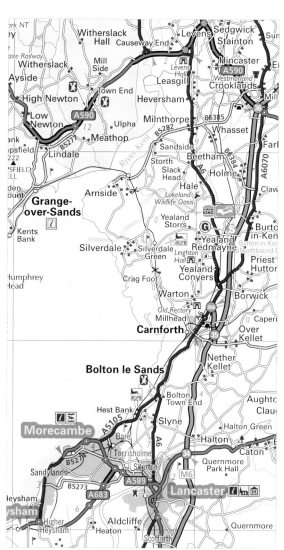

Morecambe

Morecambe is famous for its seaside promenade, which is 4 miles (6.4km) long and provides every holiday amusement you could imagine, from theatres, funfairs and amusement arcades to a modern leisure park and entertainment complex. The town's seafront renaissance has included award-winning public projects such as the Platform arts centre and the Stone Jetty, a breathtaking place to sit and watch the famous Morecambe Bay sunset. There is a new statue of the town's favourite son too – Eric Morecambe, who took his stage name from his boyhood home.

All this is a long way from Morecambe's humble origins as the little fishing village of Poulton-le-Sands, though the boats still fish locally for whitebait, cockles and shrimps. The sands are vast and flat and, though it is possible to walk across the bay to Grange, treacherous currents, quicksands and the speed of the incoming tide make this extremely dangerous without an official guide. The walk takes three hours and is subject to the weather.

Tourist Information Centres

Grange-over-Sands: Victoria Hall, Main Street (seasonal) (tel: 015395 34026
Lancaster: 29 Castle Hill (tel: 01524 32878)
Morecambe: Station Buildings, Central Promenade (tel: 01524 582808)

THE YORKSHIRE DALES

The landscape of the Yorkshire Dales National Park was formed by water and ice wearing deep into the limestone and creating gorges and waterfalls, wide valleys and gentle rivers, strange rock formations, potholes and hundreds of miles of caves and underground passages. Lush valley pastures give way to crags, grassland and moors on the hilltops.

Clapham

Clapham is idyllically situated at the foot of Ingleborough, one of the three highest peaks in the Dales. Stone cottages line the beck which flows through the village, having tumbled spectacularly down Gaping Gill pothole in a 340ft (104m) waterfall. Half an hour's walk away is Ingleborough Cave – not for the faint-hearted, but its limestone formations are worth seeing. Clapham has claims to fame. Michael Faraday, discoverer of electro-magnetism, was the son of the village blacksmith and Reginald Farrer, often regarded as one of the founding fathers of English gardening, lived at Ingleborough Hall, where his rock gardens incorporated rare and exotic plants from all over the world.

Tourist Information Centres

Hawes: Dales Countryside Museum, Station Yard (seasonal) (tel: 01969 667450)
Settle: Town Hall, Cheapside (tel: 01729 825192)

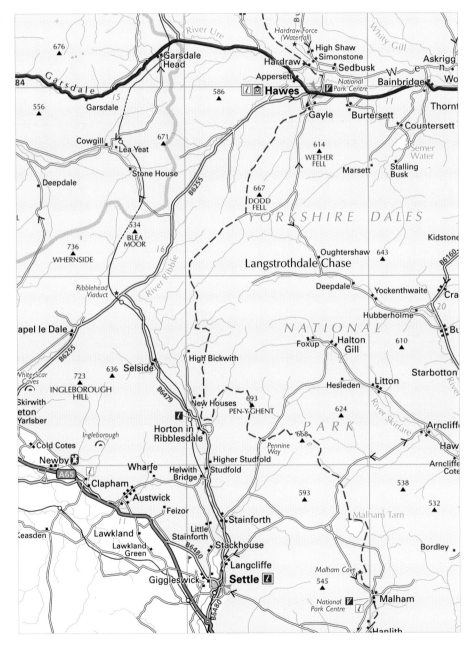

The Pennine Way and Three Peaks

Britain's first long distance footpath, the Pennine Way covers 256 miles (412km) from Derbyshire to the Scottish Border, taking in some of the wildest and most beautiful parts of the Dales. From Malham it climbs via the Cove and Tarn to the peak of Pen-y-Ghent, the 'hill of the winds', which is 2,274ft (693m) high. It then crosses Dodd Fell to Hawes, with another dramatic section on Great Shunner Fell, overlooking the unique and treacherous Buttertubs Pass, where a series of long fluted columns of limestone separate apparently bottomless holes. There are magnificent views over wild and lonely Swaledale as the walk descends to Muker before following the river up to Tan Hill, the highest inn in England. Equally strenuous is the Three Peaks challenge which takes in 5,000ft (1,524m) of climbing and 25 miles (40.2km) of walking over the three highest mountains in the Dales, Pen-y-Ghent, Whernside and Ingleborough. The hardiest of mortals can compete on foot or bicycle in the two annual Three Peaks races.

Gordale Scar

A deep funnel-shaped gorge, Gordale Scar was carved out of the limestone by melting glaciers. Following the river from Gordale Bridge, the crags close in, until, passing through a narrow entrance to the left, they open out again and the path is barred by a waterfall gushing from the rock face. The dramatic effect of the high cliffs, only 30ft (9m) apart at their base, is heightened by the tremendous overhang, beneath which you get the best view of the waterfall. Wordsworth's friend, the artist George Beaumont, rightly described it as 'beyond the range of art'.

Hardraw Force

One of England's highest waterfalls, tumbling 98ft (30m) in a single drop over a limestone crag, is a spectacular sight. It is situated behind the Green Dragon Inn at Hardraw, via a pleasant walk through a narrow wooded valley. So sheer is the drop from the overhanging rock that it is possible to walk behind the waterfall without getting wet. A challenge of a more bizarre kind was undertaken by Blondin, who crossed the gorge on a tightrope, stopping half-way to cook an omelette!

Kettlewell

This charming village, with its grey stone cottages and three inns crammed into its narrow streets, enjoys an incomparable position at the heart of Upper Wharfedale. It looks down over rich valley pastures, divided by mile upon mile of dry-stone walls. Behind the village soar the steep slopes of Buckden Pike and Great Whern-

side, over which a winding road climbs, with spectacular views, leading to the bleaker beauty of Coverdale. The pretty church contains its original Norman font, and the grave of local novelist, C J Cutcliffe Hyne, is in the churchyard.

Malham

Centred round a single stone arched bridge across Malham Beck, this is a lovely village with inns, cafés and shops. Park here to walk the mile (1.6km) upstream to Malham Cove, a spectacular natural amphitheatre of limestone crag, 330ft (100m) high and over 1,000ft (304.8m) wide, it was formed when the rocks fractured, slipped and dropped vertically. The pavement at the top is completely flat bare rock, riddled with fissures. Just north is Malham Tarn, one of only two natural lakes in the Dales; of particular scientific importance, it is now a bird sanctuary and nature reserve. The National Park Centre in the village has interesting displays on the area's history.

Settle

The start of the scenic Settle to Carlisle railway line, this small market town is an attractive tourist destination and a busy working town. It has many 17th-century buildings, including The Folly on Kirkgate, with its unusual corner windows. For a glimpse of the past visit the town's Museum of North Craven Life; for good contemporary art, visit the Linton Court Art Gallery.

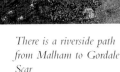

There is a riverside path from Malham to Gordale Scar

Hawes

One of the highest market towns in England, Hawes occupies a prime position in upper Wensleydale at the junction of three major valleys and is a natural tourist centre. The Dales Countryside Centre, in the Station Yard, has an extensive collection of bygones which offer an insight into the changing landscapes and the Dales communities.

Above Malham Cove is a great plateau where water erosion has revealed a rocky limestone landscape

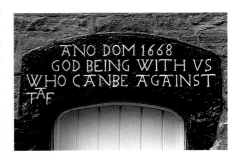

This uplifting message, over a door at Cocketts Hotel in Hawes, has greeted travellers for over three centuries

See Walk J page 288
Limestone Landscapes
Around Malham

See Walk N page 292
Up Gunnerside Gill
with Swaledale Miners

BETWEEN DALES AND MOORS

Between the Yorkshire Dales and the Great North Road (A1) are two of York-shire's most ancient settlements – Ripon and Richmond. Ripon is dominated by its beautiful cathedral, while Richmond's market place is overlooked by the keep of its castle. Around both of them are fascinating villages, delightful countryside and, at Fountains Abbey, one of the best-preserved monasteries in Europe.

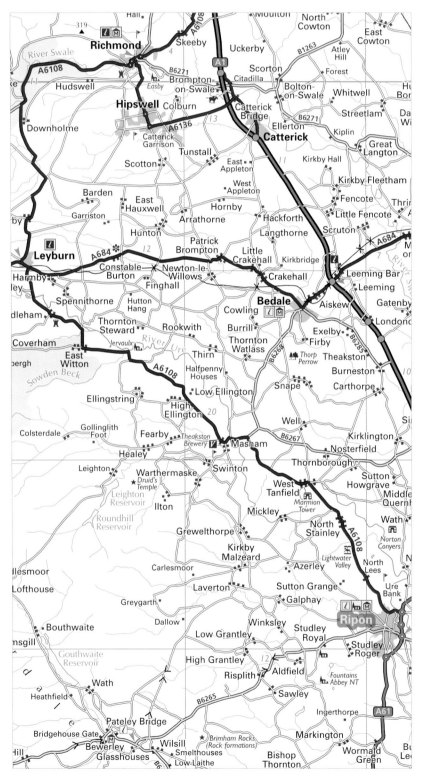

Brimham Rocks

This delightfully eccentric group of weathered rocks has long been a popular play-ground and picnic site. The formations were created over millions of years, as wind and rain transformed these out-crops of millstone grit into fantastic shapes – faces, figures and animals, which have inevitably been named. Look out for the Dancing Bear, the Sphinx and the Anvil. The Idol is a huge boulder perched incongruously on the tiniest of pedestals.

Fountains Abbey

One of the country's few World Heritage Sites, Foun-tains Abbey is arguably the best-preserved Cistercian abbey in Europe. Finding the Benedictine order too lax, a group of 12th-century monks broke away to found the Cis-tercian order. They completed the building of Fountains Abbey between 1150 and 1250. Ironically, for a commu-nity dedicated to poverty and obedience, the order went on to be very prosperous, owning farms throughout Yorkshire. The splendidly austere ruins of the abbey, on the banks of the River Skell, were incorpo-rated, in the early 18th century, into the Studley Royal estate. The abbey became the centre-piece of an elaborate water garden. With its lakes, temples, formal hedges, deer park and artfully contrived vistas, it epit-omised the Romantic ideal.

Pateley Bridge and Nidderdale

When the boundaries of the Yorkshire Dales National Park were drawn up in 1954, Nidderdale found itself on the outside. Yet the valley loses nothing in comparison with better-known dales – it is a delight all the way from bustling Pateley Bridge to the head of the dale, where a trio of reservoirs – Angram, Gouthwaite, and Scar House – were built to quench the thirst of industrial Bradford.

With its craft shops and riverside walks, Pateley Bridge is a popular destination with visitors. But it was the mining of lead – in one of the bleakest landscapes in Yorkshire – that brought prosperity to the town. Until the industry collapsed around the end of the 19th century, miners laboured in elaborate tunnels (known as 'levels') driven deep into the hillsides.

Tourist Information Centres

Richmond: Friary Gardens, Victoria Road (tel: 01748 850252)
Ripon: Minster Road (seasonal) (tel: 01765 604625)

Barnard Castle

The 'Gateway to Teesdale', Barnard Castle is a market town set in some splendidly rugged countryside. The castle, built by Bernard Baliol in the 12th century, sits on an exposed site overlooking the River Tees and County Bridge, once the site of illicit weddings. The Bowes Museum, a 'French château' in an English setting, houses an extensive collection of furniture and artworks from the second Napoleonic Empire period – collected by francophiles John and Josephine Bowes prior to the museum's opening in 1892.

Jervaulx Abbey

Cistercian monks came from France in the 12th century to found a monastic community here, in the valley of the River Ure (the name 'Jervaulx' is simply a literal translation into French of Yoredale). Though it is no match for Fountains Abbey in terms of size or setting, Jervaulx Abbey is well worth a visit. The ruins, surrounded by wooded parkland and ablaze with floral colour, exert a feeling of tranquillity that is almost tangible.

Masham

Masham (pronounce it 'Massam') is best known for a formidably strong ale from Theakstons called Old Peculier. The name refers to the Peculiar Court of Masham, first convened in the 12th century to combat outbreaks of lawlessness. Theakstons has a brewery museum, where the art of coopering (barrel-making) is demonstrated. The town has a huge market square where, every September, a two-day sheep fair is held.

Richmond

One of the few English towns to have kept its original medieval layout, Richmond is the 'capital' of beautiful Swaledale. The huge, sloping market place is overlooked by the castle, built by Earl Alan Rufus shortly after the Norman invasion; it was roofed with lead from the productive Swaledale mines. From the top of the tall keep you can see the little alleyways (known as 'wynds') leading off from the market place and some of the features that are worth a visit, including the delightful and diminutive Georgian Theatre and the Green Howards Regimental Museum.

Ripon

It was Alfred the Great who granted Ripon its charter more than 1,000 years ago, and markets are still held on Thursdays and Saturdays in the shadow of a tall obelisk. Ripon maintains much of its medieval layout, though most of the finer buildings are Georgian and Victorian. An unusual attraction is the early 19th-century prison, now the Prison and Police Museum.

A short walk from the market square, along Kirkgate, offers a surprise, as the splendid west front of the cathedral suddenly comes into view. With some parts dating from as early as AD 672, the cathedral features almost every architectural style, and contains what is believed to be the oldest Anglo-Saxon crypt in England.

Ripon is ringed by places which are well worth a visit, including Fountains Abbey to the south-west, and the splendid 17th-century Newby Hall and Gardens to the south-east. Norton Conyers, to the north, is a late medieval house with later additions, and is believed to have been the inspiration for Thornfield Hall in Charlotte Brontë's *Jane Eyre* (a family legend of a mad woman in the attic would seem to bear more than a coincidental similarity to the mad Mrs Rochester).

Also to the north is the Lightwater Valley Theme Park and Village, which includes the world's longest rollercoaster and similar thrills, along with gentler rides for the more faint-hearted. It is set in 175 acres (71ha) of country park and there is an adjacent factory shopping village.

Though it stands in ruins, Richmond Castle still has a splendid 100ft (30.5m) high keep and the well-preserved Scollards Hall, thought to be the oldest domestic building in Britain

See Walk K page 289
Ripon and its Lewis Carrol Connections

Over 370 years of occupation by one family is reflected in the pictures and furniture within Norton Conyers

IN AND AROUND YORK

To stroll around York is to feel history beneath your feet. With fascinating buildings and features from so many important periods of history, it is no surprise that the city is pencilled in on so many visitors' itineraries. To the north of York the landscape changes, from flat, arable farmland to the heather moorland and green valleys that typify the North York Moors National Park.

The Shambles in York

This short, narrow street of almost perfectly preserved medieval buildings was where the city's butchers once plied their trade and displayed their cuts of meat. The buildings huddle so close together that two attic-dwellers could shake hands across the street. The narrowness kept direct sunlight away from the meat – a wise precaution in the days before refrigeration. The butchers' shops are all gone, though many of the shop-fronts still incorporate the wooden ledges on which meat used to be displayed.

Boroughbridge

Stagecoach passengers would have heaved a sigh of relief as Boroughbridge hove into view, for this little town's main distinction was being the halfway point on the Great North Road between London and Edinburgh. Just outside the town are the Devil's Arrows, a trio of standing stones that may date from the Bronze Age.

At the nearby village of Aldborough there are the remains of *Isurium*, the most northerly of the Romans' settlements to have been built without military purpose.

Coxwold

This picturesque village of honey-coloured stone houses became the home of the Rev Laurence Sterne, best known as the author of the comic classic, *The Life and Opinions of Tristram Shandy, Gentleman.* Without false modesty he renamed his house Shandy Hall (open to the public).

Nearby Newburgh Priory was built in 1145 as an Augustinian priory; after the Dissolution of the Monasteries Henry VIII presented the building to his chaplain, who converted it into a splendid country residence. Later Oliver Cromwell's daughter lived here for a time; it is said that she secretly took his body down from the gallows and buried it in the grounds of Newburgh Priory. The house is open during early summer and Cromwellian relics are among the items on display.

Helmsley

Though it is the size of a village, Helmsley has the purposeful air of a county town – especially on Friday, market day. This is the starting point for the Cleveland Way, a long-distance walk that takes 'the long way round' the moors, ending up at Filey. Those with less energy can explore the 12th-century castle, its Norman keep still dominating the town.

Just outside Helmsley is Duncombe Park, standing in 300 acres (122ha) of parkland, which includes a spectacular early-18th century landscaped garden of 30 acres (12ha). The house, much altered since it was built in 1713, was in use as a school until the 1980s, since when it has been restored as a family home.

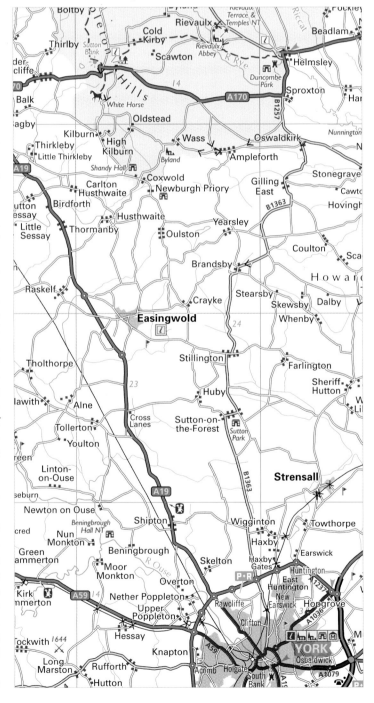

Tourist Information Centres

Helmsley: Town Hall, Market Place (seasonal) (tel: 01439 770173)
York: De Grey Rooms, Exhibitions Square (tel: 01904 621756)

A Fine Country House

The severely symmetrical brick façade of Beningbrough Hall looks out over spreading parkland and delightful walled gardens. This early Georgian country house, now looked after by the National Trust, reveals much about life here, both upstairs and down, during the 18th century. A hundred contemporary paintings, on loan from the National Portrait Galley, enhance the room settings.

Rievaulx

When Walter Espec dispatched a band of French monks to create a new community, they found the area 'fit only for wild beasts and robbers'. No matter; the monks' asceticism thrived on such challenges, and in the year 1131 they began to build what many people consider to be the finest Cistercian abbey in the country.

Rievaulx Abbey occupies a splendid wooded setting in the valley of the River Rye ('Rievaulx' is a French rendering of 'Rye Vale'). Enough remains of the Norman nave to show how the abbey would have looked all those centuries ago.

Overlooking the abbey is Rievaulx Terrace, a half-mile (0.8km) curved grassy terrace with two mock-Greek temples, which was created entirely for the views of the abbey, of Ryedale and of the Hambleton Hills beyond.

Sutton Bank

From the top of Sutton Bank you can enjoy one of the finest views in Yorkshire – on a clear day you can even see the Three Peaks of the Yorkshire Dales. This vantage point provides a sharp distinction between the flat Vale of Mowbray to the west and the Hambleton Hills to the north and east.

A delightful walk hugs the edge of Sutton Bank, passing a flying club where pencil-slim gliders are towed off the edge to exploit the thermals, and soon arriving at a much-loved landmark. The White Horse of Kilburn is a hill-figure cut into the slope by Thomas Hodgson in 1857 – his imagination having been fired by visiting the famous White Horse of Uffington in Oxfordshire.

York

The main problem for York is how to find time to see all that this remarkable city has to offer. Two historical periods – first Roman, then Viking – helped to create the York of today, leaving an astonishingly rich legacy of architectural gems, with the glory of the Minster at its heart. The Roman settlement – known as *Eboracum* – was vital to the empire right up to the time when the legions left Britain and went back to Italy.

The city is still skirted by its medieval wall, interrupted by the impressive battlements of the four gates, known as 'bars', on which the heads of traitors were once displayed. Clifford's Tower still sits on its prominent mound; here, 900 years ago, the Jews of York were slaughtered.

York boasts a remarkable collection of medieval churches, any one of which would be the architectural highlight of most other cities. But York's treasures form a long list: the Castle Museum, with artfully reconstructed streets and shops of the past, the Museum Gardens, King's Manor, the Treasurer's House, Merchant Adventurer's Hall and St William's College... all these and many, many more.

The National Railway Museum chronicles our rich railway heritage, and visitors queue around the block to climb aboard the 'time capsules' of the Jorvik Viking Centre which transport them back in time into a Viking settlement, where the sights, sounds – and even the smells – of village life have been recreated.

York Minster's stained glass windows – over 100 of them, including the magnificent Rose Window – are acknowledged as a collection of international importance

The powerful Merchant Adventurers Company built this splendid Guild Hall in the mid-14th century and it still contains furniture, pictures and paraphernalia of their business affairs

THE NORTH YORK MOORS

The most extensive area of moorland in England or Wales, the North York Moors covers 554 sq miles (892sq km) of glorious scenery. Rolling hills are ablaze with purple heather in late summer and there are pretty green valleys, with rock-strewn streams, and acres of forest. Apart from the busy seaside resorts, there are only a scattering of small market towns. Most settlements are villages, usually centred on a bridge over a river; the cottages are built of stone with distinctive red pantiled roofs. In the more remote dales and on the moortops, there are isolated farms and shooting lodges, reminders of the great estates which still own much of the land.

Bilsdale, near Hawnby, is flanked on one side by the ridge of Easterside Hill

EARLY DAYS

The earliest man-made features on the North York Moors date from the Bronze Age and are appropriately mysterious. The 40 bridestones at Nab Ridge in Bilsdale are the remains of a stone circle, 40ft (12.2m) in diameter, which may once have formed the retaining wall of a burial chamber. Above Grosmont, at High and Low Bridestones, there are remains of stone circles and some standing stones. The most dramatic group is on Bridestones Moor, on the western edge of Dalby Forest, where the huge rocks have been weathered into fantastic shapes by the elements.

The Romans also left their mark. South of Goathland, stretching across Wheeldale Moor, is one of the best-preserved examples of a Roman road in Britain, built to connect the Roman fortress of Malton with Whitby on the coast. Its culverts, kerbstones and foundations, 16ft (4.9m) wide, are visible for 16 miles (25.7km) over this remote moor. The road gave access to Roman forts, dating from AD 100, and their remains can be visited at Cawthorn Camps, to the north of Pickering. A Roman signal station, built on the cliffs at Scarborough in about AD 370, is the only one of five on the coast to have been excavated.

SAINTS AND POETS

Whitby holds a significant place in the history of early Christianity. The abbey, perched on the clifftop, was founded in AD 657 by St Hilda, and seven years later it hosted the Synod of Whitby, at which it was decided to adopt Roman, rather than Celtic practice in England. Caedmon, the first English Christian poet, appropriately had his home at the abbey. The dramatic ruins which command the coastline today are those of a much later, 13th-century foundation – on a dark night it is easy to see why Bram Stoker used it as the setting for his novel *Dracula*. St Mary's Church, reached by 199 steps from the harbour below, is a rare survivor from the 18th century, with its double-decker pulpit, galleries and box pews.

THE MIDDLE AGES

Originally a Celtic settlement founded in 270 BC, Pickering continued to thrive because it lay on the crossroads of the Malton to Whitby and Helmsley to Scarborough roads. The parish church is deservedly famous for its unusually complete set of medieval wall paintings, but it is the ruins of its motte and bailey castle which dominate this busy market town. Dating from the 12th century, the castle was reputedly used as a hunting lodge by every king from 1100 to 1400. Parts of the old Royal Forest of Pickering are still Crown Land, and there are forest drives, nature trails and picnic sites in nearby Dalby Forest.

The Normans built an even more impressive castle at Scarborough, with a curtain wall which envelopes the headland; its massive square keep, rising

Pickering Church contains some remarkably well-preserved medieval wall paintings

One of Britain's most picturesque villages, Robin Hood's Bay clings to the steep cliffs above the coast

80ft (24.4m) high, is a landmark for miles around, though the rest of the castle was almost completely destroyed during the Civil War.

SEAFARERS AND SMUGGLERS

The coastal towns of the North York Moors enjoyed their heydey in the 18th century. Whitby was then the base for a hugely successful whaling fleet, commemorated in Pannett Park Museum (there is a massive whalebone arch on the North cliff), and for colliers plying the North Sea. The Rev William Scoresby (1789–1857), son of a local whaling captain and explorer, unusually combined a career in the church with Arctic explorations, and became a leading authority on magnetism. Captain James Cook (1728–1779), the explorer and map-maker, also learnt his trade in Whitby. Though the town still has a fishing fleet and is famous for its shellfish, its importance as a port and harbour has declined.

Further down the coast, at Robin Hood's Bay, a more notorious trade was carried on. This quaint town, its cobbled streets and tiny cottages crammed into the small gap between the sea and steep cliffs, was a haven for smugglers. The only access is on foot down a long, narrow and precipitous road, though there are plenty of cafés and inns in which to break the journey.

VICTORIAN SEASIDE SPAS

It was in the 19th century that the greatest changes came to the seaside towns of Scarborough and Whitby. Scarborough had claimed healing properties for its waters, taken from the stream flowing across the South Sands, for almost 200 years. They were said to cure asthma, skin diseases and melancholy as well as to cleanse the blood and stomach. The town also lays claim to the invention of the bathing machine which enabled bathers to maintain their modesty. The craze for sea-bathing, another highly regarded cure for all manner of ills, swept the whole of the country. Anne Brontë (1820–1849), was one of many invalids who came to for the sea-cure. She died in here in 1849 and is buried in St Mary's churchyard.

Scarborough and Whitby were immensely fashionable in Victorian and Edwardian times, and many elegant buildings date from that time. Whitby's jet industry also thrived. The coal-black mineral was cut, polished and turned into mourning jewellery; it became an essential fashion item when adopted by the widowed Queen Victoria.

THE MOORS TODAY

The enduring popularity of the east coast owes much to the long sandy beaches, while the lure of the wild moorland and its communities never fades. Some of its spectacular views can be enjoyed from the steam trains of the North York Moors Railway, running 18 miles (28.9km) from Pickering to Grosmont; others can be seen

Examples of Whitby jet jewellery can be seen in the Whitby Museum

along the 93 miles (149.6km) of the Cleveland Way footpath, which skirts the northern and western edges of the moors and then follows the coast towards Scarborough.

One major attraction of the moors is the Ryedale Folk Museum in pretty Hutton-le-Hole, illustrating over 2,000 years of local history with an array of fascinating bygones. This is one of Britain's most remarkable open-air museums, with a reconstructed cruck house, Elizabethan manor and cottages from three different centuries. The museum also contains the oldest daylight photographic studio in England and a small glassmaking furnace of 1590 from Rosedale Abbey.

See Walk L page 290
In the Hole of Horcum

See Walk M page 291
High and Deep on Yorkshire's Coast

THE ISLE OF MAN

The Isle of Man is Britain in miniature, encompassing rocky cliffs, long sandy beaches, moorland and forest glens. The gulf stream warms the south and the Atlantic winds blow over the mountains of the north. Celtic and Viking civilisations have left a permanent legacy, including Tynwald (the Manx Parliament) the Manx Gaelic language and a lasting spirit of independence.

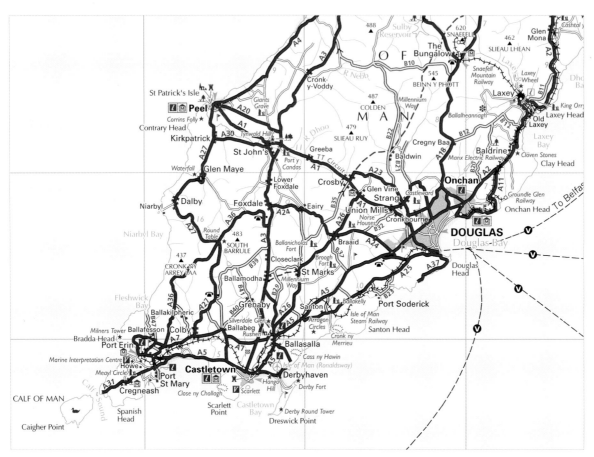

Tourist Information Centres

Ballasalla: Airport Information Desk, Ronaldsway Airport (tel: 01624 821600)
Castletown: The Old Grammar School, The Car Park (seasonal) (tel: 01624 825005)
Douglas: Sefton Tourist Information Centre, Harris Promenade (tel: 01624 686766)
Laxey: Laxey Heritage Trust, Old Fire House, near Laxey Wheel (seasonal) (tel: 01624 862007)
Onchan: Public Library, 10 Elm Tree Road (tel: 01624 621228)
Peel: Town Commissioners Office, Town Hall, Derby Road (tel: 01624 842341)
Port Erin: Commissioners Office, Station Road (tel: 01624 832298)
Port St Mary: Commissioners Office, Town Hall (tel: 01624 832101)
Ramsey: The Library, Town Hall (tel: 01624 817025)

Castletown

A gem of a town, still bustling with ordinary working life despite its venerable history, Castletown is built around a picturesque harbour at the mouth of the Silverburn. Narrow winding streets and stone cottages huddle close to the massive bulk of 600-year-old Castle Rushen, the centre of Manx government until 1874. It has also housed the island prison, lunatic asylum and barracks, as well as being the home of the Stanley family, Earls of Derby and Lords of Man. The Manx Nautical Museum includes the armed yacht *Peggy*, last in a line of locally built clippers.

Cregneish Village Folk Museum

A unique survivor of the traditional Manx way of life, this small crofting hamlet of single-storey thatched cottages, restored by the Manx Museum, overlooks the beautiful Calf Sound. The cottages contain typical furniture and everyday equipment, and demonstrations of traditional crafts take place in summer. The Meayl stone circle near by is one of several Bronze-Age sites on the island.

Douglas

The largest town on the island, spreading for 2 miles (3.2km) along the sandy curve of Douglas Bay's natural harbour, Douglas is the modern capital of Man and an internationally important finance centre. Thanks to its superb beach, mild climate and hundreds of Victorian and Edwardian hotels and guesthouses, tourism has flourished in Douglas since the mid-19th century. Ferries from Britain and Ireland

For a week in early June, the Isle of Man is taken over by the TT Races, a major event in the motorcycling year

The Calf of Man

A mile (1.6km) square and rising 400ft (121.9m) from the sea, the Calf of Man is the largest of three uninhabited islands off the southern tip of Man. Owned by the Manx Museum and National Trust since 1937, it is now a nature reserve for large colonies of puffins, kittiwakes, razorbills, guillemots and grey seals. Access for walkers, during the summer and in good weather only, is by boat from Port Erin or Port St Mary; remember to ensure that they return to pick you up! If the walk is too strenuous, boat trips round the Calf are a delightful alternative, bringing you close to the seabirds nesting on the cliffs and seal colonies on the shores; basking sharks can often be seen in the bay.

Pastures slope down to the coastline on the eastern coast of the island, with Gob ny Garvain in the distance

still dock in the harbour at the southern end of the town and horse-drawn trams carry passengers the length of the promenade in a service that began in 1876. The Manx Museum houses the treasures of the island's ancient history, while modern shops and restaurants, specialising in locally caught seafood, make this the busiest of all its towns.

Laxey

One of the island's most striking sights is the Lady Isabella, the world's largest working water wheel, built in 1854 to drain the Laxey lead mines. Dominating the narrow valley, it can be seen from many miles around, and there are fine views over the lower slopes of Snaefell and the sea from the top of the wheel. The village of Laxey consists of rows of miners' cottages, and a small section of the mine is open to the public in summer. Remnants of the old tramways which carried ore from the mines can still be seen, but Laxey station is also the starting point for the spectacular Snaefell Mountain Railway. Another traditional industry is in operation at the Laxey Woollen Mills on Glen Road, where Manx tweed is woven on handlooms.

Peel

Boasting the only cathedral on the Isle of Man, Peel is a small but busy fishing town on the west coast. A jumble of narrow

streets and cottages lead from the Market Square, with its unusual raised churchyard, down to the harbour where seals greet the fishing boats.

The dramatic ruins of Peel Castle command the coastline. Built on St Patrick's Isle and joined to the mainland by a short causeway, the castle seems part of the natural fortress of rock which gave sanctuary to monks fleeing Viking raids. A 10th-century tower, the medieval ruins of St Germain's Cathedral and burial sites within the castle precincts have provided exciting new archaeological evidence of Norse and pre-Norse Celtic settlements. *Odin's Raven*, a replica Viking ship which sailed from Norway to the Isle of Man to celebrate the island's millennium in 1979, can be seen on the quayside.

St John's

Though little more than a straggling village, St John's is physically and historically central to Manx history. Lying at the heart of the island, at the junction of all four major routes, it was the natural meeting place for Viking settlers who established their Tynwald, the independent Manx Parliament, there. Now, as then, the curious grassy mound, rising in tiers, is the centrepiece of the annual opening ceremonies, where the elected members of the House of Keys meet. Hidden in the trees behind Tynwald Green, former woollen mills are now a huge craft centre, specialising in locally produced goods.

A trip on the Snaefell Mountain Railway provides spectacular views

Manx Railways

One of the best ways of seeing the Isle of Man, if the Raad ny Foillan (Road of the Gulls) around the coastline is too arduous for your taste, is to use the railways. Sixteen steam engines, mostly built in Manchester, pull trains from Douglas to Port Erin during the summer months; this scenic route, notable for its absence of platforms, travels by the sea and passes through Castletown. A more dramatic route is taken by the Manx Electric Railway which clings precariously to the sheer cliffs of Maughold Head and Dhoon Bay as it wends its way from Douglas to Ramsey via Laxey. Best of all is the Snaefell Mountain Railway which opened in 1895 and runs from Laxey to the summit of Snaefell, 2,000ft (609.6m) above. From this vantage point you can see England, Scotland, Wales and Ireland.

THE LAKELAND OF THE POETS

*D*espite its popularity, most of this beautiful north-west corner of England retains its air of emptiness and remoteness. Narrow passes, soaring mountains, plunging waterfalls and lakes of every shape and size create a landscape which has inspired poets, writers and artists for 200 years. And in countless towns and villages you can discover the real life of Cumbria.

Just one of the many wonderful views from the Kirkstone Pass looks down over Ambleside, as the road descends towards the north end of Windermere

Dove Cottage, Grasmere. Wordsworth found the little house while on a walking tour of the Lakes with his friend, Coleridge.

Ambleside

Picturesquely situated at the head of Windermere, with mountains on three sides, this attractive Victorian town was celebrated by the Lakeland Poets. Wordsworth, Coleridge, De Quincey and Southey all lived in or near the town, making Ambleside a fashionable place to visit. A little way to the north is Rydal Mount, the home of William Wordsworth from 1813 until his death in 1850. In a wonderful setting, the house contains many of the poet's possessions and first editions of his work.

Grasmere

William Wordsworth lived at Grasmere with his sister, wife and young family from 1799 to 1808, writing some of his finest poetry in what he described as 'the loveliest spot that man hath ever found'. His home, Dove Cottage, is open to the public and an exhibition centre next door displays his manuscripts and memorabilia. In the village is the churchyard where the Wordsworths and Samuel Taylor Coleridge are buried; the studio of the Lakeland artist, W Heaton Cooper, is also worth a visit. And you can fortify yourself on the way home with some of Sarah Nelson's 'Original Celebrated Grasmere Gingerbread', baked to a traditional local recipe in the old village school.

Hawkshead

Hawkshead has a delightful network of narrow streets, with alleyways and arches, leading to the square. In Main Street is the Beatrix Potter Gallery, with a changing exhibition of illustrations from her children's books and a display about her work and life in the Lake District.

To the south-east at Near Sawrey is Hill Top, an unpretentious 17th-century farmhouse with a delightful cottage garden, where Beatrix Potter wrote and illustrated many of her books between 1905 and 1913. Hill Top has been preserved unaltered, and its particular delight is that so much is recognisable from the stories – the

Coniston and Grizedale Forest Park

The steam yacht *Gondola,* first launched in 1859 and later restored by the National Trust, runs a daily service during the summer from Coniston pier to Brantwood. It crosses the lake where Donald Campbell was killed in 1967, trying to break the speed record in his jet powered *Bluebird,* and the whole scene is dominated by the brooding mass of the mountain known as Coniston Old Man.

On the hills above Brantwood the Forestry Commission has created Grizedale Forest, the first of their enterprises which actively encouraged visitors by providing special facilities. A visitor centre illustrates the story of the forest and offers information on walks and wildlife. Grizedale has some of the best nature trails in the country (red squirrels, roe and red deer can all be seen), with forest walks, picnic areas, a tree nursery and a wildlife museum. At the heart of the woodland is the Theatre in the Forest, which hosts a variety of community events. Near by is the Gallery in the Forest, which has art, sculpture and craft exhibitions. There is also outdoor art in the form of a unique Sculpture Trail through the forest.

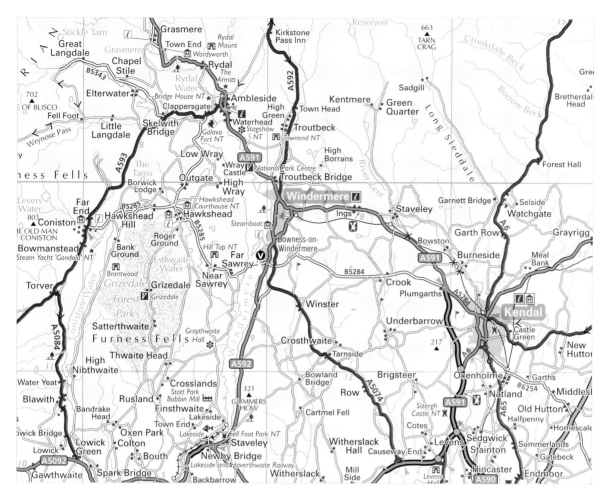

The Poets

The Lake District was an unregarded corner of England until the poets of the early-19th century Romantic movement began to celebrate its beauties. Most famous of this group of friends was William Wordsworth (1770–1850), who was appointed Poet Laureate in 1843. Settling first at Dove Cottage, Grasmere, he then moved to Rydal Mount, just outside Ambleside, where he spent the rest of his life. Samuel Taylor Coleridge (1772–1834) collaborated with him in Lyrical Ballads and spent four years at Keswick. Robert Southey (1774–1843), Wordsworth's predecessor as Poet Laureate and renowned as both a poet and biographer, lived at Greta Hall, Keswick.

See Walk P page 293
Claife Heights and the Victorian View of Windermere

See Walk R page 295
A Poet's View of the Buttermere Valley

See Walk Q page 294
The Contrasts of Upper Eskdale

Polished wood and gleaming brass at the Steamboat Museum, Bowness

Tourist Information Centres

Ambleside: Central Buildings, Market Cross (seasonal) (tel: 015394 32582)

Coniston: Main Car Park (seasonal), (tel: 015394 41533)

Grasmere: Red Bank Road (seasonal), (tel: 015394 35245)

Hawkshead: Main Car Park (seasonal), (tel: 015394 36525)

Kendal: Town Hall, Highgate, (tel: 01539 725758)

Windermere: Victoria Street, (tel: 015394 46499)

dolls that were the models for Lucinda and Jane, the grandfather clock in the tailor of Gloucester's kitchen, the garden explored by Tom Kitten and even the rhubarb patch favoured by Jemima Puddleduck.

Kendal

Once famous for its cloth and snuff, Kendal is now better known for its Mint Cake, the essential standby of hillwalkers and explorers. The steep streets of the town are dominated by the hill-top ruins of the castle where Catherine Parr, sixth and last wife of Henry VIII, was born. Narrow enclosed yards, where the weavers lived and worked, survive behind the shop fronts of Stricklandgate and Highgate. Down by the river are the grounds of Abbot Hall, now an Art Gallery with a museum of local life and industry. Kendal has remained unspoilt by tourism and is a busy working town with a weekly market.

Troutbeck

A typical Lakeland hillside village, spread out along a narrow lane, Troutbeck consists of a series of groups of farms and cottages. At the southern end is Townend, a modest farmhouse built by a yeoman farmer on

his marriage in 1625. Home to the same family for over 300 years, it remained virtually untouched by the passing years. Visiting times are limited to daylight hours as there is no electricity.

Windermere

Windermere is the largest natural freshwater lake in England, over 10 miles (16.1km) long, a mile (1.6km) wide and 200ft (61m) deep. Boating and water sport facilities here are excellent. A good place to start your visit is at the Lake District National Park Visitor Centre at Brockhole, which stands in 32 acres (13ha) of landscaped gardens on the eastern shore of the lake. As well as information about the park, there are various exhibitions, lake cruises an adventure playground and special events.

The town of Windermere grew up around the railway station, and gradually spread along the lakeside into Bowness. Dedicated to visitors, the town has a huge range of accommodation. Sight-seeing launches depart from piers at Bowness and Waterhead every half hour, and trips are also available on a Victorian steam launch from the Windermere Steamboat Museum at Bowness. Here, a historic collection of Victorian and Edwardian craft are on show, including the world's oldest steamboat.

CARLISLE AND THE WESTERN WALL

O n the border between England and Scotland, where warfare was endemic until the mid-18th century, this beautiful landscape and its sparse settlements bear the marks of continual violence. Most striking of all is Hadrian's Wall, 73 miles (117.5km) long and almost 2,000 years old, marking the northern boundary of the Roman Empire.

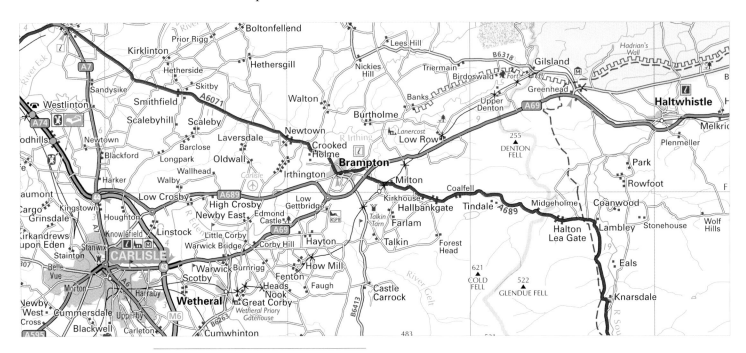

Carlisle

Known as *Luguvalium* in Roman times, Carlisle is the only historic English town or city not mentioned in the Domesday Book, because it was in Scotland at the time, on the other side of a border which has moved a number of times during the course of history. Its castle and city walls were begun by William Rufus, who recaptured it from the Scots in 1092, but for the next 700 years it was a garrison town and scene of many battles between the English and the Scots. The castle hosted parliaments under Edward I, the 'Hammer of the Scots', and medieval prisoners of war, who scratched their marks on the cell walls, were incarcerated there. In later years, another temporary lodger was Mary, Queen of Scots; Queen Mary's Tower now houses the King's Own Royal Border Regiment Museum.

After the 1745 rebellion, peace and prosperity, based on the textile trade, descended on the town. Many elegant streets and the attractive Town Hall in the Market Square date from this time. Medieval Carlisle is portrayed in the

Carlisle Castle's forbidding walls reflect a long and grim history of constant unrest

Guildhall Museum in Green Market, while the Tullie House Museum in Castle Street houses an imaginative interpretation of Border history, with a stroll through Roman Carlisle, a climb on part of Hadrian's turf wall and other displays.

Gilsland

Hadrian's Wall passes through this small village, the most westerly in Northumberland, and a section of it is in the vicarage garden. One of the best preserved milecastles on the wall, with remains of north and south gates, walls and two small barrack blocks, can be found near the railway bridge. The River Irthing flows just north of the village through a delightful wooded gorge with romantic associations – Sir Walter Scott proposed to Charlotte Carpenter at the Popping Stone.

Greenhead

There has been a river crossing at Greenhead since at least Roman times. The A69

Tourist Information Centres

Brampton: Moot Hall, Market Place (seasonal), (tel: 016977 3433)
Carlisle: Carlisle Visitor Centre, Old Town Hall, Green Market, (tel: 01228 625200)
Haltwhistle: Church Hall, Main Street, (tel: 01434 322002)

Hadrian's Wall

When the Emperor Hadrian visited Britain in AD 122 he decided to solve the problem of the troublesome northern tribes by building a wall from coast to coast. Taking advantage of a prominent natural ridge, a massive fortification some 73 miles (117.5km) long was built from a million cubic yards of stone, strengthened at key points by forts, milecastles and turrets. The project took about five years to complete, but succeeded in holding back the Picts for over 200 years. Now a World Heritage Site, the Romans' tremendous achievement can still be appreciated; substantial portions of both the stone section, running from Newcastle to Gilsland, and the turf rampart from Gilsland to Bowness, can be seen and excavations, most notably at Housesteads, have revealed the forts and living quarters of the garrisons. Other Roman sites worth visiting are Birdoswald, near Gilsland, Chesters Fort and Museum at Walwick, Corbridge, Carrawburgh and Vindolanda (Chesterholm) at Bardon Mill.

is the latest of a series of important routes crossing the Tipalt Burn, following both the Maiden Way and the Stanegate Roman road, which served Hadrian's Wall. The village lies in a small hollow beside the burn, and to the north are the picturesque ruins of medieval Thirlwell Castle, where Edward I is reputed to have stayed on one of his many campaigns against the Scots. Half a mile (0.8km) further east, next to one of the highest standing sections of Hadrian's Wall, is the unexcavated Roman fort of *Carvoran*, where a Roman Army Museum, with excellent access for disabled visitors, depicts the life and times of the Roman soldier.

Haltwhistle

A small market town serving the South Tyne valley, Haltwhistle suffered badly during the border raids of the Middle Ages. Suggestions of its violent past are to be seen everywhere. The Red Lion Inn incorporates a medieval pele tower, as does the nearby Jacobean mansion, Featherstone Castle. The Holy Cross Church is one of the most important in Northumberland. Originally built in Saxon times, on a site associated with St Aidan and St Paulinus, the present church was sensitively restored in Victorian times, but dates principally from the 13th century.

Lanercost Priory

There has been continuous worship at Lanercost Priory since the 12th century, despite Henry VIII's Dissolution of the Monasteries. Though some of the monks were executed, the nave of the old priory of Augustinian canons is now the local parish church, and many of the other orig-inal buildings are remarkably well preserved. Red sandstone blocks taken from Hadrian's Wall by the monks can still be seen in the priory remains, together with a fine collection of Roman altar stones in the undercroft.

Talkin Tarn

A 65-acre (26ha) lake, ideal for boating, fishing and swimming, lies just north of Talkin at the heart of Talkin Tarn Country Park. There are sandy bays around the tarn and a signposted nature trail leads through attractive woodland. From the top of the wooded rise behind the Victorian boathouse are some lovely views over the surrounding countryside.

Wetheral

At the centre of Wetheral is a large triangular green, edged with gracious houses built from the distinctive local red sandstone. Two buildings stand out from the rest – Eden Bank, a grandiose mock château of the 19th century, which has millstones set in its garden wall, and the elegant Crown Hotel, with a columned porch. An early five-arched railway bridge spans the wide River Eden, and from the footpaths in Wetheral woods, to the south of the village, there are charming views of the picturesque ruins of Corby Castle on the opposite bank. Near by, a 15th-century gatehouse is all that survives of the local Benedictine priory. Also overlooking the river is Holy Trinity Church, with an unusual octagonal tower and some splendid effigies.

Sections of Hadrian's wall can still be seen, including this stretch across Cawfields Crag in Northumberland

See Walk U page 298
The Edge of an Empire on Hadrian's Wall

The ancient priory gatehouse in Wetheral looks out across the River Eden towards Corby Castle

THE CITY ABOVE THE WEAR

Once at the heart of the ancient kingdom of Northumbria, Durham's importance is reflected in the fact that its cathedral and castle have been declared a World Heritage Site. Ruined abbeys and ancient churches testify to the region's role in spreading Christianity, while Roman remains and medieval castles tell the story of its often violent past.

Binchester Blocks

Fine views of Auckland Castle are seen from Binchester Blocks, less than a mile (1.6km) to the north. Excavations here have uncovered a Roman fort, *Vinovia*, built on Dere Street, the main route from York to Hadrian's Wall, in AD 80 to guard one or possibly two bridges over the River Wear. A number of buildings have been identified, the most important being a bath suite attached to the commanding officer's house, the finest of its kind in Britain.

Auckland Castle

Auckland Castle has been the country seat of the Bishops of Durham since the 12th century

An 18th-century gatehouse leads from the market square of Bishop Auckland into the 800 acres (324ha) of woodland and lawn of Bishop's Park. A Gothic-style cloister in the park is an unusual deer shelter of the same period. Home of the bishops of Durham since 1183, the present 13th-century castle (also known as the palace) is separated from the park by a screen of stone arches. Its Great Hall, state apartments and exceptional chapel, converted from a banqueting hall in 1660, are periodically open to the public. The park is open all year round.

Brancepeth

Dominated by its castle, the origins of which go back to Saxon times, Brancepeth is a delight to explore, particularly on foot. Rows of pretty Georgian cottages line the village streets, but the 12th-century church of St Brandon stands apart, in its own wooded grounds within the castle curtilage. Although badly damaged by fire in 1998, the building is being meticulously restored and still contains the tombs of the Neville family who once owned the castle. The castle itself, which is now in private hands, was virtually rebuilt in 1837 by Matthew Patterton, son of a wealthy mine owner who had purchased the property. Its distinctive 'chessmen' watchtowers are the work of his architect, John Patterson of Edinburgh.

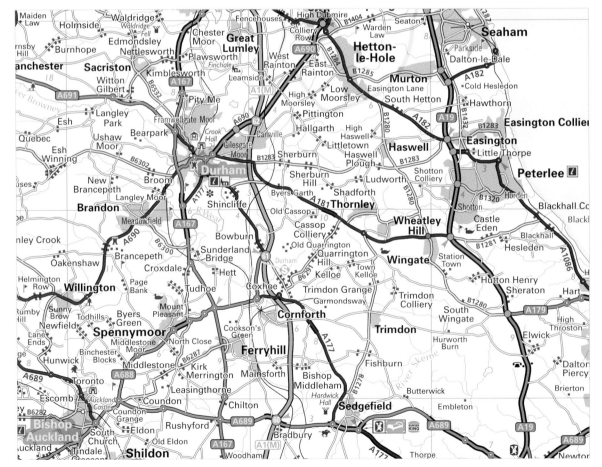

Tourist Information Centres

Durham: Market Place (tel: 0191 384 3720)
Newcastle upon Tyne: Information Centre, 132 Grainger Street (tel: 0191 277 8000)
Newcastle Airport, Woolsington (tel: 0191 214 4422)
Peterlee: 20 The Upper Chare (tel: 0191 586 4450)

Instant nostalgia for expatriot Geordies all over the world is evoked by this famous view of the Tyne, showing the High Level, Swing and Elizabeth II bridges

Durham

Built within a loop of the River Wear, on a high sandstone outcrop, Durham has one of the most dramatic skylines of any city. The cathedral and nearby castle, towering high on a bluff above the river, are an unforgettable composition of Norman splendour. The site was chosen by monks in AD 995 as a sanctuary from Viking raids for the bones of St Cuthbert, one of the founders of English Christianity. Its present cathedral, rebuilt in stone in 1093, was the seat of the wealthy Prince Bishops who enjoyed a unique position of secular and ecclesiastical power. Close by is the Norman castle which, together with most of the buildings round Palace Green and in the North and South Bailey, is now part of the famous University, England's third oldest, after Oxford and Cambridge. It contains a fascinating Oriental Museum. Predominantly a Georgian and Victorian city, Durham has many good shops, hotels and museums, and there are pleasant riverside walks and picnic places.

Finchale Priory

A reformed pirate, St Godric, founded a wooden hermitage at Finchale on the banks of the River Wear in 1110. After his death, tales of his sanctity and reports of miracles at his tomb, which is marked by a cross on the floor, brought monks from Durham Priory to found a monastery on the site in 1180. The present ruins date from the rebuilding of 1237, which proved to be too grandiose for its community to support. By the 14th century the Priory had become a holiday retreat for monks from Durham, who abandoned the refectory and greatly reduced the size of the church, keeping up only the prior's lodgings and domestic residence. Henry VIII's

Dissolution of the Monasteries in 1536 ended all monastic life here.

Peterlee

Named after Peter Lee (1864–1935), who began work underground at the age of ten and rose to be President of the International Federation of Miners, this town was built in 1950 to serve as a dormitory for the local coalfields and a centre for the surrounding villages. It claims to be the most attractive of the north-east's new towns. Lying amidst gently rolling countryside 2 miles (3.2km) from the sea, the characteristics of the site were fully exploited by the planners, who created attractively grouped housing which is well segregated from the industrial areas. Peterlee quickly established its own character and, despite the decline in mining, has succeeded in attracting new industry.

Seaham

A late Saxon church, with Roman stones in its walls and a 12th-century font, stands on the top of the limestone cliffs of Seaham. Below it is the privately operated harbour built by Lord Londonderry in 1828 for the shipment of coal from his mines in the locality. Seaham, like so much of the north-east, has suffered from the decline of the Durham coalfields and no pits now work here. The sea front is being cleaned up and new 'natural' landscapes created. To the north of the town is Seaham Hall, a white mansion, now a hospital, where Lord Byron stayed after his marriage to the heiress, Anne Millbanke, in 1815. As he separated from her the following year and left England for ever, this may account for his jaundiced comment that the coast here was dreary.

The Market Place at the heart of Durham is surrounded by ancient buildings

Newcastle upon Tyne

The commercial and industrial capital of the north-east is a grandiose city which, at the dawn of the 21st century had re-invented itself to keep pace with the region's economic changes. Ten bridges cross the River Tyne here, linking the city with the borough of Gateshead, the newest being the Millennium Bridge, which opened in 2001. George Stephenson's high-level, two-tier bridge is one of the most remarkable feats of Victorian engineering. Built in 1849 it carries both the railway and a road. Stephenson, the great railway pioneer, was born 8 miles (12.9km) west of the city at Wylam, the son of a colliery fireman. He taught himself to read and write, and went on to build the world's first public railway line and the *Rocket* locomotive. His home now belongs to the National Trust.

AS BIRDS FLYING
SO SHALL THE LORD OF HOSTS PROTECT JERUSALEM

Durham Cathedral has some wonderful stained glass windows

ALNWICK

*D*escribed as the last great wilderness in England, Northumberland encompasses the remote and empty Cheviot hills, mile upon mile of sandy beaches and rugged islands which were once the bastions of early Christianity. Hadrian's Wall, pele towers and castles bear abundant and stern witness to the centuries of violence this border country has endured. While they were once an essential means of survival, now they simply add further romance to a landscape of contrasts.

Holy Island and Chillingham Castle

Just outside the area are two very different places which are both well worth a visit. Holy Island (Lindisfarne), perhaps the most famous of all religious retreats, lies to the north of the Farne Islands. It has a ruined 11th-century priory, built on the site of St Aidan's 7th-century monastery, which was destroyed by Vikings, and a Tudor castle, restored by Sir Edward Lutyens with gardens designed by Gertrude Jekyll. Accessible only at low tides via a narrow causeway from Beal, no crossing should be attempted in the two hours before and three hours after high tide.

The ancestral home of the Earl of Tankarville, medieval Chillingham Castle is privately owned but is open to the public in summer. Here you might catch a glimpse of the unique herd of wild cattle which have roamed the estate for 700 years. With their distinctive white colouring and large horns they are believed to be similar to the oxen used by the ancient Britons. The prehistoric remains of Ross Castle, an earthwork with a double rampart, can be seen to the east of the village where the ground rises 1,000ft (304.8m), giving wonderful views all around.

Where the River Aln meets the North Sea, Alnmouth is an attractive little resort which is particularly popular with boating enthusiasts

Bamburgh Castle looks down over a superb stretch of sandy beach

Alnmouth

The quiet, pretty seaside town of Alnmouth sits where the River Aln meets the North Sea. Once a busy centre of shipbuilding and a grain port, the great storm of 1806 changed the course of the river, destroyed the Norman church and closed the harbour. Now all that remains of that industrial past are the 18th-century granaries, converted into houses which jostle for room with the shops and ancient inns in the narrow streets. The sands stretch as far as the eye can see, part of the 56 mile (90km) Northumbrian Heritage Coast.

Alnwick

Still home to the Percy family, whose ancestors ruled much of northern England for 200 years as Earls of Northumberland, Alnwick is dominated by its superb castle. A massive keep and curtain wall reflect its importance as a medieval military stronghold but the interiors, restored in the 18th and 19th centuries by Robert Adam and Anthony Salvin, are Italian Renaissance on a monumental scale. The only surviving gateway to the original walls of the town is the Hotspur Tower, built in 1450 by the son of Harry Hotspur, who was immortalised by Shakespeare in *Henry IV*. His rebellion cost the family dear, as did their

participation in Catholic uprisings from the Pilgrimage of Grace to the Gunpowder Plot, but no king could afford to ignore the powerful Percys, who were always restored to favour.

Bamburgh

One of Britain's most impressive castles, built on a huge outcrop of rock rising dramatically above the flat sandy beach, Bamburgh has a venerable history going back to at least AD 547, when it was a stronghold of Northumbrian royalty. St Aidan, a monk from Iona, first established a wooden church in Bamburgh in AD 635; its successor dates mainly from the 13th century. Grace Darling, daughter of the lighthouse keeper and heroine of the rescue of the shipwrecked *Forfarshire*, is buried in the churchyard. The cottage in which she was born is opposite the church and a Grace Darling Museum commemorates her valour.

Craster

This unspoilt fishing village centres round a tiny harbour built by the Craster family in memory of a soldier brother who was killed in 1906 fighting in the Tibetan campaign. The small local fleet fishes mainly

Lindisfarne Priory was founded in the 7th century and from it Christianity spread across much of Northern England

Berwick Upon Tweed

Fought over by English and Scots, the border town of Berwick-upon-Tweed changed hands 14 times between 1147 and 1482. The town is a product of its violent past, with fortified walls dating back to the 14th century and a ruined castle – ironically demolished not by military action but by the Victorians, who wanted to build a railway station. Fine views of the harbour and town, with its cobbled streets and jumble of houses, can be seen from the walls. The museum of the King's Own Scottish Borderers is housed in the 18th-century Berwick Barracks at Ravensdowne, the oldest purpose-built barracks in the country. The town museum and art gallery is also housed here.

for crabs, lobster and salmon. The kippers for which the town is famous are smoked in a building on the harbour, but the herrings are now purchased from Scotland. The Craster family, after whom the village is named, still live in Craster Towers, their home for the last 700 years. A dramatic but not too strenuous walk from the village leads to the ruins of Dunstanburgh Castle. Built in 1316 on a rocky promontory, which rises sheer from the sea, it has superb coastal views.

Farne Islands

Seventeen different species of seabird and a large colony of grey seals have made these treeless islands a remarkable wildlife sanctuary. Depending on the height of the tide, there are between 15 and 28 islands, of which only Inner Farne and Staple are open to visitors. Each island has rocky cliffs in the south and west and slopes gently to the sea in the north and east. Inner Farne was a favoured retreat for hermits; most famously, St Cuthbert lived there for six years and, after he became Bishop of Lindisfarne, returned to the islands to die in AD 687. A chapel to his memory is one of the few remaining buildings.

Warkworth

A horseshoe-shaped loop in the River Coquet almost encircles this pretty village, and its main street leads straight up the hill to the striking ruins of Warkworth Castle, birthplace of Harry Hotspur. The castle was owned by the Percy family for over 600 years and has a huge, cruciform keep, 12th-century Great Hall and vaulted gatehouse. The medieval stone cobbled bridge, which carried traffic over the Coquet until

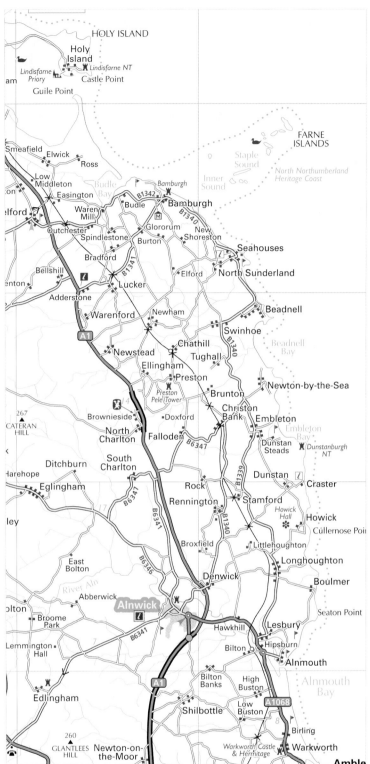

1965, provided an outer defence to the village and castle and is a rare example of a fortified bridge.

Beside the river, and only accessible by boat, are a small 14th-century hermitage and chapel, hewn out of the rockface by Sir Bertram of Bothal as a penance for accidentally killing the woman he loved. A Norman church replaced the 8th-century Saxon one, built by King Ceolwulf of Northumbria, which was destroyed by the Danes; it has the longest nave in the county and was the site of a massacre by the Scots of 300 villagers in 1174.

Tourist Information Centres
Alnwick: The Shambles (tel: 01665 510665)
Berwick-upon-Tweed: 106 Marygate (tel: 01289 330733)
Craster: Craster Car Park (seasonal) (tel: 01665 576007)

See Walk V page 299
Berwick's Bulwark Against the Scots

THE GOYT VALLEY

1 Follow the nature trail signs leading up into the forest. Soon after entering the trees join a broad path and turn right, following and eventually crossing a stream. At a sharp bend and path junction, turn right to arrive at the partly reconstructed ruins of Errwood Hall.

2 Left of the Hall ruins, up way-marked steps, continue on the woodland walk as it leads off into the trees, past some gateposts and the remains of estate workers' cottages on the edge of open country.

3 Turn right by the cottages, down to some steps which lead to a footbridge and a cross-roads of paths, where you turn left, going up through the sparse trees to contour below wooded Foxlow Edge. Beyond the trees a short detour takes you to a circular shrine, erected in 1889 by the Grimshawes in memory of their childrens' governess.

4 Climb up the steps from the shrine, back on the main path which leads up to the road ahead, which is known as The Street. This was a pack-horse route from Buxton to the west. Turn uphill on the road to its summit, known as Pym's Chair, after John Pym, the 17th-century Puritan leader.

6 From the summit, which is reached by crossing a ladder stile, drop down to a stile from which a broad green track heads left above Shooter's Clough (to the left), contouring gently down. Follow a well-marked path, reaching another path. Cross this through gateposts and continue down to the Errwood car park.

5 Cross the stile on the left of the road at Pym's Chair and walk along the 2 miles (3.2km) of partly restored path, alongside a wall to the south, to Shining Tor. At 1,834ft (559m), this is the highest point on the walk.

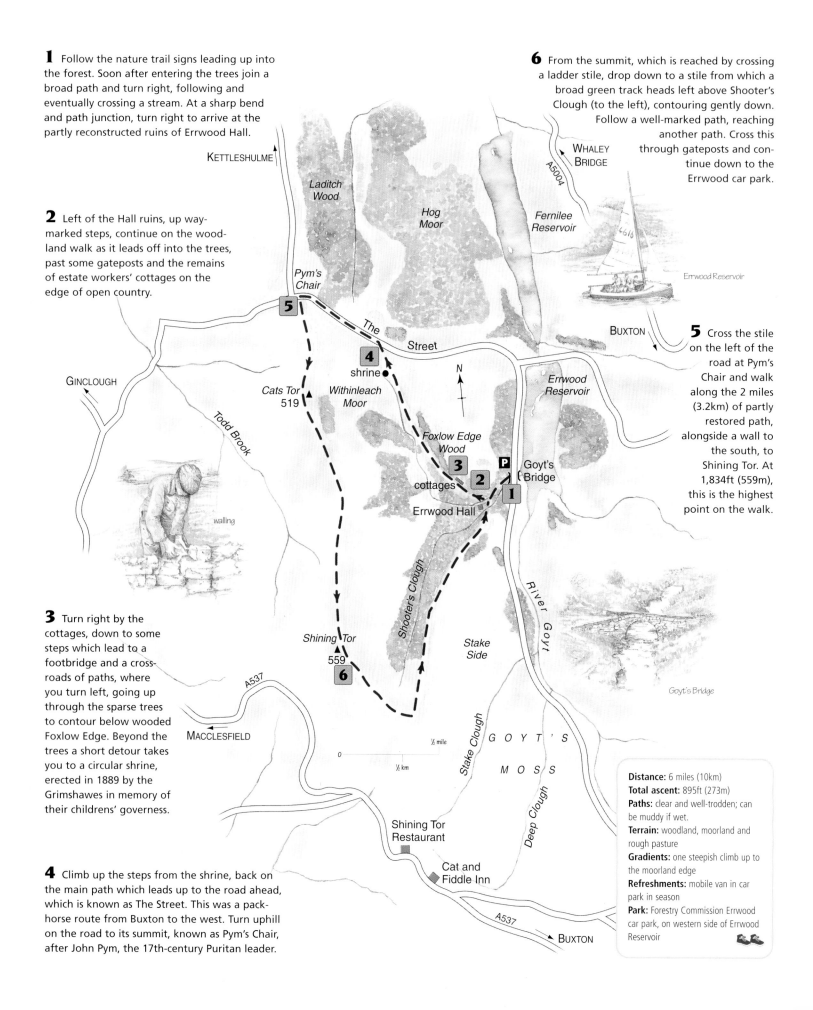

Distance: 6 miles (10km)
Total ascent: 895ft (273m)
Paths: clear and well-trodden; can be muddy if wet.
Terrain: woodland, moorland and rough pasture
Gradients: one steepish climb up to the moorland edge
Refreshments: mobile van in car park in season
Park: Forestry Commission Errwood car park, on western side of Errwood Reservoir

THE WONDERS OF THE PEAK AT CASTLETON

Distance: 5 miles (8km)
Total ascent: 1,035ft (315m)
Paths: can be muddy if wet; ridge mostly paved
Terrain: rocky start then easy going on ridge and through fields
Gradients: one steep, 1,000ft (305m) ascent to the Mam Tor ridge
Refreshments: restaurants, pubs and cafés in Castleton, picnic tables at Mam Nick
Park: main car park, Castleton

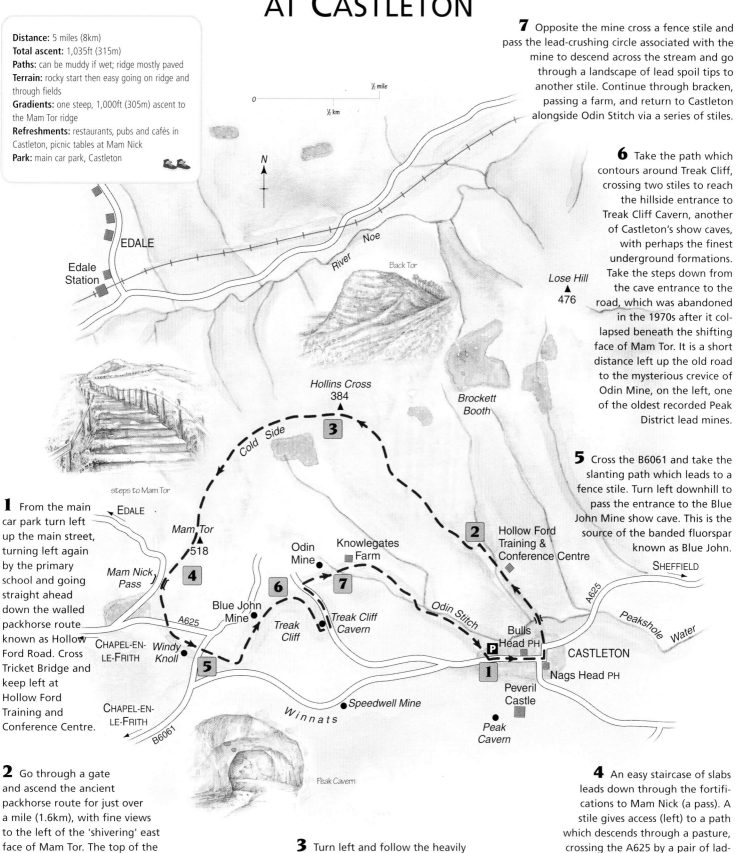

7 Opposite the mine cross a fence stile and pass the lead-crushing circle associated with the mine to descend across the stream and go through a landscape of lead spoil tips to another stile. Continue through bracken, passing a farm, and return to Castleton alongside Odin Stitch via a series of stiles.

6 Take the path which contours around Treak Cliff, crossing two stiles to reach the hillside entrance to Treak Cliff Cavern, another of Castleton's show caves, with perhaps the finest underground formations. Take the steps down from the cave entrance to the road, which was abandoned in the 1970s after it collapsed beneath the shifting face of Mam Tor. It is a short distance left up the old road to the mysterious crevice of Odin Mine, on the left, one of the oldest recorded Peak District lead mines.

5 Cross the B6061 and take the slanting path which leads to a fence stile. Turn left downhill to pass the entrance to the Blue John Mine show cave. This is the source of the banded fluorspar known as Blue John.

1 From the main car park turn left up the main street, turning left again by the primary school and going straight ahead down the walled packhorse route known as Hollow Ford Road. Cross Tricket Bridge and keep left at Hollow Ford Training and Conference Centre.

2 Go through a gate and ascend the ancient packhorse route for just over a mile (1.6km), with fine views to the left of the 'shivering' east face of Mam Tor. The top of the ridge at Hollins Cross (1,260ft/384m), is marked by a viewfinder, and has wonderful views north across the vale of Edale to the plateau of Kinder Scout, the highest point of the Peak District.

3 Turn left and follow the heavily eroded ridge path along Cold Side until you reach a newly paved section, which leads up through the embankments of the hill fort which crowns Mam Tor.

4 An easy staircase of slabs leads down through the fortifications to Mam Nick (a pass). A stile gives access (left) to a path which descends through a pasture, crossing the A625 by a pair of ladder stiles. The second stile (opposite) leads down to the Windy Knoll cave, where Victorian excavators found the bones of many prehistoric animals, including rhinoceros.

A WALK IN THE DARK PEAK

Distance: 6½ miles (10.5km)
Total ascent: 1,100ft (335m)
Paths: mainly unsurfaced, some very rough; some short road sections
Terrain: fields, peat moorlands
Gradients: very steep in parts (do the walk in reverse for a more gradual ascent)
Refreshments: Ramblers Inn, Old Nag's Head, Edale
Park: Edale car park, signed off A625

7 At Ollerbrook Farm go through the narrow stile and continue along the path ahead. Cross the railway bridge and at the road turn right to return to the car park.

1 From Edale car park, go down the steps by the toilets and turn right. Walk past the railway centre and visitor centre.

6 Follow the path as it swings to the left, away from the village, then switches to the right again, down the slope of The Nab. Climb the narrow stile and follow the track alongside the Oller Brook.

2 Just before the Old Nag's Head, turn left to follow the Upper Booth and Pennine Way sign (through the Walkers Only gate). Follow the Public Footpath direction straight ahead, ignoring the Pennine Way markers going left. Cross the steep field to the gate at the top right corner.

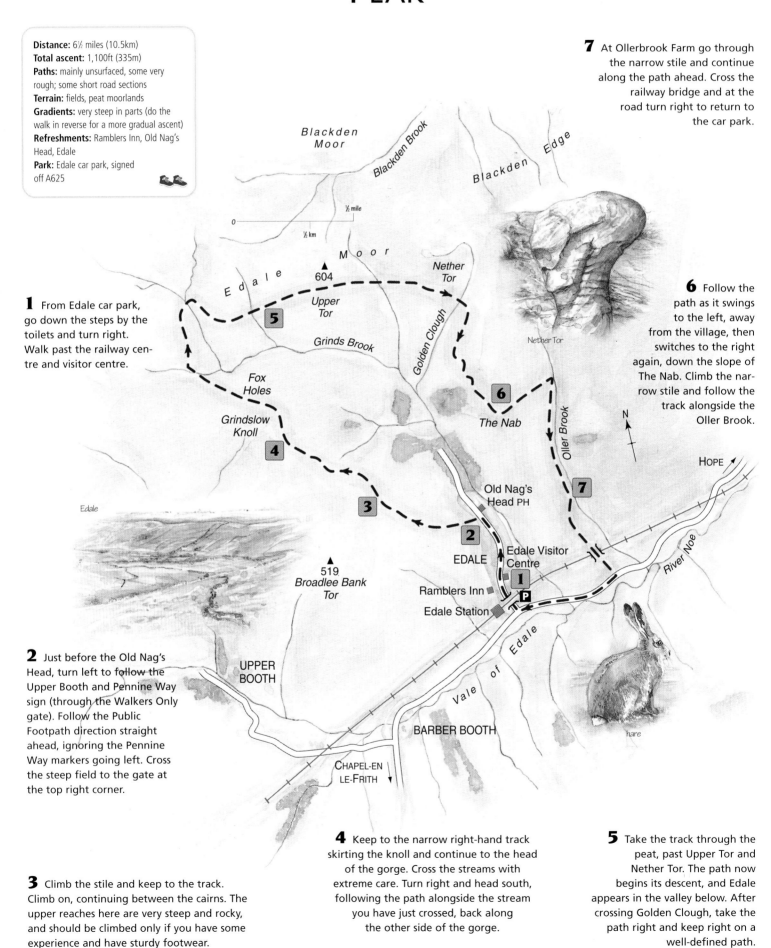

3 Climb the stile and keep to the track. Climb on, continuing between the cairns. The upper reaches here are very steep and rocky, and should be climbed only if you have some experience and have sturdy footwear.

4 Keep to the narrow right-hand track skirting the knoll and continue to the head of the gorge. Cross the streams with extreme care. Turn right and head south, following the path alongside the stream you have just crossed, back along the other side of the gorge.

5 Take the track through the peat, past Upper Tor and Nether Tor. The path now begins its descent, and Edale appears in the valley below. After crossing Golden Clough, take the path right and keep right on a well-defined path.

EYAM – THE PLAGUE VILLAGE

Distance: 5½ miles (9km)
Total ascent: 632ft (193m)
Paths: mostly good; some parts narrow, rocky
Terrain: village roads, fields, woods, unsurfaced tracks
Gradients: very steep in parts
Refreshments: tea rooms and pubs in Eyam
Park: car park opposite Eyam Museum, Hawkshill Road, Eyam (west of Chesterfield, off A623)

7 At the edge of the wood, follow the footpath along the wall to a gate. Go through the gate and take the steep path down through the wood to the road. Turn right through the gate and follow the road down to the museum and car park.

6 Retrace your steps to the signpost. Turn right, following the direction to Bretton, Hucklow and Abney. Continue along the road for some distance. At the public footpath sign, go left through the gate and cross the field towards the wood.

1 From the car park, turn left, then left again through the village, past Eyam Hall, the Plague Cottage and Eyam Church. At the square turn right up Lydgate and climb out of the village past the Lydgate Graves, then take the signed footpath to Stoney Middleton.

5 At the square, turn right, up Water Lane, and climb out of the village. At the top, follow the public footpath sign to the left. After a short distance, bear right onto a steep path up the field, and turn right through the gate at the top. Continue up the road and, at the signpost, head straight on towards Grindleford. Carry on a little further until you reach Mompesson's Well.

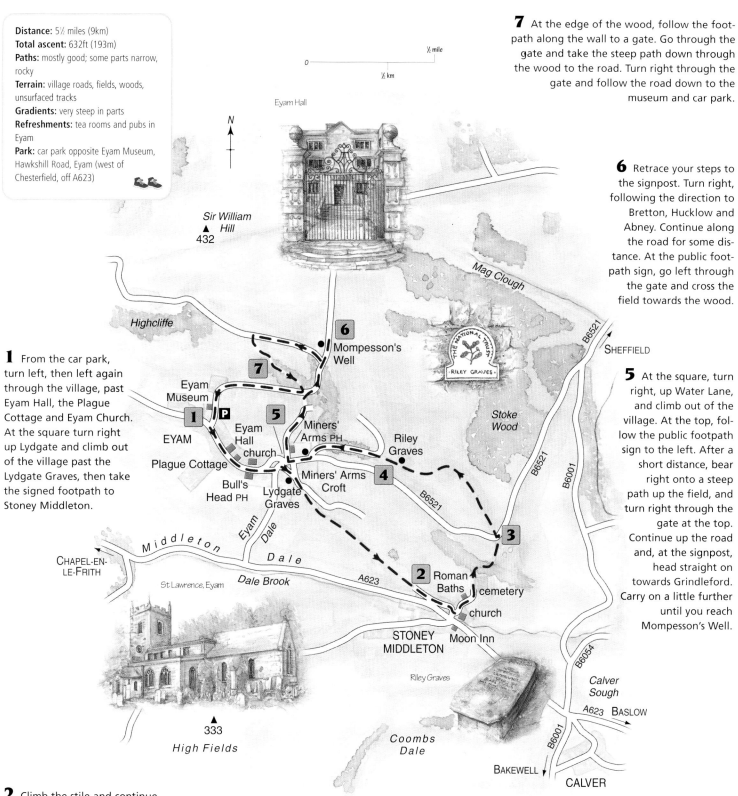

2 Climb the stile and continue along a single track road into Stoney Middleton, bearing left as you join the next road. Just before the stream, turn left towards the church. Follow the road past the Roman Baths and continue up the steep track that climbs out of the village past the cemetery.

3 At the top of the track, turn left, cross the road and pass through the narrow entrance by a gate. Follow the track alongside the stone wall. At the top corner of the field, by a trough, go through the gate ahead and continue climbing around to the right. At the top of a steep climb, turn left onto a farm track.

4 Beyond Riley Graves, continue ahead as you join the single track road that leads downhill through the trees. At the bottom, continue ahead into Eyam.

PACKHORSE TRAILS ACROSS THE PEAK

Distance: 5 miles (8km)
Total ascent: 206ft (63m)
Paths: generally good but sometimes indistinct
Terrain: moorland and woodland
Gradients: one slight climb to White Edge Moor
Refreshments: Longshaw Lodge café (seasonal), Fox House Inn or Grouse Inn
Park: Longshaw Estate National Trust car park off A625 Sheffield to Hathersage road, near Fox House Inn

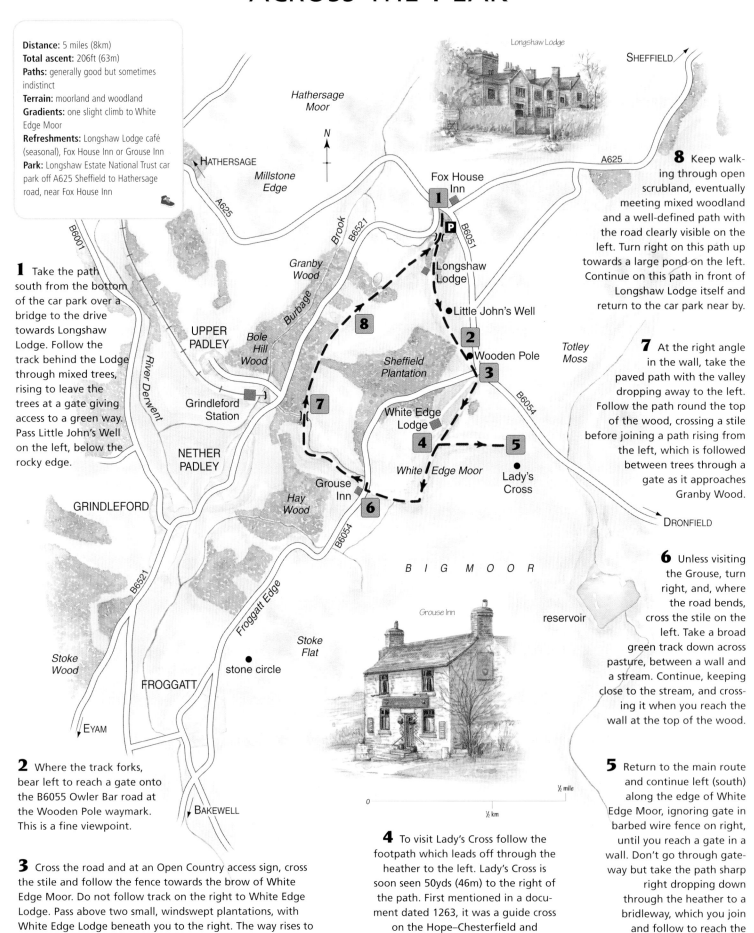

1 Take the path south from the bottom of the car park over a bridge to the drive towards Longshaw Lodge. Follow the track behind the Lodge through mixed trees, rising to leave the trees at a gate giving access to a green way. Pass Little John's Well on the left, below the rocky edge.

2 Where the track forks, bear left to reach a gate onto the B6055 Owler Bar road at the Wooden Pole waymark. This is a fine viewpoint.

3 Cross the road and at an Open Country access sign, cross the stile and follow the fence towards the brow of White Edge Moor. Do not follow track on the right to White Edge Lodge. Pass above two small, windswept plantations, with White Edge Lodge beneath you to the right. The way rises to the highest point of the walk, at 1,273ft (388m).

4 To visit Lady's Cross follow the footpath which leads off through the heather to the left. Lady's Cross is soon seen 50yds (46m) to the right of the path. First mentioned in a document dated 1263, it was a guide cross on the Hope–Chesterfield and Sheffield–Tideswell routes.

5 Return to the main route and continue left (south) along the edge of White Edge Moor, ignoring gate in barbed wire fence on right, until you reach a gate in a wall. Don't go through gateway but take the path sharp right dropping down through the heather to a bridleway, which you join and follow to reach the B6054 near the Grouse Inn.

6 Unless visiting the Grouse, turn right, and, where the road bends, cross the stile on the left. Take a broad green track down across pasture, between a wall and a stream. Continue, keeping close to the stream, and crossing it when you reach the wall at the top of the wood.

7 At the right angle in the wall, take the paved path with the valley dropping away to the left. Follow the path round the top of the wood, crossing a stile before joining a path rising from the left, which is followed between trees through a gate as it approaches Granby Wood.

8 Keep walking through open scrubland, eventually meeting mixed woodland and a well-defined path with the road clearly visible on the left. Turn right on this path up towards a large pond on the left. Continue on this path in front of Longshaw Lodge itself and return to the car park near by.

WARTIME REMAINS ON SPURN POINT

1 Walk to the far end of the car park and follow the Spurn Footpath sign, ascending the bank and turning right. Cross a bridge and stile and turn left then right, to follow waymarkers along the edge of the cliff. After passing two bird hides, follow the path right to descend beside bungalows towards the road.

2 Follow the yellow waymarkers to the left of the road, through the dunes and past the 'No Through Road' sign. The path will eventually join the road; continue along it until it veers right, when the signed footpath again goes to the left.

3 The path rejoins the road briefly, then turns off to the right, following the telegraph poles. Go over a ladder stile and towards the Heligoland Bird Trap. Go over another ladder stile to reach a signpost.

4 Follow the Seaside Path sign, crossing the road and ascending the dunes. The waymarked path follows the coastline and passes the lighthouse, eventually descending via a boardwalk to Spurn Point Car Park.

6 Go to the left of the information board at the north end of the car park, following the Riverside Path signs, past the former Low Light. The path joins the road briefly, but then goes left again, back to the Heligoland Trap. Go over the ladder stile and follow the outward route back to the car park.

5 Turn left and walk past the buildings and the jetty to explore the wartime buildings at the point, then return to the Spurn Point Car Park.

> **Distance:** 8½ miles (13.5km)
> **Total ascent:** negligible
> **Paths:** well-signed and mostly good; muddy in places; some road walking. Obey any diversions resulting from storm damage
> **Terrain:** sand-dunes and grassland
> **Gradients:** none
> **Refreshments:** seasonal at Spurn Point
> **Park:** car park, Kilnsea (east of the village, just beyond the crossroads)

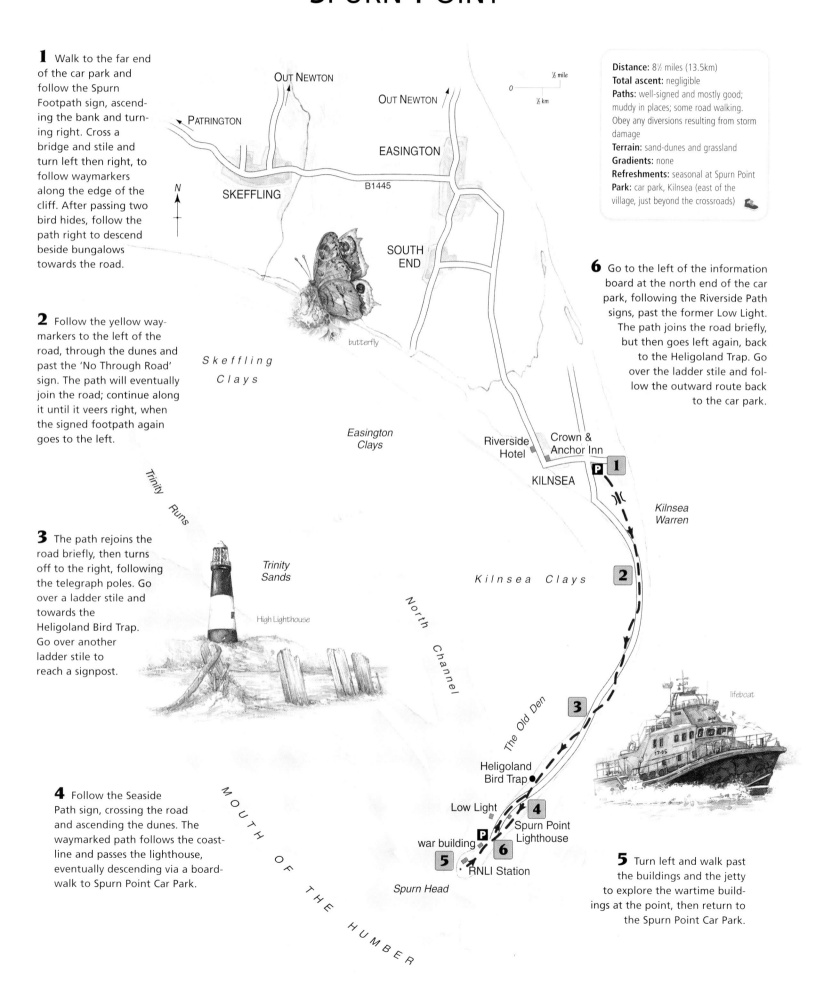

OUT NEWTON

PATRINGTON

OUT NEWTON

EASINGTON

B1445

SKEFFLING

N

SOUTH END

butterfly

Skeffling Clays

Easington Clays

Trinity Runs

Trinity Sands

High Lighthouse

North Channel

Kilnsea Clays

Riverside Hotel

Crown & Anchor Inn

KILNSEA

Kilnsea Warren

The Old Den

Heligoland Bird Trap

Low Light

Spurn Point Lighthouse

war building

RNLI Station

Spurn Head

MOUTH OF THE HUMBER

lifeboat

HAWORTH AND THE BRONTË MOORS

1 From the car park, go through gate posts opposite the museum and turn right. The lane soon becomes a paved field path that leads to the Haworth-Stanbury road. Walk left along the road and, after about 80yds (75m), take a left fork, signed to Penistone Hill. Continue along this quiet road to a T-junction.

2 Take the track straight ahead, soon signed Brontë Way and Top Withins, gradually descending to South Dean Beck where, within a few paces of the stone bridge, you'll find the Brontë Waterfall and Brontë Seat (a stone that resembles a chair). Cross the bridge and climb steeply uphill to a three-way sign.

3 Keep left, uphill, on a paved path signed to Top Withins. The path soon levels out to accompany a dry-stone wall. Cross a stile and then keep left. Cross a tiny beck on stepping stones; a steep uphill climb brings you to a way-marker by a ruined building. A short detour of 200yds (182m), left, uphill, is needed if you want to investigate the lonely ruins of Top Withins.

7 From here you retrace your outward route: walk left along the road, soon taking a stile on the right, to follow the paved field path back into Haworth.

6 Bear right along the road through Stanbury, then take the first road on the right, signed to Oxenhope, and cross the dam of Lower Laithe Reservoir. Immediately beyond the dam, bear left on a road that soon reduces to a track, uphill, to meet a road by Haworth Cemetery.

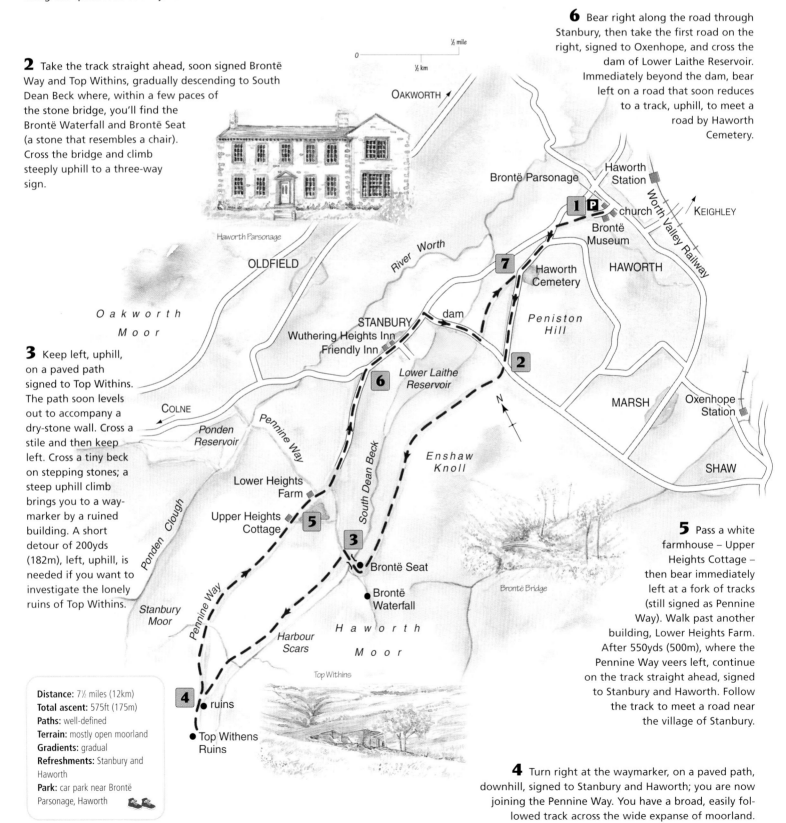

Haworth Parsonage

Top Withins

Brontë Bridge

5 Pass a white farmhouse – Upper Heights Cottage – then bear immediately left at a fork of tracks (still signed as Pennine Way). Walk past another building, Lower Heights Farm. After 550yds (500m), where the Pennine Way veers left, continue on the track straight ahead, signed to Stanbury and Haworth. Follow the track to meet a road near the village of Stanbury.

4 Turn right at the waymarker, on a paved path, downhill, signed to Stanbury and Haworth; you are now joining the Pennine Way. You have a broad, easily fol-lowed track across the wide expanse of moorland.

Distance: 7½ miles (12km)
Total ascent: 575ft (175m)
Paths: well-defined
Terrain: mostly open moorland
Gradients: gradual
Refreshments: Stanbury and Haworth
Park: car park near Brontë Parsonage, Haworth

SLAIDBURN AND THE FOREST OF BOWLAND

Distance: 11 miles (17.7km)
Total ascent: 985ft (300m)
Paths: good meadow paths, moorland roads and tracks
Terrain: wild, open moors and hillsides, with steep stream valleys
Gradients: several longish gradual climbs, and one or two short sharp ones
Refreshments: Hark to Bounty Inn, Slaidburn; village shop, Dunsop Bridge
Park: public car park on edge of Slaidburn, 9 miles (14.5km) north of Clitheroe on the B6478
Note: not recommended in poor visibility

1 Walk into the village to the Hark to Bounty Inn. From the inn turn right. Past the health centre, turn right ('Wood House' sign) on a path by Croasdale Brook, then through meadows. At a T-junction, go right down the grassy path to Myttons Farm.

8 Follow the farm track to the road, where you turn right for 600yds (548m), to reach the Hark to Bounty Inn at Slaidburn.

7 Go straight across a field, crossing first a wall stile, then a fence stile, then another wall stile. Aim diagonally right here across a field, bearing away from a fence. Keep left of a farm on your right, heading north-east until a gate and stile in a wall. Cross stile and follow the track to Pain Hill Farm. Go through farmyard, past buildings and out through a gate onto a track with several cattle grids.

2 Turn left to the road, then right for 1½ miles (2.4km) to go through a gate marked 'No vehicle access'. Turn immediately left up a bridleway, where a wall on the left soon swings away; follow the track uphill for 1 mile (1.6km) to a gate.

3 From this gate at the top of Dunsop Fell, bear diagonally right on a path, following yellow-topped marker posts for 1¼ miles (2km) down into Whitendale. Turn left on the road here beside the River Dunsop, for 3½ miles (5.6km), to Dunsop Bridge.

4 Turn left to cross the bridge then immediately left again up a marked bridleway. At Holme Head Cottages go through a gate (blue and yellow arrows). In 20yds (18m), turn right to climb steps up a steep bank. Cross a wall stile and follow telegraph poles to Beatrix.

5 At Beatrix turn left along the road. Pass houses, and take the track to Back of Hill Barn. Follow arrow waymarks down to the valley bottom, cross the stream and climb the track to Rough Syke Barn.

6 Continue uphill, keeping on the right-hand track, eastward, to go through a gate. In 150yds (137m), turn left into a walled lane, for 600yds (548m) to a road. Turn right here, and in 250 yds (229m) go left over a stile with a footpath sign.

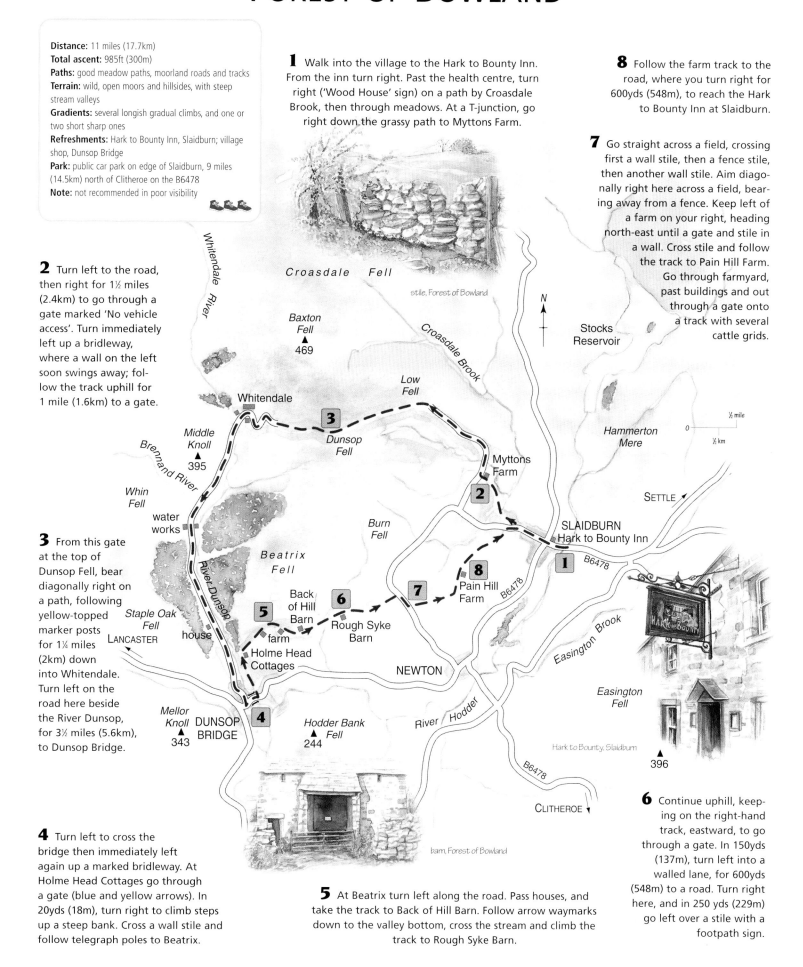

stile, Forest of Bowland

bam, Forest of Bowland

Hark to Bounty, Slaidburn

Whitendale River
Croasdale Fell
Baxton Fell ▲ 469
N
Croasdale Brook
Stocks Reservoir
Low Fell
Whitendale
Middle Knoll ▲ 395
Brennand River
Dunsop Fell
3
Myttons Farm
2
Hammerton Mere
½ mile
0
½ km
Whin Fell
water works
River Dunsop
Burn Fell
SETTLE
SLAIDBURN Hark to Bounty Inn
1 B6478
Beatrix Fell
Staple Oak Fell
LANCASTER house
5 farm
Back of Hill Barn
6
Rough Syke Barn
7
8 Pain Hill Farm
B6478
Easington Brook
Holme Head Cottages
NEWTON
Easington Fell
Mellor Knoll ▲ 343
DUNSOP BRIDGE
4
Hodder Bank ▲ Fell 244
River Hodder
Easington Fell ▲ 396
B6478
CLITHEROE

LIMESTONE LANDSCAPES AROUND MALHAM

Distance: 5 miles (8km)
Total ascent: 985ft (300m)
Paths: good; some steep, stepped sections
Terrain: limestone landscape and upland pasture
Gradients: mostly easy, apart from steps up side of cove
Refreshments: pubs and cafés, Malham
Park: car park by visitor centre, Malham

1 From the car park walk into the village. Where the road forks at the little bridge over Malham Beck, keep left, signed to Settle. About 200yds (182m) past the last building, go through a pair of gates on the right, to follow the well-trodden path towards Malham Cove. Descend to accompany Malham Beck, passing a little clapper-bridge on the way.

2 Just 300yds (274m) from the base of the cliff, take steps on the left climbing steeply to the extensive limestone pavement on top of the cove. Cross the pavement (with care) to a wall, and follow it to the left, along the dry valley of Watlowes. Beyond a wall-stile the valley narrows into a rocky gorge, that you leave by steps at the far end.

3 Take a step-stile at the top. Ignore a track to the right (signed Malham Tarn) to continue straight ahead alongside the wall. After just 30yds (27m), take a ladder stile on the left, over the wall. Follow the wall on your right; a finger post indicates Langscar Gate. Walk up to a road, cross it, and continue in the same direction, now on a rutted track. Follow the track uphill to a meeting of walls.

6 At this corner, take a gate on the right onto a field track (signed Malham 1 mile), soon enclosed between limestone walls. Follow this green lane past the water treatment works to join another, stonier track to a T-junction of tracks. Go right to return to Malham car park.

5 Go through the gate (signed to Cove Road), and follow a path downhill. Pass a way-marker sign (Malham 2 miles) and head towards Malham Cove in the distance. Descend gradually, going through a gate near where dry-stone walls meet and continuing down the broad track to a minor road. Walk right, down the road, for 200yds (182m), to a sharp hairpin bend to the left.

4 Take the gap in the walls and bear half-left to join a grassy track, uphill, to a gate in a wall. Continue in the same direction, through two more gates, after which you bear half-left towards Nappa Cross, a stone pillar on top of a wall (a medieval guide-stone). Follow the wall uphill to a gate and a three-way fingerpost. This, at 1,640ft (500m), is the highest point of the walk.

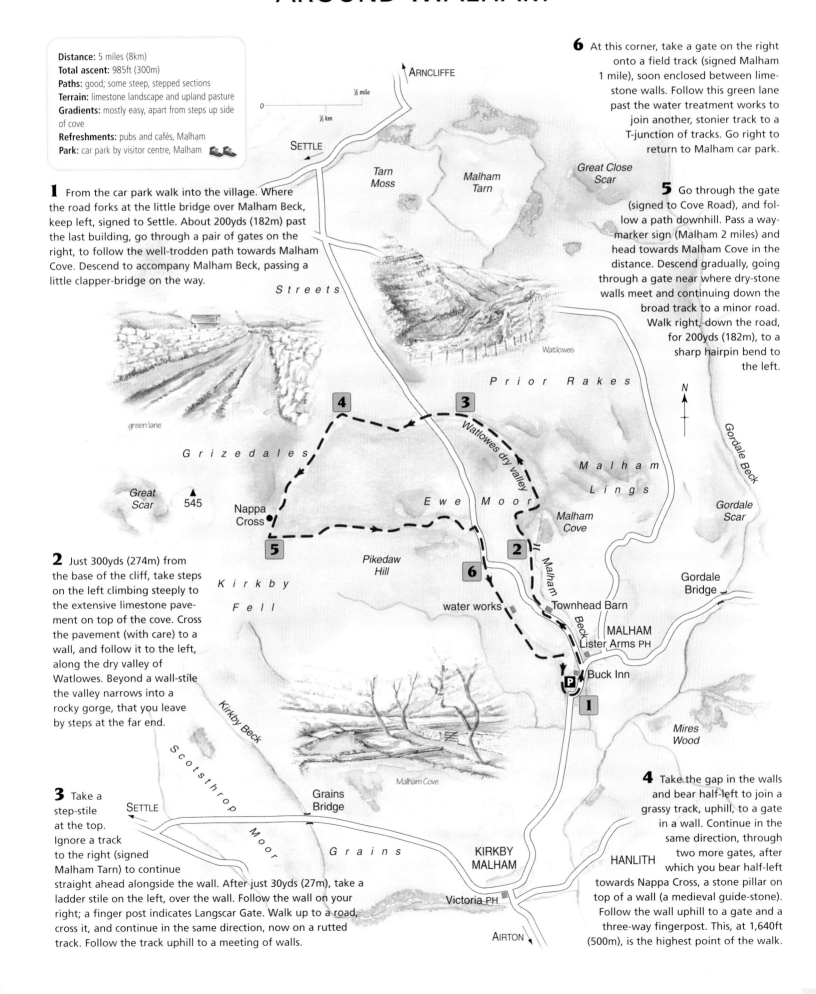

RIPON AND ITS LEWIS CARROLL CONNECTIONS

1 Leave Ripon market square by Kirkgate (near the Unicorn Hotel), and continue along to visit the cathedral and its Lewis Carroll links. Leave by the north door, near the Mothers' Union Chapel, and turn left, following the road as it curves left.

2 At the traffic lights turn left up Allhallowgate and, at the T-junction at the top, go right along North Street. 300yds (273m) on, turn left up Coltsgate Hill, continuing past the College and turning right in to Kirkby Road.

3 Walk up the hill, turning left into Lark Lane beyond the post box. At the bottom, turn right, then first left into Bishopton Road. Where the road bends left, go straight ahead down a track, then over a stile on the left. At a stone stile by the bridge turn right and walk beside the road.

8 Follow the path beside the river, down steps and past a footbridge, eventually to emerge into a minor road and then the main road. Turn left, over the bridge, and go straight on up the hill at the traffic lights, back to the market square.

7 Walk across the fields to a handgate into a lane, and turn left. As the houses begin, go left for 100yds (91m) along the lane to Hell Wath Cottage, turning right along a signed path where the metalled road ends.

6 Cross the footbridge, follow the path as it winds left, and turn right, uphill, at a crossing track. At the top of the hill turn sharp left, signed to Ripon, to reach a waymarked gate.

5 At the crossroads turn left towards the lake, and leave the metalled road to walk round the left end of the lake, over the dam and left, following the path over five stone bridges. Go through the gate in the wall, and walk along to a footbridge.

4 Where the road bends right by the caravan site, go through a kissing gate on the left and follow the footpath across the fields to Studley Roger. Cross the village street and go straight ahead, through two gates, to emerge into Studley Park, eventually turning right along the main drive.

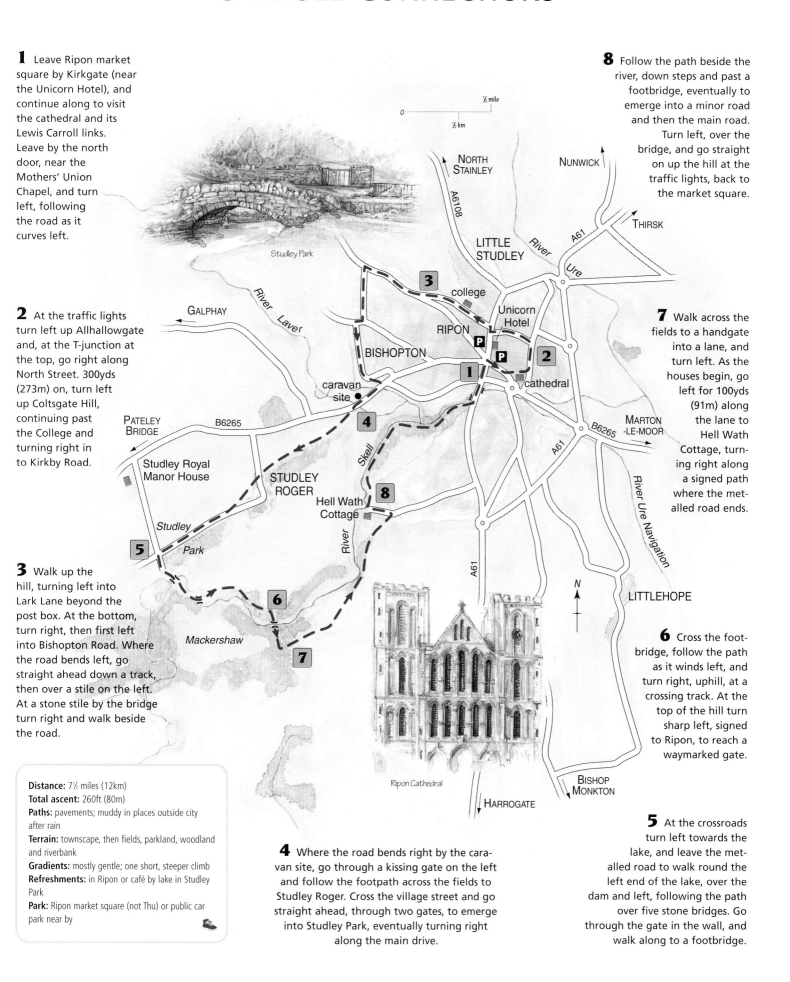

½ mile
0
½ km

NORTH STANLEY

NUNWICK

A6108

River Ure

A61

THIRSK

LITTLE STUDLEY

Studley Park

GALPHAY

River Laver

3 college

Unicorn Hotel

RIPON

2

1

P

P

cathedral

BISHOPTON

caravan site

PATELEY BRIDGE

B6265

4

MARTON -LE-MOOR

B6265

A61

Studley Royal Manor House

STUDLEY ROGER

Skell

8

Hell Wath Cottage

River Ure Navigation

5

Studley Park

River Skell

6

N

LITTLEHOPE

Mackershaw

7

A61

BISHOP MONKTON

Ripon Cathedral

HARROGATE

Distance: 7½ miles (12km)
Total ascent: 260ft (80m)
Paths: pavements; muddy in places outside city after rain
Terrain: townscape, then fields, parkland, woodland and riverbank
Gradients: mostly gentle; one short, steeper climb
Refreshments: in Ripon or café by lake in Studley Park
Park: Ripon market square (not Thu) or public car park near by

IN THE HOLE OF HORCUM

Distance: 8½ miles (13.7km)
Total ascent: 1,015ft (309m)
Paths: good tracks and woodland paths; often muddy
Terrain: moorland ridges and wooded valleys
Gradients: moderate; some steep sections
Refreshments: Levisham, or caravan in car park
Park: car park on the A169, 12 miles (19.3km) north of Pickering and 3 miles (4.8km) north of Lockton

7 At a signpost for Saltergate turn left, go over two footbridges and turn left at the waymark beyond it. The path follows the valley into the Hole of Horcum, passing a former farm-house, then ascends to a ladder stile beside the A169. Turn right to reach the car park.

6 At the top of the green take the lane to the right of the Horseshoe Inn. At a stile beside a gate across the lane, go right and descend to follow a path along the narrowing valley, beside the stream.

5 After 500yds (457m), turn right along a bridleway, going downhill and left at a crossing track. The path winds through woodland and eventually reaches a road, where you turn left up into Levisham village.

4 At the second gateway take the track uphill, through a gate into woodland. Continue uphill where a track joins from the right, turning left at a crossing track, which eventually becomes metalled.

1 From the car park cross the road and walk north, following the road's sharp left bend and then going ahead over a stile onto an uphill track as the road hairpins right. Follow this track for 2½ miles (4km), passing left of a pond, to reach signpost by a second pond.

2 Turn right (signed Station) with the pond on your right. Go ahead at a crossing track, walk beside a wall for 200yds (182m), then descend the ridge to the valley road and turn left.

3 After 200yds (182m) take a signed track to the right. Follow bridleway signs to reach a gate by a wood. The track curves through the wood to a stile, then across fields.

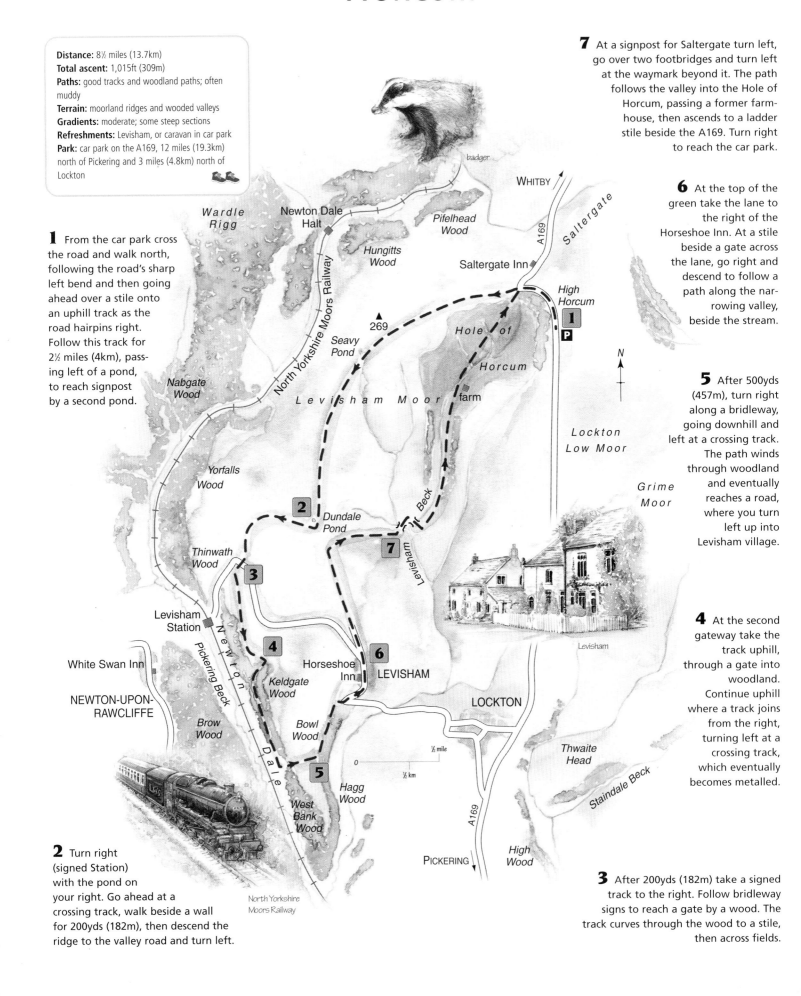

HIGH AND DEEP ON YORKSHIRE'S COAST

1 From the top of the car park walk left, past garages, along a path by allotments. Turn right up the valley and follow the footpath signs through the houses to eventually meet the main road. Cross, go over a stile, through the field and cross a track by two more stiles.

8 At a crossing track (the Cleveland Way), turn right and follow it to Staithes, following signs to Cowbar. Descend to the harbour, cross the footbridge and turn right at the main village street up to the car park.

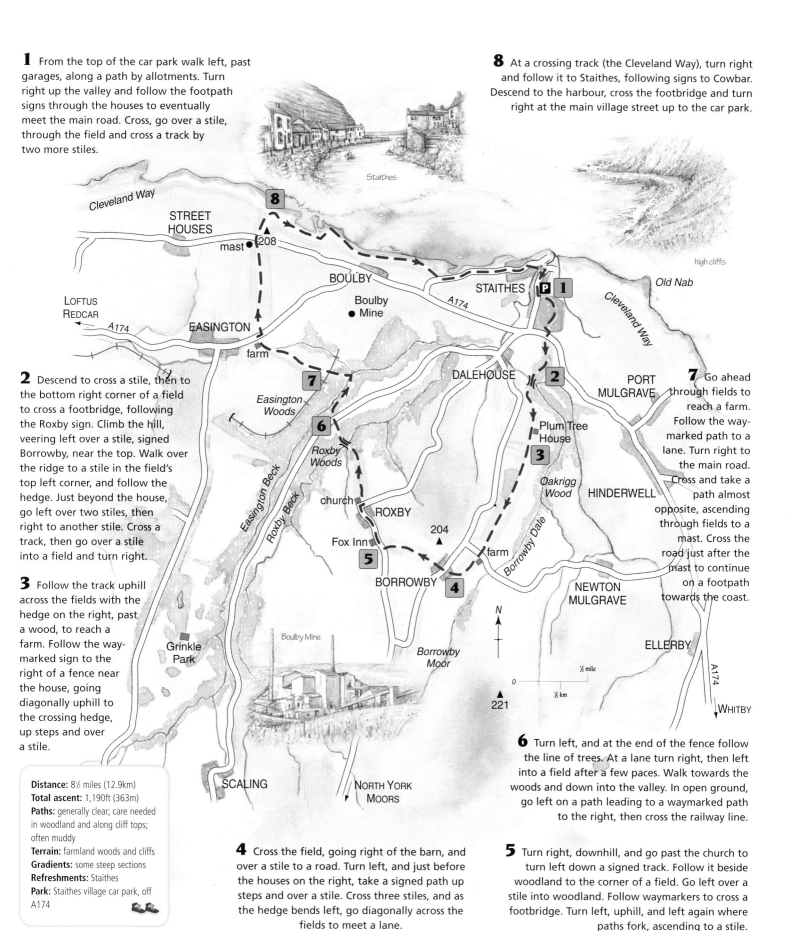

Staithes

high cliffs

Cleveland Way

STREET HOUSES

mast ● 208

BOULBY

Boulby ● Mine

STAITHES

A174

Old Nab

LOFTUS REDCAR

A174

EASINGTON

farm

DALEHOUSE

PORT MULGRAVE

Cleveland Way

Plum Tree House

Oakrigg Wood

HINDERWELL

2 Descend to cross a stile, then to the bottom right corner of a field to cross a footbridge, following the Roxby sign. Climb the hill, veering left over a stile, signed Borrowby, near the top. Walk over the ridge to a stile in the field's top left corner, and follow the hedge. Just beyond the house, go left over two stiles, then right to another stile. Cross a track, then go over a stile into a field and turn right.

Easington Woods

Roxby Woods

church

ROXBY

Fox Inn

204 ▲

Borrowby Dale

farm

NEWTON MULGRAVE

7 Go ahead through fields to reach a farm. Follow the way-marked path to a lane. Turn right to the main road. Cross and take a path almost opposite, ascending through fields to a mast. Cross the road just after the mast to continue on a footpath towards the coast.

3 Follow the track uphill across the fields with the hedge on the right, past a wood, to reach a farm. Follow the way-marked sign to the right of a fence near the house, going diagonally uphill to the crossing hedge, up steps and over a stile.

Easington Beck

Roxby Beck

Grinkle Park

BORROWBY

Boulby Mine

N

½ mile
0
½ km

▲ 221

Borrowby Moor

ELLERBY

A174

WHITBY

Distance: 8½ miles (12.9km)
Total ascent: 1,190ft (363m)
Paths: generally clear; care needed in woodland and along cliff tops; often muddy
Terrain: farmland woods and cliffs
Gradients: some steep sections
Refreshments: Staithes
Park: Staithes village car park, off A174

SCALING

NORTH YORK MOORS

6 Turn left, and at the end of the fence follow the line of trees. At a lane turn right, then left into a field after a few paces. Walk towards the woods and down into the valley. In open ground, go left on a path leading to a waymarked path to the right, then cross the railway line.

4 Cross the field, going right of the barn, and over a stile to a road. Turn left, and just before the houses on the right, take a signed path up steps and over a stile. Cross three stiles, and as the hedge bends left, go diagonally across the fields to meet a lane.

5 Turn right, downhill, and go past the church to turn left down a signed track. Follow it beside woodland to the corner of a field. Go left over a stile into woodland. Follow waymarkers to cross a footbridge. Turn left, uphill, and left again where paths fork, ascending to a stile.

UP GUNNERSIDE GILL WITH SWALEDALE MINERS

1 From the bridge in the centre of Gunnerside take the track on the eastern side up the beck, beginning opposite the Kings Head. After 100yds (91m), at a white gate, take stone steps to the right, then a walled path, emerging into open fields. The path descends to the beck as the valley broadens out. Cross a side beck on a tiny bridge, take two gap-stiles, close together, and follow a wall. Beyond two little gates you reach the beck again, and the first evidence of lead ore processing.

2 Pass two ore-dressing floors, one each side of the beck, and the entrance to a mining tunnel, known as a 'level'. Continue on the riverside path, following the yellow arrows, then go uphill, away from the beck. Cross a stile in the fence before going through a gap-stile in a wall. The path climbs gradually, as the valley becomes steeper-sided. Keep a wall to your left as the path levels out into the principal mining area.

3 Soon the Bunton mining complex comes into view. Pass through it and leave on a stony path uphill, with huge hushes on all sides. After 100yds (91m) uphill, fork left, downhill.

7 Keep left (the track soon becomes more distinct), heading for the roofs of Gunnerside that soon appear. The path gradually becomes clearer and leads you downhill. Go through a little wooden gate and back into the village.

6 Follow this track to the left, through a gate and past a little waterfall in Botcher Gill, before making a gentle descent. Across the valley the landscape changes back to a more familiar one of farms, walls and barns. When the track makes a long right turn, go left on a grassy path, by a small cairn.

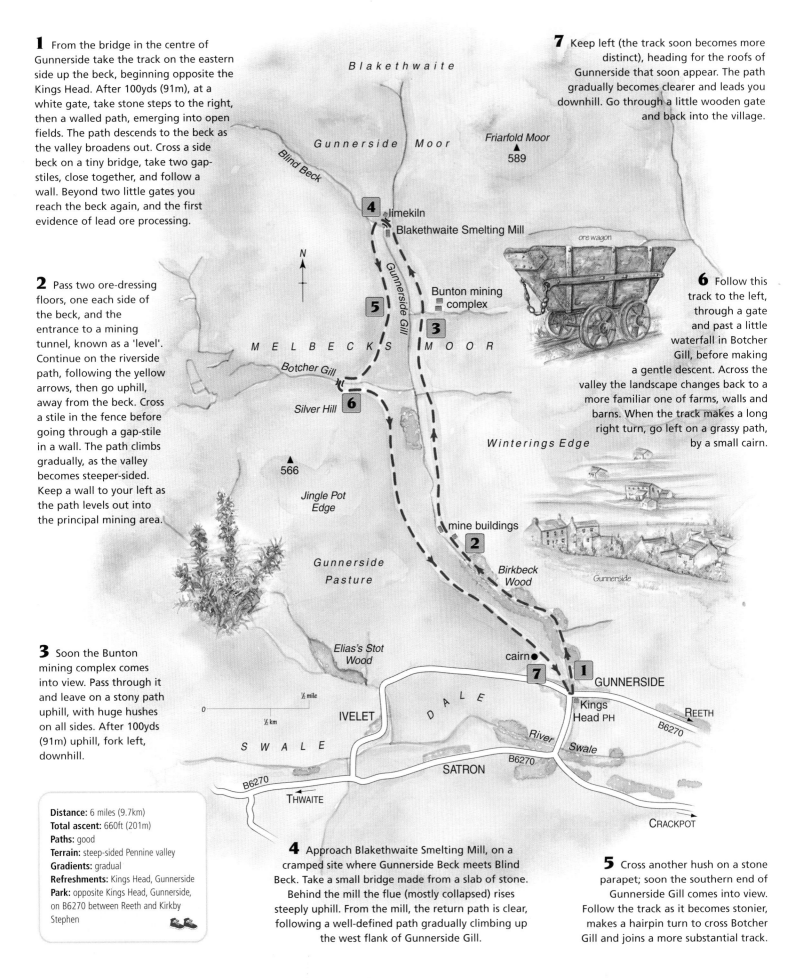

Distance: 6 miles (9.7km)
Total ascent: 660ft (201m)
Paths: good
Terrain: steep-sided Pennine valley
Gradients: gradual
Refreshments: Kings Head, Gunnerside
Park: opposite Kings Head, Gunnerside, on B6270 between Reeth and Kirkby Stephen

4 Approach Blakethwaite Smelting Mill, on a cramped site where Gunnerside Beck meets Blind Beck. Take a small bridge made from a slab of stone. Behind the mill the flue (mostly collapsed) rises steeply uphill. From the mill, the return path is clear, following a well-defined path gradually climbing up the west flank of Gunnerside Gill.

5 Cross another hush on a stone parapet; soon the southern end of Gunnerside Gill comes into view. Follow the track as it becomes stonier, makes a hairpin turn to cross Botcher Gill and joins a more substantial track.

CLAIFE HEIGHTS AND THE VICTORIAN VIEW OF WINDERMERE

1 Turn left (north) out of car park and follow the lakeside for 2 miles (3.2km). The metalled lane soon becomes an unmade track through woodland.

2 As the track approaches Belle Grange turn left just before the house up a steep and stony bridleway, signposted to Letterbarrow and Near Sawrey. Ignoring a path to the left, continue on uphill (signposted to Hawkshead) until the path levels out and reaches a broad bridleway at a complex intersection.

8 At far end of this car park, take footpath into woods and up steps to Claife Station. At top of steps turn right along the terrace walk, which drops down to the road. Turn left, then bear immediately left along a narrow lane to return to car park.

7 Turn left down the hill, then cross the road onto footpath separated from the traffic by a wall. Follow path downhill and across the road, through woodland to a car park.

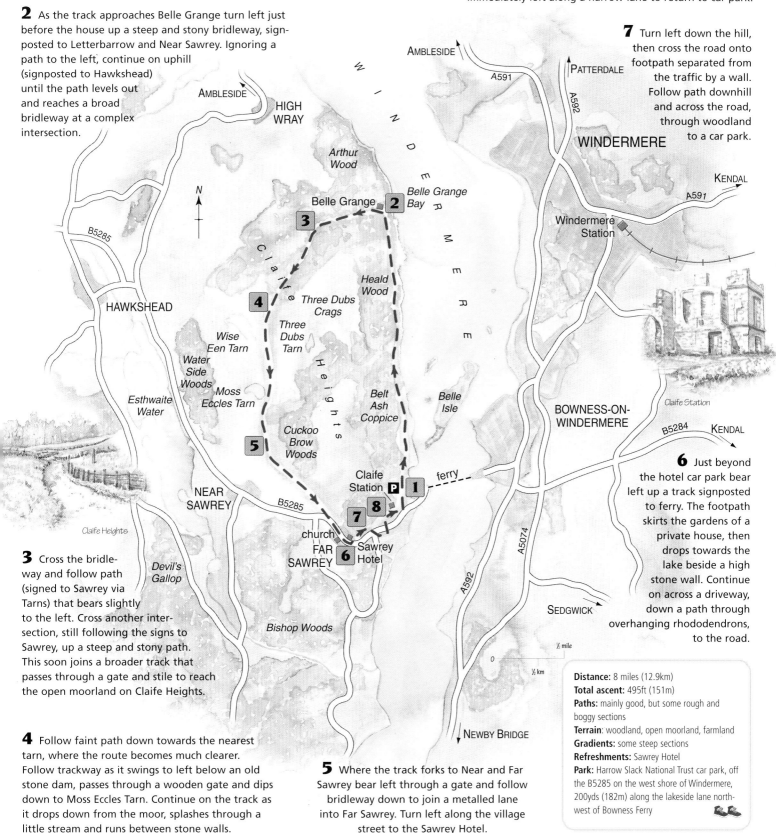

3 Cross the bridleway and follow path (signed to Sawrey via Tarns) that bears slightly to the left. Cross another intersection, still following the signs to Sawrey, up a steep and stony path. This soon joins a broader track that passes through a gate and stile to reach the open moorland on Claife Heights.

4 Follow faint path down towards the nearest tarn, where the route becomes much clearer. Follow trackway as it swings to left below an old stone dam, passes through a wooden gate and dips down to Moss Eccles Tarn. Continue on the track as it drops down from the moor, splashes through a little stream and runs between stone walls.

5 Where the track forks to Near and Far Sawrey bear left through a gate and follow bridleway down to join a metalled lane into Far Sawrey. Turn left along the village street to the Sawrey Hotel.

6 Just beyond the hotel car park bear left up a track signposted to ferry. The footpath skirts the gardens of a private house, then drops towards the lake beside a high stone wall. Continue on across a driveway, down a path through overhanging rhododendrons, to the road.

Distance: 8 miles (12.9km)
Total ascent: 495ft (151m)
Paths: mainly good, but some rough and boggy sections
Terrain: woodland, open moorland, farmland
Gradients: some steep sections
Refreshments: Sawrey Hotel
Park: Harrow Slack National Trust car park, off the B5285 on the west shore of Windermere, 200yds (182m) along the lakeside lane north-west of Bowness Ferry

THE CONTRASTS OF UPPER ESKDALE

1 Begin from a roadside parking area at the foot of Hardknott Pass, and descend to follow the access to Brotherilkeld Farm (right, by the telephone box). As you near the farm, branch left on a path parallel with the River Esk. Ignore a footbridge and continue up-river.

2 Beyond a gate follow a broad track crossing rough pasture. This leads past a series of delightful waterfalls, and ultimately arrives at Lingcove Bridge, directly below the crags of Throstle Garth.

3 Cross the bridge and climb left, still alongside, but well above, the river. Two pronounced rises follow before the path reaches Scar Lathing, where the river makes a distinct bend westwards. Cross an inflowing stream, and bear left to pass beneath Scar Lathing, beyond which lies the bleak arena of Great Moss, spread below the soaring heights of Sca Fell and the lower cliffs of Cam Spout Crag.

4 The moss is invariably waterlogged and paths sketchy, but the objective is now to cross the river. This is usually best accomplished at or just above the confluence with How Beck, and is rarely completed dryshod. Once across, head towards the base of the waterfall from How Beck, then turn left and contour along the base of a rocky slope to reach a small knoll with massive boulders, known as Sampson's Stones.

5 A short way further on a sheepfold is reached. From it a clear path begins a gentle climb away from the river into a little-known landscape of knolls, streams, low crags and bogland.

6 The path, passing below Silverybield Crag, Round Scar and Rowantree Crags, is clear throughout, but occasionally resorts to evasion tactics before breaking free of the rocks on reaching Scale Gill. Now a clear green path zigzags down through bracken, turns right at the bottom and crosses Scale Bridge, where the gill puts on an impressive show of force.

7 A short way beyond the bridge, take the lower of two ladder stiles, and follow an improving track to Taw House Farm. Immediately turn left over a ladder stile and go down an enclosed path to the footbridge across the Esk encountered at the start of the walk, and from there retrace your steps to the valley road.

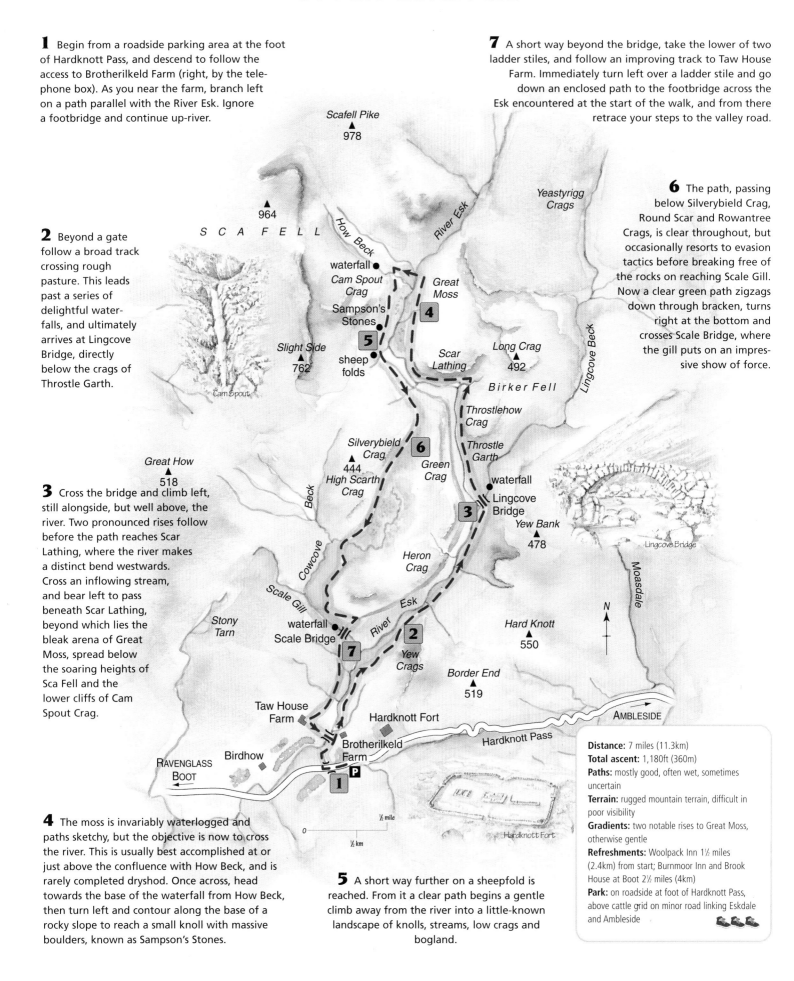

Distance: 7 miles (11.3km)
Total ascent: 1,180ft (360m)
Paths: mostly good, often wet, sometimes uncertain
Terrain: rugged mountain terrain, difficult in poor visibility
Gradients: two notable rises to Great Moss, otherwise gentle
Refreshments: Woolpack Inn 1½ miles (2.4km) from start; Burnmoor Inn and Brook House at Boot 2½ miles (4km)
Park: on roadside at foot of Hardknott Pass, above cattle grid on minor road linking Eskdale and Ambleside

A POET'S VIEW OF THE BUTTERMERE VALLEY

1 From the Bridge Hotel walk down to the left of the Fish Hotel, then through a gate, signposted to Scale Force and Scale Bridge. Go over a bridge, through a gate and turn right.

2 In ¼ mile (400m), after crossing a stream via a footbridge, take the path to the left which runs along the base of a rocky slope with occasional cairns. Eventually reach a gap in a wall. Descend to cross a footbridge. Scale Force waterfall is on your left.

3 Ascend for a few paces, then turn right, downhill, on a bank with a stream on your right. At the confluence with another stream, cross a footbridge then turn right. Later the path veers away from the stream towards the shore, then left alongside the lake.

4 Towards the end of the lake the track divides. Take the right-hand path through the gate and follow the water's edge. Go ahead at next gate and, just past a broken-down wall, turn left to pass a ruin, then aim for a group of pine trees by the shore. Pass through a kissing gate and then along a wall to a pumping station. Continue along the shore to cross a foot-bridge over a river. Later turn right over two bridges. Continue on shore path through Lanthwaite Woods and later past a boat house, then along by the lake. The path leads over several stiles and small bridges until it bears left at a wall.

5 Go through the gate and turn right onto the road to a parking area. Branch left across the hillside and soon cross the river and follow the bridleway. Go through a gate, to a footbridge. Cross over, then turn right to double-back and go down hill.

6 At the road walk left for a few paces then back up the bridle-way leading uphill and over a shoulder. Follow the path, keeping the lake on your right. When it comes back to the road, continue to a group of pine trees.

7 Pass through a kissing gate and follow the shore, then take a gravel path through woods. At the far end cross a footbridge, then go through a kissing gate. Turn left up field to another kissing gate, then immediately turn right around foot of crag. On reaching a foot-bridge, cross it and turn left, signed Buttermere village, and follow riverside path back to car park.

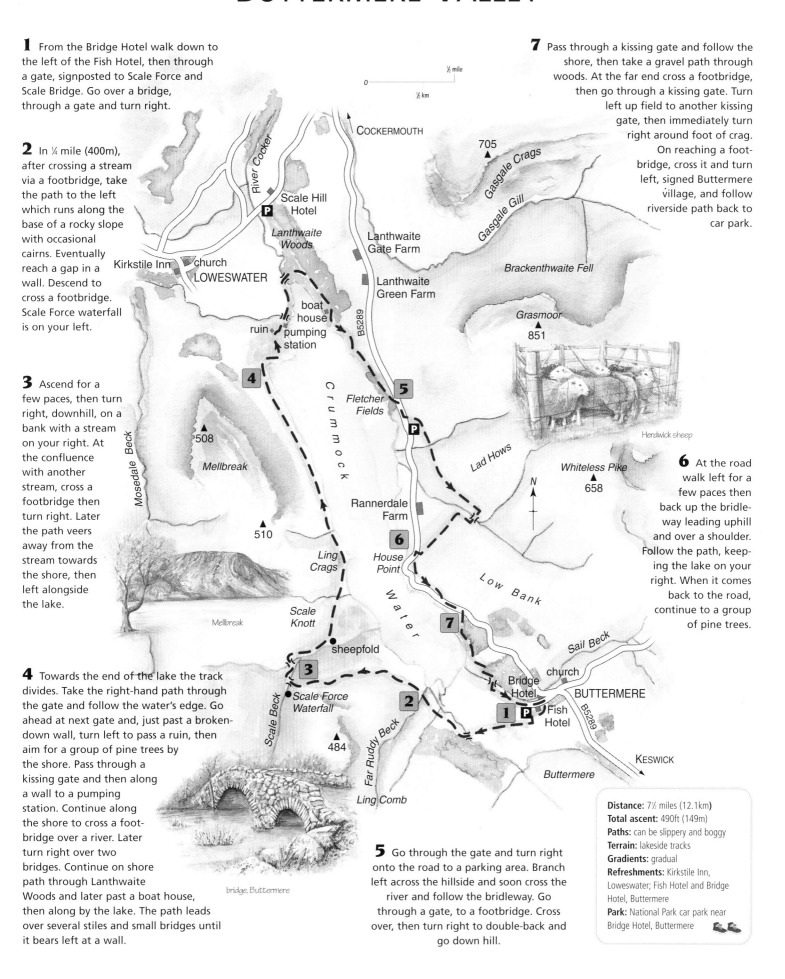

½ mile

0

½ km

COCKERMOUTH

River Cocker

Scale Hill Hotel

Lanthwaite Woods

Kirkstile Inn church LOWESWATER

boat house pumping station

ruin

Mosedale Beck

▲508

Mellbreak

510

Mellbreak

Ling Crags

Scale Knott

sheepfold

Scale Beck

Scale Force Waterfall

▲484

Ling Comb

Far Ruddy Beck

Lanthwaite Gate Farm

Lanthwaite Green Farm

B5289

Crummock

Fletcher Fields

Rannerdale Farm

House Point

Water

705 ▲

Gasgale Crags

Gasgale Gill

Brackenthwaite Fell

Grasmoor ▲ 851

Lad Hows

Whiteless Pike ▲ 658

N

Low Bank

Herdwick sheep

Sail Beck

church

Bridge Hotel

BUTTERMERE

Fish Hotel

B5289

Buttermere

KESWICK

bridge, Buttermere

Distance: 7½ miles (12.1km)
Total ascent: 490ft (149m)
Paths: can be slippery and boggy
Terrain: lakeside tracks
Gradients: gradual
Refreshments: Kirkstile Inn, Loweswater; Fish Hotel and Bridge Hotel, Buttermere
Park: National Park car park near Bridge Hotel, Buttermere

SWINDALE AND THE EASTERN FELLS

1 Leave Keld on a moorland road to Tailbert Farm. At Tailbert, abandon the road for a track across the hillside, later descending through bracken and gorse into Swindale. Cross a ford or a nearby bridge. Turn left, follow the minor road to Swindale Head Farm and go through gates onto a bridleway signed Mosedale.

2 After a final building on the left, branch left through glacial moraine, and climb through the rocky outcrops of Selside Pike. Cross open moorland to a fence at Swine Gill. Go through a gate and continue to a dilapidated building and a collapsed wall nearby.

6 When the river makes a pronounced bend to the right, move away from it to a wall. Go past Steps Hall, following a rough track towards Thornship Farm. Opposite the farm continue alongside the river to reach Keld once more.

5 Follow the road to a cattle grid. Here leave the road, turning left alongside the River Lowther. Cross a road and continue beside the river.

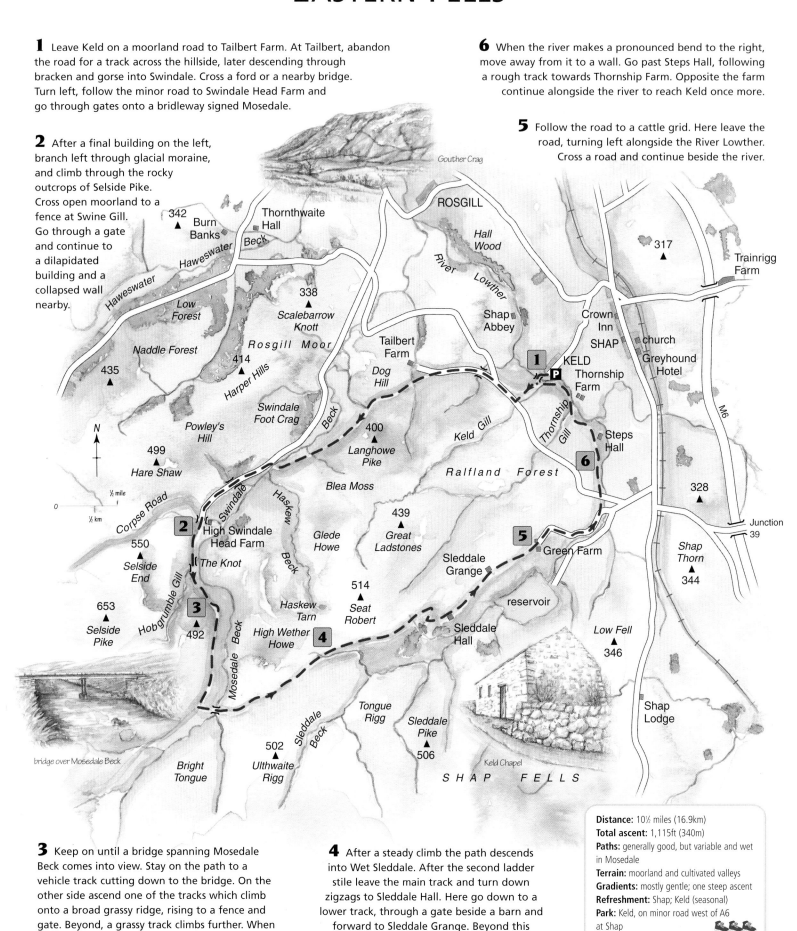

3 Keep on until a bridge spanning Mosedale Beck comes into view. Stay on the path to a vehicle track cutting down to the bridge. On the other side ascend one of the tracks which climb onto a broad grassy ridge, rising to a fence and gate. Beyond, a grassy track climbs further. When this forks, branch right.

4 After a steady climb the path descends into Wet Sleddale. After the second ladder stile leave the main track and turn down zigzags to Sleddale Hall. Here go down to a lower track, through a gate beside a barn and forward to Sleddale Grange. Beyond this follow a rough-surfaced road to Green Farm.

Distance: 10½ miles (16.9km)
Total ascent: 1,115ft (340m)
Paths: generally good, but variable and wet in Mosedale
Terrain: moorland and cultivated valleys
Gradients: mostly gentle; one steep ascent
Refreshment: Shap; Keld (seasonal)
Park: Keld, on minor road west of A6 at Shap

CROSS FELL – THE PENNINE GIANT

1 In Kirkland head up the road alongside Kirkland Beck. Beyond the last buildings a walled track heads out onto rough upland pastures, eventually looping north to skirt High Cap above Ardale Beck.

2 The gradient, nowhere unduly steep, is eased by a few bends. Within sight of the summit plateau, and not far from a bothy, the ascending track bears sharply left. Here leave it to strike eastwards on a cairned and grassy path, crossing the watershed and passing around the northern scree slopes of Cross Fell to locate the Pennine Way.

7 Onwards a broad green path descends easily through bracken to a sheepfold and across a tract of rough ground to Wythwaite Farm. At the farm turn right through gates, and follow a broad track back to Kirkland.

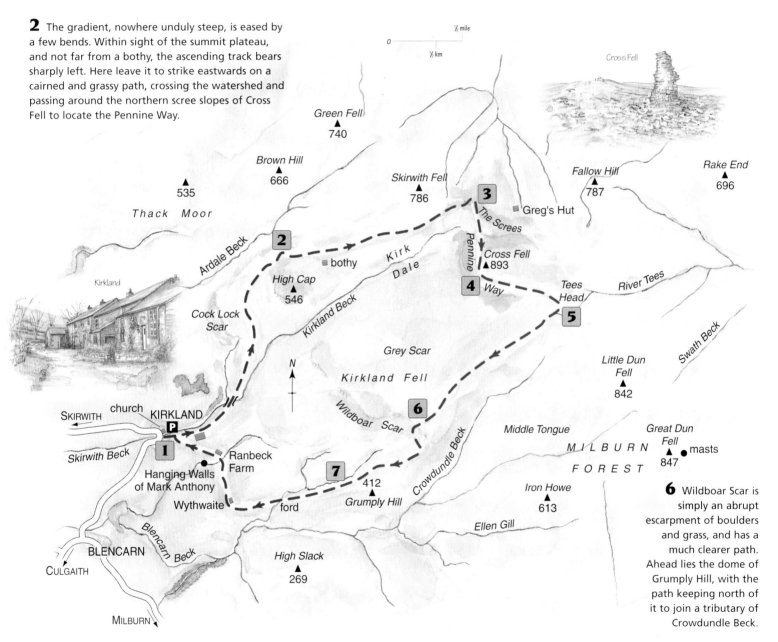

3 A waymarker indicates the line of the Pennine Way, initially wet underfoot and clear enough to follow. It soon dries out, and a few large cairns guide you to the summit shelter-cairn and trig pillar.

4 In poor visibility the surest way down is to retreat. Otherwise, press on across the summit plateau, aiming for the distant summit of Great Dun Fell and its conspicuous masts and radar station. Near the edge of the Cross Fell plateau large cairns mark the way down to Tees Head.

5 From Tees Head a cairned path, not obvious, and narrow in places, leaves the Pennine Way and heads south-west across bouldery terrain to a cairn on the edge of Wildboar Scar. If you can't locate the line of cairns leaving Tees Head, drop beneath the downfall of scree and boulders and skirt along its lower edge until cairns appear in the far distance, and head for them.

6 Wildboar Scar is simply an abrupt escarpment of boulders and grass, and has a much clearer path. Ahead lies the dome of Grumply Hill, with the path keeping north of it to join a tributary of Crowdundle Beck.

Distance: 9 miles (14.5km)
Total ascent: 2,265ft (690m)
Paths: good on ascent, thereafter sketchy
Terrain: high mountain plateau
Gradients: moderate
Refreshment: none nearby
Park: alongside river, opposite church in Kirkland, 5 miles (8km) east of A686 in Langwathby
Note: this route requires good navigational skills and should not be attempted in poor visibility

THE EDGE OF AN EMPIRE ON HADRIAN'S WALL

Distance: 6 miles (9.7 km)
Total ascent: 560ft (171m)
Paths: mostly good but can get boggy
Terrain: fields, open country
Gradients: gradual
Refreshments: Haltwhistle town centre
Park: by Haltwhistle Railway Station

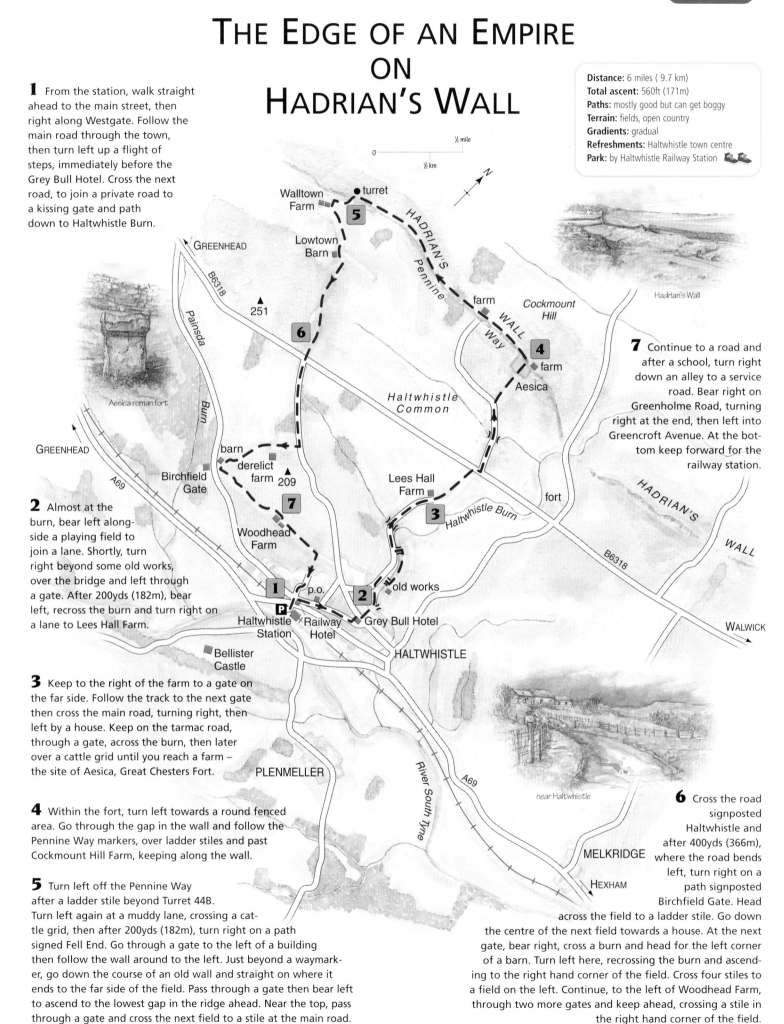

1 From the station, walk straight ahead to the main street, then right along Westgate. Follow the main road through the town, then turn left up a flight of steps, immediately before the Grey Bull Hotel. Cross the next road, to join a private road to a kissing gate and path down to Haltwhistle Burn.

2 Almost at the burn, bear left alongside a playing field to join a lane. Shortly, turn right beyond some old works, over the bridge and left through a gate. After 200yds (182m), bear left, recross the burn and turn right on a lane to Lees Hall Farm.

3 Keep to the right of the farm to a gate on the far side. Follow the track to the next gate then cross the main road, turning right, then left by a house. Keep on the tarmac road, through a gate, across the burn, then later over a cattle grid until you reach a farm – the site of Aesica, Great Chesters Fort.

4 Within the fort, turn left towards a round fenced area. Go through the gap in the wall and follow the Pennine Way markers, over ladder stiles and past Cockmount Hill Farm, keeping along the wall.

5 Turn left off the Pennine Way after a ladder stile beyond Turret 44B. Turn left again at a muddy lane, crossing a cattle grid, then after 200yds (182m), turn right on a path signed Fell End. Go through a gate to the left of a building then follow the wall around to the left. Just beyond a waymarker, go down the course of an old wall and straight on where it ends to the far side of the field. Pass through a gate then bear left to ascend to the lowest gap in the ridge ahead. Near the top, pass through a gate and cross the next field to a stile at the main road.

7 Continue to a road and after a school, turn right down an alley to a service road. Bear right on Greenholme Road, turning right at the end, then left into Greencroft Avenue. At the bottom keep forward for the railway station.

6 Cross the road signposted Haltwhistle and after 400yds (366m), where the road bends left, turn right on a path signposted Birchfield Gate. Head across the field to a ladder stile. Go down the centre of the next field towards a house. At the next gate, bear right, cross a burn and head for the left corner of a barn. Turn left here, recrossing the burn and ascending to the right hand corner of the field. Cross four stiles to a field on the left. Continue, to the left of Woodhead Farm, through two more gates and keep ahead, crossing a stile in the right hand corner of the field.

BERWICK'S BULWARK AGAINST THE SCOTS

1 From the Maltings car park go left, down the hill. At the bottom, cross the road, then keep ahead over Berwick Old Bridge. Once over, turn right. At corner of Blakewell Road take path to the right, beside the river.

2 Keep following this route by the river, taking care as it can be extremely muddy and wet and subject to high tides. Later go through a gate and follow the path, keeping to the line of the fence and up to the sewage works.

3 Go over the stile and follow the path, then go through the gate and turn left. At the next gate turn right onto the road. Go to the corner of the field and take the path along its right-hand edge, above the little hut.

4 Continue into the next field. At the end take the right-hand path and descend past a ruined hut and over a little bridge. Ascend and go over the stile to the picnic area with toilets.

5 Go over the next stile, by the main road, then turn right over the bridge. Take the footpath to the right, down the steps. Go over the stile and back along the river, keeping to the line of the hedge. After ½ mile (800m), veer right to follow a series of waymarks. At the end cross the wooden bridge then a ladder stile and ascend through woodland. At the top of the wood turn right along a woodland path. (If the tide is in, stay with the hedge on your left to cross the stone bridge and turn right into the woodland.)

6 Leaving the wood, take the paved path by the river, almost to the castle walls. At the fork, go left through the white gate and ascend with the castle walls ahead of you. Later go through another gate and cross a small park. At the main road turn right, go over the bridge, cross the road, then go left along High Greens. In 200yds (182m) turn left into Bell Tower Place then, at a school, keep right to the Bell Tower.

7 Cross the road and continue down to Berwick Holiday Centre. Turn right onto a paved path (with the golf course on your left). Later join a road, then bear right under the arch of Cow Port. Keep left and left again to the Berwick Ramparts. Follow the path to your right, passing the Powder Magazine and Coxson's Tower. Stay on the wall, with the river on your left, to Berwick Old Bridge. Turn right, up the hill to the car park.

Distance: 5 miles (8km)
Total ascent: 100ft (30m)
Paths: undefined in places; can be muddy
Terrain: fields, town
Gradients: some steps
Refreshments: plenty in town
Park: the Maltings car park, Berwick upon Tweed

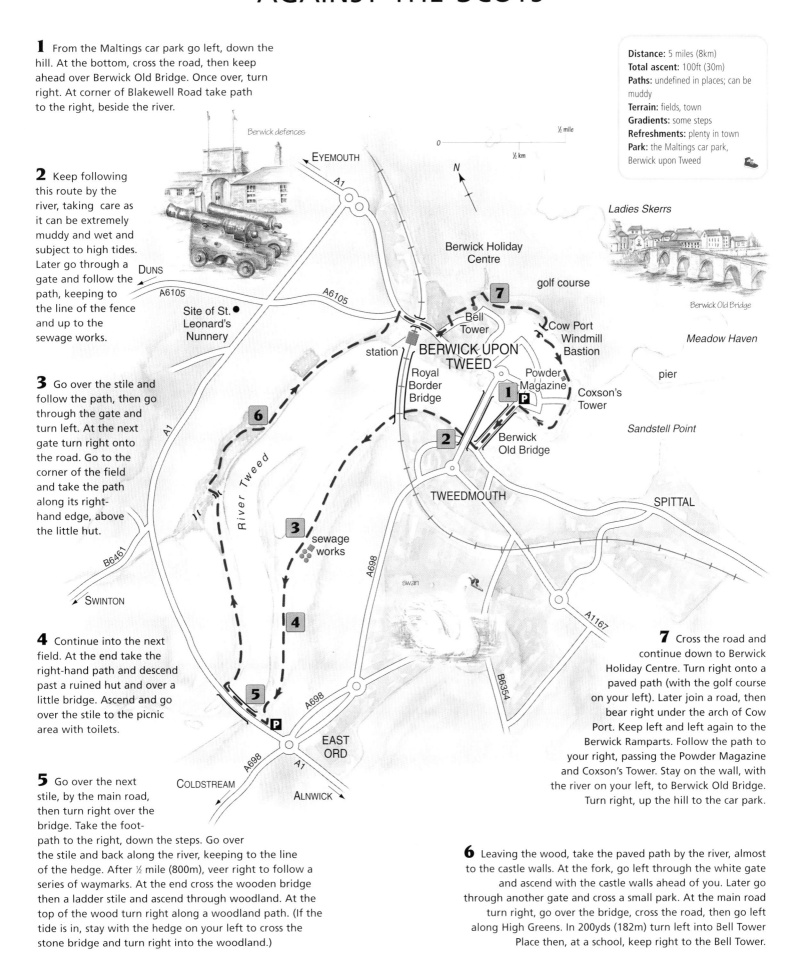

SCOTLAND

THE EMPEROR HADRIAN HAD his men build a wall from coast to coast across the top of England to keep out, or at least to regulate the passage of, the barbarians to the north. This was one in a series of border struggles which were only brought to an official end in 1706, when Scotland united with England and Wales. The arguments still rumble on, for the Scottish identity is a strong one, though the establishment of an autonomous Scottish Parliament at the devolution of 1999 went some way to fulfilling the Scots desire for independence.

The border today is further north than Hadrian's crumbled wall, but tall pele towers hidden among the trees and fierce traditions of common riding upheld in the wool towns of the Tweed Valley are reminders of later skirmishes in the eastern Lowlands. To the west, tales of raiders and pirates still colour the Galloway coastline, immortalised in the novels of S R Crockett and Sir Walter Scott. In fact, Scott, with his stirring stories of Highland heroes (and heroines), and dramatic tales of Scottish history in a romantic landscape, is frequently credited with single-handedly popularising the attractions of his native land. Certainly visitors are drawn here by the wide open spaces and magnificent landscapes, infused with a turbulent history.

Scotland's story is of a nation constantly divided against itself, for political or religious reasons. The land, scored through by the sweeping fault line of the Great Glen, lends itself to division – but this is more apparent in the people than in the landscape. The Highlanders of the north-west were Celts, eking a subsistence from their crofts and living under a system of extended family, or clanship. Those of the east and south farmed a more fertile land, and were of mixed blood that stemmed from trading with the Norse, Picts and English.

Today, of course, the Scots are largely urban, but divisions remain just below the surface. The New Town of Edinburgh has gracious Georgian buildings growing around the twin landmarks of Arthur's Seat and the old castle which still dominate the city today. Less than 50 miles (80km) away across the pinched waistline of Scotland, the industrial sprawl of Glasgow contains a contrasting and very splendid Victorian heart (along with a healthy disrespect for fancy Edinburgh 'airs'). Scotland's other great cities include St Andrews, seat of learning since 1412 and the queen of golfing resorts, and Aberdeen, capital of the northeast, a trading and fishing port which took new life from the off-shore oil industry. Between and beyond these great cities lies some of Britain's most spectacular scenery, which includes its highest mountain, deepest lake, largest trees and most remote area of wilderness. Scotland is a country of superlatives which, sadly, the Emperor Hadrian failed to appreciate.

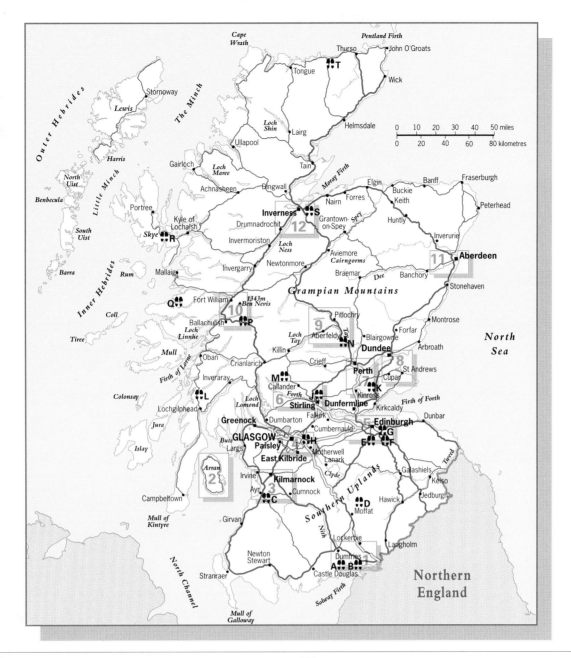

SECTION CONTENTS

FEATURES

WALKS

THE WESTERN BORDERLANDS

A land that was once in the midst of border warfare between the Scots and the English is now a haven of peace and tranquillity, with quiet roads, lush pastures, hills and woodlands. Robert Burns wrote over 100 of his poems here, Robert the Bruce began Scotland's quest for nationhood here in 1306, and countless couples plighted their troth at Gretna Green.

Caerlaverock Castle, with its mighty round towers still largely intact, is an impressive sight

The Robert Burns Centre by the banks of the River Nith

and beside the 15th-century bridge, the Old Bridge House Museum illustrates everyday life in the town.

Whitesands, is a pleasant river-front area on the east bank, while on the west bank is the 18th-century watermill which now houses the Robert Burns Centre, commemorating the poet's association with the town. He spent the last three years of his life here and his house, his mausoleum in St Michael's churchyard and the centre are all on a heritage trail.

The Dumfries Museum is the largest museum in south-west Scotland and portrays the region's history; the Camera Obscura of 1836 on the top floor gives a panoramic view of the town and surrounding countryside.

Caerlaverock

Caerlaverock Castle was built in 1290 for the Maxwells and has the unique shape of a triangular shield, fronted by a twin towered gatehouse and surrounded by a moat. In 1301 the castle was captured by Edward I, then retaken by Maxwell's forces in 1312. It's final battle was in 1640, when it fell to the Covenanters following a 13-week siege.

The Wildlife and Wetlands Trust's Reserve on the north Solway shore encompasses 1,350 acres (527ha) of saltwater marsh. It has outstanding hide and observation facilities, giving impressive views of the huge numbers of wildfowl that over-winter here, including thousands of barnacle geese. There are also pinkfooted and greylag geese, waders, whooper swans and many varieties of duck. The rare natterjack toad is another inhabitant.

Dumfries

In 1306, in what was then Greyfriars Abbey, Robert the Bruce stabbed Sir John Comyn, representative of Edward I, and began Scotland's quest for nationhood. Eight miles (12.9km) from the sea, this former seaport straddles the River Nith,

Ecclefechan

Thomas Carlyle, the essayist and historian, was born at Ecclefechan in 1795 and his grave is in the churchyard of Hoddom Castle, 2 miles (3.2km) away to the southwest. His house is now a museum with a collection of letters and other memorabilia. The Burnsward to the north of the town has a complex of early earthwork fortresses, which, as in so many other places, were later adapted by the Romans.

Gretna Green

This village in Dumfries and Galloway owes its fame to the fact that, after marriage by declaration was banned in England in 1754, it was the nearest point for runaway couples to secure a legitimate marriage under the laxer Scottish law.

The blacksmith, popularly known as 'the anvil priest', would, in front of witnesses, hear the declaration of elopers' willingness to marry. After 1856 it became necessary for one of the parties to have been resident in Scotland for 21 days prior to the ceremony, but marriage by declaration was not prohibited until 1940. Exhibitions at the Blacksmith's Shop Centre tell Gretna's story.

Scots Wha Hae

Robert Burns, Scotland's national poet, now enjoys world acclaim. His birthday on January 25th is celebrated worldwide as Burns' Night. Although he was born in Alloway, much of his important writing life was spent in Dumfries. From his farm at Ellisland, 6 miles (9.7km) north of the town, he wrote 'Tam O'Shanter' and re-penned 'Auld Lang Syne'.

For those prepared to penetrate the Scottish dialect, they will find a man ahead of his time. Despite a rakish reputation, his writing reflects a champion of noble causes and an advocate for a compassionate society.

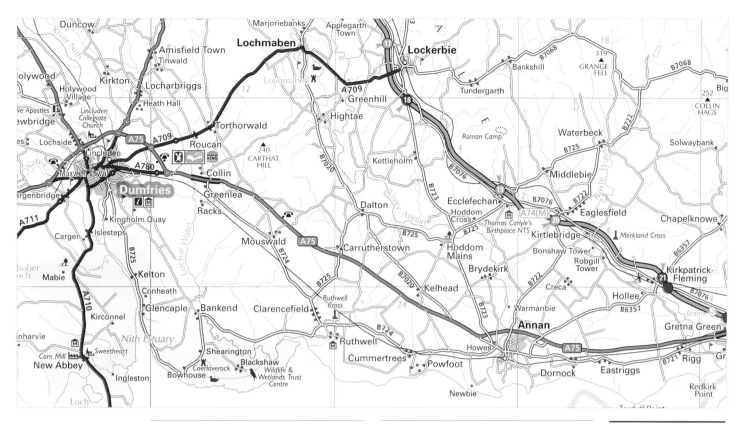

Kirkpatrick Fleming

This is where Robert the Bruce is said to have spent three months in a cave and been inspired by the unrelenting efforts of a spider. The cave, on an open cliff face, is thought to have megalithic origins. Until recently it could only be reached by a rope descent, but there is now a footpath.

Britain's worst rail disaster, in which over 200 people died, occurred at nearby Quintinshill signal box in 1915. The Station Inn contains sad reminders of the event, along with other railway memorabilia.

Lochmaben

This was the birthplace of the victor of Bannockburn, and the Latin inscription on the statue of Robert the Bruce at the head of main street reads 'From us is sprung the liberator king.' As a former headquarters for English forces, the town was a focal point in frequent border skirmishes and wars. As if that wasn't trouble enough, the town also had to endure the constant feuding between the Johnstones and the Maxwells, culminating in a final conflict beside the River Dryfe and defeat for the Maxwells. Of Lochmaben's two castles, the first, belonging to the Brus family, is now just a mound and the second is a ruin beside the loch.

New Abbey

This graceful village is dominated by the beautiful ruins of Sweetheart Abbey. It was founded in 1273 by Devorgilla Balliol to the romantic memory of her husband, John, whose embalmed heart she carried in a casket until her own death, when it was buried with her. She commemorated his name by founding Balliol College, part of Oxford University.

Close by is Shambellie House, a Victorian mansion housing a Museum of Costume. The New Abbey Corn Mill, dating from the 18th century, is restored and still grinds oatmeal on traditional stone.

Ruthwell

In an apse in Ruthwell's church stands one of Europe's finest early Christian stone crosses, dating from the 7th century. Standing 18ft (5.5m) high, it is carved with runic and Latin inscriptions around biblical scenes. It was badly damaged in 1642, but restored by the Rev Dr Henry Duncan, the parish minister. He also founded the world's first savings bank in his cottage. It succeeded, even though it was managed on draconian lines, with depositors fined for any default. The Savings Bank Museum in the reverend's former house focuses on the growth of savings banks from 1810 to the present day.

Tourist Information Centres

Castle Douglas: Markethill Car Park (seasonal) (tel: 01556 502611)
Dumfries: 64 Whitesands (tel: 01387 253862)
Gatehouse of Fleet: Car Park (seasonal) (tel: 01557 814212)
Kirkcudbright: Harbour Square (seasonal) (tel: 01557 330494)

See Walk A page 334
Four Kingdoms from Criffel

See Walk B page 335
Caerlaverock and the Rich Solney Marshes

Sweetheart Abbey's ruins include the 90ft (27m) central tower and much of the nave and transepts

THE ISLE OF ARRAN

Arran is sometimes described as 'Scotland in miniature'. It is also one of Scotland's best-kept secrets. Because it lies off the Ayrshire coast, it is easy to suppose that the island must share the gentle lowland landscape of that region. What a surprise, then, when the sharp Arran peaks come into view across the water!

Brodick

The setting of Brodick in its wide bay, backed by high peaks, with Brodick Castle rising from the trees on the lower slopes, is remarkably beautiful. The Castle, formerly owned by the Dukes of Hamilton, was taken over by the National Trust for Scotland in 1957. Retaining the warm and surprisingly intimate air of a family home, its garden is one of the most charming on the west coast, with semi-tropical plants and trees and a delightful water garden.

The award-winning Arran Heritage Museum is housed in an attractive cluster of low white buildings. It was founded by local people to show every aspect of island life in the past. Three rooms in one of the cottages are furnished as they would have been in the early 20th century and there is a forge, a dairy and an extensive archive. The original village of Brodick was on the

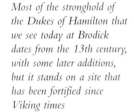

Most of the stronghold of the Dukes of Hamilton that we see today at Brodick dates from the 13th century, with some later additions, but it stands on a site that has been fortified since Viking times

north side of the bay, below the castle, and the remains of this earlier settlement can be seen at Cladach.

Corrie

Lying below the peaks of the north, Corrie was once the source of sandstone for building in the area. Seen from the sea, backed by the granite peaks and with the White Water burn flowing down to the shore, the Corrie was deservedly called one of the prettiest villages in Europe by Prime Minister Herbert Asquith.

Above the village is High Corrie, an older settlement built on an earlier shoreline – the 'raised beach' which circles much of the island. This idyllic clachan, in a natural garden of short springy turf with outcrops of rock, enjoys a delightful situation between mountain and sea.

The Glens

The Arran glens, some small and mysterious, others grand and dramatic, attract climbers, walkers and picnickers. Glen Rosa, running inland from Brodick, is a wide and peaceful valley, ideal for a gentle walk. Glen Sannox is sharper, and awe-inspiring in stormy weather. Each glen has its particular character, and the burns flowing through them are a constant pleasure; some steep as a staircase with many waterfalls, others a quiet flow of water with deep pools. A trek up the wild and lonely Catacol Glen leads to Loch Tanna.

Lochranza

Lochranza is dominated by its ruined castle, which stands on a promontory running out into the sea loch. The castle probably dates from the 13th or 14th century and was once a royal hunting lodge. In stark contrast is the newly-built distillery.

A rewarding walk from Lochranza to the Cock of Arran starts on a track, well signed, on the far side of the Chalmadale

Prehistoric Stones

Of all prehistoric sites on Arran the most impressive are those on Machrie Moor – visible even from the distant String Road in their isolated moorland setting. The site is signposted just south of Machrie on the A841, from where the standing stones are reached via an ancient track which passes through the derelict Moss Farm. The Auchgallon stone circle, dating from the Bronze Age, is the most accessible and is well preserved in an attractive situation. Unfortunately many of the ancient sites are engulfed in forestry plantations, robbing them of their former wild and open aspect. Carn Ban, probably the highest prehistoric site in Arran, is surrounded by conifer plantations, though because it stands high there are views over some of the trees. It is reached by a long and sometimes muddy walk of about 3¾ miles (6km) from the A841.

One very large stone circle is Kilpatrick Dun, thought to have been a defended farmstead about 1,800 years ago. The quiet and open position and the beautiful view north to the cliffs and fort of Drumadoon combine to make this great ring of stones and turf dyke a magical place. It is reached by a rough cart-track which starts just outside the farmyard at Kilpatrick Farm.

Arran Wildlife

In summer bird-watching tours can be arranged and offer the chance to see a golden eagle soaring above the granite cliffs. Arran's bird life is extensive and it is only necessary to pause by the shore to see a great variety of seabirds. The coast road between Brodick and Corrie runs near the water, and shelduck, eider, mallard, shags, cormorants and herons are a common sight here. A group of diving gannets, wings streamlined as they plummet from a great height into the water for fish, is a thrilling spectacle, and not unusual along the Corrie, Catacol and Pirnmill shores.

A virus took its toll of the seal population in the late 1980s, but these delightful creatures are again numerous and can be seen basking on the rocks just to the north of Brodick below the castle. Porpoises, which could once be seen rolling and leaping in the water quite near the shoreline, are now uncommon; but that immense (and harmless) creature the basking shark patrols the inshore waters from time to time. Its great dorsal fin, sailing along smoothly with only an occasional movement in the water to indicate the shark's length, is indeed an astonishing sight.

Tourist Information Centres

Brodick: The Pier (tel: 01770 302140/302401)

Arran is dotted with ancient and mysterious stones – these are known as Giant Graves

Burn. A slow, but not too steep climb above the village leads to a moorland plateau, finally dropping down to a marvellous viewpoint overlooking the Sound of Bute. The ruins of the Cock Farm are far below – in summer almost submerged in bracken – and on the lower level are the remains of the coal mines which provided fuel for the salt production in this area. This route can be retraced, or you can turn left at sea level and return to Lochranza by the coast – something of a scramble on the rocky foreshore, which can be wet and muddy approaching the village, but on a fine sunny day the views are unsurpassed and the absolute silence of this inaccessible part of the coast is truly memorable.

Mid Thundergay and Coire Fhionn Lochan

Mid Thundergay, between Lochranza and Pirnmill, is the starting point for a walk which should not be missed by anyone able to tackle a moderately steep hillside. A signpost on the A841 points to Coire Fhionn Lochan, the most picturesque of the inland lochs. Follow the burn uphill for nearly 2 miles (3km) and the lochan comes suddenly into view – clear, clean and blue in a bowl of surrounding hills. It is fringed by a narrow white gravel beach. The views are splendid, taking in the peaks of Jura and the softer hills of Islay, seen over the Mull of Kintyre.

The beautiful Arran Tapestry can be seen at the Arran Heritage Museum in Brodick

THE LAND OF ROBERT BURNS

This is probably one of the most sung songs, after 'Happy Birthday to You', but few could get past the first verse and a chorus, and fewer still could tell you what 'auld lang syne' means. Even through the dialect, the complete song portrays a sentimental celebration of enduring friendship.

Should auld acquaintance be forgot,
And never brought to mind?
Should auld acquaintance be forgot,
And days o' lang syne?

For auld lang syne, my jo,
For auld lang syne,
We'll tak a cup o' kindness yet
For auld lang syne.

And surely ye'll be your pint-stowp
And surely I'll be mine!
And we'll tak a cup o' kindness yet
For auld lang syne.

We twa hae run about the braes,
And pou'd the gowans fine
But we've wander'd mony a weary foot
Sin auld lang syne.

We twa hae paidl'd i' the burn
Frae mornin sun till dine,
But seas between us braid hae roar'd
Sin auld lang syne.

And there's a han' my trusty fiere!
And gie's a hand o' thine.
And we'll tak a right gude willy waucht
For auld lang syne.

This stretch of coastline is the playground for Glasgow and industrial south-west Scotland, with sandy beaches, first-class golf links and the promise of lively nightlife in the vibrant resort of Ayr. The undulating landscape of rich farmland is peppered with noble castles, while to the east of Kilmarnock are the deeper clefts of the Irvine Valley.

Ayr, the Burns Monument, the Brig O' Doon and pleasant gardens by the banks of the River Ayr

A replica suit of 15th-century armour from the collection at Dean castle, Kilmarnock

Ayr

With a seafront esplanade stretching for 2½ miles (4km), Ayr is famed as the favourite resort of the Clyde towns. As well as its broad beach, the town is blessed with lovely gardens and parks, and Belleisle has an aviary and two golf courses. Family outdoor recreation is its forte, but history and culture are not entirely lacking. Ayr's charter dates back to 1202, and south harbour is overlooked by the ruins of Cromwell's citadel and St John's Tower. And there is the inevitable Burns Heritage Trail. During the summer the *Waverley*, the last sea-going paddle steamer, offers popular excursions to Arran. Caledonian MacBrayne offer regular sailings year round. Ayr is Scotland's leading horse-racing venue, with both flat and national hunt meetings.

Irvine

At first glance Irvine has all the appearance of a 1960s town, but at its heart there is an old burgh with an interesting past. Until the Clyde was dredged, this was the port for Glasgow, and it is also noted for the Treaty of Irvine, signed in 1297 by William Wallace's deserters. It was also a place of inspiration – here Robert Burns, working as a flax dresser between 1781 and 1784, received the encouragement to have his work published. The Irvine Burns Club and Gallery in the restored cobbled Glasgow Vennel holds many manuscripts and first editions. Near by is Dreghorn, the birthplace of J B Dunlop, who invented the inflatable tyre.

The old harbourside district is overlooked by Seagate Castle, home to the Scottish Maritime Museum, where a collection of historic vessels includes the world's oldest clipper, the *Carrick*.

Among Irvine's modern attractions is the Magnum Leisure Centre, which offers swimming pools, ice rink, bowling, theatre and a choice of cinemas and the Big Idea, an interactive exhibit of invention and innovation, at the Harbourside.

Kilmarnock

This industrial town was once famous as the home of Johnny Walker whisky. It is also the place where John Wilson published the famous 'Kilmarnock' first edition of the poetry of Robert Burns, who is now commemorated with a new statue. Equally new is the redeveloped town centre, with its cobbled shopping mall. The leading museum is the Dick Institute, specialising in local archaeology, geology and natural

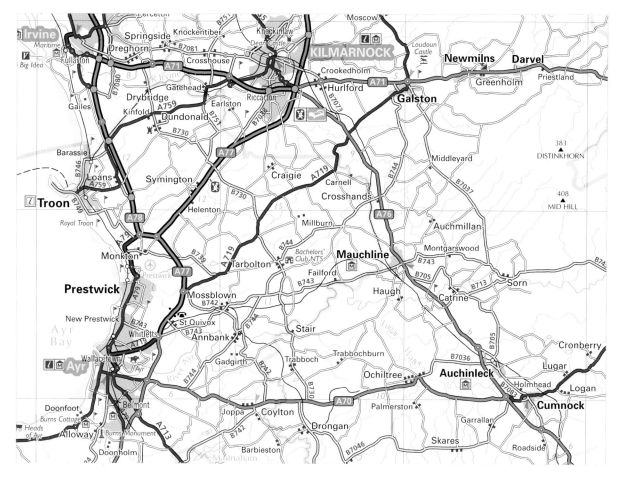

Tourist Information Centres

All telephone enquiries: 01292 678100

Personal callers:
Ayr: 39 Sandgate
Girvan: Bridge Street
Irvine: New Street
Isle of Cumbrae: 28 Stuart Street
Largs: Railway Station, Main Street

The Birthplace of Burns

The leafy suburb of Alloway at the southern edge of Ayr is where Robert Burns was born on 25 January 1759, and it attracts visitors by the coachload. The Birthplace Museum is adjacent to the white thatched cottage, built by his father, where Burns lived until he was seven years old. Near by are a cluster of Burns 'sites', including real-life landmarks from 'Tam o'Shanter', such as the Auld Brig O' Doon, over which Tam escaped the witches. The story is brought to life in the Tam o'Shanter Experience. Devotees can also seek out the Burns Monument, with its Corinthian pillars, the Auld Kirk.

history, which also has an art gallery with an important collection of paintings.

Dean Castle, the focal point of a 200-acre (81ha) country park with nature trails, started out as a 14th-century stronghold, but later developed into a palace. It contains a renowned collection of medieval ephemera, from armour and tapestries to musical instruments. The ruined Louden Castle, the place where the Act of Union was signed in 1707, is now a park.

Mauchline

Located on a rise some 8 miles (12.9km) south of Kilmarnock, this small town overlooks Mossgiel Farm, once farmed by Robert Burns. Many of his most significant works were written here, and some of the characters he wrote about now lie in the village churchyard, which was the setting for *Holy Fair*. At first glance signposts for the Burns Heritage Trail seem to outnumber the houses. They point out the Burns Museum in Castle Street, in the house he took when he married Jean Armour in 1788, the Burns Memorial Tower of 1896, Mauchline Castle and Poosie Nansie's Tavern, which is still a pub. Mauchline is also renowned for the manufacture of curling stones.

Five miles (8km) west in Tarbolton is the thatched cottage where Burns founded a debating society, the Bachelors' Club. Four miles (6.4km) to the east lies Sorn, a delightful riverside village with a 14th-century castle.

Troon

This dignified town has moved on from its fishing port origins to become a place for golf and yachting. Troon is almost surrounded by its five golf courses, the Royal Troon being the most prestigious, with its famous Postage Stamp, a par 3 short hole.

The Marine Highland Hotel is a landmark for miles around, and Troon's distinctive stalwart homes are embellished with turrets and towers. Three miles (4.8km) to the north-east are the impressive ruins of Dundonald Castle, where the Stuart dynasty was founded.

Golf attracts many visitors to Troon, who can play a different course on each weekday without having to travel too far. And it is just a short drive down the coast to Turnberry

See Walk C page 336
Burns' Alloway and the Brig O'Doon

THE 'DEAR, DIRTY CITY' ON THE CLYDE

This sprawling metropolis, famed for leading the industrial revolution, has undergone a self-imposed renaissance. Ship-building, steam locomotive works and other heavy engineering have given way to an image of art and culture. Set amongst some of the finest Victorian architecture in Britain, the reborn Glasgow offers a totally new experience in city sightseeing.

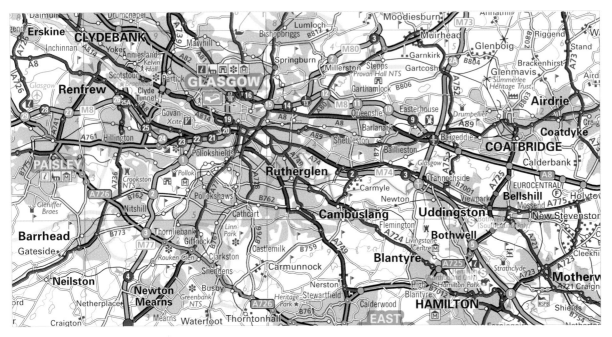

Tourist Information Centres

Glasgow: 11 George Square (tel: 0141 204 4400)
Hamilton: Road Chef Services, M74 northbound (tel: 01698 285590)
Paisley: 9a Gilmour Street (tel: 0141 889 0711)

Blantyre

The great explorer, David Livingstone, was born in Blantyre and at the age of ten worked in the local mill. The David Livingstone Centre, situated in the tenement block of his birth, traces his life in Africa and recalls his battle against slavers, his search for the source of the Nile and his famous meeting with Stanley.

To the north, standing above the Clyde, lies the breathtaking red sandstone ruin of Bothwell Castle, which saw much action during the 13th and 14th centuries. The immense circular tower tested the ingenuity of its attackers, including Edward I who, in 1301, stormed it with a siege tower taller than the battlements.

Coatbridge

Coatbridge is one of the great ironwork towns that sprang up with the Industrial Revolution. The Summerlee Heritage Trust, one of Scotland's most interesting and certainly noisiest museums, recreates an authentic look at 200 years of industrial and social history. Set in the old Summerlees ironworks of 1835, it has clattering working machinery, re-enactments, an electric tramway, a shallow mine and miners' cottages.

Glasgow

One of the most remarkable cities in Britain, Glasgow transformed its public image during the 1980s, throwing off its sometimes exaggerated reputation as a

The David Livingstone Centre, I presume. This tableau represents the explorer meeting native Africans

The Coat of Arms

The Glasgow crest features a salmon with a ring in its mouth. A curious image, until you hear the legend regarding Queen Languoreth, who, attracted by a knight, gave him a ring. The King, while resting during a hunting party, noticed the ring on the knight's finger and, suspecting an intrigue, took the ring off the sleeping knight's finger and threw it into the Clyde. He later questioned the Queen as to the whereabouts of the ring, and threatened her with death if she couldn't produce it. She pleaded with St Mungo, who sent a monk to fish the river. The first caught salmon was landed with the ring in its mouth.

Charles Rennie Mackintosh

Scotland's most famous architect, artist and designer was born in 1868. He spent most of his working life in Glasgow and was most active between 1897 and 1912. Many buildings feature his work including houses, schools and even a church. He is internationally acclaimed for transforming the Victorian influence into innovative art nouveau styles, applied to exteriors, interiors and furnishings. The Glasgow School of Art and the Willow Tearooms in Sauchiehall Street are noted achievements. A reconstruction of the interior of his own home can be viewed at the Hunterian Art Gallery.

rundown, post-industrial city and becoming known for its friendliness, vibrant arts and entertainment scene, first class shopping and superb museums and galleries.

Though Glasgow began to develop in the 18th century, through trading tobacco, cotton and sugar from America, it was the Industrial Revolution that really started its economic boom, and many of the city-centre buildings are bold statements in brick and stone of Glasgow's 19th-century prosperity and pride. In recent years the grime has been wiped away, displaying these fine buildings in all their glory, set off by exciting new architectural developments. Buildings range from the medieval splendours of the city's cathedral, founded in the 6th century by St Kentigern (St Mungo) and the most complete medieval cathedral in mainland Scotland, to the charms of the Willow Tearooms in Sauchiehall Street. These were designed by Charles Rennie MacKintosh, Glasgow's major architectural force of the early 20th century – don't miss his Glasgow School of Art or the House for an Art Lover in Bellahouston Park.

Bellahouston is only one of Glasgow's lovely parks and gardens; others include the Botanic Gardens, Greenbank and Pollok Country Park. The latter houses not only Pollok House, home to the Stirling Maxwell collection of fine and decorative arts, but also the magnificent Burrell Collection, in its purpose-built gallery. The 8,000 items were amassed by Sir William Burrell, who presented them to the city in 1944. Highlights include fine art, ceramics and superb examples of stained glass and tapestries. Other fine pictures, and much more, are found at the Kelvingrove Art Gallery and Museum, the city's main museum, the Hunterian Art Gallery and Glasgow Gallery of Modern Art.

Glasgow's history is related at the People's Palace, while Clydebuilt is a superb new interactive museum devoted to Glasgow and the Clyde. Pride of place goes to the Glasgow Science Centre, an architecturally stunning flagship attraction beside the Clyde, which celebrates science innovation with interactive exhibits, Scotland's only IMAX cinema and much more.

Hamilton

Bordering the Strathclyde Country Park, Hamilton has a history stretching back to the 6th century, but its 19th-century prosperity was firmly based on the mining

industry. The hugely rich Dukes of Hamilton were its lairds; they built the bizarre hunting lodge of Chatelherault overlooking the Clyde Valley, while the 10th Duke was buried in an Egyptian sarcophagus within the extraordinary Hamilton Mausoleum. The Low Parks Museum, occupying a fine 17th-century house, tells the story of the Dukes' and the town.

Motherwell

Motherwell (its name comes from a healing well) was once a proud industrial centre which saw its last days of steel with the closure of the Ravenscraig works. The town stands on the edge of Strathclyde Country Park, part of which is home to M & D's Theme Park, complete with thrill rides and a range of other attractions.

Paisley

This pleasing industrial town is the place where the handkerchief was invented, but more famously it has given its name to the Kashmiri teardrop design on fabrics. The Museum and Art Gallery contains some 500 shawls, reflecting the town's days as a weaving centre, and The Sma' Shot Cottages are now a museum illustrating the life of weavers and mill workers. Later the town became the world's largest manufacturer of cotton thread. The 12th-century Abbey, restored by Sir Robert Lorimer in 1897, is noted for its depictions of the life of St Mirren.

Pollock House was given to the city in 1966 after 700 years as the home of the Maxwell family. It contains the remarkable Stirling Maxwell collection of Spanish paintings

See Walk H page 341
Glasgow's Not-so-mean Streets

One of Glasgow's most famous buildings is Mackintosh's School of Art

SCOTLAND'S HISTORIC CAPITAL

*T*his is a city built on hills, and from its high crests and ridges are views which overlord its steeples, twisting medieval wynds and the neat symmetry of its delightful Georgian crescents and squares – and the freshness of the surrounding hills is ever present. From the famous castle, the boom of the 'one o'clock ' gun reverberates across the city, signalling the exact time to shipping on the Firth of Forth.

Sunset over Edinburgh, as seen from Calton Hill

Cramond

A pleasant village of white cottages and narrow alleys, Cramond is set above the anchorage where the River Almond flows into the Forth, with the uninhabited Cramond Island just offshore. The Romans established a substantial fortress at Cramond, with a small settlement including a bath house, and the ruins and outlines can be seen behind the church. To the southeast is Lauriston Castle.

Edinburgh

Scotland's capital has everything a capital city should have – a castle, a royal palace, national collections of art, splendid museums, excellent shopping, fine architecture and lovely parks. It is compact enough to explore on foot, but it's hilly, so start out on high ground, enjoy the wonderful views to the surrounding hills and the Firth of Forth, then explore downhill.

The city centre has two distinct parts. The New Town, to the north, is an architectural set-piece of Georgian townhouses lining gracious streets, squares and crescents. Princes Street, overlooking the Castle, is the main thoroughfare, a busy street with high street stores, while parallel George Street offers more up-market shopping. Charlotte Square is the jewel of the New Town, and number 7 has been restored to its late 18th-century style.

The Old Town, south and east of the castle ridge, brims with curiosity and history. Tall tenements and public buildings set in cobbled streets are the keynotes here, with atmospheric wynds and alleys to explore. It is dominated by the Castle, stategically set on an extinct volcanic plug and guarded by sentries in Scottish regimental uniform. The buildings have served various purposes over the past 900 years, with the oldest – tiny St Margaret's Chapel – dating from the 11th century. The Great Hall, with its hammerbeam ceiling, was where the Scottish Parliament met until 1639. The adjacent palace, where Mary, Queen of Scots gave birth to James VI & I, also houses Scotland's crown jewels and regalia and the Stone of Destiny, returned from Westminster Abbey in 1998.

The Edinburgh Festival

Founded in 1947, the three-week festival for the visual and performing arts which takes place every August and September, is now the world's premier cultural event. There are two distinct sides. The 'official', with set programmes for opera, ballet, dance and theatre, and the 'fringe', which of late has almost dominated the 'official'. However, each complements the other. Attendees are advised to book early, especially their accommodation.

The Military Tattoo has been a feature of the EdinburghFestival for nearly 50 years and takes place on the Esplanade of the Castle

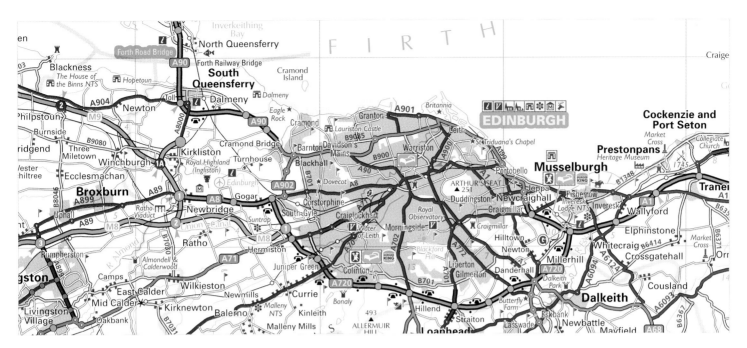

The magnificent scale of the Forth road and rail bridges can best be appreciated from the foreshore at South Queensferry

The Forth Bridges

Opened in 1890 at a cost of over £3 million, the Forth railway bridge was considered the 'Eighth Wonder of the World'. Construction began in 1882 under Sir John Fowler and Benjamin Baker, and at its height it employed 4,600 men. The viaduct, standing 157ft (47.8m) above the water, is 8,296ft (2,528.7m) long, comprising 53,000 tons of steel that require 7,000 gallons of paint. The 1½ mile (2.4km) long suspension bridge for motor traffic was opened in 1964.

The Royal Mile connects the Castle with the Palace of Holyroodhouse, the Scottish royal residence. Alongs its length, visitors can learn about the city and its citizens at the People's Story Museum, Huntly House Museum, the Writer's Museum – devoted to Burns, Scott and Stevenson – and Gladstone's Land, a restored 17th-century tenement.

There's more history at the stunning Museum of Scotland and the adjoining Royal Museum, while art lovers can head for the old masters at the National Gallery of Scotland or the National Gallery of Modern Art. State-of-the-art attractions include Dynamic Earth, Edinburgh's award-winning millennium project, which tells the story of the planet, and Shaping a Nation, a highly interactive museum celebrating Scottish creativity and innovation.

Prestonpans

Eight miles (12.9km) to the east of Edinburgh, Prestonpans takes its name from its medieval salt pans, and it has many houses dating from the 17th century. Preston

Tower is a fortified tower house with an interesting stone dovecote that could roost nearly 1,000 birds. The Mercat Cross is considered the finest in Scotland.

This was the site of the Jacobite victory of Preston Pans in 1745 (over in minutes). More recent history is on show at the Scottish Mining Museum at nearby Newtongrange, in the oldest documented coal-mining site in Britain, which has been worked for some 800 years.

South Queensferry

This delightful village, on the shore of the Forth, has the best view of the bridges, and of Inchcolm Island, with its 12th-century Abbey. As its name suggests, this was the ferry point from 1169 until the opening of the road bridge in 1964. Just outside the nearby village of Dalmeny, Dalmeny House contains the Rosebery Collections of paintings, furniture, tapestries and porcelain, while 2 miles (3.2km) west is Hopetoun House, Scotland's finest Adam mansion, with beautiful furniture and a notable collection of paintings.

Tourist Information Centres

Bo'ness: Hamilton Cottage, Union Street (tel: 01506 826626)
Edinburgh: 3 Princes Street (tel: 0131 473 3800)
Edinburgh Airport: (tel 0131 333 2167)
Musselburgh: Brunton Hall (tel: 0131 665 6597)
Old Craighall: Service Area, by Musselburgh (tel: 0131 653 6172)
Penicuik: The Library, 3 Bellman's Road (tel: 01968 72340/673286)

See Walk E page 338
Through the Wild Pentland Hills

See Walk F page 339
Mysteries of Rosslyn

See Walk G page 340
Edinburgh's Literary Past

THE WILDLIFE OF SCOTLAND

From soaring crags to misty marshland, from mountain top to coastline, from lowland plain to high moorland, the habitats of Scotland are immensely varied. Sub-tropical trees flourish less than 50 miles (80km) from the north coast in Inverewe gardens, warmed by the Gulf Stream. On the Cairngorm plateau genuine Arctic conditions, more typical of regions 1,000 (1,609km) miles north, prevail. Between these two extremes lie the high moorland, the lush glens, the rock-bound coasts and the gentle rivers that are home to many distinctive species.

Only the luckiest visitor will see Scotland's most precious treasures – the golden eagle, the osprey or the red squirrel. Nor are the fierce wild cats easy to spot in moorland and forest. Otters, too, are seldom seen, though they hunt beside the seashore of the west coast and among the islands as well as by inland burns. Despite their rarity, however, such species seem unlikely to go the way of others – wild reindeer died out here in the 12th century, the beaver probably in the 15th (though there are plans to reintroduce it), and the last wolf in Scotland was killed in 1743.

FORESTS OLD AND NEW

Many of the lost animals of Scotland needed the huge stretches of native pine forest which once covered much of Scotland. Now only one per cent of the Caledonian Forest survives, having fallen victim to man's greed for timber.

Eighteenth-century iron smelting accounted for the loss of many trees, which were felled and floated down the rivers to be burned for charcoal to fuel the furnaces. Others produced valuable timber, while deliberate clearance of forest (as well as of inhabitants) to introduce vast sheep runs accounted for much more. The bare, open, rocky landscape of much of the Highlands, although admired by visitors, is to a large extent the result of these predations.

Where there is forest today, much of it is the result of planting since the two world wars, and, although in recent years the ruler-straight edges have given way to more sensitive planting, the denseness, uniformity and blanketing effect of the trees have been much criticised. There has also been controversy over the commercial afforestation of large areas of open land, such as the unique bogland environment of the Flow Country of Sutherland and Caithness.

Where pockets of native pinewood survive – at the Black Wood of Rannoch and Rothiemurchus Forest by the Cairngorms, for example – they are magical places, with mosses, blaeberries and junipers plentiful amid the trees, and wildflowers such as wintergreens and lady's tresses.

There are ancient oak woods, too, especially in the Argyll glens towards the Atlantic coast, where gnarled trees are hung with lichens and the forest floor is home to an amazing multitude of ferns and flowers. In places, too, are survivors of ancient birch forests – among the most accessible of them is the Birks of Aberfeldy.

Upper Loch Torriden, a beautiful sea loch on the west coast, is bordered by magnificent Highland scenery

A RECORD DOZEN

The climate of Scotland is excellent for trees of all types – which may be why 12 of Britain's 30 tallest trees are here, among them a dead heat of two Douglas firs at The Hermitage in Perthshire and Dunans in Argyll, both of which measure 212ft (64.5m). Tayside also has the tallest holly and beech – both 150ft (46m) – at Hallyburton House, as well as a Sitka spruce measuring 200ft (61m) at Strathearn. Other giants are the 206ft (63m) grand fir at Strone in Argyll and a western hemlock 167ft (51m) near by at Benmore; and – a pigmy by comparison – the 98ft (30m) silver birch at Ballogie in Grampian. Scotland holds two sequoia records – for the tallest in Britain, 174ft (53m) at Strathpeffer, and for the largest, at Clunie Gardens in Tayside, with a diameter of 11ft 4in (3.5m). And as for age, the UK's oldest known tree still survives near Aberfeldy – the Fortingall Yew. It is thought to be around 1,500 years old.

At the other extreme are the miniature willow forests that clothe some Scottish mountains, high above the normal treeline. Cold and infertile, often covered with snow which may linger into the summer, these are inhospitable climates for vege-

tation. But still plants survive, often clustered in hollows or forming dense mats of green, which may suddenly burst into colourful flower in favourable conditions. Ben Lawers in Perthshire is particularly famous for the variety of its mountain flowers, including such rarities as the vivid blue alpine gentian and the drooping saxifrage.

Animals and birds, too, need to be hardy to survive the high mountain tops. The ptarmigan is one, often seen by skiers; its mottled brown plumage turns white in winter. A summer visitor, the dotterel, is much rarer; it breeds regularly in the eastern Highlands. Snow buntings also visit from their Arctic homes in the summer, but few stay to breed. The only butterfly regularly breeding here is the mountain ringlet. Mountain hares and stoats survive on the rocky slopes; they, too, go white in the winter.

MOORS AND SHORES

On lower moorland two game species come into their own – the red deer and the grouse.

Enduring symbols of the wildlife of Scotland: leaping salmon, top left, red deer, above, and the well-camouflaged ptarmigan, left

Britain's largest wild animal, the red deer was encouraged by Victorian landowners for sport, and stalking is still important in some areas. The sight of a magnificently antlered stag in a misty valley has been a favourite image of Scotland since before Landseer painted *The Monarch of the Glen*. The managed heather moors, where regular burning helps regenerate the plants, provide the habitat for many grouse – the red is the main target for sportsmen. Larger is the black grouse; each male has its territory – called a lek – where pinewoods meet moorland. The capercaillie, hunted to extinction in Scotland by 1800, was reintroduced in 1837 and is now found deep in the woodlands of the east of the country. Where bogland predominates –

in the Flow Country, for example, and on Rannoch Moor – domes of bog moss can provide striking colours in the landscape, from the brightest greens to stabbing orange and yellow. Where the bogs are wettest, plants like the cranberry gain a foothold, as well as the insect-eating sundew. Glittering dragonflies are often seen flittering over bogland.

In extreme contrast are the flower-rich sea-meadows – the machair – which lie behind many Highland beaches, and are particularly spectacular on the shores of the Outer Hebrides, where the shell sand tempers the acidity of the peat soil. Here buttercups, orchids and gentians grow in colourful profusion. The primrose banks of Barra are especially wonderful.

Birds, too, congregate on the islands. Remote St Kilda has its own species of wren, while Foula in Shetland has vast numbers of great skuas, and in the friable mountainsides of Rum in the Inner Hebrides thousands of Manx sheerwaters have their burrows. On the mainland, the cliffs of Sutherland are thronged with colonies of fulmars, kittiwakes and guillemots, the mouth of the Tay with eider duck and the Solway estuary with barnacle geese.

The leaping salmon, on its journey upstream to its spawning grounds, is king of Scottish fish, but the claims of the more prosaic sea trout and mountain trout cannot be disregarded. In deep mountain lochs the ferox trout – golden and spotted with black – keeps company with its red and black relative, the char. In the deepest of all – Loch Ness – may lurk the most mysterious of all Scotland's wildlife. If it does, it will add another aspect to the rich diversity of the country's treasures.

STIRLING AND THE TROSSACHS

'So wond'ous wild, the whole night might seem, the scenery of a feary dream.' So wrote Sir Walter Scott, who set two of his greatest works, *Rob Roy* and *The Lady of the Lake* in the Trossachs around Loch Katrine. Poets and writers have long been inspired by the scenery of hills and lochs. Coleridge, the Wordsworths, Ruskin and Hogg all succumbed to its spell.

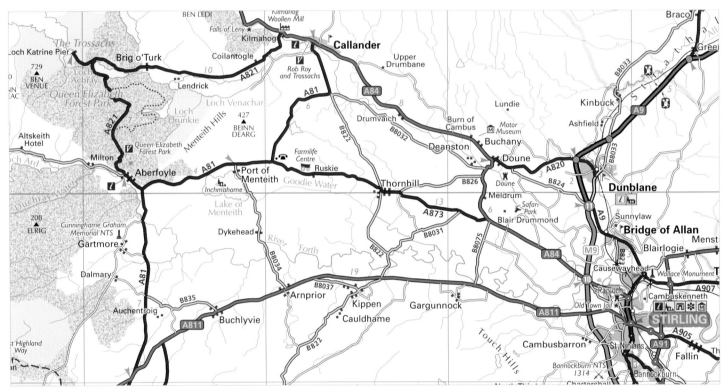

This fine bronze statue of Robert the Bruce, unveiled at the Bannockburn Heritage Centre in 1964, commemorates his great victory over the English

Aberfoyle

Tucked below the slopes of the Trossachs, Aberfoyle is a popular tourist centre. The Scottish Wool Centre here embraces every aspect of wool production, from shearing, carding and spinning to weaving and traditional knitting. The town is handy for the spectacular 67sq mile (173.5sq km) Queen Elizabeth Forest Park, which includes trails, picnic areas and wildlife lookouts. A scenic route into the Trossachs takes you over Dukes Pass, between Lochs Achray and Katrine. The Achray Forest Drive to Brig O'Turk and to the lochs of Ard and Chon is also beautiful.

Bannockburn

This suburb of Stirling was, in 1314, the site of the decisive defeat by Robert the Bruce of Edward II's English army, ten times larger than the Scots' force. The Bannockburn Heritage Centre includes an exhibition and audiovisual on the battle, outlining the confusion in the English army in the marshlands. The victory resulted in the surrender of Stirling Castle and recognition by the Pope of Robert the Bruce's kingship, culminating in Scottish independence. Though the Heritage Centre stands close to the Borderstone site, said to be Robert the Bruce's command post, the exact whereabouts of the battle ground is still disputed after all these years.

Callander

Set against a Highland backdrop, this neat market town and tourist centre, the 'gateway to the Highlands', was developed in the 18th century on forfeited Jacobite lands. The legends of its local hero, Rob Roy MacGregor, are retold in an audiovisual in the old kirk in the town centre.

Children love the Hamilton Toy Collection, while the whole family can escape the crowds on the scenic footpath to the lovely Bracklinn Falls.

Tourist Information Centres

Aberfoyle: Main Street, (seasonal) (tel: 01877 382352)
Callander: Ancaster Square (seasonal) (tel: 01877 330342)
Dunblane: Stirling Road (tel: 01786 824428)
Dunfermline: Maygate (tel: 01383 720999)
Stirling: 41 Dumbarton Road (tel: 01786 475019)
Castle Esplanade (tel: 01786 479901)

The summit of Ben An offers a wonderful view southwards across Loch Katrine and The Trossachs

Wallace and Bruce

Two of Scotland's fabled warrior heroes, who achieved their fame within sight of Stirling Castle. William Wallace, son of a Renfrewshire knight, was a resistance fighter and appointed Guardian of Scotland. His great victory in the Battle of Stirling Bridge in 1297 was short-lived. He was later captured and executed in London in 1305.

Robert the Bruce, born in 1274 of Norman ancestry, with lands in England, declared himself for Scotland and was crowned king in 1306. Even though defeated, excommunicated and outlawed, his guerrilla warfare campaign over many years culminated in victory at Bannockburn, which led to Scotland's independence in 1328. He died in Cardross Castle, possibly of leprosy, in 1329.

Doune

The awe-inspiring 14th- to 15th-century castle, with its fine tower and gatehouse, seat of the Earls of Moray, is strategically situated between the Rivers Teith and Ardoch. Two miles (3.2km) south is Blair Drummond Safari Park where visitors can drive through the wild animal reserves.

Dunblane

Though it is only a small place, Dunblane is actually a city because of its cathedral. Restored in the late-19th century, its origins go back to 1240, with foundations laid on the site of the church established by St Blane in AD 602.

Until the Reformation, Dunblane was a city of power and influence. Today it is remembered for the song, 'Jessie, the Flower of Dunblane', composed by a local weaver, and a complex tartan comprising 14 colours. Leighton Library holds 4,000 rare books, including Johnson's first dictionaries. The caves on the riverside walk to the Bridge of Allan are said to be where Robert Louis Stevenson often sought inspiration for his books. To the east lies the battlefield of Sheriffmuir, which, though an indecisive event, ended the 1715 Jacobite rebellion.

Lake of Mentieth

Scotland's only inland water not called a loch – an error by a Dutch engineer – is noted for curling in winter and fishing in the summer. The largest of the three islands on this serene loch is Inchmahome, with the ruins of an Augustinian priory. It was the hideout in 1547 of Mary, Queen of Scots, aged five, before her flight to France. The summer ferry will take you across.

Stirling

For centuries the lowest bridging point on the River Forth, Stirling, dominated by its castle, occupies the slopes of a volcanic outcrop above reclaimed marshland. A royal burgh since 1124, the city and its castle became a favourite with the Stuart monarchs, and Mary, Queen of Scots, was crowned here in 1543. Stirling is well endowed with splendid Scottish Renaissance buildings, notably Argyll's Lodgings, near the castle, and Mar's Wark, the ornate but incomplete palace of the Earl of Mar. Other landmarks include the Church of the Holy Rude, scene of James VI's coronation in 1567, Cowane's Hospital and the Tolbooth. Visitors can learn more of Stirling's history at the excellent Stirling Visitor Centre, while other attractions include the Old Town Jail, complete with living history performances, and the Smith Art Gallery and Museum.

To the north-east stands the National Wallace Monument, built in 1860 on an outcrop overlooking the scene of William Wallace's 1297 victory at Stirling Bridge. From the top of the 220ft (67m) tower there are panoramic views over the Ochil Hills and the Stirling plains, while the interior houses a Hall of Scottish heroes and gives an insight into Wallace's life.

Loch Katrine

This spectacular ten-mile (16.1km) loch is evocative of Sir Walter Scott's ballad, *The Lady of the Lake* and his novel *Rob Roy*, based on the legendary rebel. Best approached via Dukes Pass from Aberfoyle, this inspiring loch can be cruised in summer aboard the *Sir Walter Scott*, a steamer built in 1900. At the north-west end of the loch in Stronachlar is the graveyard of Clan MacGregor. Further on is Glengyle House, the birthplace of Rob Roy.

See Walk J page 342
Stirling, Cockpit of
Scottish History

THE FAIR CITY

T his area encompasses the long gone seat of the Scottish kings, which is now the 'Fair City' of Perth, and the pepperpot towers of Falkland Palace, a favourite of the Stuart monarchy. This is a historic 'royal' region of Scotland, where rich rolling farmlands, elegant fortified mansions and great country estates bask in the shelter of the Highlands.

From the top of Kinnoull Hill there is a magnificent view down over the River Tay and the Earl's Tower

Elcho Castle

This fortified mansion (pictured below, right) on the south bank of the Tay, complete with towers, turrets and crow-stepped gables, was built for the Earl of Wemyss in the late 16th century. Across the river lies 17th-century Megginch Castle, home of the Drummonds since soon after it was a built. First laid out in the 17th century, its formal gardens contain some superb and ancient holly and yew trees, a beautiful rose garden and an 18th-century physic garden incorporating astrological planting.

Falkland

Tucked beneath the Lomond Hills, this tiny Royal Burgh has over 100 listed buildings, with twisting wynds and courtyards between the cottages and sandstone town houses of the 17th to 19th centuries. Its fame and influence was at its height in the 16th and 17th centuries, when the turreted, Renaissance-style Falkland Palace, now owned by Her Majesty the Queen, was the favourite hunting lodge of the Stuart monarchs, particularly Mary, Queen of Scots. Royal monograms decorate the King's Bedchamber, while fine Flemish tapestries hang in the chapel, and a prime

feature is the tennis court of 1539, the oldest in Britain. The castle was sacked by Cromwell's forces, but restored by John Crichton Stuart in 1889, whose family still act as guardians for the Queen.

Kinross

This peaceful town on the banks of Loch Leven is surrounded by rich farmland, with the Cleish Hills in the south, the Ochills in the north and the Lomonds in the east.

The area is rich in historical sites and popular for country pursuits – the 4,000-acre (1,620ha) Loch Leven is world renowned for its fishing. The RSPB reserved at Vane Farm on the south side of the loch has hides for observing migrant geese and duck.

Close to the centre of the town, Kinross House is a Palladian-style mansion built in 1690 and noted for its formal gardens and yew hedges. Out in the loch, Castle Island, with its 14th-century fortress, is where in 1567 Mary, Queen of Scots was imprisoned until her romantic boat escape organised by Willie Douglas.

Perth

Once the capital of Scotland, this commercial centre, with its working port and fine Georgian buildings, maintains the atmosphere of a county town. Straddling the River Tay, it rose to eminence in AD 838, when Kenneth McAlpin, the first king of

Riches of The Tay

Rising in the Hills of Breadalbane, this river is Britain's largest in terms of volume, moving more water than the Severn and Thames combined. It is world famous for salmon and the coveted wild pearls from the freshwater mussel, *Unio Margaretifera*. Still fished in the traditional manner, the most exquisite pearl, known as the 'Abernethy', weighs 34 grains. The pearls vary in colour and lustre, from matt black to pink-white and white.

Rumbling Bridge

This wayside site, some 7 miles (11.3km) west of Kinross, is a long-time favourite, especially after heavy rains. The River Devon dashes over waterfalls through a deep cleft beneath the bridge, which curiously has been built over an earlier crossing, and there are footpaths and walkways along the side of the ravine. The heaviest 'rumbles' are heard to emanate from Devils Mill.

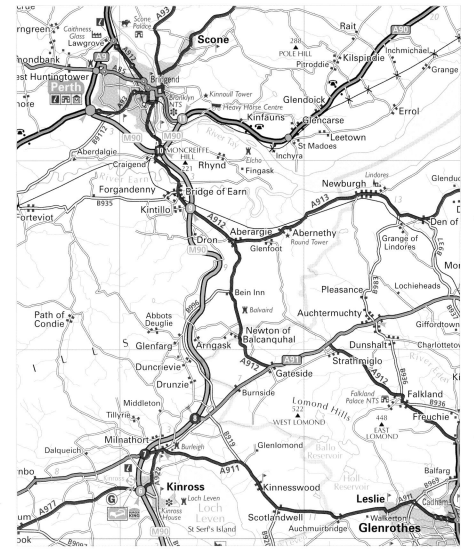

Caithness Glass

Since it was founded in 1961 in Wick, the world has taken to the hand-made paper-weights of Caithness Glass and the company now has a second factory and visitor centre 2 miles (3.2km) north of the centre of Perth. It incorporates a popular viewing gallery, from where the hand-making of their famous paperweights in abstract and modern designs, based on millefiori, can be seen. The visitor centre, with its audiovisual show, tells the story of the coloured and engraved glassware, including jewellery made from intricate multi-coloured glass canes.

The Stone of Scone

Legend has it that the Stone of Destiny was the pillow upon which Jacob had his dream. Thought to have come from the Middle East, it was brought to Scone by Kenneth McAlpin, Scotland's first king. In 1296, Edward I seized the Stone. A myth exists that the monks were forewarned, made an imitation and buried the original. The 458lb (208kg) block of hewn sandstone was taken to Westminster Abbey in London, and installed in the Coronation Chair. Since the crowning of Edward II in 1308, all monarchs have been seated above the Stone for the ceremony. In 1960 Scottish nationalists removed the Stone, which was recovered four months later from Arbroath Abbey. In 1998 it was formally returned to Scotland and can now be seen in Edinburgh Castle.

See Walk K page 343
The Lomond Hills of Fife

Formal gardens surround Kinross House, with roses and herbaceous borders enclosed by yew hedges

United Scotland, brought the legendary Stone of Destiny to nearby Scone. Kinnoull Hill, overlooking the 'Fair City' offers spectacular views to the Highlands, and across the two green parks beside the river, the North and South Inches. The North Inch was the site of the Battle of the Clane in 1396. Close by is the Black Watch Museum illustrating the proud history of this regiment, and the Fair Maid's House, one of the oldest buildings, associated with Sir Walter Scott's novel, *The Fair Maid of Perth*. The well-marked Old Perth Trail in this compact city leads through former trading streets, such as Ropemakers Close and Cow Vennel, and to the historic Church of St John (1126).

Flowers are very much part of Perth's heritage. It has been winner of the Britain in Bloom contest on more than one occasion. Bells Cherrybank Gardens, covering 18 acres (7ha), incorporates the National Heather Collection, whilst Branklyn Garden, on the eastern side of the town, is noted for its rhododendrons and alpines, and is reputed to be one of the finest small private gardens in Britain.

Scone Palace

Standing proud, just 2 miles (3.2km) north of Perth, is this imposing neo-Gothic fortified palace, built in 1803 for the Earl of Mansfield. The current structure incorporates many features from its ruined predecessor. Of great historical significance is Moot Hill, adjacent to the site of Scone Abbey, of which little can be seen today. This is where the Scottish kings were crowned under the Stone of Scone from the 9th century until its removal to London for 700 years by Edward I. The palace is splendidly furnished and has some exquisite collections, which include porcelain, china, ivory, clocks and needlework. The well laid out gardens have a children's playground, picnic area and trails.

BOTH SIDES OF THE TAY

O ver the last 1,000 years, St Andrews has led the country in 'mind, body and soul'. Throughout the Middle Ages, St Andrews was the spiritual capital and soon became the first seat of learning, with the nation's first university. It is best known today for golf, fulfilling the 'body' element. North of the river is Dundee, known for marmalade, fruit cake and *The Beano*.

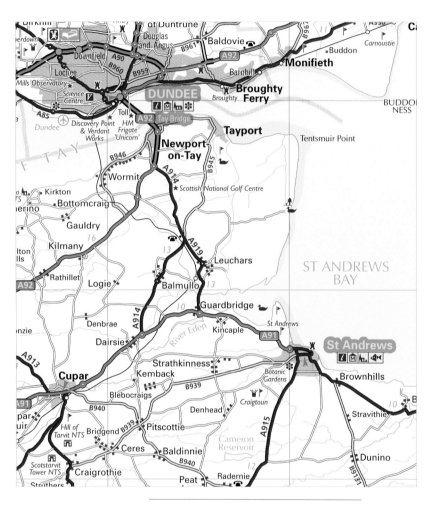

1382, this market town is one of Scotland's oldest burghs, with some atmospheric 17th- and 18th-century wynds to explore. The 1683 Mercat Cross marks the town centre; other landmarks include the 1785 parish church, whose spire dates from 1620. The graveyard contains the heads of two Covenanters involved in the murder of the Archbishop of St Andrews in 1679. Just outside town the Scottish Deer Centre fascinates wildlife enthusiasts, while devotees of country houses will enjoy Hill of Tarvit, an Edwardian mansion with fine furniture, pictures and porcelain.

Dundee

Dundee stands on the slopes of the northern shore of the estuary of the River Tay, a port and industrial city that has experienced economic ups and downs over the centuries, but has always been quick to adapt. Founded in the 12th century, the city grew rich on jute and linen manufacture and whaling, then diversified into confectionery and jam production, light industry, and, today, an increasing amount of hi-tech industry. Despite its fine Victorian buildings, this a predominantly modern-looking city, with sweeping roadways and malls.

Visitors should head for Discovery Point to see RRS *Discovery*, Captain Scott's Antarctic ship, built here in 1901, before learning all about jute at the Verdant Works, a stunning industrial museum. Elsewhere in the city, Sensation features interactive exhibits themed around the senses, while the Dundee Sweet Factory tells the story of confectionary – with plenty of free samples. East lies Broughty Ferry, a residential suburb with a good beach, picturesque castle and museum.

Golf

The world pays homage to St Andrews as the home of golf, although the game's origins may lie in the low countries. The Royal and Ancient Golf Club, founded in 1754, is the ruling body for the sport world-wide, except in the US and Mexico. Visitors can trace golf's fascinating history at the British Golf Museum at St Andrews, while players can tee off one of its five courses. The famous Old Course, founded in the mid-15th century, is unique in that evolved from 'natural' play and was never designed. The others include the New Course, over a century old, the Eden, Jubilee, Dukes' and the 9-hole Balgove. All the links are open to club golfers, but should be booked well in advance.

Ceres

Ceres is an attractive old village with 18th-century pantiled cottages and a Folk Museum in the 17th-century weigh-house, giving an insight into agricultural life in earlier times. Every June the village bursts with life when it stages the oldest Highland Games in Scotland, an event which was granted to honour the villagers, who fought at Bannockburn. At the crossroads sits a benign statue, 'The Provost', which also commemorates them.

Cupar

Set amongst a patchwork of fertile farmlands in the Lomond Hills, Cupar is crossroads for many routes. Chartered in

Tourist Information Centres

Cupar: The Granary Coal Road (seasonal) (tel: 01334 474609)
Dundee: 21 Castle Street (tel: 01382 527577)
St Andrews: 70 Market Street (tel: 01334 472021)

The Unicorn *is the oldest British warship still afloat and depicts life in the Royal Navy in the days of sail*

Tay Bridges

Two fine bridges straddle the Tay. The road bridge, started in 1963 and completed in 1966, is over a mile (1.6km) in length, and has 42 spans, with a high point of 120ft (36m) to allow passage of ships. A toll is charged.

The rail bridge, 2 miles (3.2km) west of the road bridge, is 2 miles (3.2km) long and is built on 73 piers. It was constructed between 1883 and 1888 and is only a few yards from the site of the original cast-iron bridge which collapsed within a year of its opening during the stormy night of 28 December 1879.

Leuchars

Leuchars is known mainly for its airbase, and Tornado jets thunder in the airspace above this once marshland village. The 12th-century Church of St Athernase, overlooking the village, is one of the finest examples of Norman architecture in the British Isles.

To the north, between the Tay and Eden estuaries, is the Tentsmuir Forest, covering some 15sq miles (38.8sq km) and fringed by the wide sandy Kishalfy beach. These woodlands have trails that offer plenty of opportunity for spotting a variety of wildlife, including deer.

St Andrews

The city of St Andrews attributes its founding to St Regulus (or St Rule), whose ship foundered in the 4th century whilst carrying the relics of St Andrew, the patron saint of Scotland.

Best explored on foot, the town runs almost east to west. In the east is the harbour, which in the Middle Ages thrived on trade with the low countries. Near by are the ruins of the Church of St Mary on the Rock, close to St Rule's Tower, adjacent to the cathedral ruins. The cathedral was consecrated in 1318 and was the largest in Scotland (measuring some 355ft by 160ft/108.1m by 48.7m), confirming St Andrews as the nation's spiritual centre.

The ruined castle became the Bishops Palace, notorious for its rule of terror – from the early 15th through to the mid-16th century, many martyrs to the cause of the Reformation were burnt at the stake.

John Knox, in his challenge to the old faith, brought the fight right to the archbishop. He was captured by a French squadron in 1547 defending the castle and taken to the galleys in Nantes.

The university, the first to take a female student in 1862, is the oldest in Scotland, having been founded in 1412. At the west end of St Andrews, amongst the dunes, golf evolved. The clubhouse of the world-famous Royal and Ancient overlooks the Old Course, which, like others here, is available to the public.

St Andrews Cathedral, once powerful, now stands in ruins close to the shore, its stones plundered for house-building during the 17th century

IN THE PERTHSHIRE HIGHLANDS

The Black Watch, Killiecrankie, Loch Tay, the Road to the Isles, the Grampian Mountains – all of these are names that evoke the history and beauty of Scotland and all have their links with the Perthshire Highlands, long renowned for wonderful scenery, a sense of history and Highland hospitality.

Queen's View looks down over Loch Tummel

The Atholl Highlanders on parade at Blair Castle

Aberfeldy

The River Tay at Aberfeldy is crossed by the handsome Wade's Bridge, designed by Willam Adam for General Wade in 1733. Beside it stands a tall cairn, topped by a kilted figure of a Higland soldier, which commemorates the raising of the Black Watch. On the town's eastern approach, visitors can tour a working distillery at Dewar's World of Whisky, while the town centre houses a traditional working water-mill with demonstrations of oatmeal milling. Walkers can stroll through the native birchwood of the Birks of Aber-feldy, celebrated in a poem by Robert Burns, to the enchanting Falls of Moness on the Urlar Burn.

Blair Atholl

The stone-built village of Blair Atholl clusters around the gates of Blair Castle, home to the Duke of Atholl and his Atholl Highlanders, Britain's only private army. Founded as a single fortified tower in 1269, the castle was the last British castle to be besieged – by its owner, Lord George Murray after he forfeited it for supporting the Young Pretender. It owes its present look to a restoration of 1869, which changed Georgian additions into something resembling the castle's medieval appearance. A succession of impressive rooms, from the entrance hall hung with weapons, to the drawing room, with its 18th-century decoration and the 19th-century ballroom, reflect the wealth and prestige of the Dukes, and there is fine china, furniture, portraits and costumes.

Dunkeld

Many of the small, white-painted houses around Dunkeld's attractive square owe their good repair to the National Trust for Scotland's 'Little Houses Scheme'. From beside one, the Ell House, which houses a Trust shop, a lane leads to the cathedral, invisible from most of the town. Beautifully sited beside the Tay, it dates mostly from the 14th and 15th centuries. The nave and aisles have been roofless since 1560, but the choir is now the parish church; an exhibition in the Chapter House outlines the history of the town and the cathedral. Behind the nave is the Parent Larch, sole survivor of the first group to be planted in Scotland.

Pictish Stones

Dunfallandry Stone, 2 miles (3.2km) south of Pitlochry, is an impressive example of the more than 200 Pictish stones of Scotland. The Picti – painted people – fought against the Romans, and by the 6th century Pictland occupied much of what later became Scotland. The standing stones are their most enduring legacy. They seem to have been put up between AD 550 and 850; by the mid-9th century the Picts had been overrun by the Scots and, in the north, by the Vikings. The early stones are rough slabs, simply carved, but they became more elaborate, with relief sculpture. After conversion to Christianity in the late 6th century, the Picts used their mysterious symbols alongside the cross and biblical scenes. What the symbols mean remains a mystery – they include animals, like the fine boar of Knocknagael (see Inverness, page 247) and the odd 'swimming elephant', as well as tools (hammers and anvils are quite common), mirrors, combs and Z- and V-shaped rods. Were the stones boundary markers, gravestones or monuments to alliances? No one knows.

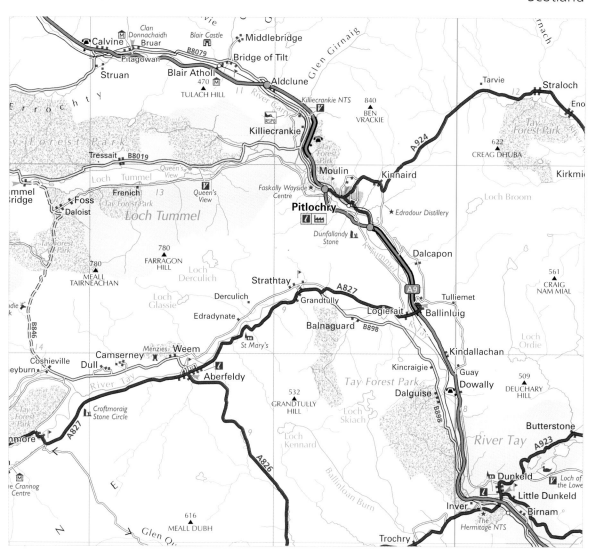

Ossian's Hall

The romantic imagination of the 18th-century was gripped by translations of Gaelic poetry from the supposed 3rd-century bard Ossian – though most of it was written by James Macpherson, a farmer's son from Kingussie. In wooded country near Dunkeld, beside the River Braan, the 4th Duke of Atholl converted a folly – then called The Hermitage – into Ossian's Hall, complete with now-vanished paintings of the bard's life. Restored by the National Trust for Scotland in 1952, it is now the focal point of woodland walks. Near by is Ossian's Cave, another Atholl folly, and, guaranteed natural, one of Scotland's two tallest Douglas firs.

Loch Tummel

The Road to the Isles winds along the north side of Loch Tummel. At Queen's View, visited by Victoria, the vista down the tree-lined loch is, justifiably, famous. The fine conical peak of Schiehallion, towards the south-west, has a place in scientific history – a determination of its mass in the 18th century led to calculations of the earth's density.

Kenmore

The pretty, planned village of Kenmore, at the eastern end of lovely Loch Tay, was built at the gateway of Taymouth Castle, the former seat of the Earls of Breadalbane. The estate village houses one of Scotland's oldest inns and is the scene on 15 January of the opening of the Tay salmon fishing season. Near by, time rolls back at the Scottish Crannog Centre, which tells the story of the daily life of prehistoric loch-dwellers.

Killiecrankie

The narrow, heavily wooded Pass of Killiecrankie was the site of the last victory of the Jacobites before their final defeat at Dunkeld during the first uprising of 1689. Under the leadership of Bonnie Dundee, they routed the English, leaving the pass a bloody and terrifying scene. One Highlander escaped pursuing Redcoats in a spectacular jump from Soldiers Leap. The Visitor Centre describes the battle and introduces the varied wildlife of the pass. s.

Pitlochry

Beautifully set on the wooded banks of the Tummel, Victorian Pitlochry is dignified and varied. Fine tweeds and woollens draw many visitors, as does the summer festival of drama and concerts. Beside the dam just upstream is a fish-ladder, installed to help migrating salmon reach their spawning grounds. Visitors can watch their progress by means of an underwater viewing chamber. The pure waters of the area have attracted two distilleries to Pitlochry, both of which welcome visitors.

Weem

Castle Menzies, west of the village of Weem, is a 16th-century tower house, complete with turrets and gables, which gives a vivid impression of the Spartan conditions the family must have endured for most of its occupation. Among the important possessions in the house are the death mask of the Young Pretender and a fearsome claymore used at Bannockburn.

Tourist Information Centres

Aberfeldy: The Square (tel: 01887 820276)
Blairgowrie: 26 Wellmeadow (tel: 01250 872960/873701)
Dunkeld: The Cross (tel: 01350 727688)
Pitlochry: 22 Atholl Road (tel: 01796 472215/472751)

See Walk N page 346
Great Birnham Wood to Dunkeld

SCOTLAND'S STRONGHOLDS

Alone piper on the ramparts of Edinburgh Castle during the Military Tattoo is for many an enduring image of the Scottish castle – massively set on an impregnable rock, battlemented and guarded with cannon, manned by fierce Highlanders urged to deeds of heroism by the call of the pipes. For others, Eilean Donan on the road to Skye is the Scottish

ROYAL FORTRESSES

The story of the Scottish castle really starts in the 13th century. Motte and bailey castles had been built to the Norman plan by the kings Alexander I and David I, who were brought up in Norman England, and these were gradually replaced by stone fortresses. Edinburghwas an early example. Continually fought over by the Scots and English, little other than the chapel survives from its earliest days. It last saw action in 1745 when the Young Pretender failed to take it but was incarcerated there instead.

Another royal castle, Stirling, 'the key to Scotland', has an equally formidable setting, and many great battles, including Bannockburn in 1314, were

castle *par excellence*, an island-held fairytale reflected in ruffled waters of a loch and backed by dramatic mountains. Or it may be the pepperpot turrets and crow-stepped gables of towering Craigievar in the gentler country of Scotland's north-east. Such is the variety of Scottish castles, reflecting the troubled history of this determinedly independent country.

Edinburgh castle, perched high on Castle Rock, has had a turbulent history

fought near by. Most of the present buildings are late medieval, and Mary, Queen of Scots was crowned here as an infant in 1543. But it was not just monarchs who built great fortresses. Wherever a suitable site was available, and circumstances demanded, the great landowners of Scotland would build.

CLAN CASTLES

The MacLeods at Dunvegan in the west of the Isle of Skye still live in their ancestral castle beside a tongue of the sea. Enlarged and made more comfortable over the centuries, it still tells of a lawless past. The family has additional protection from the Fairy Flag, possibly 7th century, which legend says will save the MacLeods from destruction on three occasions – it has already worked twice.

On the opposite side of the country St Andrews Castle was the stronghold for the powerful bishops, who were as involved in worldly politics as in prayer. As Scotland fought to retain (or recapture) its independence from England, the castle frequently changed hands, as its battered walls overlooking the sea testify.

One of the best of the early castles is set in wooded, rather undramatic country down on

the Solway Firth, south of Dumfries. Caerlaverock is a wonderful triangular castle still surrounded by the waters of its moat – the very latest in military thinking when it was built in around 1280. Captured by the English king Edward I, 'the Hammer of the Scots', in 1300, it was constantly dismantled and besieged in the Middle Ages, yet managed to retain its splendour, which was later enhanced by a splendid Renaissance façade.

Not far away to the west is a much sterner castle – the massive 14th-century tower and walls of Threave. It sits on an island in the River Dee, and was built by the appropriately named Archibald the Grim, a bastard son of Sir James Douglas. A later member of the Douglas family surrendered the castle to James II in 1455 after the king had bombarded it with the huge gun 'Mons Meg', now in Edinburgh Castle. The Douglases also held the now-ruined Tantallon Castle on the south-east corner of the Firth of Forth near North Berwick.

Some of the most impressive of Scottish castles are the result of careful restoration. Duart, on the Isle of Mull overlooking Loch Linnhe, retains 13th-century fragments, and was restored by Sir Fitzroy Maclean from 1911 onwards. It is now the home of the Clan Chief. The smaller Eilean Donan on Loch Duich was in utter ruin after bombardment from an English warship in 1719 until it was restored in 1932.

The high walls and round towers of Caerlaverock Castle, seat of the Maxwells, have stood firm since the 13th century, though the machicolations were added during the 15th century

Eilean Donan Castle poses romantically on Loch Duich, amidst wonderful mountain scenery

THE CASTLES OF MAR

Once the crowns of England and Scotland had been united by King James VI & I, a new type of castle developed – the tower house. Increasing political stability demanded increasing comfort, without altogether abandoning a defensive role. These new towers are characterised by a plain lower storey – sometimes square, but more often L- or Z-shaped. On the

Craigevar Castle is perhaps the loveliest of all the Castles of Mar

upper floors they burst into a riot of corbelled-out towers and gables to increase the amount of accommodation, though access is still usually by spiral stairways.

There are examples elsewhere, they are mostly found to the west of Aberdeen, between the Don and the Dee valleys – the former province of Mar. Among the best of the Castles of Mar is Craigievar, unaltered since it was completed in 1626. Significantly, it was built not for a monarch or a clan chief, but for one of the Jacobean nouveau riche, the Aberdeen merchant William Forbes. The largest of the Castles of Mar were Castle Fraser, Crathes and the extended Drum Castle. Glamis Castle, childhood home of Queen Elizabeth, the Queen Mother, has one of the most

prickly rooflines of all, stiff with cone-topped towerlets.

At Drumlanrig, built in the 1680s, the Douglas Dukes of Queensberry built themselves a huge square palace, which manages to combine the appearance of a medieval stronghold with an early 17th-century mansion. Like many of the inhabited Scottish castles, its interiors are a luxurious contrast to its outward appearance.

SCOTTISH BARONIAL

It was not long before the style established by the Castles of Mar began to influence architects. Inveraray Castle, designed in the mid-18th century, uses the same vocabulary of turrets

The tall tower of Balmoral Castle provides a focal point for the Scottish Baronial mansion below

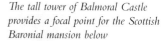

and battlements, though regulated with classical order, which also underpins superb Culzean on the Ayrshire coast, where Robert Adam's skills blend a castellated façade with wonderful Italianate interiors.

By the mid-19th century the 'Scottish Baronial' style was all the rage among the landed gentry. Blair Castle was reconstructed in the style, and so was Dunrobin. Most famous of all is Queen Victoria's Balmoral, where Prince Albert (with professional help, it must be said) provided a huge square keep with a more comfortable country house attached, tricked out in tartan in all its main apartments – the apotheosis of the Scottish castle.

FROM BEN NEVIS TO GLEN COE

Sparkling lochs and some of Scotland's highest mountains, including the towering Ben Nevis; the stunning beauty of the road to Kinlochleven; the grim story of the massacre at Glen Coe – all of these combine to make the Fort William area one of the country's most popular tourist spots. The winter sports boom has brought benefits to summertime visitors, with cable-car access to some of the mountains.

From Banavie, Ben Nevis looms on the horizon

Neptune's Staircase

The Caledonian Canal, linking Inverness with the west coast, faced its biggest challenge at Banavie, where a rise of 70ft (21.3m) in only 500 yards (457.2m) had to be negotiated. Thomas Telford designed a magnificent series of eight linked locks, dubbed 'Neptune's Staircase' by the navvies who built them – they were paid 1/6d (about 7p) a day. Work began in 1807 and lasted over three years, but it was not until 1822 that the canal opened, with a regular steamboat service between Fort William and Inverness.

Ballachulish

From 1693 until 1955 the slate quarries of Ballachulish produced millions of tons of roof slates. Today, grassy slopes have replaced the quarries besides the shores of Loch Leven and families will enjoy a visit to the Highland Mystery World, a visitor attraction complete with monsters, bogles and live performance. In South Ballachulish, near the bridge across the neck of Loch Leven, is a monument to James of the Glen, whose story inspired Robert Louis Stevenson's *Kidnapped*. Visitors can indulge themselves with a tasting tour of the confectionery factory across the bridge in North Ballachulish.

Corpach

The Caledonian Canal has its basin at Corpach, and there are stunning views along Loch Eil to Ben Nevis from the village. The Treasures of the Earth exhibition displays gems and crystals from throughout the world, including huge amethysts and emeralds, as well as prehistoric fossils and petrified trees.

Fort William

A busy tourist centre, Fort William hugs the narrow lochside strip and straggles up the hillside between Ben Nevis and Loch Linnhe. General Monk's 1655 earthwork fort and its stone replacement were sacrificed in the 19th century for the railway, which still brings visitors to the heart of the Highlands. From here you can take the scenic West Highland Railway to Mallaig.

Fort William held out against the Jacobites in both 1715 and 1745, but the West Highland Museum in Cameron Square makes much of the Pretenders' cause. Fort William is a pleasant place to stroll around – although most visitors head for the mountains, either on foot or, more easily, by the cable cars that climb the Nevis range to the north of the town.

Glen Coe

Since 6 February 1692, when the Campbells, acting for the government, slew some 40 MacDonalds, the name of Glencoe has been a byword for treachery. Slow to accept William and Mary as monarchs,

Ben Nevis

Of all 277 'munroes' (Scottish mountains over 3,000ft/914.4m), Ben Nevis is the highest. Indeed, it is the UK's highest mountain and, though it is not the most difficult to climb, it should never be attempted without making thorough preparation and wearing the right footwear and clothing. From its 4,409ft (1,344m) summit are spectacular views – the line of the Great Glen, the distant Cuillins on Skye and, very occasionally, the coast of Ireland. An observatory, now ruined, was built here in 1823 to study sun spots. For the less energetic, a drive into Glen Nevis will provide views of the mountain and ends by a waterslide. From here you can follow a rocky path through a dramatic ravine to a secret valley, closed by a waterfall, and the brave can cross the minimalist suspension bridge to the foot of Coire Dubh an Steill.

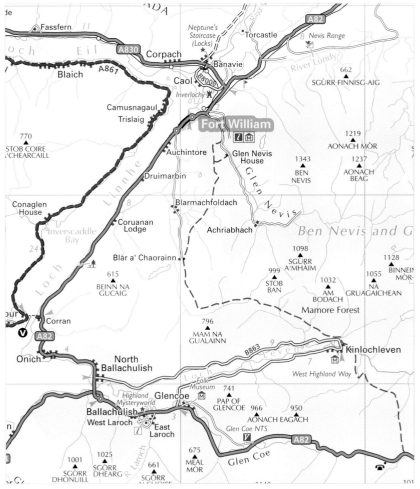

There's a fine view of the castle from nearby Primmy Hill, once used as a place of execution. Visitors can glimpse both from the comfort of the Jacobite Steam Train which covers the route from Fort William to Mallaig, one of the world's most scenic rail journeys.

Kinlochleven

The roads along the banks of Loch Leven provide some of the area's finest views of water and rugged hills, so Kinlochleven comes as a surprise. For more than 80 years the aluminium industry has provided employment here, where hydroelectricity could run the smelters cheaply. An exhibition and audio-visual display in the Visitor Centre tell about aluminium production. Not far away is the spectacular Grey Mare's Tail waterfall, and the West Highland Way long-distance trail passes close to the village.

Loch Linnhe

Loch Linnhe stretches from Fort William to Oban, more than 30 miles (48.3km), and for most of its length is backed by some of Scotland's highest mountains. A drive from Fort William down the A82 has spectacular views, but the best way to enjoy the stunning scenery is to take a cruise from Fort William. The journey takes in fish farms and islands dotted with basking seals, and offers superb views of Ben Nevis.

Neptune's Staircase represents a remarkable feat of engineering

The West Highland Way

From the outskirts of Glasgow, the West Highland Way threads 95 miles (152.9km) through Lowland and then Highland scenery to Fort William. It passes Loch Lomond and Glen Coe, following ancient routes for much of its length – drove roads (including the famous Devil's Staircase out of Glen Coe), military ways built to help suppress the clans, old coaching roads and, occasionally, disused railway lines. It is possible to walk short and spectacular sections, with the chance of seeing wildlife. To tackle the whole walk, it is best to go south to north, thus starting easy and working up to the more rugged terrain.

See Walk P page 347
The Lost Valley of Glen Coe

Tourist Information Centres

Ballachulish: (seasonal)
(tel: 01855 811296)
Fort William: Cameron Centre, Cameron Square
(tel: 01397 703781)

MacIan of Glencoe's oath of loyalty papers arrived late in Edinburgh, providing a pretext for government intervention to set an example to other recalcitrant clans. Campbell of Glenlyon and his troops were billetted on the Glencoe MacDonalds, with secret orders to 'fall upon the rebels...and put all to the sword'. Five days later, MacIan, his wife and 36 others were slaughtered in a night-time frenzy. The Glencoe Visitor Centre tells the story, and visitors can walk to Signal Rock, the Macdonald's lookout point.

Glencoe also attracts hill-walkers, climbers and mountaineers all year. The great peaks of Buchaille Etive Mhor (the Great Shepherd) and Bidean nam Bean (the Three Sisters) dominate the glen, providing an awe-inspiring backdrop for one of Scotland's most scenic glens.

Inverlochy Castle

West of Fort William, ruined Inverlochy Castle, built in the 13th century by John Comyn, Lord of Badenoch and Lochaber, stands on the banks of the River Lochy.

AROUND THE GRANITE CITY

Scotland's north-east focuses on Aberdeen, the country's third largest city, but away from the bright lights and glittering granite buildings is mellow countryside bristling with monuments to the past – stone circles, castles and industrial landmarks – as well as the lure of fine whisky.

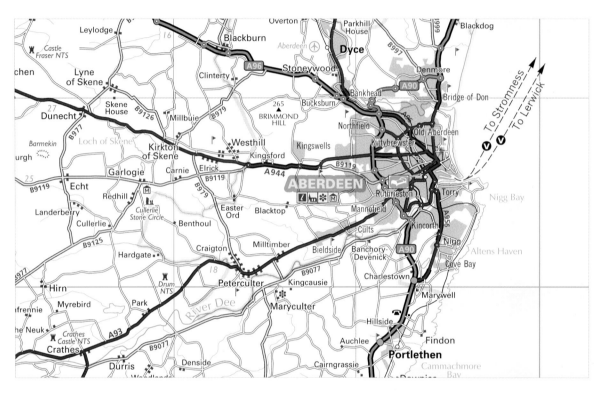

The Whisky Trail

Even more than for tartan, Scotland is known world-wide for its superb single malt whiskies. There are distilleries throughout Scotland, but half the total is to be found on the northern edge of the Grampian mountains, in the valley of the River Spey and its tributaries. The pure Highland water of the region is the basic ingredient of whisky, together with malted barley – as well as much time and care. Eight distilleries – and a cooperage, where barrels are prepared – are open to visitors and linked by The Whisky Trail, a signed route of around 70 miles (112.7km). You can see the great copper stills and learn about whisky production from start to finish, often with the help of an audio-visual programme in the visitor centre. And nearly all offer you a 'wee dram' of their product – so make sure you have a teetotal driver handy!

Aberdeen

Fish, granite and oil are for many, words that sum up Aberdeen. Fishing remains a major industry, as an early morning visit to the fish auctions will confirm. Oil, too, makes its presence felt, not just in the lights winking far out to sea in the dusk, but in the prosperity of the city. Just a stones-throw awa are the grey granite buildings that dominate the city centre – most spectacular are the early 20th-century spiky towers of the ancient Marischal College, founded in 1593.

On Union Street a colonnade heralds the Kirk of St Nicholas. There are no fewer than three cathedrals — St Mary's Roman Catholic, the Episcopal St Andrew's, where the first bishop in the United States was consecrated in 1784, and the oldest, the granite St Machar's, with its splendid heraldic ceiling, in Old Aberdeen.

Near by is King's College, founded in 1495 and, like Marischal College, now part of Aberdeen University. Its chapel, topped with an open crown, dates from around 1500. The Chanonry is the traditional home of the university's professors.

The Mercat Cross in Castlegate, at the heart of the city, has portraits of the ten Stuart monarchs of Scotland. The homes of two 16th-century Provosts of Aberdeen still survive – Provost Skene's, in Broad Street, which illustrates city life in a series of period rooms, and Provost Ross's in Shiprow, housing the fascinating Maritime Museum.

To complete Aberdeen's attractions, 2 miles (3.2km) of sandy beach stretch northward from the pier, backed by a wide promenade. Aberdeen has a wide choice of sporting and leisure activities, too, including large amusement parks and leisure centres on Beach Boulevard.

Castle Fraser

Like Crathes, one of the famous Castles of Mar which are special to this part of Scotland, Castle Fraser is a Z-plan tower house begun in 1575 and finished in 1636 for the Fraser family. Much remains to remind visitors of the castle's early history – such as the 'Laird's Lug', a tiny room high above

Castle Fraser, one of the grandest of the Castles of Mar, was built during the 16th and 17th centuries, but incorporates an earlier fortified tower house

Roses all the Way

For a city so much associated with its grey granite buildings, the flowers of Aberdeen come as a surprise. The city blazes with colour everywhere; main roads are bordered with blooms, roundabouts become luxurious gardens and streets are festooned with tubs and baskets. Most prominent of all are the roses – there are said to be 2.5 million of them. Duthie Park boasts a 'Mountain of Roses' as well as Europe's largest indoor garden. Not surprisingly, Aberdeen has won the 'Britain in Bloom' contest so often that it had to retire to give others a chance.

Cullerlie Stone Circle

Atmospherically set in remote countryside and approached through an avenue of pines, the eight boulders of the circle, the tallest around 5ft (1.5m), surround eight burial cairns. The circle, which dates from the Bronze Age, between 1500 and 1200 BC, may mark the tomb of a chief and his descendants.

the impressive Great Hall with its massive fireplace, from where the Fraser family could listen to their guests' conversations. The former chapel has its masons' calculations on the stonework.

The wooden leg of an early Victorian Fraser, as well as the lead bullet that injured him, is on show in the library, one of the rooms redecorated in the 1830s. From the roof of the castle's tallest tower are views of wooded hills and, nearer at hand, the walled garden with its fine borders.

Crathes Castle

Vibrant colour is a dominant feature both inside and outside Crathes Castle. Built on land given by Robert the Bruce to Alexander Burnett in 1323, Crathes is a romantic L-shaped tower house of gables and turrets, winding stairs and polished wood. It is famous for its painted ceilings, where elongated figures stand proudly between decorated beams swirling with leaves and flowers. This lively riot is echoed in the walled garden with its massive yews, where a succession of beautifully planned spaces offer tranquil corners and wonderful contrasts of shape and colour.

Drum Castle

Drum presents two faces to the visitor – a gaunt, battlemented tower, one of the oldest tower houses in Scotland, built in 1296, and beside it a Jacobean mansion of 1619. Oddly, the two were only joined in the 19th century when the castle was refurbished. The home of the Irvine family, it is full of solid 18th- and 19th-century furniture, as well as family portraits – don't miss the artist Hugh Irvine's Byronic self-portrait as the Angel Gabriel. The walled

gardens hold a collection of historic roses, planted in period settings, while north of the castle is the Old Wood of Drum, ancient oak woodland from the Royal Hunting Forest given to the Irvines by Robert the Bruce.

Garlogie

Garlogie, which stands in the gentle rolling landscape to the west of Aberdeen, was once the centre for a thriving wool-spinning industry. The 19th-century mills have now mostly been demolished, but the village still retains its old beam engine, the only one of its type still in situ in Scotland. Built around 1830 to supplement the original water power, the engine has been restored to working order, and an audio visual presentation gives the story of this local industry.

The beautiful gardens at Crathes Castle cover some 3 acres (1.2ha) and are sheltered by stately yew hedges that were planted in 1702

THE CAPITAL OF THE HIGHLANDS

South-west from Inverness the dark waters of Loch Ness refuse to yield up their secrets; to the east, the desolation of Culloden tells of the crushing of the clans; to the west, Beauly has links with Mary, Queen of Scots. This is quintessential Scotland – the sea, the lochs and the mountains – all converging on a congenial city.

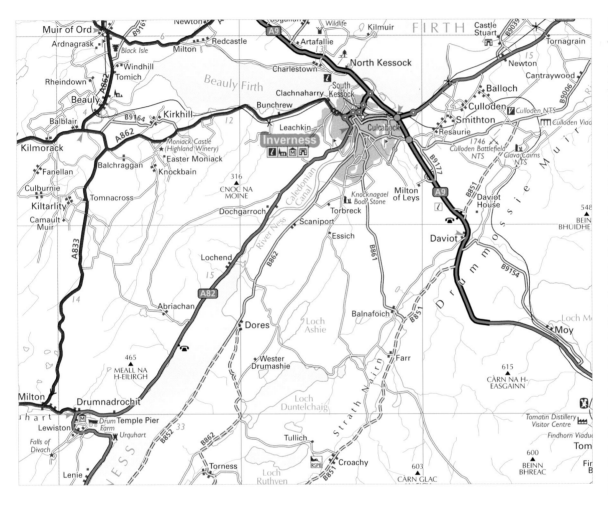

In Search of The Monster

St Columba is the first person reported to have met a monster in Loch Ness – he prevented it from eating his servant by making the sign of the cross. Quiescent for more than a millennium thereafter, 'Nessie' attracted public attention again while the main A82 road along the north side of the loch was being constructed in the 1930s. Photographs of varying authenticity, as well as inconclusive scientific research, have added to its fame – two exhibitions in Drumnadrochit, as well as millions of plastic models in souvenir shops, indicate the world-wide interest. Yet still the loch keeps its secret, aided by its 24 mile (33.8km) length and a depth in places of 900ft (274.3m).

Tourist Information Centres

Daviot Wood: A9 by Daviot (seasonal) (tel: 01463 772203)
Fort Augustus: Car Park (seasonal) (tel: 01320 366367)
Inverness: Castle Wynd (tel: 01463 234353)
North Kessock: (tel: 01463 731701)

Beauly

West of Inverness the Moray Firth becomes the Beauly Firth, fed by the River Beauly, one of Scotland's best salmon rivers, which flows through a lovely wooded strath. At the head of the Firth is the little town of Beauly – where the austere Valliscaulain monks built their priory. Only the ruins of the church, with its lovely 13th-century windows, remain. The town was laid out in 1840 by Lord Lovat; the wide central square contains a monument to the raising of the Lovat Scouts in 1905. Visitors can learn more at the Beauly Firth and Glens Trust, while the Made in Scotland exhibition offers the very best of Scottish crafts and shopping.

Kirkhill

The little village of Kirkhill lies south of the Beauly Firth, and is a good starting point for cycling or walking in this pretty wooded landscape – there are lots of way-marked trails in the area to cater for both activities.

The village is home to Highland Aromatics, where visitors can see the production of naturally-based soaps and creams. Near by is the 17th-century L-plan Moniack Castle, once a Lovat stronghold, now home to the Highlands' only winery, specialising in traditional herb and fruit wines. There are tours and tastings, and an audiovisual to explain the production process

On the south bank of the River Nairn, Clava Cairns ranks among Scotland's finest prehistoric monuments

Clava Cairns

Clava should not be missed in the excitement of nearby Culloden. Set amongst trees, this fascinating site of major archaeological importance has three principal cairns – large stone burial mounds, each surrounded by a circle of standing stones, built between about 2000 and 1500 BC. The two outer ones have stone-lined passages to the centre. The central cairn has no passage, but is unique in having odd, rough pavements radiating from it. This group is the most important of a whole series of such cairns found only in the region of the Moray Firth.

Building The Caledonian Canal

The north coast of Scotland has often proved hazardous to small boats, so the idea of avoiding that journey by constructing a canal to link the string of lochs along the Great Glen, as it slices through the Highlands from Inverness to Fort William, appealed to late-18th century minds. Surveyed in 1773, the Caledonian Canal was finally begun by Thomas Telford in 1803. The work raised the level of Loch Ness by 6ft (1.8m). When it opened in 1822 it was not deep enough, so completion was only achieved in 1847. Between the natural lochs on the 60-mile (96.6-km) route from Loch Linnhe to the Moray Firth are 22 miles (35.4km) of canal, rising through 29 locks – most spectacularly at Neptune's Staircase. The canal is mainly used by pleasure boats today, a relaxing way of seeing spectacular scenery.

Culloden

Culloden, despite its summer crowds, remains a sad and moving place. On this bleak moorland the hopes of Charles Edward Stuart to regain the throne met their end 16 April 1746 in the last major battle fought on British soil. His 5,000 Highlanders, used to savage skirmishing among the hills, faced 9,000 trained and disciplined troops under the Duke of Cumberland, and, despite courageous fighting, were swiftly defeated. The number of dead was greatly increased by 'Butcher' Cumberland's order that no prisoners should be taken. The clansmen who died are buried around the site, their graves marked with small stones. The 76 English who died lie in the Field of the English. Flags mark the disposition of the armies, and the large memorial cairn was built during the 19th century. Next to the Visitor Centre is Old Leonach Cottage, scene of a battle atrocity, restored to its 18th-century condition.

Inverness

Inverness, 'the Capital of the Highlands' and a royal burgh since the 12th century, stands on the Moray Firth. The mainly modern city centre is dominated by the castle, built and restored over the centuries. Mary, Queen of Scots hung its governor from the walls in 1562 for refusing her entry, and Bonnie Prince Charlie's troops blew it up shortly before Culloden in 1746; it was rebuilt by General Wade. The present structure is 19th century, as is the statue of Flora MacDonald in the forecourt. Below here, Inverness's museum gives an overview of local history, but visitors shouldn't miss Balnain House, a centre devoted to Scottish music. The old part of town also contains Abertarff House, a rare surviving 16th-century townhouse.

Across the river are the twin towers of St Andrew's Cathedral, consecrated in 1869 and the first cathedral to be built in Britain after the Reformation. The river banks and islands are laid out with attractive gardens, and near here is the departure point for cruises down the Caledonian Canal to Loch Ness. Dolphin and wildlife cruises also operate from Inverness harbour into the Moray Firth.

Urquhart Castle

From the promontory that Urquhart Castle occupies it is possible to see almost the full length of Loch Ness – which accounts for its popularity with monster-spotters. Ruined since it was blown up in 1692 so that it could not be used by the Jacobites, most of the visible buildings date from after 1509, when Urquhart was given by James IV to the Grant family. The medieval castle, once Scotland's largest, was captured by Edward I and then held by Robert the Bruce against Edward III. Floodlighting makes it a fine spectacle at night.

Urquhart Castle, overlooking Loch Ness, was once the largest in Scotland

Inverness Castle and its statue of Flora Macdonald make an impressive focal point for local events

See Walk S page 350
The Stuarts' Last Stand at Culloden

THE SCOTTISH HIGHLANDS AND ISLANDS

From space, Scotland north of the Forth and Clyde looks like a loosely-woven cloth – an ancient tartan perhaps – ragged at its western edge and crumpled in a series of irregular folds. Patches of smoother fabric to the north and north-east contrast with the agitation of the rest, while loose scraps and threads lie around its fringes. These are the Highlands and the Islands, where high mountains and deep glens, tumbling seas and shimmering lochs, open moorland and spreading forests lure the visitor to one of the most fascinating areas in Europe. The Highland Line – the divide between the smooth Lowlands and the sudden lifting of the mountains, and between the former Gaelic speakers and others – runs north-east from the south end of Loch Lomond to a little inland from Aberdeen, then curves around to Inverness. Across it you are in what many people regard as 'real' Scotland. Here narrow roads twist through mountain passes or beside the lochs, and towering summits rear overhead. The result of millions of years of sometimes tumultuous geological activity – faulting and folding, volcanoes and glaciers – the Highland landscape can be rugged and uncompromising, but never fails to impress.

THE ROLE OF THE ROCKS

It would be wrong to think of the area as uniformly mountainous, or that all the mountains are the same. Although large tracts both north and south of the Great Glen, a fault line, are similar in their geological formation, there are outcrops of other rock. Granite forms the most jagged peaks, like the Cairngorms, and there are basalts, chiefly in Argyll and on Skye, Mull and, most famously, at Fingal's Cave on Staffa. From the Mull of Kintyre to Aberdeen and the north-east coast, the basic rocks of the Grampians are normally smoother, rounder peaks mellowing into gentler hills in the east.

Around Inverness, north along the coast to Caithness, and out to the Orkney Islands, is easily weathered sandstone, giving the landscape a softer grain, while the deeply indented coastline from Skye northwards is mostly of heavily scarred sedimentary rocks. The Outer Hebrides are mostly low-lying. Only in Harris does the granite show through again as

Geological activity and the effects of weathering create strange rock formations and the Bannet Stane, high up in the Lomond Hills, is an exceptional example

mountains. The backbone of Shetland is rock like the Grampians, varied with sandstones and granite.

IN THE NORTHERN SEA

These distinctive landscapes give the Highlands and Islands their fascination. From the most northerly of the Shetland Islands (Muckle Flugga) south-wards, history and tradition are interwoven with the sometimes unforgiving land.

The 100 or so islands of Shetland are distinctively different from the rest of Scotland. Slashed by the sea into thousands of inlets, the rocky land is backed by huge, ever-changing skies. Birdwatchers are in their element here, and there are reminders of early settlement, like the broch on Mousa and the settlement at Jarlshof. Norse place names – *voe* and *wick* – abound, and the winter highlight of the islands is Up-Helly-Aa, when a longboat is burned in an avalanche of flaming torches.

Fair Isle, between Shetland and Orkney, is another magnet for bird-watchers – and for those determined to buy its brightly-patterned knitwear straight from the needles of traditional knitters.

Orkney is a green and fertile contrast to Shetland, and the ideal place for the study of early history, including the 60-stone Ring of Brodgar, the huge chambered tomb at Maes Howe, and the complex Skara Brae site, where ancient homes, occupied from 3100 to 2450 BC and then buried by sand, show how our remote ancestors lived. Perhaps most surprising of all is the magnificence of Kirkwall's St Magnus Cathedral, built for the Norse earls.

The huge natural harbour of Scapa Flow, where the German fleet was scuttled after its surrender in 1918, is defended by the World War II Churchill Barriers. On Lamb Holm at its eastern edge Italian prisoners of war built an emotive chapel from Nissan huts, and decorated the inside like a Mediterranean

mild landscape, though the heights of Ben Wyvis tell of the nearness of the main Highland mountains. The Black Isle, between the Cromarty and Beauly Firths, is actually a peninsula of fertile farmland; its name comes from its mild, frost-free climate that lets the winter ploughland remain dark. It is worth making the journey to Cromarty at its tip, an 18th-century seaport that has been preserved intact.

From Inverness the coast road passes through prosperous towns, with branches plunging off to fishing villages, on its way to Peterhead and Aberdeen. South-east is Strathspey, distillery country, where the magical names – including Glenlivet, Cardhu and Glenfiddich – roll smoothly off the tongue. From Grantown-on-Spey, cross the Grampian Mountains on the road through Tomintoul and Cockbridge, down into Royal Deeside. Queen Victoria first came here in 1848, and the royal family still spend summers on their

shrine. A visit to rocky Hoy provides a contrast to the rest of Orkney – the Old Man of Hoy, a rock stack in the sea, offers spectacular climbing for the really experienced. You can reach Orkney from Scrabster on the mainland.

THE FAR NORTH

On the mainland of Scotland, treeless and often windswept Caithness is the northern extremity. Its main towns, Wick and Thurso, are good bases for exploration. The undoubted attraction here, for its name, not its beauty, is John o' Groats, traditionally the top of Scotland (though Dunnet Head projects further north). The name derives from Jan de Groot, a Dutch ferryman who plied across the Pentland Firth from here to Orkney.

Westwards is the Flow Country, Europe's most important and fragile area of blanket bog, home to unique plants, animals and insects, and recently under threat from large areas of commercial forestry. Northwards, the coast is quiet and largely unvisited, with wonderful beaches and rocky inlets. Reaching Cape Wrath, the north-westerly tip of mainland

The 'water of life' is distilled in these fantastic vessels at the Glen Garioch Distillery in Oldmeldrum

Britain, involves a ferry trip and a bumpy 10-mile (16.1km) ride in a small bus, but the feeling of remoteness is worth the effort.

Turning south, the area becomes more mountainous, as the road wanders beside sea or across boggy land towards Ullapool. It passes the Inverpolly Nature Reserve, wild moorland and lochs punctuated by magnificent peaks like Suilven. Ullapool is an 18th-century planned fishing village, with a real working harbour; in winter one of the languages you may hear is Russian, spoken by visiting factory-ship crews.

GOLF AND WHISKY

On the opposite coast, the land swings south-west down from Wick to the Dornoch Firth. Helmsdale, where the Strath of Kildonan joins the coast, was built to house displaced crofters from the valley. The Dukes of Sutherland, responsible for much rural depopulation during the Clearances of the 19th century, have their ancestral home at Dunrobin Castle near

Golspie. Their wealth is evident in the sumptuous rooms and spreading Victorian gardens.

Dornoch's world-class golf course has stunning views of the Dornoch Firth. West and south is Easter Ross, a quiet,

Dunrobin Castle, seat of the Earls and Dukes of Sutherland, takes its name from Earl Robin, who built the original keep in the 13th century

Balmoral estate. Up the valley is Braemar, where the Highland Games, complete with the traditional sports like tossing the caber as well as the rather gentler pursuits of Highland dancing, have royal patronage each September. The Old Man of Lochnagar, of the Prince of Wales's children's story, lived on the nearby mountain.

SERIOUS SCENERY

West of Braemar is serious Highland scenery – the Cairngorms, Britain's highest mountain mass, with six peaks over 4,000ft (1,220m). At their heart is the Cairngorms National Nature Reserve, with its sub-Arctic plateau and rare plants and wildlife. Aviemore is regarded as the heart of the Cairngorms, a useful rather than an attractive centre, stepping off point for numerous mountain activities, including excellent winter skiing. The chair-lifts make it easy for summer visitors to ascend the mountains too.

Only the A9 road disturbs the heart of these mountains. Otherwise it is wilderness, where the waters rush foaming

A distinctive building on Mull is dwarfed by massive cliffs near Tiroran

down the mountainsides, the peaks beckon the skilled climber and birdwatchers can be content from the soft light of dawn to the gathering of dusk. These mountains can be dark, brooding and very wet and cold at times, too, and it is not just nature that has threatened the peace and tranquillity. The Perthshire Highlands remind us that, amidst all this beauty, politics have never been far away from Scottish minds. The Pass of Killiecrankie, north of Pitlochry, was the scene of bitter fighting in the 1690s in the aftermath of the abdication of King James VII & II, and at nearby Aberfeldy the Black Watch, first of the Highland Regiments, was raised to help keep the country under control.

'By Loch Tummel and Loch Rannoch and Lochaber I will go' says the song 'The Road to the Isles', but beyond Loch Rannoch, west of Pitlochry, the road disappears today in the wastes of Rannoch Moor. Better to head south-east first, alongside Loch Tay and down the Tay Valley, through Killin and Crianlarich down to Tarbet at the head of Loch Lomond. The 'bonny, bonny banks', overshadowed by Ben Lomond, are for many their first introduction to the Highlands.

SAINTS AND STUARTS

Oban on the west coast is a popular departure point both for tours on the mainland and boats to further afield. An attractive town, overlooked by the Romanesque coliseum of McCaig's Folly, it is the starting point for ferries to Colonsay, Lismore and Mull, to Coll and Tiree; if you want to visit Jura or sample whisky on Islay you will need to go to Kennacraig for the ferry. Mull has an amazingly wild coast, though it takes effort to reach it from most of the island. The central part is rather bleak, but many visitors

make straight for the holy island of Iona off Mull's western tip. It was from this magical place that St Columba spread the light of civilisation in the 6th century. It still retains its feeling of sanctity, despite the numbers of visitors who come to see the Abbey and the burial place of Scottish kings, including Duncan and Macbeth.

North of Mull, the mainland breaks down into a succession of sea-girt promontories – the Morvern, Ardnamurchan and Moidart peninsulas – each with its own character and secrets. At the top of Loch Shiel, dividing

Moidart from Sunart, is Glenfinnan, where Bonnie Prince Charlie raised his standard to mark the start of his attempt to regain the crown for the Stuarts in 1745; it ended tragically in the bloody rout of Culloden the following year. After that, everything that we recognise as typically Highland was banned – the kilt and all forms of tartan, the clan system, even the bagpipes. They returned only in the

Misty seacliffs add an air of mystery to the Isle of Skye, which is widely held to be the most beautiful of all the Scottish islands

Patches of snow mottle the green and brown of Ben Macdui, deep in the Cairngorm mountains, as viewed from Cairn Gorm

following century, after the novels of Sir Walter Scott had inspired George IV to venture north of the border in 1822, clad in a fancy-dress version of Highland costume.

OVER THE SEA

Since the completion of the toll bridge, the prosaic way to Skye is along the A87 and over the straits towards Broadford. But romantics still prefer to head for Mallaig, where both road and railway end at the ferry terminal. From here other islands of the Inner Hebrides can be reached, too. Knoydart, across Loch Nevis, is accessible only by sea, and provides wonderful walking country. Another way to reach Skye is via the tiny six-car ferry across the Sound of Sleat from Glenelg, where Gavin Maxwell's *Ring of Bright Water* was set. It is reached by the hairpin road through the Ratagain pass, with views of the Five Sisters of Kintail above

Loch Duich, rivalled in scenic splendour only by the Bealach na Ba from Kishorn to Applecross, 15 miles (24.1km) north.

However you arrive, Skye is quickly captivating. South of Broadford is Sleat, green and gentle, from which the island's mountains stand out clearly. Closer to them is Elgol, with its ferry to Loch Coruisk, isolated among the jagged Cuillins. Northward, Waternish juts towards the Outer Hebrides, sheltering Dunvegan Castle, home of the MacLeods, while Trotternish is an extraordinary landscape around the Quiraing and the Old Man of Storr.

BRITAIN'S EDGE

Beyond Skye, across the sometimes treacherous waters of The Little Minch, lie the Western Isles (Outer Hebrides). From Barra to the Butt of Lewis is

Harris tweed, sought after all over the world for its fine quality, is produced only on the island of Harris and Lewis by local people, from the wool of local sheep. Each piece of cloth bears a mark of authenticity

more than 120 miles (192km), and although the three central islands are joined by causeways, travelling the full length needs expert juggling with ferry timetables. Barra sums up the whole chain, with empty silver beaches backed by flower meadows, stretches of peat bog and small crofts.

South Uist is dotted with lochans, many of them home to a wide variety of birds. Flora Macdonald was from South Uist, and from the next island north, Benbecula, she sailed across the Minch to Skye with Bonnie Prince Charlie disguised as her maid to aid his escape after Culloden. Most of North Uist is shattered into fragments by lochs and inlets. From the west it is sometimes possible to glimpse precipitous St Kilda, 45 miles (72km) out in the Atlantic. The population was evacuated in 1933, when life became insupportable.

Largest of the Outer Hebrides is the island that comprises Harris and Lewis. Though joined, they are very different in character. Harris is mountainous, with long empty beaches and wonderful views. Lewis is flat and bare, mostly peat bogs and outcrops of rock. The capital, Stornoway, is a lively town, and centre of the prestigious Harris Tweed industry.

Away to the west is one of Scotland's most enduring and important monuments, Callanish Stone Circle, a dramatic ring of 13 tall, thin stones, some up to 15ft (4.6m) high, approached along avenues of similar stones.

An avenue of 19 monoliths and a circle of 13 stones has stood at Callanish, on the Isle of Lewis, for over 4,000 years and the site is second only to Stonehenge

It is a moving sight, very far removed from the tartan tam o'shanters and model monsters that sometimes represent the Highlands and Islands. Here, amid the bleakness of the Western Isles with only the sea and the wind for company, visitors may truly experience the reality of Scotland.

FAR-REACHING VIEWS FROM CRIFFEL

Distance: 9 miles (14.5km)
Total ascent: 1,867ft (569m)
Paths: mostly good; very boggy in winter and in wet weather
Terrain: road, fields, woodland, heather moorland and farm tracks
Gradients: very steep up Criffel
Refreshments: Abbey Tea Room at car park.
Park: Sweetheart Abbey car park off A710 in New Abbey

1 From the car park at Sweetheart Abbey, turn left onto the main road. Leave the village past the petrol station and over a bridge. Pass the farm roads for Lochhill and Ingleston Ford and later a gaily painted bus shelter.

2 300yds (274m) beyond the bus shelter, turn right at the signpost for Ardwall and Ardwall Mains to the parking area for Criffel. You could start and finish your walk here but you would miss the walk down the far side of Knockendoch. Follow the Forestry Commission sign – 'Criffel Walk 2 miles'.

3 Go through the metal gate on the left, walk for 70yds (64m) on a rough farm track and turn right, following the track between two dry-stone walls to the foot of the hill. At the end, pass beside a gate across the track.

8 Go through several gates, cross a burn, then bear right until eventually the track joins the drive to Barbeth Farm. This leads into the village. Follow the road ahead to the main road, emerging at the petrol station. Turn left and follow the road round to the car park at Sweetheart Abbey.

7 Descend Knockendoch via the path which continues from the summit in the direction you have been travelling. Cross the stile where a fence meets a dry-stone wall part-way down. Continue with the wall on your right and later, near a plantation of larches, veer to the left to a forestry track and turn right.

6 Follow the well-trodden path to Criffel summit, with its trig point and cairn. From the cairn, head (north-west then north) across some rough ground for the wide ridge which runs from Criffel to Knockendoch until you intersect a narrow path leading down, then back up to Knockendoch summit.

5 Mostly the path follows the course of a stream uphill. Cross two forestry roads. At the top of the treeline there is a fence and a stile leading onto the hillside. To your right is Knockendoch; to the left, Criffel.

4 The forestry road curves to your left but take a rough trodden path to the right marked Criffel Walk. The path up through the woods is rough, uneven and narrow with lots of large boulders to clamber over, but plainly visible and easy to follow.

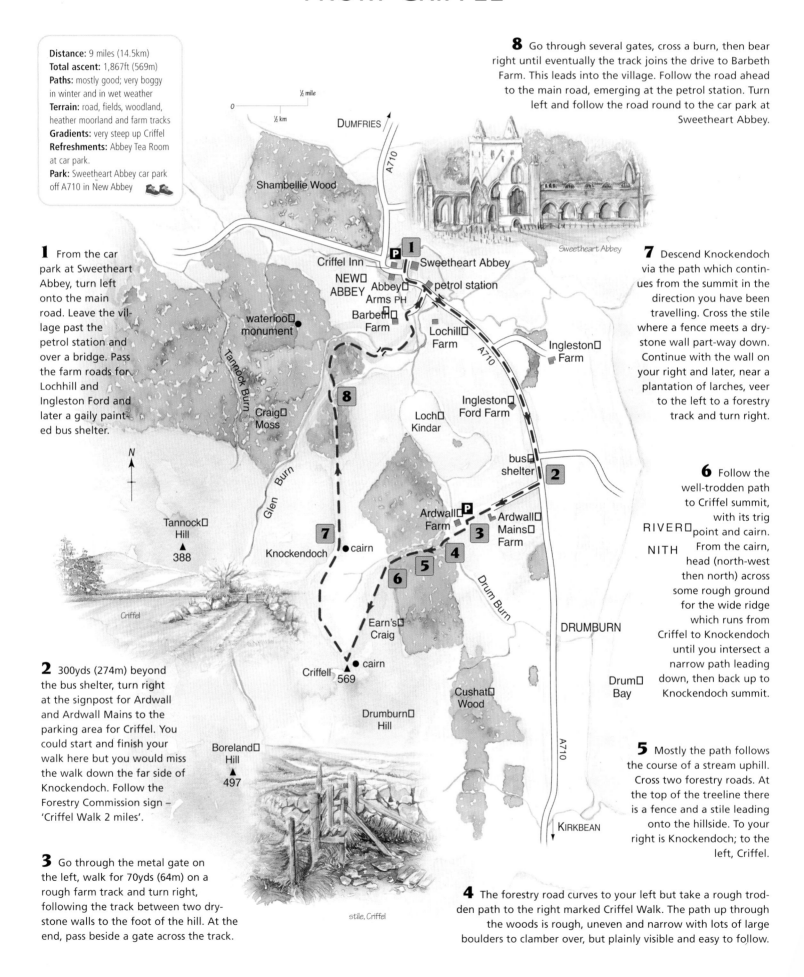

½ mile

DUMFRIES

Shambellie Wood

Sweetheart Abbey

Criffel Inn

NEW ABBEY

Abbey Arms PH

petrol station

Sweetheart Abbey

Barbeth Farm

waterloo monument

Lochill Farm

Ingleston Farm

Tannock Burn

Craig Moss

Ingleston Ford Farm

Loch Kindar

RIVER NITH

Glen Burn

bus shelter

Tannock Hill
▲ 388

Ardwall Farm

Ardwall Mains Farm

Knockendoch

cairn

Drum Burn

DRUMBURN

Earn's Craig

Drum Bay

Criffel

Criffell
569

cairn

Cushat Wood

Drumburn Hill

Boreland Hill
▲ 497

A710

KIRKBEAN

Criffel

stile, Criffel

CAERLAVEROCK AND THE RICH SOLWAY MARSHES

1 From the car park, turn back along the approach road for ½ mile (800m) then turn left, passing Scottish National Heritage's information point on your left.

2 In 300yds (275m), bear left by a house, along a hedged track to the edge of the Merse (saltmarsh). Turn right before the next fence and keep left for 150yds (136m) then turn right along a low bank for 1 mile (1.6km). Near the end, veer left to cross two wooden bridges and then a stile.

Distance: 6 miles (9.5km)
Total ascent: 310ft (95m)
Path: country roads, lanes and foreshore tracks; very muddy after rain
Terrain: flat estuary foreshore, saltmarsh, grassland
Gradients: one fairly gentle hill
Refreshments: tearoom at Caerlaverock Castle
Park: car park at the Wildfowl and Wetlands Trust's East Park Centre at Caerlaverock, signposted off the B725 9 miles (14.5km) south of Dumfries.
Note: entrance fees are charged for entry to the Wildfowl and Wetland Trust facilities and Caerlaverock Castle

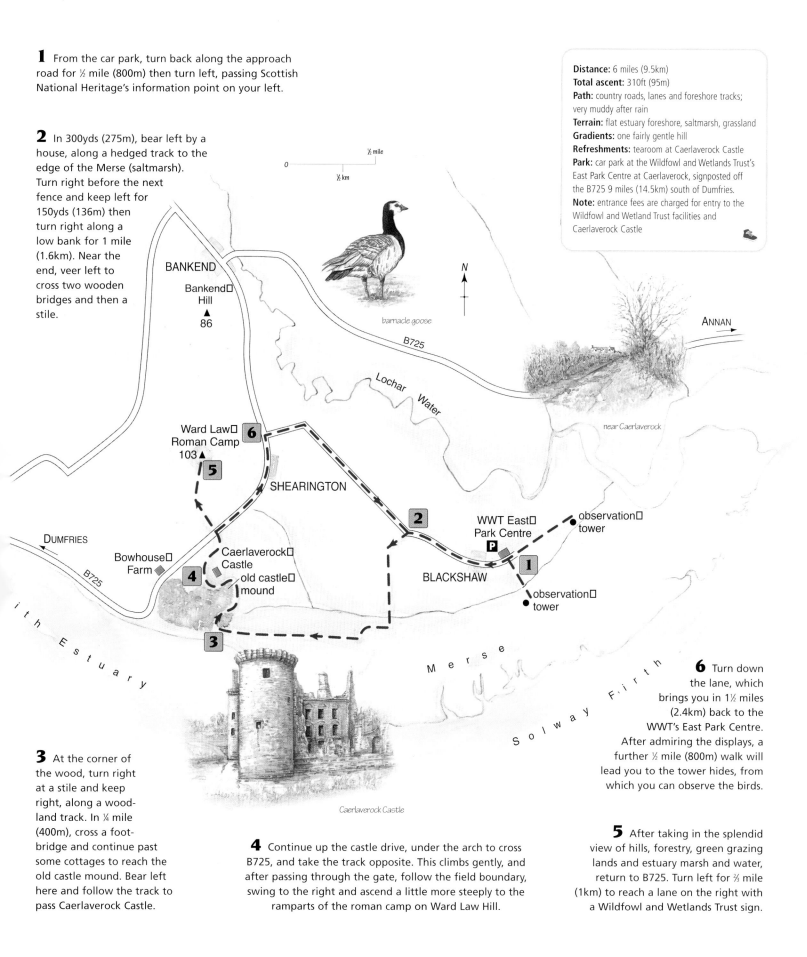

barnacle goose

near Caerlaverock

BANKEND

Bankend Hill
▲ 86

B725

Lochar Water

ANNAN

Ward Law Roman Camp
103 ▲ **6**
5

SHEARINGTON

2

WWT East Park Centre
P

observation tower

DUMFRIES

Bowhouse Farm

Caerlaverock Castle
old castle mound

4

1

BLACKSHAW

observation tower

B725

Solway Firth Estuary

3

M e r s e

S o l w a y   F i r t h

Caerlaverock Castle

3 At the corner of the wood, turn right at a stile and keep right, along a woodland track. In ¼ mile (400m), cross a footbridge and continue past some cottages to reach the old castle mound. Bear left here and follow the track to pass Caerlaverock Castle.

4 Continue up the castle drive, under the arch to cross B725, and take the track opposite. This climbs gently, and after passing through the gate, follow the field boundary, swing to the right and ascend a little more steeply to the ramparts of the roman camp on Ward Law Hill.

6 Turn down the lane, which brings you in 1½ miles (2.4km) back to the WWT's East Park Centre. After admiring the displays, a further ½ mile (800m) walk will lead you to the tower hides, from which you can observe the birds.

5 After taking in the splendid view of hills, forestry, green grazing lands and estuary marsh and water, return to B725. Turn left for ⅔ mile (1km) to reach a lane on the right with a Wildfowl and Wetlands Trust sign.

BURNS' ALLOWAY AND THE BRIG O' DOON

1 From Tam O'Shanter Experience, walk to end of car park, furthest from entry road. Go right down path into Burns Monument Gardens. Follow path anti-clockwise around monument then towards Auld Brig (Brig o'Doon) ahead. Visit Statues House, then continue to top of steps down to right. Descend to road, turn right and cross over. Just short of large white hotel, go down steps on left into Riverside Gardens.

2 Walk around gardens by river towards Auld Brig. Leave by steps back up to road, turn right and cross Auld Brig. Continue up path, under old railway bridge to top, swinging right on to main road.

3 Turn right and follow main road back over river. Just over newer bridge, cross over and turn left, up steps, into Auld Alloway Kirkyard (opposite parish church) to Burns' parents' graves.

Distance: 7 miles (11.3km)
Total ascent: negligible
Paths: good; can be muddy
Terrain: old railway, fields, beach, golf course and woodland
Gradients: some steps
Refreshments: visitor centre at car park
Park: Tam O'Shanter Experience car park, Alloway, near Ayr

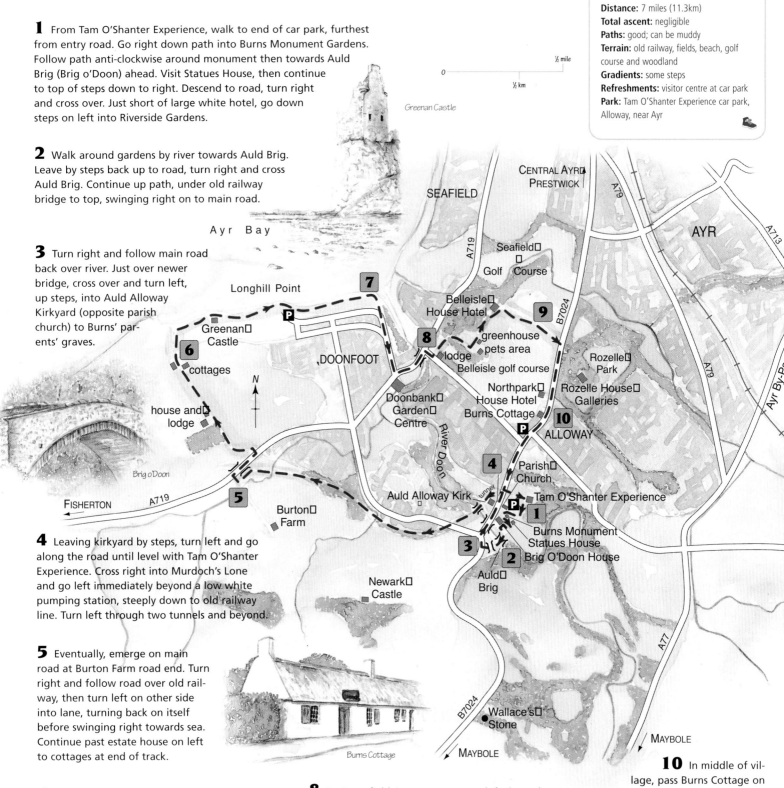

Greenan Castle

Ayr Bay

Longhill Point

AYR

SEAFIELD

CENTRAL AYR
PRESTWICK

Seafield
Golf Course

Belleisle
House Hotel

greenhouse
pets area

lodge
Belleisle golf course

Rozelle
Park

Rozelle House
Galleries

Northpark
House Hotel
Burns Cottage

DOONFOOT

Greenan
Castle

cottages

house and
lodge

Doonbank
Garden
Centre

ALLOWAY

Brig o'Doon

FISHERTON   A719

River Doon

Parish
Church

Auld Alloway Kirk   tunnel

Tam O'Shanter Experience

Burton
Farm

Newark
Castle

Auld
Brig

Burns Monument
Statues House

Brig O'Doon House

Wallace's
Stone

MAYBOLE

MAYBOLE

Burns Cottage

4 Leaving kirkyard by steps, turn left and go along the road until level with Tam O'Shanter Experience. Cross right into Murdoch's Lone and go left immediately beyond a low white pumping station, steeply down to old railway line. Turn left through two tunnels and beyond.

5 Eventually, emerge on main road at Burton Farm road end. Turn right and follow road over old railway, then turn left on other side into lane, turning back on itself before swinging right towards sea. Continue past estate house on left to cottages at end of track.

6 Go between cottages and leave lane as it swings right, going through gate and down field, through gate to beach. Turn right along beach past Greenan Castle and car park to river mouth.

7 Turn right up road with river to left, to T-junction, opposite garden centre. Turn left over river bridge and cross road, turning right into Greenfield Avenue.

8 As Greenfield Avenue curves, go left through gates by lodge into Belleisle Park. Continue with golf course on right, through trees and then curve off right to pets area. Just before this, turn left into walled garden and carry on into second garden with large greenhouse. Leave by path from far left corner, up to rear of Belleisle House Hotel. Pass in front of golf shop and in 150yds (136m) turn right across golf course, following signs to Practice Area.

10 In middle of village, pass Burns Cottage on right and continue on main road (B7024) past cricket ground to return to Tam O'Shanter Experience on left.

9 At path's end, go through green gates to main road and turn right. Follow past Rozelle Park on left and Northpark House Hotel on right, until road curves right into Alloway.

MAGIC WATERS FROM HART FELL

1 From Annan Water Hall, follow the signpost to Hartfell Spa. Follow the path along the Auchencat Burn, then through a gate in a dry stone wall. The track heads up away from the burn. Beyond the next wall, the first waymarker can be seen.

2 The path continues along the edge of the hill. Go through the gate in the wall and keep the fence on your right. Cross the stile at the next waymarker.

3 Descend to the burn and cross two bridges made from telegraph poles. Ignore the third bridge. A small sign points the way to the spa. The glen starts to widen at the next waymarker.

4 Head towards the narrow ravine for ½ mile (800m), past some sheep pens on the right and across another path. As you ascend, the ravine narrows just before a rocky outcrop on the left. The spa is on the right. Retrace your steps to the sheep pens.

5 Turn left up the main valley to a wire fence after ½ mile (800m). Head left along it and ascend to an opening. Turn right then ascend north-eastwards across featureless terrain for ¾ mile (1.2km) to a small cairn on Arthur's Seat. Beyond it, continue north-easterly to pick up a track to Hart Fell summit.

Distance: 7 miles (11.3km)
Total ascent: 2,400ft (732m)
Paths: generally good but indistinct in places
Terrain: fields, riverbank and grassy mountain
Gradients: slight to moderate; one very steep section
Refreshments: Star Hotel, Moffat
Park: Annan Water Hall, near head of minor road north of A701 in Moffat

9 Keep ahead, passing farm sheds on your left. Cross two cattle grids to reach the lane. Turn left along the lane to return to Annan Water Hall.

8 Bear right on a track for 100yds (91m), then bear left to a gate. Beyond, cross a plank bridge and continue across a field to the left hand corner of a wooded ravine. Keep ahead, with the wood on your right to reach a gate to the right of a grey-roofed shed. Continue down the track to the next gate by a bridge.

7 Towards the end of the ridge, bear right to a sheep pen then descend on a faint track ahead, in the direction of Annan Water Hall, to a gate.

6 Return by way of Arthur's Seat to the gap in the wire fence. Take the path directly ahead and in 100yds (91m), take the right fork.

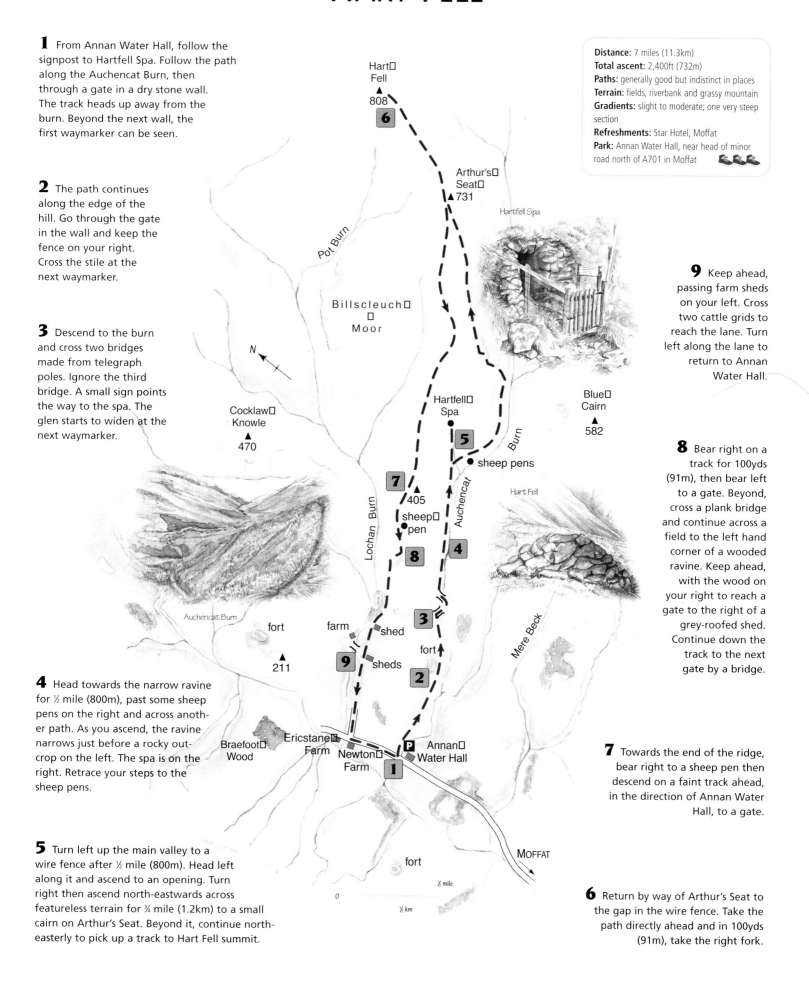

Hart Fell 808

Arthur's Seat 731

Hartfell Spa

Pot Burn

Billscleuch Moor

Cocklaw Knowle 470

Hartfell Spa

Blue Cairn 582

sheep pens

Auchencat Burn

Hart Fell

405

sheep pen

Lochan Burn

Mere Beck

Auchencat Burn

fort

farm

shed

fort

sheds

Braefoot Wood

Ericstane Farm

Newton Farm

Annan Water Hall

211

fort

MOFFAT

N

0   ½ mile
    ½ km

THROUGH THE WILD PENTLAND HILLS

1 From the car park, pass an information board on your left, turn left up the track, then immediately right along a footpath (Nine Mile Burn and Glencorse). After ¼ mile (400m), cross a stile and turn left into Bavelaw. Cross over a bridge and pass through the white gate to go uphill through an avenue of trees. Turn left at the junction, then follow drive to right. As the drive turns into private grounds of Bavelaw Castle, go straight ahead to a gate out onto moorland.

7 Beyond the cottage, follow the path to the right at the head of Harlaw Reservoir and, after crossing a dam, follow the track around to the left and along the shore. After ½ mile (800m), turn right along the side of a concrete spillway and follow the path as it swings left by Threipmuir Reservoir. Veering from the bank, the path turns right just before a hut. Pass through a gate and continue along a cinder track, which, after passing through another gate, continues to the car park.

6 Cross the stile and continue downhill across moorland. Further down the slopes, ignore a path to Currie and go straight ahead, crossing a stile and then along field paths to a T-junction. Turn right towards a belt of trees, then turn left, just before a gate, to a road. Follow the track to Warlaw House Rangers Centre (displays on local wildlife), passing through a gate to the cottage and ignoring sign to Balerno.

5 Turn left through a gate, following a footpath signed to Balerno by Harlaw. After 300yds (275m) continue ahead, ignoring path to right. Continue up the valley, known as Maiden's Cleuch, to a stone stile near the summit of the pass.

4 Crossing a wooden bridge in front of the house, turn right down the lane, following the shore of Loganlea Reservoir and then Logan Burn down to Glencorse Reservoir. Continue along the lakeside for ½ mile (800m) until the shore is lined by pine trees.

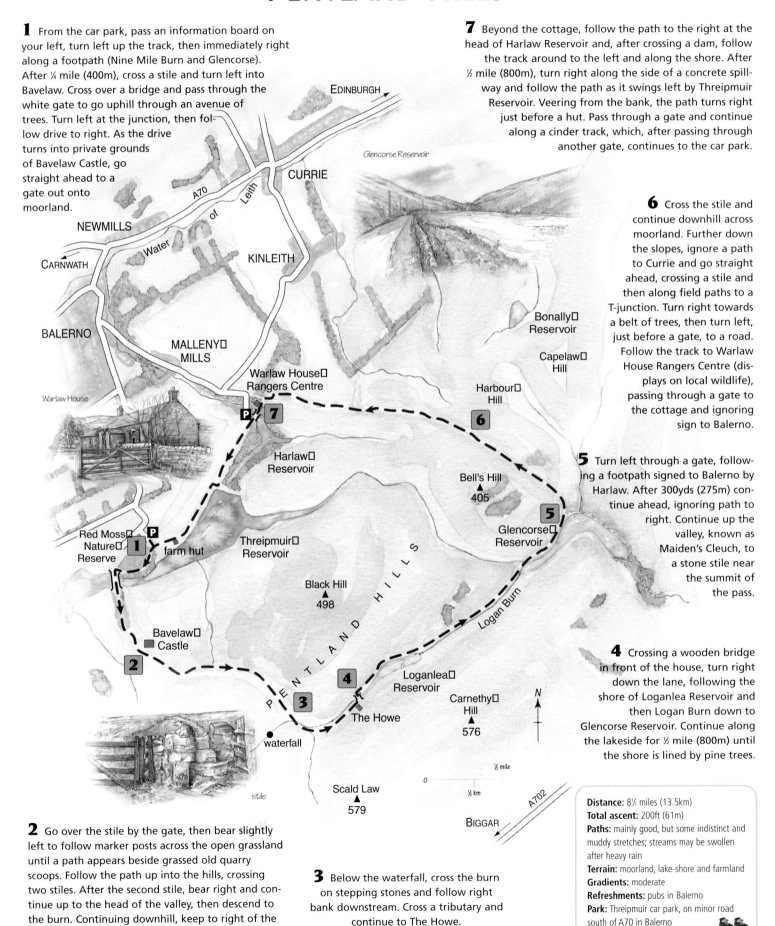

2 Go over the stile by the gate, then bear slightly left to follow marker posts across the open grassland until a path appears beside grassed old quarry scoops. Follow the path up into the hills, crossing two stiles. After the second stile, bear right and continue up to the head of the valley, then descend to the burn. Continuing downhill, keep to right of the burn until it meets a larger one by a waterfall.

3 Below the waterfall, cross the burn on stepping stones and follow right bank downstream. Cross a tributary and continue to The Howe.

Distance: 8½ miles (13.5km)
Total ascent: 200ft (61m)
Paths: mainly good, but some indistinct and muddy stretches; streams may be swollen after heavy rain
Terrain: moorland, lake-shore and farmland
Gradients: moderate
Refreshments: pubs in Balerno
Park: Threipmuir car park, on minor road south of A70 in Balerno

THE MYSTERIES OF ROSSLYN

1 From the car park, take the path leading towards the river and cross the metal footbridge. Follow the path uphill and pass under the arch of the castle bridge. At the T-junction, turn left along Gardener's Brae.

5 From the cairn, continue along the road into Roslin itself. At the end of the road, follow the signs to the left, to Rosslyn Chapel. From the chapel, retrace your steps, then turn left towards the cemeteries and left again between the cemeteries, towards the castle. Return from the castle to the steps on the left, which will return you to the car park.

2 Follow the path along the side of the river. This will take you uphill to a wall on the left. Keep the wall on your left as you follow the path back down towards the river, then continue over three stiles.

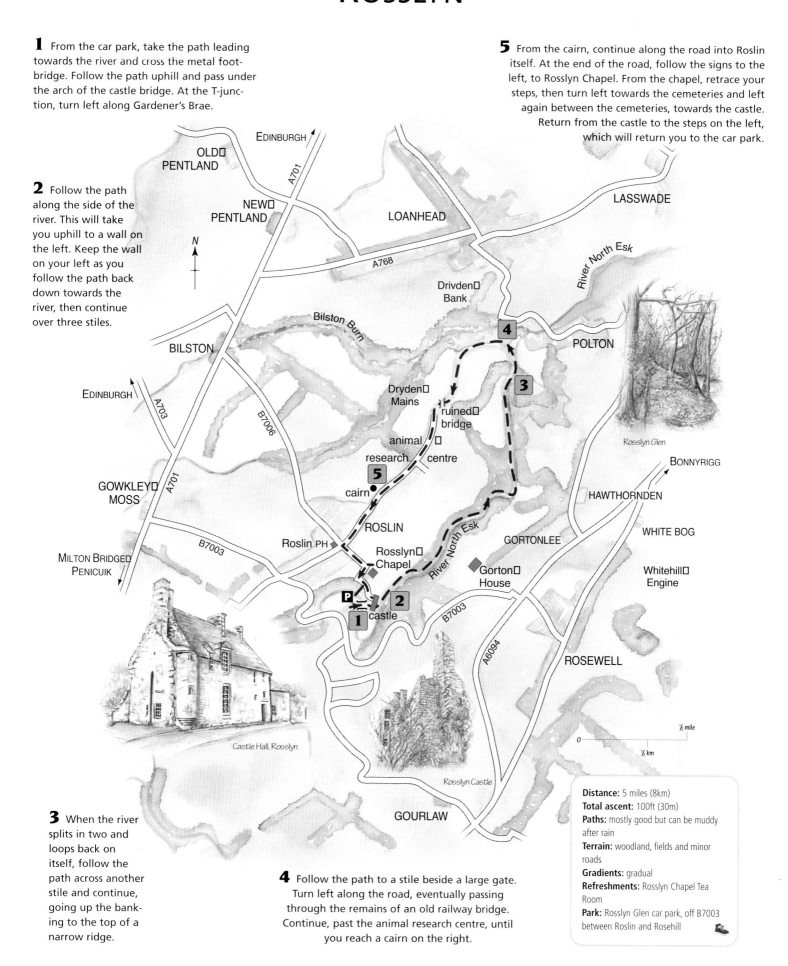

Castle Hall, Rosslyn

Rosslyn Glen

Rosslyn Castle

3 When the river splits in two and loops back on itself, follow the path across another stile and continue, going up the banking to the top of a narrow ridge.

4 Follow the path to a stile beside a large gate. Turn left along the road, eventually passing through the remains of an old railway bridge. Continue, past the animal research centre, until you reach a cairn on the right.

Distance: 5 miles (8km)
Total ascent: 100ft (30m)
Paths: mostly good but can be muddy after rain
Terrain: woodland, fields and minor roads
Gradients: gradual
Refreshments: Rosslyn Chapel Tea Room
Park: Rosslyn Glen car park, off B7003 between Roslin and Rosehill

EDINBURGH'S LITERARY PAST

Start: Edinburgh Waverley railway station
Distance: 5 miles (8km)
Paths: pavements throughout
Terrain: city streets
Gradients: a few short, steep sections
Refreshments: plenty in city centre
Park: Waverley Station

1 From Waverley Station, turn right, then left into Princes Street. Walk down to the Scott Monument, cross over, continue down Princes Street, then right into Frederick Street. Take the second turning on your left, George Street, then next left into Castle Street.

2 Walk down and cross, turning right into Rose Street. Continue along Rose Street to the end. At this junction, turn right and right again, into George Street. Cross over and turn left down North Castle Street until you reach Queen Street. Cross over, turn left, then right down Wemyss Place and right into Heriot Row.

3 Walk down Heriot Row to Dundas Street, turn left, cross over, then right into Great King Street. Cross at the end, then turn sharp right into Nelson Street, then left into Drummond Place. Follow Drummond Place into London Street, then turn right, up Broughton Street. Keep going to the main road junction at the top of the hill, then turn left into Picardy Place.

4 Cross the road opposite the Playhouse, turn left, then right at the roundabout with the clock and immediately right up Blenheim Place. Take the path on the right by Greenside Church, climbing up to Calton Hill. Taking the the left hand path, walk across towards the Edinburgh Experience and descend by the path leading to Waterloo Place.

5 Turn right, cross over then turn left at the Balmoral Hotel and up North Bridge. Turn left down the High Street (Royal Mile) and walk down to Holyrood Palace. Walk back up the other side of the road.

6 Turn left along Melbourne Place (George IV Bridge). Cross over and walk down to the statue of Greyfriars Bobby on the corner. Go sharp right down Candlemaker Row, then left into the Grassmarket.

7 Go right up West Bow into Victoria Street. Opposite Byzantium Market, go up the steps leading to Castlehill and the castle. Walk up to the Castle Esplanade to enjoy the views, then return down the hill of Lawnmarket until you reach Bank Street on the left.

8 Turn left along Bank Street, following the road down and keeping walking down the hill until you reach Princes Street. Turn right and walk back to Waverley Station.

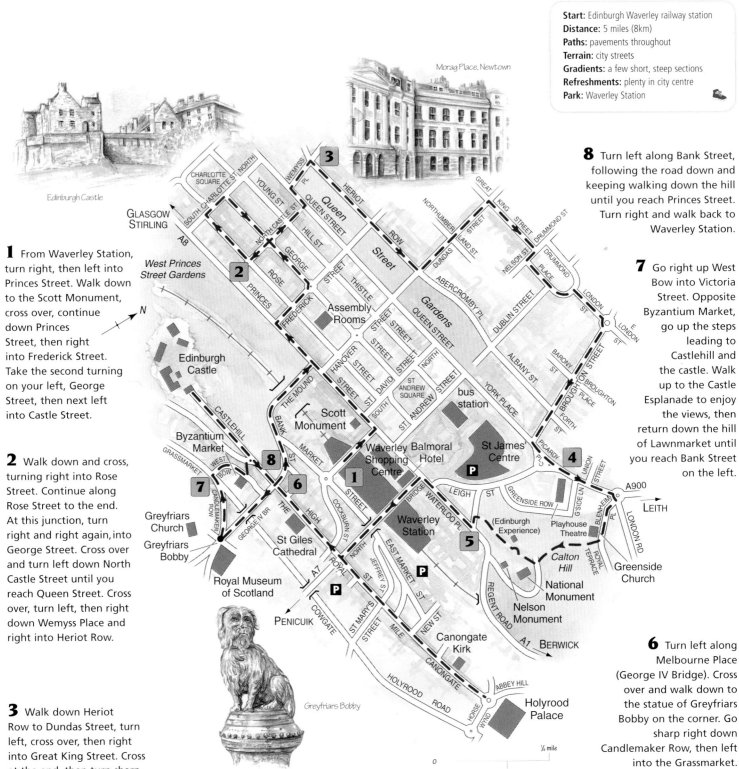

Morag Place, Newtown

Edinburgh Castle

Greyfriars Bobby

¼ mile

0

¼ km

GLASGOW'S NOT-SO-MEAN STREETS

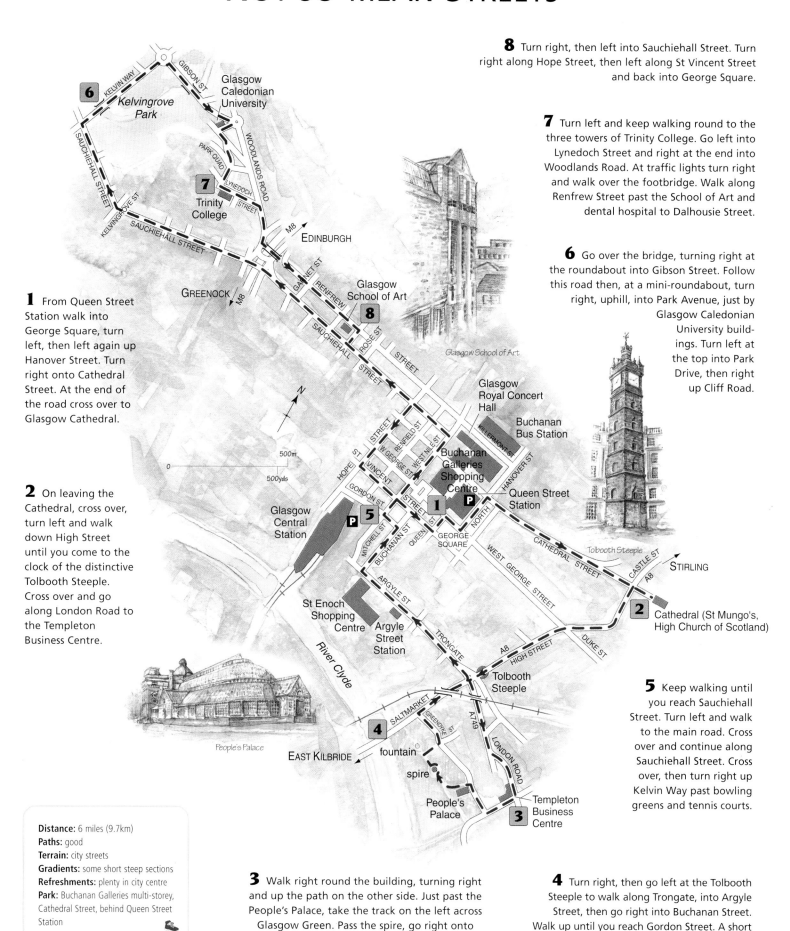

Glasgow School of Art

People's Palace

8 Turn right, then left into Sauchiehall Street. Turn right along Hope Street, then left along St Vincent Street and back into George Square.

7 Turn left and keep walking round to the three towers of Trinity College. Go left into Lynedoch Street and right at the end into Woodlands Road. At traffic lights turn right and walk over the footbridge. Walk along Renfrew Street past the School of Art and dental hospital to Dalhousie Street.

6 Go over the bridge, turning right at the roundabout into Gibson Street. Follow this road then, at a mini-roundabout, turn right, uphill, into Park Avenue, just by Glasgow Caledonian University buildings. Turn left at the top into Park Drive, then right up Cliff Road.

1 From Queen Street Station walk into George Square, turn left, then left again up Hanover Street. Turn right onto Cathedral Street. At the end of the road cross over to Glasgow Cathedral.

2 On leaving the Cathedral, cross over, turn left and walk down High Street until you come to the clock of the distinctive Tolbooth Steeple. Cross over and go along London Road to the Templeton Business Centre.

Cathedral (St Mungo's, High Church of Scotland)

5 Keep walking until you reach Sauchiehall Street. Turn left and walk to the main road. Cross over and continue along Sauchiehall Street. Cross over, then turn right up Kelvin Way past bowling greens and tennis courts.

Distance: 6 miles (9.7km)
Paths: good
Terrain: city streets
Gradients: some short steep sections
Refreshments: plenty in city centre
Park: Buchanan Galleries multi-storey, Cathedral Street, behind Queen Street Station

3 Walk right round the building, turning right and up the path on the other side. Just past the People's Palace, take the track on the left across Glasgow Green. Pass the spire, go right onto Greendyke Street then left to Saltmarket.

4 Turn right, then go left at the Tolbooth Steeple to walk along Trongate, into Argyle Street, then go right into Buchanan Street. Walk up until you reach Gordon Street. A short way along turn right into West Nile Street.

STIRLING, COCKPIT OF SCOTTISH HISTORY

1 From the castle car park, head downhill, passing the visitor centre on your left. Follow the sign to the right for the Back Walk, passing the old Grammar School, now a hotel called the Portcullis. On the Back Walk, the cemetery is to the left and the Pyramid to the right.

2 Turn into the cemetery by the iron gates opposite the Pyramid. Climb the Ladies' Rock for a view over the historic sites of Stirling and the Forth Valley and exit by the back gate. Turn right and continue until you see a fork to the left.

3 Ignore the steps to the left and take the path alongside as far as a narrow tarmac road. Cross the road via two kissing gates and continue on the path, ignoring two forks to the left and passing Gowan Hill with a pair of cannons on top.

4 Continue on the path, ignoring a right uphill fork. At the houses turn left down a lane with the Wallace Monument ahead in the distance. At the T-junction bear left on a lane, then take the narrow, grassy track on your left up to Gowan Hill.

5 Return to the lane and continue to the main road. Cross and turn left, heading through the pedestrian underpass. Old Stirling Bridge is to your left and accessible through the hospital grounds. Retrace your steps from the bridge and turn left into an underpass to the centre of the roundabout. Turn left again through another underpass which exits beyond the road bridge.

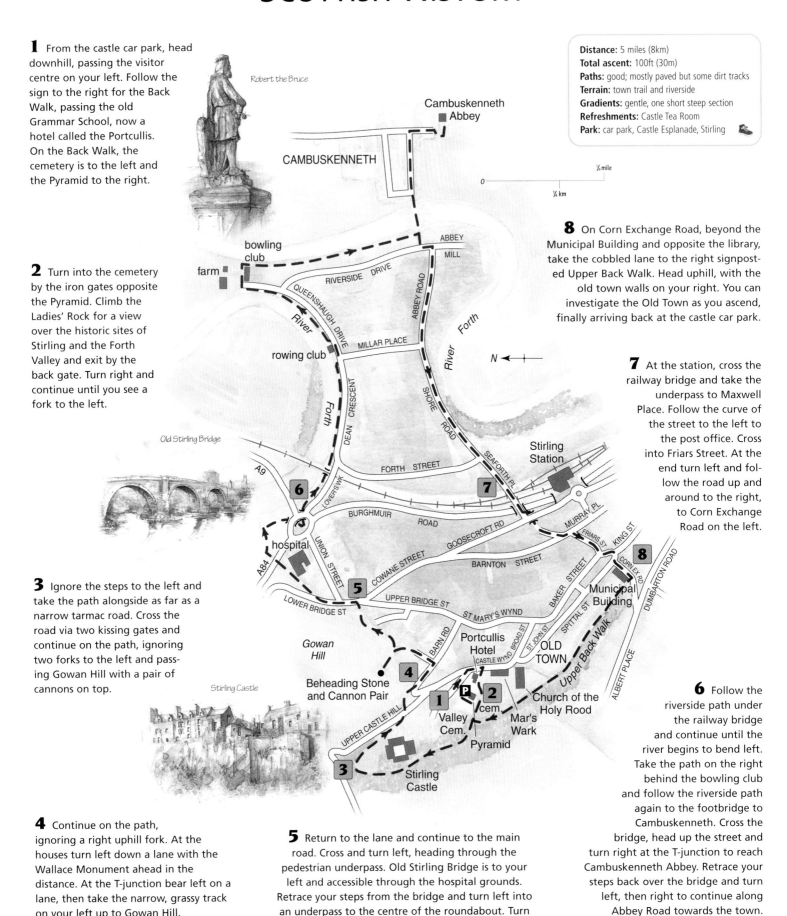

Robert the Bruce

Old Stirling Bridge

Stirling Castle

Distance: 5 miles (8km)
Total ascent: 100ft (30m)
Paths: good; mostly paved but some dirt tracks
Terrain: town trail and riverside
Gradients: gentle, one short steep section
Refreshments: Castle Tea Room
Park: car park, Castle Esplanade, Stirling

8 On Corn Exchange Road, beyond the Municipal Building and opposite the library, take the cobbled lane to the right signposted Upper Back Walk. Head uphill, with the old town walls on your right. You can investigate the Old Town as you ascend, finally arriving back at the castle car park.

7 At the station, cross the railway bridge and take the underpass to Maxwell Place. Follow the curve of the street to the left to the post office. Cross into Friars Street. At the end turn left and follow the road up and around to the right, to Corn Exchange Road on the left.

6 Follow the riverside path under the railway bridge and continue until the river begins to bend left. Take the path on the right behind the bowling club and follow the riverside path again to the footbridge to Cambuskenneth. Cross the bridge, head up the street and turn right at the T-junction to reach Cambuskenneth Abbey. Retrace your steps back over the bridge and turn left, then right to continue along Abbey Road towards the town.

THE LOMOND HILLS OF FIFE

2 Follow the diversion signs to the right of the hill and part-way round turn left up a narrow path to the summit. Retrace your steps to the diversion sign and continue round the front of the hill.

1 Follow the sign to West Lomond. Go up some steps, cross a stile and turn left. At the top of the field go through a gap in the wall, turn right, through another wall, and turn left onto the path to West Lomond.

3 Follow the track as it bears away from the hill to a stile where three fences meet. Cross this and head downhill beside the cut of the stream. Cross a plank bridge and another stile on your right then turn left following the line of the wall.

4 At the bottom of the field go left through a kissing-gate and follow the path towards the edge of the wood. A kissing-gate on the right leads you across a bridge and to a road through the wood.

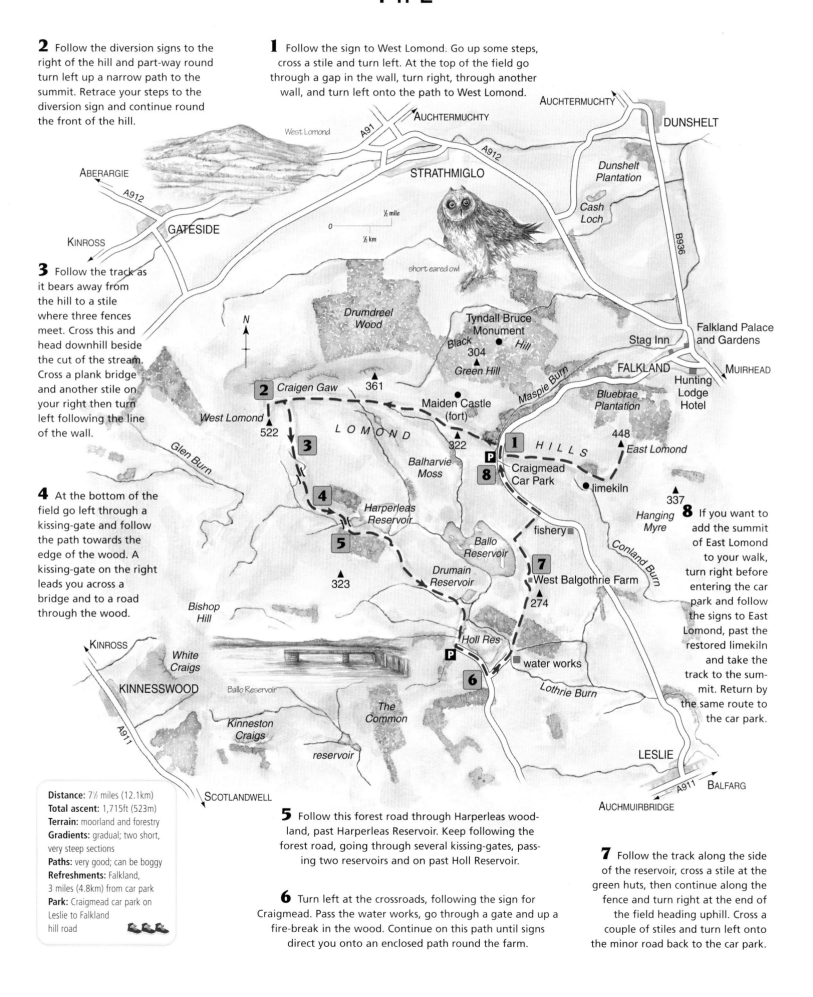

Distance: 7½ miles (12.1km)
Total ascent: 1,715ft (523m)
Terrain: moorland and forestry
Gradients: gradual; two short, very steep sections
Paths: very good; can be boggy
Refreshments: Falkland, 3 miles (4.8km) from car park
Park: Craigmead car park on Leslie to Falkland hill road

5 Follow this forest road through Harperleas woodland, past Harperleas Reservoir. Keep following the forest road, going through several kissing-gates, passing two reservoirs and on past Holl Reservoir.

6 Turn left at the crossroads, following the sign for Craigmead. Pass the water works, go through a gate and up a fire-break in the wood. Continue on this path until signs direct you onto an enclosed path round the farm.

7 Follow the track along the side of the reservoir, cross a stile at the green huts, then continue along the fence and turn right at the end of the field heading uphill. Cross a couple of stiles and turn left onto the minor road back to the car park.

8 If you want to add the summit of East Lomond to your walk, turn right before entering the car park and follow the signs to East Lomond, past the restored limekiln and take the track to the summit. Return by the same route to the car park.

ALONG KILMARTIN GLEN

1 Leaving the car park, cross the lane and take the footpath bridge over the stream. Passing Nether Largie Standing Stones, continue on the footpath to a lane beside Temple Wood stone circle.

2 Facing the stone circle, turn right along the lane, passing Nether Largie chambered cairn on your right. At the junction by Kilmartin school, continue straight ahead along a track (old coach road), passing two more cairns that form part of the linear cemetery. After 1 mile (1.6km), as the track crosses the stream, continue across a junction towards the quarry.

Distance: 9 miles (14.5km)
Total ascent: 200ft (61m)
Paths: mostly tracks and forest roads
Terrain: fields and forest
Gradients: moderate
Refreshments: Kilmartin House vistor centre; Kilmartin Hotel
Park: Lady Glassary Wood car park, on junction of A816 and B8025, 1 mile (1.6km) south of Kilmartin

5 Continue on down the track, with views of Kilmartin Glen ahead. When you reach the quarry, continue straight ahead to rejoin the outbound route (at stage 3). At the quarry exit, bear right along the coach road to return to Nether Largie Standing Stones and the car park.

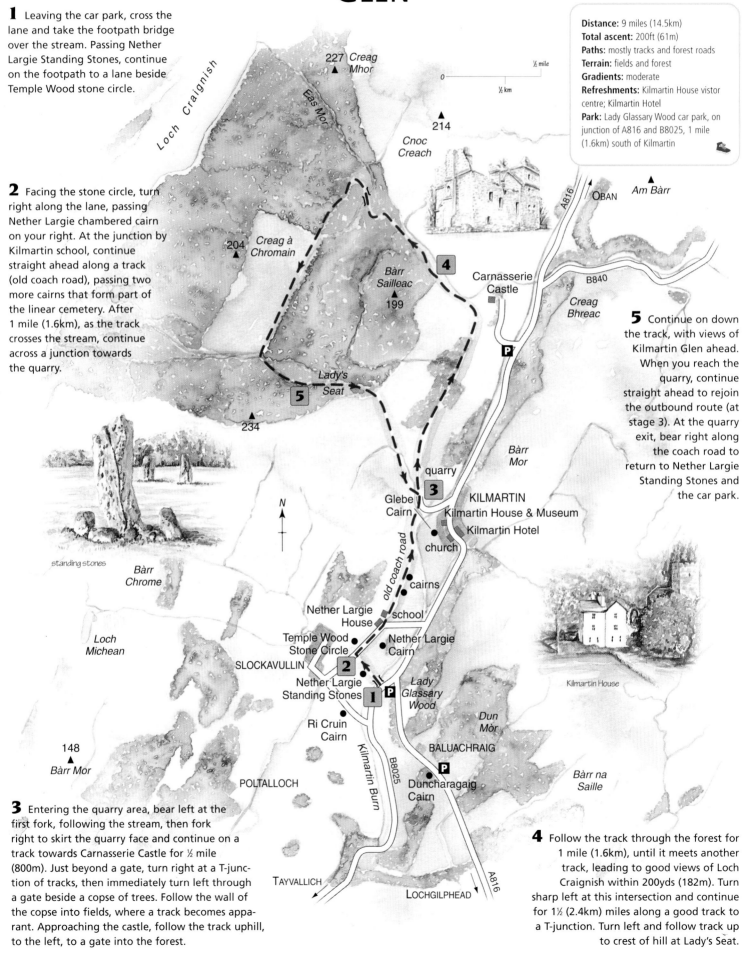

3 Entering the quarry area, bear left at the first fork, following the stream, then fork right to skirt the quarry face and continue on a track towards Carnasserie Castle for ½ mile (800m). Just beyond a gate, turn right at a T-junction of tracks, then immediately turn left through a gate beside a copse of trees. Follow the wall of the copse into fields, where a track becomes apparant. Approaching the castle, follow the track uphill, to the left, to a gate into the forest.

4 Follow the track through the forest for 1 mile (1.6km), until it meets another track, leading to good views of Loch Craignish within 200yds (182m). Turn sharp left at this intersection and continue for 1½ (2.4km) miles along a good track to a T-junction. Turn left and follow track up to crest of hill at Lady's Seat.

THE BRAES OF BALQUHIDDER

Distance: 7 miles (11.3km)
Total ascent: 1,750ft (533m)
Paths: good but boggy on hillside
Terrain: mostly forestry roads;
some hillside
Gradients: moderate to steep
Refreshments: Kingshouse Hotel
Park: Balquhidder church,
Balquhidder, off A84 between
Callander and Lochearnhead

8 Eventually this road turns back on itself and goes downhill to join the road beside the burn. Turn left, continuing past the bridge on your right and the water works back to Balquhidder church and the car park.

7 This road is at a higher altitude and will let you see all of the glen before you. After about 1 mile (1.6km) or so look for the magnificent view to your right over Loch Voil and the Braes of Balquhidder.

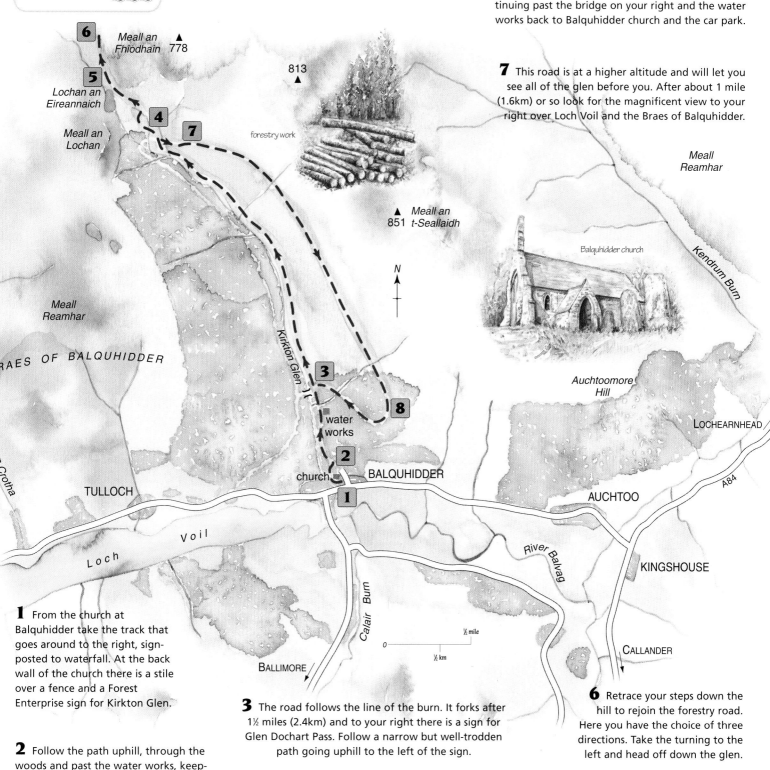

1 From the church at Balquhidder take the track that goes around to the right, signposted to waterfall. At the back wall of the church there is a stile over a fence and a Forest Enterprise sign for Kirkton Glen.

2 Follow the path uphill, through the woods and past the water works, keeping the burn on your left. A newly made logging road crosses the burn from the left. Continue uphill with burn on the left. There has been a lot of felling work here and it is now possible to see the shape of the Glen.

3 The road follows the line of the burn. It forks after 1½ miles (2.4km) and to your right there is a sign for Glen Dochart Pass. Follow a narrow but well-trodden path going uphill to the left of the sign.

4 Follow the path, crossing the burn at a fence then over the fence at a stile further up, and head for a range of crags as the path becomes indistinct. Follow it as it turns right then curve up to the left through the crags to the Lochan an Eireannaich.

6 Retrace your steps down the hill to rejoin the forestry road. Here you have the choice of three directions. Take the turning to the left and head off down the glen.

5 From here cut across the shoulder of Meall an Fhiodhain, the hill on your right, keeping to the high ground and going through a ruined fence. Your reward is the spectacular view along the course of the Ledcharrie Burn to Glen Dochart.

GREAT BIRNAM WOOD TO DUNKELD

2 Cross the bridge and walk down the steps on the left-hand side of the bridge. At the bottom follow the path to the right, downstream along the river. Just past the Birnam Oak turn up the steps signposted to Birnam, following the path round to the road. Cross to the Beatrix Potter Garden. Leaving there, turn left along the main road.

1 From the car park at Dunkeld walk along Athol Street and turn right into High Street. From the square you can investigate the fountain, rectory, cathedral and surrounding historic buildings. Retrace your steps to Athol Street and turn right.

Distance: 6 miles (9.7km)
Total ascent: 200ft (61m)
Paths: good; can be muddy after rain
Terrain: woodland with some riverbank and pavements
Gradients: gradual
Refreshments: Birnam Hotel, opposite Beatrix Potter Garden
Park: car park at end of Athol Street

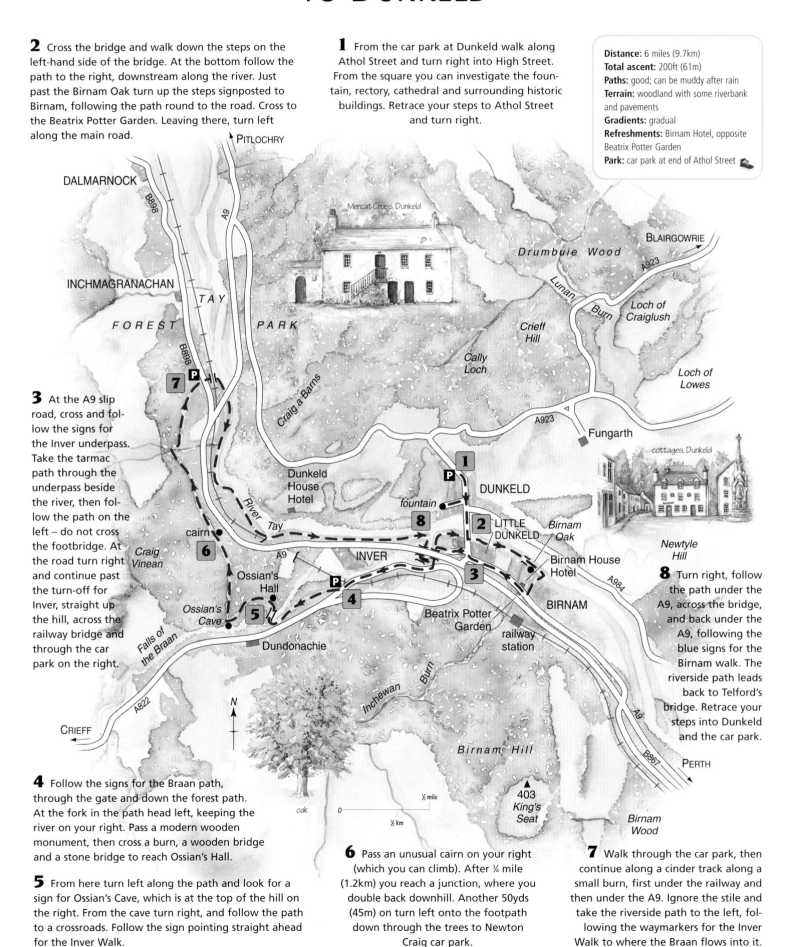

3 At the A9 slip road, cross and follow the signs for the Inver underpass. Take the tarmac path through the underpass beside the river, then follow the path on the left – do not cross the footbridge. At the road turn right and continue past the turn-off for Inver, straight up the hill, across the railway bridge and through the car park on the right.

4 Follow the signs for the Braan path, through the gate and down the forest path. At the fork in the path head left, keeping the river on your right. Pass a modern wooden monument, then cross a burn, a wooden bridge and a stone bridge to reach Ossian's Hall.

5 From here turn left along the path and look for a sign for Ossian's Cave, which is at the top of the hill on the right. From the cave turn right, and follow the path to a crossroads. Follow the sign pointing straight ahead for the Inver Walk.

6 Pass an unusual cairn on your right (which you can climb). After ¾ mile (1.2km) you reach a junction, where you double back downhill. Another 50yds (45m) on turn left onto the footpath down through the trees to Newton Craig car park.

7 Walk through the car park, then continue along a cinder track along a small burn, first under the railway and then under the A9. Ignore the stile and take the riverside path to the left, following the waymarkers for the Inver Walk to where the Braan flows into it.

8 Turn right, follow the path under the A9, across the bridge, and back under the A9, following the blue signs for the Birnam walk. The riverside path leads back to Telford's bridge. Retrace your steps into Dunkeld and the car park.

THE LOST VALLEY OF GLEN COE

1 Start on the path leading down from the car park, to join the main path through the Pass of Glencoe. Walk down east, then turn south to cross the footbridge over the River Coe, located just downstream of the Meeting of Three Waters. Climb the opposite bank, go through the birch scrub and up over a ladder stile at fencing.

2 After a further 100yds (91m) or so, leave the main path and climb a zigzagging path rising steeply off to the right. This leads up to the higher path, the one above the tree-fringed gorge of the Allt Coire Gabhail. Having enjoyed a gentle stroll for a while, and just before a large boulder, descend through the trees to make the crossing of the river. Take care traversing a few awkward rocks and roots on the way down.

3 Stepping stones make the river crossing easy. Continue the climb up along the left bank, clambering over an outcrop of rocks before reaching the point overlooking the distinctively flat, alluvial plain of the Coire Gabhail (Lost Valley).

4 From the northern edge of this hidden valley, follow the path along the left-hand side of the flat area, to where the valley narrows and the river is again visible.

5 Cross the stream and then turn right on the opposite bank and walk back along the west side of the alluvial deposits, to reach a huge glacial erratic boulder by the trees.

6 From this prominent landmark (fun to scramble on), walk up the bank behind to reach the start of stage 4. Retrace footsteps in descent to make the river crossing again (from stage 3). For variation, return to the beginning of stage 2 by descending the better-defined path, the one that is lower and closest to the river. From here, head back across the River Coe and up to the car park, in reverse of stage 1.

Distance: 3½ miles (5.6km)
Total ascent: 855ft (261m)
Paths: rough but clearly defined on ascent; less obvious on the short circuit around the Lost Valley
Terrain: confined, steep-sided gorge through woodland giving way to more open mountainous aspect at the top
Gradients: short but steep over rocks although no serious difficulties
Refreshments: Clachaig Inn, 3 miles (4.8km) west of car park
Park: westernmost car park in the Pass of Glencoe on A82 between Tyndrum and Ballachulish

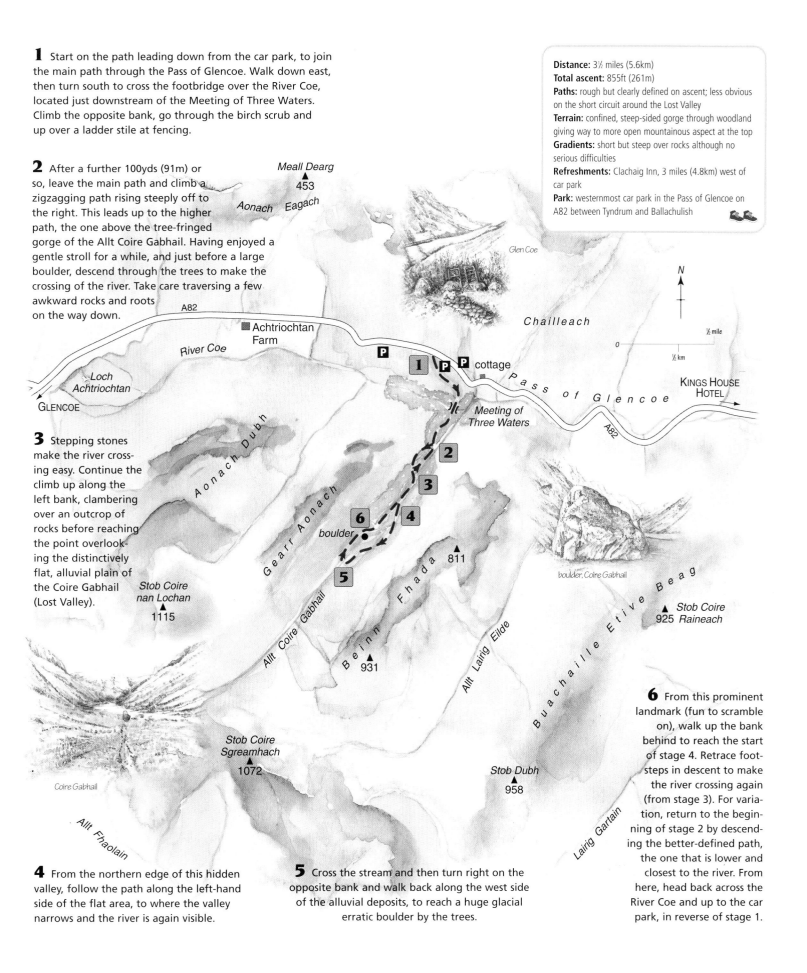

Meall Dearg 453
Aonach Eagach
Glen Coe
Chailleach
N
½ mile
½ km
A82
Achtriochtan Farm
River Coe
Loch Achtriochtan
GLENCOE
cottage
Pass of Glencoe
KINGS HOUSE HOTEL
Meeting of Three Waters
A82
Aonach Dubh
Gearr Aonach
boulder
Allt Coire Gabhail
Stob Coire nan Lochan 1115
Beinn Fhada 811
boulder, Coire Gabhail
Buachaille Etive Beag
Stob Coire 925 Raineach
Allt Lairig Eilde
931
Stob Coire Sgreamhach 1072
Stob Dubh 958
Coire Gabhail
Allt Fhaolain
Lairig Gartain

REMOTE MOIDART'S CITADEL

1 Turn right out of the car park, passing through a gate to follow the shoreline path.

5 Cross a field at the bottom of the valley, go over a stile and turn right along the road to return to the car park.

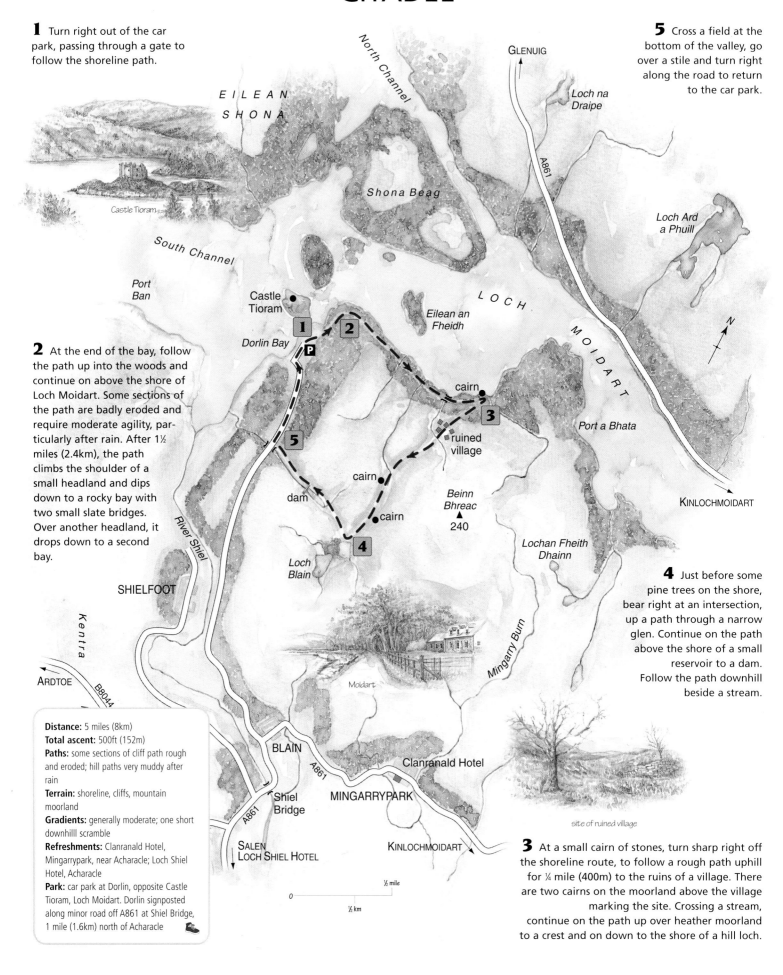

Castle Tioram

EILEAN SHONA

North Channel

GLENUIG

Loch na Draipe

Shona Beag

Loch Ard a Phuill

South Channel

LOCH

MOIDART

Port Ban

Castle Tioram

Eilean an Fheidh

Dorlin Bay

1

2

cairn

3

Port a Bhata

2 At the end of the bay, follow the path up into the woods and continue on above the shore of Loch Moidart. Some sections of the path are badly eroded and require moderate agility, particularly after rain. After 1½ miles (2.4km), the path climbs the shoulder of a small headland and dips down to a rocky bay with two small slate bridges. Over another headland, it drops down to a second bay.

5

ruined village

cairn

KINLOCHMOIDART

dam

4

cairn

Beinn Bhreac ▲ 240

Lochan Fheith Dhainn

River Shiel

Loch Blain

4 Just before some pine trees on the shore, bear right at an intersection, up a path through a narrow glen. Continue on the path above the shore of a small reservoir to a dam. Follow the path downhill beside a stream.

SHIELFOOT

Kentra

ARDTOE

B8044

Mingarry Burn

Moidart

site of ruined village

Distance: 5 miles (8km)
Total ascent: 500ft (152m)
Paths: some sections of cliff path rough and eroded; hill paths very muddy after rain
Terrain: shoreline, cliffs, mountain moorland
Gradients: generally moderate; one short downhilll scramble
Refreshments: Clanranald Hotel, Mingarrypark, near Acharacle; Loch Shiel Hotel, Acharacle
Park: car park at Dorlin, opposite Castle Tioram, Loch Moidart. Dorlin signposted along minor road off A861 at Shiel Bridge, 1 mile (1.6km) north of Acharacle

BLAIN

A861

Clanranald Hotel

Shiel Bridge

MINGARRYPARK

SALEN
LOCH SHIEL HOTEL

KINLOCHMOIDART

½ mile

0

½ km

3 At a small cairn of stones, turn sharp right off the shoreline route, to follow a rough path uphill for ¼ mile (400m) to the ruins of a village. There are two cairns on the moorland above the village marking the site. Crossing a stream, continue on the path up over heather moorland to a crest and on down to the shore of a hill loch.

DEEP IN THE CUILLINS OF SKYE

1 From the Sligachan Hotel, walk along the A863 for about 200yds (182m). Take one of the paths on the left, opposite the top of a slip road to the hotel. Most lead across boggy ground to cross the Allt Dearg Mor at the footbridge. Walk south on the gently rising footpath towards Sgurr nan Gillean, the easternmost peak of the mountains seen clearly on the skyline ahead.

5 The path ends at Loch a' Bhasteir, the tiny body of water held in the secluded recesses of Coire a' Bhasteir, from where you can retrace your steps back to Sligachan. **This upper leg of the walk provides some challenging and exposed walking and should only be attempted by those with experience of walking in the mountains.**

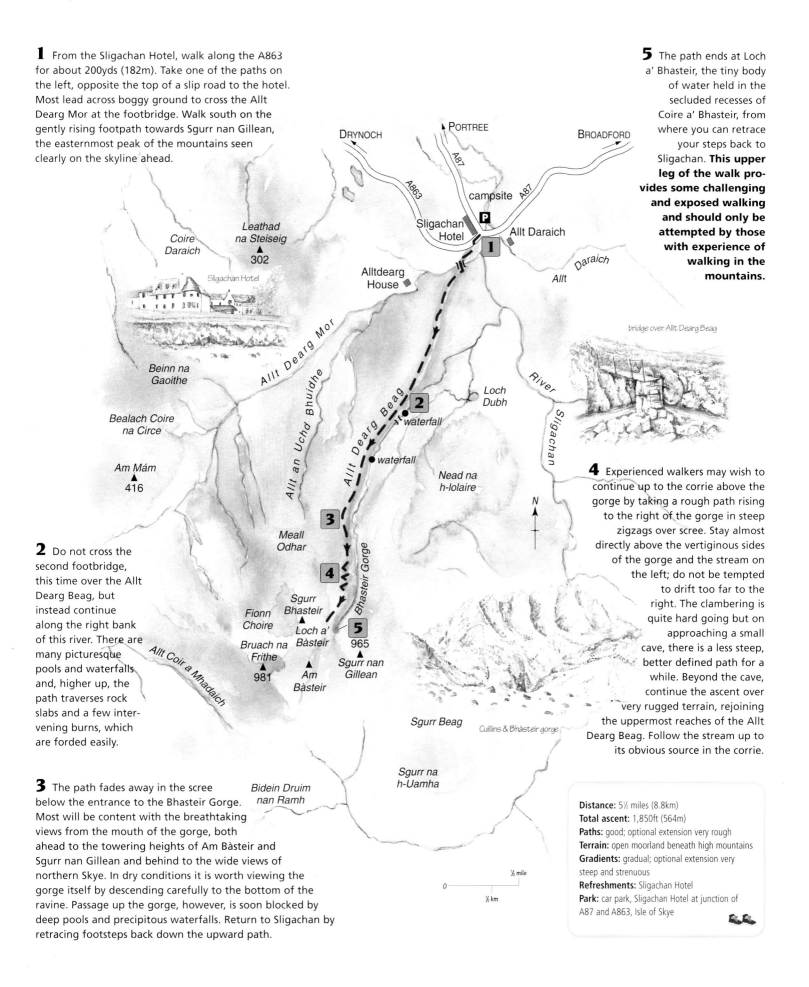

bridge over Allt Dearg Beag

4 Experienced walkers may wish to continue up to the corrie above the gorge by taking a rough path rising to the right of the gorge in steep zigzags over scree. Stay almost directly above the vertiginous sides of the gorge and the stream on the left; do not be tempted to drift too far to the right. The clambering is quite hard going but on approaching a small cave, there is a less steep, better defined path for a while. Beyond the cave, continue the ascent over very rugged terrain, rejoining the uppermost reaches of the Allt Dearg Beag. Follow the stream up to its obvious source in the corrie.

2 Do not cross the second footbridge, this time over the Allt Dearg Beag, but instead continue along the right bank of this river. There are many picturesque pools and waterfalls and, higher up, the path traverses rock slabs and a few intervening burns, which are forded easily.

3 The path fades away in the scree below the entrance to the Bhasteir Gorge. Most will be content with the breathtaking views from the mouth of the gorge, both ahead to the towering heights of Am Bàsteir and Sgurr nan Gillean and behind to the wide views of northern Skye. In dry conditions it is worth viewing the gorge itself by descending carefully to the bottom of the ravine. Passage up the gorge, however, is soon blocked by deep pools and precipitous waterfalls. Return to Sligachan by retracing footsteps back down the upward path.

Distance: 5½ miles (8.8km)
Total ascent: 1,850ft (564m)
Paths: good; optional extension very rough
Terrain: open moorland beneath high mountains
Gradients: gradual; optional extension very steep and strenuous
Refreshments: Sligachan Hotel
Park: car park, Sligachan Hotel at junction of A87 and A863, Isle of Skye

THE STUARTS' LAST STAND AT CULLODEN

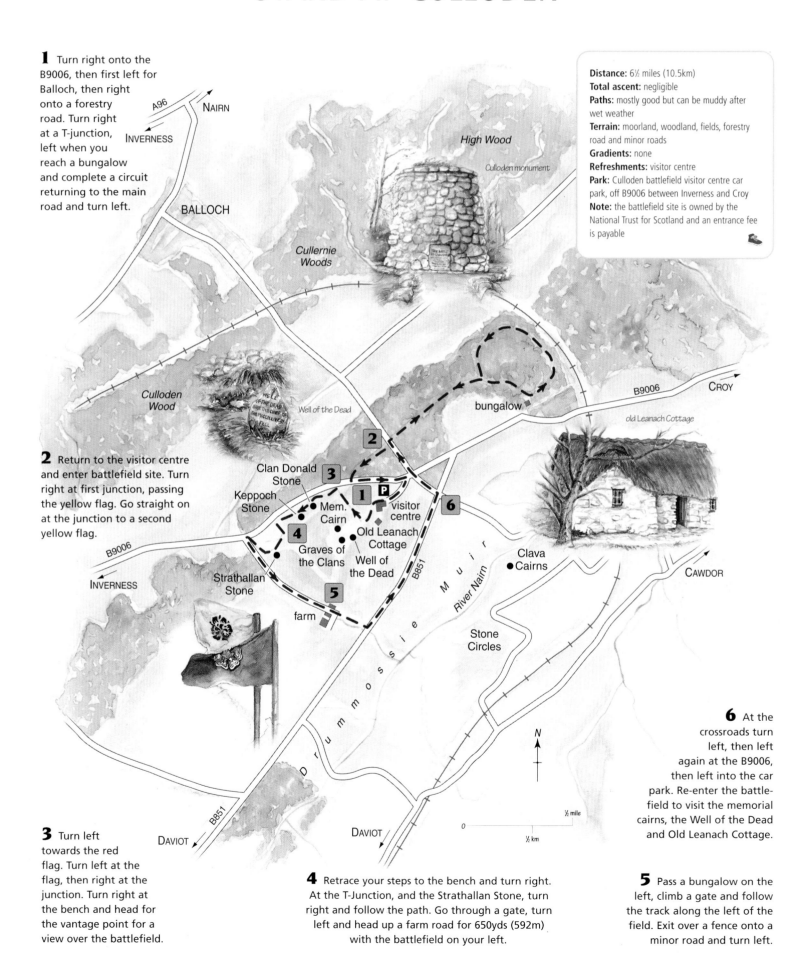

1 Turn right onto the B9006, then first left for Balloch, then right onto a forestry road. Turn right at a T-junction, left when you reach a bungalow and complete a circuit returning to the main road and turn left.

A96   NAIRN

INVERNESS

High Wood

Culloden monument

BALLOCH

Cullernie Woods

Distance: 6½ miles (10.5km)
Total ascent: negligible
Paths: mostly good but can be muddy after wet weather
Terrain: moorland, woodland, fields, forestry road and minor roads
Gradients: none
Refreshments: visitor centre
Park: Culloden battlefield visitor centre car park, off B9006 between Inverness and Croy
Note: the battlefield site is owned by the National Trust for Scotland and an entrance fee is payable

Culloden Wood

WELL OF THE DEAD

Well of the Dead

bungalow

B9006   CROY

old Leanach Cottage

2 Return to the visitor centre and enter battlefield site. Turn right at first junction, passing the yellow flag. Go straight on at the junction to a second yellow flag.

2

Clan Donald Stone

3

Keppoch Stone

1 P

visitor centre

6

Mem. Cairn

Old Leanach Cottage

4

Graves of the Clans

Well of the Dead

Clava ● Cairns

B9006

INVERNESS

Strathallan Stone

5

farm

Drummossie Muir

River Nairn

CAWDOR

Stone Circles

B851

N

6 At the crossroads turn left, then left again at the B9006, then left into the car park. Re-enter the battlefield to visit the memorial cairns, the Well of the Dead and Old Leanach Cottage.

B851

DAVIOT

DAVIOT

½ mile

0

½ km

3 Turn left towards the red flag. Turn left at the flag, then right at the junction. Turn right at the bench and head for the vantage point for a view over the battlefield.

4 Retrace your steps to the bench and turn right. At the T-Junction, and the Strathallan Stone, turn right and follow the path. Go through a gate, turn left and head up a farm road for 650yds (592m) with the battlefield on your left.

5 Pass a bungalow on the left, climb a gate and follow the track along the left of the field. Exit over a fence onto a minor road and turn left.

THE FLOW COUNTRY

1 From the lay-by to the south-east of Melvich, cross the road and head up a farm track to the left of a small loch. The track goes through a gate and curves to the left behind a derelict cottage. You will encounter two gates across the track close together.

2 Midway between the two gates, take the rough peat-cutters track that goes uphill on your left. Continue to follow this track, keeping left when it forks, until it disappears. Then continue in this direction heading for the highest point, where you will see Loch Sgiathanach slightly to your left.

3 Head for the left-hand edge of the loch and follow the course of the Allt a Ghlasraich burn, which flows from here to Achridigill Loch.

4 Where the burn meets the loch, turn 90 degrees to the right. You should be heading to the mid-point between two small hills. Loch Baligill lies at the foot of the hills. Follow the shore-line along the right-hand side of the loch.

5 At the end of the loch, turn right and, keeping the hills on your left, head for the highest point in front of you. Climb a short, steep slope and from the top you should see the hill of Cnoc Eipteil ahead of you.

Distance: 8 miles (12.8km)
Total ascent: 500ft (152m)
Paths: some good but others very boggy or indistinct
Terrain: extensive peatbog, hillside
Gradients: moderate to steep
Refreshments: Melvich Hotel
Park: lay-by on A836 south-east of Melvich
Note: this is remote and difficult terrain and the walk should not be attempted in wet weather or poor visibility

8 If you don't spot it, walk in that direction and eventually you will cut across it. This track will take you back to the main road. Turn right and follow the road through the village and beyond, to where you started.

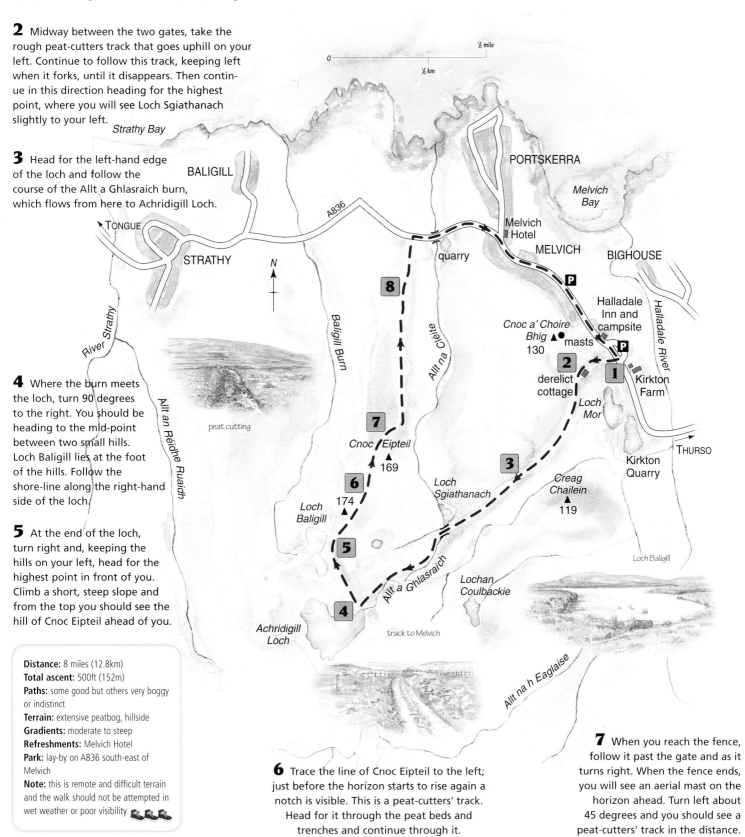

6 Trace the line of Cnoc Eipteil to the left; just before the horizon starts to rise again a notch is visible. This is a peat-cutters' track. Head for it through the peat beds and trenches and continue through it.

7 When you reach the fence, follow it past the gate and as it turns right. When the fence ends, you will see an aerial mast on the horizon ahead. Turn left about 45 degrees and you should see a peat-cutters' track in the distance.

ACKNOWLEDGEMENTS

The Automobile Association wishes to thank the following photographers, libraries and associations for their assistance in the preparation of this book.

V. BATES 270tl, 270b;
BRITISH WATERWAYS MUSUEM 154t, 155c;
S. L. DAY 42t; FLEET AIR ARM MUSEUM 39t;
IMAGES COLOUR LIBRARY F/Cover;
THE MANSELL COLLECTION 26tl, 26tr, 27tl, 27bl;
MUSEUM OF RURAL LIFE 168t;
NATURE PHOTOGRAPHERS LTD 252t (P R Sterry), 313tl (C Palmer), 313tr (W S Paton), 313b (P R Sterry);
PICTURES COLOUR LIBRARY LTD 117b, 117r, 177bl;
REX FEATURES LTD 118r (N Jorgensen);
SPECTRUM COLOUR LIBRARY 80, 81t, 81b, 116l, 176t, 177br.

ILLUSTRATED MAPS: chrisorr.com

The remaining pictures are held in the Association's own library (AA PHOTO LIBRARY) with contributions from the following photographers:

M. ADLEMAN 110b; M. ALEXANDER 302t, 302br, 303, 322b; M. ALLWOOD-COPPIN 214; P. ATHIE 217t, 222br; A. BAKER 40b, 46t, 124, 162t, 162b, 163t, 165r, 166br, 318, 319b; P. BAKER 14, 15tl, 21, 24t, 25, 27br, 28, 29b, 30, 31t, 31b, 32l, 32r, 34b, 41tr, 77t, 78b, 82, 85t, 86t, 89, 90, 91b, 106br, 112, 126b, 145r, 146tr, 146b, 148t, 149r, 150/1, 152t, 154b, 155t, 170t, 171b, 172, 175, 176b, 179tl, 179bl, 179br, 180b, 253b, 265tr; V. & S. BATES 219b; J. BEAZLEY 275b, 276, 277tr, 279, 317, 323c, 329tr; M. BIRKITT 37tl, 42, 110t, 111l, 111r, 150b, 151l, 151r, 152b, 153l, 156l, 165l, 166bl, 171t, 173t, 173b, 174t, 174b, 177c, 180t, 181b, 252b; E. BOWNESS 272b, 274b; P. BROWN 76l; D. BURCHILL 254t; I. BURGUM 50b, 51b, 149l, 201t, 202/3, 203b, 207b, 211b, 218t, 220br; J. CARNIE 305b, 308, 332/3; D. CORRANCE 322t; D. CROUCHER 74, 96b, 98b, 105t; R. CZEJA 39b, 260t, 260b; S. L. DAY 37b, 144bl, 169tl, 169tr, 213bl, 246t, 246bl, 247, 248t, 248bl, 251l, 251r, 254bl, 254br, 255, 257tr, 257b, 261, 272t, 311, 314, 316t, 320t, 324, 325; M. DENT 309br; R. EAMES 223; R. J. EDWARDS 164b; E. ELLINGTON 323t, 331t, 331b; R. G. ELLIOTT 310, 326, 332bl, 333b; P. ENTICKNAP 34t, 94, 95t, 118c; R. FLETCHER 42/3; D. FORSS 72b, 73, 75t, 76r, 77b, 78t, 83b, 85b, 86b, 87l, 87r, 88b, 95br, 96t, 97l, 98tl, 98tr, 100t, 102t, 102b, 103t, 103b, 106, 114/5, 164t; S. GIBSON PHOTOGRAPHY 306b, 309t, 309bl; J. GRAVELL 196, 197t; V. GREAVES 178t; J. HENDERSON 329tl, 329b; A. J. HOPKINS 153r, 253t, 253br, 275t; C. JONES 198t, 198b, 201b, 211t, 212, 214/5, 215l, 215r, 217br, 218b, 220t, 220bl; A. LAWSON 16r, 81c, 109b; C. LEES 277tl, 278t, 278b; S. & O. MATHEWS 44bl, 46b, 48t, 72t, 83l, 88t, 97r, 101l, 106bl, 113tr, 113br, 145b, 156r, 157bl, 157br, 158, 159tl, 159bl, 160b, 161b, 163b, 213tr, 268b; E. MEACHER 41b, 44br, 49; J. MILLER B/cover, 79r; C. & A. MOLYNEUX 222br; C. MOLYNEUX 209t, 209cl, 219t, 221; J. MORRISON 250, 263br, 268t, 269t; R. MORT 117t, 118tl, 123l, 127bl; R. MOSS 15tr, 15b, 16l, 17r, 19t, 19bl, 19br, 20, 22l, 23t, 24b; J. MOTTERSHAW 265b, 269b; R. NEWTON 26b, 33l, 33r, 36r, 42b, 47, 146tl, 148b, 213br, 267b, 269c; C. NICHOLLS 50t; D. NOBLE 91t; K. PATERSON 304, 305t; A. PERKINS 169b; N. RAY 12, 17l, 38; G. ROWATT 265tl; P. SHARPE 271, 302bl, 306t, 307; M. SHORT 109t, 144br, 168br, 206, 210bl; B. SMITH 101r; A. SOUTER 44t; F. STEPHENSON 48b, 147l, 147t; R. STRANGE 107, 113bl, 116r, 119tr, 120t, 121tl, 122t, 125t, 125b; R. SURMAN 159tr, 161t; D. TARN 263t, 263bl; T. TEEGAN 23b, 40t; T. D. TIMMS 207t; M. TRELAWNY 79l, 100b, 119br, 120br, 121b, 126t, 127br, 159br; A. TRYNOR 155b, 170b; R. VICTOR 123r; W. VOYSEY 22r, 27tr, 29t, 35, 36l, 37tr, 41tl, 44b, 75b, 84/5, 92t, 92b, 93t, 93b, 99, 103c, 104, 105c, 105b, 119cl, 122b, 127t, 168bl; R. WEIR 315, 319t, 320b, 323b, 327b, 330, 331c; J. WELSH 144t, 248br; L. WHITWAM 166t, 177t, 222t, 246br, 249, 257tr, 259t, 259b, 267t, 277b; H. WILLIAMS 51t, 204tl, 204b, 205, 210br, 217bl; P. WILSON 113cb, 125c; T. WOODCOCK 120bl, 121tr, 157t, 258; J. WYAND 46c; T. WYLES 119bl;

Produced by AA Publishing.

Material in this book first appeared in *AA Illustrated Guide to Britain* (1996) and *AA Book of Britain's Walks* (1999).

Original contributors: Tony Aldous, Chris Bagshaw, Juliet Barker, Nick Channer, Christine Collins, Paddy Dillon, Martin Dunning, Rebecca Ford, John Gilham, David Hancock, Des Hannigan, Christopher Knowles, Alison Layland, Laurence Main, Guy Mansell, Terry Marsh, Julie Meech, John Morrison, Paul Murphy, Brian Pearce, Richard Sale, Hamish Scott, Roly Smith, Christopher Somerville, Hugh Taylor & Moira McCrossan, Hilary Weston, Stephen Whitehorn, Angela Wigglesworth, Nia Williams, David Winpenny.

Verifiers of this updated edition: Chris Bagshaw, Des Hannigan, Alison Layland, Penny Phenix, Sally Roy, Hilary Weston.

Published by AA Publishing, a trading name of Automobile Association Developments Limited, whose registered office is Millstream, Maidenhead Road, Windsor, Berkshire, SL4 5GD; registered number 1878835.

Find out more about the AA on www.theAA.com

Hardback ISBN 0 7495 3201 7
Paperback ISBN 0 7495 3152 5

A CIP catalogue record for this book is available from the British Library.

Colour Repro by Chromagraphics, Singapore
Printing by Oriental Press, Dubai

CONTENTS

REGIONS AND COUNTIES

In this book mainland Britain has been divided into six regions as shown on the colour-coded map, opposite. A map of each individual region appears at the beginning of the appropriate section, indicating the location of the walks within the region.

The numbers listed below and shown opposite correspond to the major town, city or landscape feature around which each road map extract is based.

- Inverness
- 12
- 11 Aberdeen
- Fort William
- 10
- 9
- Dundee
- 7 8
- 6
- Edinburgh
- Glasgow
- 5
- 4
- 2
- 3
- 14
- 1
- 12 Newcastle upon Tyne
- Carlisle
- 13
- 11
- 6 7 8 9
- 10
- 4 5
- Leeds Hull
- Liverpool Manchester
- 1 2 3 14
- 10 11 Chester
- 12
- Nottingham
- 15 16
- Shrewsbury 12 13 10 Norwich 11
- 9 Leicester
- 7 3 Birmingham 9
- 6 2 4 5 Cambridge
- 8 1 6 8
- 4 7
- 5
- 1 17 16 Oxford 17
- Swansea 16
- 2 Bristol 15 14 15 18 LONDON
- 3 14 13 9 8
- Cardiff 11 13 11 12 7 6
- 6 12 10 Southampton
- 13 2 3 4 5
- 8 Bournemouth Brighton
- Exeter 7 9 10 1
- 5 4
- 3 Plymouth
- 2
- 1

ABOUT THIS BOOK

In this book the country is divided into six regional sections, each of which opens with an introduction and a map showing the extent of the total area covered by that chapter. Within the regional chapters, each featured location occupies a double-page spread, with the appropriate extract of AA mapping, generally at a scale of 1:200,000 (for an explanation of symbols used on the maps, see opposite). The text highlights places of interest around the main location – selected towns, cities and landscape features – which are arranged in alphabetical order. Panels in the margins of these pages give information about additional points of interest, which can include some historical background, or special attractions. Contact details for the local tourist information offices are included; these can provide further information, tell you what's on and perhaps help with finding accommodation.

Interspersed between these pages about key places are features which explore topics that are linked to the region, from literary associations to wildlife. The pages in the London section consist entirely of special features about particular aspects of the nation's capital.

At the end of each regional chapter is a section containing recommended, specially mapped walks in the area. The route of each walk, cross-referenced from main text pages where appropriate, is shown on an illustrated map, and directions to help you follow the walk are given clearly in numbered sections around the edge of the map. We recommend that you use this information in conjunction with a more detailed map produced for walkers by, for example, Ordnance Survey or Harvey Map Services.

A panel with each walk details the total distance, terrain, conditions underfoot and any special conditions that apply, such as restricted access or entrance fees. We also suggest where you might park your car, and these suggestions have been chosen to minimise the impact of leaving cars parked in the countryside. They do no imply that motorists have a guaranteed right to park in the places suggested, and we ask that you park with due consideration for others. Refreshment places mentioned in the text have been suggested by our researchers for their convenience to the route; they may or may not carry an AA classification.

The walks are graded to indicate their relative difficulty: one boot symbol for easy, two for moderate and three for the hardest, either because they include a lot of ascent, cover greater distances, or are over mountainous or otherwise difficult terrain. All the walks are on rights of way, permissive paths or on routes where de facto access for walkers is accepted. On routes in England and Wales which are not on legal rights of way, but where access for walkers is allowed by local agreements, no implication of a right of way is intended. It is important that you remain fully aware of your own capabilities when undertaking the walks, and be mindful of weather conditions, particularly when tackling walks at higher altitudes where conditions can change rapidly.

MOTORING INFORMATION

Motorway with number	M4
Motorway junction with and without number	11
Motorway junction with limited access	3
Motorway service area	S Fleet
Motorway and junction under construction	
Primary route single/dual carriageway	A3
Primary route service area	S Grantham North
Primary route destination	BATH
Other A road single/dual carriageway	A1123
B road single/dual carriageway	B2070
Unclassified road single/dual carriageway	
Roundabout	
Interchange	
Narrow primary, other A or B road with passing places (Scotland)	
Road under construction	
Road tunnel	
Steep gradient (arrows point downhill)	

MOTORING INFORMATION

Road toll	Toll
Distance in miles between symbols	5
Vehicle ferry - Great Britain	V
Vehicle ferry - Continental	BERGEN V
International freight terminal	F
Airport	
Heliport	H
Railway line/in tunnel	
Railway station and level crossing	
Tourist railway	
AA telephone	
Urban area/village	
Spot height in metres	628
River, canal, lake	
Sandy beach	
National boundary	

TOURIST INFORMATION

Tourist Information Centre	i
Tourist Information Centre (seasonal)	i
Abbey, cathedral or priory	
Ruined abbey, cathedral or priory	
Castle	
Historic house or building	
Museum or art gallery	M
Industrial interest	
Aqueduct or viaduct	
Garden	
Arboretum	
Vineyard	
Country park	
Agricultural showground	
Theme park	
Farm or animal centre	
Zoological or wildlife collection	
Bird collection	
Aquarium	
Nature reserve	
RSPB site	RSPB
Forest drive	
National trail	
Viewpoint	
Picnic site	
Hill fort	
Roman antiquity	

TOURIST INFORMATION

Prehistoric monument	
Battle site with year	1066
Steam centre (railway)	
Cave	
Windmill	
Golf course	
County cricket ground	
Rugby Union national stadium	
International athletics stadium	
Horse racing	
Show jumping/equestrian circuit	
Motor racing circuit	
Air show venue	
Ski slope - natural	
Ski slope - artificial	
National Trust property	NT
National Trust for Scotland property	NTS
Other place of interest	
Boxed symbols indicate attractions within urban areas	
National Park (England & Wales)	
National Scenic Area (Scotland)	
Forest Park	
Heritage Coast	
Little Chef Restaurant (7am-10pm)	
Travelodge	
Little Chef Restaurant and Travelodge	
Granada Burger King site